# Søren Kierkegaard's Journals and Papers

# SØREN KIERKEGAARD'S
# JOURNALS AND
# PAPERS
### Volume 6, Autobiographical
### Part Two   1848–1855

EDITED AND TRANSLATED BY

## Howard V. Hong and Edna H. Hong

ASSISTED BY GREGOR MALANTSCHUK

# INDIANA UNIVERSITY PRESS
#### BLOOMINGTON AND LONDON

*This book has been brought to publication with the assistance of a grant from Carlsberg Fondet.*

**Library of Congress Cataloging in Publication Data**

Kierkegaard, Søren Aabye, 1813–1855.
Søren Kierkegaard's journals and papers.

Translation of portions of the 20 volume Danish work published 1909–48 under title: Papirer.
Includes bibliographies.
1. Philosophy—Collected works. I. Hong, Howard Vincent, 1912–  ed.  II. Hong, Edna (Hatlestad) 1913–  ed.  III. Malantschuk, Gregor.
B4372.E5H66  1967        198'.9        67–13025
ISBN 0–253–18245–X (vol. 6)
        0–253–18239–5 (complete set, vols. 1–7)
1 2 3 4 5 81 80 79 78 77

# Contents

# Chronology

vii

*1835*

Summer in north Sjælland.

*1837*

Between May 8 and May 12    On a visit to the Rørdams in Frederiks-
berg meets Regine Olsen for the first time (see II A 67, 68).

Autumn    Begins teaching Latin for a term in Borgerdydskolen.
Sept. 1    Moves from home to Løvstræde 7.

*1838*

"The Battle between the Old and the New Soap-Cellars" (a
philosophical comedy drafted but not completed or published; see *Pap.* II B 1–21).

May 19    About 10:30 A.M. S.K.'s entry concerning "an indescribable
joy" (see II A 228).

Aug. 8/9    Father dies, 2:00 A.M.
Aug. 14    Father buried in family plot in Assistents Cemetery.
Sept. 7    Publication of *From the Papers of One Still Living, published
against his will by S. Kierkegaard.* (About H. C. Andersen as a
novelist, with special reference to his latest work, *Only a Fiddler.*)

*1840*

Feb. 1    Census list gives address as Kultorvet 132 (now 11).
Apr. or Oct.    Moves to Nørregade 230A (now 38).
June 2    Presents his request for examination to theological faculty.
July 3    Completes examination for degree (*magna cum laude*).
July 19–Aug. 6    Journey to ancestral home in Jutland.
Sept. 8    Proposes to Regine Olsen.
Sept. 10 Becomes engaged to Regine.
Oct. 8    First number of *Corsaren* (*The Corsair*) published by M.
Goldschmidt.
Nov. 17 Enters the Pastoral Seminary.

*1841*

Jan. 12    Preaches sermon in Holmens Kirke (see II C 1).
July 16    Dissertation for the *Magister* degree, *The Concept of Irony, with
Constant Reference to Socrates,* accepted.

Aug. 11 Returns Regine Olsen's engagement ring.

Sept. 16 Dissertation printed.

Sept. 28 10 A.M.–2:00 P.M., 4:00 P.M.–7:30 P.M. Defends his dissertation. (In 1854 *Magister* degrees came to be regarded and named officially as doctoral degrees such as they are now.)

Oct. 11 Engagement with Regine Olsen broken.

Oct. 25 Leaves Copenhagen for Berlin, where he attends Schelling's lectures.

### *1842*

March 6 Returns to Copenhagen.

Nov. 11 S.K.'s brother Peter Christian Kierkegaard ordained. *Johannes Climacus, or De omnibus dubitandum est* begun but not completed or published.

### *1843*

Feb. 20 *Either/Or,* edited by Victor Eremita, published.

May 8 Leaves for short visit to Berlin.

May 16 *Two Upbuilding [Edifying] Discourses,* by S. Kierkegaard, published.

July Learns of Regine's engagement to Johan Frederik Schlegel.

Oct. 16 *Repetition,* by Constantin Constantius; *Fear and Trembling,* by Johannes de Silentio; and *Three Upbuilding [Edifying] Discourses,* by S. Kierkegaard, published.

Dec. 6 *Four Upbuilding [Edifying] Discourses,* by S. Kierkegaard, published.

### *1844*

Feb. 24 Preaches terminal sermon in Trinitatis Kirke.

March 5 *Two Upbuilding [Edifying] Discourses,* by S. Kierkegaard, published.

June 8 *Three Upbuilding [Edifying] Discourses,* by S. Kierkegaard, published.

June 13 *Philosophical Fragments,* by Johannes Climacus, published.

June 17 *The Concept of Anxiety [Dread],* by Vigilius Haufniensis; and *Prefaces,* by Nicolaus Notabene, published.

Aug. 31 *Four Upbuilding [Edifying] Discourses,* by S. Kierkegaard, published.

Oct. 16 Moves from Nørregade 230A (now 38) to house at Nytorv 2, Copenhagen.

*1845*

Apr. 29   *Three Discourses on Imagined Occasions,* by S. Kierkegaard, published.

Apr. 30   *Stages on Life's Way,* edited by Hilarius Bogbinder, published.

May 13–24   Journey to Berlin.

May 29   *Eighteen Upbuilding [Edifying] Discourses* (from 1842–43), by S. Kierkegaard, published.

Dec. 27   Article "The Activity of a Travelling Esthetician . . .," containing references to P. L. Møller and *The Corsair,* by Frater Taciturnus, published in *Fædrelandet* [*The Fatherland*].

*1846*

Jan. 2   First attack on S.K. in *The Corsair.*

Jan. 10   S.K.'s reply by Frater Taciturnus in *Fædrelandet.*

Feb. 7   Considers qualifying himself for ordination (VII$^1$ A 4).

Feb. 27   *Concluding Unscientific Postscript,* by Johannes Climacus, published.

Mar. 9   "Report" (*The Corsair*) begun in first NB Journal (VII$^1$ A 98 ).

Mar. 30   *Two Ages: the Age of Revolution and the Present Age. A Literary Review* [*The Present Age* is part of this work], by S. Kierkegaard, published.

May 2–16   Visit to Berlin.

June 12   Acquires Magister A. P. Adler's books: *Studier og Exempler, Fors øg til en kort systematisk Fremstilling of Christendommen i dens Logik,* and *Theologiske Studier.*

Oct. 2   Goldschmidt resigns as editor of *The Corsair.*

Oct. 7   Goldschmidt travels to Germany and Italy.

*1847*

Jan. 24   S.K. writes: "God be praised that I was subjected to the attack of the rabble. I have now had time to arrive at the conviction that it was a melancholy thought to want to live in a vicarage, doing penance in an out-of-the-way place, forgotten. I now have made up my mind quite otherwise" (VII$^1$ A 229).
Date of preface to *The Book on Adler* [*On Authority and Revelation*], not published; ms. in *Papirer* (VII$^2$ B 235–70; VIII$^2$ B 1–27).
Drafts of lectures on communication (VIII$^2$ B 79–89), not published or delivered.

Mar. 13  *Upbuilding Discourses in Various Spirits,* by S. Kierkegaard, published.

Sept. 29  *Works of Love,* by S. Kierkegaard, published.

Nov. 3  Regine Olsen marries Johan Frederik Schlegel.

Dec. 24  Sells house on Nytorv.

*1848*

Jan. 28  Leases apartment at Tornebuskegade and Rosenborggade 156A (now 7) for April occupancy.

Apr. 19  S.K. notes: "My whole nature is changed. My concealment and inclosing reserve are broken—I am free to speak" (VIII[1] A 640).

Apr. 24  "No, no, my inclosing reserve still cannot be broken, at least not now" (VIII[1] A 645).

Apr. 26  *Christian Discourses,* by S. Kierkegaard, published.

July 24–27  *The Crisis and a Crisis in the Life of an Actress,* by Inter et Inter, published.

Aug.  Notes that his health is poor and is convinced that he will die (IX A 216).

Reflections on direct and indirect communication (IX A 218, 221–24, 233–35).

Sept. 1  Preaches in Vor Frue Kirke (IX A 266–69, 272).

Nov.  *The Point of View for My Work as an Author* "as good as finished" (IX A 293); published posthumously in 1859 by S.K.'s brother, Peter Christian Kierkegaard.

"Armed Neutrality," by S. Kierkegaard, "written toward the end of 1848 and the beginning of 1849" (X[5] B 105–10) but not published.

*1849*

May 14  Second edition of *Either/Or;* and *The Lily of the Field and the Bird of the Air,* by S. Kierkegaard, published.

May 19  *Two Minor Ethical-Religious Essays,* by H. H., published.

June 25–26  Councillor Olsen (Regine's father) dies.

July 30  *The Sickness unto Death,* by Anti-Climacus, published.

Nov. 13  *Three Discourses at the Communion on Fridays,* by S. Kierkegaard, published.

*1850*

Apr. 18  Moves to Nørregade 43 (now 35), Copenhagen.

Sept. 27 *Practice [Training] in Christianity,* by Anti-Climacus, published.
Dec. 20 *An Upbuilding [Edifying] Discourse,* by S. Kierkegaard, published.

*1851*

*Veiviser* (directory) listing for 1851: Østerbro 108A (torn down).
Jan. 31 "An Open Letter ... Dr. Rudelbach," by S. Kierkegaard, published.
Aug. 7 *On My Work as an Author;* and *Two Discourses at the Communion on Fridays,* by S. Kierkegaard, published.
Sept. 10 *For Self-Examination,* by S. Kierkegaard, published.

*1851–52*

*Judge for Yourselves!,* by S. Kierkegaard, written. Published posthumously, 1876.
*Veiviser* listing for 1852–55; Klædeboderne 5–6 (now Skindergade 38).

*1854*

Jan. 30 Bishop Mynster dies.
Apr. 15 H. Martensen named Bishop.
Dec. 18 S.K. begins polemic against Bishop Martensen in *Fædrelandet.*

*1855*

Jan.–May Polemic continues.
May 24 *This Must Be Said; So Let It Now Be Said,* by S. Kierkegaard, advertised as published.
First number of *The Moment.*
June 16 *Christ's Judgment on Official Christianity,* by S. Kierkegaard, published.
Sept. 3 *The Unchangeableness of God. A Discourse,* by S. Kierkegaard, published.
Sept. 25 Ninth and last number of *The Moment* published; number 10 published posthumously. S.K. writes his last journal entry (XI² A 439).
Oct. 12 Enters Frederiks Hospital.
Nov. 11 Dies.
Nov. 18 Is buried in Assistents Cemetery, Copenhagen.

# Translators' Preface

With Volumes 5 and 6, the work on the text of *Søren Kierkegaard's Journals and Papers* is completed—eighteen years after the task was undertaken. We are deeply grateful to the many persons who in various ways have given encouragement and assistance from the fifties on into the seventies.

Dr. Gregor Malantschuk of the University of Copenhagen has continued to share with us the fruits of his lifetime of penetrating study of all of Kierkegaard's works. For the support of this international collaboration we acknowledge the assistance of Rask-Ørsted Fondet and Carlsberg Fondet. The translations of Kierkegaard's letters included in this volume are the collaborative work of the editors and of Dr. Henrik Rosenmeier, University of Copenhagen, who is presently preparing a full volume of letters and documents.

The year 1972–73 was a year of concentration on Volumes 5 and 6. We acknowledge with thanks a sabbatical leave granted by St. Olaf College, as well as the quarters arranged by the college for the Kierkegaard Library, a research and publication grant from the National Endowment for the Humanities, the courtesies and facilities of the Kierkegaard Bibliotek of the University of Copenhagen, and guest-scholar quarters at Nyhavn 18 provided by Danmarks Nationalbank. This superb contributive constellation made possible an unprecedented year of undispersed time and effort, resulting in a certain quality of work, we trust, and in an earlier completion of the whole task. We are also indebted to Gyldendal Forlag of Copenhagen for permission to use the text of the *Papirer* and to absorb the editors' notes, and to Munksgaard Forlag of Copenhagen for similar permission regarding *Breve og Aktstykker vedrørende Søren Kierkegaard*.

Dr. Rune Engebretson has generously provided translations of the German passages in the text and Professor Emeritus Bert Narveson the translations from Greek and Latin. Nathaniel Hong has meticulously checked the apparatus, and Todd Nichol and John Hendricks have carefully read the entire manuscript. Grethe Kjær has again given valuable counsel and assistance in numerous ways. Dorothy Bolton and Ann Søvik had a share in the typing. Members of the Indiana University Press have consummated their part in this long publication process. To all these colleagues and to friends and son we are permanently and gratefully beholden.

*Kierkegaard Library*                                         H.V.H.
*St. Olaf College*                                            E.H.H.
*Northfield, Minnesota*

A history of Kierkegaard's journals and papers and a full account of the principles of this selection from them are given in the translators' preface to Volume I. Briefly, the entries in the first four volumes of this edition are arranged topically, and chronologically within each topic. Volumes 5 and 6 contain the autobiographical selections. Volume 7 will contain a complete index and composite collation.

The entries in Volumes 5 and 6 are arranged in as rigorous a chronological order as possible, given the many undated and loose items. This has required an interleaving of entries from sections A, B, and C in the Danish edition of *Papirer*. A collation of entries in the present volume with the standard designations in the *Papirer* is provided at the end of the volume.

Within the entries, a series of five periods indicates omissions or breaks in the Danish text as it stands. A series of three periods is used in the few instances of the translators' omissions.

Brackets are used in the text to enclose certain Danish terms just translated or to enclose references and formulations supplied by the translators.

Footnote numbers in the text refer to the editors' notes, which appear in serial order at the end of the volumes. Kierkegaard's notes and marginal comments appear at the bottom of the particular page, at the end of the entry, in the following entry, or in a few special cases as a bracketed insertion within an entry.

Kierkegaard's consciously developed punctuation (VIII$^1$ A 33–38) has been retained to a large extent. This is evident in the use of the colon and the dash and a minimal use of question and quotation marks. Pedagogical-stylistic characteristics (change of pace, variation of sentence-length, and the architecture of sentences and paragraphs) have also been carried over in the main. They are intended as an invitation to reflection and rereading—ideally, aloud.

# Søren Kierkegaard's Journals and Papers

# VII. WITHOUT AUTHORITY—THE CORRECTIVE
## MAY 1848–1851

« **6141**

A whole country is Christian; there are several million Christians, 10,000 preachers, and there is constant talk about faith, faith.

Let us take a look at it! Moses is commanded by God to be an instrument by which a miracle is to be performed. (We only imagine the torture, what a maiming it must be for an individual to be used in that way—we imagine it but do not grasp it.) Moses is willing, he strikes the rock, but doubtingly, and as punishment—we imagine it, as punishment he does not get to enter the promised land.

And this terribly strenuous life! What a scale it is on, this life that overwhelms me and makes me a nothing beside a Moses—and this life is lived by every man in Christendom!

IX A 8   *n.d.,* 1848

« **6142**

If I should need a new pseudonym in the future, he shall be called: Anticlimacus.[1806] And then he must be recklessly ironical and humorous.

IX A 9   *n.d.,* 1848

« **6143**

The secrecy with which a passion can dwell in a person who is closed up within himself is very remarkable. A quiet, modest, but very competent practicing lawyer, a man who commands great confidence and in whom one must have unqualified confidence. He comes to see me one day, and it turns out that for twenty years he has been the most ardent lottery player: he brings along a compilation of combinations and calculations which I literally did not dare look at because it made me dizzy.

This cannot be used, however, since he is an actual person. I do not actually know his name, although I know him well, and if I did know it I would not record it.

IX A 10   *n.d.,* 1848

3

« **6144**

Strangely enough, Socrates[1807] always spoke of having learned from a woman. O, I, too, can say that I owe my best to a girl.[1808] I did not learn it from her directly, but she was the occasion.

IX A 18   *n.d.,*   1848

« **6145**

When one himself realizes that his life is retrogression and not progress and that this is the very condition, precisely this, which one before God is supposed to work for with all his sagacity—then he can speak with no one. Everyone else inversely understands what happens to a person (what one freely and voluntarily works for with God's help), thinks he grieves over it, wants it taken away. —But God comforts beyond measure, he strengthens, he fills a person with joy!

IX A 23   *n.d.,*   1848

« **6146**

If I had just one-tenth of my capabilities, had more pride, stood less in fear and trembling before God: then I would get along well in the world. The point is that in everything I undertake, the thought that always possesses me in the presence of the lowliest man or the most distinguished, is that I am before God. The very thought that I might allow myself to ignore a single human being! —And just this is my misfortune. Without a doubt, and I dare maintain this in eternity, all my trouble with men is caused by my not being aristocratic and exclusive—which neither the people of status nor those with no status can grasp. But there is one who knows it along with me. But justify myself? No, that I cannot do. Before God I am within my rights when I remain silent. After all, I do not demand an easy life; on the contrary, I console myself that the sufferings of these times[1809] (which I have understood as my penance, also as the meaning of Christianity) will benefit those with whom I live; an awakening will surely come, God will surely place an accent upon my life—when it is over, not before. My life must not be another unchristian edition of the essentially Christian, so that one will benefit from it even during his own life. Christ's self-denial is unto death;[1810] otherwise it is no different from the secular.

IX A 25   *n.d.,*   1848

« **6147**

Strangely enough, the very moment I had written the above, I quite by chance opened Plutarch's moral writings,[1811] which I had not read for a long time, and opened the book to the essay on talkativeness, where I read a passage in chapter 12, marked in my copy:

> *Die Meernadeln, und die Ottern sagt man, zersterben beim Ge-*
> *bären; so richten auch Geheimnisse, welche entfallen, den zu*
> *Grunde, welcher sie nicht bei sich halten konnte.*[1812]

IX A 26 *n.d.*, 1848

« **6148**

The same work,[1813] chapter 13:

> *Ganz artig war die Antwort, die Archelaus einem geschwätzigen*
> *Barbier gab, als dieser ihm das Handtuch unlegte und ihn fragte,*
> *wie soll ich Dich rasiren:* Stillschweigend, *erwiderte der*
> *König.*[1814]

IX A 27 *n.d.*, 1848

« **6149** *Come unto me all you who labor and are
heavy laden!*[1815]

Seven New Discourses
*In margin:* See journal NB⁴, p. 163 [i.e., VIII¹ A 637–39].
No. 1. The Invitation
*In margin:* See p. 12 [i.e., IX A 16].
No. 2. The Hesitation

Is it not true, my listener, that you do not want me to deceive you, you do not want me to coax you to tears like a languishing zither player —you want me to speak the truth. Then why the hesitation? It is because of the one who speaks these words, not as if he were not man in order to do it or even more surely God in order to keep what he promises. No, in that respect there are no misgivings at all. But look more closely at him—he is a scorned and abandoned man, an object of pity on the streets. He is greeted out of a kind of pity, for he is excluded from the synagogue; no one wants anything to do with him; anyone who has anything to lose, the least to lose, shuns him, only flagrant sinners with whom no one wants to associate, reformatory prisoners and the like, only lepers whose society no one would seek at any price, despised tax collectors—and then a few stray individuals of the lowest class and who called themselves his apostles. But to be helped in this way—indeed, it is better to keep the toothache, if it is a toothache you have, it is better to keep it just as it is than to be helped in this way —this, you see, is why these words sound like paganism's holy words: *procul o procul est profani.*[1816] But the difference is that he invites; yet his invitation is so earnest that in another sense he scares away.

No. 3. The Invitation

And in this way it should continue to alternate until number seven ends with the Invitation.

IX A 33    n.d.,  1848

### « 6150

It is really impossible to explain Mynster. In one paragraph[1817] he can speak of the dreadful confusion prevailing in the world as if it were the end of Christianity. Then in the next the subject is—that *therefore* the great festivals are to remind us of what we owe to Christianity. For example, now Pentecost. He preaches a sermon about it. Then he goes home. On the whole he handles his office like a lawyer bureaucrat.

No, the very confusion of the times constitute an examination of the lives we live, and here Mynster is without a compass. His greatness is a personal virtuosity *à la* Goethe. That is why he maintains a certain dignity. But his life actually does not express anything.

He has always been very fond of "these quiet hours in holy places"[1818] because: (1) he distributes the religious as an ingredient in life, not as the absolute, (2) he takes a thousand things into account and wants to be sure of them before he opens his mouth (in short, his discourse has to be a masterpiece and delivering it a triumph), (3) he personally wants to protect himself and remain aloof. —It would be impossible, yes, most impossible of all, for Mynster to preach in the public square. And yet preaching in churches has practically become paganism and theatricality, and Luther was very right in declaring that preaching should really not be done in churches.

In paganism the theater was worship—in Christendom the churches have generally become the theater. How? In this way: it is pleasant, even enjoyable, to commune with the highest once a week by way of the imagination. No more than that. And that actually has become the norm for sermons in Denmark. Hence the artistic distance —even in the most bungled sermons.

IX A 39    n.d.,  1848

### « 6151

It is, after all, very comical that a man, a clergyman, "in quiet hours"[1819] describes the confusion of the age, confusion appalling as perhaps never before, that is, confusion so dreadful that if the same man used twenty-four hours of every day simply and solely for this, toiling and moiling with no other goal but this, his effort would still be a drop in the sea compared to the immensity of the confusion. —It is, then, very comical that this man thinks he has said it in "one quiet hour" once a year, thinks he has done his part and has accomplished something. Merciful God, if my life were at stake, I could not understand it. —Alas, alas, and when I consider that Bishop Mynster is the one who did it this last festival day[1820] (second Pentecost day), not disdaining a purely rhetorical device, too, a flattering of the nationalism now in vogue—I could weep, and in any case I must say there is aroused in me what Mynster himself in his younger days talked about, a longing for a better world.

The whole thing pains me indescribably. When I look at Mynster —and he has the appearance of earnestness itself—this peerless *Erscheinung*[1821] will always be unforgettable—and yet I would regard myself as an irresponsible visionary if I could ever think of behaving that way.

But it must be remembered that Mynster is an old man, and that he has once and for all settled down to being an optimist and has wanted to make Christendom out to be an assembly of Christians. That was a lie, and now it is all too starkly clear. But that is why this reminiscence appears so contradictory.

IX A 41   *n.d.*, 1848

« **6152**

God be praised, there will be time in eternity to think every thought through to the smallest particular. There, thinking will not mean anything but to think; it will not mean earning a living, acquiring honors and status—and being understood by others—by means of a few half-digested thoughts.

My season of penitence is no doubt soon over. I have nothing to complain about; in an understanding with God I realize why I suffer —and I give thanks. I am living—and with God's help I shall die in the faith that when I am dead (and it cannot happen before, for then it would not be penitence to the end) He will place the stamp of Governance upon my life so that it will be useful and lead men to be aware of God and of how frivolously they prevent themselves from leading the highest life, a life in fellowship with God.

It is not because I imagined myself to be better than other men that I chose this life which I have continually felt to be my allotted task. It was because I felt more wretched—and a greater sinner.

This is why I conduct my life in rigorous repudiation of any worldly recompense—and this is why I have been quite consistently (in the spirit of Christianity) treated badly, loathed, scorned, exposed to every crudity, while exclusive circles rejoice in silent envy.

There is no point in speaking about this to anyone. There is a time to be silent.[1822] The supreme prototype demonstrates that. He was silent.[1823] I have learned it from a lesser one, for Socrates,[1824] after all, had it in his power to save his life—by flattering the people.

IX A 42   *n.d.*, 1848

« **6153**

But even if I were to consider my life as an author altogether isolated from the rest of my life—there nevertheless is a dubious aspect to it, namely, the fact that I have had the privilege of being able to live independently. I am fully aware of this and for that reason feel exceedingly inferior to men who have been able to develop an authentic life of the mind and spirit in actual poverty. Back in antiquity this was the great thing, even more so in Christendom. If it had not been for my melancholy, all my mental-physical wretchedness, I might perhaps have attempted to risk such a life. Whereas I now humble myself under my preferential treatment which, like my wretchedness but in another sense, has taught me to be satisfied with a humble station in life.

But from the beginning I was never able to think like this, for just when the need was greatest, help was nearest, and just when things were blackest for me in my wretchedness, God did for me and continues to do for me, as I repeatedly say, that which inexpressibly exceeded anything I ever expected.

By the help of God I will never forget my miserable condition and how I felt it—so my inability to find words for my gratitude to God is easy to understand. The injustices of men against me and all that have no bearing on the cause; that, after all, is part of my task, what I may call my commission. If men were to kill me, my gratitude to God would remain the same; it is simply part of the cause which he in his indescribable love permitted me to serve—I who looked upon myself as a poor wretch who would only make others unhappy and could only be a burden and almost a curse to those with whom I entered into a closer relationship.

IX A 43   *n.d.*, 1848

« **6154**

*Periissem, nisi periissem*[1825] still is and will be my life motto. This is why I have been able to endure what long since would have killed someone else who was not dead.

IX A 48   *n.d.*, 1848

« **6155**

One thing I do have to my credit—I am not responsible for the birth of anyone—there are, to be sure, too many of them, and yet this is the only thing that concerns the majority of people—having children.[1826]

IX A 50   *n.d.*, 1848

« **6156**

By the help of God my life will contribute a little bit to putting an end to the appalling wickedness of deluding men by the millions into thinking that they are Christians and of achieving status in the world by means of proclaiming Christianity. Really and truly, Pilate was more worthy of respect than a Christian secularism of that sort. Pilate at least did not profit from being a friend of Christ's.

IX A 53   *n.d.*, 1848

« **6157**

Originally I had thought to end my work as an author with *Concluding Unscientific Postscript*, to withdraw to the country,[1827] and in quiet unobtrusiveness to sorrow over my sins. The fear and trembling in my soul about being a Christian, my penitence, seem to me to be sufficient suffering. I had almost forgotten that being a Christian is and should be a thing of scorn in the world, like unto him, my Lord and Master, who was spit upon: then Governance came to my assistance again. I became aware of it and now stay where I am. God in heaven, who has reason to be disgusted with me because I am a sinner, has nevertheless not rejected what I, humanly speaking, honestly intended. Yet before God even my best work is still a bit squalid.

IX A 54   *n.d.*, 1848

« **6158**

I blame no man for anything; they have not understood me. Yet even now I cannot get away from the thought I have had from the beginning: does not every man in his quiet mind think about God. I

have never ignored any man, the humblest farmhand or housemaid—
for he who is "before God" must simultaneously shudder deep in his
soul at the thought: suppose now that God in recompense ignored me.
My misfortune is and remains that, humanly speaking, I have made
much too much of men. Perhaps I have seemed to ignore them—alas,
it was simply because I scarcely dared let it be known how much they
lay on my heart—lest I should be regarded as mad.

Merely to have forgotten to greet a housemaid has disquieted me
as if I had committed a crime, as if God would have to abandon me.

I have seen duty in every situation, and God has been there with
me—but no one seems to have had any obligation to me.

IX A 55   *n.d.,* 1848

« **6159**

If I had never loved God before, everything he has done for me
during the time I have been the victim of coarse brutality, mistreated
for the gratification of envy, is so unbelievably and unspeakably a
pledge of his love, that he is love, that, God be praised, I feel very
strongly that I can spend a whole eternity doing nothing else but
thanking him.[1828]

IX A 62   *n.d.,* 1848

« **6160**

I feel no bitterness at all at the thought of all the indignities I have
suffered and all the times I have been betrayed; I never think of escap-
ing all of this all at once, so to speak, by death. If there is time and place
for joking in eternity, I am sure that the thought of my thin legs and
my ridiculed trousers[1829] will be a source of salutary amusement to me.
It is a blessed thing to dare say: What I have suffered in that respect
I have suffered in God's name for a good cause and because, humanly
speaking, I did a good deed in a truly unselfish sacrifice. This I dare
say—directly to God—I am more sure of this than I am sure that I live,
more sure than of anything else, for I already feel that he will answer:
Yes, my dear child, you are right, and he will add: Everything negative,
when you sinned, when you were wrong, has been forgiven you in
Christ.

I have never been a Diogenes, have never bordered on cynicism;
I have dressed properly and decently—I am not guilty for a whole
country's being a madhouse. I have been able to crack jokes with an
individual over my thin legs—but when it is the rabble, the utterly

brutish humanity, the rowdies, silly women, school children, and apprentices who abuse me: that is the meanness and lack of character of a people directed against one who truly merits something from his people. The most tiresome aspect is that I am the only one who has the right to joke, but on those terms I cannot and will not joke. And yet I need the refreshment of laughter so often. But then, alas, that the one who is clearly the wittiest in a little country is the only one who is not witty—but the riffraff and the fools are all witty and ironic.

IX A 64   n.d., 1848

« **6161**

I almost feel an urge to say not one single word more except: Amen, for I am overwhelmed with gratitude for what Governance has done for me. That everything actually can turn out for a man this way —I know of nothing that has happened to me of which I poetically might not say it is the only thing which is appropriate to my nature and disposition; I am in want of nothing. I became unhappy in love, but it is impossible for me to conceive that I could be happy without having to become someone else. My unhappiness became my blessing. I am saved, humanly speaking, by one who is dead and gone, my father, but it is impossible for me to conceive of any living person's being able to save me. Then I became an author, precisely according to my potentialities; then I was persecuted—but without it my life would not have been my own. Melancholy shadows everything in my life, but that, too, is an indescribable blessing. That is precisely how I became myself by the indescribable grace and help of God; I could almost be tempted to say by his partiality, if this were not less to me than the blessed thought which I believe and which puts my mind at rest: that he loves every man in the same way.

In all literalness I have lived with God as one lives with a father. Amen.

IX A 65   n.d., 1848

« **6162**

If I dared become reconciled with her,[1830] this would be my only wish, would be a deep joy to me. But I bear a responsibility for her marriage. If she found out for certain from me how I did love her and do love her, she would repent of her marriage. Her sustaining thought is that no matter how much she saw in me and admired me and loved me, I nevertheless treated her shabbily. She was not sufficiently religious to stand alone in an unhappy love—I have never dared help her directly; that has cost me enough suffering.

IX A 66   *n.d.,*   1848

« **6163**

If I had not found my melancholy and depression to be nothing but a blessing, it would have been impossible to live without her.[1831] The few scattered days I have been, humanly speaking, really happy, I always have longed indescribably for her, her whom I have loved so dearly and who also with her pleading moved me so deeply. But my melancholy and spiritual suffering have made me, humanly speaking, continually unhappy—and thus I had no joy to share with her. But I dare write no entries about her—as long as I live I bear responsibility for her future.

IX A 67   *n.d.,*   1848

« **6164**

I am indebted to my father for everything from the very beginning. Melancholy as he was, when he saw me melancholy, he appealed to me: Be sure that you really love Jesus Christ.

IX A 68   *n.d.,*   1848

« **6165**

How wonderful that very early in my life (that is, in my youth after my father's death), when I was independent and had no thought of looking for a position, when I went around in a depression and regarded myself as the most wretched of all men—how wonderful that I nevertheless prayed every morning that God would give me the strength for the task you yourself would assign to me. Thinking about this now, how in the world did I ever think of praying like that! And how true it has turned out to be that I got work to do which was assigned to me by God himself.

IX A 69   *n.d.,*   1848

« **6166**

But my father's death[1832] was also a frightfully disturbing event for me; how much so I have never told a single person. After all, my whole past life was so encompassed in the blackest depression and the fog of profoundest brooding wretchedness that it is no wonder I was as I was. But all this remains my secret. On someone else it may not have made so deep an impression, but my imagination—and especially at an early stage when it still had no tasks to apply itself to. A primitive

depression like that, a huge dowry of distress, and in the profoundest
sense the sad fate of being brought up as a child by a melancholy old
man—and then with the native virtuosity of being able to deceive everyone into thinking me a jolly good fellow—and then that God in heaven
has helped me as he has.

IX A 70   *n.d.,*  1848

« **6167**

How wonderful that all this which for some centuries now has
been an enigma, something one does not know whether he should
laugh or cry about—namely, that God intervenes in the world and helps
a man so that he actually has nothing to do but obey[*]—how wonderful
that all this happens to me, I who have always gone around feeling so
wretched and unhappy, and I, who, if I am anything at all, am the most
dialectical of those with whom I live.

Everything my father told me is true.[1833] "There are sins which a
man can be saved from only by extraordinary divine help." Humanly
speaking, I owe everything to my father. In every way he has made me
as unhappy as possible, made my youth incomparable anguish, made
me inwardly almost scandalized by Christianity, or indeed scandalized,
even though I decided out of respect for it never to say a word about
it to any man, and out of love for my father to present Christianity as
truthfully as possible in contrast to the nonsense which is called Christianity in Christendom—and yet my father was the most affectionate of
fathers, and my longing for him was and is sincere, and no day goes
by that I am not reminded of him morning and evening.

Only now have I reached the point where everything is clear to
me. Just as a woman becomes quiet and serious when she feels that she
is pregnant and thinks of nothing but the child, so also I at present
have seen enough in the world, and my task is now clear to me—
whether I live an hour more or a hundred years, my task is there before
me just the same.

[*] *In margin:* and that God is willing to help every man in the same
way if only one does not completely forget him or keep oneself a
Sunday's distance away from him.

IX A 71   *n.d.,*  1848

« **6168**

It is a matter neither more nor less than an auditing [*Revision*] of
Christianity; it is a matter of getting rid of 1800 years as if they had
never been.[1834] I believe fully and firmly that I shall succeed; the whole

thing is as clear as day to me. Yet I note all the more soberly that if there is the very slightest impatience and self-assertiveness, then I shall not be able to do it, then my thought will be confused.

I get up in the morning and thank God—then I begin to work. At a definite time in the evening I break off, thank God—and then I sleep. This is the way I live, although not without assaults of depression and sadness, yet essentially in the most blissful enchantment day in and day out. Alas, and so I live in Copenhagen—and in Copenhagen am the only one who is not serious, the only one who bestows no benefits and accomplishes nothing, a half-mad eccentric. That is how the crowd judges me, and the few who see a bit more deeply really have nothing against this being the general estimate of me.

IX A 72    n.d., 1848

### « 6169

He who from childhood has never had an idea of Christianity—and has such things happen to him—must necessarily shatter, become anxious and afraid for himself. I feel so at peace, for only now am I at home, with the old and familiar.

IX A 73    n.d., 1848

### « 6170

Humanly speaking, my misfortune is that I am not sufficiently corporeal; my intense inwardness (and this is the God-relationship, where in fear and trembling I constantly feel like a nothing, not to mention the pain of repentance) trembles in practically the least thing I undertake; I wonder whether God will not be angry with me and let me go. This is why I am so uneasy in my relations, particularly to all who are called suffering mankind, all who are more lowly than I. And God knows how it goes, that I am accused of pride and egotism.

But no matter how blessed it is to be before God in this way, from the other side it is enormously strenuous. That is why I feel so unhappy and have felt so unhappy in comparison with other men. To be a strong, healthy man who could take part in everything, who had physical energy and a carefree mind—O, how often in earlier years I desired that for myself. In my youth my agony was dreadful.

IX A 74    n.d., 1848

### « 6171

What Bishop Mynster[1835] has sown I am harvesting. For Bishop Mynster has proclaimed true Christianity—but in an unchristian way, has derived great advantage from it, has enjoyed all the good things

of life because of it, has gained enormous prestige, and also has in-
gratiated himself by making Christianity into "the gentle comfort" etc.

As a result he in many ways has distilled Christianity out of the
country. Then when the one who is supposed to move forward with
the task and the specific orders to observe the way, that is: to reflect
doubly, then it becomes outright martyrdom. And Bishop Mynster is
responsible for this. Such a person would always have opposition, but
it would not have needed to become a martyrdom if Mynster had not
gone in advance.

This being the case, I have worked against myself by strengthening Bishop Mynster, but Governance certainly is aware of why I did it
and will also know how to show me why it was good. If I had not done
it, I perhaps would have gotten away with a good bargain.

IX A 81   n.d., 1848

### « 6172

Bishop Mynster's[1836] service to Christianity is essentially that,
through his outstanding personality, his culture, his superiority in
distinguished and most distinguished circles, he has created the fashion or more solemn way of regarding Christianity as something no
deep and earnest person (how flattering to the persons concerned!)
could do without.

However, this service, eternally and Christianly understood, is
dubious, for Christianity is something much too distinguished to need
patronage.

And yet in his earnestness there is something of a mélange—so
touched, so profoundly moved by the thought of those glorious ones
—and so sensitive when it comes to the part where this should be made
earnest by minimizing oneself just a little bit.

IX A 83   n.d., 1848

### « 6173

And yet I love Bishop Mynster;[1837] it is my only wish to do everything to reinforce the esteem for him, for I have admired him and,
humanly speaking, do admire him; and every time I am able to do
anything for his benefit, I think of my father, whom it pleases, I believe.

IX A 85   n.d., 1848

### « 6174

It seems to me that I have written things which must move stones
to tears—but it moves my contemporaries only—to insults and envy.

IX A 86   n.d., 1848

### « 6175 *From* The Diary of an English Physician[1838]

The scene where he visits a poor wretched scholar dying in extreme poverty and says to him: You yourself surely are not to blame for your poverty, you surely have nothing to reproach yourself about. A hypocritical, sanctimonious Doctor! How pleasantly cruel to enjoy his own righteousness that way.[1839]

IX A 87    *n.d.,* 1848

### « 6176

Peter[1840] knows that my finances[1841] are in a precarious state, he knows that it is up and down with my health, he knows or has some notion of how strenuous it is to do what I am doing in a context of fools and daily abuse—since that time I have not heard a word from him. He probably has become utterly afraid, and pusillanimous as he has always been, he no doubt is sitting there very self-satisfied at the thought that this is God's punishment upon me. O, he is a mollycoddle, and conceited to boot; he receives all the tokens of respect from those Grundt-vigians and it is all "so loving" and so lovable.

It is beyond me how a man can be like that. If one actually realizes that a man is having a bad time, it seems to me that all other considerations must disappear. His past difficulties with the Bishop[1842] had scarcely begun before I got busy and wrote to him again and again. But the orthodoxy which does not have a bold childlike confidence toward God but regards him as a tyrant one flatters rather than worships in love—those people always have a kind of joy when they believe that now God is punishing someone else.

Enough of that—I feel the same toward my brother as always. As usual the one to whom God grants the extraordinary is misunderstood, especially by friends and relatives. Basically, Peter has always regarded himself as better than I and pettily [regarded me] as the prodigal brother. He is right in so thinking, for he has always been more upright than I. His relation to Father, for example, was that of an upright son —mine, on the other hand, was often blameworthy: ah, but yet Peter has never loved Father as I did. Peter never brought grief to Father, to say nothing of the grief I brought him, but then Peter has long since forgotten Father, while I remember him every day, unconditionally every day since that August 9, 1838,[1843] and will remember him until a blessed reunion in the hereafter. And so it is in all my relationships.

—A long time went by during which I was essentially regarded as a bright fellow gone to ruin—Peter, on the other hand, was always the upright one. Then I became a scoundrel (every third person must have thought so)—Peter is, and it is true, the upright one; in the light of contrast he is the lovable one. Then I turn over a new leaf. Peter cannot understand me: he looks anxiously and fearfully at me. In any case he is waiting now for me to seek his confidence. And this I simply cannot do. He is getting a little offended. No wonder the whole relationship is so wrong.

IX A 99   *n.d.*, 1848

« **6177**

It is God who has humbled me in this way, but truly it was for my own good. This whole troublesome affair with people would have made me only prouder and more defiant, for I would have felt my superiority to a dreadful degree. But the fact that my financial situation[1844] was precarious weakened me somewhat, and in that weakness, as a penitent I bore my troubled responsibility before God for what I myself had done wrong. That is the basis of the humility so salutary for me.

But the world missed the point; it did not perceive that from the beginning I was a penitent. It has thought me a proud person who would become fearful and step aside; alas, I am a penitent who humbly remains on the spot—for it is not the world I care about, it is God. I was a penitent when I put the first line in print, and I am that now.

IX A 100   *n.d.*, 1848

« **6178**

My father died—then I got another father in his place: God in heaven—and then I discovered that my first father actually had been my stepfather[1845] and only figuratively my first father.

IX A 106   *n.d.*, 1848

« **6179**

Reply: "O, how hard it is to be as old as the eternal makes a person when he is still a man, man most of all, and when all existence speaks to him in the language of youth. I loved a young girl, lovely was she, and so young (how blissful it must be to be so young!) and persuasive and inviting: O dreadful sorrow: I was an eternity too old for her."

IX A 108   *n.d.*, 1848

## « 6180

I have read somewhere in Plutarch (*Moral Epistles,* [1846] in my own copy of the little German translation it was volume III; as far as I can remember I opened the book at random and therefore did not note it down) an anecdote which illustrates very well that there can be a double reason for shaking and trembling, that it can also express strength. The story goes that a person who sometimes would shake when making his appearance (in a crucial moment or some such) answered: Yes, if the body knew in what danger it was going to be, it would shake even more.

IX A 122   n.d.,  1848

## « 6181

Humorous lines: "And then God will say to me: God knows you are right, or what am I saying, I know that you are right."

IX A 123   n.d.,  1848

## « 6182

No doubt there has been many a one who has done irreparable harm in the world with his talking about being the extraordinary. But the question is whether I am doing harm by constantly saying and believing that every man knows what I know.

It does not surprise me that someone who considers my life will think me mad, for how many would agree with me, I wonder, in the view of life that to be sacrificed is the highest victory, and that this is Christianity.

IX A 125   n.d.,  1848

## « 6183

Lines: Ah, to be caught up into the third heaven[1847] just *once* in a whole lifetime—and as a memento of that to keep a thorn which reminds one perhaps *many times* every day.

IX A 128   n.d.,  1848

## « 6184

In human weakness, this is the proper motto for my life: No one puts a new patch on an old garment. —The opposite is the wisdom of the prudent, who therefore are on good terms with the present moment, that is, they place their little smidge of improvement directly upon the established order.

IX A 129   n.d.,  1848

### « 6185

Very strange! In one of my first conversations with her,[1848] when I was deeply moved and my whole being was profoundly agitated, I told her that in every generation there were a few individuals who were destined to be sacrificed for others. She scarcely understood what I was talking about and perhaps I myself scarcely understood (and in any case really only about my own inner suffering), least of all that it would begin with her having to suffer. But just her spontaneous, youthful happiness alongside my dreadful melancholy, and in a relationship such as that, was bound to teach me to understand myself, for I had never suspected before how melancholy I was, I had no proper criterion of how happy a person can be.

By being sacrificed I meant that my suffering and anguish would make for resourcefulness in digging out the truth which could then benefit other men.

So God has gently led me farther and farther, and now I stand at the point where it is also true externally that there are men who are sacrificed for others.

IX A 130   *n.d.,* 1848

### « 6186

There is a prophetic word by her[1849] about me: You will definitely end up becoming a Jesuit. In the romanticism of youthful imagination Jesuitism is the striving whose $\tau\acute{\epsilon}\lambda o\varsigma$[1850] goes far beyond the understanding of this youthfulness.

IX A 131   *n.d.,* 1848

### « 6187

But nothing about my relation to her[1851] may be written down. I bear responsibility for the rest of her whole life, and therefore even now any direct information would cause endless confusion.

IX A 132   *n.d.,* 1848

### « 6188

. . . . . If one looks around at people, it is fine that there is someone who is able to say, "I am only thirty-four years old and am already department head. I am only twenty-nine and already have a big business etc." It is fine that every individual has a successful, comfortable life; God grant that every individual has it or still might get it. But, Good Lord, when it comes to being a nation, we are, after all, a little people; consequently there ought to be some concern in every generation about having something to show, a little something of which the nation could say: This I do have. But in this respect the situation in Denmark is utterly hopeless. In the end mediocrity and finite prudence about earthly advantage will be deified, and it will be regarded as immoral not to have earthly advantage from one's efforts.

But it is not true that every individual who has made his life secure is supposed to insist defiantly that this kind of striving is the earnestness of life and that belonging to an idea is fanaticism—just the opposite, an admission must be made.

But even worse, as far as distinction and greatness are concerned, Denmark is able to tolerate only possibility, not actuality. It can tolerate a man of whom it can be said: he could—woe unto him if he does it.

IX A 134   *n.d.*, 1848

« **6189**

This is what I mainly do in the book "Come to me, all you"[1852] etc.: I place what is said on Sunday together with what one says and does the rest of the week. Contrasted in this way, the cleavage shows up, and all the mendacity in their Sunday preaching.

IX A 135   *n.d.*, 1848

« **6190**

Proverbs 14:13: The heart of the ungodly man, even when it laughs, is sad. I found this quoted in *Kirketidenden*[1853] (III, no. 44, p. 710), in Lütken's account of his wife Cornelia's life.

IX A 137   *n.d.*, 1848

« **6191**

Perhaps someone or other who smugly thinks he understands life has in the past said: It is beneath Magister Kierkegaard's dignity to demean himself by getting mixed up in all this wretchedness of rabble barbarism.[1854] O, how elevated. No, I would say that it is beneath my dignity to have lived in such demoralized times and to have remained silent in order to maintain trimness and neatness in a worldly sense, but instead all the reek and stench of rabble barbarism is, in an eternal sense, my adornment.

This, too, is a scurvy human invention, that it is supposed to be a great thing to avoid getting mixed up in evil in order not to be exposed to the consequences. No thanks! The world always wants to have two advantages: first to sneak away from any inconvenience and then in addition to be admired for it, for that is greatness! But I am not so easily deceived.

IX A 139   *n.d.,* 1848

« **6192**

What I have said to myself about myself is true—I am a kind of secret agent[1855] in the highest service. The police use secret agents, too. It is not always just the men with the best and purest lives who are selected for this, quite the reverse; the police use the ingenuity of cunning, wily criminals, at the same time forcing them with the consciousness of *vita ante acta.* [1856] Alas, God uses sinners in the same way. But the police do not think of reforming their secret agents. God does. At the same time as he mercifully uses such a man, he educates and reforms him. But the consciousness of *vita ante acta* here again influences unconditional obedience, because such a man, humbled and crushed, must admit that if a man could claim anything of God at all, he himself has absolutely no claim to make but must only submit to everything and yet be grateful for merciful punishment.

IX A 142   *n.d.,* 1848

« **6193**

Humorous[1857] lines: I know very well that I may die, but I think like this, one day more or fifty years less is all the same to me.

IX A 144   *n.d.,* 1848

« **6194**

My health is failing day by day; soon I may very well be released, but I do not fear death; just like the Roman soldiers, I have learned that there are worse things.[1858]

IX A 492   *n.d.,* 1848

« **6195**

I as an author am a penitent, but if I let men perceive this, I would *eo ipso* not be a penitent; then they perhaps might even esteem me, that is, I would win them over directly, that is, I would deceive them.

IX A 150   *n.d.,* 1848

« **6196**

One single vote, absolute, without
any further additions.

As a political author Sibbern[1859] is different from Gert W.[1860] only in that he[*] never shaves the beard off anyone but only pesters people with talk. There is something sad that a man in such a distinguished position in the state, a teacher at the university, consequently a man who is responsibly committed to set a good example[†] for young people, like a low-comedy character who fools around in dance halls and other such places, fools around as an author in a certain class of newspapers that belong in the basement of literature. As far as S. is concerned, one is certainly obliged to yield to grief.

In the latest number of *Aftenbladet*[1861] he orientates us for the thirty-seventh time[1862] to the domestic situation—for S. always feels called to give orientation. In a slightly more fantastic costume than the careless jumble of old and new in which he usually goes about, he appears as a prophet. He predicts a reaction against the present administration, a frightful reaction, as frightful as possible, that is, from all four corners of the world. The first corner is the old bureaucratic competence. Praise be to it![‡] The second corner is really curious: *Nord og Syd*[1863]—for a corner, especially a corner of the world, with "North and South" corners also, is really a remarkable corner. And then two more corners are added, making six corners. What dreadful confusion! How fortunate that S. knows where to go for comfort amid the confusion that possibly could ensue in the dreadful moment when the storm begins simultaneously in all four of the other world's—six corners. In that event he entrusts himself to "the editor of *Adresseavisen* and *Flyveposten.*"

This can be called *orientation* in the state of affairs, but perhaps in all this Sibbernism it has never been demonstrated clearly that he has been called to orientate, and that is why we emphasize it.

In any case, perhaps this little account of Sibbernism may contribute to orientating us to Sibbern once and for all: that as a political vagrant he is a complete Gert W., which also accounts for his drinking "Dus" with the executioner[1864]—the wretched discarded tool of literary despicableness and envy—or as Sibbern calls his Du-brother, student Goldschmidt: the young genius.[1865] These two understand each other—of course, not the lovable, remarkable thinker, Councillor Sibbern, but the political Simple-Peter [*corrected from:* naughty] Sibbern—and the naughty boy of literature Goldschmidt—who make a practice of handing each other compliments—alas, what a miracle it is, they already have accepted honor from each other many times.

[*] *In margin:* cannot even shave but only pester people.

[†] *In margin:* that is, as a vagrant and loafer slouches around in the dance halls.

[‡] First of all comes the first corner—that it functions in the regular way it does is all to its credit.

IX A 493   *n.d.,* 1848

« **6197**

Dear *Conferentsraad,* [1866]

I am sure you will easily remember that excellent passage in Holberg[1867] in which Pernille says of Gert W. that if one sewed his mouth shut, he would teach himself to speak with his nostrils. How splendid! It is so descriptive, so graphic, for when a person closes his mouth and tries to speak anyway, then his cheeks become inflated, and one cannot help but get the impression that the words must escape through his nostrils. Furthermore, there is infinite *vis comica*[1868] in this "to teach himself how to" with his nostrils. It is a superb expression for the infinity of need. It may take him ages, perhaps many years—it makes no difference, it does not matter, provided only that he succeeds—for even though it were the last day of his life, he would faithfully persist in "teaching himself." Only he who has an infinite goal dedicates himself in this way, and only he who strives infinitely is able to persist in this way. So also with G. W., but only with respect to that which for him is the sole goal: to be able to speak with his nostrils, assuming that his mouth has been sewn shut. And suppose that he succeeded, succeeded beyond all expectation, and instead of speaking with only one mouth could now speak with two—since he has, after all, two nostrils. What joy! Not even the inventor of that machine[1869] with which one writes and makes copies at the same time, in other words, with which one may write in duplicate, could be as happy as G. W. would be— although it would be horrible for the neighborhood if this infinitely garrulous person were now to have, as we speak of a double-barreled rifle, a double-barreled mouth with which to speak.

But to the point. As with G. W.'s need to talk, so also with my longing for and need to walk with you, sir. And as that is not possible, there is no other way than to teach myself to walk with you in writing.

With this my letter ends. It is brief; hence it may be taken to correspond with the manner of walking with you that occurs when I call at Kannikestræde,[1870] ring the bell, and the porter says, "The *Conferentsraad* is not at home." At some other time I may perhaps write you a letter that will deal with another manner of walking with you, as when the porter in reply to my question says, "Yes," and I hurry upstairs to the second floor where a young lady[1871] informs me that the *Conferentsraad* is not at home after all. Eventually I will finally get to walk with you. But in our present manner of walking that event will not occur, and that is the reason I now, thinking about this, beg pardon in the event that *Conferentsraad* R. should find himself sitting and waiting at some prearranged time and that scoundrel, Magister K., should fail to show up.

And so, for now—but no! After all, we did not go walking, and so I cannot thank you for the walk. And yet it seems as if I had been walking with you, and exactly as if I were standing and taking my leave of you and saying, "Please take care of yourself, my dear *Conferentsraad;* stay in good health; you have actually grown younger in the short time I have known you." And now, enjoying the real surroundings, relaxing in the company of selected poets of several nations—why should you not grow younger every day to the unspeakable joy of that circle for whom the high noon of your health is the only determination of time that is of any real interest?

And then, when you once more return to town, when my time begins with the advent of fall, then I shall probably be so fortunate as to see you, I who in my remote solitude yet remain

Your<br>S. Kierkegaard

N.B. In testimony whereof I hereby declare (what I cannot know is how you will take [this]—alas, perhaps as a piece of good luck) that this letter may well be the last one. Once I get a pen in my hand, it says many things I must be careful to retract.

*Letters,* no. 180 [July, 1848]

### « 6198

I concede that I began my work as an author with an advantage: being regarded as something of a villain but extremely brilliant—that is, a salon hero, a real favorite of the times. There was a bit of untruth in it—but otherwise I would not have gotten people along with me. As they gradually became aware that this was not quite the case, they fell away and continue to fall away. If it gets to be known that I am working out my salvation in fear and trembling, then it is goodbye to the world's favors.

But here lurked the secret agent.[1872]—And that went unobserved.
For someone to be first of all a dissipated sensualist, a party-lion, and
then many years later, as they say, to become a saint, this does not
capture men. But they are not at all accustomed to having a penitent,
a preacher of repentance, begin in the costume of a party-lion as a kind
of cautionary measure.

This has also served to provide me with an almost prodigious
knowledge of men.

IX A 155   n.d., 1848

« **6199**

When everyone in a little country reaches an agreement to regard
what any other just tolerably cultured person can see is coarseness,
vulgarity—not wittiness—to regard it as wittiness, and as a consequence
the highest levels of society read such things and are witness to it and
as a consequence the young women of the most refined families allude
to it without blushing: then the country *eo ipso* has foundered, it is
guilty of treason against itself and against all the goodness and nobility
it had, and prevents itself from achieving it in the future.

IX A 156   n.d., 1848

« **6200**

The only way to get air is to die; in that same instant I will be in
my ideality, for the trouble with me is that I am too ideally developed
to live in a market town.[1873] How disgusting to live in a situation where
the only thing that can help me is to die. Every day I live, I become
more of a burden to the envy of this market town.

IX A 159   n.d., 1848

« **6201**

As early as the article "Public Confession"[1874] there was a signal
shot (I was at the time finished with the manuscript of *Either/Or,* and
immediately after that followed *Either/Or;* the article was also a mystifi-
cation: after having disavowed the authorship of the many newspaper
articles, which, to be sure, no one had attributed to me, I ended by
asking people never to regard anything as mine that was not signed by
me, and that was just the time I planned to begin using a pseudonym)
suggesting that Professor Heiberg was the literary figure I wanted to
protect; he and Mynster both were mentioned there and as unmistaka-
bly as possible. But then Heiberg himself came along with his imperti-
nent and foppish reivew of *Either/Or,*[1875] also with a careless promise

which he never kept. Then the opposition of his clique, his attempt at the silent treatment, fakery in such a small literature—all this gave the occasion for rabble barbarism to emerge so strongly. I was the one who could and should strike but could not because I constantly had to keep the way clear for a possible polemic against Heiberg. Finally I struck at the barbarism—and Heiberg left me in the lurch. Prior to that time it had often been whispered about that I approved or indulged that revolt. Now one got an insight into the affair—but Heiberg thought: Now if Kierkegaard could get shafted, it would be a good thing. Pfui!

IX A 166    *n.d.,*  1848

### « 6202  *What I Have Written in Papers*[1876]

In *Flyveposten:*
  An article
  "Yet Another Defense of Woman's Eminent Talents"[1877]
Three political articles
  "*Kjøbenhavnpostens* Morning Observations"[1878]
  "On *Fædrelandets* Polemic"[1879]
  "To Orla Lehmann"[1880]
In *Fædrelandet:*
  "Public Confession"[1881]
  "Who Is the Author of *Either/Or*" over the
    signature FF[1882]
  Then a little article about the sermon in
    *Either/Or* and one I had given in the seminary[1883]
  "A Fleeting Comment on a Detail in *Don Juan*"[1884]
  "A Declaration and a Little More"[1885]
  And then the two articles by Frater Taciturnus.[1886]

IX A 167    *n.d.,*  1848

### « 6203

. . . . . O, one can be cruel in many ways. A tyrant can have a person mistreated cruelly. But one also can be cruel in another way, for example, as one person has been cruel to me. With tears in his eyes and on his knees he[1887] begged me for Jesus Christ's sake to do what I could not do—O, it was very cruel; I have never gotten over it! What, after all, is cruelest, to choose to be the cruel one—or to impugn another as being very cruel!

IX A 168    *n.d.,*  1848

« **6204**

Even if Denmark would do it, it is highly questionable whether it could rectify the wrong it has done me. That I am an author who definitely will bring honor to Denmark is indisputable; that I have lived *qua* author practically at my own expense with no subsidy from the government or the nation,[1888] saw it through, continued producing even without the least literary assistance from a journal because I saw what a small country it was—and then to be treated this way, my major work not even reviewed[1889]—and the machinery of the total plan hardly suspected—and then its author singled out by rabble barbarism to be recognized by every shoemaker's apprentice, who in the name of "public opinion" insults him on the street (for the press, after all, is the organ of public opinion): No, no, Denmark has condemned itself.

IX A 169   *n.d.*, 1848

« **6205**

. . . . . Thus in a certain sense I began my activity as an author with a *falsum* or with a *pia fraus*.[1890] The situation is that in so-called established Christendom men are so fixed in the fantasy that they are Christian that if they are to be made aware at all many an art will have to be employed. If someone who does not have a reputation of being an author begins right off as a Christian author, he will not get a hearing from his contemporaries. They are immediately on their guard, saying, "That's not for us" etc.

I began as an estheticist—and then, although approaching the religious with perhaps uncustomary alacrity, I denied being a Christian, and so on.

This is the way I present myself as an author to my contemporaries —and in any case this is the way I belong to history. My thought is that here I am permitted and able to speak of myself only as an author. I do not believe that my personality, my personal life, and what I consider my shortcomings are of any concern to the public. I am an author, and who I am and what my endowments are I know well enough. I have submitted to everything that could serve my cause.

I ask the more competent ones in particular to be slow to judge the capabilities and the use of capabilities which do not appear every day—I ask this especially of the more competent, for there is no use in requesting this of fools. But as a rule every more competent person has respect for himself and for his judgments—and for just this reason I request him to judge carefully.

It is Christianity that I have presented and still want to present; to this every hour of my day has been and is directed.

IX A 171     *n.d.*, 1848

### « 6206

*In margin of 6205* (IX A 171):

It was essential for me to learn to know the age. Perhaps the age found it quite easy to form a picture of this author: that intellectually he was an exceptionally gifted person, dedicated to pleasure and wallowing in a life of luxury. Ah, it was mistaken. It never dreamed that the author of *Either/Or* had said goodbye to the world long before, that he spent much of the day in fear and trembling reading devotional books, in prayer and supplication. Least of all did it think that he was and is conscious of himself as a penitent from the very first line he wrote.

IX A 172     *n.d.*

### « 6207

Yet in a certain sense it is unwillingly and only with great reluctance that I explain the coherence of my whole endeavor.[1891] Mainly for one reason, because despite all my, humanly speaking, enormous reflective and systematizing powers, a third power, Governance, constantly intervenes, and while I, by means of reflection, grasp many relations, he has me in his power and leads me in such a way that it is always afterwards that I understand best how precisely that serves my cause.

IX A 173     *n.d.*, 1848

### « 6208

And then to have to live in such a small country! Eventually I become almost revolting to myself because I feel my disproportion. It is, indeed, as if I were staggeringly vain. And yet it is not entirely so, but in a large country I would more or less disappear.

IX A 174     *n.d.*, 1848

### « 6209

I have been thinking these days of having the little article: "The Crisis in the Life of an Actress" printed in *Fædrelandet*.[1892] The reasons *for* doing it are the following. There are some minor reasons, but they have persuasive power, and therefore I must first subject them to a critique. I believe I owe it to Mrs. Heiberg,[1893] partly also because of the piece about Mrs. Nielsen[1894] at one time. I would like to poke Heiberg a little again. This way certain things can be said which I otherwise could not say so lightly and conversationally. It would make me happy to humor Gjødwad,[1895] who has asked for it. And then the main reason that argues for it: I have been occupied now for such a long time exclusively with the religious and perhaps people will try to make out that I have changed, have become earnest (which I was not previously), that the literary attack has made me sanctimonious, in short, they will make my religiousness out to be the sort of thing people turn to in old age. This is a heresy I consider extremely essential to counteract. The nerve in all my work as an author actually is here, that I was essentially religious when I wrote *Either/Or*.[1896] Therefore, I have thought that it could be useful in order once again to show the possibility. I regard this as my task, always to be capable of what the vanity and secular mindedness of the world hankers after as supreme, and from which point of view they patronizingly look down on the religious as something for run-down subjects—always to be capable but not essentially to will it. The world is sometimes so insipid that if it believes that one who proclaims the religious is someone who cannot produce the esthetic it pays no attention to the religious.

This is a very important reason *pro*. But the *contra* speaks. I now have gone so decisively into the essentially Christian, have presented much of it so forcibly and earnestly that no doubt there are some who have been influenced by it. These people might be almost scandalized to hear that I had serialized a piece about an actress. And surely one has a responsibility to such people.

Allowing the article to be published will mean that perhaps someone will be made aware of the essentially Christian simply by avidly reading that little serialized article. But there may also be the one who is almost offended.

Furthermore, at the moment I have no religious book ready for the printer that would come out at the same time.

Therefore it must not be published. My position is too earnest; a little dialectical mistake could do irreparable harm. An article in a newspaper, particularly about Mrs. Heiberg, creates much more of a sensation than big books.

It is now a matter of faithfulness in serving my cause. There may have been crucial significance in beginning as I began, but not any more. And the article itself is in fact much older.

N.B. This whole matter is interpreted to be conceitedness; it is reflection which wants to make me so extraordinary, instead of placing my confidence in God and being the person I am.

[*A page removed*] it to Gjødwad—and then I left it alone, and became very sick in the afternoon—ah, I would rather write a folio than publish a page.

But now it must come out whatever happens; I will bitterly regret having remained suspended in reflection.

IX A 175    *n.d.*, 1848

« **6210** *N.B.*

July 20

And now the doctrine of the forgiveness of sins must come forth in earnest.

The title can be:

The Radical Cure

or

The Forgiveness of Sins and the Atonement

It may be best to write a smaller book prior to this one
"Blessed is he who is not offended in me."[1897]
[*In margin:* See journal NB², p. 250 (i.e., VIII¹ A 381).]
This will be an appendix to "Come to me."[1898] It will be shorter discourses, one for every time Christ said these words. Thus at the same time a complete development of the concept "offense" will be developed, since Christ himself knew best where the possibility of offense lies.

In every discourse, therefore, the occasion, the setting, the situation, and the one addressed will be emphasized.

It will be best to arrange these discourses quite simply in chronological order. The simpler the better. They could also be arranged according to the development of the concept to be used as the basis.

IX A 176    July 20, 1848

« **6211**

No, no, the little article must be published.[1899] I am a prey to nothing else than melancholy reflection. Lately I have been possessed with the thought that I am going to die soon, and therefore I have continually produced and produced in the hope that it will not be published until after my death. Then the thought of publishing this little article awakens; it appeals to me very much; Gjødwad[1900] gets the same idea at the same time. I hope it is a hint from Governance—and then, my melancholy reflection changed what was undeniably a trifle, an innocent matter, a little joy I had wished to have by making a few people happy—my melancholy reflection transformed that into something so big that it seemed as if I would create a scandal, as if God might abandon me. It is indolence, melancholy, nothing more nor less. I have pondered publication of one of the manuscripts already finished. But no, I have the fixed idea that I am going to die, and I coddle myself by shunning the inconvenience and trouble of publishing.

The point is that the issue is too minor, I dare not entreat God's help—but that is wrong. If I remain suspended in reflection, I will lose myself. I will never come out of it. And my relation to Gjødwad, who knows of the article, is a perpetually open sore which will be a frightful drain on me since I actually have nothing with which to counter his requests but a despondent whim.

As far as offense is concerned, let me above all not pass myself off as more religious than I am or be credited with any kind of pietistic excess. Before God I have been able to justify writing it. Well, now I can and will publish it, for I must be honest. Granted that I would not do it again—but it is, after all, an older work. That is why the article is dated: Summer, 1847, and therefore all that troubled doubt is removed.

So in God's name—O, it is difficult to use God's name in connection with such a minor thing. But it is really a much different issue, that of being true to myself, of having the bold confidence before God to be myself and take everything from his hand.

Perhaps it will turn out in the end just as I began, that I will have joy in having done it.

IX A 178   *n.d.,* 1848

« **6212**

Furthermore, this whole question of the possibility of offense[1901] is something that just happened to occur to me momentarily, something I had never before thought of, something quite foreign to my nature, conflicting with what I may call the clue to my assisting role in relation to Christianity. It must be emphasized once again that I have not changed over the years but that originally it was my honest intention to serve Christianity.

From now on begins a decisive presentation of the essentially Christian in a stricter sense than before—and thus I do not dare do more—and it follows as a matter of course that I will not have time or energy, either, to present anything esthetic.

But the worst thing at this point seems to be that I have gotten this matter so confused in reflection that I am at my wit's end. Therefore even if there had been no other reason for it, I had to act. Nothing exhausts me so terribly as negative decisions, to be ready to do something, consequently to have found it completely right, desirable, etc., and then suddenly a mass of thoughts drifts in, almost overcoming me. It is not right that something which in itself is unimportant and has been pondered suddenly should be able to acquire such horrible reality [*Realitet*]. It is a sign that the reflection has become sick. If this is so, there must be action in order to save life. Then indolence is ready to make one think that the negative was, after all, better—but that is an outright lie. The only right thing is to flee to God—and to act.

IX A 179   *n.d.*,  1848

« **6213**

It was good that I carried out my intention,[1902] and Pfui! on me for having to be shaken up this way, for swelling up this way in the dropsy of despondent reflection. But that was why I was not allowed to get away before I did as I should. I would have regretted it in a thousand ways had I not done it, caused myself horrible torment, and deadened or stupified myself.

Before pushing on for the last time it was important and appropriate to my nature once more to place a decoy in the course, to tempt, and as far as possible to give a presentable impression of my differential virtuosity.[1903]

I have the honor of serving the contemned and disdained cause of Christianity. But there must be no possibility of the illusion that I fled to Christianity because I was no longer able to move about and handle myself with esthetic ease. O, no, by the help of God it must be made impossible for the world to do that. Yet I am not the parading victor who enjoys condemning the world in this way—ah, in other ways I am far, far more humble.

[*In margin:* Psalm 116:10: I believe, therefore I speak, but I am very humble.]

But now, as I begin for the last time, I feel much more joy in advancing toward what awaits me, for I am committed to being sacrificed[1904]—if it is required. But I also would like to avoid having a man like Professor Heiberg complain that I have not done everything possible for him and his.[1905]

But here I put an end to these entries. They are too extensive, and yet they do not exhaust what I carry around inside of me, where before God I understand myself far more easily because there I am able to get everything together at one time, and yet in the end I understand myself best by leaving everything to him.

IX A 180    *n.d.*, 1848

« **6214**

I need encouragement, humanly speaking—perhaps it will come. But maybe it is not encouragement I need after all, but a new shock or rap on the knuckles so that I will be able to pull even harder—perhaps it will come.

IX A 183    *n.d.*, 1848

« **6215**

The trouble with the whole affair about the little article[1906] was that I originally thought it a little thing I could take care of on my own. Therefore it seems to me easier to publish a book, a very important book, for then it is assumed right away in the beginning that I resort to God. But it is so very difficult to ask God for help to do a trifling thing as a trifling thing. But God can help here as well, for in his divinity his love is still more human than that of the best human being.

IX A 184    *n.d.*, 1848

« **6216**

Although I work extremely hard as an author and see very well both what God gives and what he makes out of it, which I do not always understand in spite of my reflective powers, my true test is in being the poor, insignificant, sinful man that I am, to be that before God—my work as an author I actually do not dare talk about; in a way it is not my own.

IX A 185    *n.d.*, 1848

« **6217**

Now I perhaps could publish a little collection of all the short articles (but with their respective signatures or pseudonymous names) which I have written up until now (mainly so as to protect myself against being regarded as author of what I have not written and so that I might exist *in toto*). This would show that I have not written occasional-claptrap.

It could be called

Previously Published
Minor Writings[1907]
By
S.K.

A preface to the book should be as unpretentious as possible. It possibly might seem pretentious to publish a collection of small articles such as these. But [they would show] that I did it in order to exist as I in fact do exist as an author down to the least little line, and I hope that one who has followed me with particular attention would like to own this little book as well.

Then I will have withdrawn[1908] once and for all from periodical literature. Every line I have written will then exist in book form.

IX A 186   *n.d.,* 1848

**« 6218**

Lest it seem strange that I was prompted in any way to publish separately the little article "The Crisis and a Crisis"[1909] etc., the pseudonym should be kept, but the thing is dedicated to Professor Heiberg.

To

Professor J. L. Heiberg[1910]

Denmark's esthetician

dedicated

by

a subordinate esthetician,

the author

God knows that I have always thought well of Heiberg, sticking as always to my first impression. But his treatment of me is not defensible. And even after that time I have still done what could be done to maintain him essentially in a position of honor.

IX A 187   *n.d.*, 1848

« **6219**

Praise God, it is just the opposite with Bishop Mynster. He was a rural pastor, became an assistant pastor, an altogether regular man of the cloth, and preached every Sunday year in and year out—and the church was attended as it should be. Now he is an old man; he has had his day, and his position does not allow him to preach more than every fourth Sunday—and now his church does not have the unusual attendance as before. In a certain sense, praise God. These are the proper proportions. It is apparent that he has not been aided and abetted by any illusions. On the contrary, he now has the illusion working against him that he is an old man and therefore can never do any harm preaching only every fourth Sunday.

But it is bad enough in Christendom that being a clergyman is a salaried profession, this is one illusion; still worse and altogether un-christian is the illusion of elegance and unusualness which indulges and flirts with the lethargy of the senses and conjures up an appearance of tremendous piety—because such a preacher as this has the church chock full to overflowing.

IX A 188   *n.d.*, 1848

« **6220**

It was really fortunate that I finally did publish that little article,[1911] thereby remaining true to myself to the last, so that my life may not become a detriment rather than a benefit.

If I had died without doing it, I am convinced that in the horrible irresponsible confusing of concepts in our day some would have stepped forward and gabbled up something about my being an apostle. Good God, instead of being a positive influence and holding the essentially Christian in a position of honor, I would have ruined it. What a charming kinship for the apostle: that a person like me was also an apostle. What a charming fruit of my life to help establish the masterful category: such a one also is an apostle and so on.

From the very beginning I have kept an Argus eye on that confusion, that horrible confusion. In such a garrulous time as ours, which flirts with everything—if it merely spots someone somewhat different from the clergy—O, the creation of confusion lies perpetually imminent. Did not Magister Adler[1912] aspire to this? I have worked against this with fear and trembling. To that end my continual use of the phrase: without authority; to that end the essay on the difference between a genius and an apostle.[1913] But all that still would not have helped—so now an article about an actress.

As a man I am personally a poor unhappy child whom a despondent old man in his love made as unhappy as possible—and whom God then took in hand and for whom he has done "so indescribably, O, so indescribably more than I ever expected," and so indescribably that I long only for the stillness of eternity in order to do nothing but give thanks. As a man I am personally in more than an ordinary sense a sinner who has traveled a long way on the road to perdition, whose conversion all too frequently was and is characterized by relapse—a sinner who nevertheless believes that all his sins are forgiven in Christ, even if he must bear the consequence of punishment, a sinner who longs for eternity in order to thank Him and His love.

As an author I am a somewhat strange kind of genius—no more and no less, unconditionally without authority, and therefore continually under orders to annihilate himself so that he does not become an authority to anyone. What is most unusual, in case anyone wants to know, is that I have just as much imagination as I have dialectical talent and the reverse, and in addition that my thinking is essentially present tense.

IX A 189   *n.d.*, 1848

« **6221**

I probably do not have long to live, but whether I have an hour or seventy years, my choice is made, to present Christianity at all times (except for the time out I must take for recreation, but for that I ask God's permission). It is all too true that essentially it has been abolished. In this connection I am like a secret agent.[1914]

IX A 190   *n.d.*, 1848

« **6222**

Alas, it goes with me and so it will go with me and my age as it did with my father. I gave him much grief—then he died, and I inherited him. The age is doing its part to torment me—that alone torments the best energies out of me—then I will die—and the age will inherit me.

There will come a time when a Dane will be proud of me *qua* author —and therefore at bottom proud that they mistreated me.

IX A 203   *n.d.*, 1848

« **6223**

That little article[1915] was all right. The most decisive consequences will come later. But then perhaps the habit of thinking that I have become earnest will be broken and the collision will be all the more violent. Those who live esthetically here at home have no doubt given up reading me since I "have gone religious and do not write anything but sermon books." Now maybe they will peek into the next book, hoping to find something for them—and perhaps I will get the attention of one or two of them and help him to wound himself.

This explains why the more stoutly orthodox, Rudelbach,[1916] too, influence only a small circle, because they have no resources for nipping into the common life of the people. The orthodox write only for and talk only to the orthodox, and that is that. They pay no attention at all to the fact that a whole country calls itself and imagines itself to be Christian, and to the whole business of Christendom.

IX A 205   *n.d.*, 1848

« **6224**

To reduplicate [*reduplicere*] is to be what one says. Men are therefore better served by someone who does not speak in lofty strains but is what he says. I have never had the nerve to say that the world is evil. I make a distinction and say: Christianity teaches that the world is evil. But I do not dare say it, for that I am far from being sufficiently pure. But I have said: the world is mediocre, and my life expresses exactly that. But many a greenhorn of a clergyman stands and thunders that the world is evil—and what does his life in fact express. —I have never had the nerve to say that I would venture everything for Christianity. I still am not strong enough for that. I begin with something smaller. I know that I have ventured various things and I think and believe that God will educate me and teach me to venture more. But Mynster[1917] weeps at the thought that he is willing to sacrifice everything, that even if everyone falls away he will stand fast. God knows what he has ventured. One should never talk that way. The little bit of fever for an hour on Sunday only leaves more languor and indolence. A person should never talk about doing what he has not done. One may say: Christianity demands it, but since I am not tested in this way I dare say nothing of myself. I have always been independent, therefore I have always talked with great caution about the cares of livelihood. I am often reminded that I really have no experience, that here I speak as a poet.[1918]

O that there were truth in communication between man and man! One person defends Christianity, another attacks Christianity, and after all is said and done, when it comes to auditing their existences, neither one nor the other cares much about Christianity—perhaps it is their career.

For my part, I have a thorn in the flesh[1919] from my early years. If I had not had it, I would easily have been far gone in worldliness. But I cannot, even if I wanted to very much. So I have no meritorious- ness whatsoever, for what is meritorious about going along the right way when one is riding in a go-cart or about a horse's following the track when it is bridled with a sharp bit.

IX A 208   n.d., 1848

« **6225**

The evil principle in the world still is, as I have always maintained, the crowd—and blather. Nothing is as demoralizing as blathering gos- sip. When I think of all the cackling about my legs and trousers![1920] Here everybody agrees—their Excellencies and the shoemakers' ap- prentices, and the street sweeper who stops sweeping just to have a look, and the maids, and the shopkeepers, and the fine young ladies, and the young scholars, and so on. And if I had a friend to whom I had remarked, "This certainly is annoying," he would have answered, "It's nothing at all"—and then we would have walked arm in arm, but he— absorbed in looking at my legs and trousers.

IX A 209   n.d., 1848

« **6226**

Everything else I would have been able to endure, would have been able to endure the attacks of men far more easily (for where that is concerned I am adequately conscious of my superiority)—if my finan- cial future did not distress me.[1921]

IX A 211   n.d., 1848

« **6227**

I cannot repeat enough what I so frequently have said: I am a poet, but a very special kind, for I am by nature dialectical, and as a rule dialectic is precisely what is alien to the poet. Assigned from childhood to a life of torment that perhaps few can even conceive of, plunged into the deepest despondency, and from this despondency again into despair, I came to understand myself by writing. It was the ethical that inspired me—alas, me, who was painfully prevented from realizing it fully because I was unhappily set outside of the universally human. If I had been able to achieve it, I no doubt would have become terribly proud. Thus I related to Christianity again. It was my plan as soon as *Either/Or* was published to seek a call to a rural parish and sorrow over my sins. I could not suppress my creativity, I followed it—naturally it moved into the religious. Then I understood that my task was to do penance by serving the truth in such a way that it virtually became burdensome, humanly speaking, a thankless labor of sacrificing every-thing. That is how I serve Christianity—in all my wretchedness happy in the thought of the indescribable good God has done for me, far beyond my expectations.

The situation calls for Christianity to be presented once again without scaling down and accommodation, and since the situation is in Christendom: indirectly.[*] I must be kept out of it: the awakening will be all the greater. Men love direct communication because it makes for comfortableness, and communicators love it because it makes life less strenuous, since they always get a few to join them and thus escape the strain of solitariness.

Thus do I live, convinced that God will place the stamp of Govern-ance on my efforts—as soon as I am dead, not before—this is all con-nected with penitence and the magnitude of the plan. I live in this faith and hope to God to die in it. If he wants it otherwise, he will surely take care of that himself; I do not dare do otherwise.

IX A 213   *n.d.,*   1848

« **6228**

[*]*In margin:* but not as one who enthusiastically proclaims Chris-tianity but as a dialectician does it, in Socratically starving the life out of all the illusions in which Christendom has run aground. For it is not that Christianity is not proclaimed, but it is Christendom which has become sheer expertise in transforming it into illusion and thus evad-ing it.

IX A 214   *n.d.*

« **6229**

Yes, it had to be this way. I have not become a religious author; I was that: simultaneously with *Either/Or* appeared two upbuilding discourses—now after two years of writing only religious books there appears a little article about an actress.[1922]

Now there is a moment, a point of rest; by this step I have learned to know myself and very concretely.

So the publication must proceed (that is, of course I have more, I have finished what is to be used: (1) A Cycle of Ethical-Religious Essays, (2) The Sickness unto Death, (3) Come unto Me All You . . . . .), if I do not happen to die beforehand. My health is very poor, and the thought of dying has gotten the upperhand with me as I use this half year to sorrow for my sins and work further in the presentation of Christianity. Perhaps it is a despondent thought, perhaps also because I have become disinclined to make the finite decisions involved in publication—in any case I have now been prodded by it.

The next publication will be very decisive for my inner life. I always have held on to the remote possibility of seeking a pastoral call[1923] if the worst comes to worst financially.[1924] When I publish the last books, this may well be denied me even if I were to seek it, so the problem will not be as before, if I do dare to undertake it, but rather that it will not even be given to me.

This is one more heavy burden added to my inner suffering and outer mistreatment, but no doubt it will be beneficial so that I do not rush on but come to need God more and more. For the more God entrusts to me, the more burdens he lays upon me.

So the work goes on, given time, if I do not die before that, carrying the enormous voltage of reflection as I virtually do every moment—and yet trustful as a child in my inner being. O, I can never sufficiently thank God for what he has done and is doing for me, so indescribably much more than I had expected, he who helps one, step by step, if one honestly tells him the situation and then allows himself to be helped, helps one by taking away the burdens one may not be able to bear, helps one little by little to carry the burdens from which one once shrank. He who loves God is loved forth[1925] by God in such a way that this is an education. At all times there is a world of help possible, because for God everything is possible: if I have done something wrong, even though I honestly considered it, there is at all times a world of help, because for God everything is possible—how blessed that he is also love, that for the loved one everything is possible, and that he for whom everything is possible is love. And if I stumble, if sin wins a temporary victory over me, O, at all times for the honest penitent there is a world of help in the Atonement for all our sins with him our Savior and Redeemer.

To be surrounded everywhere by love in this way, O, who would not feel blessed in the midst of all his sufferings, which no doubt come so that one may not take salvation in vain but also to make one even more blissfully aware of salvation.

IX A 216 *n.d.,* 1848

« **6230**

How often this same thing has happened to me that now has happened to me again! I am submerged in the deepest suffering of despondency, so tied up in mental knots that I cannot get free, and since it is all connected with my personal life I suffer indescribably. And then after a short time, like an abscess it comes to a head and breaks—and inside is the loveliest and richest creativity—and the very thing I must use at the moment.

I have been experiencing much spiritual trial [*Anfægtelse*] thinking about how far one dares to withhold direct communication.[1926] O, there are perhaps few men who have any idea of the fear and trembling involved in having lightness enough to be able to be something else [in order] to act in the service of the truth—and then, then to sit in fear and trembling lest one do anyone harm, all the while understanding that this is the truest way to help another.[1927]

And then this is the very thing I will use in characterizing offense[1928] with respect to the God-man. My life is often readjusted in this way. I suffer as a man can suffer in indescribable despondency— as always it has something to do with my life—and then it is just what I need to use.

But while the suffering lasts, it is often extremely painful. Yet, believing, one learns little by little by the help of God to remain with God even in the moment of suffering, or to come back to God as quickly as possible when it seems as if he had abandoned one for a brief moment during one's suffering. It has to be this way, for if a person could have God right there with him during the suffering, he would not suffer at all.

IX A 217 *n.d.,* 1848

« **6231**

It was a good thing that I published that little article[1929] and came under tension. If I had not published it, I would have gone on living in a certain ambiguity about the future use of indirect communication.

Now it is clear to me that henceforth it will be indefensible to use it.

The awakening effect is rooted in God's having given me power to live as a riddle—but not any longer, lest the awakening effect end by being confusing.

The thing to do now is to take over unambiguously the maieutic structure of the past, to step forth definitely and directly in character, as one who has wanted and wants to serve the cause of Christianity.

If I had not published that little article, indirect communication would have continued to hover vaguely before me as a possibility and I would not have gotten the idea that I dare not use it.

I dare not say of myself that I have had a clear panorama of the whole plan of production from the outset; I must rather say, as I have continually acknowledged, that I myself have been brought up or educated and developed in the process of my work, that personally I have become committed more and more to Christianity than I was. Nevertheless this remains fixed, that I began with the deepest religious impression, alas, yes, I who when I began bore the tremendous responsibility of the life of another human being and understood it as God's punishment upon me.

IX A 218    n.d., 1848

### « 6232

The thought that I would soon die, the thought in which I have rested, has now been disturbed by the publication of that little article;[1930] it would disturb me if this were to be the last thing I publish.

But on the other hand the thought of dying now was only a gloomy notion—how good then that I published that little article. This very thing had to be probed—and the publication of the article served to do this.

IX A 219    n.d., 1848

### « 6233

*In margin of 6232* (IX A 219):
But in my case there is R. Nielsen[1931] as one who can provide explanation.

IX A 220    n.d.

### « 6234

But on the other hand, the understanding, reflection, is also a gift of God. What shall one do with it, how dispose of it if one is not to use it? And if one then uses it in fear and trembling not for his own advantage but to serve the truth, if one uses it that way in fear and trembling and furthermore believing that it still is God who determines the issue in its eternal significance, venturing in trust in him, and with unconditional obedience yielding to what he makes of it: is this not fear of God and serving God the way a man of reflection can, in a somewhat different way than the spontaneously immediate person, but perhaps more ardently. But if that is the case, does not a maieutic element enter into the relation to other men or to various other men. For the maieutic is really only the expression for a superiority between man and man. That it exists cannot be denied—but existence presses far more powerfully upon the superior one precisely because he is a maieutic (for he has the responsibility) than upon the other.

As far as I am concerned, there has been no lack of witness. All my upbuilding discourses are in fact in the form of direct communication. Consequently there can be a question only about this, something that has occupied me for a long time (already back in earlier journals[1932]): should I for once definitely explain myself as author, what I declare myself to be, how I from the beginning understand myself to be a religious author.

But now is not the time to do it, I am also somewhat strained at the moment. I need more physical recreation.

IX A 222     *n.d.*, 1848

« 6235

But if someone says: If a man is so devout in his inmost being, wills the good to that extent, then let him say it quite directly; if God wants him to be honored and esteemed for it, then let him accept it—this is the simplest.

But who is speaking? He who dares say of himself that by means of revelations God immediately determines for him what he must do —yes, such a person is able to act with unmitigated immediacy.

It holds true of everyone else that God does not immediately determine for him in that way; he must himself deliberate, choose; the relationship between God and him is still through reflection, be it more or less.

Now I am at that point. Reflection then discovers that to serve the good in truth also implies avoiding the appearance of doing it, in order to have no advantage from it. This is self-denial, which reflection devises, which immediacy (also that with relative reflection) actually does not know, for self-denial is a [yield of] reflection.

What do we do now? Is a man not just as responsible to God for the use of his reflection as for everything else; when he is able to understand something to be right, is he not obligated to God to do it, even if this self-denial leads out into the painfulness of sufferings, a weight of responsibility of which the immediate person has no intimation?

Or is reflection in itself evil? By no means. It is evil when it is selfish: either finite reflection which covets the advantages of finitude, or reflection selfishly terminating in the infatuation of the self with itself.

But it is quite another matter—and this is precisely the duty—when reflection humbles itself under the hand of God, submits everything to God (because everything it encompasses is still nothing to God), does not find pleasure in being concealed but, humbled before God, understands that God, any second he wants to, can annihilate reflection, by means of which one avoids that appearance of willing the good, while on the other hand reflection cannot act any other way than it does. And it is also quite another matter when reflection humbly confesses that it quite literally is brought up by God for whom it is more or less a child and whom it needs every moment. —But among men there is a difference in that one man has more reflection than another. But is reflection's fear of God therefore less because its language is somewhat different from what is commonly called the language of spontaneity or immediacy (we are not speaking here of one who has an exceptional call), because the language of reflection has one more extension?

The danger is that reflection wants to please itself and end in itself instead of ending in worship. But God-fearing reflection does not do this, it easily understands and with much fear and trembling that God is the Almighty who, any second he wants to, can draw the threads in such a way that a man's reflection cannot remain hidden. But reflection itself dares not do this, for it understands avoidance of the appearance of willing the good to be the true form of the good. On the other hand, the fact that God is along in this way prevents all self-complacency.

But then is there not still some meritoriousness in the relationship to God? How? Suppose now that a particular reflective estimate of reflection were—humanly speaking—superior: What then? Who is it who gabbles this standard for reflection into the God-relationship.

Before God even the most brilliant human wisdom is still nonsense, but it does not follow that a man, if he has this reflection, is supposed to stop using it; he must simply learn humility before God and then do what he unselfishly acknowledges to be the wisest thing, but without forgetting that when God looks at it, it is quite possible he will regard it as very stupid.

Furthermore, how could it become meritoriousness when reflection early and late presents itself before God and consequently again and again and a thousand times must learn to realize its inferiority? And finally, if reflection, which is in fact part of a man, consequently is in a sinner, must flee to grace every moment, simply because reflection itself grasps that before God it infinitely needs grace and mercy: how does it then become meritoriousness?

No, this is all in order. But on the other hand, it still stands that there must at some time be a definite and direct communication of how I understand myself or my authorship.

And at present I need recreation and rest.

IX A 223   *n.d.*, 1848

« **6236**

In many ways Christendom could benefit even from the experience (actually it is probably the only remedy) of killing someone for the sake of Christ just so as to get its eyes open to what Christianity is. But I do not have the physical strength for that, perhaps not the courage either, and finally, I am a dialectician who, it is true, can do a great deal when it comes to thinking and the interior life and can also stimulate an awakening but not in a situation which is not really appropriate for the dialectical.

IX A 225   *n.d.*, 1848

« **6237**

|  | **Instructive** |
| [*In margin:* | **Instructive** |
|  | **for** |
|  | **My Work as an Author**] |

In order to get men along, one may (out of consideration for what men are like these days and what one is himself) reduce the Christian requirements, reduce Christianity, make concessions in that direction. This way one gets to be the most earnest Christian himself and wins many such people over to Christianity. This does irreparable harm, and it is inconceivable that anyone has dared to take this responsibility upon himself, for it is winning men over to Christianity by doing away with Christianity.

One may, however, do the reverse and present Christianity without such deference, and then, lest one seem to be judging others, judge oneself as being so far behind that one can scarcely claim the name of Christian, yet deeply desires to become a Christian and strives to be that. This is the right way. In due time it may have a resemblance to the relation of Socratic ignorance to the glut of human knowledge.

And this is the point in the change from the time when Christianity was embattled with paganism; then to become a Christian was relatively quicker, in order to be used promptly as a warrior in the service of Christianity. But in Christendom there is a quite different kind of peacefulness for the inwardly directed struggle to become and be a Christian. Now becoming a Christian is such an enormous task (because this task has now been cast into reflection) that one scarcely dares call himself a Christian but says only that he aspires to be that, loves it, battling all day long for that alone.

Here is an analogy. First of all, in antiquity, came the wise men (σο-φοὶ.) Then came a time when no one dared call himself wise, when Pythagoras therefore invented the more modest name, φιλόσοφοι, and why? Because the task had become infinitely greater. Those σο-φοὶ were essentially the wise men of immediacy. Reflection's definition of what it really is to be wise began, quite properly, with first of all making the task so enormous that in relation to it there was only a relationship of reflection, and yet it was far more strenuous to become a φιλόσοφος than to be a σοφός.[1933]

With this interpretation, I believe I can defend going ahead and declaring that Christendom has abolished Christianity. It is neither my intention nor my task to insult or personally agitate and attack one single man. If so, I no longer understand myself. Here it is not a matter of getting the teacher dismissed etc. O, no. It is a purely ideal task: casting Christianity completely and wholly into reflection.[1934]

I may well drop under this task, but God be praised that he has let me see this and become essentially prepared for it already. However much I suffer, his goodness and love constantly overwhelm me. And when my head is weary of all this intense reflection, when my soul is weary of all the misunderstandings and insults and mistreatment by men, he grants me the ability to rest in the concise thought that he is love, that Christ died for me as well—and then I begin my work again and God is with me once again.

It is true that Christianity seems to be inimical to men, but that is because man, the natural man, is lazy and weak and sensate, and Christianity is the absolute. What the natural man understands by human love is nothing more nor less than this: Be lenient with yourself and with us. If a man will cling to God, repent of his sloth as soon as it asserts itself, and not conceitedly delude himself that God has to be remodeled after him but just the opposite, then Christianity is in fact love. But it certainly is not this wretched silliness that human sympathy and stupidity have made it out to be.

IX A 226  n.d.,  1848

« **6238** *N.B. N.B.*

Yes, it was a good thing to publish that little article. I began with *Either/Or* and two upbuilding discourses; now it ends, after the whole upbuilding series—with a little esthetic essay. It expresses: that it was the upbuilding, the religious, which should advance, and that now the esthetic has been traversed; they are inversely related, or it is something of an inverse confrontation, to show that the writer was not an esthetic author who in the course of time grew old and for that reason became religious.

But it is not really to my credit; it is Governance who has held me in rein with the help of an extreme depression and a troubled conscience.

But there still would have been something lacking if the little article had not come out, the illusion would have been established that it was I who essentially had changed over the years, and then a very important point in the whole productivity would have been lost.

It is true I have been educated by this writing, have developed more and more religiously—but in a decisive way I had experienced the pressures which turned me away from the world before I began writing *Either/Or.* Even then my only wish was to do, as decisively as possible, something good to compensate, if possible in another way, for what I personally had committed. That I have developed more and more religiously is seen in my now saying goodbye to the esthetic, because I do not know where I would find the time that I could, would, might fill up with work on esthetic writings.

My energies, that is, my physical energies, are declining; the state of my health varies terribly. I hardly see my way even to publishing the essentially decisive works I have ready ("A Cycle of Essays," "The Sickness unto Death," "Come All You Who Labor and Are Heavy Laden," "Blessed Is He Who Is Not Offended"[1936]). It is my opinion that here I am allowed to present Christianity once again and in such a way that a whole development can be based on it. The emphasis upon the situation of contemporaneity, that Christ's life is infinitely more important than the result; unrecognizability is the incognito in relation to the God-man; the impossibility of direct communication etc.—in my opinion all the articles contain such a wealth of ideas that again and again I cannot praise God enough for having granted me so infinitely much more than I had expected. And I am convinced that it will serve for the inward deepening of Christianity—for it has been taken in vain, made too mild, so that people have forgotten what grace is; for the more rigorous it is, the more grace becomes manifest as grace and not a sort of human sympathy.

Just one wish for this endeavor of mine if I happen to be separated from it. I live in the faith that God will place the accent of Governance on the life of an extremely unhappy, humanly understood, man who nevertheless by the help of God has felt indescribably blessed—but my wish is that now R. Nielsen[1937] might be relied on. The same cause which has cost me my health and an enormous strain, the same cause which as long as I live occasions only insults and humiliation, the same cause, as soon as I am dead, will be a triumphant affair!—if only he does not sell too cheap.

So I turn to the other side,[1938] forgetting all these many thoughts, mindful only of my sins and entrusting myself to the Atonement of Jesus Christ.

IX A 227    *n.d.*,    1848

« **6239**

The relationship to R. Nielsen[1939] in this matter[1940] has made me very uneasy in fear and trembling. I had given R. N. a direct communication. But on the other hand, to what extent R. N. had really understood me, to what extent he was capable of venturing something for the truth, is not at all clear to me. Here was the opportunity to make a test, and I felt that I owed it to the cause, to him, and to myself. Fortunately he was staying in the country. He has maintained constantly that he understood the esthetic to have been used as an enticement and an incognito. He has also maintained that he understood that it always depended entirely upon involvement. But whether that is entirely true he never did really put to the test. He scarcely understood the significance of *Either/Or* and of the two upbuilding discourses.[1941] Not until much later, especially when I became an exclusively religious author, and when I drew him to me did he understand it. Well, fine, that means he did not understand it in the form of reduplication; he understood it as a direct communication, that I explained to him that it was done that way. We must now find out; the question of what he thinks of this seemingly suddenly esthetic article about an actress must be put to him. Furthermore, the article contains a little allusion to Martensen.[1942] If R. Nielsen in some way wants to avoid holding a judgment in common with the persons concerned, that is up to him. In brief, for a moment he must stand entirely alone so that I can see where we are. It is something entirely different to talk afterwards about this reduplication, consequently in direct form, than to have to pass judgment at the moment oneself.

O, it is very strenuous to serve the truth in self-denial. I had given many people in many ways the impression that I was a devotional author—and then to disturb this impression myself.[1943] I did cherish R. Nielsen's having understood me as much as he did—and then to have to lose all this.

Yes, it is very strenuous to serve the truth in this way, constantly exposing oneself to misunderstanding—in order if possible to keep men awake, in order that the religious may not again become an indolent habit, and it might be like that for R. N. I must in fear and trembling let God judge between him and me, so that he does not attach himself too much to me but to God. But, humanly speaking, it is hard for me to work against myself in this way simply in order to serve the truth.

It is good that I did it. It has matured me exceedingly much. As so often happens, so here again the *summa summarum* of actuality becomes a triviality—but again and again I am educated by God and formed by possibility.[1944] Many a time it is almost mad, this disproportion—the corresponding actuality and the possibility by which I am educated.

And now the point has been reached for a direct communication and conception of my work as an author. What I have to say about the esthetic and myself as a religious author[1945] who has used it would otherwise have become to a certain degree an assertion—that little article is an entirely different kind of argument for testimony and confrontation.

Thus in a sense I am a poor child, in another sense a poor sinful man—but one whom God educates. And therefore I can never sufficiently thank God for all the indescribable good he has done for me.

O, R. N. scarcely dreams of how he has occupied me on this occasion, and why? Because he has become involved in my God-relation. That is infinitely crucial. In this way I am strong and weak. Actually there is not a man living with whom I would not dare to take this up, relying on my superiority over him—and any man, whoever he is, who comes in touch with my God-relationship, becomes a prodigious concern to me.

IX A 229   n.d.,  1848

« **6240**

That was a strong gust—but what I have learned!

IX A 230   n.d.,  1848

« **6241**

Mynster[1946] has let down Christianity in these two ways. (1) He has converted it from divine compassion and "the truth" to human sympathy, gentle, friendly, loving consolation for the suffering, which we all need since we all suffer a lot and even the happiest person does not know when he will suffer. (2) By making the relationship of the proclaimer purely human: the most talented shall be the most prominent, have the most honor and prestige—instead of the essentially Christian principle: the true servant of the Word must suffer, and the more true he is the more he will suffer.

IX A 236   n.d.,  1848

« **6242** *N.B. N.B.*

Strange, strange about that little article[1947]—that I was so close to being carried away and forgetting myself. When one is overstrained as I was, it is easy to forget momentarily the dialectical outline of a colossal structure such as my authorship. That is why Governance helps me.

Right now the totality is dialectically right. *Either/Or* and the two upbuilding discourses*[1948]—*Concluding Postscript*—for two years only upbuilding discourses and then a little article about an actress. The illusion that I happened to get older and for that reason became a decisively religious author has been made impossible. If I had died beforehand, then the writing I did those two years would have been made ambiguous and the totality unsteady.

In a certain sense, of course, my concern is superfluous when I consider the world of actuality in which I live—for as a matter of fact I have not found many dialecticians.

*In margin:* *Note. And these two discourses quite properly did not appear at the same time as *Either/Or* but a few months later—just as this little article now.

IX A 241    *n.d.,* 1848

« **6243**

Far be it from me to insist that I am a superlative Christian—among real Christians, but in relation to Christendom I still am ahead in that I know what it is all about. It may be assumed that most people have never gotten any impression of what Christianity is and therefore have not even detected the possibility of offense. What I know is not to my credit but is actually due to my father's upbringing.

There must once again be some single persons. It may have been quite all right for Luther[1949] to marry, but if he had been married he would never have become Luther. There must be single persons particularly in these times, for the evil that must be fought hides in the "crowd" and in prudence and in fear of men. Nowadays it is conceivable that a wife could even reconcile herself to the thought that her husband would risk sacrificing himself in battle with a great power— a king, for example, or an emperor. *Warum?* Because it appeals to her imagination. But to expose oneself to people's gossip, to be laughed to scorn by them, that is something from which a woman's nature shrinks. She perhaps would have the fortitude to think of him beheaded by the state—but mistreated by the rabble, laughed and scorned by the crowd—no, no, that she cannot endure. Here a woman will beseech and implore the man for God's sake not to expose himself to that; she will tearfully maintain that she cannot bear to see him mistreated that way, will beg for the sake of their children, so that they may not have to suffer the torture of having the father abused in this way, and of being the children of such a father.

And how entrenched this evil is in the daily press! And almost all journalists are unmarried persons—and is it not apparent, then, that there must be unmarried persons to serve the good.

IX A 243    *n.d.,* 1848

« **6244**

My martyrdom is a martyrdom of reflection, is the martyrdom which can manifest itself in the world after reflection has come to occupy the place of spontaneous, immediate passion. The painfulness consists in being bereft of all pathos: it is child's play, nothing. And therefore without question men shrink from no martyrdom more than from this.

IX A 251   n.d., 1848

### « 6245 *From on High He Will Draw All Men to Himself*[1950]

Seven Discourses at the Communion on Fridays

No. 1 lies finished in the tall cupboard.[1951]

No. 2 To draw is a compound concept (two factors), especially when it involves drawing a free being (who in fact is himself to *choose*).

Thus there is here: lowliness and elevation,

not *lowliness* alone or *elevation* alone.

No. 3 That you must first of all feel yourself drawn to him in his lowliness—otherwise it is a delusion because of elevation.

No. 4 Use this as a criterion for the Christianity that is in you: Do you feel drawn to him more by lowliness or by elevation.

—

—

No. 7 The prayer: Draw me to yourself;[1952] the different ways in which it can be said by various people.

Parents on behalf of the baby

The young man at the beginning of life

The sinner entering the path of conversion

The sufferer in his last hours

("Oft filled

With tears,

I now the last

Can see" etc.[1953]).

The elderly person—as an oldster. who happy in God

is separated from the world.

And we would wish the same for everybody.

IX A 255   n.d., 1848

### « 6246

R. Nielsen[1954] is a curious fellow. We had an agreement or understanding that there should be a relationship between us but that it by no means must become a coterie. But what is a coterie? It implies an advance agreement among the persons concerned about future action and a mutual judgment about what has been done, which is then broadcast. Consequently that must not be done. So I write a note to him, an altogether proper one, and yet—and this certainly was not unfortunate—yet done in such a way that it was sufficient to maintain the relationship while it became an alienating factor with respect to that little thing I wrote,[1955] something of such great importance to my whole authorship that I scarcely dared communicate anything about it directly right away. Had I done so, I would have lost myself, become saddled with an inconsistency which I perhaps never would have lived down. But R. N. was offended—and then chooses not to answer at all, so I actually had to believe that he had not received the letter.

And he was the one who almost imploringly wanted to make me an apostle!—something I quite properly would have nothing to do with. But it did not help. On the other hand, a little precautionary measure, then everything becomes clear. God knows whether it was his idea that I should be the apostle and he disciple No. 1. God knows if he has developed so profoundly that he actually could be in earnest about suffering in the world.

IX A 258   *n.d.*, 1848

« **6247**

Nothing can be done for her.[1956] God knows how willingly I would, both for my sake, and if she so desires, for hers.

She would be completely unhinged if she found out the real truth of the matter. The keystone of her marriage is and will continue to be that I am a villain or at least someone who wanted to be important in the world.

I began thinking of her situation again during those incredible days (especially Thursday or the night from Wednesday to Thursday [*changed from:* Thursday to Friday] when I had not prayed for R. N.[1957] because I had been a little impatient with him but felt it a terrible sin against him and promptly took him into my God-relationship again) Thursday, Friday, Saturday, August 24, 25, 26. On Saturday (August 26) I drove to Fredensborg. An unexplainable presentiment took me there, I was so happy and almost sure of meeting the family there—and that an attempt must be made. I arrived there. No one was there. I took my usual walk, talked with Thomas or whatever his name is, the solitary sailor, who remarked that it was the first time I had been in Fredriksborg this year, which was true. I asked him casually *en passant* if Councillor Olsen[1958] had been there much this year. He answered: No, only once, on First Easter Day.

Then I went up to Kold's[1959] again, sat and ate—a man walked by the window: it was Councillor Olsen.

He is the only one I safely dare become reconciled with, for here there is no danger as with the girl. I was about to leave, but I walked just once down Skipper-Alleen with the purpose of going there just this once and then, if we did not meet, giving up the attempt on that occasion. But sure enough, I do meet him. I go up to him and say: Good day, Councillor Olsen, let us talk together. He took off his hat and greeted me but then brushed me aside and said: I do not wish to speak with you. O, there were tears in his eyes, and he spoke these words with tormented feeling. I went toward him, but the man started to run so fast that, even if I had wanted to, it would have been impossible to catch up with him. But I did manage to say this much, and he heard it: Now I make you responsible for not listening to me.

For the time being nothing more can be done.

IX A 262    n.d., 1848

« 6248

Now I see my way to writing a short and an as earnest as possible explanation of my previous authorship,[1960] which is necessary before a transition to the next. And why do I see my way to doing it now? Simply because I am now clear about the relation between direct communication and decisive Christianity. For this very reason I now am able to illuminate and interpret indirect communication. Earlier I had been continually unclear. For one always must be over and beyond what he wants to interpret. Previously I had been uncertain about the whole thing, because I was not myself clear and basically maintained the connection with indirect communication. This relation would have altogether ruined the entire presentation.

IX A 265    n.d., 1848

« 6249

The Friday sermon[1961] I gave today was one I had previously worked out in its essential features. I find this better than to do it at the last minute under the stimulus of creativity. It is so easy then for something esthetic to creep in.

It originally was scheduled to be given January 14, 1848, but there was no communion either in Frue or in Helliggeistes Kirke.

IX A 271    n.d., 1848

« **6250**

How willingly I would do everything for her, both for her sake and for mine, but it cannot be done; I dare not, I fear her unreckoning passionateness if she gets the least thing to go on! I actually am guaranteeing her marriage; God knows what a terrible strain it is. And what I have endured I best perceive from the indirect indication that for the first time now, after seven years, I dare confide on paper my thoughts about her.

[*In margin:* See journal NB⁵, p. 65 bottom (i.e., IX A 66)].

Steps were taken at the time to break the engagement, and in a manner as humiliating to me and as sympathetic to her as possible; so it was easy enough to see that it was despondency. I did everything to spare her the slightest humiliation; thus I was the superior one etc. Here lies her guilt, her only guilt, for apart from this I know best how innocently she has suffered, how frightfully, I who have had to suffer as the cause of it. But here lie her guilt and essentially her self-love. She took my despondency in vain—she thought it was possible to alarm me into giving in. Being somewhat imaginative, also, perhaps not essentially, but now that she was distraught, she assured me that if I could convince her that I was a villain she would submit readily to the whole thing. That is, she had some idea of my despondency. She ought to have given in at that time, accepted her suffering, accepted separation from me in such a moderate way, because I was despondent. She overstepped the bounds of what one person has a right to do to another, she troubled me terribly, she did not consider that behind my enormous despondency lay an equally great resiliency. It emerged. The scale she herself evoked; it had been set.

The trouble is that she was especially proud of her relationship to me. In that connection a little explanation now perhaps would ease and enhance her marriage.¹⁹⁶² God knows how willingly I would have done it; what a constant torment it has been to me that she should be humiliated because of me, even though I did everything to prevent it. But nevertheless the guilt is mine, for my guilt toward her is so great that it swallows her guilt toward me.

As soon as I die (which I continually expect to happen soon), she of course will be reinstated in her rights. Everything is ready for that. Her name will belong to my authorship and be remembered as long as I am remembered. But while I am alive—if she has not changed much—she is a very dangerous person.

For me it was an indescribable relief, for the actual situation was never too burdensome for me, but it has been dreadful to keep her in possibility that way. But that is the condition for her marriage.

IX A 276   *n.d.*, 1848

« **6251**

No one wants to learn anything; there are thousands and thousands who want to be flattered.

IX A 281   *n.d.*, 1848

« **6252**

I could almost be tempted to ask: Why was I brought up in Christianity? Except for that, it would never have occurred to me to establish such a standard for my life. Humanly speaking, how would it cross any man's mind that his life destiny was to be sacrificed? I would have used my copious endowment of sagacity—and then I would have come to lead the very opposite kind of life.

It does not help to speak with someone. For the majority would see me in terms of my sagacity and then barely understand that—i.e., how cleverly I could have acted. But not the next—my not daring to use the least bit of this sagacity.

A thoroughly Christian Christian I have not seen. The highest examples I have seen are some few of what I call human-lovable Christianity. But here the authentic qualification of the absolute is missing. It is more a quiet human kindliness, sympathetic concern, and the like, which of course was also found in paganism.

The Christian requirement of sacrifice stops at no point. One gives up everything, unconditionally everything, chooses God, holds to God. Enormous task, how rarely, how rarely does it happen. And yet Christianity does not stop here. I seem to hear such a man say: Well, now, I choose God—and forsake everything. But then—then God can surely be depended upon, then he will certainly not abandon me. Here we have the ultimate. The prototype teaches that Christian suffering also includes God's abandoning you right in your heaviest suffering. Frightful! And this is the teaching those job-holding men call the mild doctrine of truth.

A Christian pastor I have never known. The whole battle of orthodoxy and heterodoxy has no useful purpose whatsoever.

But now as to my situation. Without being so bold as to maintain that I am a fairly perfect Christian, I have existentially striven to express something of what is distinctive to Christianity, that there is some absolute—and I am regarded as mad, proud, selfish. Most ridiculous of all is that the setting is in Christendom and that there are 1,000 preachers, approximately 2 million Christians, and they all flatly regard me as mad.

IX A 283   *n.d.,*   1848

« **6253**

On this point I am stymied. If I open myself to others, then, *ipso facto,* my life is less strenuous. Humanly speaking (that is, in the sense of human self-love), men have a right to demand this of me, but over against God do I have the right to do it? I can see with half an eye that, far out as I myself am, I gain no one; for me to open myself will mean that I get dragged under. On the other hand my progress forward is certain destruction. But is there, then, not an absolute? Here it is again. The moment I lay my life out in relativities, I am understood, and in a deeper sense my cause is lost—humanly speaking it is then won.

The only true way of expressing that there is an absolute is to become its martyr or a martyr to it. It is this way even in whole-hearted erotic love.

The human race is so far from the ideal that in a few generations there is occasionally one who more or less expresses that there is an absolute, and he is trampled upon by the generation.

IX A 285   *n.d.,*   1848

« **6254**

This is how I actually am treated in Copenhagen. I am regarded as a kind of Englishman, a half-mad eccentric, with whom we jolly well all, society people and street urchins, think to have their fun. My literary activity, that enormous productivity, so intense that it seems it must move stones, portions of which not a single contemporary is able to compete with, to say nothing of its totality, that literary activity is regarded as a kind of hobby *ad modum*[1963] fishing and such. Those who are able to produce something themselves envy me and are silent—the others understand nothing. I do not receive the support of one single word in the form of reviews and the like. Minor prophets plunder me in silly lectures at meetings and the like but do not mention my name. No, that is unnecessary.

Consequently that hobby is regarded as a lark. The game is really to see if they can drive me crazy—that would be great sport—or get me to decamp, that would be great sport.

Behind all this is a tremendous impression of what I am, of the extraordinariness granted to me, but the envy of a market town fosters the desire that my having such advantages be, if possible, a greater torment than being the most wretched of all; and everything is left up to the capriciousness of the market town.

A somewhat more lenient version is this. I am supposed to be a genius, but such an introverted genius that I can see and hear nothing. All this sport is something the market town is supposed to share in common (society people in common with the commoners and they with the street urchins), something which consequently is nothing.

Well, let it be! When I was a child I was taught that they spit upon Christ.[1964] Now, I am a poor insignificant man and a sinner and no doubt will get off more leniently. This, you see, is the Christian syllogism and not the preacher-nonsense which says: Be a nice, good, altruistic man and men will love you—for Christ, who was love, was loved by men.

Generally speaking, there no doubt will be no one in eternity who will be judged as severely as those professional pastors. From the point of view of eternity, they are what public prostitutes are in temporality.

IX A 288    *n.d.*, 1848

« **6255**

. . . That it was an age of disintegration,[1965] an esthetic, enervating disintegration, and therefore, before there could be any question of even introducing the religious, the ethically strengthening, *Either/Or* had to precede, so that *maieutically* a beginning might be made with esthetic writings (the pseudonyms) in order if possible to get hold of men, which after all comes first before there can even be any thought of moving them over into the religious, and in this way it was also assured that in the sense of reflection the religious would be employed with dialectical care. That it was an age of disintegration—that "the System" itself signified, not as the systematicians were pleased to understand, that the consummation had been achieved, but that "the System" itself, as an overripe fruit, pointed to decline. That it was an age of disintegration—and consequently not as the politicians were pleased to think, that "government" was the evil, an assumption which would have been a curious contradiction from the standpoint of "the single individual," but that "the crowd," "the public," etc. were the

evil,* which corresponds consistently with "the single individual."
That it was a time of disintegration—that it was not nationalities that
should be advanced but Christianity† in relation to "the single individual," that no particular group or class could be the issue but "the
crowd," and the task: to change it into single individuals. That it was
an age of disintegration—all existence as if in the clutch of a dizziness
induced and in intensification fed by wanting continually to aid the
movement with the momentary, that is, with finite cleverness and with
the numerical, which simply feeds the sickness, a dizziness induced and
fed by the impatience of the moment demanding to see effects at the
moment, whereas what was required was the very opposite: the eternal
and "the single individual." That it was an age of disintegration—a
crucial age, that history was about to take a turn, that the problem was
to have heard correctly, to be in happy rapport with the times and the
turn which was supposed to be made: that it was the ethical, the
ethical-religious, that should be advanced, but that above all the problem was to watch, with what one could call the self-love of the true or
zeal for itself and its heterogeneity, lest the ethical again get garbled
up with the old,‡ which meant particularly that it hinged *not on teaching*
the ethical but on accentuating the ethical ethically, on again mounting
the qualitative force of the ethical—in qualitative contrast to the system, informational instruction, and everything pertaining to them—
and at the same time to support it with personal existing, which,
however, at the time meant to hide in the circumspect incognito of an
idea. This, all of which is implied in "the single individual" as well as
in the use made of this category, places the writing into another
sphere, for "that single individual" will become an historical *point de
vue*.

The author does not call himself a "witness to the truth" because
of this, even though in view of the fact that the whole authorship,

*In margin:* *Note. And now in 1848 it presumably is well understood, now when the
one thing needful, indispensable, can be named in a single word: government.

*In margin:* †Note. Even now in 1848, up to the present time, it does indeed look as if
everything were politics, but it will no doubt appear that the catastrophe corresponds
inversely [*changed from:* the future will correspond inversely] to the Reformation: then
everything appeared to be a religious movement and became politics; now everything
appears to be politics but will become a religious movement.

*In margin:* ‡Note. This is expressed (just to mention one pseudonym), but of course
in character, therefore humorously, in Johannes Climacus's standing motto:[1966] 'Better
well hung than ill wed,' which he himself comments upon, saying: Better well hung than
by an unfortunate marriage to be brought into systematic affinities with all the world.

understood as a totality, is as one thought, the thought of the religious, it could be said without falsity of the author that he *qua* author "in purity of heart has willed only one thing."[1967] By such [*changed from:* "witness to the truth"] is not meant everyone who says something true; no, thanks, then we would have enough witnesses for the truth. No, in a "witness to the truth" consideration must be given ethically to personal existing in relation to what is said, whether the personal existing expresses what is said—a consideration which, it is altogether true, the systematic and informational instruction and the characterlessness of the age have altogether wrongly abolished. The author's life has indeed expressed rather accurately that which was ethically accentuated: to be an individual [*changed from:* "the single individual"]; he has stood alone,[1968] completely alone, whereas in the world around almost everything was the setting up, setting down, and setting aside of committees. He has stood completely alone and labored alone on such a scale that he, the solitary person, was like an epigram over his contemporaries, whose activity in large part consisted in the setting up, setting down, and setting aside of committees. . . .

IX B 63:7   *n.d.*, 1848

« **6256**

What lay at the root of the catastrophe will then become apparent, that it is the opposite of the Reformation, which appeared to be a religious movement and proved to be political;[1969] now everything appears to be politics but will turn out to be a religious movement. And when this becomes apparent, then (whether or not this is considered necessary in time) it will also become apparent that what is needed is "pastors." *There* is where the battle will be; if there is to be genuine victory, it must come about through pastors. Neither soldiers nor police nor diplomats nor political planners will achieve it. "Pastors" are what will be needed: pastors who, possessing the desirable scientific-scholarly education, yet in contrast to the scientific game of counting, are practiced in what could be called spiritual guerrilla skirmishing, in doing battle not so much with scientific-scholarly attacks and problems as with the human passions; pastors who are able to split up "the crowd" and turn it into individuals; pastors who would not set up too great study-requirements and would want nothing less than to dominate; pastors who, if possible, are powerfully eloquent but are no less eloquent in keeping silent and enduring without complaining; pastors who, if possible, know the human heart but are no less learned in refraining from judging and denouncing; pastors who know how to use authority through the art of making sacrifices; pastors who are disciplined and educated and are prepared to obey and to suffer, so they would be able to mitigate, admonish, build up, move, but also to constrain—not with force, anything but, no, constrain by their own obedience, and above all patiently, to suffer all the rudeness of the sick without being disturbed, no more than the physician is disturbed by the patient's abusive language and kicks during the operation. For the generation is sick, spiritually, sick unto death. But just as a patient, when he himself is supposed to point to the area where he suffers, frequently points to an utterly wrong place, so also with the generation. It believes—yes, it is both laughable and lamentable—it believes that a new administration will help. But as a matter of fact it is the eternal that is needed. Some stronger evidence is needed than socialism's belief* that God is the evil, and so it says itself, for the demonic always contains the truth in reverse. It is eternity that is needed, and the physician must—even if in another sense yet as once was the custom in the past—prescribe: the pastor.

This is my view or conception of the age, the view of an insignificant man who has something of the poet in him but otherwise is a philosopher, but—yes, how often I have repeated what to me is so important and crucial, my first declaration about myself—"without authority."[1970]

*In margin:* *that frightful sigh (from hell) uttered by socialism: God is the evil; just get rid of him and we will get relief. Thus it says what it needs itself.

$X^6$ B 40   *n.d.,*  1848(?)–49

« **6257**

"Christian" *pastors*[1971] are what will be needed, also with respect to one of the greatest of all dangers, which is far closer than one possibly can believe—namely, that when the catastrophe spreads and turns into a religious movement (and the strength in *communism* obviously is the same ingredient demonically potential in religiousness, even Christian religiousness), then, like mushrooms after a rain, demonically tainted characters will appear who soon will presumptuously make themselves apostles on a par with "the apostles," a few also assuming the task of perfecting Christianity, soon even becoming religious founders themselves, inventors of a new religion which will gratify the times and the world in a completely different way from Christianity's "asceticism." The age for scientific-scholarly attacks on Christianity was already over before 1848, we were already far into the age of attacks of passion, attacks by the offended. But these are not the most dangerous; the most dangerous comes when the demonics themselves become apostles—something like thieves passing themselves off as policemen—even founders of religion, who will get a dreadful foothold in an age which is critical in such a way that from the standpoint of the eternal it is eternally true to say of it: What is needed is religiousness—that is, true religiousness; whereas from the standpoint of the demonic, the same age says about itself: It is religiousness we need—namely demonic religiousness.

This is my view or conception of the age, the view of an insignificant man who has something of the poet in him but otherwise is a kind of philosopher, but—yes, how often I have repeated and emphasized what is so important and crucial, my first declaration about myself—"without authority."[1972] S.K.

X⁶ B 41    n.d., 1848

« 6258

I am still very exhausted, but I have also almost reached the goal. The work *The Point of View for My Work as an Author*[1973] is now as good as finished. Relying upon what I have done in existential action in the past to justify my productivity, in the recent period I have been only a writer. My mind and spirit are strong enough, but regrettably all too strong for my body. In one sense it is my mind and spirit that help me to endure such poor health; in another sense it is my mind and spirit that overwhelm my body.

IX A 293    n.d., 1848

« 6259

From an appendix (4) to "The Point of View for My Work as an Author," which was not used.[1974]

My heart has expanded, not as if it ever had been constricted in my breast, but the inner intensity which has been my life and which I believed would be my death has gotten a breathing spell, the dialectical bond has been broken, I dare to speak openly.[1975]

I love my fatherland—it is true that I have not gone to war—but I believe I have served it in another way and I believe I am right in thinking that Denmark must seek its strength in the spirit and the mind. I am proud of my mother tongue whose secrets I know, the language I treat more lovingly than a flutist his instrument.

I can honestly say that I have loved every man; no matter how many have been my enemies, I have had no enemy. As I remarked in the book,[1976] I have never known thoughts and ideas not to present themselves. But I have known something else. If, on my way home after a walk—during which I would meditate and gather ideas—overwhelmed with ideas ready to be written down and in a sense so weak that I could scarcely walk (one who has had anything to do with ideas knows what this means)—then if a poor man on the way spoke to me and in my enthusiasm over the ideas I had no time to speak with him—when I got home all the ideas would be gone, and I would sink into the most dreadful spiritual tribulation at the thought that God could do to me what I had done to that man. But if I took time to talk with the poor man and listened to him, things never went that way. When I arrived at home everything was there and ready. All assurances are disdained these days—and yet the best assurance that a man loves men is and will be that God is as close as life to him, which is the case with me almost every moment.

IX A 298   *n.d.*, 1848

« **6260**

Now it seems as if I am going to be on good terms with the exclusive people, partly because they themselves have become polemical; now they are or think that they are in the minority, and I, well, if my genius can be said to be connected with anything, it is with being in the minority.

IX A 307   *n.d.*, 1848

« **6261**

If I were not personally a penitent there might have been moments when I would have been offended by Christianity, but I dare not breathe a word about it. And afterwards I am reconciled to what otherwise would have offended me. This is how I understand Peter's words:[1977] To whom shall we go. Usually these words are declaimed sentimentally by the clergy. I understand them to mean that the consciousness of sin binds a man to Christianity.

That is how I understand myself as well. But is it not a peculiar explanation to say that I am now so conscious of myself as a sinner that I dare do nothing else? To a certain extent, yes, for I make no secret of the fact that I have sinned in a way different from what is usually meant by being a sinner. But on the other hand I have perhaps also had the prerequisites for discovering and understanding offense in a quite different way. And since it is God who binds each and every individual to God through the consciousness of sin, it must no doubt be assumed that he determines the collisions for each and every individual. In this way, it is still the consciousness of sin which binds men to Christianity. Everyone not bound in this way is not Christianly bound; all that sentimental talk about its being deep and elevated and a friend etc. is rubbish. The correlations are: if I were not personally conscious of being a sinner, I would have to be offended with Christianity. The consciousness of sin shuts my mouth so that in spite of the possibility of offense I choose to believe. The relationship has to be that penetrating. Christianity repels in order to attract. But Christianity has been diluted, the aspect of Christianity which, so to speak, turns a man upside down, has been diluted, and therefore the impetus of sin-consciousness is not needed to drive one into it—that is, it is all sentimentality.

IX A 310    *n.d.*, 1848

« **6262**

They say that a person who is going to console others must himself have suffered. Fine, that is the case with me. I perhaps have suffered so much that I am more likely to dismay others. But, after all, I can keep that to myself and then perhaps my consoling will become all the more inward, fed by this hidden fire. As a matter of fact, I do know how to console; as my physician says, no one he knows is as capable of it as I am. And so I do it. I also know that it will not miscarry. The sufferer will feel relieved and will take a great liking to me. But the trouble is that I also know that this is not Christianity. I take it from another flask. It is poetry with an invigorating addition of the ethical. But Christianity it is not. As a rule Christianity is dismaying rather than consoling. Even I, who have been brought so far out, can scarcely bear Christianity's consolation—and then the average man! But if I am a Christian clergyman, I am obliged to bring consolation in the Christian way. The question remains whether I would have the courage to be Christianly cruel. The thing is: momentary relief is always human sympathy. A whimpering mother who coddles her child has the most sympathy, but we find fault with that. She has the most sympathy, always helps at the moment, therefore cannot educate. Then come the dimensions of the universally human. But Christianity goes further qualitatively and educates with the help of eternity and to eternity. Therein lies the dismaying aspect of Christianity's help, for when a person suffers, Christianity's help begins by turning the whole temporal life into suffering.

The more quickly help comes, the more inferior and meaningless the education; for this very reason Christianity denies all temporal help —in order to educate for eternity. But to be denied all temporal help, to proclaim all temporal life to be destined for suffering, is of course worse than every particular suffering in temporal life or makes it worse for the sufferer.

Now, do I have (as a human being) the right to do this to another man, even if I could be Christianly cruel? On the other hand, if I am a Christian pastor, I must be that.

When it comes to children, we adults deny that the child is right when it complains because help has been denied momentarily so that the child will be educated and learn to help himself. But we adults are related to eternity (as a child to the adult). When we ourselves are the adults (for eternity, after all, is not visible among us as a father or teacher to the child), we apply our own criteria. But this means essentially the abolition of Christianity.

It is certainly true that I have never seen a single man who really applied the Christian criterion—but we are all Christians!

IX A 312   n.d., 1848

« **6263**

Only patience and faith! However distressing it is to live as I am living right now, completely superfluous, seemingly only for the amusement of the rabble, for the refreshment of envy, and for the strengthening of mediocrity—it comes again, just that will serve to give me and my cause a better recommendation in the future than the bravos of the critics.

This is why I in a sense feel alien among my contemporaries, for I understand that when all is said and done, even if they were to make a big fuss over me, my cause would be ruined.

IX A 321   n.d., 1848

« **6264**

It is curious that today in Arndt's *True Christianity*[1978] I read a line which is just like my description of the confusion of our age, but the author probably did not mean the same by it as I.

It reads (p. 225): *Wenn anders das Haupt und nicht die Füsse im Lande regieren.*[1979] It reminds me very much of the postscript[1980] to the second essay in *A Cycle of Ethical-Religious Essays.*

IX A 338    n.d., 1848

### « 6265

Counsel, guidance I almost never find. The few outstanding religious individualities usually are rooted in spontaneity or immediacy. A person like that is spontaneously enthusiastic; he is convinced that he will soon be victorious, so (—spontaneously—*) convinced of the rightness of his cause that he has the fixed idea that if he merely gets it publicized it will be accepted with open arms. In this kind of enthusiasm he talks to the others, he sweeps them off their feet, since spontaneous enthusiasm always charms. So they storm ahead—and now comes the opposition. Perhaps the leader does weather the battle gallantly, but from him I learn nothing of what occupies me—the beginning.

For in reflection everything looks different. In reflection a person understands in advance that the danger must come, knows its consequences exactly. He sees it every moment and step by step. On the other hand, he cannot sweep anyone off his feet, for if anyone wants to attach himself to the reflective person, he must above all make that one aware of the danger, thus warn, repel—instead of charm him.

*In margin:* *Note. For in reflection he can also be convinced of the rightness of his cause without necessarily being ignorant of the nature of the world or lacking an essential view of life—and truth.

IX A 343    n.d., 1848

### « 6266

But whatever happens or however it turns out, I hope to God that my daily prayer for a long time now will be granted, that my last words when I for the last time have repented my sin and received the gracious forgiveness of my sins, consequently my last words as a dying man, will be words of gratitude for the indescribable good he has done for me, far more than I ever expected. And this is eternally true. For what I am suffering either has its basis in my sin and my sins or it is what it is simply because God has done so extraordinarily much for me. The consequence of that in this world can be nothing else but to suffer. By this it becomes altogether sure and true that God has done the extraordinary for a person.

IX A 371   n.d., 1848

« **6267**

Dear Professor,[1981]

Please permit me to thank you once again for my carpenter.[1982] Once more he is what he had the honor to be for twenty-five years, a worker with heart and soul, a worker who, although he thinks while he works, does not make the mistake of wanting to make thinking his work. For this reason I hope that I in turn am not making a mistake in thinking him essentially cured. I have allowed him to go on living with me, because I felt it would distress him very much to have to move now.

Thus everything is in order. But indeed—as you yourself said when I last had the pleasure of speaking with you, which I appreciated and appreciate as added proof of your kindness to me—indeed, you will please remember, if that time ever comes and he has a relapse: then I am to inform you at once, and then he will be admitted to the hospital as quickly as possible.

In conclusion, please allow me to add special emphasis here to that "Your" with which I would sign every letter to you,

Your gratefully obliged

S. Kierkegaard

*Letters*, no. 192   [1848]

« **6268**

When I sold the house[1983] I considered putting an end to writing, traveling for two years abroad, and then coming home and becoming a pastor. I had, in fact, made about 2,200 rix-dollars on the place.

But then it dawned on me: But why do you want to travel abroad? To interrupt your work and get some recreation. But you know from experience that you are never so productive as when you are abroad in the extreme isolation in which you live there, so when you return from your travels in two years you will have a staggering amount of manuscripts.

So I rented rooms,[1984] an apartment which had tempted me in a very curious way for a long time and which I frequently had told myself was the only one I could like.

This plan to travel for two years was no doubt just a whim. The fact is that I had a complete book[1985] ready to publish, and, as I said, by going abroad the sluice gates of my productivity would be opened.

But it was the thought of traveling for two years that prompted me to take the cash I got from the sale of the house, which in general I had decided to leave alone, and buy government bonds—the most stupid thing I ever did and which I probably should regard as a lesson, for I have now lost about 700 rix-dollars on them. [*In margin:* For the rest of the cash I later bought shares, on which I perhaps have not lost anything.]

So I rented that apartment, printed *Christian Discourses,* and sat in the middle of the proof-reading when the whole confusion started— Anders[1986] was taken from me: and it was fortunate that I had the apartment.

I moved in. In one sense I suffered greatly because the apartment proved to be unsuitable. But on the other hand here, too, Governance came to my assistance and turned my mistake into a good. If anything helps me to be less productive and diminish my momentum and in general limit me, it is finite anxieties and inconveniences.

In that residence, however, I have written some of the best things I have written;[1987] but in this connection I have had constant occasion to practice pianissimo the idea of halting my productivity or in any case to pay more attention to my livelihood. It would never have happened abroad, where, far from all distractions, less despondent, I would have plunged into the most enormous productivity.

Last summer I drew R. Nielsen[1988] a little closer to me; that means that I reduce my writing and yet do little to put an end to my endeavor.

If I could travel without becoming productive, travel and travel for some time, it perhaps would be a good thing. But a prolonged sojourn in one place makes me more productive than ever. I have been much better off learning a little by not having Anders and other such conveniences which perhaps encourage the writing too much.

I wanted to travel for two years; among other things, I was also sick and tired of this whole mess[1989] in Copenhagen. But it would not help. I am well suited to seeing things like this through, if only I stay patiently where I am.

But the economic situation in these confused times has been a drain on me in various ways. It is no doubt good that I became aware of it in time. It also helps burn out whatever selfishness there is in me and my work: for my position as author is in fact becoming serious enough.

IX A 375   *n.d.*, 1848

« **6269**

"A little while" and "At last"![1990]
A Discourse

That these words say one and the same thing; it depends entirely on how close the eternal is. If it is very close, then all our suffering and unhappiness and wretchedness is "a little while"; if it is far away, we sigh "at last."

IX A 379   *n.d.*, 1848

« **6270**

They preach about the rich man and Lazarus.[1991] They preach that one should be compassionate. But I almost never find presented the double danger involved here. On the other hand, be genuinely compassionate, have money to give to the poor, and not only that but truly have a heart in your bosom, be kind to every poor and needy person —and this certainly is required to be truly compassionate—either so unhappy deep down inside of you or so sad that earthly honor and status do not tempt you and consequently you are willing to be greeted by the poor and you respond in a friendly manner (not aloofly, in the third person *en passant,* but affectionately as one greets an acquaintance), be willing to talk with the poor on the street, be willing to let yourself be addressed by him on the street: in short, be in truth tender and compassionate—and you will see that if you enjoy any kind of reputation for being out of the ordinary or unusual you will be laughed at and ridiculed for doing it; and if you enjoy this out-of-the-ordinary reputation, you will be regarded as extremely strange and your behavior very peculiar. The frivolous majority will grin every time they see you standing in conversation with a poor man, and if this becomes known about you perhaps also through the press (which, after all, works for the well-being of the simple classes!), it perhaps will end with the rabble insulting you, the shrewd fellows who aspire to finite goals will consider you mad, not so much because you give money this way as because you are losing and diminishing your reputation, since, of course, poor people do not always have tact enough to avoid placing you in peculiar situations. And the exclusive ones, who have a bit more understanding, swiftly take in the awkwardness of the situation, quickly avert their eyes so as not to see you, and with the full marching equipment of their worldly honor and status pass by—an object of the startled crowd's deference. A man of such distinction would be able to weep on Sunday as he preaches about compassion. He will rapturously declare that Christianity does not establish a separation as if we should be holy only on Sunday; no, Christianity should penetrate the whole of life, the everyday as well. And if tomorrow you were to consult him about what you should do in a particular case or other, well, let us not speak about the advice he would give. And he will not blush when he does it, for he is no hypocrite—he is merely a sentimental blabber who on Sunday piously entertains himself and the congregation with the diversion of these exalted feelings, while on Monday it quite literally never occurs to him to think of what he himself said yesterday.

This I have seen; and however disgusted I sometimes get at life when I think of this, one thing comforts me: by seeing this and at such close hand I learn to understand Christianity. Fortunately something like this has happened to me many times: I have experienced something, a relationship, and have myself mused and pondered on it, and not until later have I thought—but that, indeed, is the teaching of Christianity. Most people do the opposite, they lecture on Christian doctrine and do not perceive how they themselves act or how things go in the world. It is different with me, if I do say it myself. I am eminently attentive to how things go in the world. I experience now that things do go in a certain way—and only then do I come to consider: Yes, but that is precisely the shape of things that Christianity teaches.

IX A 381    n.d., 1848

« **6271** *N.B.*

Perhaps it would be best to publish all the last four books ("The Sickness unto Death,"[1992] "Come to Me,"[1993] "Blessed Is He Who Is Not Offended,"[1994] "Armed Neutrality"[1995]) in one volume under the title

*Collected Works of Fulfilment*
[*Fuldendelsens samtlige Værker**]

with "The Sickness unto Death" as Part I. The second part would be called "An Attempt to Introduce Christianity into Christendom" and below: poetic—without authority.[1996] "Come to Me" and "Blessed Is He Who Is Not Offended" would be entered as subdivisions. Perhaps there could also be a third part,[1997] which I am now writing,† but in that case Discourse No. 1 would be a kind of introduction which is not counted.

And then it should be concluded.

*In margin:* *Perhaps rather: *Collected Works of Consummation* and the volume should be quarto.

†"From on High He Will Draw All Men unto Himself." The three: "Come to Me," "Blessed Is He Who Is Not Offended," and "From on High," would then have a separate title-page: poetic attempt—without authority.

IX A 390    n.d.,  1848

### « 6272

If I lived in a rigorously religious period when, as in times past, a person realized that Christianity means that all this earthly life must be suffering, I would more easily discover if there is a little element of self-torment in my religiousness. But I am unable to find any help in the secular indifference in which Christendom lives now, for however unsound it is, a little bit of self-torment is far preferable to this paganism which, while wanting to be Christian, is also this shameless lack of concern.

IX A 393    n.d.,  1848

### « 6273

I could be tempted to say that I have taken one examination more than most people, although it is true enough that this examination is of such a nature that one or another has submitted to it who otherwise is not an examinee—I allowed the ardor of my feelings to be examined by a woman. Whatever I have suffered because I staked everything on that desire and once again staked everything on it since she asked for it, and yet once again staked everything on it, I who must bear the responsibility and be the agent—I still had strength enough, in order to mitigate the affair for her,[1998] to give the impression that I was a villain, a deceiver. Thus a murder was placed upon my conscience; it was said and repeated as solemnly as possible, that this would be her death. Therefore this girl was the examiner. One and a half years later she was engaged again[1999]—since that time I have scarcely spoken to a young girl, and no thought has been more alien to my soul than to want to fall in love again or even to think about it.

If at times it has satisfied my anger to be like an epigram over my contemporaries, here I have learned how woeful it is to be an epigram in that way.

IX A 408    n.d.,  1848

« **6274**

It is appalling to think even for one single moment about the dark background of my life right from its earliest beginning. The anxiety with which my father filled my soul, his own frightful depression, a lot of which I cannot even write down. I acquired an anxiety about Christianity and yet felt powerfully attracted to it. And then what I suffered later from Peter[2000] when he became morbidly religious.

As mentioned, it is frightful to think for a single moment of the kind of life I have led in my most hidden inwardness, literally never a word about it spoken to a single human being, of course, not even daring to write down the least thing about it—and then that I have been able to encase that life in an exterior existence of zest for life and cheerfulness.

Therefore how true it is what I so often have said of myself, that as Scheherezade saved her life by telling stories, I save my life or keep alive by being productive.[2001]

IX A 411    n.d.,  1848

« **6275** [*N.B. N.B.*]

If anyone were to say: "But if your conception of what it is to be a Christian is right, then there are as good as no Christians, or at most no more than there were in the first generation—twelve." To that I would answer: No, you give my descriptive art or power too much credit. I am not able to draw up the past so that it becomes altogether present in that way. If anyone could do that, I also think the result would be that becoming or being a Christian would be as rare a thing as in the first generation, or in any case in the first generation after Christ's death.

If then the same person went on to say: "Then being a Christian would be such a rarity—it is indeed absurd." Then I would reply: Why do you talk that way? I wonder if it is not because you want to impress me by means of the human sympathy which holds that Christianity must be scaled down in such a way that practically everybody becomes a Christian. But if human sympathy is to be the authority that judges Christianity or the truth, what then is one to think of Christ—why did He not scale down, or, not to speak of Him, then the apostles, why did they not scale down but jacked up the price as high as possible by getting themselves killed instead of scaling it down. [*In margin:* Human sympathy is a scaling down of the requirement; divine sympathy arranges the requirement in such a way that it is not a matter of individual differences, but every man is capable of it.] No, Christianity is the absolute, and the absolute *must* hold; even if 100 million rebel or shout or scream: We cannot—the absolute must hold, must not be scaled down, and it must take hold by letting itself be put to death. And precisely this discipline could well be needed in our time to teach that there is an ought that refuses to have its corners filed with angles to please men, but absolutely will prevail.

That is how I would talk. Having said that, I would add: But as for the rest, I also am a human being, a poor humble man; I do not pretend to be such a Christian myself, and yet I trust that God will show me his grace as a Christian. But of course there is one thing I will not do, either, I do not feel the need to go further than being a Christian.

But when a whole generation, like the most recent, has the rashness to dare to ignore Christianity, to want to go further: then it is high time that the ideal comes along or is presented in order to pass judgment.

And here is where I believe the merit lies, or not my merit but the singularity granted me. I have won a victory, but it is not as when someone wins a battle against tyrants and the next year he or someone else has to begin from the beginning. No, the battle I have won consists in successfully establishing the categories of what it is to be a Christian so firmly, in nailing them down in such a way, that no dialectician can get them loose. I am in the right in seeing that what should be maintained again is not Christianity but being a Christian, and then the concept of contemporaneity, and then the possibility of offense, and then at the top, the highest of all concepts, the concept of faith.

But first of all rigorousness, the rigorousness of the ideal, then mildness. I myself need to be spoken to gently as much as anyone, my soul is very much inclined to speak gently—but in confused times the first things must be first so that mildness does not get to be sluggish indulgence.

How strenuous, how enormously strenuous this task of bringing forward the ideal has been, I myself know best. The fear and trembling, the sleeplessness in venturing far out, losing all sight of finiteness, of keeping up this increasing pace year in and year out, it is dreadful. But God be praised who has given me the strength for it.

I have no right to jack up the price of being Christian this way for one who is downcast (and God knows how it goes against my nature to do it). But in the face of all this brazen impudence which wants to go further than being Christian, I have the permission to do it, yes, it is God-pleasing that it be done, and therefore it is granted to me to be able to do it. I have not trifled with it, have not taken it in vain, have not played the game of myself personally being this ideal Christian who judges everyone; no, I have first and foremost humbled myself under it. But it is also true that I have not wanted, that is, have not dared, to pay any attention to a whining human sympathy that is all mixed up.

IX A 413   n.d., 1848

« 6276

The difference between Jewish piety and Christian piety is that Christian piety understands straightway that it has to suffer. We read the psalms of David: the whole struggle, aided by spontaneous good health, the expectation that God will smash his enemies, hold back their attack, etc., is really not Christian piety. That is the way the natural man behaves, but the Christian knows that being a Christian means to suffer and therefore relates himself at once to the suffering, occupying himself only with suffering in the true God-pleasing way.

At best these words are added: Is it possible that I might avoid it —but this thought gains no dominion.

IX A 416   n.d., 1848

« 6277 *"Let not the heart in sorrow sin"*[2002]

Under this title I would like to write a few discourses[2003] dealing with the most beautiful and noble, humanly speaking, forms of despair: unhappy love, grief over the death of a beloved, sorrow at not having achieved one's proper place in the world, the forms the "poet" loves and which only Christianity dares to call sin, while the human attitude is that the lives of such people are infinitely more worthwhile than the millions that make up the prosy-pack.

IX A 421   n.d., 1848

« 6278 *"Let not the heart in sorrow sin"*[2004]

### Seven Discourses

Here the finest, humanly speaking, the most lovable forms of despair (which is the "poets' " ultimate) are to be treated—for example, unhappy love, grief over one who is dead, grief over not having achieved one's destiny in life.

Perhaps the three or four themes left over from "Notes in the Strife of Suffering,"[2005] which are some place in a journal [i.e., VIII$^1$ A 500], could be combined with these. Each discourse would first of all develop or describe the particular sorrow which it is to treat; then the admonition: Let not the heart in sorrow sin—consider this: and now the theme. For example, about one who is dead—description—let not the heart in sorrow sin—consider this: the joy in the fact that *at last* and *for a little while*[2006] are identical (but this is used lyrically in another piece, "From on High He Will Draw All to Himself"[2007]); or consider this: the joy in the fact that it is for joy that one does not believe the highest etc.[2008]

But perhaps (instead of leading backward by means of joyful thoughts) it would be better to concentrate attention constantly on the infinite distinction between sorrow and sin, after each discourse show explicitly how this sorrow is sin, or can become that by a hair's breadth.

IX A 498   *n.d.*, 1848

« **6279**

*Addition to 6278* (IX A 498):
            *Let Not the Heart in Sorrow Sin*[2009]
            [*Changed from:* Sorrow in Sin]
                      Introduction

My Listener, do you almost shudder at these words, are you seized by the anxiety that of all sins this sin might be the most dreadful. You find it almost superfluous, you look around involuntarily to see if there could be someone like this, you think of the people you have learned to know, whether among them there could be anyone like this who hides this very sin in his conscience.

If you do, you make a mistake. There is perhaps no sin as common as this one, which the old poet[2010] has described in such a way and so excellently that he did not need to say more to be remembered; no doubt there is scarcely a man who has not once in his life (if not all his life) sinned in this way, in the time of sorrow—and indeed every man has sorrow in this life. But not only this; this sin is also so well-regarded among men that it is even praised and extolled. Ask "the poet" what it is that especially inspires him to songs which praise heroes and heroines—it is this very sin of the heart in sorrow. It is in fact the highest form of despair. When Juliet kills herself, or Brutus, or, if it does not go so far, when a man's mood is such that every one of his words betrays that he believes that for him and his pain, his sorrow, there is no cure either in heaven or on earth, neither from God nor with men, neither in time nor eternity—well, that is precisely when the poet becomes inspired, and it is precisely then that he has let the heart sin in sorrow.

IX A 499   *n.d.*, 1848

« **6280**

*Addition to 6279* (IX A 498):
*Let Not the Heart in Sorrow Sin*
Seven Discourses

No. 1 Let not the heart in sorrow sin   so
    you abandon **faith** *in God*

No. 2 Let not the heart in sorrow sin   so
    you abandon **faith** *in men*

No. 3 Let not the heart in sorrow sin   so
    you abandon the **hope** *of eternity*

No. 4 Let not the heart in sorrow sin   so
    you abandon **hope** *for this life*

No. 5 Let not the heart in sorrow sin   so
    you abandon **love** *to God*

No. 6 Let not the heart in sorrow sin   so
    you abandon **love** *to men*

No. 7 Let not the heart in sorrow sin   so
    you abandon **love** *to yourself*

IX A 500   *n.d.*, 1848

« **6281**

Mynster's whole sermon[2011] about Christ's relationship to his friends is really a web of deceit. To call Christ's relationship one of friendship and to use the occasion to preach about making friends! Can anything more polemical be imagined than being forced to sort through a whole contemporary age that way in order eventually to find a few from the most simple class. If Mynster, instead of becoming what he is, perhaps with the help of friendship, had followed Christ's example and held to the truth so rigorously that his relationship to all who could be called his equals became polemical and he eventually found an apprentice shoemaker and apprentice tailor who became his closest friends—I wonder if Bishop Mynster would not have split his sides laughing at the friendship.

IX A 428   n.d., 1848

« **6282**

How strange, after all, are the outlook of the moment and the outlook of history. In a way it was just plain cowardice for men to speak about *The Corsair* as nothing at all, but although that is not the case, the majority honestly believe that *The Corsair* will be forgotten quickly; all the other papers look down on it in this respect and console themselves that they belong to history. But if I were to express my opinion to the contrary, this would be interpreted as my supposed instability. And yet *sie irren*.[2012] It is the history of the disintegration of Denmark we are living—and *The Corsair* is the normal phenomenon of one sort and the March ministry[2013] another, but *The Corsair* has a longer life and covers an enormous area. In a certain sense it was important, that is, in the realm of evil—and to history it is in a certain sense indifferent whether it is good or evil if only it is important, carried through with talent, consistency, and boldness. Up to a point *The Corsair* has understood this, and therefore its attempt at being a sort of moral enterprise in which ethical satire would be beneficial to the good (à la Aristophanes). I regard it as very important to have gotten this lie exposed, and I was successful in doing it. But, on the other hand, Goldschmidt[2014] was in one sense right over against most of his contemporaries, for their supposed disregard was an untruth, insofar as the issue was one about talent, an attempt to ascribe falsely to themselves the ability to overlook his talent because he misused it. I consider it important to my whole historical position that it be scrupulously maintained that I regard the two articles[2015] as belonging unconditionally to my total literary activity. Therefore, I must also see about doing what I thought of earlier, getting the newspaper articles I have written published in a separate little book.[2016]

IX A 432   n.d., 1848

« **6283**

Through my writings I hope to achieve the following: to leave behind me so accurate a characterization of Christianity and its relationships in the world that an enthusiastic, noble-minded young person will be able to find in it a map of relationships as accurate as any topographical map from the most famous institutes. I have not had the help of such an author. The old Church Fathers lacked one aspect, they did not know the world.

IX A 448   *n.d.,*  1848

« **6284**

In this, too, as in everything else, we were very different; she[2017] wishes or had wished to shine in the world—and I with my despondency and gloomy views on suffering and of having to suffer. For the time being, she no doubt would have been satisfied with her relationship to me, who at first would have gratified her in terms of shining. But when it got to be an earnest matter with my receding into unimportance or my plunging into actual suffering and into Christian suffering, where there is no honor or status to be gained, then she easily would have lost her good humor. And I—I never would have become myself.

IX A 451   *n.d.,*  1848

« **6285**

But it is very wearing, it is a school for patience, to be reminded again and again, day after day, year after year, of the same old thing (now by a child, now by a shoemaker's boy, a brewery hand, a student, a burgher, etc. etc.) of my poor skinny legs.[2018] And then these collisions of reflection everywhere, that at the same time I am supposed to express that I am a sort of esteemed figure among the people etc. etc. And then to be so extraordinarily endowed that I can keep on producing—for if I were a simple citizen, all this mistreatment would be unthinkable, they would be tired of it all in just a week.

This is how distinction is recognized in the market town Copenhagen. An unselfishness of endeavor which is not to be found here, a talent which seeks its equal, a primitive Christian willingness to be equal with everybody: qualities which it seems to me must needs touch the little nation which I truly do not harm: this is how it is rewarded.

How easy the whole thing would be if there were only a few who could do the dance steps with me, but there is no one with the courage to swing so high, and the stage is too small; that is why all oppress me since all are more or less accomplices. Even the individual who in the beginning was most indignant obviously has become insensitive over the years and in the end condemns me.

Why do I take it, why did I not travel long ago? For the time being I cannot do otherwise; I am convinced that I would repent of my journey abroad as unfaithfulness to my idea; I must stay on the spot as long as possible, believingly assured that Governance will let the emphasis fall on my life when I have seen it through and let all this serve to illuminate Christianity and be of service to the cause I have the honor to serve.

IX A 458   *n.d.*, 1848

« **6286**

To some extent I do have it in my power to put an end to this whole unpleasantness[2019] here at home: one simple turn, and I will be able to win men to my side, but I dare not do it. If help comes, I will rejoice, but I dare do nothing but what I have been doing all the time, present my cause clearly, vividly, convincingly—but no private hand-shaking to get people to do something in my behalf.

IX A 463   *n.d.*, 1848

« **6287**

I cannot very well discuss my innermost feelings with anyone, for what in so many ways cheers me up, my trained eye for the historical perspective, which, besides my faith, already sees the rightness of my cause: all this I cannot very well open up to others—in a way they are interlopers and would not be able to share it with me.

IX A 467   *n.d.*, 1848

« **6288**

The only person I can say I envy is he, when he comes, whom I call my reader, who in peace and quiet will be able to sit and purely intellectually enjoy the immensely comic drama I have allowed Copenhagen to perform just by living here. No doubt I perceive the worth of this drama better than he, but I have had a bitterness and loathsomeness in daily life, as well as the new misunderstanding of people not daring to laugh along with me because they are suspicious and cannot get it into their heads that in all this unpleasantness I still could have an eye for the comic. From a poetic point of view, it is not at all interesting. Yes, poetically it is all wrong for this drama to go on being performed every single day year after year; poetically it must be ab-breviated. So it will be for my reader. But in and with the dailiness begins the religious, and this is how I interpret my life: this immensely comic drama is for me a martyrdom. But one thing is sure, if I were not convinced of being under infinite religious obligations, I would be inclined to go away to some solitary spot and sit down and laugh and laugh—even though it would pain me that this *Krähwinckel*[2020] is my beloved native land, this residence of a prostituted bourgeois mentality is my beloved Copenhagen.

IX A 471    *n.d.*, 1848

« **6289**

In relation to all my contemporaries, things will probably go as they did with my engagement and prior to that with my father and at every crucial point in my life. A young girl says a word to me, a word that does not have great significance for her (for she was not very religiously mature)—and she produces an enormous effect,[2021] although she has no inkling of it and marries again.[2022] In the same way my contemporaries presumably have fancied they can have a little sport with me. They do not realize that because of my imagination and my upbringing religiously to obey orders to the uttermost, the matter becomes completely different. Things will go with my contemporaries as with that girl: suddenly they will discover what they have caused, and only afterwards will they come to repent.

IX A 473    *n.d.*, 1848

« **6290**

More and more God becomes my only comfort. To whom should I turn? The general opinion about my life is not entirely true, and therefore it is not easy for people to be reconciled to me. They consider me a visionary and that it is ambition which drives me on. Good Lord, to be ambitious in Denmark! What honor, indeed, does this little speck have to give me, I who as author had essentially taken a place of honor even with my first book. But if I were to tell men bluntly what motivates me, that I know very well that with every forward step I take I am working against myself, they promptly would call me crazy.

IX A 484    *n.d.*, 1848

« **6291**

If my despondency has misled me in any way, it may have been to make me to look upon what perhaps was only unhappy suffering, spiritual trial, as guilt and sin. This is a frightful misunderstanding in one sense, namely, it is the sign of almost demented anguish; but even if I went too far in that respect, it has nevertheless been helpful to me.

IX A 488    *n.d.*, 1848

« **6292**

"Phister as Scipio"[2023]
Fair Copy

Written the end of 1848

Can be signed
Procul
IX B 67   *n.d.,* 1848

« **6293**

*Mr. Phister*
*as Captain Scipio*[2024]
(in the musical *Ludovic*)

A recollection and
for recollection. . . .

December, 1848     Procul
IX B 68   December, 1848

« **6294**

Dear Julie,[2025]

It is obvious that we wronged your little son[2026] today, for we walked too fast, and we, or I, am to blame for his beginning to cry, which from a child's point of view he was completely justified in doing. It is for this reason that I am writing and sending the accompanying parcel.

You see, with respect to the world—by which, according to Balle's Catechism,[2027] is understood heaven and earth and all therein contained, but by which I more or less understand all the human multitudes therein contained—my advice to everybody is to let the world "be blown," each to the best of his ability. Perhaps you remember one of Grimm's fairy tales.[2028] As usual, someone is setting out into the world. He walks and walks and keeps getting farther and farther away until he stops by a mill. Said *in parenthesi,* one may perceive in this how easy, but in another sense how difficult, nay impossible, it is to go out in search of adventure when one lives in Copenhagen, for in order to set out on an adventure one would first of all have to set out through the city gates, and yet it is of course impossible to walk through those gates without having come to a mill. In other words, the mill lies too close for it to be the occasion of any adventure. And herein lies the difference between actuality and the fairy tale, in proximity and distance. Given distance, infinite distance, then you have a fairy tale, for then any object—be it a mill, a horse, a sheep, a moo-cow, yes, be it even that which at times may cause most sadness in the real world, a human being—takes on a fairy tale aspect, as does the mill in this fairy tale. So the wanderer stops by the mill. He is surprised to discover that the mill is turning under full sail—although there is no wind at all. (Here one must agree with the wanderer, for I almost do believe that one would be surprised oneself if this happened with the mill on the city wall directly across from where one lives.) Now the wanderer proceeds. Nine miles farther on he encounters a man who is closing one nostril with his finger while blowing through the other—on that mill! And that is how it came to pass that it was turning under full sail. Thus, not even using both nostrils, but with a finger phlegmatically closing one nostril, one should, while blowing through the other, say, "The whole world be blown!"

However, a little child—indeed, be it ever so tiny, the least offense against this little child—indeed, be it ever so tiny—when I have offended against this little one, that is a very serious matter for me, something about which I cannot say "be blown!" I am very reluctant to have the sun set before I have made up for it, but at this time of year when the days are so short, the sun could easily set before I could possibly have made amends. But since our civic lives are so wisely arranged that the night watchman does not sing out the passing of the day until it is eight o'clock, I may after all manage to do it before the sun sets. For the town council and the police, and hence also the night watchman, constitute authority, and although it is not astronomical, it is still authority, and to children something very close to astronomical authority, whereas their elders, who have hardened themselves against all authority, no longer arrange their going to bed according to the night watchman's bidding, but the children probably still do so.

Please, then, give my love to the little fellow and present him with this box of toys from the strange man who walked too fast for him today. And you, my dear Julie, you who—yes, that certainly suffices as punishment for your having walked so *fast* today—you who have now been forced to go all the more *slowly* as you have had to spell your way slowly through my illegible handwriting, receive in conclusion an assurance of the devotion with which I remain your wholly devoted

Cousin
S.K.

[Address:]
To
Mrs. Julie Thomsen.
Accompanying small parcel

*Letters*, no. 195 [1848]

« **6295**

Dear Peter,[2029]

Happy New Year! I never go calling to offer my New Year greet-
ings and send them in writing only rarely and as an exception—but you
are among the exceptions. In recent years I have often thought of you,
and I intend to do likewise in this one. Among the other thoughts or
considerations I often have had and intend to go on having about you
is this: that reconciled to your fate,[2030] with patience and quiet devotion, you carry out as important a task as the rest of us who perform
on a larger or smaller stage, engage in important business, build
houses, write copious books, and God knows what. Undeniably your
stage is the smallest, that of solitude and inwardness—but *summa summarum,* as it says in Ecclesiastes,[2031] when all is said and done, what
matters most is inwardness—and when everything has been forgotten,
it is inwardness that still matters.

I wrote this some days ago, was interrupted, and did not manage
to conclude it. Today your father[2032] visited me, and that circumstance
once more reminded me to complete or at least put an end to what I
had begun. For there was something more I wanted to add. If I were
to give you any advice about life, or taking into consideration your
special circumstances, were to commend to you a rule for your life,
then I would say: Above all do not forget your duty to love yourself;
do not permit the fact that you have been set apart from life in a way,
been prevented from participating actively in it, and that you are
superfluous in the obtuse eyes of a busy world, above all do not permit
this to deprive you of your idea of yourself, as if your life, if lived in
inwardness, did not have just as much meaning and worth as that of
any other human being in the loving eyes of an all-wise Governance,
and considerably more than the busy, busier, busiest haste of busyness—busy with wasting life and losing itself.

Take care of yourself in the new year. If you would enjoy visiting
me once in a while, please do come. You are welcome.

Your Cousin
S.K.

Perhaps you yourself will notice that many days have now gone by since your father visited me; so once more some time has passed before you finally get this letter.

[Address:]
To
Mr. Peter Kierkegaard

*Letters,* no. 196  [1848]

« **6296**

[Copy of *Det nye Testament*[2033] (Copenhagen: 1820), *ASKB* 33, with numerous marginal markings and notations.]

$x^6$ C 1  *n.d.,* 1849–52(?)

« **6297**

[Copy of Alphons von Liguori, *Vollständiges Betrachtungs-und Gebet-buch* (Aachen: 1840), *ASKB* 264, with considerable marginal side-lining.]

$x^6$ C 2  *n.d.,* 1849–52

« **6298**

The joy of being a child I have never had. The frightful torments I experienced disturbed the peacefulness which must belong to being a child, to have in one's hands the capacity to be occupied etc., to give his father joy, for my inner unrest had the effect that I was always, always, outside myself.

But on not rare occasions it seems as if my childhood had come back again, for unhappy as my father made me, it seems as if I now experience being a child in my relationship to God, as if all my early life was misspent so dreadfully in order that I should experience it more truly the second time in my relationship to God.

$x^1$ A 8  *n.d.,* 1849

« **6299**

In Denmark, of course, there is no discerning judgment, no real criterion for an artist, a poet, a philosopher, etc. The few that we are, all of whom know each other, all play along in the equality game, and therefore the criterion is: Is he popular or not. We are just like school boys—who are in fact all each other's equal—who merely use the criterion: Is he popular or not. That is why living here in Denmark is so pleasant for all those who are nothing, for they do in fact play along and we are all equal. But it goes all the worse for the few who are something.

Hostrup[2034] has never really earned any position, but the public has built him up. And now I am convinced that he is being dumped again, and why? Is it because he has written something worse than usual? No, it is because of a little article[2035] he wrote criticizing the drama director Lange, of which the public will say: I don't like Hostrup for that.

X¹ A 9   n.d., 1849

« **6300**

If I had not been brought up strictly in Christianity, had not had all my mental and spiritual suffering, beginning in childhood and intensified at just the time I began my career, had I not experienced that and yet had known what I know, I would have become a poet, and I actually would have become an interesting poet $\kappa\alpha\tau$' $\dot{\epsilon}\xi o\chi\dot{\eta}\nu$.[2036] There has hardly been a poet before me who has known about life and especially about religion as profoundly as I do.

But here is where I turn aside, and my position is that old one in *Either/Or*: I do not want to be a poet such as A describes from one angle and B in a far deeper sense confirms, yes, declares it to be the only one of A's many ideas that he confirms entirely.[2037]

What is it to be a poet? It is to have one's own personal life, one's actuality, in categories completely different from those of one's poetical production, to be related to the ideal only in imagination, so that one's personal life is more or less a satire on the poetry and on oneself. In this sense all modern thinkers, even the outstanding ones (I mean the Germans, for there simply are no Danish thinkers), are poets. And on the whole this is the maximum to be seen in life. Most men live utterly destitute of ideas; some few relate poetically to the ideal but deny it in their personal lives. Pastors likewise are poets, and since they are pastors they are "deceivers," as Socrates[2038] once called poets, in a much deeper way than poets are.

But here as everywhere demoralization has come about through the disappearance of position no. 1 and the assumption of position no. 1 by no. 2. Relating oneself to the ideal in one's personal life is never seen. Such a life is the life of the witness to the truth. This rubric disappeared long ago, and preachers, philosophy professors, and poets have taken over the place of servants of the truth, whereby they no doubt are served very well—but they do not serve the truth.

X¹ A 11   n.d., 1849

### « 6301

The true is really always defenseless in this world, where there very rarely are even ten who have the capability, the time, the diligence, and the moral character to follow through in pursuing the truth —but here in the world the mob of contemporaries is the judge, and they are far too confused to understand the truth but understand untruth very easily. I have regarded it as my religious duty to draw a person[2039] to me in order not to leave out the human tribunal completely. He now gets communications from me which he otherwise would never get—and gets them privately. Here again is the possibility that I may become completely defenseless. If vanity and a secular mentality run away with him, he will publish this in a confused form as his own and will create an enormous furor. My efforts at reclamation would be useless. Alas, and a person who is already married, a professor, a knight—what real hope is there of his competence to serve the truth, in a more profound sense what fondness can he have for an undertaking in which all these qualifications are just so many N.B.'s, while at any moment he can turn to the other side, where these are substantiations.

$x^1$ A 14   *n.d.*, 1849

### « 6302

If that which one has to communicate is, for example, a conception of something historical or the like, it may be a good thing for someone else to arrive at the same conception, and all one has to do is simply to work to get this idea acknowledged. But if the point of a person's activity is to do what is true: then one additional assistant professor[2040] is just a new calamity, and not least when he gets assistance privately and confidentially.

$x^1$ A 15   *n.d.*, 1849

### « 6303

[*Five pages removed from the journal*] . . . . . everything reminiscent of her is to be found. A small bundle of letters which I wrote from Berlin to Emil Boesen but which later were returned to me by him may be found in a sealed package in a drawer, labeled "to be destroyed after my death."

Nothing can be done for her;[2041] I dare not risk it, she obviously cannot bear the truth. She can endure it, perhaps find happiness, if she still believes that I aspired to greatness and therefore abandoned her, actually did not love her; but the religious element would disturb the whole thing right away. I am certain that, loving as always, she lovingly forgives me, carries no rancor against me, but if she were to understand me, she could not go on, for what keeps her going is the thought that, conceding me everything (as far as talents are concerned), she still believes that she treated me far better than I treated her.

X¹ A 23   *n.d.*, 1849

« **6304**

No, nothing can be done for her.[2042] Schlegel[2043] has in a way been somewhat successful, becoming head of a department already at so young an age. This will comfort her as providential approval of her marriage. She will be reconciled with her fate, lovingly will forgive me, with the interpretation that no matter how exceptionally endowed I was, I nevertheless was untrue to her and she was the faithful and loving one. She at times may feel that what has happened to me of late is a punishment for me and sometimes may consider she was lucky, after all, not to be included in it. In that way everything will be mitigated. I am becoming a fading memory which eventually will visit her rarely and then with a touch of sadness because it gratifies her not to condemn me, and because it gratifies her that I still am unmarried.

All this would be disturbed if in any way she learns the true state of affairs, for she has no intimation of the specifically religious. At that moment she would have a different understanding of the situation, would reproach herself for having treated me unjustly, would lose her self-image and her feeling of superiority over me, and then she would be confused, her imagination would take over again, and then—yes, then all is lost.

X¹ A 24   *n.d.*, 1849

« **6305**

An example of rhetorical fraud. Bishop Mynster's sermon for Second Christmas Day, "The Accomplishments of Christ's Witnesses."[2044]

P. 70. "If we, my listeners, had been present at this scene, would it not have struck us as utterly pitiable." But then we simply would have been present as spectators. Here is the untruth; he forgets that if we had been present—that is, contemporary, we would have been among the persecutors.

X¹ A 33   *n.d.*, 1849

« 6306

Could be a little pseudonymous article.
*Who Is To Proclaim Christianity?*
Either God himself, an apostle—or an authentic sinner.

An authentic sinner, someone who essentially understands that he is a sinner—not a preacher-platitude about universal human imperfection—his only passion is repentance. Humanly he is in despair, but Christianly he is saved, for he is a believer; humanly repentance is his only passion, but the Atonement is his consolation. As the hungry man greedily devours bread, so the hunger of repentance within him devours the Atonement; just as it is a matter of life or death to the hungry man if he does not get food, so it is life and death to him if he does not hear the Atonement.

The life of such a sinner is rigorous. For example, he cannot marry. Or should he perhaps fall in love and unite with a girl in order to repent together, this should be the significance of the marriage. And if one's only passion is repentance—then to give a child life, a child who should innocently rejoice in life and have the right to do so. No, he will say, if Christianity commanded marriage it would be madness. I know well enough that those who have such a lively interest in falling in love, and this is human, have gotten Christianity to be interested in it also, but it is easy to see that Christianity does not command marriage.

Consequently he is the person who can proclaim Christianity! But now suppose—how shall I say it, shall I say it is one of his fine traits or that it is, from a Christian point of view, an imperfection—suppose he really has an eye for the beauty in ordinary human life as this is lived amiably in a kind of innocence. He sees very well that they actually are not living in Christian categories, but he does not have the heart to disturb them. Here, you see, is the monastery, not as select exclusiveness, but as a kind of penitentiary. He would desire to enter something like this and be silent—and yet, Christianly understood, he is precisely the one who can proclaim Christianity. It is as if Christianity did not fit into the world.

$X^5$ A 158   *n.d.*, 1849

« 6307

For this is then the *summa summarum*[2045] of the wisdom of men nowadays, of the entire age and almost all individuals: human authority. If men agree with me, if I have the majority on my side, then who the devil will hurt a hair on my head, that is, God does not exist—and then we are all Christians. For me, out of fear of God and God's judgment, to endure the persecution of the majority—that would certainly be madness, and also untruth, for *vox populi* is indeed *vox dei*, [2046] that is, there is no God—and then we are all Christians. To relinquish what is certain, the certainty of my having won (and for this it is required that I have the majority on my side), in exchange for what is uncertain, is surely madness, for suppose that there were no God, that is, that there is no God (for when the hypothetical proposition by comparison with one's life, which expresses that no God exists, is formulated that way, it is a denial; otherwise, when the hypothetical proposition by collation with a life which existentially through sacrifice and renunciation expresses that there is a God, it is positive, affirmative, and thus it is clear that there is nothing incorrect in the hypothetical proposition but that one's life is decisive)[2047]—and then we are all Christians.

Rise aloft as high as you can and (somewhat à la Satan—in Job—and a spectator) look out over men, and you will discover that you find no one whose wisdom, existentially, is not this. Eliminate, as far as possible, curiosity about others, turn your gaze entirely in upon yourself, but then let your life express (which is an obvious consequence) that a God does exist, and you will learn, learn in all seriousness, what the wisdom of the majority is, for they will scarcely give you any peace.

$X^1$ A 37   *n.d.*, 1849

« **6308**

I will hardly be able to carry out the whole project. It is too much for one man. Precisely because it centered upon reflecting Christianity out of an extreme sophistication, refinement, scholarly-scientific confusion, etc., I myself had to have all that refinement, sensitive in one sense as a poet, pure intellect as a thinker. But for the next part there must be physical strength and another kind of rigorous upbringing: to be able to live on little, not to need many creature-comforts, to be able to apply some of one's mind to this self-discipline.

Take a strong, healthy child and train him in this kind of self-mastery. In a few well-spent years he will have mastered my whole movement of thought; he will not need a tenth of my mental concentration and effort, nor the kind of talents I have had and which were particularly necessary for the first attack. But he will be the man who is needed: tough, rigorous, and yet adequately armed dialectically.

But I do indeed dare say that the work I have done was herculean.

For this I have had the decisive presuppositions, wonderfully good fortune, and blessing, but I do not have the prerequisites for the next part. I would have to become a child again and above all, not a child of old age,[2048] for such children often are physically weak; I would have to have better physical health and much less imagination and dialectic.

$X^1$ A 39    *n.d.,* 1849

« **6309**

It is miserable, as I once said to Christian VIII,[2049] it is miserable to be a genius in a market town. Of course I said it in such a way that it was a compliment to him. I said: Your Majesty's only misfortune is that your wisdom and intelligence are too great and the country too little; it is a misfortune to be a genius in a market town. To which he replied: Then one can do all the more for the individuals. That was the first time I talked with him. He said many flattering things to me and asked me to visit him, to which I replied: Your Majesty, I visit no one. He said: Yes, but I know that you will not object if I send for you, to which I replied: "I am your subject. Your Majesty has but to command, but like for like—I make one condition." "Well, and what is that?" "That I be permitted to speak with you alone." With that he offered me his hand and we parted. At the beginning of the conversation he also said something to me about my having so many ideas that perhaps I could turn some over to him. I replied that I regarded my entire work to be beneficial also to any government, but the point of it was that I was and would remain a private citizen, since otherwise a mean-spirited interpretation would be insinuated. And moreover I added: "I have the honor of serving a higher power, on which I have staked my life."

As I came through the door and gave my name, he said: I am especially happy to see you; I have heard so many good things about you. To which I replied (having, of course, sat in the anteroom in fear and trembling, not knowing whether I would come through the door on my head or on my feet [someone standing out there asked me if I was going to bow three times when I entered, and I responded that it was ridiculous to ask me that question; an old courtier could decide such things in advance, but I did not know whether I would come in on my head or on my feet], but upon entering I approached so close to him that he stepped back and fixed his eyes upon me, and there I promptly saw what I wanted to see): "And I, Your Majesty, I have always said to myself that in the end the man you will get along with best will be the King, because for that to happen I must have someone with enough intelligence for it and of such high standing that it would never occur to him to be small-minded toward me."

On the whole our conversations were well worth writing down.

X[1] A 41   *n.d.*, 1849

### « 6310

The second time I talked with Christian VIII was at Sorgenfri[2050] many months later. In a certain sense, however, his conversation was not particularly significant for me, for he wanted me to do the talking. But it was exhilarating to speak with him, and I have never seen an elderly man so animated, so stimulated, almost like a woman. He had a kind of spiritual and mental voluptuousness. I saw at once that this could be dangerous for me and therefore as circumspectly as possible maintained distance between us. Face to face with a king I found it unseemly to use my eccentricity as an excuse for not coming and therefore employed another tactic—namely, that I was in poor health. Christian VIII was a splendidly gifted man but actually had lost control of his considerable intelligence, which lacked a moral background equal to it. If he had lived in a southern country, I imagine Christian VIII would have been sure booty for a cunning religious. No woman would have gotten real power over him, not even the most superbly endowed woman; for one thing he was too smart for that, and for another he had a bit of the masculine superstition that men are smarter than women. But a Jesuit—he could have turned and twisted Christian VIII, but of course it would have been necessary for this Jesuit to have had the interesting at his command, for that was what he actually was gasping for. But charming, extraordinarily acute, with a rare eye for what could please and gladden the individual, that very individual in particular—that he was.

So I went in. He said: "It is a long time since I have seen you here." Still standing in the door, I answered: "Perhaps Your Majesty will first and foremost allow me to explain. I beg Your Majesty to rest assured that I appreciate very much the grace and favor you show me, but I am in poor health and this is why I come so infrequently; I cannot bear this waiting in the anteroom, it exhausts me." He responded that I did not need to wait but that in any case I could write to him. I thanked him for that. Then we started to converse, for a time walking about as we did so. He always preferred talking about governmental matters or commenting in general on one or another political issue. That day he turned the conversation to communism, about which he obviously was anxious and afraid. I explained that, as I understood it, the whole movement confronting us would be a movement that would not touch the kings at all. It would be a class conflict, but it would always be to the interests of the conflicting parties to get on well with the monarch. The problems were ancient ones returning again, and thus it was easy to see that in a way the king would come to stand outside them. It would be like household disputes between the basement and the first floor, between these two and the second floor, etc., but the landlord would not be attacked. Next I spoke of how to do battle with "the crowd": just remain completely calm; [I said] that "the crowd" was like a woman, whom one never engaged in direct battle, but indirectly, helped it get carried away, and since it lacks thought, it always would lose in time—but just stand firm. At this point he said: "Yes, a king especially ought to do that." To that I gave no reply. Then I said that the whole age needed upbringing and that what took the form of violence in a large country became rudeness in Denmark. Then he paid some compliments to my intellect etc., and I used the situation to say: Your Majesty, you see best in me that what I am saying is true, for everything about me essentially may be credited to my being well brought up and thus really to my father. Then we talked a bit about Guizot[2051] and an attack which had just been made on him. I showed the shabbiness in the equivocation that although modern states have actually elevated scandal to an official magnitude with the correlative tactic of ignoring it, suddenly one day people take it into their heads to say that such an attack must be serious. "I am thinking of Guizot; he has read the attack, then does no more than glance in the mirror to reassure himself that his smile and appearance are quite normal— and then, then people come up with the idea that it is supposed to be serious; and if at some other time he had taken an attack like that seriously, he would have been ridiculed as a country squire who was unaccustomed to life in the big city."

[*In margin:* Then he talked a little about Sorø,[2052] gave a lecture of sorts on it, and questioned me: I answered that I had never given Sorø much thought. He asked if I might not want to have an appointment there. Now I knew that he had been fishing that very morning and therefore alluded to it in my answer. That in addition to the regular lines fishermen liked to have an odd little line on which they sometimes caught the best fish—I was an odd little line like that.]

Then he thanked me for the book I had brought him the last

time;[2053] he had read some of it—"It was very profound but over his head." I replied: "Of course Your Majesty does not have time to read books, nor is what I write intended for you. But on the other hand you recently had the natural scientists[2054] visit you; that appeals to you, appeals to your sense for beauty." He obviously was a bit affronted by this and said: Yes, yes, but the other can also be very good.

Several times I made as if to leave and said I did not wish to detain him longer. Each time he replied: Yes, I have plenty of time. The third time this happened I said: Your Majesty realizes that I have plenty of time; I was afraid that Your Majesty did not have the time. I learned later from a more experienced man to whom I told this that I had behaved like a bumpkin, that trying to be polite this way in the presence of a king is actually being impolite, since one merely has to wait until he bows.

Eventually I took my leave. He said he would be especially glad to see me. Thereupon he made a move with his hand, which I realized from my last visit meant that he wanted to offer me his hand, but since the same man had told me that it was the custom to kiss the hand offered by a king and since I could not feel comfortable doing that, I pretended that I did not understand and bowed.

Meanwhile I vowed to visit him as infrequently as possible.

The third time I visited him was at Sorgenfri; I brought him a copy of *Works of Love*. Pastor Ibsen[2055] had told me that he had somehow gotten the idea fixed in his head that he could not understand me and that I would not get it out again. I had this in mind. I entered, handed him the book. He glanced at it, noted the organization of Part One (You *shall* love, you shall love *your neighbor, you* shall love your neighbor) and grasped it immediately; he really was very intelligent. Thereupon I took the book from him again and asked his permission to read a passage aloud to him, and chose the first portion[2056] (p. 150). It moved him, easily moved as he generally was.

Next he walked to the window, and I followed him. He began talking about his government. I told him that obviously I could tell him a thing or two which he otherwise might not get to know, for I could tell him how he appeared from the street. "But shall I speak or shall I not, for if I am to speak, then I must speak quite openly and directly." He replied: "By all means do." So I told him that he had let himself be seduced by his personal gifts, that in this respect a king was somewhat like a woman, who ought to hide her personal talents and simply be a housewife—and be simply the king. I have often reflected on what a king should be. In the first place, he very well could be ugly. In the next place he should be deaf and blind, or at least pretend to be, for it simplified many difficulties; a foolish or inopportune remark, just because it is said to the king, acquires a kind of significance which is brushed aside best by an "I beg your pardon," signifying that the king did not hear it. Finally a king must not say much but have an aphorism he uses on every occasion and which as a consequence says nothing. He laughed and said: A delightful description of a king. Then I said: "Yes, it is true, and one thing more, a king must see to it that he is sick occasionally so that he arouses sympathy," whereupon he burst out with a strange interjection of almost joy and jubilation: Aha, that is why you talk about being in poor health. You want to make yourself interesting.

Yes, it is definitely the case; he could become so excited that talking with him was really like talking to a woman. Then I pointed out to him that he had done himself damage with his audiences, that he became too personally involved with every Tom, Dick, and Harry, thus alienating the upper official class who became impatient with this haphazard sort of extraneous influence, that after all he must realize that it was impossible to rule by talking with each of his subjects. He did not take into consideration that everyone he talked to this way went out and gossiped about it. That the error was apparent this very moment when I stood talking this way with him, even though I was an exception, since I felt religiously committed to keep secret every word. (It is in fact true, that as long as he lived I did not speak of it to a person, and after his death to only one and very fragmentarily.) He responded that I must not believe that he was led astray only by his possible talents but that when he ascended the throne he believed that to be a king could no longer be a matter of prestige, but that he had gradually changed his view.

I had said that I had had occasion to make some of these observations the very first day he ascended the throne. He answered: That is so, that was the time there was a general assembly[2057] of which you were the president. —What a memory he had. —Just then a door to an adjoining room opened and was immediately closed again. I stepped back. He went to the door, saying: That must be the Queen; she is so eager to see you; I shall fetch her. He returned leading the Queen by the hand, and I bowed. That was essentially a discourtesy to the Queen, who really did not get a chance to make an elegant impression, she even looked insignificant—but is there any other possibility when a Queen makes such an entrance.

[*In margin:* The King then showed the Queen the copy of the new book, which led me to say: Your Majesty embarrasses me for not having brought along a copy for the Queen. He answered: Ah, but we two can be satisfied with one.]

The Queen said that she recognized me, for she once had seen me on the embankment (where I ran off and left Tryde[2058] high and dry), that she had read a part of "your *Either and Or* but could not understand it." I replied: Your Majesty realizes that it is too bad for me. But there was something more unusual in the situation. Christian VIII promptly heard the mistake, *"Either and Or,"* and I certainly did hear it, too. It amazed me to hear the Queen say precisely what seamstresses etc. say. The King looked at me; I avoided his glance. After speaking a few more words, the King said to the Queen: Is Juliana alone in your apartment? She said "yes"—and then left.

I continued conversation with the King. He asked if I did not plan to take a journey this year. I answered that if I did it would be a very short one, and to Berlin. "You no doubt have many interesting acquaintances there." "No, your Majesty, I live in complete isolation in Berlin and work harder than ever." "But then you could just as well travel to Smørum-Ovre"[2059] (and he laughed at his own witticism). "No, Your Majesty, whether I go to Smørum-Ovre or to Smørum-Nedre, I do not gain an incognito, a hiding place of 400,000 people." That was a little sarcastic, and he answered: Yes, quite right.

Then he asked me about Schelling.[2060] With a few strokes I tried to give him a quick impression. He then inquired about Schelling's personal attitude to the court, his reputation at the university. I said that the same thing was happening to Schelling as to the Rhine at its mouth—it becomes stagnant water—in the same way he is deteriorating into a character of a royal Prussian "excellency." I talked a bit more about how Hegelian philosophy had been the state philosophy, and now Schelling was supposed to be that.

My last visit was an example of Christian VIII's sensitivity in displaying an awareness tailored to the particular individual, making it something of a family visit.

I did not speak with him after that. I had firmly decided to visit him as infrequently as possible, preferably when I had a book to bring him. But I do not repent visiting him; I have fond memories of my visits. If he had lived longer, it would not have been good for me, for he really could not appreciate anyone's being a private person; he considered it a king's prerogative unequivocally to point out to everyone his task. Thus it was at the time I began thinking of taking an official appointment that I first went to him.

The whole relationship is a delightful memory to me; he had no opportunity to get anything but an altogether encouraging impression of me, and I continually regarded him as kindness and vivacity personified.

$X^1$ A 42   *n.d.*, 1849

« 6311

Besides, in a certain sense I am much indebted to Christian VIII for something, namely the pleasant, salutary impression of life he has conveyed to me. I have always been much too disinclined to care about the finite; if my expeditions to see the King had taken an unfortunate turn, the effect certainly would have been to make me more indolent. The very opposite was the case. The relationship was beneficial to me in another sense as well. Environed by all the rabble barbarism and by so much petty envy, without having any supportive illusions, I was then and am a strictly private individual, and had become, because of the wretched atmosphere in Denmark and because of my preeminence, an eccentric in the eyes of the masses, since they could not understand me. In a way it was a good thing, too, that the envious upper class, who secretly always have exploited the vulgarity directed against me, got a little difficulty to bite on. For that reason my life had to be accentuated a little. My relationship to the king was of some importance for that. In a certain sense it is just the task for me: only one human being, an absolute monarch, and Christian VIII at that. I readily perceived that the relationship could have become dangerous for me, that Christian VIII could get to relish me too much; that is why I was extremely circumspect, as anyone certainly will admit who knows how he liked me. On the other hand, the relationship was so advanced that at any chosen moment I could have made something of it if necessary.

Christian VIII was only intelligent enough to be almost superstitious about his own intelligence, and therefore when he got the impression of a superior intelligence he became almost fantastic—he constantly feared ghosts. He did not have strong nerves, his life had left its mark on his whole mental-spiritual make-up, he lacked ethical backbone, the religious had practically only an esthetic effect on him —and that was the nature of his intelligence. It is easy to see that such a constitution is unbalanced, and it is a likely prey to duplicity, but please note, in the most delightful and pleasant way. Basically he was very domineering. His preference for other associations to the official ones was a deception perpetrated by his cunning and caution. He was afraid of anyone with real character. If such a person was also visibly strong and muscular, so to speak, he kept him at a distance. But an inflexible character concealed in a flexible cunning and imagination—that was his limit. This X he could not cope with, and as if by a law of nature he would be in the power of a man like that.

Generally speaking, Christian VIII has provided me with many psychological observations. Perhaps a psychologist ought to pay special attention to kings, especially absolute kings, for the more free a man is, the less[2061] enmeshed he is in finite concerns and considerations, the more there is to know in the man.

$X^1$ A 43   *n.d.*, 1849

« 6312

For

*The Collected Works of Consummation*[2062]
There could be a very brief preface.

Just as a cabinet minister steps down and becomes a private citizen, so I cease to be an author[2063] and lay down my pen—I actually have had a portfolio.

Just one word more, but no, no more words now, for now I have laid down my pen.

$X^1$ A 45   *n.d.*, 1849

« 6313

On the whole it is dreadful to think about what is going to become of the next generation after the way it has been brought up, when with the help of the press it has literally been the case that parents and children have collaborated in playing childish pranks. For *The Corsair* was something different. In my day we lads did things like that together in school, but of course we were afraid that the teachers or parents would find out. But nowadays the parents themselves set the pattern for the children, making it altogether official. And the schoolmaster himself is afraid of it, as, for example, that spineless fellow M. Hammerich,[2064] who preferred to let a teacher (Høedt[2065]) leave the school because he had been persecuted by *The Corsair* and the pupils brought it along to school. What a generation!

$X^1$ A 46   *n.d.*, 1849

### « 6314

There is something tragic-comic in my situation with R. Nielsen.[2066] Gradually he has read his way into my books so that every once in a while there comes an illustration, a brilliant observation, which I recognize and could quote from the text, but he does not seem to notice it.

$$x^1 \text{ A } 52 \quad n.d., \text{ 1849}$$

### « 6315

It could be rhetorically beautiful and moving to end a discourse, as is frequently done, with a verse from an old hymn, and then, just when the listener is sure it is all finished, lyrically but briefly exegete the particular words.

For example, the discourse is over, and now comes "a verse from an old hymn":[2067]

> And when the world's comfort is no longer there
> Then you become to me twice as fair . . .

and so it will in fact be, yes, so it has to be; for when the vinegar poured for us gets more sour and the gall more bitter, the tiniest bit of comfort which we scarcely tasted in our happier days when we fed on confections becomes twice as sweet. It is not intrinsically sweeter, but the vinegar is more sour and the gall more bitter. Consequently

> And when the world's comfort is no longer there
> Then you become to me twice as fair.
> O, Jesus, all poor sinners' friend,
> Draw me wholly to yourself again.
> [*In margin:* Brorson, no. 1104, 9.]

$$x^1 \text{ A } 53 \quad n.d., \text{ 1849}$$

### « 6316

In fact it could be beautiful to take a single verse this way and gradually weave it into a lyrical commentary.

#### Example

My attentive listeners: In the hymnody of an earlier period it was customary to portray the soul's relationship to Christ as a conversation, using the metaphor of the relationship between a bride and groom. The soul was the bride and was often called the Shulammite maiden.[2068]

There is the case of an old hymn in which the soul (the bride) is portrayed as having become impatient, and, no longer able to carry on in the sufferings of life, it impatiently waits for the hour of deliverance. Christ is portrayed as speaking to the bride and saying:

[*In margin:* It is from Brorson's *Svanesang*, no. 49, 1, p. 867,[2069] but I quote it a bit differently, dropping the first line and drawing the next two lines down to the fourth.]

> "When the air is still so bright
> With the shivering-cold of winter's might"

Consequently it is still midwinter, it is a long time yet until spring, therefore it is impatience to want to have spring now, there is much more to endure before the hour of deliverance comes, in fact the suffering perhaps has just now really begun. The air is still full of snow; indeed, it is not only cold, it is so cold that one shivers, distressingly cold, for cold does not always make one shiver. Therefore the poet has created a new word: shivering-cold. [*In margin:* It is early winter, the "winter's snow" is still a long way off, it remains tormentingly in the air, thus the uncomfortably cold air that makes one shiver: shivering-cold.] Therefore

> "When the air is still so bright
> With the shivering-cold of winter's might
> Why then do you open the window?"

Thus the bride is portrayed as sitting by the window, opening the window; but anyone who opens the window at that time of year is waiting impatiently, is asking every hour, every minute for a change. And it is still mid-winter.

> "Why do you open the window
> And always stare up into the sky."

As if spring had to come, spring forth as a bud from the stem; and "always" stare—it is much too early! or—and "always" stare, that is, continues to stare: O, then you will keep on staring for a long time, while you simply grow more impatient, making the long time even longer and the winter even colder and the air even more distressing with its shivering cold. Therefore

> Why do you open the window
> And always stare up into the sky?

Why do you do it again and again,
My Shulammite maiden?

$X^1$ A 54   *n.d.*, 1849

« 6317 *N.B. N.B.*

The question is: When should all the latest books be published! I cannot thank God enough for having finished them, and if I had not had the tension of additional mental anguish I perhaps would never have completed them, because once I have come out of the momentum of writing, I never get into it again in the same way. This time I succeeded, and for me it is enough that they exist, finished in fair copy, containing the completion and the entire structure of the whole, going as far as I in fact could go in my attempt to introduce Christianity into Christendom—but, please note, "poetically, without authority," for, as I have always maintained, I am no apostle, I am a poetic-dialectical genius, personally and religiously a penitent.

But when shall they be published? If I publish them while I am still in the position of heterogeneity maintained up till now—that is, independent, free, unrestricted, floating—if I publish them while still maintaining this mode of life, all the extremely exact dialectical categories and determinations in the books will be of little help in defending myself against unhappy confusions, and I will nevertheless be confused with such a one.

But if I had gotten myself a position in the established order first of all, then my life would be a hindrance to a misunderstanding like that. But if I had held such a position, I would not have written the books, of that I am sincerely convinced, and it is really easy to understand. But now it is done and the delay is simply a matter of publishing.

My situation will place me personally under the same "judgment," as everyone else, the judgment upon Christendom contained in these books. It is precisely this which will prevent my being confused with an apostle or someone like that. The books are poetically written, as if by an apostle, but I have stepped aside—no, I am not the apostle, anything but, I am the poet and a penitent.

I have always kept my eyes open for that reef, being confused with an apostle. If that enters in, then I have spoiled my work and am guilty of disloyalty.

Without a doubt Governance has supported me beyond telling; that I myself knew best of all, but not in such an extraordinary way as if I had a special relationship to God.

The influence of this whole *"monumentum ære perennius"*[2070] will be purely ideal. It is like a judgment, but I am not "the judge"; I submit myself to the judgment.[2071]

$X^1$ A 56   *n.d.*, 1849

« **6318**

The person who lives in a very restricted context (*Stilleben*[2072]) very easily falls into the trap of wanting to apply the God-relationship or place God into relation to the least triviality, for example that it is God's punishment that it is smoky today, that yesterday the food was scorched, or on each and every occasion one is prompted to think of God. The entire opening portion of Tieck's novel *Jahrmarkt*[2073] takes this up very well.

Those who live in the hurly-burly of the world very easily fall into the trap of getting no occasion in which there is genuine pathos and earnestness in the thought of God or in thinking through the conception of God. They have so many concepts and experiences dancing along that everything is immediately placed under rubrics and nothing really makes a pathos-filled impression. A pastor, for example, who conducts ten funerals every day, twenty marriages every Sunday, baptizes babies by the dozen, in short, never takes off his robe.

Therefore a good measure of the ethical earnestness of a pastor is the pathos with which he is able to invest each of these repetitious ceremonies. This is the case with Bishop Mynster and this really makes him far greater than all his eloquence.

As a preacher Mynster undeniably has something in common with that brand of wisdom and virtuosity exemplified by the ingenious housewife who is also a lady and has some style and knows how to give the impression that there is a superabundance on the table even though this is not the case. I cannot forget the virtuosity with which my aunt on Kjøbmagergade could say: Won't you have another little piece of chicken—when there was perhaps a wing, which we all naturally passed on saying: No thanks, I am well satisfied—and it was almost as if we were all really satisfied. Mynster's strength is his way of officiating and preaching, and this, although for him a moral *virtu*osity,[2074] at times achieves the level of an artistic masterpiece, which for a quick imagination is reminiscent of the miracle with the three small loaves. Of course this is not a deception but a noble wisdom; in a religious sense there is an insatiability which is anything but religious.

$X^1$ A 58   *n.d.*, 1849

### « 6319

In view of the fact that Peter[2075] is my brother and obviously has the religious qualifications to enable him to pass judgment,[2076] and also because I still have the responsibility for placing him in such a situation that when I am dead and the dialectical riddle of my life of self-denial has been solved, and the pain of my life can be used as a clue, he will then have the humiliation of actually having judged me wrongly—I have gently reminded him, but with extreme circumspection, that he should watch his step.

But, as he says, he has enough confidence in his judgment. So it is up to him. I did not do it for my own sake. I understand him very well, that he really is still unable to interpret my life as anything but a reckless striving to be great.

That, of course, comes easy, for we have long been familiar with that sort of thing; it is so easy to think that way instead of venturing just a little way into the intellectual exertions contained in my books, particularly since they do indicate the fine line between egotism and what can be true self-denial. To a great extent my essentiality as an author consists in practically having discovered: sympathetic passion.[2077]

But all that takes effort; it is much handier to interpret my life that way, so self-complacently to regard one's own *Stilleben*[2078] as religiously superior.

To me he is an example and proof that a man does not understand more than his life expresses. This explains his opinion that the opposition I have had of late is nemesis or God's punishment.

As far as I am concerned it is a matter of indifference, but my responsibility, if I have any, I have taken care of.

$x^1$ A 61   *n.d.,* 1849

### « 6320

It is a rather strange title: *Wisdom for a Penny Bought with a Million of "Repentance."* It is by a R. Green,[2079] published toward the end of the sixteenth century. Mentioned by Ben Jonson in his work *Epicoene,* translated by Tieck in his collected works,[2080] II, p. 371, first column in a note.

$x^1$ A 63   *n.d.,* 1849

### « 6321 *Lines for a Poetic Individual*

For any person who has made gossip his profession and living etc. (for example, Goldschmidt[2081]) to be considered as belonging to the community again, it should be required that he first and foremost unconditionally apologize at least once a year for as many years as he has carried on the profession. He also could be required to give back the money he has made—Judas did that; after all, he gave back the thirty shekels.

X[1] A 67   n.d., 1849

« **6322**

In the *Kirketidende*[2082] (for Feb. 2, 1849) I see in a sort of review of Birchedahl's[2083] sermons that he will not recognize a state church at all and battles it in his sermons. Excellent, here again we have one of those confused phenomena—he ought to perceive that the first thing he would have to do would be to resign his position as pastor in the state church, give up his livelihood. But of course he would have an easy answer to that: Then I would have nothing to live on. And of course that can be understood by the whole world, which sees nothing wrong with earning one's bread and butter but considers what I say to be an exaggeration. But there is no doubt that Birchedahl should do it for his own sake in order to see whether or not his conviction is so firm that he could make a sacrifice for it.

X[1] A 71   n.d., 1849

« **6323**

The same objection which the Judge in *Either/Or*[2084] uses to trap A (confronting him with a young man who wants to talk with him, instead of lecturing and admonishing him—very moving—see especially the second essay in part II), the same objection is made by life itself against the person who wants to enter into decisive religious categories of which cruelty is one aspect. Life prompts one to become aware of the many, many less endowed, weak, simple men, women, and children, the sick and the sorrowful, etc., who live among us. Life says to the religious: Confronted by all these people, can you have the heart to jack up the price[2085] of the religious, of salvation, as high as you are doing, you cruel person. And if the religious person is truly religious and consequently has love in his heart, this objection will make a deep impression on him, one who wants so much to be with those who suffer, whose only joy and consolation, after all, is to comfort those who suffer.

But the objection is the spiritual trial of "human sympathy." What does the prototype teach? Was Christ lenient with himself, or the others. Was it human sympathy to say to the person who was willing to follow him but merely asked to bury his father first: Let the dead bury their dead.[2086] Humanly speaking, is it not cruel, humanly speaking almost shocking, to forbid him something that is a matter of piety? We do not say that Christ, after all, was high and mighty and therefore there must not be any meddling in sympathy; that is a misunderstanding, for Christ was not high and mighty, but He was love and the greater His love the less His cruelty would have to be. Not so, Christ is the absolute, and this cruelty is inseparable from the absolute. Nor is there the slightest trace of human sympathy in his reply to poor Peter: Get behind me, Satan.[2087] After all, Peter meant the best for Christ in his own way, that is, in human sympathy—and then to treat him that way.

The point is that the religious person unconditionally shall and must have sympathy for all the weak; he wants to be with them, comfort them, and all that, but he does not dare do it—that is, he does not dare center his life in this sympathy so that instead of remaining true to God he scales down and remains in the religiosity of sympathy.

As soon as a religious person ceases to comprehend it this way: I dare not, I cannot do otherwise (that is, he is in the power of the absolute, absolute obedience is demanded of him), he will be sidetracked and will remain in the religiosity of sympathy.

The danger for the religious person who is in the religiousness of the absolute is, of course, self-righteousness, that he becomes arrogant instead of pious, that he wants to be better than other men or puts God, as it were, in his debt, or at least has a self-satisfied consciousness of having done his part.

For this reason such a religious person will usually have a secret strain, comparable to Paul's "thorn in the flesh,"[2088] which gives him the bold confidence to go on, because it teaches him that he is nothing and truly makes this truth in him. No one can venture out into absolute religiousness on his own; he must begin in an altogether singular understanding with God. Under other circumstances, that which in absolute religiousness is dialectically cruel becomes outright cruelty, sin, guilt.

X¹ A 72   n.d., 1849

« 6324

Strangely enough, the Chinese have the same custom as the Jews. Confucius's name is *Khu* or *Ju,* but when the name appears in the sacred books, the people are forbidden to utter it—it is recommended instead that they read it as *Mou*. It is exactly the same as with *Jehovah*. The loose way in which the name of Christ is used in Christendom is really all wrong. Curiously, I have personally experienced long periods in which I have been unable to mention Christ's name to anyone because I regard it as too solemn. I have expressed this, also, in the "psychological experiment," where Quidam[2089] says (p. 254 bottom) that the girl has pledged herself to him with the name which he does not dare utter, that is, the name of Christ.

See *China, historisch-malerisch*,[2090] Karlsruhe, p. 223.

'x¹ A 73 *n.d.*, 1849

« **6325** *Deliberations*

It is clear that once again my prudence and my melancholy have wanted to deceive me.

I practically had decided not to publish anything but the second edition of *Either/Or*.[2091] (1) The situation at present is so painful and confused, and then to have to say what I must say and in the end be notorious and branded as I am—yes, almost any danger is possible, and in fact it is almost as if one hurled himself into it—and I think that right now I need a little peace and quiet. (2) My financial situation[2092] makes it necessary, even obligatory, to think of an appointment. But if in one way or another I become the extraordinary to my contemporaries, that itself would possibly be a hindrance to me. —Then, too, my understanding tells me that it would be humble of me not to publish even what I have ready. (3) It would be almost uncomfortable to live if men in any way have the emotion-charged notion that I am something extraordinary. —But in that case I could, after all, travel a bit.

But the answer to all that must be that it is prompted by nothing but prudence and melancholy. As far as danger is concerned, the magnitude of it only makes it more of a duty not to plunge into it but trusting in God to venture into it; if I remain silent, there will be no danger. —As far as getting an appointment is concerned, that again would be a luxury. But the whole thing is just a possibility for me, a possibility which looks as if it were something as long as it is used merely to disturb me and prevent me from acting in the opposite direction. But if it becomes something in earnest, then I see dubious aspects arising again: ergo, it is an evasion. The big question is whether or not I am qualified for an appointment. Suppose I got an appointment and just what I wanted—but I prudently had refrained from acting decisively in the most crucial moment of my life—what then? Well, it would immediately become a torment to me, like a punishment placed upon me, as if I had sneaked or done it on the sly, deceived God, deceived him about the inner truth of my whole authorship, as if I had let it stand ambiguously in abeyance so that its completion would not hinder my getting an appointment or make too much trouble for me. And how would that help me in my position? Furthermore, it must be remembered that publishing the two books[2093] in question would not make it at all impossible for me to get an appointment;[2094] on the contrary, in one sense it would make it much easier, inasmuch as it would make me stand out more clearly as a religious author. But, to be sure, this possibility is literally not mine to decide, not until I have ventured to do what according to my understanding would add to my difficulties. Consequently this possibility is only in God's hands. But if he so wills—and I have ventured what I should: then I can accept it serenely. As far as the humbleness of refraining from publishing is concerned, this has little meaning since the publishing itself will be bitter enough for me.

I have another concern regarding "The Point of View for My Work as an Author": that in some way I might have said too much about myself, or whether in some way God might want me to be silent about something. On the first point I have emphasized as decisively as possible in "A Cycle of Ethical-Religious Essays" that I am without authority; furthermore it is stated in the book that I am a penitent,[2095] that my entire activity as an author is my own upbringing or education.[2096] That I am *like* a secret agent[2097] in a higher service. Finally, in "Armed Neutrality," every misunderstanding, as if I were an apostle, has been forestalled as decisively as possible. More I cannot do; these are the most important stipulations. Moreover, by reading the book through again I can take care—and I am fully convinced that God once again will watch over me—that no word escapes me which makes me into too much, since God and I know how deeply inadequate I am in my innermost being and how concerned I am that I do not forfeit the meaning of my life by the slightest word to that effect.

With respect to God's wanting me to suppress what is most important, it must be mentioned that the actual motive for that idea is the fearful judgment of the understanding that such an admission would prevent me from getting an appointment, together with the fact that my whole reserved nature is far too disposed toward silence and subtlety. But I do owe it to the established order to make an accurate account of myself before taking any appointment. In one sense my total outlook has been in the service of the established order, altogether conservative, and I would regard it as a gross misunderstanding on the part of the established if it refused to accept me as an appointee. On the other hand there is still a possibility of such a misunderstanding if I publish the books. I ought to expose myself to that danger.

Therefore, it is rather that I owe it to God, myself, the established, and my cause to publish the two books under consideration.

Finally, there is the most crucial point. The second edition of *Either/Or* is coming out. But since that time I have stepped out in the character of a religious author: how do I now dare let it be published without a careful explanation; it would surely cause offense.

With regard to the idea, which I have had all along, of keeping back completed works in order to slow down my productivity, I do have four works[2098] held in abeyance.

Therefore I really must thank God for being constrained eventually into a decision; it is compassion on the part of Governance. I had gotten too much into the habit of pushing decisions aside, of writing but otherwise diverting my mind with possibilities: on the one hand to travel, on the other to seek an appointment. In the midst of all this, time slipped by; even if I kept on writing, I nevertheless was in another sense slack.

At the moment my melancholy raises so many horrendous possibilities that I neither can nor will record them. The only way to fight such things is to say: Hold your tongue, and to look away from them and look only to God. And yet I have a presentiment, or an intimation of faith, that this step, far from becoming the ruination of me, humanly speaking, will make my future happier and easier. Exhausted as I am, very concerned as I always have been, suffering of late in many ways, I could use some encouragement, humanly speaking; humanly speaking, I can say no more, for it may well be that if I just move out I will have more powers. But the point is that because of this presentiment I truly cannot act; thus if it turns out that way, it really will be a gift of God's love and in one respect unexpected, for I must act by virtue of the very opposite, that everything grows dark around me, and that I nevertheless go on with it.

$X^1$ A 74  *n.d.*, 1849

« 6326

My depression actually has gotten an all too frightful upper hand over me. Most likely much of what appals me is, as usual, imaginary, largely because I have not breathed freely for a long time but have been troubled by finite concerns, which is not the case with me ordinarily. But whether it is imaginary or not, it is very exhausting when one is obliged to act, to lift the pillar of reflection as I must do.

There must be action simply in order to save life; then God will bring—yes, how can I say it, no, it is eternally true, God will bring the best out of it. This matter of the appointment is a lazy possibility that merely will hinder me in the other.

$X^1$ A 77   *n.d.*, 1849

« 6327        *N.B.*        *N.B.*
                    *N.B.*

"The Point of View for My Work as an Author" must not be published,[2099] no, no!

(1) And this is the deciding factor (never mind all those ideas I had about endangering my future and my bread and butter): I cannot tell the full truth about myself. Even in the very first manuscript (which I wrote without any thought at all of publishing) I was unable to stress the primary factor: that I am a penitent, and that this explains me at the deepest level. But when I took the manuscript out with the thought of publishing it, I was obliged to make a few small changes, for in spite of everything it was cast too intensely to be published. But I can and will speak of the extraordinary gifts entrusted to me only if I can give the same strong emphasis (which I feel myself when I reflect on the subject) to my sin and guilt. Not to do so would be taking the extraordinary in vain.

(2) I cannot quite say that my work as an author is a sacrifice. It is true I have been unspeakably unhappy ever since I was a child, but I nevertheless acknowledge that the solution God found of letting me become an author has been a rich, rich pleasure to me. I may be sacrificed, but my authorship is not a sacrifice; it is, in fact, what I unconditionally prefer to keep on being.

Thus I cannot tell the full truth here, either, for I cannot speak this way in print about my torment and wretchedness—when the pleasure is really predominant.

But perhaps I have had my head somewhat in the clouds and possibly could have deceived myself about the extent to which, if it came to that, I would really prefer being slain to being obliged to seek a quieter, more tranquil activity.

(3) Once I have articulated the extraordinary in me, even with all the guardedness I have used, then I will be stuck with it, and it will be

a torment and a fearful responsibility to go on living if I am pathetically looked upon solemnly as someone extraordinary.

(4) The fact that I cannot give the full truth in portraying myself signifies that essentially I am a poet—and here I shall remain.

————

But the situation is this: the past year (when I wrote that piece) was a hard one for me; I have suffered greatly. The treatment by rabble barbarism has interfered somewhat with my incognito and tended to force me to be direct instead of dialectical as I have always been, to force me out beyond myself. My incognito was to be a sort of nobody, peculiar, odd-looking, with thin legs, an idler, and all that. All this was of my own free will. Now the rabble have been trained to stare at me inhumanly and mimic me, day after day, with the result that I have become fed up with my incognito. So I was in danger of making a complete turnabout.

This must not happen, and I thank God that it was precluded and that I did not go ahead and publish "The Point of View for my Work as an Author" (indeed, there always was something in me that opposed it).

The book itself is true and in my opinion masterly. But a book like that can be published only after my death. If my sin and guilt, my intrinsic misery, the fact that I am a penitent are stressed a bit more pointedly, then it will be a true picture. But I must be careful about the idea of dying, lest I go and do something with the thought of dying in half a year and then live to be eighty-two.[2100] No, one finishes a book like that, puts it away in a drawer, sealed and marked: To be opened after my death.

————

And now suppose, speaking quite humanly, that I ventured too little, that I could have ventured a bit farther. In that case the good lord, God in heaven who is love, my Father in heaven, who forgives me my sins for the sake of Christ, he surely will forgive me this as well. After all, he is not a cruel master, not a jealous lover, but the loving Father. To him I dare say: I do not presume to venture more, I have a fear of becoming false, of being brash toward you. I would rather stick with my incognito and let everyone think what he pleases about me than solemnly become somebody, an extraordinary. There is no one to whom I can make myself completely understood, because that which is crucial in my possible extraordinariness is that I cannot, after all, discuss my sin and guilt.

So God surely will turn it all into good for me.

———

Moreover, what I have written[2101] can very well be used—if I do indeed continue to be an author—but then I must assign it to a poet, a pseudonym.

For example—

by
the poet Johannes de Silentio
edited
by
Søren Kierkegaard

But this is the best proof that "The Point of View for My Work as an Author" cannot be published. It must be made into something by a third party: A Possible Explanation of Magister Kierkegaard's Authorship, that is, so it is no longer the same book at all. For the point of it was my personal story.

———

And then I must go abroad in the spring.

———

But it was due to God's solicitude that I was flushed out of this indolent productivity, producing and producing (and in one sense superbly), but I never took the trouble to think about publishing, partly because I was hoping for death.

X[1] A 78   n.d., 1849

« 6328

Luther's sermon[2102] on the Epistle for Septuagesima Sunday, which I read just today (according to plan), was very impressive. I was moved by the first point, that only *one* found the jewel, but even more by the next—to miss the mark, which Luther develops beautifully right at the beginning.

X[1] A 80   n.d., 1849

« **6329**

[*In margin:* N.B.]

Incidentally, the "supplements"[2103] to "The Point of View" could very well be published and separately. They will then be read considerably. In fact, I now will and should get more involved in the times.

$x^1$ A 84   *n.d.,* 1849

« **6330**

"The Seducer's Diary" had to come first in order to shed light on the "Psychological Experiment."[2104] The latter lies in the confinium between the interesting and the religious. If "The Seducer's Diary" had not come out first, the result would have been that the reading world would have found it interesting. "The Seducer's Diary" was a help, and now it was found to be boring—quite rightly so, for it is the religious. Frater Taciturnus himself gives the same explanation.[2105]

$x^1$ A 88   *n.d.,* 1849

« **6331**

The fashion designer (in *Stages*)[2106] gets the idea of starting a fashionable boutique, one section devoted entirely to dressing corpses; thus for the corpse to be dressed in vogue is equivalent to being buried in Christian ground, that is, the latest interpretation.

$x^5$ A 152   *n.d.,* 1849

« **6332**

If I wanted to tell about it, a whole book could be written on how ingeniously I have fooled people about my pattern of life.

During the time I was reading proof on *Either/Or* and writing upbuilding discourses I had almost no time to walk the streets.[2107] I then used another method. Every evening when I left home exhausted and ate at Mini's, I stopped at the theater for ten minutes—not one minute more. Familiar as I was, I counted on there being several gossips at the theater who would say: Every single night he goes to the theater; he does not do another thing. O, you darling gossips, thank you—without you I could never have achieved what I wanted.

I did it also for the sake of my former betrothed. It was my melancholy wish to be scorned if possible, merely to serve her, merely to help her offer me proper resistance. Thus there was within me unanimous agreement from all sides with respect to impairing my public image this way.

$x^5$ A 153   *n.d.*, 1849

« 6333

What I am afflicted with is a mixture of a kind of modesty and a kind of pride. When it comes to finite things I am unable to take advantage or look to my own advantage; I am ashamed to protest being cheated—I am embarrassed on behalf of the other person. And yet I am well aware of it, but there is also a certain pride over the fact that for me it is actually enough to have perceived it.

$x^1$ A 89   *n.d.*, 1849

« 6334

What I have written about Adler[2108] perhaps could be published separately under the title: "A Literary Review,"[2109] and the longer preface[2110] to "A Cycle of Ethical-Religious Essays" could be used here.

$x^1$ A 90   *n.d.*, 1849

« 6335

No, "such an extraordinary" [2111] I certainly am not. Partly because I have not collided with the established order but with the universally-human (a suffering which has often happened to a genius), partly because I am a penitent, and finally, the extraordinary in me is so remote from producing anything new that, just the opposite, I am suited to preserving the established order.

Now I see it more clearly—that, rightly understood, I am or ought to be the movement, the awakening, only in a soft and dormant period (for I am the more ideal established order), but in rebellious times I am quite clearly conservative. What R. Nielsen[2112] said is quite true—that in a way Bishop Mynster[2113] regards me as an exaggeration—in peace-time; but now he thinks that I am more suitable.

$x^1$ A 92   *n.d.*, 1849

« 6336          *N.B.*          *N.B.*
                    *N.B.*

Great care must be taken now; there must be a new direction.

There are three possibilities open to me. (1) To step forth directly and decisively into the world of actuality in the character of the extraordinary, disregarding the fact that I am essentially a poet, that essentially I have related poetically to it (even though I am unusually ethical for a poet in the sense of an emphasis upon willing to be what is poetized), disregarding the fact that I have an accidental advantage: private means. —This would be false on my part and is therefore an impossibility. (2) To draw everything poetical back into myself as a poet and then arrange my total personal life as a poet, seek a poet-distance in order to avoid any occasion for confusion as to whether I am existentially what is poetized. (3) To seek an appointment,[2114] as I originally intended.

But my financial problem, especially in these confused times,[2115] has taken a bit out of me. With this advantage I wanted to be able to keep on my feet in spite of all the mistreatment from people and to be approximately what has been poetized, but this concern has gnawed at the dialectical elasticity of my mind and spirit, and the mistreatment and all the loathsomeness I put up with has made me a little impatient, to the point where I almost went ahead and declared something about myself (of course still dialectical enough so that I would not say I was that but that I had been), something which, to be sure, is not untrue but which I have regarded religiously as my duty to preserve in self-denial and therefore in all consistency I cannot make public the basis of it, however surreptitiously.

For this reason no. 2 of "A Cycle of Ethical-Religious Essays"[2116] (the universal—the single individual—the special individual) cannot come out, either. Despite all disclaimers it will be understood as being about me. But it does also contain the explanation of "The Seducer's Diary,"[2117] although it probably will not be understood that way, but rather as being about my exposure of myself to the rabble.

$X^1$ A 94   n.d., 1849

« **6337**

And then perhaps, as stated frequently, all the writings[2118] that lie finished (the most valuable I have produced) can also be used, but, for God's sake, in such a way as to guarantee that they are kept poetic, as poetic awakening.

$X^1$ A 95   n.d., 1849

« **6338**              ***N.B.***        ***N.B.***
                        ***N.B.***

What a moody oddity I am. Today I take out what I wrote recently to see if it were the case that it said too much. And there on it stands already: poetical, without authority.

$X^1$ A 100   n.d., 1849

« **6339**

It could be droll to give a play three titles.

He Laughs Best Who Laughs Last
or
He Laughs Last Who Laughs Best
or
*Wie es euch gefällt*[2119]
A Comedy
or
Musical
or
Fruit Montage
in Three Acts

Nonsensical, but obviously there are possibilities here for some lines à la Falstaff. That crazy third title or Fruit Montage is characteristic of him. In his abusive works as well as in his comparisons, when there already has been a plenitude of lunacy, along comes one more which is utterly mad. Things of this nature happen in life. I have a childhood memory (one of Wahlgreen's boys; they lived with Agerskov at Blegdam 8)—after having exhausted all his invective against another boy in a fit of bad temper, finally pausing for a moment, he then cried out desperately, half ecstatically: You canary!

$X^1$ A 104    *n.d.,* 1849

« **6340**

So it goes. I posed the problem, the problem which confronts the whole generation: equality between man and man. I posed it in action here in Copenhagen. That is something quite different from writing a few words about it; I expressed some approximation of it with my life. In an *essentially Christian* sense I leveled,[2120] but not in a mutinous way against position and power, which I have maintained with all my might.

But people do not grasp this, but they do talk—and I become the victim; and I am supposed to have been guilty of pride, I who have fought sacrificially for equality.

And the result. Well, the result is quite simply that if I had not been as profoundly influenced religiously as I am, I might have withdrawn and sought company—with the exclusive set—that is, I would have become proud.

O, you fools!

$X^1$ A 107    *n.d.,* 1849

« **6341**

I have become involved with R. Nielsen[2121] because I considered it my religious duty to have at least one man, so that it could not be said that I bypassed completely this claim.

Of course he can be of no benefit to me ultimately: he is too heavy, too thick-skinned, too spoiled by the age of Christian VIII. Were I to become secular-minded, he naturally would be of advantage to me.

I have been obliged to be a little distant with him, for otherwise he prattles pleasantly about my cause, my cause which either should be intensified unconditionally or hidden in deepest silence.

$X^1$ A 110  *n.d.,* 1849

« **6342**

R. Nielsen[2122] can understand me up to a point, but he cannot resist himself, is fascinated by all this profundity, hurries home, jots it down, and communicates it—instead of first acting upon it himself. His communication of the truth will never in all eternity become action.

$X^1$ A 111  *n.d.,* 1849

« **6343**     *N.B. N.B.*

It is absolutely certain that I am not "such an extraordinary"[2123] as presented in No. 2.[2124] I have never clashed with the established order, have always been basically conservative. In breaking an engagement I have clashed—but as an individual—with something universally human. But this really does not concern any other man; it is not a collision with the historical as an established order, the kind of collision embodying the dialectic of bringing forth something new. But I have never claimed to have that. Moreover, I have done everything lest my example, my collision, should harm anyone, *as if* there were something great in not getting married.

$X^1$ A 112  *n.d.,* 1849

« **6344**     *N.B. N.B.*

I can truthfully say that I have worked in the service of the established order.

And even if pressed forward to becoming a reformer according to my own highest possible standards, I would still be in the service of the established order, for I regard "the crowd" as the evil. If I should fall, I must fall—I have opposed it and will continue to oppose it, supporting the government with all my powers.

But insofar as I touch on that odious traffic in [ecclesiastical] jobs, it is not, again, with the idea that anyone's living should be taken away from one single solitary person, or that anyone should become anxious and for that reason give it up. What I am fighting for on this point (still very secondary) is, again, a conception, how one views his job, that one admits to himself that to have it is an alleviation, an accommodation, but does not shamelessly turn the thing around and turn "bread-and-butter" into earnestness—and Christ and the apostles into visionaries.

What I said to Christian VIII is really true—that I certainly believe I have been of benefit to the established order, but it is also true what I said to him about the point of the whole thing being that I am a private individual.[2125] For an awakening was needed, and the established order needed rehabilitation in such shabby times, when everything is explained by low motives and when the competent state employee is in one sense diminished by saying: He is in the paid service of the state.

$X^1$ A 113    n.d., 1849

« 6345               *N.B.*          *N.B.*
                         *N.B.*

It is awkward to publish even the least little thing that remotely explains the extraordinary. True enough, I am not such a person,[2126] but from that, but from that it does not follow, in spite of all the excluding elements, that I will be so regarded [as not being an extraordinary]. But if part of being an extraordinary is to hide the fact, I ought not give any telegraphic signals of that kind.

My only characteristic of extraordinariness is that I am a penitent. It is impossible now to explain this in such a way that the accent falls in the right place. For what does the world really care about such things if it can only get to stare at the extraordinary. But if I cannot say A, then I cannot say B, either.

No doubt there is something sad here. My life, my work as an author, will be explained *höchstens* as a special kind of genius, by no means as serious and by no means as consistent as the lives of various others. None of my contemporaries penetrates more deeply than this. I am the only one who can explain it (for here to explain is to have made the discovery, to have discovered capacities which do not exist as such for others)—alas, and I am silent. It is as though someone had a great treasure and hid it so securely that he threw the key away.

What troubles me is whether or not I have the right to do this, whether in relation to God this silence is permissible, whether it is permissible to let a productivity which is so infinitely indebted to Him for its ingenuity remain an enigma and for many somewhat odd. And why? In part because the author considers this to be self-denial and in part because he feels unable to assume every misunderstanding in actual life resulting from giving an explanation.

$$X^1 A 115 \quad n.d., 1849$$

« **6346**              *N.B.*        *N.B.*
                           *N.B.*

"A Cycle of Minor Ethical-Religious Essays,"[2127] if that which deals with Adler is omitted (and it definitely must be omitted, for to come in contact with him is completely senseless, and furthermore it perhaps is also unfair to treat a contemporary merely psychologically this way), has the defect that what as parts in a total study does not draw attention to itself (and originally this was the case) will draw far too much attention to itself and thereby to me. Although originally an independent work, the same applies to no. 3, a more recent work.

But if no. 2 and no. 3,[2128] which are about Adler, are also to be omitted, then "A Cycle" cannot be published at all.

Besides, there should be some stress on a second edition of *Either/ Or*. Therefore either—as I previously thought—a quarto with all the most recent writing or only a small fragment of it, but, please note, to constitute a proper contrast to *Either/Or*. The "Three Notes"[2129] on my work as an author were intended for that, and this has a strong appeal to me.

If I do nothing at all directly to assure a full understanding of my whole authorship (by publishing "The Point of View for My Work as an Author") or do not even give an indirect sign (by publishing "A Cycle" etc.)—then what? Then there will be no judgment at all on my authorship in its totality, for no one has sufficient faith or time or competence to look for a comprehensive plan in the entire production. Consequently the verdict will be that I have changed somehow over the years.

So it will be. This distresses me. I am deeply convinced that this is not the case, that there is an integral comprehensiveness in the whole production (by the special assistance of Governance), and that there certainly is something else to be said about it than this meager comment that the author has changed.

I keep this hidden deep within, where there is also something in contrast: the sense in which I was more guilty than other men.

These proportions strongly appr 1 to me. I am averse to being regarded with any kind of sympathy or to representing myself as the extraordinary.

This suits me completely. So the best incognito I can choose is quite simply to take an appointment.

The enticing aspect of the total productivity (that it is esthetic—but also religious) will be very faintly intimated by the "Three Notes." For that matter, if something is to function enticingly, it is wrong to explain it. A fisherman would not tell the fish about his bait, saying "This is bait." And finally, if everything else pointed to the appropriateness of communicating something about the integral comprehensiveness, I cannot emphasize enough that Governance actually is the directing power and that in so many ways I do not understand until afterwards.

This is written on Shrove-Monday. A year ago today I decided to publish *Christian Discourses;*[2130] this year I am inclined to the very opposite.

For a moment I would like to bring a bit of mildness and friendliness into the whole thing. This can best be achieved by a second edition of *Either/Or*[2131] and then the "Three Notes." In fact it would be odd right now when I am thinking of stopping writing[2132] to commence a polemic in which I do not wish to engage by replying (a polemic which is unavoidable because of no. 1 and no. 2 in "A Cycle").

Let there be moderation on my part: if someone wants a fight, then in a concealed way I certainly am well-armed.[2133]

$x^1$ A 116   February 19, 1849

« 6347                   *N.B.*        *N.B.*
                              *N.B.*

[*In margin:*
N.B.    N.B.
N.B.]

My task was to pose this riddle of awakening: a balanced esthetic and religious productivity, simultaneously.

This has been done. There is a balance even in quantity. *Concluding Postscript* is the midpoint.

The "Three Notes" swing it into the purely religious.

What comes next cannot be added impatiently as a conclusion.

For dialectically it is precisely right that this be the end. What comes next would be the beginning of something new.

x¹ A 118   *n.d.*, 1849

« **6348**

A martyrdom of laughter is what I really have suffered. Anything more than this and more profound than this I dare not say of myself: I am a martyr of laughter; but not everyone who suffers being laughed at, even for an idea, is therefore a martyr of laughter in the strict sense. For example, when a thoroughly earnest man suffers it in a good cause, he does not have the deeper relationship to the martyrdom he suffers. But I am a martyr of laughter and my life has been designed for that; I understand myself so completely as such that it is as if I now understood myself for the first time—on the other hand I would find it difficult to understand myself becoming successful in the world. No, in the martyrdom of laughter I recognize myself again. To be able to become just that, I am the wittiest of all, possessing a superlative sense of comedy, could myself have represented laughter on an unsurpassed scale, could also deceptively have lured men out upon thin ice by doing that, thereby becoming what the age demanded—this superiority, this self-determination is the criterion of the more ideal martyrdom. Quite rightly, I had to direct the laughter upon myself[2134] (as Ney[2135] directed the soldiers who shot him). And the one who must carry out the order would gladly have been my lieutenant, and it certainly never occurred to him to do otherwise than give me place no. 1.

x¹ A 120   *n.d.*, 1849

« **6349**

*Climacus and Anticlimacus*
*A Dialectical Discovery*
*by*
*Anticlimacus*

*Postscript*

I, Anticlimachus, who wrote this little book (a poor, simple, mere man just like most everybody else) was born in Copenhagen and am just about, yes, exactly, the same age as Johannes Climachus, with whom I in one sense have very much, have everything in common, but from whom in another sense I am utterly different. He explicitly says of himself that he is not a Christian;[2136] this is infuriating. I, too, have been so infuriated about it that I—if anyone could somehow trick me into saying it—say just the opposite, or because I say just the opposite about myself I could become furious about what he says of himself. I say, in fact, that I am an extraordinary Christian such as there has never been, but, please note, I am that in hidden inwardness. I shall see to it that no one, not one, detects anything, even the slightest, but profess I can, and I can profess (but I cannot *really* profess, for then, after all, I would violate the secret's hiding-place) that in hidden inwardness I am, as I said, an extraordinary Christian such as there has never been.

The reader, who in addition to being my friend is also a friend of understanding, will also readily perceive that, despite my extraordinary Christianity, there is something malevolent in me. For it is sufficiently clear that I have taken this position simply out of spite against Johannes. Had I come first, I would have said of myself what he now says of himself and then he would have been compelled to say of me what I say of him.

For we are related to each other, but we are not twins, we are opposites. Between us there is a deep, a fundamental relationship, but despite the most desperate efforts on both sides we never get any farther, any closer, than to a *repelling contact.* There is a point and an instant at which we touch, but at the same instant we fly from each other with the speed of infinity. Like two eagles plunging from a mountain top toward one point, or like one eagle plunging down from the top of a cliff and a predatory fish shooting from the ocean's depth to the surface with the same speed, we two both seek the same point; there is a contact, and at the same instant we rush from each other, each to his extremity.

The point we are seeking is this: simply and plainly to be a genuine Christian. There is a contact, but at the same instant we fly from each other: Johannes says that he is not a Christian, and I say that I am an extraordinary Christian such as there has never been, but, please note, in hidden inwardness.

If it should happen sometime that we switched identities at the instant of contact, so that I would say of myself what Johannes says of himself and conversely, it would make no difference. Just one thing is impossible—that we both say the same thing about ourselves; on the other hand it is possible that we both could vanish.

Actually, we do not exist, but he who does come to be simply and plainly a genuine Christian will be able to speak of us two brothers—opposites—just as the sailor speaks of the twins by which he steers. Just as the sailor tells about the fantastic things he has seen, so also the person who has come to be simply and plainly a genuine Christian will be able to tell about the fantastic things he has seen. Perhaps there are lies in what the sailor tells—this will not be true of what the genuine Christian tells of us, for it is true that we two brothers are fantastic figures, but it is also true that *he* has seen us.

Anti-C. [sic]

$X^6$ B 48    *n.d.*, 1849

« **6350**

The "Postscript" by Anticlimachus[2137] could well make a complete little book under the title:

Climachus and Anticlimachus

for Climachus is already known and the idea implicit here (by placing the two together) is authentically dialectical.

$X^1$ A 121    *n.d.*, 1849

« **6351** *My Last Word About Goldschmidt*[2138]

If I were to speak, I would say something like this. I have nothing to reproach him for. I must reproach myself for wronging myself out of perhaps exaggerated good nature and kindness, for having too much faith in him and hoping for some hidden good in him, for doing him the wrong of putting him to the test so that this had to come out in the open in a decisive way.

Everyone regarded him with contempt; none of those with whom I had any connection associated with him. That was the judgment passed on him, and I thought that it possibly was an injustice to him. He wished to become an author and with that in mind turned to me. I honestly and sympathetically did everything to encourage him and to tear him away if possible from the aberration and perdition of *The Corsair.*

I laid myself open to the possibility (so in fact several have told me) that many would take exception to my greeting or accompanying that man on the streets. I laid myself open to the circulation by certain envious circles of the opinion that I secretly humored rabble-irony.

I had entertained the thought of becoming more involved with him. But before that happened there had to be a test. Would he, in connection with the only object of his admiration and with what he himself had said in print, have the courage and self-respect to say either: No, I will not attack him, or: I will attack the little article[2139] he has written but not the earlier books I personally have admired and immortalized and to which I really am deeply indebted.

He did not stand the test. For me it became—if it must be called punishment—a punishment for being the only person here at home who did Goldschmidt the wrong of having too much faith in him and of hoping that there was something good hidden deep down in the man.

An Eastern proverb[2140] says: He who first praises and then berates someone lies two times. That was the snare I stretched for him—an exaggeration, *ach ja,* I could have been satisfied with the positive assurance of all the others that he was contemptible.

X¹ A 123   *n.d.,* 1849

« 6352                   *N.B.*        *N.B.*
                              *N.B.*

It is really unnecessary for me to give information about myself in direct communication for the sake of my contemporaries. It is not essentially a case of their misunderstanding me but is simply their rudeness, flouting, and envy.

To say something about myself as author *in toto* is difficult for me, because I never can emphasize strongly enough the part of Governance or my deepest conception about the whole matter. That is something that cannot be done until I am dead.

Self-denial requires the consistency of silence on this subject.

The only misgiving has to do with the God-relationship, whether I do not owe it to him to speak. One can deceive by being a hypocrite. But it is also a deceit to encourage and confirm people in an opinion which underrates one as much as possible. Here is the dialectical point, for if I declare the extraordinary about myself with respect to talents etc., yes with respect to being an author—I still cannot say anything about what to me is absolutely a part of it: all my wretchedness, my sin, etc. But if I cannot do that, then the extraordinary is taken in vain and gives a false picture of me.

X¹ A 126   *n.d.,* 1849

« 6353

Mohammed protests with all his might against being regarded as a poet and the Koran as a poem; he wants to be a prophet. [*In margin:* See Goethe, *Westöstlicher Divan, Sämtl. W.,*[2141] VI, pp. 33 ff.] I protest with all my might at being regarded as a prophet and want only to be a poet.

X¹ A 130   *n.d.,* 1849

« **6354**

(That I voluntarily exposed myself to ridicule)[2142]

. . . . . In this respect there is something that filled my soul with sadness. What is called the ordinary class, the common man, has rarely had and in Copenhagen has rarely had anyone who has Christianly loved him more disinterestedly than I have. On the other hand, here as everywhere, we have plenty of those, who in the capacity of journalists, want to make money on him—in exchange for false ideas which can only make him unhappy and make the relationship between class and class more bitter, plenty of those who in the capacity of agitators and the like want to exploit his numbers in order to help him get shot down, while from a loftier position an erroneous view is held and it is said: The simple class is demoralized; they must be shot down. No, no, no—the tragedy of the whole thing lies at the feet of the bourgeois, and if anyone is to be shot down, then let it be the journalists for the manner in which they have wanted to exploit the ordinary class and profit from them. God in heaven knows that blood-thirst is alien to my soul, and I believe that I also have a concept of a responsibility to God that is appalling, but yet, yet I would in the name of God take the responsibility for giving the order to fire if I first of all, with the precaution of a most anxious conscience, had convinced myself that there was not one single other man facing the rifles—yes, not one single living creature other than—journalists. This is said of the class. There have been, and according to a quite different standard, honorable and excellent princes and clergy—and yet at the time and with a certain truth it was said, consequently of the whole class—evil comes from the princes, from the clergy.

$X^1$ A 131    *n.d.*, 1849

« **6355**

Like everything else in the Middle Ages, the origin of indulgences etc.—their degeneration is something else again—was a childish misunderstanding. By reading this and that prayer so and so often one then received so and so much indulgence (for example, see Liguori, *Betrachtungen und Gebetbuch*,[2143] Aachen, 1840, p. 599 note). But did not my father do the same with me when I was a child? He promised me a rix-dollar if I read one of Mynster's sermons aloud for him, and four rix-dollars if I would write up the sermon I had heard in church. True enough, I did not do it; I even remember pointing out that it was wrong to want to tempt me in that manner, because he knew I would like to have the money. But it was not really my father's fault but mine that

I never have been a child. For a child, who after all does not have a better sense of things of supreme importance, this method is not at all wrong; one counts on the child's gradually coming under the power of higher conceptions and having at a later time occasion to appropriate them personally in a more profound sense.

$X^1$ A 137   *n.d.,* 1849

« 6356        *N.B.*                    *N.B.*

*N.B.*        *N.B.*

*N.B.*

It is true that my original intention was always to try to get appointed to a small rural parish.[2144] But at the time I was actually thinking of it as a contrast to having become, despite my efforts, successful in the world as an author. Now the situation is entirely different, my circumstances so unrewarding, that for the time it is appropriate especially for a penitent to stay where he is. Humanly speaking, if it were up to me I would give it up, for the generation in which I live is a miserable one indeed when an author of my competence and my self-dedication is treated in this way. I have no interest whatsoever in fighting with them, for in fact there is hardly one I really can say has the competence to judge me. Christianly speaking, my only concern is obedience to God.

It is also true, as I have always said, that the place was unoccupied: an author who knew how to stop. Right. But I was bound to the idea of trying to introduce Christianity into Christendom, albeit poetically and without authority (namely, not making myself a missionary). That, too, has been carried out. But the trouble is that it nauseates me to have to say one more word to this generation, a word which merely will cost me new sacrifices and expose me to new nastiness. And if it is printed, it can just as well lie until after my death. But Christianly, the only question is that of obedience. If it had anything to do with this kind of nastiness, Christ would never have kept his mouth closed.

It is difficult to know whether it is more humiliating to declare right out that I can no longer afford to be an author and now take on the burden of the finite or to lay myself wide open to all that may follow if I publish something but, please note, not making myself an extraordinary who acquires a few disciples.

Finally, there is one thing to remember—that my original thought must still be subject to a certain control. How many times have I not said that a warship does not get its orders until it is out at sea, and thus it may be entirely in order for me to go farther as an author than I had originally intended, especially since I have become an author in an entirely different sense, for originally I thought of being an author as an escape, something temporary, from going to the country as a pastor. But has not my situation already changed in that *qua* author I have begun to work for the religious. At first I planned to stop immediately after *Either/Or*. That was actually the original idea. But productivity took hold of me. Then I planned to stop with the *Concluding Postscript*. But what happens, I get involved in all that rabble persecution, and that was the very thing that made me remain on the spot. Now, I said to myself, now it can no longer be a matter of abandoning splendid conditions, no, now it is a situation for a penitent. Then I was going to end with *Christian Discourses* and travel, but I did not get to travel— and 1848 was the year of my richest productivity. Thus Governance himself has kept me in the harness. I ask myself: Do you believe that out in the rural parish you would have been able to write three religious books[2145] such as the three following *Concluding Postcript?* And I am obliged to answer: No! It was the tension of actuality which put new strength into my instrument, forced me to publish even more. And so again in 1848.

Moreover, now it is only a question of publishing a few short ethical-religious essays—and three friendly notes. But as I said, I have become sickened at the thought of having to address what I say to such an age, to which, humanly speaking, the only proper response would be silence.

I must travel in the spring.

$X^1$ A 138  *n.d.*, 1849

« 6357  *N.B.*

"In every one of the pseudonymous works the theme of 'the single individual' appears"[2146]—yes, certainly, and the following is one of several ways: the pseudonymous writers concentrate upon working out the universal, the single individual [*den Enkelte*], the special individual [*den særlige Enkelte*], the exception, in order to find the meaning of the special individual in his suffering and his extraordinariness.

The Judge in *Either/Or* had already posed this with respect to the exception from being married.

Then came *Fear and Trembling—Repetition,* the psychological experiment[2147]—all commentaries on the category: the single individual.

But in relation to the reading public, the pseudonymous writers themselves as well as the books affirm the category of the single individual.

$X^1$ A 139  *n.d.*, 1849

« **6358**                               *N.B.*

The beginning of my authorship is indirectly explained in something correlative, the essay "The Dialectical Relations: the Universal, the Single Individual, the Special Individual."[2148] The more recent direction is indirectly explained in the essay "Has a Man the Right To Let Himself Be Put To Death for the Truth?"[2149]

$X^1$ A 140   *n.d.*, 1849

« **6359**

The words from Philippians[2150] could be the text for a Friday-sermon.

"For me to live is Christ"; but no more, not the next phrase, "to die is gain."

$X^1$ A 143   *n.d.*, 1849

« **6360**                               *N.B.*

An understanding of the totality of my work as an author, its maieutic purpose, etc. requires also an understanding of my personal existence [*Existeren*] as an author, what I *qua* author have done with my personal existence to support it, illuminate it, conceal it, give it direction, etc., something which is more complicated than and just as interesting as the whole literary activity. Ideally the whole thing goes back to "the single individual" [*den Enkelte*], who is not I in an empirical sense but is the author.

That Socrates belonged together with what he taught, that his teaching ended in him, that he himself was his teaching, in the setting of actuality was himself artistically[2151] a product of that which he taught—we have learned to rattle this off by rote but have scarcely understood it. Even the systematicians talk this way about Socrates. But nowadays everything is supposed to be objective. And if someone were to use his own peson maieutically, this would be labeled "à la Andersen."[2152]

All this is part of an illumination of my position in the development. Objectivity is believed to be superior to subjectivity, but it is just the opposite; that is to say, an objectivity which is within a corresponding subjectivity is the finale. The system was an inhuman something to which no human being could correspond as author and executer.

$X^1$ A 146   *n.d.*, 1849

« 6361                    *N.B.*        *N.B.*
                                *N.B.*

It will never do to let the second edition of *Either/Or*[2153] be published without something accompanying it. Somehow the accent must be that I have made up my mind about being a religious author.

To be sure, my seeking an ecclesiastical post[2154] also stresses this, but it can be interpreted as something that came later.

Therefore, do I have the right (partly out of concern lest I say too much about myself, partly because of a disinclination to expose myself to possible annoyances) to allow what I have written to be vague, lie in abeyance as something indefinite and thus as being much less than it is, although it no doubt will embitter various people to have to realize that there is such ingeniousness in the whole [authorship]. It is, in fact, comfortable to regard me as a kind of half-mad genius—it is a strain to have to become aware of the more extraordinary.

And all this concern about an appointment and livelihood is both depressing and exaggerated. And a second question arises: Will I be able to endure living if I must confess to myself that I have acted prudently and avoided the danger which the truth could have required me to confront.

Furthermore, the other books ("The Sickness unto Death," "Come to Me," "Blessed Is He Who Is not Offended"[2155]) are extremely valuable.[2156] In one[2157] of them in particular it was granted to me to illuminate Christianity on a scale greater than I had ever dreamed possible; crucial categories are directly disclosed there. Consequently it must be published. But if I publish nothing at present, I will again have the last card.

"The Point of View" cannot be published.

I must travel.

But the second editon of *Either/Or* is a critical point (as I did in fact regard it originally and wrote "The Point of View" to be published simultaneously with it and otherwise would scarcely have been in earnest about publishing the second edition)—it will never come again. If this opportunity is not utilized, everything I have written, viewed as a totality, will be dragged down into the esthetic.

                                        X[1] A 147   *n.d.*, 1849

« **6362**

The actual Johannes Climacus[2158] (author of *Scala Paradisi*) says: There are but few saints; if we wish to become saintly and saved, we must live as do the few.

See Liguori, *Betrachtungs und Gebetbuch*[2159] (Aachen: 1840), p. 570.

$X^1$ A 151    *n.d.*, 1849

« **6363**

[*In margin:*—N.B. An observation concerning two passages in note no. 2 of the three friendly notes.[2160]]

Although "the pseudonyms expected to get only a few readers," it can still be quite all right for the esthetic productivity "to be used maieutically to get hold of men." For one thing, the human crowd is inquisitive about esthetic productions; another matter is the concept of "readers" that the pseudonyms must advance. How many readers *Either/Or* has had—and yet how few readers it has had, or how little it has come to be "read"!

$X^1$ A 152    *n.d.*, 1849

« **6364**

And is it then a joy to me to introduce something like this into the world? Quite as if I were not a man—I who have so much of the poet in me.

But I am a penitent. And I cannot comprehend that it would please God if I were to begin flagellating myself (as the Middle Ages piously believed), but certainly it can please God that the truth be spoken. It is just the task for a penitent. That which I say, from a divine point of view, is the truth, this is eternally certain. But the point is that the truth, divinely speaking, is, humanly speaking, inimical to what it is to be human.

Christ was himself God, he could not propound anything else than the divine truth. The apostles were called by him. But in the course of time (I cannot understand it in any other way) there has to be a penitent to present the truth in this way, for only a penitent can be so anxious and fearful before God that he dares say nothing else but that which, humanly speaking, makes himself and everybody else unhappy.

$X^1$ A 156    *n.d.*, 1849

« **6365**

[*In margin:* N.B.–]

A literary form I could use in the future would be to publish the books as if they had been written fifty years ago.

$X^1$ A 158   *n.d.*, 1849

« **6366**          *N.B.   N.B.*

As yet I have not said a direct word about myself: the postscript to *Concluding Postscript* contains nothing of the sort; all I did was to assume responsibility for the pseudonyms and speak *hypothetically* ("according to what I have understood"[2161]) about their ideas. The information given in *Concluding Postscript*[2162] about the structure of the pseudonyms is by a third party. The conclusion of *Works of Love*[2163] ("The Work of Love in Praising Love") contains nothing direct about me; on the contrary, it says that "the most selfish person" "may be the one who undertakes to praise love."[2164] The review of *Two Ages*[2165] has one little hint about me, but that again is not direct communication but is concealed by making it seem as if I had learned it from the novel.

$X^1$ A 161   *n.d.*, 1849

« **6367**

The title page of each of the later books has:

"*poetic*"—to signify that I do not pass myself off as being an extraordinary Christian or as being what I describe. "Without authority" —to indicate that I do not put others under any obligation or judge others. "For inward awakening"—to show that I have nothing to do with external changes or that kind of reformation.

$X^1$ A 162   *n.d.*, 1849

« **6368** *A Comment on the Book*

"Come to Me All You" etc.[2166]

There is no specific reference to Christ's entry into Jerusalem, but then on the whole there is no reference to the historical.

The poetic character in the book (and therein is the stimulus to an awakening) is in the stamp of modernity it has, without, however, missing the points. Yes, it even became a matter of not holding too scrupulously to the historical facts because they have become trivialized to people who have heard them since childhood.

As far as the entry is concerned, it is a fairly isolated curcumstance, nor can it be regarded entirely as a triumphal procession. A man who is so despised (that allowing oneself to be helped by him is punished by exclusion from the synagogue [*in margin:* for this reason the parents of the man blind from birth do not dare say anything about the one who helped their son[2167]]; so despised that it says, "I wonder if any of the teachers of the people listen to him, but the mob";[2168] so despised that he must seek or seeks the company of sinners and tax collectors etc.)—any entry he makes must be understood more as a disturbance than a prestigious affair. [*In margin:* Luke 19:37 says the whole multitude of the disciples praised God etc., but how many, in fact, are the whole multitude of the disciples; and furthermore they were disciples, after all, and this proves nothing about how the people regarded Christ.]

With poetic propriety I have construed his life as having two phases. The first phase in which his reputation is a problem and there is a controversy about him. The second in which the crowds are influenced by the judgment made on him by those of position and reputation.

But, to repeat, the center of interest in my book is not in a scrupulous correctness about the facts (although, please note, there is nothing that directly controverts anything factual) but in a modernity, that it happens right before our eyes in the dress of our day.

What is presented is the absolute existing in the medium of actuality and in a form of a single human being who is like one of us. This is the paradox. The particular factual details and words are utilized as cues and therefore have the opposite effect they usually have. As a rule people cling to the purely historical; here the book ventures to interpret this poetically in such a manner that the way the particular sacred words are used provides the commentary on them.

It was just the right thing to do. It would have disturbed the effect if I had stuck too scrupulously to the historical.

$x^1$ A 163   *n.d.,*  1849

« 6369

The temporal and the earthly, which seek to hold one back, seem so important at the moment (all the possible dangers and sacrifices etc. are so great), and when at the point of death one comes to review his life, then one will see that what held him back was so very insignificant, and yet it is one and the same. One ought to be fearful of this inversion.

$x^1$ A 166   *n.d.,*  1849

« 6370                        *N.B.*        *N.B.*

                                  *N.B.*

                       *N.B.*        *N.B.*

I ought to see that, as usual, I have received my orders out on the open sea, that things are laid out for me to go forward, that the catastrophe in 1848[2169] also has significance for me.

If anyone in Denmark (yes, I wish I knew if there were really many in any other country) is prepared to be sacrificed, it is I. I have always understood this but ought to continue to understand it. If I had understood from the beginning what I understand now, I would not have been able to persevere. This is how Governance disciplines. But therefore I should obediently and gratefully accept this understanding.

It is my prudence which shrinks back somewhat—in order to help me, in the eternal sense, to be deceived.

Just have faith and confidence; God tests no man beyond his powers.

The other day I went to Mynster[2170] and casually mentioned an appointment at the pastoral seminary. It helps. If it were offered to me, I would scarcely be tempted. But it is good that I did it, that I do not have to feel that I plunged myself into great decisions because I was too proud to seek an appointment. But God knows that this is very far from being my case.

$X^1$ A 167    *n.d.,* 1849

« 6371

Humanly speaking, it is obvious that my misfortune is that I have been brought up so rigorously in Christianity—and then that I have to live in so-called Christendom. To have to go through a martyrdom with all the sensitivity of a poetic soul is frightful enough. But I always see before my eyes that Christ is being spat upon.[2171] Why then does the world suppose it is frightening me off when all it does is thrust forward. I perhaps could renounce various things readily enough if it is a matter of abandoning something spendid in order to seek the essentially Christian. But as soon as the world beckons to me in the direction of persecution, I promptly follow the beckoning—there I would dare not give way.

$X^1$ A 169    *n.d.,* 1849

« 6372                    *N.B.*        *N.B.*

                         *N.B.*        *N.B.*

O, to what dangers it is possible to lay oneself open! Danger, after all, is just my element.

But there is one danger, or more correctly, there is something which runs against the constitution of my whole personality, is really in revolutionary opposition to it, and that is to be obliged to speak about my interior life, about my relationship to God. It would distress me to make that step and I would simply beg to be excused. I have been and am willing to risk anything, but this is something else—it is not a polemic but a submission.

It is really for this reason that the publishing of my most recent books costs me so much suffering.

Yet it may well be my duty to God. To have to talk about how I spend my time in prayer, how I literally live in relationship to God as a child to a father (mother) etc. O, this—if I dare say so—this letting down my guard is so hard, so hard for me; it seems to me as if my interior life were too true to me to talk about it.

And yet it is perhaps my duty to God, and the hiddenness of my interior life may be something God has accommodatingly permitted me to have until I have grown strong enough to speak out about it. My unhappy childhood, my abysmal mental depression, the wretchedness of my personal life until I became an author, all this has contributed to developing my hidden interiority. I can quite literally say that in this regard never in my life have I ever spoken to one single person the way two people ordinarily speak together—I have always kept my interior life to myself, even when I spoke more confidentially; and confidentially I have never been able to speak.

Until now God has permitted this, but in one respect it is for me a kind of coddling. God has been so good, so loving to me, that I truly can say that my association with Him has been my only confidential relationship, and He, in all my misery He has permitted me to find the strength to endure it, yes, to find blessing in it.

But when I am to speak about my interior life to others, I am appalled, lest I say too little or too much, yes, just speaking about it seems to me to be, as mentioned, an untruth. In God's confidence I can struggle with men, can submit even to being put to death, but I cannot endure being enthusiastically regarded by men as the extraordinary—to me it is like death. Although under ordinary circumstances I would not have thought of traveling, now I would have to travel far, far away, and if possible remain abroad.

$X^1 A 183$   n.d., 1849

« **6373**

Voluntarily exposing myself to attack by *The Corsair*[2172] is no doubt the most intensive thing along the order of genius that I have done. It will have results in all my writing, will be extremely important for my whole task with respect to Christianity and to my elucidation of Christianity, to casting it entirely into reflection.[2173]

It is frequently said that if Christ came to the world now he would once again be crucified. This is not entirely true. The world has changed; it is now immersed in "understanding." Therefore Christ would be ridiculed, treated as a mad man, but a mad man at whom one laughs.

The antinomy must now be resolved: that one *shall* believe that which derision can render ridiculous, which one can see done in a secular and earthly way. This is an even higher accentuation than *credo quia absurdum*.[2174] To the simple man it simply says: All you have to do is believe. To the comprehending understanding it says: It is diametrically opposed to the understanding, but you *shall* believe. Here the *shall* is stronger just because it is in opposition to something. In relation to the most caustic mockery of intellectuality it says: Well now, seen from your point of view it is ridiculous, extremely ridiculous, the most ridiculous of all—but you *shall* believe; it is a matter of heaven or hell, you *shall*. This is a frightful *shall* precisely because it makes such a great concession to the opposition.

I now understand better and better the original and profound relationship I have to the comic, and this will be useful to me in illuminating Christianity.

For this reason it is appropriate for my own fragment of life to express this dialectic: that I have allowed myself to be laughed at—but what I say is true.

When no concession at all is made to the opposition, then the *shall* related to it is not nearly so strong. The greater the concession, the more frightful this *shall*. The concession is, so to speak, the height of the shower bath.

Therefore the one who is to present Christianity must eminently have what the most caustic scoffer has at his disposal—precisely in order to pose this: *shall.*

x¹ A 187   n.d., 1849

« **6374**

What if I wrote at the back of the second edition of *Either/Or:*[2175]

Postscript

I hereby retract this book. It was a necessary deception in order, if possible, to deceive men into the religious, which has continually been my task all along. Maieutically it certainly has had its influence. Yet I do not need to retract it, for I have never claimed to be its author.

x¹ 192   n.d., 1849

« **6375**

As far as I know no one has yet thought of writing a farce:

A play in 5 1/2 or almost 6 acts.

x¹ A 199   n.d., 1849

« **6376**                    ***N.B.***

[In margin: N.B.]

Why I Did not Go abroad in the Spring of 1848

In recent days I have had the persistent thought that it would have been better for me if I had gone abroad in the spring a year ago, because however much I have been built up and enriched in the past year, it has also taken a lot out of me.

When I sold the house[2176] in December of 1847 it was my thought to take an extensive journey in the spring of 1848. That is why I let time slip by and did not rent an apartment. Meanwhile it became clear to me that if I planned to give up being an author altogether, it would not help very much to travel, in fact, just the opposite, for I am never so productive as when I travel abroad. So time went by; then an apartment in the corner of Tornebuskegaden[2177] became vacant, an apartment I have liked from the moment it was built. I decided to rent it and then take a shorter trip in the spring and summer. So time went by. Then I began the publication of *Christian Discourses.*[2178] While I sat reading the proof, the insurrection in Holstein[2179] and all that trouble broke out. To travel now was impossible, and not to have an apartment to move into at this time would certainly have been very disturbing.

So I moved in. But the apartment was extremely unsuitable, and the confused financial conditions[2180] as well as many other things were a drain on me. However, it was precisely during that time that I wrote some of the best things I have done.[2181]

Suppose I had taken my departure earlier (which, incidentally, was impossible, since, after all, I had to publish *Christian Discourses* first), it would have ended with my prompt return, for to experience a financial crisis like that one abroad would have been even more frightful.

Thus it was in no way a fault of mine that I did not go abroad.

But what has preoccupied me is this: how altogether singular that every time I get serious about ceasing to be an author, something happens to make me keep on and I simply get a new, a richer stretch of creativity. Such was the case again this time. But I have suffered so much in other respects that I have become a bit impatient, and this impatience has certainly nurtured my melancholy notion that it would have been better if I had traveled, something I was prevented by circumstance from doing.

In other respects it is also a testing of patience to be developing as I am in greater ideality—and then to undergo the painfulness of these days and these daily troubles. Ideally, as a believer I comprehend my significance more and more; at the moment it seems more and more as if I were superfluous. I almost despair of bringing thoughts to bear at this moment, but on the other hand I can be mistreated by the rabble every day, and every day have new occasion to be reminded of the financial situation.

But *summa summarum:*[2182] I cannot thank God sufficiently for the indescribable good he has done for me, far more than I expected.

X¹ A 202   *n.d.,* 1849

« **6377**

Goldschmidt[2183] has two very important strengths: he is despised, and he is an object of pity. The first he arrived at by way of *The Corsair,* the second, by *The Jew.*[2184] In a demoralized world this is the most secure position. He occupies the point from which all attacks can be launched on men of honor and repute, men who are feared, but where he himself cannot be attacked—the very idea is an impossibility. He is despised—that is already a very secure position, although it is conceivable that indignation could mount to the point where he would begin to feel it; but *ach wei mir,*[2185] he is the object of pity, after all, he has described so movingly what he has suffered as a Jew.

X¹ A 206   *n.d.,* 1849

« **6378**

But if someone says: The trouble is that you have become too involved with the common man,[2186] that you have wanted to exist—if not as author, then personally—for them, my answer is: I know that it is more prudent to live in concealment—but what is Christianity, then? And when Mynster,[2187] for example, boasts of the wisdom of his hidden life (not the life hid in Christ) in the secrecy of elite social circles, he satirizes himself dreadfully.

X[1] A 228   *n.d.*, 1849

« **6379**

How sad that this, also—yes, God knows it is certainly preposterous—this big fuss about my trousers[2188] is also connected (symbolically) in a melancholy way with the melancholy of my life. It is not true that there is anything at all conspicuous about them, and it is a lie that I myself in any way arranged or intended to draw attention to my clothes. But the matter is quite simple. If one pays any attention to people's dress, he discovers that older people like to wear shorter trousers. Young people, youth, have a natural interest in clothes and especially the legs. Older people think only of comfort and of anything but how they look.

My father was an old man; I never knew him otherwise. The fundamental misfortune of my whole life is that I was confused with being an old man, and this appeared also in my clothes. I remember very well how distressed I was, from childhood on, to have to wear such short trousers. I remember, too, my brother-in-law Christian's[2189] constant teasing.

Then I became a student, but a youth I never was. I never received a youthful impression of life (that a long life stretches out ahead of one, because for me there literally was never more than half a year, and hardly that) which leads a person to have interest and pleasure in his appearance. I consoled myself in another way. My mind developed prodigiously, and I thought about such things least of all. But, just as in other things I abided by the customs of my father's house, eating dinner at a fixed time in the evening etc. etc., so also in the matter of clothes. They remained essentially unchanged, so that I may truthfully say that when they attack the way I dress they actually are attacking my deceased father. Inclined to melancholy, given to irony, I recognized that in suffering I had been an old man at the age of eight—and that I never had been young; intellectually well-endowed, I elevated myself ironically over everything connected with the animal aspects of being human. But that I should ever become the object of a literary attack in this respect, and that thousands should take this very seriously as an attack upon my character—no, this I never dreamed.

$X^1$ A 234   *n.d.,*   1849

« **6380**

If someone wanted to publish my journals after my death, it could be done under the title:

The Book of the Judge.

$X^1$ A 239   *n.d.,*   1849

« **6381**

Right Reverend Bishop:[2190]

When it comes to receiving a gift from you I hope never to grow older, but I also hope that you will not take amiss the juvenile, almost childish way in which I thank you again and again. I dare not be profuse, as gratitude loves to be, or rather, not *here.* For in the quiet of my mind where "recollection" completely hides all the particulars that "memory" now and then piece by piece has transmitted to it, there indeed is the proper place for the profusion of grateful recollection and faithful memory. *Here,* however, the greatest possible brevity, and therefore I beg you to forget it at once if I have been too profuse after all.

With deep veneration,
S. Kierkegaard

[Address:]
To
His Excellency
The Right Reverend Bishop, Dr. Mynster
Grand Cross of *Dannebrog,* Member of *Dannebrog,* a.o.
The Bishop's Residence

*Letters,* no. 243   [1849]

« **6382**

I feel inexpressibly weak; it seems to me that death must soon put an end to this affair. As a matter of fact, a dead man is just what Copenhagen and Denmark need if there is going to be any end at all to this infamous meanness, envy, and derision.[2191] So I do not complain, even if it seems a hard fate that I, who in any other country would have made a considerable fortune and been regarded as a genius of the first rank with an extensive, penetrating influence, by being born in a demoralized provincial town quite logically turned out to be a sort of Mad Meyer, notorious, insulted by every guttersnipe (quite literally), even by criminals—while the envy at the top secretly rejoiced and delighted in its victory. I do not complain, despite the indictment that literally every single person has kept absolutely silent the three years that this has gone on every day. I do not complain. The ancients entertained themselves by having men fight with wild animals; the villainy of our age is more refined. But victims have fallen and tears have been shed silently by women (the wives and daughters etc. of the persecuted), and meanwhile the derisive laughter and the subscription list mounted. The victims turned aside and died, the women hid their tears, and no one paid any attention, for those who were suffering of course did everything to hide. Then I offered myself as a victim.[2192] I dared think I was a little too big for Denmark for the way in which I meet my death to go unnoticed. Only a dead man can stop and avenge baseness of the kind in which a whole country is more or less guilty. But avenged you will be, all you who have suffered. I feel inexpressibly satisfied that I, if anyone, have found the specific life-task that is utterly appropriate to all my personal qualifications. It was convenient enough for my contemporaries to let me put a stop to the evil, to let me with all my sacrifices guarantee P. L. Møller and Goldschmidt's restraint[2193]—and at the same time to satisfy their envy by my having to suffer what I have had to suffer, augmented by being regarded as mad by the notables for being willing to expose myself to such a thing. Retribution is coming.

And so I turn to the other side,[2194] reflecting with much fear and trembling on my personal life and its sins, but hoping and believing that for Christ's sake God will forgive me—and then "*ein seliger Sprung in die Ewigkeit.*"[2195]

X[1] A 247   *n.d.,* 1849

« 6383

The "Three Notes"[2196] shall not be published, either. Nothing is to be declared directly about me; if anything is to be said, much more should be said, "The Point of View"[2197] should be published. But all such writing shall lie there finished, just as it is, until after my death.

About my personal life, and directly, nothing is to be said: (1) because after all I am essentially a poet; but there is always something enigmatical in a poet's personality and therefore he must not be presented as, and above all he must not confuse himself with, an authentically ethical character in the most rigorous sense. (2) Insofar as I am a little more than a poet, I am essentially a penitent, but I cannot speak directly of that and therefore also cannot discuss any possible extraordinariness granted me. (3) I cannot make sure for myself and for my communication that the emphasis will fall strongly enough upon God. (4) It is an inconsistency in connection with self-denial.

Therefore, to want to do it would be on my part: (1) a piece of recklessness, wanting to speak about myself at this time, as if either I were about to die tomorrow or it had been decided that I would stop being an author, since neither is the case. (2) It would be arbitrariness and impatience (the result of my having been the one who suffered) for me to want to decide my own fate in advance or to contribute to my being forced farther into the character of a martyr, even if I secretly am that but without demanding the satisfaction of being regarded as one.

It was a godsend that I did not do it, that I did not publish the "Notes" or that God did not permit it to happen. It would have disturbed my life in every way, whether I continue to be an author at present or am put to something else. Therefore I actually have to repent the time I spent bumbling around tinkering with the "Notes," one word here and a word there. I have suffered a great deal, but God is helping me also to learn something.

How much God is the one directing the whole thing I see best in the manner in which the discourses about the lily and the bird[2198] came into being at the time—just what I needed! God be praised! Without being contentious against men and without talking about myself, I managed to say what ought to be said, but in a moving, gentle, uplifting way.

And now to travel; I must get away from here both for a moment's recreation and for a longer period, for it is all involved with my still being essentially a poet.

If I am to make any direct communication about myself personally, I must be forced to it from the outside, although with difficulty, since my creativity is actually not my own but a higher power's.

$X^1$ A 250   *n.d.*, 1849

« **6384**

O, but it is still inconceivable and at times I am overwhelmed when I suddenly think about it: that I, who in my melancholy and my understanding of what is essentially Christian, found my only joy in expressing equality with all men and therefore exposed myself to the disfavor of the elite—that I, I in particular, that I was persecuted by the simple class for my pride, that I, I in particular, that I became the victim which the whole trend of the times craves—and thus I was precisely the one who expressed it long before the problem emerged.

It can hurt when I think about how I was forced to change in some ways, it can hurt deeply. I who previously had a genial greeting for every working man and to everyone a friendly word, an expression of recognition for everyone—I am now a man of few words, evasive, alter my manner of greeting people somewhat, look half absent-mindedly at the one who greets me (alas, I who loved to be the first to greet!) and greet impersonally. I am obliged to do it; I must deliberately remind myself to do it—for I cannot be the savior of the world, and if I do not continue somewhat this way it will end with my being put to death.

From this it is easy to see that the tragedy of journalism is always the same, that it says what it says in such a way that, if there was nothing to it before, it turns into something. For now there is something to my being proud. But whose fault is it? The journalists'! If I look at everyone with open, genial eyes—then I detect those grinning fools by the dozens: ergo, I must (in self-defense)—keep my eyes to myself. If I am willing as before to have a friendly word for everyone, then I am promptly surrounded by a bunch of those tittering oafs: ergo, I must (in self-defense) proudly be a man of few words. The result of this conflict is that I accentuate all the more the individuals who are devoted to me or for whom I have a special affection—and in this way (yes, it is in self-defense) I have been obliged to change.

One thing I have learned, however: the essentially Christian collision. This collision was not originally within my scope. I owe it solely to my conflict with the crowd. My collision is genuinely Christian. I am persecuted—because I was good-natured.

It is not simply that the world wants to be deceived,[2199] that is, that one gets farthest ahead (in the secular world) by deceiving; no, it *insists* on being deceived, becomes enraged when one does not deceive it.

Proudly hold men in contempt—and they love you—love them, and they hate you.

But I ought not be discouraged; however, the situation is all too demented, and therefore I must pull back somewhat. The fact that the press is involved makes the evil frightfully powerful. If the press were not involved, I could still place some hope in my personal powers. But it is a dreadful thing that every week or every day in the twinkling of an eye one man can get 40,000 to 50,000 men to say and think the same thing. And it is impossible to get hold of the one who is personally guilty, and the thousands he incites against one are in a sense not guilty.

Woe to the daily press! If Christ came to the world today, as sure as I live he would not attack the high priests etc.—he would attack the journalists.

$$X^1 \text{ A } 258 \quad n.d., \ 1849$$

« 6385

Governance really does know how to relate every man's collision to his capacities. The collisions in my life[2200]—very likely because I have been granted unusual capacities—have a potentiation which has given them great import for me and has led me to recognize at once my identity, my personal peculiarities; thus I can correlate the nature of my collisions with my spiritual and intellectual characteristics, and it is also certain that such collisions occur very seldom.

My erotic collision had the potentiation that it was not some other force that separated us, nor was it the girl herself who made the break with me, but it was I myself who was obliged to demolish an authentic love. Thus, in addition to my own erotic pain, I felt sympathetic pain for her whom I made unhappy and eventually the anguish of responsibility doubly sharpened by the fact that it was my melancholy and repentance for my earlier life which made me do what I did. Without a doubt this is as complicated an erotic collision as possible.

My other collision is with the world. Here again the potentiation is that I am the one who voluntarily exposed myself to the whole thing.[2201] Incidentally, the collision with "the crowd" was already a potentiation; but of course there is not one single man with whom I could collide in such a way that it could enter my mind that it had any great significance or was an equal struggle.

My superiority in relation to the universally human is promptly manifested in the collisions of my life by the "spiritual trial" [Anfægtelse] that always accompanies them. The spiritual trial is due to the fact that I myself am the one who acts. I myself must take the decisive step; I myself must expose myself to the suffering. Precisely this unsolicited movement becomes the spiritual trial, which always voices the thought: has not too much been ventured. That is, in every one of my collisions there is also a collision with God or a struggle with God. It is precisely this aspect of the collision which makes my suffering so frightfully earnest.

Just imagine how changed my life would have been if it had been a girl who chose not to love me and broke up with me—I think I would have kicked over the traces as a prank. But I did not do it—for I was obliged to be the one who acted and had to strive with God: frightful collision. Imagine that it was one single man who attacked me in print: I believe that in the same moment he would have fallen over me and broken his neck. But "the crowd" is in itself already a strenuous collision of quite another sort. And yet this, too, does not amount to much; but I myself was the one who acted, I struggled with God: frightful collision!

But this again witnesses to the fact that I relate to the essentially Christian, for these are genuinely religious and Christian collisions.

$x^1$ A 260   *n.d.*, 1849

« **6386**

If there is anything called necessity in an individuality, then in mine it is to be where the danger is. Thus it was possible that I was the only one in a whole generation who perceived the wrong and hurled myself against the rabble-barbarism and the ridicule and ventured out into a danger—which supposedly was no danger at all! You fools, or, more correctly, you equivocators! No, there is no danger as feared in the world as just this danger of laughter, and how it was feared here in Denmark and here in Copenhagen I know best of all, I who associated with everybody and am indeed something of a connoisseur of men; I knew how it was and is feared by the boldest journalists and public personalities, I knew that it was cowardice that kept everyone silent. That was how I found out that this danger, which in addition is profoundly congruous with my personal individuality, was a danger for me. It is the only danger I have found in Denmark to match my capacities. A polemic with Heiberg[2202]—that would have been a joke, and even if he had had ten others along, it would not have become serious and would soon have been forgotten. But now it is in its fourth year—and Copenhagen is still interested in my trousers and legs[2203] as passionately as in Tivoli, the masques at the Casino,[2204] or the war.[2205]

« **6387**
*N.B.*

X¹ A 262   *n.d.*, 1849

All the treatises (associated with Adler) in "A Cycle" etc.[2206] could well be published. But they are to be published separately, each by itself, or at most two together, and by the pseudonyms HH, FF, PP.[2207] They could then, like guerrillas, accompany the publication of the three books for awakening.[2208] But precisely because their role is to be guerrillas, they must appear in as small doses as possible.

« **6388**
*N.B.*

X¹ A 263   *n.d.*, 1849

I have made one final attempt to say a word about myself and my whole authorship. I have written "A Supplement" which should be called "The Accounting"[2209] and should follow the "Discourses."[2210] I think it is a masterpiece, but that is of no importance—it cannot be done [published].

The point is that I perceive with extraordinary clarity the infinitely ingenious thought present in the totality of the authorship. Humanly speaking, now would be just the right time, now when the second printing of *Either/Or*[2211] appears. It would be splendid. But there is something false in it.

*For I am a genius of such a kind that I cannot just directly and personally assume the whole thing without encroaching on Governance.* Every genius is preponderantly immanence and immediacy; he has no "why"; but once again it is my genius that lets me see clearly, afterwards, the infinite "why" in the whole, but this is Governance's doing. *On the other hand, I am not a religious person of such a kind that I can directly assign everything to God.*

Therefore not a word. If anything is to be said, then just that. Or if the world wants to extort a statement and explanation from me, then this.

I suffer indescribably every time I have begun to consider publishing something about myself and the authorship. My soul becomes restless, my mind is not content to be producing, as it is generally; I regard every word with horrible suffering, think of it constantly, even outside of my time for work; my praying becomes sickly and distracted, for every trifle becomes excessively important as soon as it gets tied in with this. As soon as I leave it alone, either produce it with the idea of not publishing, or produce something else, then I am calm immediately, my mind is at rest, as it is now in having written and in intending to publish the "Three Godly Discourses."[2212]

Suddenly to want to assume this enormous productivity as one single thought is too much—although I see very well that it is that. Yet I do not believe that I was motivated by vanity. It is originally a religious thought—I intended to attribute it to God. But this is why everything is now ready—until after my death.

I cannot assume it personally in this way. It is true, for example, that when I began as an author I was "religiously resolved," but this must be understood in another way. *Either/Or,* especially "The Seducer's Diary," was written for her sake,[2213] in order to clear her out of the relationship. On the whole, the very mark of my genius is that Governance broadens and radicalizes whatever concerns me personally. I remember what a pseudonymous writer[2214] said about Socrates: ". . . his whole life was personal preoccupation with himself, and then Governance comes and adds world-historical significance to it." To take another example—I am polemical by nature, and I understood the concept of "that single individual" [*hiin Enkelte*] early. However, when I wrote it for the first time (in *Two Upbuilding Discourses*[2215]), I was thinking particularly of *my* reader, for this book contained a little hint to her, and until later it was for me very true personally that I sought only one single reader. Gradually this thought was taken over. But here again Governance's part is so infinite.

The rest of the things written can very well be published. But not one word about myself.

I must take a journey.

x[1] A 266   *n.d.,* 1849

### « 6389 *A Poetic View of Myself*

[*In margin:* Used as "an accompanying paper" with "The Accounting."[2216]]

. . . . . If, however, someone were to say to me: You who for a long time now have lived and go on living every day surrounded by the drivel, ridicule, and cruel treatment etc. of these thousands of people —it seems to me that there is something artificial in the silence you steadily maintain about all this, or in the tranquillity with which you talk about yourself, as if you were untouched by the wretchedness of life [*changed to:* all these matters], I would answer him like this.

In the first place, when I speak, there is a very exalted person listening[2217]—incidentally, this is the case with every human being, but the majority do not bear it in mind—there is a very exalted person listening: God in heaven; he sits in heaven and listens to what every person says. I bear this in mind. No wonder then that what I say has a certain formality and solemnity. Moreover, I am not speaking with those thousands, but with the single individual before God—thus it is rather to be wondered at that what I say is not infinitely more formal and solemn.

Secondly, already as a small child[2218] I was told—and as solemnly as possible—that "the crowds" spit upon Christ, who was in fact the truth [*in margin:* that *they* spit on Christ, that *the crowd* ("those who passed by"[2219]) spit on him and said: Fie on you]. This I have hid deep in my heart [*penciled in margin:* even though there have been moments, yes, times, when I seemed to have forgotten it, it has always come back to me as my first thought]. In order better to conceal the fact that I hid this thought deep in my soul, I have even concealed it under the most opposite exterior, for I was afraid that I would forget it too soon, that it would be tricked out of me and be like a blank cartridge. This thought is my life [*in margin:* although the task so far has been intellectual but fought religiously], and aided by it I also promptly and readily understood that simple wise man[2220] who occupied me so much in my youth, that martyr of *intellectuality,* whom "numbers," "the crowd" persecuted and condemned to death. I know for certain that I am on the right road—the drivel, derision, and bestiality of "the crowd" are the best possible proofs of that. No wonder, then, that what I say has a certain formality and solemnity and has, as I do, a tranquillity, for the road I am taking is right, I am on the right road, even though far behind. Assuming that those who after *voluntarily* suffering for a long time the cruelty, mistreatment, and vilification of their contemporaries (consequently after being, as it were, salted,[2221] for "every sacrifice ought to be salted"), then after having been mocked, spit upon (consequently after having accepted the last dedication beforehand)—assuming that they end up being crucified or beheaded or burned or broken on the wheel—assuming, then, that in the Christian order of precedence these are in first rank, which certainly is indisputable—I believe that without saying too much about myself I am just about in the lowest class, the eighth class. No doubt I will rise no higher. A teacher's comment on one of his pupils is appropriate to my life, the only thing lacking is that it was not written about me: "He is going backward, but not without great diligence." Certainly this was an unsuitable expression by the teacher. Only in a very special situation such as my own can such a judgment be expressed appropriately. Yet "not without great diligence" is perhaps saying too little, for I am applying myself very diligently, am extremely busy and hard-working, and I am going backwards for sure, and it is also certain that the more diligent I am the more I go backwards—thus I am in truth going backwards with great diligence. In this way I hope to enter into eternity, and from a philosophical point of view how would it be possible to enter into eternity except by going backwards; from an essentially Christian point of view, how would it be possible to enter into eternity except though the backward movement[2222] of one's affairs. After all, Christ, who was the truth, was spit upon—and if I forgot everything, I do not forget, just as up to now I never have forgotten for a moment, what was said to me as a child and the impression it made on the child. It sometimes happens that a child while still in the cradle is pledged [*forloves*] to the one who someday will be his wife or her husband: religiously understood, I was pre-pledged [*for-lovet*[2223]] early in childhood. Ah, I have paid dearly for at one time misinterpreting my life and forgetting—that I was pledged. On the other hand, I once experienced in my life the most beautiful, blessed, and to me indescribably fulfilling satisfaction because in the step I took at that time, in the danger I voluntarily exposed myself to at that time, I completely understood myself and realized that I was pre-pledged. Pledged, betrothed to the love which, despite all my errors and sins, has surrounded me from the beginning until this moment, surrounded me, of whom it can be said with complete truth that he sinned much, but of whom it perhaps may not be completely false to say: he loved much[2224]—surrounded by a love which infinitely exceeds my understanding, a fatherly love "compared to which the most loving father is but a stepfather."[2225]

Just one thing more, something upon which, if possible, I, with a dying man's last will, put the strongest, most earnest emphasis. I no doubt have a grave and sad advantage (when I consider myself in relationship to those glorious ones, to whom I stand in only the most distant possible relationship, down below as the very lowest in the lowest class, in eighth class), yet in one respect an advantage over them with respect to being able to hold out. For it seems to me that if one is himself pure, perfect, and holy, the opposition of the world (to the truth) would make a person so sad that he quickly would die of sadness. But I am not a saintly person, I am a penitent, for whom it can be indescribably suitable to suffer and for whom, precisely as a penitent, there is a satisfaction in suffering. Yes, if I were a contemporary of a more pure man, I would be happy to turn all the scorn and mistreatment of "the crowd" from him to me. I look upon it as an advantage that I, who have the honor of serving the truth by personally being a penitent (for what I may have done wrong earlier and for what offense I personally have committed) in this way (but only in this way), that I find human mistreatment to be in the right place when it is turned against me. [*In margin:* And I certainly have been extraordinarily successful in my deception, which to a certain degree may have been the invention of mental depression, the deception of being regarded as the most frivolous of all.]

$x^1$ A 272    *n.d.*, 1849

« 6390                                    *N.B.*

No, absolutely right, not one word is to be said about me personally, above all not with respect to assuming the whole authorship as my idea and goal; no matter how much I demur in the presentation itself, it is not sufficient—I must be silent. For everything would become false if I were to consolidate the whole course of the foregoing the moment I came out decisively as a religion author.

No, I am a poet. My writing is essentially my own development; just as juice is pressed from fruit, Governance time and again and in a wonderful way has pressed me into a necessary situation precisely in order to make me as productive as I should be.

Right now I actually am at the point where it could be a matter of stepping forth in character,[2226] but this would be something new and ought not be confused with assuming as my own everything I wrote previously, all the more so since I have thought constantly of stopping.

I am a poet. I shall go abroad. It is the economic situation[2227] which prevents it. Independence was the support I needed, and the fact that I had it is perhaps to blame for my actually being a poet. Now I understand it. Now just patience.

$x^1$ A 273    *n.d.*, 1849

« 6391

April 25

God be praised, now I understand myself. It is good that I did not go abroad a year ago this spring and perhaps become distracted on the journey or wrongly productive, and furthermore what I have suffered the past year has been supremely beneficial even though terrible.

Never have I had such an abundance of ideas—and with all the qualifications I stand now in a certain sense as at the beginning. It is Christianity I shall set forth, and what I have to do in this respect is already κατὰ δύναμιν[2228] present in me, but it will be abundantly sufficient for the longest life.

There is only one humiliation *qua* author that I must take, like everything else, from God's hand—and personally I have always been deeply humbled—and that is that I may not venture myself to express in actuality that which I present and according to the criteria I set forth, as if I myself were the ideal. Here I am obliged to admit to being predominantly a poet and thinker; mental depression and impatience and anxiety had nearly driven me too far out, which would have ended with my cracking up. It was also (something I realized earlier but not as clearly as now) a misunderstanding of all my qualifications; it was a superhuman task which perhaps never will be worked out: with my temperament, my imagination, my poetic aptitude for description, and then *also* to want to be that existentially. As a rule the hero comes first, or the ethical character, and then the poet—I wanted to be both; at the same time as I needed the "poet's" tranquillity and remoteness from life—and the thinker's composure, at the same time I wanted to be, right in the middle of actuality, that which I wrote and thought. Self-tormenting as I have always been, in my depression and very likely, too, with an admixture of pride, I devised this task to plague me. God has helped me, and as always in every possible way.

It is now so very clear to me, all that I realized earlier about how God has led me to this task: to illuminate Christianity, to depict the ideal of the Christian. That I myself should be that, I did not consider at the time, for I believed that I was about to die.

When that did not happen and I did not die, I momentarily started to misjudge myself. It seemed to me that the world, or Denmark, needed a martyr. What I had written was all ready and I actually thought of underscoring, if possible, what I had written in the most decisive way by being put to death.

The misunderstanding, or the potential wound to myself, was that I was incapable of doing it.

Now everything is in order. I have to withdraw a step from this wanting personally to be what is presented, and then the task is mine. I will put all the more pressure on Christendom. I became the unhappy lover with respect to becoming personally the ideal Christian, and therefore I became its poet.[2229] I will never forget this humiliation and to that extent will be unlike the usual orator who wantonly confuses talking about something with being it. I did not get married, but I became the most enthusiastic champion of marriage.[2230] So also in a similar way with the second task. I do not have the strength to become a witness to the truth who is put to death for the truth. Nor do I have the temperament for it. I remain a poet and a thinker; for that I was born, but in relation to Christianity and the ideal for being a Christian. I perhaps can bring a minor sacrifice or two, but essentially I relate myself to being a witness for the truth in the true humility of confessing that in the strictest sense I am not a witness to the truth. My admitting this is the truth in me. But the fact that it is true in me produces a pain which is precisely the condition for the poet's and the philosopher's creativity.

I have ventured much farther out than a poet usually does. This too was necessary in order to accomplish the task: Christianity, the ideal for being a Christian.

Just as the sigh of a poet's own unhappy love is heard in his song,[2231] so also in all my enthusiastic discourse about the ideal for being a Christian my sigh will be heard: Alas, I am not one, I am only a Christian poet and thinker.

$X^1$ A 281    April 25, 1849

« **6392**

From a letter of thanks to Councillor Ørsted[2232] for the third volume of his book on the constitution, but the letter was not sent.

. . . . ."I wonder, is it the same with horses?"[2233]

It seems to me there is something, to speak as a Greek, something divine in this Socratic question, and not least in this incomparable comparison—with horses.

From another angle as well, for these days one is tempted actually to abandon talking about human beings in order to devote oneself to talking about horses, or, when the discussion is about human beings the talk is just like that about horses. At any rate I have found extreme satisfaction in the fact that a state (Genoa) has finally succeeded in finding the type of prime minister for our day: a *hackney cabman!*[2234] Truly, if he cannot, he who is accustomed to associate with horses, if he cannot rule men—then no one can.

A hackney cabman! How witty actual life is! I do not believe that it would occur even to the wittiest poet to use a hackney cabman à la Aristophanes. He perhaps would have used a barber, a rope-maker, a brush-maker, a flunked student, a janitor, a part-time waiter, a delivery boy, a pauper, etc., but he would not have thought of a hackney cabman. Aristophanes himself used a sausage peddler in *The Knights*, [2235] but did not think of a hackney cabman! This can be explained by the fact that there were no hackney cabmen in Greece then, but even if there had been, Aristophanes perhaps would not have thought of using one. And if it had occurred to him, he perhaps would not have used him, and perhaps he would have been right, for very likely, despite all their excesses, men were somewhat more human then than they are now.

In a certain sense, "the hackney cabman" has reconciled me with life again, for now my mind is at ease. In my apartness from life I time and again do get to know according to the barber that somewhere in Europe a professor has become a prime minister, or a person with an M. A. degree, a bachelor of laws, an academic virtuoso, an attorney, etc. At times I was indignant, at times I had to laugh, but my soul found no rest, no complete satisfaction, either in indignation or in laughter. Finally came—the hackney cabman. Eureka, I shouted. When one goes traveling to discover America—and sees land, when in the midst of chaotic times one discovers—the law—then one's mind is set at ease. That very same moment I fell poetically in love with the hackney cabman or what I could be tempted to call *my* hackney cabman. Now it was my wish—ah, and all the greater the disappointment, for actuality did not have what it promised!—my wish was that the hackney cabman might succeed in hurling his two colleagues from power, in overthrowing them, and in setting himself up as dictator in Genoa, and next, that by force of arms or in some other way he might succeed in gradually subduing all Europe under his paternal and wise hackney-cabman reign. What would one not give to see all Europe or the reins of the government in all Europe in the hands of—a hackney cabman!

$X^1$ A 289    *n.d.*, 1849

« 6393

If anything should be said about my activity as an author, it could be done in such a way that a third person is formed, the author, who would be a synthesis of myself and the pseudonym, and he would speak directly about it. Then only an introduction would be needed, in which this author would be introduced, and then he would say everything in the first person. The introduction would point out that the whole authorship is a unity; but I would not be the pseudonym, nor the pseudonym I; therefore this "author" would be a synthesis of the pseudonym and me.

$X^1$ A 300   *n.d.*, 1849

« **6394**

Pfui, pfui, that my fear of danger, hypochondria, and distrustfulness of God led me to want to make myself out to be far inferior to what I have been given. As if arrogating something to oneself were only a matter of defrauding the truth, as if making oneself out to be inferior were not a matter of defrauding God and the truth, and yet it seemed to me to be so humble. O, hypochondria, hypochondria!

Humanly speaking, there really is no pleasure or joy in having to be the extraordinary in such cramped quarters as Denmark; it gets to be a martyrdom. But now, now, after God has inundated me with kindness, granted me so indescribably much more than I expected, now when he (both by means of the abundance he has showered on me during the year past—and its sufferings) has led me to understand my destiny (true enough, it is different from what I originally supposed, but things had already worked out earlier in such a way that all my religious writings, yes, everything I wrote after *Either/Or*, are not as I originally planned and presumably I could not have understood everything right away), should I now blink, shrewdly take it all back because of apprehensions about making ends meet and become a poet —that is, religiously understood, a deceiver. No, no, from the very beginning I had no such ideas: either an author in character—or a country pastor, and then not a word more from me ever, but not a poet, not an author on the side.

The future looks dark, and yet I am so at peace.

This day, my birthday, will be an unforgettable day for me!

$X^1$ A 309   *n.d.* [May 5], 1849

« **6395**

When all is said and done, a play such as "The World Wants To Be Deceived"[2236] or its existence is a dreadful judgment on or a confession of the corruption of the age. Corrupt ages have been seen before, and every age is more or less corrupt. But then there was also someone or other who profoundly perceived the corruption of the age

—and he emancipated himself from it, dissented, perhaps became the victim, *eh bien*, [2237] but also the sign that there was still some truth left.

But for a penetrating, authentic, completely realistic understanding of the corruption of the age to become, not a call to repentance, but a witty stage play with the basic theme that this is the way the world is and we are all the same, one person is no better than the next—so clear the decks, let's have a good time over it—good God, how awful!

And then that such a society is permitted to call itself Christian. But then, of course, like everything else it is a lie which everyone uses (as Scribe says) but no one is deceived by, since everyone knows that it is a lie—it is a lie, the only truthful thing about it is that the clergy have their bread and butter.

O, that I then could become so depressed that out of fear of God, out of fear that I would arrogate something to myself, I wanted to be —a poet. A poet! Really, one poet more at this time is just as insane as if someone were to avail himself of the moment to get married at the very time his house is on fire. A poet at this time! What is needed now, if possible by the thousands, is martyrs, the authentic rescuers. Nevertheless, I have been afraid of aiming too high and then later doing damage because I was unable to do it. But this is despondency. After all, I can take being mistreated, grossly mistreated—but I do not require the other.

How easy it would have been, too, to have fooled away my life in the miserable old rut, just taking care of myself, living in respectable obscurity—truly a respectable obscurity when one despicably uses obscurity to avoid dangers. Therefore, whatever the cost, I am grateful and thank my God that I became aware, that my first care and training has been at the hands of bestiality, so that I should not arrive in eternity and then perceive—how I had frittered my life away in respectable obscurity.

At times I can become almost anxious and afraid on behalf of the man when I think of Bishop Mynster. He is seventy-two now and soon will go to his—judgment. And what harm he has done to Christianity by conjuring up a false appearance—in order that he could sit and reign. His sermons are very much in order—but in eternity he will not preach, there he will be judged.

My one constant thought is that I may never get so busy that I forget to sorrow over my sins and reflect on my personal guilt. O, it is so very difficult for a penitent to proceed resolutely, because he continually feels paralyzed by the thought that he is a penitent.

$x^1$ A 320   *n.d.,* 1849

« 6396

As far as my writing is concerned, the world-movement or the conflict is between two conceptions: the interesting and the simple. The age has been carried away by the interesting and still is; the movement should be made to the simple.

Therefore I was in eminent possession of the interesting (it was this which the age demanded). There is hardly an author, and certainly none in Denmark, who can dispute my precedence in the sense of being essentially the only one of the kind as author, the interesting one.

By falsifying my task I would have become the hero and idol of the moment; in that case I would in fact have abandoned the movement toward the simple and transformed all my power into the interesting and into the moment. I remained, eternally understood, faithful to my task and became the martyr of the moment, and precisely this is evidence that I remained true to the task.

God be praised; I owe it all to him.

On my part there is nothing at all meritorious in the whole thing. For one thing, I have been a genius who frequently did not understand having done the right thing until afterwards, and for another, I have been bound, as if in the service of a higher power, by a congenital melancholy and a tormenting thorn in the flesh, as well as by being personally a penitent.

$x^1$ A 322   *n.d.,* 1849

« 6397

It might be very good sometime to write a book entitled:
The Life of Christ<br>
portrayed<br>
by              S. Kierkegaard<br>
Joh. de Cruce   An Eyewitness
It might not be so good to use a pseudonym here.

$x^1$ A 323   *n.d.,* 1849

« 6398

Somewhere[2238] there must be an aphorism by me which reads something like this:

There is some consolation in the fact that language has so many words like nonsense, drivel, rubbish, chitchat, gossip, prattle, chatter, jabber, etc., for if there were no such word at all in the language, one would have to fear that everything is gossip. The alarming thing is not that there are so many words in the language to describe something like this; it would be alarming if there was not one single word for it.

$x^1$ A 325   *n.d.,* 1849

« **6399**

How witty a typographical error can be![2239] In the second of the two minor essays, instead of "the gift of being able to work miracles" it reads "the inconvenience."[2240]

$x^1$ A 336   *n.d.,* 1849

« **6400**

*The first essay* (of "Two Minor Essays")[2241] is poetic, but in the same sense as a Platonic dialogue. A personality like that is created in order to avoid pure abstraction, the informational approach. But no more. The novelistic in him, incidentally, is of no value, only his thought content. A work of this nature corresponds to the unity of "thinker" and "poet." Someone like that is different from abstract thinkers in that he has a poetic element at his service, but he differs from a poet in that he essentially stresses the thought content.

$x^1$ A 338   *n.d.,* 1849

« **6401** *My Tragedy, Humanly Speaking,*

is simply that I have been a genius, that I have had a strict upbringing in Christianity, that I have had money.

Without the first, I of course would not have begun with a gigantic jump but gradually, my motives would have been cluttered; without the second I would not have had the idea of suffering which made me decide to act against prudence; without the third I would have been unable to gain position.

All these three things, of which the first two actually are advantages, have become my misfortune, for people regard truth and piety as pride and vanity.

$x^1$ A 342   *n.d.,* 1849

« **6402**

R. Nielsen's book[2242] is out. Realizing the wrong I have suffered in the interest of truth, realizing my mastery of the circumstances, he still thought, as I suspected, that if he only enlisted my support and I stayed by him somewhat—that it could be done, that he could even gain importance, perhaps be a success.

That was the enthusiasm for the rightness of my cause.

In fact, he did come to the right one.

The writings are plundered in many ways, the pseudonyms most of all, which he never cites, perhaps with deliberate shrewdness, as the least read.

And then my conversations!

$X^1$ A 343  *n.d.,*  1849

« **6403**

*Polemika*

R. Nielsen[2243]

by

Johannes Climacus

Writing exercises in character that are not to be used.

$X^6$ B 83  *n.d.,*  1849

« **6404**

*Addition to 6403* ($X^6$ B 83): This book[2244] seems to be intended to be an *Either/Or;** perhaps it will be only a neither/nor.

It is mainly Johannes Climacus[2245] who is used, and he is the only one who is not cited.

The author has simply spoiled the whole thing with all that scholarly apparatus and detail. Inquiries of this kind must be settled *in toto,* not by dealing with the individual miracle.

Johannes Climacus correctly perceived that the task was one for a poet-philosopher.[2246] The hero of faith—the atheist—the speculative thinker—and then Johannes Climacus on the outside because of not even being a Christian himself.[2247]

Considered as a whole, the entire book is a slavish imitation.

Moreover, there is an incredible number of minute imitations, poor imitations. For example, the description of faith in the beginning, that the believer stands on his head, which is straight out of *Fear and Trembling.* [2248]

As a thinker the author, compared to Johannes Climacus, has produced nothing new, and as a poet he has produced nothing at all. Then what is the purpose of the book. On such a small literary scene as the Danish a book like this is close to a forgery. It would have been more seemly for the author to take his place as a reviewer of Johannes Climacus instead of running up a new structure which *essentially* is a plagiarism. [*In penciled parentheses:* The only thing lacking is that the author had been aided in private by Magister Kierkegaard.]

However, perhaps the book will be a success. After all, it has happened before that an imitator has stood alongside the original— and the imitator made a big success with the mess he made of what in its true and essential form cost the former his life.

*Note. Even the preface is a bit too reminiscent of Victor Eremita's preface to his *Either/Or:*[2249] that whether the esthete or the ethicist is right is not decided—that it is a process—which again is a bit too reminiscent of Johannes Climacus, who calls his book: a contribution.[2250]

$x^6$ B 84   *n.d.,* 1849

### « 6405

*In margin of 6404* ($x^6$ B 84):
Used in particular: Johannes Climacus.[2251] The doctrine of the paradox. The whole decisive new direction: not to comprehend faith but to comprehend oneself in believing, not to comprehend the paradox, but to comprehend that one cannot comprehend the paradox. The leap.[2252]

Becoming open and making manifest.[2253]
The hero of faith in *Fear and Trembling.*[2254]

$x^6$ B 85   *n.d.*

### « 6406

*Addition to 6403* ($x^6$ B 83):
The author battles mediocrity—in part with borrowed weapons. What mediocrity! Mediocrity is precisely his position, if one knows the literary scene at all.

With respect to the dialectic of points of view, the contours, structure, design, and imaginative passion are the main thing; the scholarly details (scrutinizing every miracle, for example) are hindrances. To jumble this together is mediocrity. But the author probably had an apparatus lying around which should be used and decided to do it this way. This is mediocrity.

This is mediocrity: to want to be along a little bit in those certain things requiring complete capability.

The whole thing is mediocre, even this: the discourses are addressed to the public; these are lectures that have been "heard by an illustrious audience,"[2255] dedicated to the Queen, who no doubt has paid for the whole thing, and which are now being published; special care is taken to include a quotation from every one of our famous authors etc.

The only danger this author has had was to risk taking his position from the pseudonyms; he avoided this danger by a private relationship to Magister Kierkegaard. What he says about John the Baptist[2256] is touching: he was not the man who knew all about changing his point of view—the systematician R. Nielsen[2257] knows how to do that.

x⁶ B 86    n.d., 1849

### « 6407  *The Total Production with the Addition of the Two Essays by H. H.*[2258]

The authorship conceived as a whole (as found in "One Note Concerning My Work as an Author,"[2259] "Three Notes Concerning My Work as an Author,"[2260]) and "The Point of View for My Work as an Author"[2261] points definitively to "Discourses at the Communion on Fridays."[2262]

The same applies to the whole structure. "Three Godly Discourses"[2263] comes later and is supposed to accompany the second edition of *Either/Or* and mark the distinction between what is offered with the left and what is offered with the right. "Two Minor Ethical-Religious Essays"[2264] does not belong to the authorship in the same way; they are not an element in it but a point of view. If there is to be a halt, it will be like a period one projects in advance in order to have a stopping place. It also contains an apparent and an actual eminence: a martyr, yes, an apostle—and a genius. If any information about me is to be sought in the essays, then it is this: that I am a genius—not an apostle, not a martyr. The apparent eminence is included in order to determine all the more accurately the actual one: for most men the word "genius" is so indiscriminate that it can mean anything; for that very reason it was important to define this concept, as the two essays do by means of defining that which is infinitely qualitatively higher.

Thus the "Two Minor Essays" appropriately has the character of a signal. But it is dialectical. It could signify: here is the stopping place; and then could signify: here is the beginning—but always in such a way that above all I take precautions not to occasion any conceptual confusion but remain true to myself in being no more or no less than a genius, or in being a poet and thinker with a quantitative "more" not customary in a poet and thinker with respect to being what one writes and thinks about. A quantitative "more," not a qualitative "more," for the qualitative "more" is: the witness to the truth, the martyr—which I am not. And even qualitatively higher is the apostle, which I have not fancied myself to be any more than that I am a bird. I shall guard myself against blasphemy and against profanely confusing the religious sphere, which I devoutly am doing my uttermost to uphold and secure against prostitution by confused and arrogant thinking.

X¹ A 351   *n.d.,*  1849

« **6408**

To "deceive" takes an infinite virtuosity in deception. One thinks he has definite information about the deception and next time for sure he will catch the deceiver—but ignores the fact that the next time his deception will be something new. He is the opposite of Stupid Gottlieb; at times it seems as if Stupid Gottlieb[2265] will catch him. Stupid Gottlieb dutifully, faithfully, and obediently does the next time exactly what he was told to do the previous time. With respect to the deceiver people are like Stupid Gottlieb; they think that the deceiver will do the same thing next time—and they are tricked.

Seen in terms of the idea, this is the maieutic, which serves just to develop the other.

X¹ A 366   *n.d.,*  1849

« **6409**

If I were asked how, apart from my relationship to God, I was disciplined to be an author, I would answer: By an old man, to whom I am most grateful, and by a young girl,[2266] to whom I am most indebted—to that unity of age and youth, of the severity of winter and the gentleness of summer which must also have been a natural potentiality within me; the former disciplined me with his noble wisdom, the other with her loving unwisdom.

X¹ A 374   *n.d.,*  1849

« **6410** *Something about the play*
*"The Sisters on Fir-Tree Mountain"*[2267]

In the preface the author says that the idea was not borrowed from a fairy tale, but neither is it his own. This is a curious kind of honesty and perhaps, after all, dishonesty. It is honest to say that it is not his own, it is dishonest not to say more. For if he gave his source and the more pertinent particulars—perhaps, who knows, perhaps he both owed another more than one thinks, and perhaps he used badly that which he borrowed.

Instead of getting married, a girl became avaricious—sits upon the mountain and spins gold—this is detected twenty-five years later at the other sister's silver wedding (incidentally, it could have been quaint to make it fifty years because of the golden wedding). The miner explains that it is not only on account of this girl but of many that he, lost in something abstract (or the like), actually does not live but merely wastes his life. The idea is that there is an abstract life which means simply to lose life.

Fine. That may very well be what was borrowed, the part about the abstract life. What has the poet done with it? He has taken a particular example, and what? Avarice—how thoughtless. If one wishes to pinpoint discerningly the falsity in abstract life, then one must select something essentially innocent. The avaricious maiden's defect is not abstract life—but avarice.

Thus the author has picked a wrong example. Thereupon he makes, as they say, a universal of the particular and puts it in the mouth of the miner. But it is precisely that which is not illuminated by the example, for the example was erroneously selected.

On the other hand, if one wishes to validate the concrete life in contrast to the abstract, then one must see to it that he does not go too far afield. For the authentic religious life, in contrast to what people generally understand by concretion and what this poet no doubt understands by it—is an abstract life: to suffer, to "be sacrificed."

This the poet has had no inkling of at all. For example, he has neither grasped how the problem should be placed in proper relation to the ethical, which will forbid not only the sin but also an abstract life, nor in contrast to the religious, which in a completely different sense affirms the abstract life. From a categorical point of view, the author has bungled in every respect; his categories are confused.

Now take a look at the pseudonyms. On the assumption that the life most men "live" and live concretely and that in this sense of concretion life is also wasted, the attempt here is to achieve the legitimate abstract life. For this purpose there is used: (a) an esthetic eccentric whose very defect is an erroneous abstract life, without being essentially sinful—and (b) the ethicist, but in such a way that he points to the religious.

This is the process in all the pseudonyms' endeavors.

But, of course, such a grand endeavor is probably also an abstract life—but is it more concrete to seize with muddled categories a particular idea, to turn the whole thing wrong, to confuse all the spheres—and then "momentarily" make a big hit as a profound thinker.

Were I to take a particular example for the pseudonyms, I could use the passage in *Either/Or*[2268] where the esthete divides men into two classes, those who work in order to live and those who do not need to, and then show that it would be a self-contradiction if the purpose of life is supposed to be to work in order to live, since the purpose of living, after all, cannot be to produce the prerequisites for living.

On this basis the piece could be constructed. But then the piece would also have to point out the religious. In *Either/Or* the ethicist rounds off life with marriage, but the whole work is also only an element in the endeavor.

Obviously there should have been three sisters, a third, a Christian "Mary"; then the play would have had value. [*In margin:* or an "Anna" (patience in expectation[2269]) in order to show the abstraction of the religious life to be true abstraction.]

Here Quidam of the psychological experiment has the great merit of making clear that "the desire" must be preserved in suffering. The ethicist rightfully condemns waiting for hallucinations and wasting life as being esthetically eccentric, but from behind the ethical emerges the religious again: that to live abstractly (ideally) is to live. Only one man has lived absolutely ideally abstractly in this way: the God-man.

O, but what do they know, these poets who pose as being so profound!

$X^1$ A 377   *n.d.*, 1849

### « 6411

It has always been difficult for me to present Christianity in its true rigorousness, for it seemed to be that way only for me, for me because I had sinned more than others. It has always been my desire to be rigorous with myself in order to be all the more lenient with others, but this is still only a misunderstanding, for it was most rigorous in the Holy One himself. But just as a parent does not consider a child's possible iota of guilt worth mentioning, so in comparison to me other men have always seemed to me to be innocent.

$X^1$ A 381   *n.d.*, 1849

« 6412

There is something sad in hearing Mynster (as today in Pentecost vespers), who has adhered to the secular mentality as much as anyone, begin on the text[2270] about the little flock to whom it pleases the Father to give the kingdom etc. Essentially it is no different from the time when Heiberg,[2271] the public's foster father, became polemical because he got into a quarrel with the public.

In the same sermon,[2272] like a background bass, was the idea that he had been consistent enough to join the minority in parliament. Good Lord, is that anything to get excited about, himself maintaining silence and associating with the biggest names. No, Mynster has never had an inkling of what Christian polemic is; he is pampered and spoiled, mainly by being an orator—there is perhaps nothing which so spoils and corrupts a man. Promptly to become emotional in the pulpit —instead of acting in actuality—and then to have it seem to the person himself and the audience as if the man had acted. Yes, Plato[2273] and Socrates were right: banish poets and also orators from the state.

On the whole, the Greek concept of a philosopher (that is, a thinker in ethical character[2274]) is much more appropriate to the communication of the essentially Christian than this spineless concept: an orator, a declaimer—instead of an implementer.

$X^1$ A 385   n.d., 1849

« 6413

Each of the writers here at home received a copy of *Either/Or*.[2275] I felt it was my duty, and I could do it at this time, for now there can be no apparent notion of trying in this way to create a coterie for a book—for the book, after all, is old, its peak is passed. They of course received the copy from Victor Eremita.[2276] As far as Oehlenschläger[2277] and Winther[2278] are concerned, I was happy to send them copies, for I admire them. I was happy to send one to Hertz[2279] as well, for he has significance and there is something charming about the man.

$X^1$ A 402   n.d., 1849

« 6414                    *N.B.*          *N.B.*
                              *N.B.*

I dare not ruminate any more about publishing the books that are finished, and I cannot justify it. What troubles me is my economic concern for the future; the depressing thought that I might situate myself too high; the earthly consideration that I possibly might hinder myself in getting an official appointment.

Well, God certainly is a long way from compelling me against my will, I can readily be free—but humbly, almost penitently, I must rather feel ashamed of having consumed myself in melancholy and reflection for such a long time and almost prefer to have God forcibly constrain me to do what he wants me to do freely.

I do fervently thank God that he has not let me escape but has made me stick to the one and the same idea; for the worldly evasions and excuses (I cannot, it is too high for me, too much, etc. etc.) look so good at the moment, especially together with thousands and thousands who probably are of the same opinion. But in eternity—if I died tomorrow—O, the time for regret, for recollection will be so long. To have enjoyed the moment, to have been prudential in the moment cannot be recollected in eternity—no, that is impossible, after all, it is most alien to eternity—but to have denied oneself in the moment, that can be recollected in eternity.

$X^1$ A 404   *n.d.*, 1849

« **6415**

God knows whether I may not have been a little too thin-skinned about not wanting to have one single adherent![2280] For even though I were actually to die right now, or suppose even that I were put to death for my idea, and in this way escaped the difficulties involved in acquiring adherents: it must, after all, occur in a second generation if it all is not to relapse into itself; and am I myself then in some way too good to suffer and endure the inconvenience of having adherents, who always more or less bungle the idea.

It seems as if I have loved myself only or mainly in the idea: insisting that my life express the idea without considering that if the truth or something true is to get into the world, it must put up with its communication to others and then tolerate its becoming precisely thereby less true, that all who get it second hand depreciate its value. But nevertheless should one not love them so much that one speaks it plainly to them just the same.

Take the supreme example: if Christ, who was truth, had insisted absolutely upon not exposing truth to any misinterpretation, refused to become involved in any accommodation: then his whole life would have been one single monologue.

The point is that I have too profoundly understood that truth does not win by means of adherents but constantly suffers loss the more it acquires. My life's thought was the extreme consequence of that.

However, I do not believe there was any egotism involved. In the first place, my melancholy must be taken into consideration—my idea that I am a penitent. Furthermore, that the alternative (to accommodate) had not occurred to me previously. In the third place: why is the appearance maintained that all as such are Christians? An illusion like that can be destroyed only by indirect polemic, and that was my intention, and that was why I had to be so consistent and so inflexible in my consistency.

$x^1$ A 406   *n.d.,* 1849

« **6416**

Just as the Guadalquibir River plunges into the earth somewhere and then comes out again, so I must now plunge into pseudonymity, but I also understand now how I will emerge again under my own name. The important thing left is to do something about seeking an appointment and then travel.

(1) The three small ethical-religious essays[2281] will be anonymous; this was the earlier stipulation. (2) "The Sickness unto Death" will be pseudonymous and is to be gone through so that my name and the like are not in it. (3) The three works, "Come to Me," "Blessed Is He Who Is not Offended," and "From on High He Will Draw All Men to Himself" will be pseudonymous. Either all three in one volume under the common title, "Practice in Christianity, Essay by ———," or each one separately. They are to be checked so that my name and anything about me etc. are excluded, which is the case with number three. (4) Everything under the titles "The Point of View for My Work as an Author," "A Note," "Three Notes,"[2282] and "Armed Neutrality"* cannot conceivably be published.

*See this journal, p. 157 [i.e. $x^1$ A 450].

These writings properly remain pseudonymous. Here there is the dialectical tension and tightening with respect to the doctrine of sin and redemption, and then I begin with my own name in a simple upbuilding discourse. But it is one thing for a work of such a dialectical nature to appear pseudonymously and something quite different if it appears over my name, in character, as the finale of the whole effort.

After all, there is no hurry about publishing. But if it is to be in character and as a finale, it must be done as soon as possible, something which has pained me frightfully and which has now become almost an impossibility, because today, June 4, I spoke with Reitzel,[2283] who said he dared not take on anything new for publication. On the whole the man has plagued me unbearably with his miseries, which perhaps are exaggerated anyway.

A battle of ideas has taken place here. In actuality the whole matter of publishing with or without my name perhaps would have been a bagatelle. But to me in my ideality it is a very taxing problem so that above all I do not falsely hold myself back or falsely go too far but in truth understand myself and continue to be myself.

I have struggled and suffered fearfully. Yet one who fights for the "You shall" as I do must also suffer at this point. But yet at times I probably have not been far from pressing this "You shall" in an almost melancholy-maniacal way. But now I understand myself. You shall— this is eternally true—but it is not less true and it is also a "You shall" that with God you shall understand your limits and beyond them you shall not go or you shall abandon such desires.

But, gracious God, how I have suffered and how I have struggled. Yet it is my consolation that the God of love will let this be to my good, and in a certain sense it consoles me that I have endured this suffering, because in this very suffering I have become convinced of the way I am to turn.

My misfortune always has been that it is so difficult for me to take an appointment. My melancholy, which is almost a quiet derangement, has been a hindrance to me all along, my consciousness of sin, too. This has aided me continually in venturing, for it has assured me that I was at least not being guided by vanity and the like. But now in God's name I must turn in this direction.

Strangely enough, incidentally, I have written so much in journal NB[10] [i.e., *Pap.*, x¹ A 82–294] and in this journal [NB[11], *Pap.*, x¹ A 296– 541], but there is on a loose sheet something I have not wished to enter in the journal and which I still really regard as the most decisive [factor] and also one of the earliest—I now end with precisely this.

x¹ A 422    June 4, 1849

« **6417**

*Addition to 6415* (x¹ A 422): *ad* journal NB[11], p. 127 [i.e., x¹ A 422].

If "From on High He Will Draw All Men to Himself"[2284] is to be pseudonymous, then the first discourse will have to be omitted, since it actually was preached by me in Frue Kirke. Or with a note which just as well admits the truth promptly and candidly. This discourse is a kind of plagiarism. It is a discourse delivered in Frue Kirke by Magister Kierkegaard. I believe it is reproduced fairly accurately, and I beg the Magister's forgiveness for having published it, but this discourse has substantially determined the whole book—thus in a way belongs with it. The author, who so frequently has had to tolerate being used, no doubt will easily put up with this. —Then I could answer that I really have no objection except that by appearing in this connection it really has become something different.

But perhaps it is better to omit it; such jesting could easily be misunderstood.

$X^1$ A 423   *n.d.*, 1849

« **6418**

This is the loose sheet mentioned on page 129 of this journal [$X^1$ A 422]. To be written transversely in the journal.

If I had the means, I would venture further out—of course, not with the intention of being put to death (for that, after all, is sinful), but nevertheless, with that possibility in mind, believing that eventually my life might take a still higher turn.

Now I cannot, and I cannot defend venturing in the way which would give my life such a turn that I really would not recognize myself, whereas I fully recognize myself in the kind of persecution, if it may be called that, which I have suffered. Yes, from earliest childhood I have had the presentiment in my soul that things would turn out this way for me, that in a certain sense I should be regarded even with a certain solemnity as somewhat extraordinary and yet be laughed at and regarded as a bit mad.

Now I cannot. Now all my original plans go against me: to be a writer for only a few years and then seek an appointment,[2285] to practice the art of being able to stop—all the more so since it was my intention, never as definite as last year when I sold the house and made a little on it, to stop in earnest (I did not even rent rooms; this I did only much later) and to travel; and the Friday-discourses[2286] have always seemed to me to be a suitable terminating point. Perhaps I should have done that. I suffered much in 1848, but I also learned much and in that case [traveling] I would scarcely have learned to know myself in this way.

Now I cannot. Suddenly to be forced to sustain a very perceptible financial loss,[2287] perhaps at a time when I am about to take the most decisive step—and then perhaps not be put to death anyway and then to bungle the whole cause and myself—no, that I cannot do. To my mind it would be tempting God if I, spoiled by having had financial means, were now, with this new danger, to venture to a degree previously untried.

In addition, I now have a misgiving about myself which I would not have if I had financial means: is there possibly a connection between this almost martyr-impatience of mine and another kind of impatience, my shrinking from the humiliating task of actively seeking an appointment and from the humiliation implicit in all such things and in the whole mode of life. Moreover, I do have perhaps a trace of life-weariness. Perhaps it is also an exaggeration in the direction of expressing that I have suffered injustice and therefore could wish that they would put me to death.

Finally, there is a big question whether I, with my differential mental and spiritual capacities,[2288] am not intended to live, because the more there is of scientific scholarship and the like, the less relevant it is to work in that way.

Finally, it is part of being human not to become the very highest which he has envisioned—patience and humility in this respect. But he will be wounded by this highest, and that I have been, through having been so close to it in thought.

Consequently I do not take the least little step in that direction.

$x^1$ A 424   *n.d.*, 1849

### « 6419

[*In margin:* A motto which relates to the three books: *Practice in Christianity.*]

The motto that appears in one of the latest journals [i.e., $x^1$ A 251] and which is supposed to appear in the edition of the three books (*Practice in Christianity*) is an authentic motto for my endeavor— I do not feel strong enough to imitate you to the point where I die for you or your cause; I am content to do something less, in adoration to thank you that you would die for me.

$x^1$ A 425   *n.d.*, 1849

### « 6420

There is a something appalling, an extremely concentrated sadness, in one single phrase in the first essay by H. H., right at the

beginning of the introduction.[2289] Already as a child he was an old man
. . . . . he went on living, he never became younger. This almost insane
inversion, a child who never became young, a child who was already
an old man and never became younger. What a terrible expression for
terrible suffering.

And yet there is the difference that when he does, as we assume,
grow old, he is not at all as old—because, as an old man to be old as
an old man is old is not the same as to be, as a child, old as an old man
is old.

$X^1$ A 441    n.d., 1849

« **6421**

"Armed Neutrality" can best be published as an appendix when
the three works[2290] are published as one ("Practice in Christianity, a
Venture"), but of course pseudonymously by the same pseudonym.

A pseudonym is excellent for accentuating a point, a stance, a
position. He is a poetic person. Therefore it is not as if I personally
said: This is what I am fighting for—which indeed could become a duty
almost for my entire life, but which external conditions could make it
impossible for me to fulfil, if, for example, I find it necessary to use
most of my time to work for a living.

$X^1$ A 450    n.d., 1849

« **6422**

Curiously enough, in the *Three Godly Discourses*[2291] I attributed to
Paul the words of Peter:[2292] "Cast all your cares upon God."

$X^1$ A 469    n.d., 1849

« **6423**

[*Crossed out:*]
My misfortune or what makes my life so difficult is that I am
stretched one key higher than other men and where I am and what I
do are concerned not only with the particular but always with a principle and idea as well. The most the majority do is to think about which
girl they should marry; I had to think about marriage. So it is in
everything.

It is basically the same with me now. The most the majority do is
to think of which appointment they should seek, and I am at present
deeply involved in the tension, in the battle of ideas, the question of
principles, concerning the extent to which these so-called Christian
professions are legitimate from the essentially Christian point of
view.[2293]

No doubt what makes me unpopular is not so much the difficulty of my books as it is my personal life, the fact that even with all my endeavors I do not amount to anything (the finite teleology), do not make money, do not get appointed to a job, do not become a Knight of Denmark, but in every way amount to nothing and on top of that am derided. To my mind this is what is great about me if there is anything great. And this costs me struggle and strain, for I, too, am flesh and blood—and yet this is precisely why I am unappreciated and mistreated.

$x^1$ A 476    *n.d.*, 1849

### « 6424

What actually has made me a religious speaker? The fact that I am a listener. That is, my life was so complicated and intense that I truly felt the *need* to hear words of guidance. I listened and listened, but if what I heard was supposed to be Christianity, then there was no help for me. So I became a speaker myself. This accounts for my knowing with certainty what our pastors seldom know, that there is *one* who benefits from these discourses: I myself. I am the exact opposite of other speakers: they are preoccupied with speaking to others—I speak to myself. And it is also a fact that insofar as others think it impossible to benefit from my discourses, then it must be because their lives are far too superficial, all too lacking in intensity, insulated from dangers.

$x^1$ A 483    *n.d.*, 1849

### « 6425

Why is it that children who are brought up strictly do not cry when they fall and hurt themselves? Because they know that if the parents find out they will get a beating to boot. Therefore why? Because the pain of the fall is not final and definitive to them. And why is it that an older generation brought up in rigorous piety can endure so much without complaining? Because of their conception that God's punishment would swiftly come, consequently because the pain itself was not the final and definitive thing, but the punishment was the derivative.[2294]

Why is it that today, and in particular the more externally favored a man is, the more he suffers under even the slightest hardship. Because no higher, no ethical idea, derivative and vivifying, intervenes.

Yesterday I read about the following case in one of our newspapers. A workman's wife comes home and finds that her husband has hanged himself. Imagine her horror. She takes him down and then must turn and look after her baby crying in the cradle. She then runs to get help. She finds that two doctors are not at home, then goes to a woman she knows to ask for advice; finally gets hold of a barber—of course it is too late. And then what? Just listen. She is brought to trial for not having exercised proper vigilance in trying to revive him. Merciful God! But something else occurred to me. Suppose this terrible thing had happened in a more prosperous family—what grief there would have been, and rightly so, but perhaps also the heartbreaking grief that would elicit expressions of sympathy. But the poor wretched woman. Yes, she can thank the justice for getting something else to think about, she gets, as we said, a trial and is fined ten rix-dollars. One thing is sure, this is a splendid derivative device—but justice!

$X^1$ A 488   *n.d.,* 1849

« 6426

Monday, June 25

Pfui, pfui!

So I wanted or rather thought it necessary to act circumspectly and make sure of an appointment[2295] first of all and then publish the books[2296] pseudonymously. A splendid interpretation of "Seek first the kingdom of God!" What good would it have done me if I had collapsed under the weight of having acted circumspectly and then would have had to resign from my position anyway. All my apprehension about being denied an appointment is no doubt hypochondria. No doubt all my other apprehensions are also to a large extent mixed with hypochondria, but however heavily it weighs upon me, the action still must not be prudential.

This came alive for me yesterday (Sunday). It has bothered me for a long time that I had considered stopping my publishing in order to take steps to arrange an appointment for myself. Of late one of my own phrases has come to mind spontaneously—that God is not served by men who snap in the crucial moment. I have been troubled by something I read somewhere in Fenelon, that it must be frightful for a man "from whom God had expected more or upon whom God had counted for a decision of greater amplitude." On the other hand I was struck by what I read today in Fenelon,[2297] part 2, p. 26 (Claudius's translation). And especially what I read yesterday in Tersteegen's Christmas sermon,[2298] p. 141. "The wise men went another way," for we should always be ready to follow God's guidance.

The whole matter of its being a higher course than I had considered is no doubt true, but then a man ought not demand that the whole thing be transparent to him right away. And has not my idea been changed little by little, has not the intervention of Governance made me an author in a completely different sense than I originally had in mind. What was my original thought? Allow me to backtrack scrupulously in time. What was my thought when I left her? It was: I am a penitent; marriage is an impossibility; there will always be a shadow to make it unhappy and that also protests the wedding. On the other hand —and God knows I thought of this too, even though I wanted to forget it or pretended to have forgotten it—on the other hand, the decisively religious life, for which I feel a need and for which I as a penitent must have the possibility if I want to be honest with God, cannot be combined with marriage. If God is going to bring my sins down upon me, I must not through falsification be in the situation of having to ask God to spare me for the sake of another person, another human being to whom I have in that case been joined by a falsification. That is, my life must either become a despairing hedonism—or an existence as unconditionally consistent as possible.

And for me (**N.B.**) to stop at this time and beget a heresy and deceive God, him who like a father gently has led me farther and farther out into decisions I would have been unable to endure if I had understood everything at once. O, pfui on me! And because I have hesitated so long, everything has become more difficult.

$x^1$ A 494    June 25, 1849

« **6427**

*In margin of 6426* ($x^1$ A 494):
*Later Observation*

**N.B.**    But obviously something is still overlooked here, that then I still had the idea of being an author without financial worries, and in any case would be able to get a pastoral appointment*[2299] whenever I wanted it.

$x^1$ A 495    *n.d.*, 1849

« **6428**

*Addition to 6427* [$x^1$ A 495 in margin of $x^1$ A 494]:
*Later Observation*

*Yes, and that is very crucial, for actually that is just where the trouble lies. But here, too, as happens so frequently when I write this way, there is a certain editing, that is, there is, as here, a τέλος in the interpretation which forces me to act.

x¹ A 496    n.d., 1849

« **6429**

*Addition to 6426* (x¹ A 494):

*Historical Note.* To make sure it is not because I shrink from taking a step in the opposite direction, the day before yesterday (Saturday) (after failing to meet with Mynster on Friday), I went to see Madvig but did not meet him. That was perhaps fortunate. For I may say in my defense that this time, as usual, I considered taking this step but always with the possibility of getting the momentum to act in the opposite direction; in other words, this is intrinsic to my nature because when something that tempts me as possibility turns out to be capable of realization, it turns into something else.* So I did not get to see Madvig.[2300] Now Mynster[2301] was left. How reluctantly I went to him, for I have indeed noticed how uneasy he is with me, especially since R. Nielsen's book[2302] and the little anonymous piece[2303] which he certainly has read. Three weeks ago I visited him—I immediately saw how things stood with us and merely exchanged two words with him, pacing up and down the floor, quite contrary to custom. He, however, repeated again and again: Dear friend, dear friend—but refused to enter into conversation. That was why I reluctantly brought myself to go to him. But I did go on Friday; scrupulous as I am, I regarded it as my duty not to spare myself lest I start worrying about it afterward. Friday he was administering communion. I wanted to visit him on Saturday, but he was going to preach on Sunday and I knew that he would rather not talk with anyone. Today (Monday) I visited him. Just as I thought: "How do you do, dear friend"—and "Dear friend"—and then he said that he had no time to talk with me—"I am speaking plainly." I understood him. But I also understood how to collect myself and thanked him for showing such confidence in me. He repeated this. "Dear friend" six or seven times, I am sure, clapped me on the shoulders, and patted me—meaning that he is afraid to talk with me because he is afraid to get too involved with me. To be sure he said: Come again another time, but since he realizes very well that it cannot be this week, after which he leaves to make his official visits, it is easy to understand, after all. But thank God I did it and did not spare myself. But thank God I did not get to talk with him. For even if I actually was merely exploring the possibility of arranging an appointment[2304] prior to making a definite decision, who knows, it could be very risky for me. However, my past life certainly has taught me the opposite. The very day I decided in earnest to break the engagement in the afternoon, in the forenoon of that day I said just the opposite —and had I not done so, I would not have had the strength to do the opposite in the afternoon. It is due to the fact that I am almost sheer reflection. But no doubt it is best for me that it happened as it did. A positive predisposition to agree with my idea could have helped me. If that had happened, I most likely would have gained the strength to abandon it in order to do just the opposite. But if opposition to my idea of getting an appointment had been indicated, such a situation could very easily have an adverse effect upon me and induce me to apply additional energy to accomplishing its possibility—for its realization always would be subject to one final consideration. An unsuccessful attempt along that line perhaps could give me a distaste for that which really preoccupies me.

x[1] A 497   n.d., 1849

« **6430**

*In margin of 6429* (x[1] A 497):

*Yes, it is true. Would to God I had been offered an appointment, for then it very likely would be far easier to understand that I cannot accept it. But here comes my self-tormenting again; if it is not offered to me, then I fear that I do not take the necessary steps in order to safeguard myself.

x[1] A 498   n.d.

« **6431**

The other alternative[2305] is perhaps more rash, perhaps bolder, perhaps a more daring venture, but this does not make it more true for me—and to be true is of first importance.

If I consider my own personal life, am I then a Christian or is my personal life purely a poet-existence, even with an addition of something demonic. In that case the idea would be to take such an enormous risk that I thereby make myself so unhappy that I would get into the situation for really becoming a Christian. But does this give me the right to do it dramatically so that the Christendom of a whole country gets involved. Is there not something desperate in the whole thing, something like the treachery of starting a fire in order to throw oneself into the arms of God—perhaps, for perhaps it would nevertheless turn out that I would not become a Christian.

All this about my person as author cannot be used at all, for it is clear that it only will involve me more in the interesting instead of getting me out of it, and this is also the effect it will have on my contemporaries. The simple transition is utterly elementary: to be silent and then to see about getting an appointment.

There is no question but that I will stop being an author now, but I would still like to dispense with the interesting: put down the period myself and officially in character. The simple way to do it is to cross over to the new in complete silence; this solemn determination to put down a period is an extremely dangerous thing; the elemental point is that there in fact comes to be a period.

I regret—and I blame myself for it—that in several previous entries in this journal there are attempts to exalt myself, for which God will forgive me.

Until now I have been a poet, absolutely nothing else, and it is a desperate struggle to will to go out beyond my limits.

The work "Practice in Christianity" has great personal significance for me—does it follow that I should publish it right away? Perhaps I am one of the few who need such strong remedies—and should I, then, instead of benefiting from it and myself beginning in real earnestness to become a Christian, should I first publish it? Fantastic!

The work and other works are ready; perhaps the time may come when it is suitable and I have the strength to do it and when it is truth in me.

In many ways it is true that the entire authorship is my upbringing or education—well, does that mean that instead of being in earnest about becoming a true Christian I am to become a phenomenon in the world?

CONSEQUENTLY *The Sickness unto Death* appears at this time, but pseudonymously and with me as editor. It is said to be "for upbuilding." This is more than my category, the poet-category: upbuilding.[2306]

Just as the Guadalquibir River (this occurred to me earlier and is somewhere in the journal [i.e., IX A 422] plunges down somewhere into the earth, so is there also a stretch, the upbuilding, which carries my name. There is something (the esthetic) which is lower and is pseudonymous and something which is higher and is also pseudonymous, because as a person I do not correspond to it.

The pseudonym is Johannes Anticlimacus in contrast to Climacus,[2307] who said he was not a Christian. Anticlimacus is the opposite extreme: a Christian on an extraordinary level—but I myself manage to be only a very simple Christian.

"Practice in Christianity" can be published in the same way, but there is no hurry.

But nothing about my personality as a writer; it is false to want to anticipate during one's lifetime—this merely converts a person into the interesting.

On the whole, I must now venture in quite different directions. I must dare to believe that through Christ I can be saved from the power of melancholy in which I have lived; and I must try to be more economical.

x¹ A 510    n.d., 1849

### « 6432

The wrong way is much too close, wanting to reform, to arouse the whole world—instead of oneself, and this certainly is the wrong way for hotheads with a lot of imagination.

I have also had a tendency toward it, almost demonically[2308] wanting to force myself to be stronger than I am. Just as sanguine men are required to hate themselves, perhaps it is necessary for me to love myself and renounce this gloomy self-hatred which can even become almost pleasurable.

I also have the fault that I constantly escort myself in the role of a writer and then almost desperately demand of myself that I act in character. That is why I need humiliation at this point. I was humbled at the time by the engagement, having to break it jolted my pride.

x¹ A 513    n.d., 1849

### « 6433

*[In margin:* About Anti-Climacus]

Johannes Climacus and Anti-Climacus have several things in common; but the difference is that whereas Johannes Climacus places himself so low that he even says himself that he is not a Christian, one seems to be able to detect in Anti-Climacus that he regards himself to be a Christian on an extraordinarily high level [*in margin:* see p. 260, p. 267 (i.e., x¹ A 530, 536], at times also seems to believe that Christianity really is only for geniuses, using the word in a non-intellectual sense.

His personal guilt, then, is to confuse himself with ideality (this is the demonic in him), but his portrayal of ideality can be absolutely sound, and I bow to it.

I would place myself higher than Johannes Climacus, lower than Anti-Climacus.

X[1] A 517   *n.d.*, 1849

« **6434**

Dear friend,[2309]

Your note[2310] of Friday of last week duly received. It may perhaps have escaped you that the association of ideas from omnibus to omnibus is evoked in the maxim *de omnibus dubitandum*.[2311] Hence when Johannes de Silentio[2312] calls the system "an omnibus," it must be understood as having a double meaning.

I am sending along a new book.[2313] Presumably you will have no difficulty in discovering why this pseudonym is called *Anti*-Climacus, in which respect he is quite different from Johannes Climacus, with whom he certainly does have something in common (as they do also share parts of a name), but from whom he differs very essentially in that J. Cl. humorously denies that he himself is Christian and, in consequence, can only make indirect attacks, and, in consequence, as a humorist must take it all back—while Anti-Climacus is very far from denying that he himself is Christian, which is evident in the direct attack. There is no more space here, except for this:

Yours,

S.K.

*Letters,* no. 213   July, 1849

« **6435**

It was, after all, a desperate notion and also somewhat demonic, the whole idea which I long ago abandoned of publishing everything, including the part about my authorship, in one volume.[2314]

As a matter of fact something different took place. All the suffering involved in the work of reflection of late actually has been a personal awakening for me.

Now I am able to say that Christ has come in this way to reveal to me that Savior is to be understood as one who helps a person out of his misery and not simply one who helps a person bear it.

But the point is that I have never been able to take command of myself in the ordinary human sense because of my unfortunate melancholia, which at one point was a kind of partial madness.

Thus my only possibility was to function simply as spirit, and that is why I could be only an author.

At last I was ready to stake everything (the consequence of working in this way) and then of my own volition retire, again because I inhumanly have been able to work only as spirit, that is, in the third person.

All my inner torment, together with my brilliance and the treatment I have suffered, brought me to the point where it seemed as if I myself were a governing force to organize an awakening.

To be able and to be allowed to do this for the truth has been my only satisfaction, my only comfort.

Now Governance has intervened and required me in self-denial to abandon that bold but also demonic idea.

It will help me if God will enable me to work more humanly so that I do not always need to make myself a third person, so that I personally can enter into things.

$$X^1 \text{ A } 519 \quad n.d., \text{ 1849}$$

### « 6436

[*In margin:* About *The Sickness unto Death*]

The book is characterized as being "for upbuilding";[2315] the preface speaks of it as upbuilding.[2316] It really should say: for awakening. [*In margin:* see p. 259 in this journal (i.e., $X^1$ A 529)]. This is its basic character, and this is the forward step in the writings. Essentially it is also for awakening, but this does not need to be said yet. This will come out decisively for the first time in the next book, "Practice in Christianity."

$$X^1 \text{ A } 520 \quad n.d., \text{ 1849}$$

### « 6437

[*In margin:* About a postscript to *The Sickness unto Death.*]

At first I thought of a postscript by the editor. But for one thing it is plain to see that I personally am a part of the book—for example, the part about the religious poet;[2317] for another, I am afraid I thereby will contradict the argument in another book (in one of those which make up "Practice in Christianity")[2318] about making observations instead of preaching.

[*In margin:* Such a postscript is completely inappropriate to the tone of the book, and in the long run humility of that sort might rather almost embitter.]

In any case, the sketches for this postscript[2319] are in my desk.

X¹ A 525   *n.d.,* 1849

« **6438**

[*In margin:* The title of the book: *The Sickness unto Death.*]
It finally came to bear the inscription:

For upbuilding and awakening.[2320]

This "for awakening" actually is the "more" that came out of the year 1848, but it is also the "more" that is so much higher than my own person that I use a pseudonym for it. [*In margin:* See p. 253 in this journal (i.e., X¹ A 520).]

I use only the poetic designation: "upbuilding," never "for up-building."[2321]

X¹ A 529   *n.d.,* 1849

« **6439**

[*In margin:* A passage in the preface to the book *The Sickness unto Death.*]

To the closing passage, "but that the form is what it is,"[2322] I have thought of adding:

apart from the fact that it is also rooted in my being who I am.

But this would be going too far in transforming a fictitious character into actuality; a fictitious character has no possibility other than the one he has; he cannot declare that he could also speak in another way and yet be the same; he has no identity which encompasses many possibilities.

On the other hand, the fact that he says: "It is at least well considered"—is proper, for it may very well be that, although it is his only form. For him to say: "It is psychologically correct" is a double blow, for it is also psychologically correct with respect to Anti-Climacus.

Climacus is lower, denies he is a Christian.[2323] Anti-Climacus is higher, a Christian on an extraordinarily high level. [*In margin:* see p. 249 (i.e., X¹ A 517).] With Climacus everything drowns in humor;[2324] therefore he himself retracts his book.[2325] Anti-Climacus is thetical.

X¹ A 530   *n.d.,* 1849

« **6440**

[*In margin:* The significance of the pseudonyms.]

*The Significance of the Pseudonyms*

All communication of truth has become abstract: the public has become the authority; the newspapers call themselves the editorial staff; the professor calls himself speculation; the pastor is meditation, no man, none, dares to say *I*.

But since without qualification the first prerequisite for the communication of truth is personality, since "truth" cannot possibly be served by ventriloquism, personality has to come to the fore again.

But in these circumstances, since the world was so corrupted by never hearing an *I*, it was impossible to begin at once with one's own *I*. So it became my task to create author-personalities and let them enter in the actuality of life in order to get men a bit accustomed to hearing discourse in the first person.

Thus my task is no doubt only that of a forerunner until he comes who in the strictest sense says: *I*.

But to make a turn away from this inhuman abstraction to personality—that is my task.

$X^1$ A 531   *n.d.*, 1849

### « 6441

[*In margin:* the eulogy[2326] on Bishop Mynster by F. F.[2327]]

This eulogy is given on the presupposition that "state church," "established Christendom" are valid concepts. That from a Christian standpoint this must be denied is an entirely different matter. But if these concepts are assumed to have reality (and this ought to be assumed in a conception of Bishop Mynster, since it is reasonable, after all, to conceive a man according to his own idea and thought), then he is great and admirable. On the other hand, Bishop Mynster can be attacked only if one attacks these two concepts.

$X^1$ A 535   *n.d.*

### « 6442

[*In margin:* About Anti-Climacus]

If I have represented a person so low that he even denied being a Christian[2328] [*In margin:* see p. 249 (i.e., $X^1$ A 517)], then the opposite also ought to be represented. And Christendom does indeed greatly need to hear the voice of such a judge—but I will not pass myself off as the judge, and therefore he also judges me, which is easy enough and quite appropriate, for anyone who cannot present ideality so high that he is judged by it himself must have a poor understanding of it.

$X^1$ A 536   *n.d.*

### « 6443

There is no Christianity in the land—and then a synodical meeting is called![2329] It will probably be of the same nature as parents-teachers'

meetings; problems will come up about louvres in the church to venti-
late the air, whether to abolish the collection plate—whether the pastor
should not have different garb, perhaps also have a ring in his nose.

$X^1$ A 538 *n.d.*, 1849

### « 6444 *De se ipso*[2330]

Actually, something else will happen than what I originally had in
mind.

When I began as the author of *Either/Or,* I no doubt had a far
more profound impression of the *terror* of Christianity than any clergyman in the country. I had a fear and trembling such as perhaps no one
else had. Not that I therefore wanted to relinquish Christianity. No, I
had another interpretation of it. For one thing I had in fact learned
very early that there are men who seem to be selected for suffering,
and, for another thing, I was conscious of having sinned much, and
therefore supposed that Christianity had to appear to me in the form
of this terror. But how cruel and false of you, I thought, if you use it
to terrify others, perhaps upset ever so many happy, loving lives that
may very well be truly Christian. It was as alien as possible to my nature
to want to terrify others, since I both sadly and perhaps also a bit
proudly found my joy in comforting others and in being gentleness
itself to them—forgetting the terror in my own interior being.

So my idea was to give my contemporaries (whether or not they
themselves would want to understand[2331]) a hint in humorous form (in
order to achieve a lighter tone) that a much greater pressure was
needed[2332]—but then no more; I aimed to keep my heavy burden to
myself, as my cross. I have often taken exception to anyone who was
a sinner in the strictest sense and then promptly got busy terrifying
others. Here is where *Concluding Postscript* comes in.

Then I was horrified to see what was understood by a Christian
state (this I saw especially in 1848); I saw how the ones who were
supposed to rule, both in Church and State, hid themselves like cow-
ards while barbarism boldly and brazenly raged; and I experienced
how a truly unselfish and God-fearing endeavor (and my endeavor as
an author was that) is rewarded in the Christian state.

That seals my fate. Now it is up to my contemporaries how they
will list the cost of being a Christian, how terrifying they will make it.
I surely will be given the strength for it—I almost said "unfortunately."
I really do not say this in pride. I both have been and am willing to pray
to God to exempt me from this terrible business; furthermore, I am
human myself and also love, humanly speaking, to live happily here on

earth. But if what one sees all over Europe is Christendom, a Christian state, then I propose to start here in Denmark to list the price for being Christian in such a way that the whole concept—state church, official appointments, livelihood—bursts open.

I dare not do otherwise, for I am a penitent from whom God can demand everything. I also write under a pseudonym because I am a penitent. Nevertheless, I will be persecuted, but I am secure against any honor and esteem that from another side could fall to me.

For some years now I have been so inured to bearing the treachery and ingratitude of a little country, the envy of the elite and the insults of the rabble that I perhaps—for want to anything better—am qualified to proclaim Christianity. Bishop Mynster can keep his velvet robe and Grand Cross.[2333]

X[1] A 541    *n.d.*, 1849

« **6445**

Thank God I did not publish the book about my work as an author or in any way try to push myself to be more than I am.

*The Sickness unto Death* is now printed, and pseudonymously, by Anti-Climacus.

"Practice in Christianity" will also be pseudonymous. I now understand myself completely.

The point in the whole thing is this: there is a zenith of Christianity in ethical rigorousness and this must at least be heard. But no more. It must be left to everyone's conscience to decide whether he is capable of building the tower so high.

But heard it must be. But the trouble is simply that practically all Christendom and all the clergy, too, live not only in secular prudence at best but also in such a way that they brazenly boast about it and as a consequence must interpret the life of Christ to be fanaticism.

This is why the other must be heard, heard if possible as a voice in the clouds, heard as the flight of wild birds over the heads of the tame ones.

But no more. That is why it must be pseudonymous and I merely the editor.

Ah, but what I suffered before arriving at this, something which was essentially clear to me earlier but I had to understand again.

God will certainly look after the rest for me.

If I now continue to be an author, the subject must be "sin" and "reconciliation" in such a way that in an upbuilding discourse I would now make use of the fact that the pseudonym has appropriately raised the price.

For this pseudonyms will be used continually. I entertained this idea once before, particularly regarding that to which Anti-Climacus is assigned,[2334] and it is somewhere in the journals, no doubt in NB[10] [i.e., $x^1$ A 422].

The fearful stress and strain I have experienced lately are due to my wanting to overexert myself and wanting too much, and then I myself perceived that it was too much, and therefore I did not carry it out, but then again I was unable to let the possibility go and to my own torment held myself on the spearhead of possibility—something, incidentally, that without any merit on my part has been an extremely beneficial discipline for me.

Now there has been action, and now I can breathe.

It was a sound idea: to stop my productivity by once again using a pseudonym. Like the river Guadalquibir—this simile appeals to me very much.

So not a word about myself with respect to the total authorship; such a word will change everything and misrepresent me.

$x^1$ A 546   *n.d.*, 1849

« **6446**

It is absolutely right—a pseudonym[2335] had to be used.

When the demands of ideality are to be presented at their maximum, then one must take extreme care not to be confused with them himself, as if he himself were the ideal.

Protestations could be used to avoid this. But the only sure way is this redoubling.

The difference from the earlier pseudonyms is simply but essentially this, that I do not retract the whole thing humorously but identify myself as one who is striving.

$x^1$ A 548   *n.d.*, 1849

« **6447**

[*In margin:* About the review of H. H.'s book[2336] in *Kirketidenden*]

The little book by H. H. is reviewed in *Kirketidenden*[2337] (Saturday, July 21). The opinion is that it is by "a very young author who has read Mag. Kierkegaard." Splendid. What a critic! This little book is very significant. It contains the key to the greatest potentiality of all my writing, but not the one at which I have been aiming. And the second essay contains the most important of all the ethical-religious concepts, the one I have deliberately omitted until its appearance there.

But I will not say anything about the book. Because to me, as I expressed earlier somewhere [i.e., $x^1$ A 351], it is a false point of view, signifying that I will take another direction.

Perhaps it is even a feint on the part of the reviewer to lure me out onto thin ice.

If anything is to be written about this review, it must be done with the idea that I would stand up in defense of that "young man" and that the reviewer has done him an injustice. If it could be of any joy or compensation to him—who is a very young man according to the expert reviewer—then I can assure him that I have read the little book with unusual interest and found that it grasped a point (the sympathetic collision) which as far as I know no one here at home has grasped with the exception of my pseudonyms, and found that it properly grasped and also explained the perhaps most important ethical-religious concept: authority.[2338] Assuming, as the expert reviewer says, that he is a very young man, I would say to him: Young friend, keep on writing. Without reservations you are the one I would entrust with the continuation of my work.

But nothing will be done; I will not elaborate the point. It is just for a little fun.

$x^1$ A 551   *n.d.*, 1849

« **6448**

[*In margin:* Martensen's *Dogmatics*[2339]]

While all existence is disintegrating, while anyone with eyes must see that all this about millions of Christians is a sham, that if anything Christianity has vanished from the world, Martensen sits and organizes a dogmatic system. What does it mean that he undertakes something like this? As far as faith is concerned, it says that everything in the country is just as it should be, we are all Christians; there is no danger afoot here, we have the opportunity to indulge in scholarship. Since everything else is as it should be, the most important matter confronting us now is to determine where the angels are to be placed in the system, and things like that.

$x^1$ A 553   *n.d.*, 1849

« **6449**

[*In margin:* Martensen's *Dogmatics*[2340]]

It is really ridiculous! There has been talk of the system and scientificity and about scientificity etc., and then finally comes the system. Merciful God, my most popular book is more stringent in definition of concepts, and my pseudonym Johannes Climacus is seven times as stringent in definition of concepts. Martensen's *Dogmatics* is, after all, a popular piece lacking the powerful imagination or something similar which could give it that kind of a worth; and the only scholarliness I have discovered in it is that it is divided into paragraphs. He has no more categories than Mynster. Strangely enough, Mynster is frequently quoted—and as a dogmatician. And at one time it was Mynster whom "the system" was going to overthrow.

$x^1$ A 556   *n.d.*, 1849

« **6450**

So I turn off the tap; that means the pseudonym Anti-Climacus, a halt.

An awakening[2341] is the final goal, but that is too high for me personally—I am too much of a poet.

$x^1$ A 557   *n.d.*, 1849

« **6451**

Now *The Sickness unto Death*[2342] is published and pseudonymously, putting an end to the confounded torment of undertaking too great a task: wishing to publish everything at one time, including what I wrote about the authorship, and, so to speak, taking the desperate step of setting fire to established Christianity.

Now the question of when the three other books[2343] come out is of less importance (and the one about my authorship will not appear at all), for now there is no question of the force of one single blow.

Now I will rest and be more calm.

$x^1$ A 567   *n.d.*, 1849

« **6452**

I did not learn that Olsen[2344] was dead until I was talking with Luno[2345] about printing *The Sickness unto Death*. I was so reluctant to impair the impact of my dealings at the printing house that I went ahead with the printing. Furthermore, I was so shaken by the far too much thinking I have done of late that I finally feared completely losing grip on myself.

x¹ A 568    n.d., 1849

« 6453

*In margin of 6452* (x¹ A 568)*:*
Councillor Olsen[2346] is dead.

This will certainly lead her to think in a special way of her relationship to me. If so, I owe it to her to bring up the matter again. Governance, too, indicates to me that this is the time for it. My most difficult period is always from August 9 to September 10. I have always had something against summer. And now, at the time when I am physically at my weakest, come the anniversaries of my father's death and, September 10, of my engagement.

x¹ A 569    n.d., 1849

« 6454

[*In margin:* about "her."[2347]]
Where "she" is concerned, I am, as ever, but even more fervently if possible, ready and willing to do everything that could comfort her and cheer her up. But I am continually afraid of her passion. I am the guaranty of her marriage. If she finds out the real truth of my relationship to her she suddenly may get a distaste for marriage—alas, I know her far too well. And either she is essentially unchanged, and then it is extremely dangerous, or she has changed so essentially that it will not mean much to her if I make any approach.[2348]

The Sunday after the Councillor's death[2349] she was in church (Helliggeistes-Kirke) with her whole family. I was there too. Contrary to her custom, she left immediately after the sermon, something she usually does not do, since she always remains and sings a hymn, whereas way back as far as I can remember I have had a habit of leaving immediately. As I said, she left immediately, accompanied by Schlegel.[2350] She was just in time so that we almost met when I came down from the gallery. She perhaps expected me to greet her, but I averted my eyes. A purely accidental reason also made it impossible to get further involved at the time, even if I had wanted to.

Perhaps it is good that I had all that trouble at the printer's during that time, for otherwise I perhaps would have gone ahead and made a move—directly contrary to my previous understanding that her father was the only one with whom I could wish and dare to become involved.

She no doubt thinks the opposite, perhaps believes that he has stood in the way of my making a move toward her.

God knows how much I long to be, humanly speaking, gentle to her, but I dare not. And in many ways it also seems as if Governance wants to prevent it—perhaps knowing the consequences—for it was a purely accidental circumstance that made it impossible for me to speak to them that time. The next time [2351] when Kolthoff[2352] preached I was in Helliggeistes-Kirke, but she was not.

*X*[1] A 570   *n.d.,* 1849

« **6455**

If it could be done and if I had not virtually ceased being an author, it would give me much joy to dedicate one of my books[2353] to the memory of Councillor Olsen.[2354] In fact, for that purpose the book "From on High He will Draw All to Himself" could provide the opportunity.

*X*[1] A 571   *n.d.,* 1849

« **6456**

The trouble with Martensen[2355] is this perpetual talking about Kant, Hegel, Schelling, etc. It provides a guaranty that there must be something to what he says. It is similar to the journalistic practice of writing in the name of the public.

*X*[1] A 576   *n.d.,* 1849

« **6457**

[*In margin:* The three godly discourses (*The Lily and the Bird*) and *The Sickness unto Death* with respect to time of writing.]

It must be remembered that the three godly discourses about the lily and the bird are the last thing I wrote. They were finished May 5, 1849. *The Sickness unto Death* is from the middle of 1848.

*X*[1] A 583   *n.d.,* 1849

« **6458**

What an accomplishment the *Concluding Postscript* is; there is more than enough for three professors. But of course the author was someone who did not have a career position and did not seem to want to have one; there was nothing worthy of becoming a paragraph in the system—well, then, it is nothing at all.

The book came out in Denmark. It was not mentioned anywhere at all.[2356] Perhaps fifty copies were sold, thus the publishing costs for me, including the proofreader's fee (100 rix-dollars), came to about 400 or 500 rix-dollars, plus my time and work. And in the meantime I am caricatured by a scandal sheet that in the same little country has 3,000 subscribers, and another paper (also with wide circulation, *Flyveposten*) continues the discussion about my trousers.[2357]

$$X^1 \text{ A } 584 \quad n.d., \text{ } 1849$$

### « 6459

I am like a chaplain in a monastery, a spiritual adviser to the solitary etc.–but I cannot involve myself in the nonsense that is now called piety, religiosity. Spiritual trial [*Anfægtelse*] is literally never spoken of any more.

$$X^1 \text{ A } 586 \quad n.d., \text{ } 1849$$

### « 6460

[*In margin:* Martensen]
It is characteristic of Martensen[2358] that he never quotes the younger Fichte, Baader, Günther, but constantly quotes Schleiermacher, whom he corrects. This means that he directly capitalizes upon what has appeared since Schleiermacher and also profits by correcting Schleiermacher.

$$X^1 \text{ A } 588 \quad n.d.$$

### « 6461

The two works by Anti-Climacus[2359] ("Practice in Christianity") can be published immediately.

With this the writing stops;[2360] essentially it has already stopped (that which is wholly mine) with "The Friday Discourses."[2361] The pseudonymous writer[2362] at the end is a higher level, which I can only suggest. The second-round pseudonymity is precisely the expression for the halt. *Qua* author I am like the river Guadalquibir, which at some place plunges under the earth; there is a stretch which is mine: the upbuilding;[2363] behind and ahead lie the lower and the higher pseudonymities: the upbuilding is mine, not the esthetic, not [the pseudonymous works] for upbuilding either, and even less those for awakening.[2364]

$$X^1 \text{ A } 593 \quad n.d., \text{ } 1849$$

### « 6462

Anti-Climacus will be the higher pseudonym,[2365] and thus the piece "Climacus and Anti-Climacus" [i.e., $X^6$ B 48] cannot be used, unless it should be by a new pseudonym. That means that I cannot be the author of the piece.

But, on examining it, I see that this was never the intention. The piece is by Anti-Climacus himself. It may well be done. Nevertheless, perhaps a new pseudonym is better.

$x^1$ A 594    *n.d.*, 1849

« **6463**

The concept "Christendom," "established Christendom," is what has to be reformed (the single individual).

What is needed is the maieutic. It is not at all a matter of getting any change in externals, not that I, for example, get hundreds to imitate me in what before God I have realized; it is a matter of men being guided to an awareness that every individual is to seek the primitive God-relationship.

A flanking manoeuvre can be made against the clergy on the point that they have become all too secularized, but not personal attacks on individual clergymen; yet it must not be done in such a way that external changes seem to be recommended.

It was impatience on my part suddenly to want to abandon indirect communication and personally take over the whole thing in the capacity of an extraordinary. In spite of all my disclaimers and stipulations there still would be confusion about such a step.

$x^1$ A 598    *n.d.*, 1849

« **6464**

"Practice in Christianity" will be the last to be published. There I shall end for now.

Consequently the year 1848 will be included, since the things by Anti-Climacus[2366] are all from 1848. The remainder is from 1849. According to decision current writing will be shelved.

If "Practice in Christianity" is published, what has been intimated many places elsewhere will be carried out—in all earnestness to set forth the possibility of offense. This is also related essentially to my task, which is continually to jack up the price[2367] by bringing a dialectic to bear. But for this reason, too, a pseudonym must be used. That which represents the dialectical element has always been by a pseudonym. To want to make it my own would be both untrue and an all too frightful and violent means of awakening.

$x^1$ A 615    *n.d.*, 1849

« **6465**

[*In margin:* Martensen]

Martensen can lecture on anything. In his *Dogmatics,*[2368] p. 456: "The more fervently and powerfully faith is proclaimed in the world, the more it becomes the signal for opposition, and the world is constrained to manifest its enmity to the truth, which becomes effective by means of this very opposition." That is all very well and good for rote-reading—but now take Martensen's life: he is in collusion with speculation, floridly courts the favors of philosophy, makes accommodations, etc., etc.—and this he himself alludes to as wisdom in contrast to the paradox. But faith cannot be proclaimed powerfully without the paradox, and the paradox is precisely what tenses the world in torment, so that deliberately or against its will it must reveal itself.

This, you see, may be called a professor, in contrast to a thinker.

$x^1$ A 616   *n.d.,*  1849

« **6466**

[*In margin: The Basic Shift in Modern Christendom*]

As I have demonstrated on all sides, all modern Christendom is a shifting of the essentially Christian back into the esthetic. Another shift is that the conception of the preparatory condition for becoming a Christian has been broadened in a completely confusing way. Thousands of men who are a long, long way from having an impression of Christianity stand on the same level as a catechumen and summarily have been made Christians. In this fashion there has been such an advance that if such people are supposed to be Christians, then an indifferent catechumen is an outstanding Christian. And this is just about the way it is in "established Christendom." Just as everywhere else, first place has been allowed to vanish; third place, which otherwise is alien here, has been promoted to an actual position, and class 2 becomes number 1. The apostles, the no. 1 Christians, the witnesses to the truth, etc. become fanatics.

$x^1$ A 617   *n.d.,*  1849

« **6467** *My Writings Considered as a "Corrective"*[2369] *to the Established*

The designation "corrective" is a category of reflection just as: here-there, right-left.

The person who is to provide the "corrective" must study the weak sides of the established scrupulously and penetratingly and then one-sidedly present the opposite—with expert one-sidedness. Precisely in this consists the corrective, and in this also the resignation in the one who is going to do it. In a certain sense the corrective is expended on the established.

If this is done properly, then a presumably sharp head can come along and object that "the corrective" is one-sided and get the public to believe there is something in what he says. Ye gods! Nothing is easier for the one providing the corrective than to add the other side; but then, right there, it ceases to be the corrective and itself becomes established order. Therefore an objection of this nature comes from a person utterly lacking the resignation required to provide "the corrective" and without even the patience to comprehend this.

$X^1$ A 640   n.d., 1849

« **6468**

The "thorn in the flesh" must be struggled against by yielding, not by kicking against the goads[2370] (against which Paul seems to have kicked so hard that as a result he kept the thorn in the flesh); sin must be struggled against with all the combative power one has.

Thus one of the most difficult collisions occurs when a person finds some ambiguity at this point, to what extent it is the thorn in the flesh or it is sin.

$X^1$ A 643   n.d., 1849

« **6469**

It would seem easier to proclaim Christianity to those who lead happy lives, are healthy and prosperous, enjoy life—than to proclaim it to cripples, the sick, malcontents, etc., but in another sense it probably is far more difficult.

The point is that we are not very careful about what Christianity is. If Christianity is to be preached in truth to the happy, those who enjoy life, then Christianity becomes a kind of cruelty. And on the other hand it is far easier to proclaim the consolation of Christianity —to cripples.

But the point is that people would rather enjoy life etc.—and that is why they are even afraid to look at a cripple, an insane person, a beggar; they wish to keep on being ignorant of him—and then to proclaim Christianity to—the favored!

O, I have seen this much too close at hand. My own soul has been in fear and trembling and I have therefore actually needed Christianity

—and then a young, light-hearted girl. Yes, when a hardened sinner in the last days of his life suddenly awakens to repentance and the pangs of sin-consciousness, send for me—with God's help I will be sure to preach. But a young, light-hearted, lovable girl, as yet without any deep impression—and then Christianity! Here I did not know how to preach. And yet she is no doubt much, much purer than I.

But then is not Christianity for all, is it only for those who are sick and full of sorrow, for those who labor and are heavy laden?

Is it a mistake to want to make everybody Christians?

These problems have occupied me very much. I sometimes use the advice I give myself: Does it concern you? Do you not need Christianity? Then I answer Yes, and look after myself.

$X^1$ A 644   *n.d.*, 1849

« 6470

[*In margin:* About "her"[2371]]

Now that the Councillor is dead,[2372] it is not impossible that she thinks that some approach[2373] could take place from my side; in that case she would have considered the Councillor to have been the real hindrance to me. This certainly is a misunderstanding. The Councillor was the very one with whom I desired reconciliation and therefore also sought it.[2374] Reconciliation with him had no dangerous and serious consequences whatsoever, and in my eyes the offended father was the object of very serious concern.

But if she really does wish it, how gladly I would be reconciled with her. She has suffered for my sake, suffered what must be the deepest humiliation to a young girl, even if I did everything to alleviate the humiliation, and also proposed that she be the one to break the engagement—she has suffered for my sake, and God knows how much I want to make all possible amends. For my own sake as well: the easier the conditions on which she can be married to another, the easier my personal life will be. In a way my personal relationship to God is a reduplication of my relationship to her.

But on the other hand, if she finds out that I was motivated in the past by considerations of religion and suffering, I run the risk of her suddenly yielding to despair over her marriage. It is an awkward matter, "that it would be the death of her,"[2375] and she is the married one; an awkward matter that I was "a scoundrel"—and now it must be seen in a quite different light. And even if I could do all this for her so gently that there would be no danger in this respect—I know very well her vehemence and passionate nature. As I have said to myself before, I am the guaranty of her marriage.

But if she herself takes the bold risk of being the one who requests it, then I will consider myself obligated in God's name to do what I so gladly would do. In that case the chief responsibility will not be mine. By getting married she has emancipated herself from being unconditionally under my responsibility.

Moreover, one thing is sure, my relationship to her has been a very personal contemporaneous course in getting to understand what faith is. For in this relationship I know very well how what seems to be is just the opposite of what lies at the base. The fact that I have gone through this experience has helped me in my own faith-relationship to God. Although my life goes against me and the world is sheer opposition, I nevertheless do have faith. If one has no such experience, in his relationship to God he will promptly want to have a direct understanding and not the understanding of faith.

Moreover, it is quite fitting that just when I was ready to diminish my existential momentum as author the thought of having a direct understanding has been placed right before me.

$x^1$ A 648   n.d., 1849

« **6471**

My Relationship to "Her"[2376]
August 24, 1849

somewhat poetic
$x^5$ A 148   August 24, 1849

« **6472**

1. [*In margin:* **NB**
   Scattered here and there in the more recent journals, those from this year and a year ago, there are a few comments about her.]

2. *Infandum me jubes, Regina, renovare dolorem.* [2377]

3. Regine Olsen. —I saw her for the first time at Rørdams.[2378] It was there that I really saw her in the early days before I visited the [Olsen] family. (In a way I have a certain responsibility toward Bollette Rørdam; as it happens I was really impressed with her earlier and perhaps interested her also, even if in all innocence and purely intellectually.)

Even before my father died my mind was made up about her. He died. I studied for the examination.[2379] During all that time I let her life become entwined in mine.

4. She is also responsible for the remark[2380] about me: It no doubt will end with your becoming a Jesuit.

5. In the summer of 1840 I took the final university examination in theology.

Right away I made a visit to the house. I journeyed to Jutland[2381] and perhaps even then was trying to draw her to me a little (for example, by lending them books in my absence and by encouraging them to read a certain passage in a particular book).

I returned in August. Strictly speaking, the time from August 9 to September can be said to be the period in which I drew closer to her.

September 8 I left home determined to resolve the whole thing. We met on the street outside their house.[2382] She said that there was no one at home. I was rash enough to take this as just the invitation I needed. I went in with her. There we stood, the two of us, alone in the parlor. She was somewhat restless. I asked her to play the piano for me as she usually did. She does so, but it does not interest me. I suddenly take the music book, shut it not without a certain vehemence, throw it on the piano, and say: O, what do I care about music; it is you I seek, for two years I have been seeking you. She was silent. I did nothing, however, to fascinate her; I even warned her against myself, about my melancholy. And when she spoke of a relationship to Schlegel,[2383] I said: Let that relationship be a parenthesis, for after all I do have the first priority. [In margin: N.B. The tenth must have been the earliest she spoke about Schlegel, because on the eighth she did not say a word.] She remained virtually silent. I finally left, for I was uneasy lest someone come and find the two of us and her so agitated. I went immediately to her father. I know that I was dreadfully afraid that I had made too strong an impression on her and also that my visit might in some way occasion a misunderstanding, even damage her reputation.

Her father said neither yes nor no, but I readily perceived that he was willing. I asked for an interview, which took place September 10 in the afternoon. I did not say one single word to fascinate her—she said yes.

Immediately I assumed a relationship to the whole family. I turned my virtuosity toward her father in particular, whom I always had liked very much anyway.

But to the central issue: the next day I saw that I had made a mistake. Penitent that I was, my *vita ante acta*, [2384] my melancholy—that was sufficient.

I suffered indescribably during that time.

She seemed to notice nothing. On the contrary, she finally became so presumptuous that she once declared that she had accepted me out of pity[2385]—in short, I have scarcely known such presumption.

In a way this got to be the danger. If she takes it so lightly, I thought to myself, that, as she herself once said, "if she believed I came out of habit, she would promptly break the engagement," if she takes it that lightly then I am reinforced. I calmed down. In another sense I confess my weakness, that for a moment she did make me angry.

Now I exerted all my powers—she yields in earnest and behaves the very opposite, with extreme devotion and adoration. Up to a point it was my fault or I bear the responsibility for it, because—seeing all too clearly the difficulty of the relationship and perceiving that it would take enormous energy to overcome my melancholy, if that were at all possible—I had said to her: Be submissive, with pride you will make my cause easy. Utterly truthful words, honest with regard to her, and sadly treasonable with regard to me.

Of course my depression returned, for I acquired the greatest possible "responsibility" for her devotion; whereas her pride freed me more or less from "responsibility"—I saw the break coming. My judgment is and my thought was that it was God's punishment upon me.

I cannot quite understand the purely erotic impact she made on me. It is true that she had yielded to me almost adoringly, pleaded with me to love her, and this had so affected me that I would risk anything and everything for her. But however much I loved her, it seems I continually wanted to conceal from myself how much she actually affected me, which really does not seem appropriate to erotic love.

6. If I had not been a penitent, if I had not had my *vita ante acta*, if I had not had my depression—marriage to her would have made me happier than I had ever dreamed of becoming. But being the person I unfortunately am, I must say that I could become happier in my unhappiness without her than with her—she had touched me deeply, and I willingly, or even more than willingly, would have done everything.

7. [*In margin:* She did, however, sense my predicament somewhat. For frequently she would say: You will never be happy anyway,

so it cannot make any difference to you if I am permitted to stay with you. Once she also told me that she would never ask me anything if she only might be with me.]

8. But there was a divine protest, so it seemed to me. Marriage. I would have to keep too much from her, base the whole marriage on a lie.

I wrote to her and sent back her ring. The note is found verbatim in "The Psychological Experiment."[2386] I deliberately made it purely historical, for I have spoken to no one about it, not one single person, I who am more silent than the grave. If she should happen to see the book, I simply wanted her to be reminded of it.

9. [*In margin:* Some of the lines are also factual. For example, the one about its not being quite as stated, that one gets fat when he marries,[2387] that I knew a person (here I mentioned my father to alter the story) who was married twice and did not get fat. The lines: that one can break an engagement in two ways, with the help of love as well as the help of respect. Her remark: I really believe that you are mad.[2388]]

10. What does she do? In feminine despair she goes too far. She obviously knew that I was melancholy and meant to make me extremely uneasy. The opposite happened. To be sure she made me extremely uneasy, but now my nature reared up like a giant to shake her off. There was only one thing to do: to repulse her with all my power.

It was a frightfully painful time—to have to be so cruel and to love as I did. She fought like a lioness; if I had not believed there was divine opposition, she would have won.

11. [*In margin:* During these two months of deception I intermittently took the precaution to say directly to her: Give up, let me go; you cannot endure it. To which she answered passionately that she would rather endure everything than let me go.

To spare her all the humiliation, I offered to give the affair the turn that it was she who was breaking up with me. She would not have it; she answered that if she could endure the other she could endure this, too, and not unsocratically remarked that very likely no one would let her detect anything in her presence and what they said about her in her absence would make no difference.]

12. Then the break came, just about two months later. She was heartbroken. For the first time in my life I scolded. It was the only thing to do.

From her I went straight to the theater because I was to meet Emil Boesen[2389] (this is the foundation for the story told around town that I am supposed to have said to the family as I took out my watch that if they had anything more to say they had better hurry, for I was going to the theater). The act was over. As I was leaving the second section, the Councillor came from the first and said: May I speak with you. I accompanied him home. She is in despair. He said: It will be the death of her; she is utterly desperate. I said: I will try to calm her, but the matter is settled. He said: I am a proud man; this is hard, but I plead with you not to break up with her. Truly, he was great; he jolted me. But I stuck to my resolve. I ate supper with the family, spoke with her when I left. The next morning I received a letter from her saying that she had not slept that night, that I must come and see her. I went and made her see reason. She asked me: Will you never marry. I answered: Yes, in ten years, when I have had my fling; I will have to have a lusty young girl to rejuvenate me. A necessary cruelty. Then she said to me: Forgive me for what I have done to you. I answered: It was I, after all, who should ask that. She said: Promise to think of me. I did so. She said: Kiss me. I did—but without passion. Merciful God!

13. [*In margin:* She took out a piece of paper on which there were some words by me and which she usually carried on her breast; she took it and tore it into small pieces, saying: So you have been playing a dreadful game with me.]

14. [*In margin:* She said: Do you not like me at all. I answered: Well, if you keep on this way I will not like you.]

15. [*In margin:* She said: If only it will not be too late when you regret it—she was referring to death. I had to make a cruel joke and asked if she meant that I would turn out as Wilhelm in *Lenore.*[2390]]

16. [*In margin:* To extricate myself from the relationship as a scoundrel, if possible an arch-scoundrel, was the only thing to do to buoy her up and give her momentum for a marriage, but it was also studied gallantry. Deft as I was, it really would have been easy to pull out of it on cheaper terms. —The young man with Constantin Constantius has interpreted this conduct as gallantry,[2391] and I agree with him.]

17. So we parted. [*In margin:* It is true. That day when I picked up and left her, I wrote a letter to the Councillor which was returned unopened.] I spent the nights crying in my bed. But in the daytime I was my usual self, more flippant and witty than even necessary. My brother told me he would go to the family and prove to them that I was not a scoundrel. I said: If you do, I'll blow your brains out. The best proof of how deeply concerned I was.

I went to Berlin.[2392] I suffered exceedingly. I was reminded of her every day. Up to this day I have unconditionally kept my resolve to pray for her at least once every day, often twice, besides thinking about her as usual.

18. When the bond was broken, I thought to myself: Either you will plunge into wild diversion—or absolute religiousness of a kind quite different from the preacher-blend.

"The Seducer's Diary"[2393] was written for her sake, to repulse. The preface to the two upbuilding discourses[2394] is intended for her, as are many other things: the date of the book,[2395] the dedication to father.[2396] And in the book itself there is a slight hint about giving up, that one loses the beloved only if one gets him to act against his conviction. She has read it—that I know from Sibbern.[2397]

19. [*In margin:* "The Seducer's Diary" was definitely intended to repulse—and I know very well the agonies I went through when it was published, because my thought and object was to arouse everybody's indignation against me, something that surely did misfire, especially as far as the public was concerned, which jubilantly accepted me, something that has contributed to my scorn of the public—but insofar as anyone was prompted or happened to think about "her," it was also the most studied gallantry imaginable. To be selected by a seducer is for a woman what it is for a fruit to be pecked by a bird—for the bird is the connoisseur. A "lover," after all, is blind, his judgment is not objective, he perhaps sees charms and differences which simply are not there. But a seducer is a connoisseur. And now "the seducer," the absolute connoisseur—and then the one single girl: truly, it was the greatest gallantry imaginable, but too profound to become popular; it would not have been a greater gallantry even to have that one and only girl reform "the seducer," for in that very moment he will become the "lover," blind, and his judgment unreliable. What are all those songs of the poets who have *directly* sung the praises of and idolized the

beloved—and have themselves been "the lover"—what trustworthiness is there in their eulogies? No, "the seducer"—and then one single girl.]

20. I was in Berlin just half a year. I had planned to travel for a year and a half. She must have observed that I came back so quickly. It is quite true that she did look for me after Mynster's sermon on Easter. I avoided her in order to alienate her lest she become convinced that I thought about her while I was abroad. Besides, Sibbern had told me that she herself had said that she could not bear to see me. Now I saw that this was not true, but I had to believe that she could not bear to talk with me.

No doubt the decisive turn in her life was made under my auspices. Shortly before her engagement to Schlegel her eyes met mine in church. I did not avoid her gaze. She nodded twice. I shook my head, signifying: You must give me up. Then she nodded again, and I nodded as friendly as possible, meaning: I still love you.

After her engagement to Schlegel,[2398] she met me on the street, greeted me as friendly and charmingly as possible. I did not understand her, for at the time I did not know of her engagement. I looked questioningly at her and shook my head. No doubt she thought that I knew about it and sought my approval.

On the day which was bright for her[2399] I sat in Frelsers Kirke.

21. [*In margin:* See some place in journal NB[12] (i.e. $x^1$ A 648) toward the middle.]

Now the Councillor is dead. Possibly she may still hope to get to see me again, establish a relationship again,[2400] an innocent, affectionate relationship. O, the dear girl, God knows that I want to see her more than ever, to talk to her, and to make her happy, and if she needs it, inspire her. What would I not do if I dared, dared adorn her in her lifetime with the adornment of historical fame which is sure to be hers.[*] She shall take rank among women, and it is important that I formulate the matter. For otherwise the marriage becomes dubious and I a satire—I remain unmarried, whereas she was going to die of love.

22. [*]*In margin:* And it would no doubt make her happy to be famous—she who once in her late youth wished to be an actress, to shine in the world; the resurrection of honor, she who was proud.]

23. O, how happy it would make me to talk with her, and how it

would alleviate my God-relationship. In possibility she is difficult for me; in actuality, easy.

But I dare not. She once showed me how far she can go beyond bounds. A marriage will not truly bind her if her passion is kindled again. And the very fact that my position is so good is dangerous, dangerous. Yes, if I actually had been a scoundrel, the situation would be easier.

Her relationship to Schlegel is no security. Suppose that somehow she shrewdly surmised that this was the only way she could possibly establish a relationship to me again, for if she were unmarried, the question of a marriage would never come up again. Suppose that she thought that I wanted her to marry Schlegel and that was why I talked so much about him those last two months, even if teasingly and jokingly, and that she should take him. And it was indeed my intention and wish. But in that case I mean more to her than her relationship to Schlegel.

If God permits her to get the idea of herself asking me to talk with her, then I will risk it. Make me happy—yes, that it surely will. But only in that case do I dare do it. The relationship would then be perfect. A brotherly relationship to her would be a great, great joy to me!*

24. [*In margin:* *What joy for me to be able to make her happy, she who has suffered so much for my sake! And how hard it is to have to go on being cruel this way. How almost treacherous to do everything to draw her into a marriage and then let her sit there. Suppose she has perceived her marriage as a possibility of a sisterly relationship to me, in whom she presumably has seen a purely intellectual magnitude! But I cannot justify taking the step. She once showed me that she dares to go too far, and on the other hand, by marrying she has indeed actually emancipated herself.]

25. When I lived in the second floor apartment at Nørregade[2401] I had a tall palisander cupboard[2402] made. It is my own design, prompted by something my beloved said in her agony. She said that she would thank me her whole life if she might live in a little cupboard and stay with me.[2403] Because of that, it is made without shelves. —In it everything is carefully kept, everything reminiscent of her and that will remind her of me. There is also a copy of the pseudonymous works for her. Regularly only two copies of these were on vellum—one for her and one for me.

Among my papers there will also be found a letter about her that is intended to be opened after my death. The books will be dedicated to her and to my dead father together: my teachers, an old man's noble wisdom, and a woman's lovable injudiciousness.

Truly the cause of religion and especially of Christianity needs a single person, but what a prolix story my upbringing makes, how amazingly dialectical!

But if she does not think of it, I must give up the idea. Incidentally, it is strange she has not learned to know me well enough to know that for me everything depends on responsibility. That is why I also wanted so much that she had been the one who broke the engagement.

But now she no doubt is happily married to Schlegel; he has been successful,[2404] and this will hearten her as a sign of Governance's approval of their union. In a certain sense the world is against me; perhaps she interprets this as something of a punishment imposed on me. But the opposition of the world might well give me new worth in her eyes, and that would be dangerous.

_____

26. Insofar as what Miss Dencker[2405] told me is true (and I have sometimes used Miss Dencker to convey what I wanted to say, all with the aim of consolidating her marriage), that she has said "that what she was angry about with me was not that I broke the engagement but the way I did it," then this demonstrates that she has a fairly large share of that feminine forgetfulness which is part of immediacy. She forgets that two months prior to the decisive break she received a disengagement letter worded as humbly as possible for me—there certainly was nothing to criticize about the way in which it was done. But then it was she who, failing to make the break, lashed out so despairingly that I had to pull out the whole alphabet. She forgets that she herself said that if I could convince her that I was a scoundrel, she would be reconciled to the whole affair. And now she complains about the manner, probably "the scoundrel manner." Moreover, if that manner had not been used, we very likely would still be in the process of breaking up. To that extent it is all right to complain about "the way," for I would have succeeded in no other way.

_____

27. In a certain sense a woman is a terrifying being. There is a form of devotion that dismays me because it is so contrary to my

nature: it is femininely-ruthless womanly devotion, terrifying because the womanliness in one sense is so powerfully bound by regard for custom. But if it is disrupted—and the other party is a dialectician with a morbid imagination and a heavy religious burden: truly it is terrifying.

———

28. As far as I myself am concerned, I have learned this, that there has been not a little of the self-torment in me. Presumably this will be changed now.

———

29. [*In margin:* And it is also clear that if a relationship is reestablished, I definitely would begin by scolding her. For in order to help her I resigned myself to looking like a scoundrel in the eyes of others, and I did everything to promote this. But she does bear a great responsibility. It was no merit on her part that I was not driven to downright desperation. And however endearing her despair and however willing and eager I am to forgive and forget as if it never happened, it nevertheless will be said to her if the relationship should be reestablished and if there is to be any truth in it.]

30. As far as Cornelia[2406] is concerned, at the time her engagement in a sense distressed me. She possessed a rare and genuine womanliness. Just this one trait of genuine feminine simplicity. When all the clever ones readily perceived that I was a scoundrel and every clever head flattered himself on being completely able to understand it, she said: I cannot understand Magister Kierkegaard, but nevertheless I believe that he is a good man. Truly a powerful statement, and I was indeed impressed. Ideally Cornelia belongs in the class with Regine. That is where she should have been, and she would have been immortalized poetically. Now she in a way is lost.

Regine should and ought to be married. This is the only thing that is poetically true. And if she herself were to tell me that she did it out of bitterness toward me etc., I would say: Fiddlesticks! What does a little miss like that know about what she does. You have done a very extraordinary thing, you have done me a kindness, have helped me precisely by this step you have taken. And thus I know that you did it out of love for me, even if you would insist that you had never thought of it. But tell me, was it becoming of you to act in a pettily, frivolously feminine style, or do you believe that I am capable of petty thoughts. The pettiness is the only thing I cannot understand. From the historical point of view of a dullard, she has a point against her: her marriage. My interpretation, which unconditionally is the only true one, makes it what it is: a plus. In the first relationship she ranks high because of her faith: to have sufficient womanliness to believe a man who treated her and confounds everything for her this way. In the second relationship she ranks high by having correctly grasped the point that she had to get married. It is this which can be misconstrued so easily. Looked at in this way, it pains me that I now have the advantage, I, the unmarried one, and that I cannot establish her in her rightful place with my interpretation that this was exactly what she should do.

X⁵ A 149   n.d., 1849

« **6473**

*Addition to 6471, 6472* (X⁵ A 148–49):

*An Accounting*

1. She may have thought something like this. He really loves me; he is engaged to me. I love him only too much; what in all the world, then, is the sense of this collision. It must be madness, a mental depression bordering on madness. *Ergo,* I will concentrate everything on driving it away. Excellent, from a feminine point of view, completely true—but being religiously undeveloped, she was bound to be oblivious to its being a religious collision, and least of all to suspect this kind of a religious collision. Everything is fine and she is splendid in the feminine intrepidity with which she charges ahead. Moreover I myself in a way prompted her to this. I knew that if she were to become dangerous to me, but in a way to her advantage, as she deserved, the lovable creature, the affair would have to be as costly as possible for me, and then she would be careful to use a devotion in her struggle. This she did, the lovely child, and superbly as a woman.

As for me, the law for my whole life, the law that applies at all the decisive points in my life, is this: just as that general²⁴⁰⁷ who personally gave the order when he was to be shot, so I personally have always given the order when I was to be wounded. But the skirmish itself, which she had to wage, was in the grand style and admirable. In a way I put the bow in her hand, set the arrow, showed her how to aim—my idea was—and it was love—either I become yours or you will be allowed to wound me so deeply, wound me in my melancholy and in my

God-relationship so deeply that I, although parted from you, yet remain yours.

What a model of unhappy love. It is not like Goethe's Frederikke,[2408] for example, who rejects every marriage because to have loved Goethe must needs be enough for a girl. My life, which accentuates her, is just the opposite. It is I who do everything, everything to get her married.

A collision such as this is unimaginable if it is not a religious collision. For if it was my pride etc. my self-indulgence, etc., then it would be impossible for my life ever to express that I accentuate her as the one and only.

She marries[2409]—and now the relationship is altogether normal.

———

2. Of her there is nothing to say, not one word, not a single word, except to her honor and praise—especially since the moment her presumption became transfigured as devotedness. She was a lovely child with a lovable nature, just as if designed so that a melancholy such as mine could have its only joy in enchanting her.

How lovely she was that first time I saw her,[2410] truly lovable, lovable in her devotedness, touching, magnificently impressive in her sorrow, not without loftiness in the final moment of parting, childlike first and last, and in spite of her clever little head,* I always found one thing about her which alone would be sufficient for perpetual praise: silence and inwardness, and she had one power: a beseeching look when she pleaded which could melt a stone; and it was a joy to enchant her life, it was happiness to see her indescribable happiness.

3. *Note. I am indebted to her for the story about a girl and a fellow who were talking about another girl who had broken up with her sweetheart, and she added: How amazing, for he had such nice clothes. —She also told the story about Mrs. Münter who ran away with Pollon and went to her husband herself and said: Well, it is just as well for me to tell you myself: I am married to Pollon.

4. It was an outrageous wrong to her to tear her out of her relationship to me in a terrible scene that seemed calculated to destroy the impression she had made. God forgive me! I had to offend her and leave her in order to help her if at all possible—I had to be cruel the last two months. That was perhaps the most difficult part of it for me. I had to keep on being cruel, truly with the most honest intention. She

no doubt suffered indescribably during that time; she wanted to forgive me!

She was the beloved. My life will unconditionally accent her life, my literary work is to be regarded as a monument to her honor and praise. I take her along into history. And I who sadly had only one single desire—to enchant her—*there* it will not be denied to me. There I will be walking by her side; like a master of ceremonies I will lead her in triumph and say: Please make way for her, for "our own dear little Regine."

————

5. I once prayed to God for her as for a gift, the most cherished gift; at the time I glimpsed the possibility of carrying out a marriage. I also thanked God for her as for a gift; later I had to regard her as God's punishment on me—but always I have committed her to God and have honestly persisted in doing this, even when, all too desperate, she did everything to make me feel my superiority.

And indeed God does punish frightfully! What an appalling punishment for a troubled conscience! To hold this lovely child in one's hand, to be able to enchant her life, to see her indescribable happiness, for the melancholy man the highest happiness—and then to become aware of this inner voice of judgment: "You must let her go," it is your punishment, and it will be intensified by seeing all her anguish, intensified by her prayers and tears, she who does not suspect that it is your punishment but believes that it is your hardness of heart* which has to be touched.

6. [*In margin:* *Note. This in fact was what she really believed, for she told me many times that my pride was to blame for my wanting to leave her. She also told me that I actually was not a good man, but she nevertheless could not stop loving me and pleaded that she might stay with me.]

7. For me the content of that year of being engaged was essentially the agonizing deliberations of a troubled conscience: do you dare to be engaged, do you dare to marry—alas, in the meantime the lovely child was at my side and was—my betrothed! I was as old as an old man, she as young as a child, but I had capacities—alas, almost so much the worse—for enchanting her, and when I had some faint hope I could not deny myself the joy of enchanting her, who was a lovable child, continues to be a child, and despite all her sufferings was still a child when

we parted. Yet the relationship had to be broken, and I had to be cruel in order to help her—this is "fear and trembling." So frightful did the relationship become that finally the erotic aspect seemed to be absent because the nightmare shifted the relationship into other categories. I was so much an old man that she became like a beloved child whose sex was more or less of no importance. This is "fear and trembling." And I dare maintain that I wanted the marriage more fervently than she; in the purely human sense it signified for me (like those demoniacs in the fairy tale[2411]) my salvation. But I could not enter that harbor; I was to be used in another way. Thus what she said in her anguish was puzzling; she did not understand it herself, but I all the more: After all, you cannot know if it might not be good for you to let me stay with you. This, you see, is fear and trembling.

$X^5$ A 150   *n.d.*, 1849

## « 6474  *A Final Version of a Catastrophe in My Public Life*

Rabble barbarism has won out in Copenhagen and has made headway in Denmark; all who should be authorities, journalists,[2412] even the police, despaired and said that there is nothing to be done here, and the rabble barbarism increased and of course was triumphant. And yet it was said continually, but as a wish, a *pium desiderium:*[2413] It is intolerable, something ought to be done about it.

Now the question was whether or not there was in the land an esteemed younger man—for an older one would not be of use in such a situation, for it would immediately be said: He is too old, he does not understand this modern age—an esteemed younger man who dared to do something.

Such a one there was and just one: "the great pseudonym," without reservation a most esteemed name and without spot or stain to date—and venerated by that very rabble barbarism, which shrewdly preferred to have a friendship in that quarter.[2414]

But it would have been absurd for "the great pseudonym" suddenly to be false to himself and have prior consultation with others. Therefore he does it without preliminaries, but with religious resolve.

What he actually had to do, his task, was this: would he be able to give the affair such a mighty turn with a few words that he could manage to impress editors themselves.

This he succeeded in doing. It is a historic fact. Goldschmidt[2415] lost his nerve and went abroad. P. L. Møller[2416] came out very shamefacedly under his own name and bowed; later he too went abroad. *The Corsair* got the worst of it and in a way was "never itself again."

Now the question was: what price would this altruistic person have to pay for taking this step, for quite understandably payment must be made.

Here was the task for the contemporaries who occupy themselves with regulating the opinions of the more educated classes (the better type of journalists). Their task was to second the step and show that it was unselfish, the only thing there was to do, almost heroic.

They were all silent. This was the betrayal. And I saw at once that little by little my relation to the citizenry[2417] would be lost irretrievably.

Meanwhile I calmly held my position and was basically victorious. I actually had never realized how strong and religiously undergirded I was.

If I had had sufficient financial assets[2418] and could have looked ahead without any worries on that score, or if my whole life had been stabilized, nothing more would have been necessary; all alone I was unqualifiedly the strongest.

Everything that distinguishes itself in the world is usually betrayed by contemporaries. But my betrayal at the hands of my contemporaries was of a baser sort because it constituted a double betrayal.

It is the more reputable people who actually have betrayed me.

Moreover, it should be noted (this is characteristic of me) that regardless of how difficult my position was, I asked the journalists I knew not to get involved in it. That is true; I asked them or advised them not to—but what I thought privately is something else. My cause was clean, dedicated to God—one does not then personally beg for help.

Wretched age! The possibility of which I otherwise had continually assured myself—that of living an agreeable rural life when I retire from writing, situated not a little above a rural pastor's modest position because of my literary reputation—is lost; it is hard for such a marked man to live in the country.

X[1] A 653   n.d., 1849

## « 6475 *A Theological Point of View*

What men find so very difficult about Christianity is this matter of becoming a Christian in earnest—actually dying to the world in this life —in this life actually renouncing flesh and blood, a successful career, honor, reputation, etc. What is done, then? The whole scene is transferred to purgatory, to the hereafter[2419]—*there* is the monastery, *there* is the dying to the world—well, thanks, a dead man will usually be extravagant in salting and smoking himself, in abstaining from marriage and the like. Meanwhile there stands all Christendom with all its millions of Christians on this side of the grave—and the many fine livings and high offices—it surely is tough on them.

That kind of dogmatizing, which is a total satire on Christendom and the best indirect proof that Johannes Climacus is right, is not only heard with deep admiration in *ex cathedra* lectures by a thinker for thinkers; it also would be heard with great jubilation on a dance floor, delivered by a dancer to his partners in the dance: Enjoy life in the springtime of your life[2420]—when you are dead, enter a monastery.

Johannes Climacus has shown that the fundamental confusion in all modern speculation is to have pulled back the essentially Christian one whole sphere, down into the esthetic.[2421] Here the projected "in perspective" dislocation of the essentially Christian is, if possible, even more demented. The whole thing becomes apocalyptic; the scene is completely shifted to the next world, there one becomes a Christian, there one dies to the world, etc. And strangely enough, this demented *changement*[2422] is proposed at the very time when the whole matter of the hereafter is not far from being left open to question. Dogmatizing of that sort certainly must satisfy the age in every way, because it does simply want to smuggle Christianity out of the way but still also wants to keep on the one hand a relationship of possibility (as inconveniencing as possible) to it, and on the other hand wants to preserve all those good jobs and official positions.

For example, Martensen, the profound M., who has already found a connoisseur in the no less profound Frederikke Bremer,[2423] who profoundly prophesies that Martensen's *Dogmatik* will regenerate all scientific scholarship in the North, perhaps also in *North* America, where the forerunner, the traveling Fr. B. has now gone. Not only this, the no less profound—despite its superficial appearance (*Erscheinung*)—*Berlingske Tidende,* or wholesaler Nathanson,[2424] who according to his own words (on another occasion[2425]) "has bestowed," as one sees, is bestowing, and probably will continue to bestow upon "Danish literature his special attention," says of Martensen's *Dogmatik* that one feels conviction in every line. Alas, I have now learned otherwise, that the only proof of a conviction is one's life. But are you quite sure, now, Mr. Wholesaler, do you dare say: By God. Think carefully now; you will see for yourself how important taking this oath could be, since this involves nothing less than—as Frederikke B. prophesies—the rebirth of theological scholarship in the North, and to which we add (what modesty no doubt has prevented Frederikke B. from adding) in North

America. Do you dare, Mr. Wholesaler, do you dare say: By God. In view of the great importance of taking this oath, you yourself will perceive how important it is to do everything as solemnly as possible before proceeding to take the oath. [*Along the margin:* For even if I, too, who have learned otherwise, that the only proof that one actually has a conviction is one's life, if I, too, in return for your munificent bestowal, were willing to bestow upon you the taking of the oath, the public, the common good, as Holberg[2426] says, will of course scarcely do it.]

> A disciple of Johannes
> Climacus
> $X^6$ B 105   *n.d.,* 1849

« **6476**

[*In margin:* About "her"[2427]]

Aug. 26, 1849
It would be most desirable to be completely free in my relationship to her for a moment in order to see what power she actually has. Basically she has so taken possession of me with her appeals and tears that I have taken her into my relationship to God and keep her there.

Her appealing but also too intense feminine submissiveness was disturbing to a melancholy such as mine. Her rash supplication to me in Jesus' name to remain with her was disturbing to an anguished conscience such as mine, which all too willingly would do everything for her but in its contrition cannot do it, an anguished conscience which itself knows best how profoundly, how exceedingly great is its need for gentleness—and then whenever my faith is weak it is tortured by the thought that I have been cruel to her.

It is a dreadful torment, augmented by the great capabilities entrusted to me. Truly, when Providence gave the man strength and the woman weakness, whom did he make the stronger? The terrible thing about getting involved with a woman is that she yields through weakness and then—then one battles with himself, with his own power.

$X^1$ A 659   August 26, 1849

« **6477** *My Position in Regard to What Will*
*Become the Situation in the Near Future*

Presumably the Church is to be reformed now; synods are supposed to be held, there is to be balloting, etc.

Even the strictest orthodox, even Rudelbach,[2428] seem to want to take the position of relating themselves directly to all this and to do everything to make it as orthodox as possible.

I have always carried out flank attacks, wounding from behind. At the very time that our most important task is supposed to be to reform the Church, I come with a contribution[2429] which screws up the price of being a Christian so high that it is doubtful that in the most rigorous sense there is a single true Christian living.

This is troublesome! Undeniably! But it is also sad and ridiculous that there is no awareness of what constitutes the basic corruption.

My continual task has been that of delaying—it is something like tapping a man on the shoulder when he is ready to jump and saying to him: May I have a word with you?

Right there is my point of coincidence with Mynster. This is the genuinely derivative means. But the fact is that in a certain sense Mynster is afraid of such derivative means,[2430] especially when it is my hand. He himself has used it a little, but as a prudent official—here it is used by one who is nothing (one of those dangerous, suspicious people) and is used with absolute teleology.

Yet it may well turn out that Mynster is not the victim, if he will only be circumspect, keep quiet, and act calmly. I have always given my activity a turn as if I were a complete subordinate who operates under Mynster's supreme auspices and have given the impression that he nods his supreme approval and that this is decisive.

In a certain sense there is an uneasiness in this lest there occur, so to speak, a blink of the eye, a touch of uncertainty in the face.

My task quite rightly is entirely dialectical, and I cannot get away from the thought that I ought not get into a struggle with one who reminds me of my father.

x¹ A 660   n.d., 1849

« 6478

[*In margin:* About "her"[2431] forgiveness.]

If I sincerely ask her forgiveness and obtain her sincere forgiveness, I must also sincerely justify myself and tell all. If I do that, she will first of all get a correct understanding of how she was loved, of how I was and have been true to her, of what I have suffered, of how the very deception, the cruelty were solicitude—and then, then suppose that she suddenly conceives a dislike for her marriage and begins where we left off in the first course, since I did in fact ask her forgiveness two months before the actual breaking of the engagement. Anyone who knows how she talked about Schlegel[2432] in the past, that is, how disparagingly (it must be remembered that the situation of my being the one who suggested she take Schlegel must, after all, really exasperate her and make her lose patience), will always have misgivings.

Her forgiveness cannot make my life any easier. When all is said and done, it really is not she who binds me but I myself who bind myself with her. The wound I received at her hand but that was directed by me was and must remain a religious wound—it is the relationship to God which is binding.

On the other hand, if I were to follow through in the deception and suddenly act as one who has been a scoundrel and now has repented of it, then I will deceive her and her forgiveness will be a mockery.

Being an affectionate woman, she no doubt is now content in her marriage. She interprets it this way. I was a man of exceptional talent in a sense too high for her. But then I would not have been the loyal one either. I had a bolder, more ambitious goal—she would have to fall. But I did love her, she will tell herself, and I will piously forgive him, yes, pray to God for him. In this there is femininely some sense. Her way of maintaining herself in relation to me is simply to be the pious, devout one and thus better than I. If I now come with my explanation of the pious one, everything will perhaps be disturbed.

It is plain that my relationship is a God-relationship.

But I ought to renounce all self-torment. My self-torment has been that I have wanted, to the point of despair, for her to understand me completely. But perhaps this is not God's will at all; he holds me in relationship to him by this very misunderstanding, and I rest meekly in his hand because whenever I have little faith, I anxiously wonder whether I could do something to make her understand me. When I trustingly close my eyes and am silent, I am at peace; as soon as I cease to do that, the misunderstanding torments me, because, after all, in my relationship to her every immediacy, every externality, is against me.

Now, if she herself were to demand an explanation from me, I would risk it. I would do it in such a way that I would make it plain to her: there is in this one factor of which I cannot speak, and you must not ask it of me but must forgive me for not being able to speak of it. Other than that I would tell her the truth, and here I believe that there would be a degree of understanding that perhaps could even give her joy. I can truthfully say: she was the beloved, the only one, and that

I loved her more and more, and that she was the beloved when I left her, that I will love no other. Then, as to a certain point, I must beg her to believe me. If she is woman enough for that, then the explanation is almost total. But if it were possible that she would turn dialectical and begin to ponder over such a demented collision, she would be unhinged. As long as she can hold to this—that I was, if not an evil man, at least a man intoxicated with high flying ideas—then there is no collision; but if I turn out to be religiously motivated, then there is a collision.

I have borne the responsibility for her to the point of bearing responsibility for her life. For a long time now she has had the support of a marriage. For what wrong I did in venturing into a relationship I could not realize, I have suffered my punishment, and if I have not suffered enough, or if I have suffered it, in any case I must ask God for forgiveness. To give her an explanation, insofar as it is possible, can be dangerous for her, can disturb the illusion of her marriage, can be dangerous for me, can alter my relationship to God. And even if this were not so, there is still one more consideration, consideration for Schlegel, who deserves every circumspection.

But, as was said, the fact that it can be dangerous does not mean that it absolutely must not occur, for sometimes the most proper thing to do can be dangerous. If she asks for it, the risk will be taken. God knows there is nothing I would like better.

Perhaps it eventually will be clear to me that I might dare to take the first step, but the main thing, after all, is my personal relationship to God, and, after all, she is married.

$X^1$ A 661    *n.d.,* 1849

« **6479**

[*In margin:* "Her[2433] Relationship to Me"]

I should and must have my freedom; even on the most reasonable terms it perhaps would still have been punishment enough to my pride to have ventured into something I could not realize. Consequently I should and must have my freedom.[*]

Perhaps to a point she herself ought to have understood this a little and made my situation a bit easier, perhaps.

Alas, but she was so young, and she was so lovingly devoted to me —O, all too humbly submissive to entertain the thought of taking sides against me. Furthermore, she was in a difficult position. She certainly must have had a prior conception of how furiously embittered the

Councillor,[2434] the fearful one in the eyes of the family, would become. Furthermore, she perhaps had wronged Schlegel[2435] somewhat by taking me—and now this catastrophe. Finally, I myself have dialectically made the affair difficult for her. I could have demanded my freedom more directly, either in a moderately religious way or a little more persuasively. But I deliberately did not do so, I had a very particular reason for not getting married; I was not stranded by her but by marriage itself, and on religious grounds. It was indefensible to let her remain unmarried for the same reason—and that would have happened if I had used altogether direct communication, for then I would have imprisoned her to me forever.

Consequently she is utterly and completely without guilt—after all, should not innocence be guiltless! In any case it is impossible to see her fragment of guilt if one looks simultaneously at my enormous guilt in "sweeping her along with me out into the current"—alas, these words remind me of the very beginning of our engagement when it was so clear to me that I had done just this. But at the time in her overweening confidence she made me feel so secure that I almost began to regard the danger as insignificant since she took the matter so lightly.

My guilt is that I swept her out into the current, and her guilt is really no guilt, even though she ought to have perceived earlier that it was impossible for her to struggle through and get what she wished, for I was too strong. But here, too, she is without guilt, for in fact I myself gave her the hint[†] to use submission in her struggle, for I knew this would be most dangerous to me, as it has in fact been. But consequently she is innocent; yet I constantly reminded her to submit because she could not possibly stand against me.

$$x^1 \text{ A } 663 \quad n.d., 1849$$

« 6480

[*]*In margin of 6479* (x[1] A 663):
And certainly getting my freedom was also the only suitable thing for her. She would have been unhinged and in a very short time she would have run herself ragged, overstrained herself, because she had such a prodigious impression of me and wanted if possible, to match something more ideal. Meanwhile I with my intellectual activity and my dreadful closedupness would have been living in a world of my own. How mad, to be wasted on me, how mad, all for nothing, or that in this way she would become a tremendously agonizing burden to me—which she neither should nor ought to be. I still retained, for all that, the

torments of my interior life. Now if I had dared marry her in such a way that my innermost self would have been shut off from her and dared to apply all my resources to charming her and making her happy: truly, this would have been my highest wish. But the marriage vow obligates me to be completely open, convicts me if I do not do so, demands that I lead her into my deepest inner self; well, at that very moment the relationship will be an absurdity and she will be insanely wasted upon me, wasted on me, will make my life all the more tormented by having to see her suffering. —She can greatly enrich Schlegel's[2436] life, she can make him happy; he will adore and thank her. She may retain a secret pain with regard to her relationship to me, but in the profoundest sense just this may make her more ideal and the relationship may actually correspond to her nature, in which there was still a good deal of pride.

If femininely she had been content with my first proposal to break the engagement, which was composed as humbly as possible and in which I asked her forgiveness—the relationship would never have become so dreadful. In her despair she went beyond her limits and in despair wanted to force me beyond my own: now the relationship became frightful. There was only one thing to do, absolutely only one thing to do, to undergird her with a deception. This I did, without sparing myself. But thereby the affair became for me a single combat with God. At any moment God can fill me with anxiety over not having her forgiveness—and in that I am, humanly speaking, as guiltless as possible. If I were to ask her forgiveness now, I run the old risk that, discovering that she was nevertheless loved, she will cast herself in despair upon me again.

In a certain sense it is fortunate to be a woman. She suspects nothing of all this, "she does not complain that I broke up with her, but about the way in which I did it."

x[1] A 664    n.d.

« **6481**

*In margin of 6479* (x[1] A 663):
†Note.
And why was it fair and square of me to give her the hint? Because I was not the Lord God but was myself struggling with a higher power, and in my inward struggle her struggle with me was reflected; so it was important both for her sake and mine that the affair did not become too easy for me.

x[1] A 665    n.d.

## « 6482

[*In margin:* My relationship to her[2437]]

*My Relationship to Her*

My basic guilt is to have swept her along.

### Phase I

The engagement. I, essentially turned inward, suffering the anguish of mental depression and of conscience for having "swept her along"; naturally, in my relationship to her, love and solicitude, perhaps too much, but I was already a penitent. In other respects I was not at all attentive to her, as if there could be any difficulty with her.

### Phase II

She goes ahead in boundless overweening confidence. At the same time I am not essentially depressed about the matter, and the pangs of conscience have no connection with it. I breathe as lightly as usual.

Here is part of my guilt. I ought to have used the opportunity to let her break off; then it would have been the victory of her overweening confidence.

But the matter was too earnest for me, whether I would be able to actualize the marriage, and besides there was something childish in her presumptuous confidence.

In any case, in a way I now had myself in hand—and I approached the matter more from her side.

### Phase III

She yields and is transfigured into the most lovable creature.

Simultaneously I am assailed for the second time by my first feelings, intensified by the responsibility which has increased now with her feminine, almost worshipful devotion.

### Phase IV

I see that there must be a separation.

Here—honest with her and traitorous to myself—I advise her not to attempt to fight with the weapon of pride, for that would make it much easier for me, but with submission.

But there must be a break—I send her back her ring in a letter, which word for word is printed in the "Psychological Experiment."[2438]

### Phase V

Instead of letting the decision rest, she goes to my room in my absence and writes an utterly despairing note in which she beseeches me for Jesus' sake and the memory of my dead father not to leave her.

Then there was nothing for me to do but to go to the extreme and, if possible, support her with a deception, do everything to repel her in order to incite her pride again.

Then two months later I broke the relationship a second time.[2439]

$X^1$ A 667   *n.d.*, 1849

## « 6483 *About "Her"*[2440]

Now, except at particular times, there must be no more thinking about this. Otherwise the throes of self-torment will be in full course. Furthermore, the explanation, the more concrete explanation, which I conceal deep within, the one which actually involves an even more definite horror for me—this I am not writing down.

For me this relationship signifies God's punishment. It became terrible because in her despair she cast herself upon me so forcefully that she weighs heavily on my sympathy and on my God-relationship. The affair will certainly follow me through my whole life, even though it will come to be understood somewhat differently in relation to my whole development.

The main thing now is to remember to thank God again and again for "having given the explanation himself" by letting her get married and thereby alleviating the situation.

My prayer is that I may be able—if she desires it—to give her some joy in return for what she has innocently suffered for my sake—some joy, but, please note, of the kind which truly will benefit her.

Perhaps the day will come when she will have forgotten me completely, perhaps; in any case it is an open matter! At one time she cast herself upon me and upon my relationship to God in such a way that I will carry her the rest of my life.

But I must guard myself against surrendering to self-torment.

$X^1$ A 668   *n.d.*, 1849

## « 6484

I could almost say that my genius has really been my suffering. In any case it has supported me the way a life-jacket supports a swimmer.

To have a strong body and then just intellectually have to maintain merely the idea, for example, that death is a certainty at any time—well, thanks, generally that is reserved only for preacher-prattle.

But there is no difficulty for one as weak as I am.

Every day I live is an occasion for wonder. Doomed as I am—and yet I go on living! Yes, my life is like a satire on what it is to be a man.

But this gives credence to what I write. Actually it is all too true that men are too physically strong to allow them to get involved with such matters.

### « **6485**

Strangely enough, early in my engagement I frequently touched on the theme that there have been men whose very significance was to be sacrificed for others. Just as in a shipment of fruit some are likely to be bruised because, for one thing, they must bear the pressure of the others and, for another, ward off the pressure on the others: so in every generation there are some who are sacrificed for the race.

I had an early inexplicable presentiment that this was my destiny, but now, right now, it has become very clear to me that this is my destiny—and why, just because I became engaged, consequently just because I stepped out of character and wanted to extend myself in life instead of remaining an intensive point. That particular thought and the fact that it became so palpable to me was the indirect evidence that I must get out of that relationship.

But what a strange reduplication; alas, it almost seems as if she has been sacrificed for me!

### « **6486**

It is not only true that the mistreatment I have experienced at the hands of rabble barbarism has profoundly influenced my development, but it is certainly also responsible for a tone my environment would not have provided otherwise: the kind of lyric entitled *The Lily and the Bird.* [2441]

Dialectically this mistreatment has also enriched me with the essential conflict between Christianity and the world, something that otherwise would have escaped me in my preoccupation with internal problems.

The shaping element in this suffering has once again been that I have been the superior one, yet in combat with a weaker element which in a sense is stronger. If I take each individual in the crowd, how in the world could it ever occur to me to battle with him; and yet it can be a very onerous task to battle the crowd. But on the other hand it may become idealizing and tinged with sadness simply because I feel all too clearly my disproportionate superiority, plus my having been well-

disposed toward these people—and yet in another sense, in a far inferior, vapid sense, the "crowd" is far, far the stronger.

Once again it is my relationship to God which really must be
developed. When one strives with a man who is either actually, in the
ideal sense, one's superior or equal, the relationship to God is eclipsed
and completely forgotten. But no battle is so likely to develop a man
spiritually as a conflict in which he is the stronger, and the weaker one
in another sense is the stronger. The fact that I actually am unable to
find an appropriate opponent signifies that God wants to use this
conflict to develop my God-relationship.

X¹ A 676   n.d., 1849

### « 6487

"Practice in Christianity"[2442] certainly should be published under
a pseudonym. It is the dialectical element and would be much too
strong if I brought it out personally.

So *The Sickness unto Death,*[2443] "Practice in Christianity," "The
Point of View for My Work as an Author,"[2444] and "Three Notes"[2445]
belong to the year 1848.

To 1849 "From on High He will Draw All unto Himself,"[2446]
"Armed Neutrality,"[2447] and other small things, including the one
about Phister.[2448]

Even if I wanted to publish "From on High" under my name, it
is nevertheless definite that the conception of my writings finally gath-
ers itself together in the "Discourses for Communion on Fridays,"[2449]
for "The Point of View," after all, is from 1848.

> N.B. And in order that "From on High," which is some-
> what polemical, not be the last work, some additional
> discourses for the Communion on Fridays could be writ-
> ten, a second series of them. One is already as good as
> finished, and some suggestions for a few more are in one
> of the new folders bookbinder Møller has made.

X¹ A 678   n.d., 1849

### « 6488

Sept. 7

[*In margin:* About her]

About "Her"[2450]

This girl must needs become very costly to me, or I had to make
her very costly to me religiously.

She herself implored me with tears and supplications (for the sake of Jesus Christ, in memory of my dead father) not to forsake her; otherwise I could do anything, anything at all with her; she wholeheartedly would put up with everything and still thank me all her life for the greatest of blessings, her relationship to me. The father, who explained my behavior as eccentricity, begged and beseeched me not to leave her: "She was wholeheartedly willing to put up with everything." As far as he himself and the rest of the family were concerned, he promised me most solemnly that if I wished it to be that way, neither he nor any member of his family would ever set foot in my house; as soon as I married her she would be completely in my hands, as if she had neither relatives nor friends.

So I could have married her (disregarding my inner problems) in a convenient way; I could have put everything under obligation in gratitude, could even have been an utter tyrant, always having this frightful method of coercion that, after all, I had done her a good deed. If I really had done that, I would have been a scoundrel; shamefully, outrageously shamefully, I would have exploited a young girl's agony which brought her to say what never ought to have or could have been meant that way. She was not wrong in thinking that if I only decided to marry her, I certainly would do everything I could to make her life worth living, that is, she had faith in me.

Suppose I had married her. Let us assume it. What then? In the course of a half year or less she would have been unhinged. There is —and this is both the good and the bad in me—something spectral about me, something no one can endure who has to see me every day and have a real relationship to me. Yes, in the light overcoat in which I am usually seen, it is another matter. But at home it will be evident that basically I live in a spirit world. I was engaged to her for one year, and she really did not know me. —Consequently she would have been shattered. She probably would have bungled my life as well, for I always was overstraining myself with her because in reality she was in a sense too light for me. I was too heavy for her and she too light for me, but both factors can very well lead to overstrain. Very likely I would not have amounted to anything or perhaps I may have developed just the same, but she would have been a torment to me simply because I would see that she was altogether wrongly situated through her being married to me. —Then she would have died and all would be over. To take her along into history as my wife—no, it cannot be. It is all right for her to become Madam and Mrs., but no longer may she be maintained in the character of being my beloved; it must be set forth as a story of an unhappy love, and for me she will remain the beloved "to whom I owe everything": then history will take her along —on this I will give instructions to history.

It is all very simple. My understanding told me clearly that what I wanted to do was right, the only right thing to do. But if my conscience had not kept its grip on me, she would have won. Solely on the strength of my understanding I could not have risked defying her tears, her supplications, her father's sufferings, my own wish—and I would have given in. But I was obliged to fight the matter through on a higher plane, and that accounts for my inflexibility, which was interpreted as heartlessness. On the other hand, if it had not been a matter of conscience for me, the affair would never have become as extreme as it did; I very likely would have surrendered earlier. She actually would have sacrificed herself much too intensely and there would always be the question of whether she could recover from it.

My understanding told me. She can marry Schlegel.[2451] She herself admitted to me later that if I had not come along when I did, she no doubt would have become engaged to Schlegel. Thus everything was as it should be. Who knows, the little girl who thought that my pride was to blame for forsaking her, who knows, perhaps it was her pride that made her prefer me at the time. After what she had gone through with me, the relationship to Schlegel could indeed be beautiful. So she got a man, a good man whom she had once loved. She would be installed in her rights as a woman, for her life would have great meaning to him; he would gratefully appreciate every day and every hour of their life together and all her loveliness and lovableness. If he does not, he is a fool. Alas, after all I am somewhat spectral, and it would have been far more frightful to live with me day in and day out in my home. —Thus her relationship to me once again would be beautifully ordered. She did not become the beggar in my house, but the beloved, the one and only beloved. And so it is that she belongs to history.

I do not cling especially tightly to life but would just as soon die; her situation the day I die will be enviable. She is happily married and her life has a significance to her husband that is rare for a wife, for no doubt he comes little short of idolizing her—and then too, my life expresses that she was the only beloved, and my whole author-existence will accent her. If not before, she will understand me in eternity.

[*A page removed from the journal*[2452]]

But as for myself, it becomes more and more clear to me that it is Governance who used her to capture me. The possibility of her—it was that which was supposed to develop me, and then responsibility in the God-relationship.

I was meant to be captured. And I had to be captured in such a manner that, in the deepest sense, I had to come into conflict with myself. For that reason the other party had to be someone who in a sense was nobody, an object and yet not an object, an inexplicable something who by capitulating brought me to do battle with myself. It took a woman to do that, a woman who femininely uses weakness as a weapon. And she had to be lovely in order to be able to affect me all the more—thus all the more assuredly bringing me to do battle with myself. She had to be young so that the father, regarding her practically as a child, felt all the more called upon to put the whole responsibility on me.

So it was that I was captured, or I was forced to make myself captive in the God-relationship. After it happened, it was as if Governance said: As far as she is concerned, she will be taken care of; she will come out of this all right. But you are trapped. She can neither release you nor bind you; nothing can change the picture, for you are trapped in the responsibility and captive to me.

$x^2$ A 3   Sept. 7, 1849

« **6489** *The Past Summer,*

as was the intention, lent support to my considered duty to stop writing now; it has been constantly distressing, creating a new external torment whenever one was over and done with.

The war took Anders[2453] from me; my feeling about my house suffered and even more so because of Strube's[2454] most regrettable illness; I wanted to be far away, and yet it was impossible for me to leave.

Then, too, all my financial worries,[2455] and the calamity that before one knows a thing about it there is probably an income tax.

Then, too, Reitzel[2456] has not been dependable. When being an author involves the self-sacrifices it has for me, putting my own money into it as I am now doing, perhaps ruining my future, then not even to have an accommodating publisher but to be choked and stifled by his concerns and misgivings, his unreasonableness in asking me to have one or two sheets printed each week and have the book come out at a more opportune time of the year. All of which then turned out to be a lie—but under the circumstances it is agonizing to go through such things.

And then the tanner with whom I live during the summer has plagued me with odors. Many, many times I have had to use sheer mental power not to get sick out of impatience. Abused in many ways by rabble barbarism and snoopy inquisitiveness, I have found my home to be a comfort, having a pleasant home was my greatest earthly encouragement. With that in mind I rented a splendid and very expensive apartment—and then to have to pay 200 rix-dollars[2457] and have to suffer this way.[*]

In addition, I have had scruples again and again about publishing what I have finished writing.

To find any diversion in Copenhagen is practically impossible, since the minute I show myself I promptly am assaulted by pecky, tiresome, snoopy inquisitiveness.

Through all this I have suffered the usual discomfort summer has for me.

Then Councillor Olsen died, and I acquired new concerns.[2458]

During all this I have had to deny myself what really gives me strength: I have not dared to start any new writing project, to say nothing of giving it momentum and impetus. I have decided to stop writing. And yet to write is actually my life.

Of course my mental depression has had a free hand such as it usually does not have, for when I write I forget everything.

It truly has been a difficult time for me. I look upon it simply as a practice in patience and hope that as such it truly will be of benefit for me. However painful it is, it may help me become more concrete.

But may I never forget to thank God for the indescribable good he has done for me, far more than I had expected. And that blessed thought that is original and primary in my soul must always stay there —that God is love and his wisdom is infinite, his possibilities are limitless; and where I have scarcely one possibility, he has a million!

$x^2$ A 10   *n.d.,* 1849

« 6490

[*]*In margin of 6489* ($x^2$ A 10):

Besides that, I also have been terribly hindered by my relationship to R. Nielsen;[2459] my own interpretation of that is as follows. Through him I come in contact with the confounded geniality which chatters and chatters and makes arrangements with publishers in advance and uses, God knows, a half year, I believe, to print a little book[2460]—and meanwhile I would just like him to get it out. And then he finally gets it out, but for the most part only confusion results.

$$x^2 \text{ A } 11 \quad n.d.$$

« 6491

O, once I am dead, *Fear and Trembling* alone will be enough for an imperishable name as an author. Then it will read, translated into foreign languages as well. The reader will almost shrink from the frightful pathos in the book. But when it was written, when the person thought to be the author was going about in the incognito of an idler, appearing to be flippancy, wittiness, and irresponsibility personified, no one was able to grasp its earnestness. O, you fools, the book was never as earnest as then. Precisely that was the authentic expression of the horror.

For the author to appear earnest would have diminished the horror. The reduplication is what is monstrous in the horror.

But when I am dead, an imaginary character will be conjured up for me, a dark, somber figure—and then the book will be terrifying.

But in calling attention to the difference between the poet and the hero[2461] a truth has already been said. There is a predominating poetic strain in me, and yet the real hoax was that *Fear and Trembling* actually reproduced my own life. This aspect of the book was intimated in the first hint [i.e., IV A 76] about it in the oldest journal, the one in octavo, that is, the oldest journal from the time of my literary activity.

$$x^2 \text{ A } 15 \quad n.d., \; 1849$$

« 6492

At times I am buoyed up by the thought that the thorn or spike I have in the flesh, a suffering I try to bear patiently, will itself be or will help me to be a thorn in the eye of the world.

$$x^2 \text{ A } 20 \quad n.d., \; 1849$$

« 6493

Frederikke Bremer will become popular in various circles because of this interpretation.[2462]

I live on here now, having voluntarily exposed myself to and continuing to endure the prolonged and yet perhaps the most bitter of martyrdoms, the martyrdom of ridicule[2463] (doubly painful because the context is so limited and because the measure of my endowments and achievements is generally recognized). With frightful mental and spiritual strenuousness I endure by continued writing in the face of constant financial sacrifices[2464]—and yet it is well known that I have not dropped one single comment on the situation. Frederikke's version is that I am so sickly and irritable that I can become bitter if the sun does not shine when I want it to. You smug spinster, you silly tramp, you have hit it! Various circles that are perhaps not so different will be united by this interpretation. On the one side Martensen,[2465] Paulli,[2466] Heiberg,[2467] etc., on the other, Goldschmidt,[2468] P. L. Møller.[2469] It was a wonderful old world—Martensen may witness "for God and his conscience"; did he not become Bishop and swathed in velvet and did not Frederikke run to him every day and read his *Dogmatik*,[2470] of which she got proof sheets (this is a well-known fact). And Goldschmidt may declare: It was a wonderful old world, I always had 3,000 subscribers. Tutti, it was a wonderful world; only Magister Kierkegaard was so sickly and irritable that he could get bitter if the sun did not shine when he wanted it to.

$x^2$ A 25   *n.d.*, 1849

### « 6494 *Discourses for Fridays*[2471]

This can be the regular form of writing
Three Discourses for the Communion on Fridays
No. 1. Luke 7:47. "He who is forgiven little, loves little."
No. 2. I Peter 4:7.[2472] Love covers a multitude of sins.
At "the altar" it is especially true that "love," namely Christ's love, covers a multitude of sins. In the strictest sense Christ's reconciliation was a work of love or "the Work of Love" κατ' ἐξοχήν.[2473]
No. 3. I Corinthians 11:31,32.
Can be used another time.

$x^2$ A 39   *n.d.*, 1849

### « 6495

*In margin of 6494* ($x^2$ A 39):
No. 3. Luke 24:31 could be used. The very fact that he becomes invisible to me is the sign that I recognize him: he is indeed the object of faith, a sign of contradiction, in a certain sense must become invisible before I recognize him. He is the prototype, must therefore become invisible so that the imitator can be like him.

At the altar he is invisibly present and yet verse 30 says that it was when he blessed the bread, broke it, and gave it to them that they recognized him.

$x^2$ A 40   *n.d.*

« 6496

It is certainly not unusual in this world to see a person who believes that he himself does not need rigorous Christianity but that he must be rigorous with others. In my own life I have not and perhaps never will get beyond the point of "fear and trembling," literally positive that everyone else will very likely be saved—but not I. Also in another sense, I always have been afraid to depict the rigorousness of Christianity, for to me it seems that it is too rigorous and that, considering my life, I need that kind of rigor, but others do not. As soon as anyone appealed to me personally, I promptly would mitigate it considerably and be as lenient as possible—but I myself do not escape the rigorousness.

$$X^2 \text{ A } 44 \quad n.d., \ 1849$$

« 6497 *My Position*

I depict what Christianity is; I am unusually well qualified to do that and quite literally understand it to be my calling, to which I have been led in the most amazing way from the beginning.

I do it in partially poetic[2474] form.

Now it depends on how the age will take it, and my fate also depends upon that.

If it remains calm, quietly lets itself be influenced by it, the relationship will be as genial as possible.

If not, if it turns and challenges me, in one sense the age will get the worst of it, for then I must stay put. What happens to my depiction will be my direct evidence against Christendom. Then everything will be raised one power in rigorousness, making it more rigorous for me, of course, but I must certainly be included.

I have never passed myself off as the extraordinary Christian. My situation really is not unlike that of a man well known for his intelligence and talents along certain lines, who is arrested by a prince and told: I want you to interpret a certain matter. If you do as I desire, you will be well off. You will have enough time for rest and recreation, but you also must work diligently and industriously a suitable time each day. I truly do feel that I have a strangely childlike relationship such as this to Governance. I get certain free hours every day for diversion, and I never think of it as being anything but entirely permissible and of Governance's wanting anything less than the greatest possible human happiness for me. But no more. Incidentally, if I do not do what is wanted, Governance has frightful means of constraining me.

And this is how I live in this boundless world. When I make the mistake of looking at others and seeing how they live, busily occupied with operating in the moment and for finite goals, I shudder. But I am secure and happy in my faith.

$x^2$ A 45     *n.d.,* 1849

« **6498**

There is something indescribably sad about my life. I wanted to live with the simple man; it gratified me immeasurably to be concerned, friendly, kind, and attentive to that social class which simply is forgotten in the so-called "Christian state." In many ways what I could do was insignificant, but to just that kind of people it can be significant, nevertheless. Let me take an example of the people I know by the score. An oldish woman from Amager sits in Buegangen and sells fruit; she has an old mother whom I sometimes have helped a little. When I greet her, I essentially am not doing anything—but yet it would please her, it would cheer her up that every morning a man whom she must regard as well off came along and never forgot to say "good-morning" to her and sometimes also spoke a few words with her. Really, what the state needs is just the kind of idler I was if it is to recompense in the smallest way for the scandalous wrongness of its existence. For everyone clutches at the higher, the more distinguished relativities in society—and when people reach that point, who cares about the common man of the land. An idler like that is necessary, or many of them; he is a copula. To the social class that generally has to stand and wait in anterooms and hardly gets permission to say a word, how encouraging in many ways that there is a man they invariably see on the street, a man they may approach and talk to freely, a man with hundreds of eyes particularly for the sufferings of that social class—and I was that man—and that in addition this is a man who has established himself in the elite world.

O, even if it was motivated in part by melancholy, it nevertheless is Christianity.

All this is now virtually destroyed.[2475] To that social class I now am a sort of half-looney—I cannot be of any good to them. Now I, too, must avert my eyes and be aloof, lest I end up like a Mad Maier[2476] with a veritable crowd collecting around me.

It all comes from the journalism which is published to protect the common man—against the elite.

This, you see, is the result of having a situation in the country where "boys judge us."[2477] A really clever fellow,[2478] a young man, who—not in connection with his crimes, for here I have only been an admonisher for him and have cautioned him, but in connection with a perhaps better possibility—sat as a learner at my feet (and this he will scarcely deny), and he has 3,000 subscribers in a country where I have 50 purchasers.[2479]

But, but, here it comes again. I will be understood, perhaps while I still live, and perhaps far sooner than I think—and as soon as this understanding is established a bit, I am convinced that there will not be anybody so hard of heart that he will not be affected by my life— and then the fact that I have endured this will once again be beneficial to me—or not to me but to my cause. The common man is my task, even if I continually have had to make a stand at the very top level of the cultured and distinguished world.

And among other things my life eventually will have the recompense that it is not so much the distinguished who wrong the poor as all their counselors and heroes.

$X^2$ A 48   *n.d.*, 1849

« **6499**

Equality is what the world wants, love to the neighbor—and yet I am persecuted because I lived and live on the streets.[2480] If there was any purpose to it at all, it was to weaken the secular mentality petrified in relativities. By being that $\mu\epsilon\tau\acute{a}\beta\alpha\sigma\iota\varsigma$ $\epsilon\acute{\iota}\varsigma$ $\check{a}\lambda\lambda o$ $\gamma\acute{\epsilon}\nu o\varsigma$,[2481] that is, into the existential, my daily existence or a daily existence such as that is worth much more than ten or twenty newspaper articles and a whole journal, which pontificate but existentially remain in the old ways.

The reason I was misunderstood was, for one thing, that I did what I did for religious motives and not to serve an esteemed cultured public.[2482] That is why I cannot defend myself either, for in doing so I concede to the public.

But my life will involve the most precise, existential police-operation in the Christian spirit; everything on all sides will be arranged to illuminate the theme: by what right does Denmark, especially Copenhagen, call itself Christian, by what right do 1,000 career men make Christianity into a living and nothing else? My life will also be a complete existential study on human selfishness and the deceit and hypocrisy carried on in the name of Christianity.

$X^2$ A 56   *n.d.*, 1849

### « 6500  *Something about Myself Which Must Be Steadfastly Maintained*

I have never claimed and I do not claim to be a Christian to any extraordinary degree.[2483] Definitely not. If I, with my imagination and my passions etc. had been a man in the ordinary sense, no doubt I would even have forgotten Christianity altogether. But I am tied and bound to tormenting wretchedness, like a bird with clipped wings, but I still retain all my seemingly extraordinary mental powers. But the very simplest qualifications for being an ordinary human being, these are the very ones denied to me, while the extraordinary in another sense is granted me. Thus I am brought to a halt once and for all, can be made conscious of my chains at any hour of the day if need be. But otherwise I have been equipped with great capacities, have been well brought up in Christianity from childhood, and furthermore have all the qualifications for it—and then it has become my task to present Christianity. But free, free as a man ordinarily is, that I have never been. As a matter of fact, I was brought up too rigorously in Christianity; it actually has been an offense to me—but free I have never been, not so free that I could ever cast it into oblivion; for when one expects to die tomorrow and today feels—perhaps many times—how unhappily bound he is: then there is no space for oblivion. I fully recognize how very much has been done for me; it is true of me that I cannot thank God sufficiently for all that he has granted to me and for giving me, the most wretched of all, a meaning which I discern best of all. I also have been increasingly mollified, through a religious understanding of my life—but, O, what would I not have given, especially in my younger days, to be an ordinary person for just half a year! All my eccentricity, O, it is nothing but a cleverly devised hoax to conceal my misery. What cost me in private the bitterest tears and plunged me into despair I explained away as pride and all that.

I do not claim and never have claimed that I did not get married because doing so is contrary to Christianity, as if my being unmarried were, from a Christian point of view, a perfection in me. Far from it. Had I been an ordinary human being, the danger for me no doubt would have been something else, that of being taken up too much with women, and I possibly could have been a seducer. But one thing for sure, I most joyfully would have married my fiancée; God knew how much I wanted to; but here again my wretchedness intrudes. So I remained unmarried, and I got the opportunity to reflect upon what Christianity actually has meant in commending the unmarried state.

I do not claim and have never claimed that it is a Christian perfection on my part not to try to get a position, as if that were the reason I did not do it. Far from it. From the time my financial situation became difficult and also earlier I very easily could have accepted a position. It always has been very easy for me to get along with people, and accustomed as I am to being circumscribed, it never occurred to me that it might be burdensome for me. But here comes my wretchedness again: I cannot because I am not an ordinary person, because my mental depression borders on insanity, something I no doubt can hide as long as I am independent, but which makes me unfit for service where I myself cannot control everything. People think it is pride: well, that is the old story. Therefore, I have had to persevere in uncertainty and have had good opportunity to reflect upon what Christianity actually means by having something against bureaucratic office.

This all explains why I always assume a poetic relation[2484] in my presentation of Christianity. In a certain sense I am being constrained continually against my will—and in the process I discover the essentially Christian. In this way I seem to be freed from the danger that what I think of could be vanity. I have not rejected marriage out of vanity, far from it; it has its warmest advocate in me.[2485] I have not rejected a position out of vanity, far from it, I would rather have had it. It seems to me that if I could get more peace and tranquillity this way and foresee a longer life in such a context, I could do some greater things: perhaps it is a delusion, but that is how it sometimes looks to me. —That is why I dare not require that others do what I am doing, for one thing is certain: I did not have the strength either to abstain from marriage or from seeking a position, but I have been constrained. But this also is true, that what I present is Christianity. Neither should I be accused of partiality, of not being able to see the other side, for the other side has in me its most ardent spokesman.

$x^2$ A 61   *n.d.,* 1849

« **6501** *On the Year 1848*

In one sense 1848 has raised me to another level. Another sense has shattered me, that is, it has shattered me religiously, or to say it in my own language: God has run me ragged. He has let me take on a task which even trusting in him I can not raise to its highest form; I must take it in a lower form. For this reason the matter actually has contributed inversely to my religious or further religious development. In one sense I want so much to venture; my imagination beckons and goads me, but I will simply have to agree to venture in a lower form. Without a doubt it is the most perfect and the truest thing I have written;[2486] but it must not be interpreted as if I am supposed to be the one who almost censoriously bursts in upon everybody else—no, I must first be disciplined myself by the same thing; there perhaps is no one who is permitted to humble himself as deeply under it as I do before I am permitted to publish it. I, the author, who myself am nothing (the highest) must not be permitted to publish it under my own name,[2487] for the work is itself a judgment. In one way or another I first must have arranged myself in life some way or other and have conceded that I am weak like everyone else—then I can publish it. But that which tempts my imagination is to get permission to do it before I, humanly speaking, can pay the price. Quite true, the blow would then be all the more powerful, but I would also gain a false high position. It is poetry[2488]—and therefore my life, to my humiliation, must demonstrably express the opposite, the inferior. Or should I also be an ascetic who can live on water and bread. —And yet this mortification, I would willingly submit to, if only I am able to undertake an appointment. In a still deeper sense this is my difficulty. And there may be still greater humiliation here before it becomes possible, if it becomes possible.

Economic concerns[2489] came suddenly and all too close. I cannot bear two such disparate burdens, the hostility of the world and concern for the future, at the same time. My idea when I rented the apartment in Tornebuskegaden was to live there a half year, quietly reflecting on my life, and then seek an appointment.[2490]

Then suddenly everything was thrown into confusion. In a matter of months I was in the situation where tomorrow, perhaps, I would not own a thing but be literally in financial straits. It was a severe drain on me. My spirit reacted all the more strongly. I wrote more than ever, but more than ever like a dying man. Without question, in the context of Christian truth it certainly is the highest that has been granted to me. But in another sense it is too high for me to appropriate right off in life and walk in character.[2491]

This is the deeper significance of the new pseudonym,[2492] which is higher than I am myself.

O, I know I have not spared myself; even to the point of strain I have wanted to force myself to venture something rash,[2493] but I cannot do it, I cannot justify it.

This is how Governance continually keeps his hand on me—and governs. I had never considered getting a new pseudonym. And yet the new pseudonym—but note well that it is higher than my personal existence—precisely that is the truth of my nature, it is the expression for the limits of my nature. Otherwise I would finally become veritably more than human.

$x^2$ A 66    *n.d.,* 1849

« **6502 *About Her***[2494]

As stated earlier [i.e., $x^2$ A 648] it is not improbable that now, after her father's death, she is expecting an approach.

Without my doing anything, such as deviating from my ordinary pattern, she more than once has managed to pass so close to me that it was almost a confrontation. But I cannot very well make the first step.[2495] After all, I really do not have any direct information about her situation, and by getting married her life expresses that she has forgotten the story. Suppose that, even if not completely forgotten, it were forgotten in such a way that raking up the past would be dangerous. And then there is Schlegel;[2496] it is almost unfair to him for me to be put in the same play. And yet it worries me that I may be unkindly cruel to her—how sadly true, my love once was that terrible thing: kind cruelty! And just as the bogeyman in the fairy tale thirsts for blood, so I thirst to do all I possibly can to make amends to her—they really thought that I was proud—well, thanks for that—so proud that I left my honor in the lurch—no, but it would be of satisfaction to me if sometime I might be allowed to show the world how proud I am by making her everything. Ye gods, from a human point of view it is a fairly modest request for a renowned man such as I am now to venture to be allowed to take an unobtrusive place as a kind of unhappy lover alongside the girl who beseechingly begged that she might be his maidservant. And yet I ask nothing more, except that it must be abundantly clear that I have God's approval to act in this direction. Irony was once part and parcel of my nature, but here it approaches sadness —how ironic to imagine myself religiously fulfilled by being a kind of unhappy lover.

But what a wonderful and yet moving pattern! Ordinarily it goes like this. Either it is the girl who cannot be satisfied with the inferior but snatches after the more glamorous—and then there is an inoffensive fellow (but the more mediocre) who loved her before. She still feels kindly toward him and he is allowed to trot humbly alongside as an unhappy lover toward whom one feels somewhat kindly. Or it may be this way: he is the famous figure etc., and he lets a girl sit and twiddle her thumbs remembering him while he marries a more distinguished girl.

And yet nothing fits me better than this very relationship. To trot along as an unhappy lover on the left side of a girl who has rejected my love: no, that will not do for me. But to trot alongside the girl whose love I truly did not reject but was forced to make it seem as if I, humanly speaking, rejected it: yes, this is the task for me. Yet may not danger be involved in such a relationship. Perhaps she never did love me as much as she admired me, and I perhaps never loved her erotically as much as I can truthfully say I was moved in the most beautiful way by the lovable child. Furthermore, if I understand that it can be done, then the power whose sanction I have received will also hold his hand protectingly over us. But it would be an alleviation for me—God knows if I would recognize myself again—if I, all too frightfully rehearsed in the kind of love which looks like cruelty, were permitted for once to express a line, a friendship, a bit more directly.

$x^2$ A 68   *n.d.*, 1849

« **6503**

Luther's sermon[2497] on the Gospel for New Year's Day contains the authentic Christian distinction, the stringent assertion that:

Christ is not a savior for this life but for eternal life. Yes, what is more—and Luther says this, too, in the same place—he is the very opposite of a savior for this life; for Luther declares that in this life—precisely to express that he is no savior for this life—he lets those who believe in him slog along as if in a bog.

Incidentally, here one sees the distinction between Jewish and Christian piety, for Jewish piety wants a savior for this life.

But in Christendom Christ has been completely transformed into merely human pity.

But it is my view that the most rigorous must really be heard, that men must not be permitted to cross it out and ignore it, that it must be heard so that men can humble themselves under it, but not proclaimed in such a way that men are cruelly driven to want to be spirit according to a frightful criterion.

Here is where I differ from Mynster[2498] and the like; he wants to suppress it completely. I want to have it said; and furthermore I am willing to declare that when I say it it is only poetic,[2499] since my life is far from being that spiritual.

On the whole I believe that this is the ethical respect which has to be introduced. Wherever I describe what is higher than my own personal life, I have to add explicitly: I am only a poet. Where my own personal life expresses what I speak about, there I use and should use a certain kind of authority. But if what I describe is higher than my life, then for the sake of truth I must admit that I am only a poet. And above all I must not suppress the highest and make my little no. 2 or no. 3 or no. 10 into the highest.

Mynster may have some justification for everything he says about the necessity for moderation etc—but, but the highest must not be suppressed in the name of moderation. No, it must be presented in all its demand and men must then be told: If you cannot do it, then entrust yourself to God, confess your weakness: he is no cruel Lord, he has great compassion. But you are not permitted to be ignorant of the highest aspects of God's requirement.

If a young girl were to ask me if I regard not marrying as superior to marrying and if so she would forego it, I would answer: If you are in love, if it truly is your dearest wish to be united with the beloved, then simply say so to God, and I would joyfully conduct the wedding ceremony and do everything to make it the best. But you must know that God could require that you should renounce this happiness also.

$x^2$ A 75   *n.d.,* 1849

### « 6504 *A Sigh!*

O, the way I lived with the common man: there perhaps is not one in the whole generation who could do it, and how few are they who understand him and understand the callousness and cruelty of class distinctions that ordinarily underlie associations with the common man. And then to have this forbidden to me, to have it regarded as ridiculously overplaying the part, and that I cannot ever do anything more for the common man, because for him I exist as a sort of half-looney. And that this has come about by means of those "who take the part of the common man against the aristocrats."[2500]

O, how tragic!

$x^2$ A 88   *n.d.,* 1849

### « 6505 *About the Completed Unpublished Writing*[2501] *and Myself*

The difficulty in publishing anything about the authorship is and remains that, without my knowing it or knowing it positively, I really have been used, and now for the first time I understand and comprehend the whole—but then I cannot, after all, say: *I*. At most I can say (that is, given my scrupulous demand for the truth): this is how I now understand the productivity of the past.* The flaw, again, is that if I do not do it myself, there is no one who can present it, for no one knows it the way I do.[2502] No one can explain the structure of the whole as I can.

But this is my limitation—I am a pseudonym. Fervently, incitingly, I present the ideal, and when the listener or reader is moved to tears, then I still have one job left: to say, "I am not that, my life is not like that."[2503]

Quite true: I feel I would be able to be more effective if at this moment someone stepped forward and spoke in his own name and gesticulated with his life: but perhaps Governance does not think this way—I must in truth learn that there is something higher which I perhaps am able to think but do not dare venture.

"From on High He Will Draw All to Himself" must be done pseudonymously.[†2504]

*Note. The truest statement, however, is that there is an "also,"[2505] because I have understood part from the beginning and always understood in advance before I did it.

$x^2$ A 89   *n.d.*, 1849

« **6506**

*In margin of 6505* ($x^2$ A 89):

†On a scrap of gray paper enclosed with this manuscript there is a note to the effect that in one way this book contains a dialectical heresy; to be specific, one of the Expositions[2506] (no. 5 or 6) develops the point that preaching in our day has become impersonal, and this is stated by a pseudonym! But for one thing this is my limit, I can go no further than to call attention to this,[2507] and for another, I am, after all, the responsible publisher, and as a matter of fact people will regard it as being said by me. The more which is there is really this: that while it is true the speaker is a nobody, a pseudonym, the publisher is an actual person and recognizes that he is judged by what the pseudonym says.

$x^2$ A 90   *n.d.*

« **6507**

If my suffering, my frailty, were not the condition for my intellectual work, then of course I would still make an attempt to deal with it by an ordinary medical approach. There is just no point in suffering as I suffer and not do a thing about it if one's life has no significance anyway. But here is the secret: the significance of my life corresponds directly to my suffering.

$x^2$ A 92   *n.d.,*  1849

« **6508**

It would indeed be appropriate for me to come out directly and admit how I regard the poetic element[2508] in me, despite my being a religious author—that from a religious point of view it is an imperfection, but I still cannot avoid it, and no doubt most of my contemporaries are unable to, either.

$x^2$ A 94   *n.d.,*  1849

« **6509**

Incidentally, the nonsense they said about me in other respects has been long forgotten and makes no difference. But it has had the effect that for the lowest class I live under a nickname,[2509] am tagged by one comical oddity or another which I am forced to carry (for I cannot in fact put off my legs[2510]—that is, I no doubt may do so in the grave)—in that way my life is a daily martyrdom. Even the elite have the power any time they are so inclined to let me understand that this is how the rabble look upon me. Such a martyrdom is not the easiest. My fame is utilized to sustain the insults.

It is both laughable and lamentable, but one thing is sure, it would be a relief if I could get Goldschmidt[2511] to write, for example, about my suit-coat, my vest, my hat, so my legs could get a little peace.

$x^2$ A 101   *n.d.,*  1849

« **6510**

It is really a blessing and a comfort to me right now to know before God that I suffered in leaving her, that it was sheer suffering. What strength it gives me! In fact, if I had left her out of selfishness and an ambition to be a glittering success, my life would have been inevitable despair. Right now I am very serene; where under other conditions I would say: I have lost, now I say: I have won. I know that basically there is not one single person who would not be appalled and moved to deepest compassion if he really knew, quite literally, how I have suffered. But it was precisely that which intensified the pain, knowing that I was a sure prey to pity—and that is why I did everything I could to keep it entirely under cover, and I succeeded.

The suffering was dreadful; depressed as I was, I realized my misery to be greatly intensified by having made her unhappy—and then, suddenly, a wealth burst from my soul which appalls me when I look back upon it.

This is the real basis of my power; my suffering is my superiority; there is also something terrible in the awareness that undergirding me and my relation to a contemporary there is a diametrically opposite understanding of myself before God.

Very likely the same thing will happen to me that happened to others before me: sooner or later they will think that they understand me by means of *the results*. O, but then I was all alone in my misery, so miserable that I cannot even get my pen to write about it, although I knew and remember it all too well. Then I stood all alone—not like one who is suffering, no, with a young girl's indictment that I would be the death of her,[2512] with a father surviving as if she were already dead, with a family's curse upon me, with human speech and everything hostile to me! If at that time I could not have walked around and talked with peddler-women and cab-drivers etc., I could not have survived. I was struck by what I read about Napoleon when crossing the Alps, that he was preoccupied, like someone in a dream, and talked preferably with his guide, discussing the latter's domestic affairs. That is to be expected. Napoleon, after all, was carrying around a plan for the world; I carry only a deep melancholy, about as deep as possible.

$X^2$ A 105    *n.d., 1849*

### « 6511 *About Myself as Author*

Once again I have reached the point where I was last summer,[2513] the most intensive, the richest time I have experienced, where I understood myself to be what I must call a poet[2514] of the religious, not however that my personal life should express the opposite—no, I strive continually, but that I am a "poet" expresses that I do not confuse myself with the ideal.

My task was to cast Christianity into reflection,[2515] not poetically to idealize (for the essentially Christian, after all, is itself the ideal) but with poetic fervor to present the total ideality at its most ideal—always ending with: I am not that, but I strive. If the latter does not prove correct and is not true about me, then everything is cast in intellectual form and falls short.

Given the momentum of my writing a year ago I also managed to comprehend the total authorship and myself. I realized that I was a poetic reflector of Christianity with the capacity to set forth the Christian qualifications in all their ideality; I realized how in wonderful ways I had been led into this early in my life. I realized—and God be praised I still realize it unaltered—that I can never thank God sufficiently for the good he has done for me, indescribably much more than I had expected. All this I realized, and the total structure of the authorship, and I put it all down in the book about my work as an author.[2516]

Then for a time I misunderstood myself, although not for long. I wanted to publish this book. The understanding of my life as an author and of myself was, if I may say so, a gift of Governance to me, encouraging me to go ahead with becoming more truly a Christian— and the misunderstanding was that I wanted to publish it, forgetting that this would be an overstepping of my limits. If I state that I am this poetic reflector and venturer, then I am making myself out to be more than I say I am: in one way or another I myself get to be the ideal and claim to be it. The whole thing would then be in the realm of the interesting, and my contemporaries would then be made fellow-conspirators in my intrigue—but I have no right at all to call it that, for it is also my development.

In the most curious ways I have been prevented from publishing. And now the turn has been made, the new pseudonym established. I deserve no credit whatsoever, because once again it seems that a Governance has helped me do the right thing.

Many times I was all set to publish the writings about myself, but —no. I was able to write them with the same calmness I customarily have in my work, but the minute I took them out with the thought of publishing them, I felt uneasy, an overstraining I had never sensed before.

That was my boundary. To publish them would have produced a great confusion. Despite all the disclaimers in the writings, it would not have been possible to prevent my being regarded as an extraordinary Christian, instead of being only a genius; eventually I perhaps would have made the error of regarding myself as an extraordinary Christian. The truth of the matter, however, which I have learned by the very writing of these books, is that I am far, far from being an extraordinary Christian, that there is still an element of the poetic in me which from a Christian point of view is a minus. Publishing them would have been a bewildering poet-confusion. In one sense the understanding I arrived at elevated me to a perception of what extraordinary endowments had been granted to me, and how an infinitely loving

Governance had been leading me from the very beginning, but at the same time and in another way it humbled me by giving me to understand how far I still was from being a Christian in a stricter sense. But this very perception was gained through the suffering of wanting to publish but not being able to do it. If I had not been hindered, if I had been permitted to storm ahead with the publishing, a confused darkness undoubtedly would have entered my soul.

If things take such a turn that a contemporary demands an explanation from me, I certainly could give it, but not until I first ask permission to speak quite unguardedly. It is a different matter if I, so requested, explain the enterprise itself, how I now understand myself, what the end will be despite all my objections: to press on to my goal with the transformation of my own life.

$X^2$ A 106   *n.d.*, 1849

### « 6512  *Example of Horror in a Situation*

In a boat on the seething, foaming sea there is but one man, a pilot or whomever you want to imagine. Calmly he sits in the end of the boat, his hand on the rudder, while the boat sails along in proudest flight. Then it is lifted up on the crest of a burgeoning wave—the spectators on shore gasp in admiration; the pilot himself is calm and almost seems to enjoy the excitement of the shuddering. Suddenly he notices a little tremor in his hand, telling him: either your hand has gone lame or the boat is not responding to the rudder. It would have been impossible to see this even if one had sat calmly alongside of him as the calmest observer—and without altering his quiet, composed posture, he plunges into the abyss.

The horror consists in concentration of the horror in one single almost unnoticeable point, that the horror is really given no expression at all, that he does not make the slightest change in his daring, calm, and composed posture and yet is so crippled that he plunges to disaster. The very horror is that the horror is not manifested in any way, not so much as in a movement of the arm.

$X^2$ A 109   *n.d.*, 1849

### « 6513

From one angle something may be immodest, from another angle, the opposite may be immodest.

If a man were granted one wish and he wished for a kingdom, he perhaps would be called immodest. But if a man were permitted to wish and he said: Well, I really do not have anything to wish for, except that I wish I had put on overshoes today instead of rubbers—this, in fact, is being immodest, for it actually signifies that one is very well off (unless one is mentally deranged or insane). But if a person is very well off and merely lacks his galoshes in place of his rubbers—and then if a spirit came along and granted him a wish, he would turn away from the spirit, turn to God and say: No, indeed, I will not make a wish, but I will thank God for all the good things he has done for me.

$x^2$ A 110 *n.d.,* 1849

« **6514**

This is why I am so indescribably happy in the midst of all my sufferings. My imagination almost swoons to think of the millions of possibilities that God has at every moment. I do something wrong. I am aware of it at once. What is to be done now? My gloomy imagination instantly perceives the possibility that this little mistake can ruin everything. But then, the very same moment, I say to God: *Bitte, bitte;*[2517] I made a mistake; but even if I am a pest, an impudent pest, O God, make something good out of this very mistake. And then (God who has millions of possibilities at every moment), then the circumstances are combined somewhat differently and, so it is. This very mistake proves to be the right thing. That is how I pray to God. And that is how I get more joy out of this mistake than out of the most proper thing I ever did.

$x^2$ A 112 *n.d.,* 1849

« **6515**

About the *Three Discourses on Fridays*[2518] (The High Priest, The Publican, and The Woman Who Was a Sinner)—they are related to the last pseudonym, Anti-Climacus.[2519]

$x^2$ A 126 *n.d.,* 1849

« **6516**

There was some truth in Peter's[2520] comment once that religiously the difference between him and me was that he considered the relationship to God as one of being loved and I as one of loving. This was not a completely new observation to me; I frequently have pondered whether or not God is far too infinitely elevated for a man to dare love him—but it does, after all, stand there: You shall love the Lord your God. Furthermore, I myself have always maintained that it is God who does everything for me.

Nevertheless this is not an infelicitous way of indicating the difference between us two. In fact, Peter has never been mentally-spiritually young; the religious made a morbid impact on him; he became so anxious and afraid before God that he is stuck in this pusillanimity—and God knows whether he ever will really be stirred up to dare believe that God loves him. I have never been young physically. But mentally-spiritually I have been a youth in the best sense of the word. Overwhelmed by God, shattered until I felt even less than a sparrow before him, I nevertheless received a positive bold confidence to dare youthfully to become involved with God; I have childishly been able to get it through my head that God's infinity is manifested precisely in his being able to be concerned about the very least; I was childishly able to imagine piously that he was not irked when in connection with an honest endeavor I said: *Bitte, bitte,*[2521] do not refuse me, O you infinite one, you for whom I am in another sense less than nothing at every second.

This is youthfulness, this is childlikeness, but it is fundamental to my nature. What a blessing to me that it has been so natural and *geläufigt*[2522] for me to understand this, to have at my finger tips the understanding that the more infinite one is—the less he is able to be concerned with little things—O, no, I have never been that commonsensical! —No, the more infinite one is the more he can and will concern himself with little things. I literally believed that he was concerned about every single sparrow—literally, of course, for it was extremely important to me, since in another sense I continually have regarded myself as a sparrow or less.

Call it crazy, but in my final moment I am going to pray to God for permission to thank him once again for making me crazy this way. In fact, it is doubtful whether anyone whom God has not made crazy like this really has ever realized that he exists before God.

Moreover, I readily recall what I so frequently recall—that in the relationship to God progress in one sense means that the longer one lives with him the farther he feels himself to be away from him in one sense, for, after all, he is infinitely more elevated.[2523] As a child one lives with him cheerfully and without ceremony; as a youth, one believes that it still can be done if one really tries: alas, as an adult one perceives that he is far too infinite for him—however, there is a not unimportant difference if one has been a child and a youth or started right away with what belongs to the aged.

$X^2$ A 134   *n.d.,* 1849

« **6517** *The Turn in the Authorship, How the New Pseudonym (Anti-Climacus) Was Introduced*

My intention was to publish all the completed manuscripts in one volume,[2524] all under my name—and then to make a clean break.

This was a drastic idea, and I suffered indescribably in persistently wanting to cling to it; I penciled notes here and there (especially in the books about the authorship), at the same time continually overtaxing myself on the whole project, especially on the added point that I should existentially alter my course and yet in a way conceal that there was something false about my stepping forth in character on such a scale—by withdrawing entirely.

Finally it became clear to me that I definitely had to consider my future and that it was beyond my ability to undertake both at once—to concentrate on a literary enterprise like that and also to have financial difficulties. So I decided to lay aside everything I had finished writing until a more propitious time—and then not to write anymore and to make a move to get an appointment.

Then the idea came to me again that it might be unjustifiable for me to let these writings just lie there, and I also became somewhat impatient when I thought of how difficult it is for me to get to be an office holder, even if willing to do everything, and so I make futile visits to both Madvig and Mynster.[2525] Then I tackled the matter again—send the first part of the manuscript to the printer under my name, making it possible now to undertake the whole project. My idea was to let actuality put the pressure on me and to get a close perspective of the matter, and I committed myself to God and his help.

Meanwhile Councillor Olsen[2526] died, raising a host of difficulties —I realized also that it was rash and unconscionable to instigate a *coup* of that nature—with the result that *The Sickness unto Death* was made pseudonymous.

This led me to understand myself and my limitations; I gained an ingeniousness with respect to the structure of the authorship, which again is not original to me; I realized that it was practically desperation on my part to want to venture that far out toward being an apostle of sorts, and in so curious a manner that I simultaneously would break off and with the same step possibly wipe out my future.

If this had not happened, if I had let all that I had written just lie there, I no doubt would have come back every week to the thought of carrying out that stupid idea, and I probably would have unhinged myself, for it still would not have been carried out.

Now the writing has begun to move, the pseudonym is established, I can breathe again and am released from the ghost of overstrain.

$x^2$ A 147   *n.d.*, 1849

### « 6518

*Note.* Recently a new pseudonym appeared: Anti-Climacus. But this simply implies a halt; this is how one goes about dialectically effecting a halt: one points to something higher that examines a person critically and forces him back within his boundaries.

October, 1849

The note which accompanies the final draft in the mahogany chest reads something like this.

$x^5$ B 206   October, 1849

### « 6519

About the *Three Discourses* (The High Priest, The Publican, The Woman Who Was a Sinner)

They are now delivered to the printer.

(1) I must have a fulcrum, but I cannot use a pseudonym as a fulcrum; they are parallel to Anti-Climacus;[2527] and the position of "Discourses at the Communion on Fridays" is once and for all designated as the fulcrum of the authorship.

(2) Since at this time there is an emphasis on my pseudonym (Climacus), it is important for the stress to be in the direction of upbuilding.

Again, what love on the part of Governance, that what I need and must use always lies finished and ready.

(3) The preface is reminiscent of the two upbuilding discourses of 1843, because to me it is very important to emphasize that I began at the outset as a religious author; it is of importance for the repetition [*Repetitionen*].[2528]

$x^2$ A 148   *n.d.*, 1849

### « 6520 *About My Authorship as a Totality*

In a certain sense there is a problem of choice for my contemporaries: They must choose either to make the esthetic the total idea and interpret everything in that way or choose the religious. Precisely in this there is something awakening.

X² A 150    *n.d.,* 1849

## « 6521 *A New View of the Pastor—the Poet*²⁵²⁹ *in the Sphere of Religion*

Christianity has of course known very well what it wanted. It wants to be proclaimed by witnesses—that is, by men who proclaim the teaching and also existentially express it.

The prevailing modern notion of a pastor is a complete misunderstanding. Since pastors probably should also express the essentially Christian, they have quite rightly discovered how to relax the requirement, abolish the ideal.

What is to be done now? Yes, now we must prepare for another tactical advance.

First a detachment of poets; almost sinking under the demands of the ideal, with the glow of a certain unhappy love they set forth the ideal. Present-day pastors may now take the second rank.

These religious poets must have the particular ability to do the kind of writing that helps people out into the current.

When this has happened, when a generation has grown up which from childhood on has received the pathos-filled impression of an existential expression of the ideal, the monastery and genuine witnesses of the truth will both come again.

This is how far behind the cause of Christianity is in our time.

The first and foremost task is to create pathos, with the superiority of intelligence, imagination, penetration, to guarantee pathos for the existential, which "the understanding" has reduced to the ludicrous.

Here is my task. A young man, an utterly simple man can be used for the highest level of the existential—for that the ethical alone is the sole requirement. But when "the understanding" and the power of the understanding have triumphed in the world and made the genuinely existential almost ludicrous, then neither a young man nor a simple man is able to cut through. Then there must first be a maieutic, an old man in a certain sense, eminently possessing all the gifts of mind and spirit—and these he applies to create pathos for the pathos-filled life.

Any young girl can truly fall in love. But imagine an age which has sunk to such depths of commonsensicality that all the brilliant minds etc. applied their talents to making love ludicrous—then no young girl is able to cut through. There must first of all be an older person who can crush this commonsensicality and create pathos—and then, hail to thee, O youth, whoever you are—then there is a place for youth's in a sense far inferior powers. And yet in one sense the relation is such, as it always is in the pseudonymous works, that the young person stands higher than the older one.[2530]

Alas, my own life demonstrates this. Only now do I see where the turn must be made—now after almost overstraining myself for seven years, now when I must begin to carry a new kind of burden, concern for making ends meet.[2531] O, why was there no older person who related to me as I do to the youth.

Yet in a certain degree I myself do belong to the old, but I guarantee pathos.

Mynster's[2532] error was not the prudence etc. he has used. No, the error was that, enchanted by the workings of his prudence in the world of temporality, enchanted by his power and influence, he actually let the ideal vanish. Were there in Mynster's preaching but one thing—a constant and deep sorrow over not having been spiritual enough to become a martyr, I would have approved of him; I would then have said of him what I say of myself: He did not become a martyr, but he is able to bring forth martyrs.

No one can take what he has not been given—and neither can I. I also am marked by having been born in Christendom, spoiled in my upbringing, etc. If I had not been brought up in Christianity, if I had stood outside Christianity, it might perhaps have the power to swing me a stage higher, if, note well, Christianity itself were represented as in its earliest time, when there was pathos in abundance.

But no one can take what has not been given to him.

How true it is to me now that all my recent productivity has actually been my personal upbringing, my humiliation. Youthfully I have dared—then it was granted to me to put forth the requirement of ideality in an eminent sense*—and quite rightly I am the one who feels humbled under it and learns in a still deeper sense to resort to grace. Moreover this which I now again have experienced even more personally has already been called to mind in the works themselves, for Anti-Climacus says in the moral to "Come to Me All Who Labor and Are Heavy Laden":[2533] The prototype must be presented so ideally that you are humbled by it and learn to flee to the prototype, but in an entirely different sense—namely, as to the merciful one.

But all must relate themselves to the ideal; and no matter how far below and how far away I am, there must still be in my glance and in my sighing a direction which indicates that I also am related to the ideal—only in that way am I one who strives.

And then, as Anti-Climacus says: then no overrash impetuosity.

Yet how different to begin as a young man can begin, and then in the best years of his life still to have belonged to the old.

One thing remains—we are still all saved by grace.

$$X^2 \text{ A } 157 \quad n.d., \quad 1849$$

« 6522

*In margin of 6521* ($X^2$ A 157):

*Note. Apart from what always, of course, takes precedence, the solicitude of Governance, which accounts for the fact that I always understand best afterwards,[2534] the success of my presentation is connected with: (1) the injustice and mistreatment I have suffered as an author, something that has all the stronger impact because of my polemical nature, (2) my mental depression, (3) my religious attitude and inner sufferings, (4) also the conception I have that as a penitent I must venture, just because of that, what others do not venture. But I must be very cautious on that last point, for it is extremely difficult to know oneself and not confuse boldness with really being willing to suffer.

$$X^2 \text{ A } 158 \quad n.d.$$

« 6523

[*In margin:* The Position of Christianity at the Present Moment]

*The Position of Christianity at the Present Moment*

Actually, the revolution is much closer than we think. The last band of free-thinkers (Feuerbach[2535] and all related to him) has attacked or tackled the matter far more cleverly than formerly, for if you look more closely, you will see that they actually have taken upon themselves the task of defending Christianity against contemporary Christians. The point is that established Christendom is demoralized, in the profoundest sense all respect for Christianity's existential commitments has been lost (for assurances of respect amount to nothing). Now Feuerbach is saying: No, wait a minute—if you are going to be allowed to go on living as you are living, then you also have to admit that you are not Christians. Feuerbach has understood the requirements but cannot force himself to submit to them—ergo, he prefers to renounce being a Christian. And now, no matter how great a responsibility he must bear, he takes a position that is not unsound, that is, it is wrong of established Christendom to say that Feuerbach is attacking Christianity; it is not true, he is attacking the Christians by demonstrating that their lives do not correspond to the teachings of Christianity. [*In margin:* This is why one may say of Feuerbach: *ab hoste consilium.* [2536]] This is quite different. It may very well be that he is a *malitieus dæmon*,[2537] but he is useful for tactical purposes.

What Christianity needs for certain is traitors. Christendom has insidiously betrayed Christianity by not wanting to be truly Christian but to have the appearance of being so. Now traitors are needed.

But this concept, traitors, is dialectical. The devil also, so to speak, has his traitors, his spies, who do not attack Christianity, but attack the Christians—with the express purpose of getting more and more to fall away. God, too, has his traitors: God-fearing traitors, who in unconditional obedience to him simply and sincerely present Christianity in order that for once people may get to know what Christianity is. I am sure that established Christendom regards them as traitors, since Christendom has taken illegal possession of Christianity by a colossal forgery.

Strangely enough, I always understand best afterwards. Dialectically Johannes Climacus[2538] is in fact so radical a defense of Christianity that to many it may seem like an attack. This book makes one feel that it is Christendom that has betrayed Christianity.

This book has an extraordinary future.

And I, the author, am in a way held up to ridicule as always. I manage to do things the entire significance of which I do not understand until later. This I have seen again and again. For that very reason I cannot become serious in the trivial sense in which serious people are serious, for I realize that I am nothing. There is an infinite power which, as it were, helps me; when I turn to it, I pray—this certainly is earnestness; but when I turn to myself, I almost have to laugh at the thought that I, a wretched nobody etc., seem to be so important. I cannot quite make myself intelligible to others, for whatever I write they promptly categorize as pertaining to me. In my own consciousness, where I understand the way things really hang together, at every alternate moment jest can scarcely be avoided. But it is a pious jest, for precisely in smiling at myself in my nothingness there is again an expression of devotion. To use a metaphor and example, it is as if a little girl were loved by someone whom she feels to be very superior to her intellectually. In the ordinary sense of the word this relationship does not become serious. The like for like that provides finite security and earnestness is lacking. She cannot help smiling at herself when she thinks of being loved by—him, and yet she feels blissful during every moment of his visit. Nor does she dare tell herself "in earnest": He loves me, for she will say: My relationship to him is actually nothing; he would do no wrong whatsoever in leaving me this moment, for there is no relationship between us, but the relationship is blissful as long as it lasts.

But my relationship has the peculiar quality of being reflective, so that I do not see it until later—see, there I have been helped again. I take my pen, commend myself to God, work hard, etc., in short, do the best I can with the meager human means. The pen moves briskly across the paper. I feel that what I am writing is all my own. And then, long afterwards, I profoundly understand what I wrote and see that I received help.

It is easy to see that dialectically Johannes Climacus's defense of Christianity is as radical as it can be, for dialectically the defense and the attack are within a single hair of being one.

"Johannes Climacus" was actually a contemplative piece, for when I wrote it I was contemplating the possibility of not letting myself be taken over by Christianity, even if it was my most honest intention to devote my whole life and daily diligence to the cause of Christianity, to do everything, to do nothing else but to expound and interpret it, even though I were to become like, be like the legendary Wandering Jew—myself not a Christian in the final and most decisive sense of the word and yet leading others to Christianity.

$x^2$ A 163   *n.d.*, 1849

« **6524**

A line by Thomas à Kempis[2539] which perhaps could be used as a motto sometime. He says of Paul: Therefore he turned everything over to God, who knows all, and defended himself solely by means of patience and humility. . . . . He did defend himself now and then so that the weak would not be offended by his silence.

Book III, chapter 36, para. 2, or in my little edition, p. 131.

$x^2$ A 167   *n.d.*, 1849

« **6525** *The Significance of the Whole Authorship*

is its *calling attention* to the essentially Christian.

Attention is not supposed to be called to me, and yet it is to existence as a person that attention is to be called, or to the crucial significance of existence as a person for the essentially Christian.

Therefore, my existence as a person is also utilized, but always in order to point beyond me at the decisive moment: I am not that.[2540]

To call attention this way is to place the essentially Christian in the relationship of possibility to men, to show them how far we all are from being Christian.

$x^2$ A 174   *n.d.*, 1849

### « 6526  *The New Pseudonym Anti-Climacus*

Since all the writing under the title *Practice in Christianity* was poetic,[2541] it was understood from the very first that I had to take great pains not to become confused with an analogy to an apostle. Generally my hypochondria has also had a part in all the later works, for even though things undeniably have become more clear, they were not understood this way from the beginning.

When the section "Come to Me All Who Labor etc." was written, "Poetic Venture—Without Authority—For Inward Deepening in Christianity" was placed on the title page at the outset. And then came my name. And the same with the others.

But as time went on, it became clear to me (in this connection see journal NB[11] or NB[12] [i.e., $x^1$ A 295–541; $x^1$ A 542–682 and $x^2$ A 1–68], but more particularly NB[11]) that if possible there must be an even stronger declaration that it was poetic—and that it was best to have a new pseudonym. This became clear to me. Meanwhile I wanted to wait and see, during which time I suffered very much, constantly undertaking too much with the whole writing project and tormented by the fixed and desperate idea of publishing it all in one swoop and then leaping aside and vanishing, something I basically understood could not be done but which nevertheless captivated my imagination so that I really did not want to give up the possibility, although it became more and more apparent that if I were to get air, there would have to be a break.

Finally I decided to lay the whole project aside and seek an appointment; and when that had been done, I would publish gradually, in small lots, what was completed.

I then went to Madvig and Mynster[2542] and met neither of them; then I was strongly influenced in the opposite direction and took it to be a hint from Governance that I was about to make a mistake, that I simply should venture everything. Now came the reaction. I wrote to the printer and engaged the compositor and said that they "should go ahead." I get word from the printer[2543] that all is clear and could they have the manuscript. At the very same time I learn that Councillor Olsen[2544] has died. That affected me strongly; if I had known about it before I wrote to the printer, it would have prompted a postponement. But now, after so frequently being on the verge of it, fearfully over-taxed as I was, I was afraid I would be incapacitated if I backed out after taking this step.

I was under great strain and slept badly, and, strangely enough, a phrase came to my mind, as if I myself were hurling myself into disaster.

In the morning I pondered the matter again. It seemed to me that I had to act. Then I decided to submit the whole matter to God: to send the first manuscript (*The Sickness unto Death*) to the printer without saying anything about what else there was to be printed. My intention was to allow actuality to test me; it was possible that the sum total could be printed, and it was possible that there could be a turning aside.

Under that tension I began to see that it should be published under a pseudonym, something I understood earlier but postponed doing because it could be done at any time.

In the middle of the typesetting there was trouble with Reitzel, making me extremely impatient. Once again I had the thought of withdrawing the whole manuscript, laying it aside, and waiting once again to see if I should have everything published at the same time, and without the pseudonymity, for the pseudonymity was not established as yet, inasmuch as the title page was not printed, because, contrary to my practice, I had originally ordered it to be printed last. I went to the printer. It was too late. The composition was as good as finished.

So the pseudonym was established. That is how one is helped and helps himself when it is so difficult to act.

$X^2$ A 177   *n.d.*, 1849

« 6527

Basically people would rather have a fanatic who says that he himself is the ideal (then they can either parade with him or promptly part company with him, saying, and rightly so—he wants to be Christ) than one who honestly strives, who humbly does not call himself more than a poet,[2545] and confesses how infinitely far behind he is. The contemporaries cannot get rid of him as promptly or quickly; he can become a continual disturbance to his contemporaries.

$X^2$ A 183   *n.d.*, 1849

« 6528 *The New Pseudonym (Anti-Climacus)*

The fact that there is a pseudonym is the qualitative expression that it is a poet-communication, that it is not I who speaks but another, that it is addressed to me just as much as to others; it is as if a spirit speaks and I get the inconvenience of being the editor. What he has to say is something we men prefer to have cast into oblivion. But it must be heard nevertheless. Not that everyone should do it, nor that salvation depends upon my doing it—O, no. I realize, after all, that my life does not express it either, but I humble myself under it; I regard this as an indulgence, and my life is restless.

With respect to ethical-religious communication (that is, along the lines of depicting the requirement of ideality—which is different from grace and what is involved in it, different in that rigorousness creates a tension to the point that one feels the need of grace, without, however, being permitted to take it in vain), I am not permitted to communicate more than I, the speaker, am, that is, in my own factual first person, no more than my life existentially but fairly well conforms to. If I place the requirement higher, I must express that this presentation is a poetic one. It is altogether appropriate for me to present it, for it may influence another to strive more, and I myself define myself as one who is striving in relation to it, thereby distinguishing myself from the typical poet, to whom it never occurs to strive personally toward the ideal he presents.

Incidentally, it is a terrible thing for the requirements of the ideal to be presented by men who never give a thought to whether their lives express it or not. That I have been aware is indicated by my calling this a poetic communication—even though I am striving.

That the communication is poetic may be expressed *either* in the form of a declaration by the speaker saying in his own person: This is poetic communication, that is, what I am saying is not poetic, for what I am saying is the very truth, but the fact that I am saying it constitutes the poetic aspect, or *qua* author he can do it with the help of pseudonyms, as I have done now for the first time[2546] in order to make matters clear.

But the difference between such a speaker-author—and a typical poet—is that the speaker and author himself defines himself as striving in relation to what is being communicated.

And this whole distinction pertaining to poet-communication is related again to Christianity's basic category, that Christianity is an existence-communication [*Existents-Meddelelse*] and not doctrine, as Christianity has unchristianly and meaninglessly been made to be, so that the question in relation to a doctrine is simply: Is my interpretation of the doctrine true, the true interpretation, or not, like, for example, an interpretation of Plato's philosophy. No, the question is: Does or does not my personal life express what is communicated. As long as my life expresses what is communicated, I am a teacher; when this is not the case, I am obliged to add: What I say is certainly true, but my saying it is the poetic aspect; consequently it is a poet-communication which, however, is meaningful both for keeping me awake and keeping me striving, and, if possible, for awakening others.

———

In book no. $1^{2547}$ ("Come to Me All Who Labor and Are Heavy Laden") the *qualitative* rigor is Christianly untrue in one sense (because it is almost solely metaphysical)—the affirmation that Christ came to the world because he was the absolute, not out of human compassion or for any other reason, an affirmation which corresponds with the absolute "You shall." At the same time it holds true Christianly on the other side that Christ came to the world out of love *in order to* save the world. The fact that He was obliged to break the world, as it were, the fact that, humanly speaking, enormous suffering comes from accepting him, certainly are due to his being the absolute, but joy over the fact that he came *in order to* save must completely surmount all this suffering. These two affirmations (He came because he was the absolute, and He came out of love *in order to* save the world) make the difference between Christianity being proclaimed in "law" or in "grace."

In book no. 2 ("Blessed Is He Who Is Not Offended") the qualitative rigor is the *necessity* with which the offense is joined together with all that is essentially Christian.

In book no. 3 ("From on High He Will Draw All unto Himself") the *qualitative* rigor is the *necessity* with which abasement is joined to being Christian, that unconditionally every true Christian is abased in this world.

$$x^2 \text{ A } 184 \quad n.d., \ 1849$$

« 6529

So much is certain, the preacher-talk which sentimentally longs to be contemporary with Christ certainly must cease. My formula is: I will be honest, I will admit that if I had been contemporary with you, I too certainly would have betrayed you. Incidentally, this has already been stated in one of the Friday discourses in the first collection.[2548]

$x^2$ A 191    *n.d.*, 1849

## « 6530 *Pseudonymous Publication of the Writings about My Work as an Author*

But it is not necessary to publish them pseudonymously, it is not even right to do so, inasmuch as the matter does not become sufficiently simple.

The category: that I myself am the one who has been educated, that it all is my own education,[2549] is decisive enough.

The first idea to publish all the books (including those which have become pseudonymous) in my name and in one volume[2550] along with the writings about my work as an author was still vague and unclear (as it was impatient), because the writings about my work as an author go only to the Friday discourses in *Christian Discourses* and therefore no impression is conveyed of the whole new productivity contained in the same volume.

No, the new pseudonym, *Anti-Climacus*—who in the dialectical sphere makes a new dialectical contribution which must be resolved by an upbuilding discourse on "grace"—provides "the halt." And within the halt, then, comes the communication about my work as an author.

$x^2$ A 192    *n.d.*, 1849

## « 6531 *About Myself*

The thought of publishing all the writings in one swoop under my name,[2551] and thereby with the greatest possible impetus, and then jumping back without really ever knowing where, without regard for the consequences I would invite by such a step, other than wanting to live in retirement: this was sheer, desperate impatience.

My task has never been to bring down the established order but constantly to infuse inwardness into it.

From the beginning I perceived the wrongness of it, but it momentarily tempted my imagination and was related to a poet-impatience.

My task always has been difficult. With my sights on a brash scientific scholarship, a brash culture, etc., which wants to go even farther[2552] than Christianity, I jack up the requirements of ideality[2553] so high—and at the same time I also have a great responsibility, since I have the most intense sympathy for the common man, woman, etc., and I do not want to make them anxious.

On the whole, the woman is and ought to be a corrective in

proclaiming the ethical-religious. One must not make it rigorous for men and have another kind for women, but in making it rigorous one ought to respect the woman as an authority also and temper it through assistance from that source. And for the sake of the cause, a woman perhaps may lift the burden just as well as a man precisely because she has fewer ideas and also fewer half-ideas than the man, and thus more feeling, imagination, and passion.

$X^2$ A 193   *n.d.,* 1849

« 6532

As a rule the religious ought to be kept just as mild as rigorous. God wants to be the ruler, but in the form of grace, concession, etc.: he wants to handle a person as carefully and as solicitously as possible. To suffer ought to be a joy, a matter of honor; one comes to God and asks permission—and God says: Yes, indeed, my little friend. But of course it does not follow from this that one may not suffer. On the contrary, in the profoundest sense one may suffer indescribably, have his thorn in the flesh as well, but despite this, assuming that this suffering cannot be taken away, one can find joy in getting permission to be active in this way, to live for an idea.

It is different with "the apostle": he is constrained.

Here I thoroughly understand why it is so important that I hold myself back and do all I can to prevent being confused with something à la an apostle: precisely because I am able to provide a point from which the qualifications of an apostle may in some measure be scrutinized. But what disarray if I myself were to cause the confusion.

It is not at all surprising that Socrates made such a deep impression upon me.

It may be said that there is something Socratic in me.

Indirect communication was my native element. By means of the very things I experienced, went through, and thought through last summer with respect to direct communication, I have set aside a direct communication (the one on my work as an author, with the category: it is all my education) and have also acquired a deeper understanding of indirect communication, the new pseudonymity.

There is something inexplicably felicitous in the antithesis: Climacus—Anti-Climacus, I recognize so much of myself and my nature in it that if someone else had invented it I would believe that he had secretly observed my inner being. —The merit is not mine, for I did not originally think of it.

$X^2$ A 195   *n.d.,* 1849

« **6533**

*The category* for my undertaking is: to *make men aware* of the essentially Christian, but this accounts for the repeated statement: I am not that,[2554] for otherwise there is confusion. My task is to get men deceived—within the meaning of truth—into religious commitment, which they have cast off, but I do not have authority; instead of authority I use the very opposite, I say: the whole undertaking is for my own discipline and education.[2555] This again is a genuinely Socratic approach. Just as he was the ignorant one, so here: instead of being the teacher, I am the one who is being educated.

$x^2$ A 196   *n.d.,*  1849

« **6534**

[*In margin:* Concerning the Preface to "Practice in Christianity"]

It is also part of my task to present the essentially Christian so high that I judge myself—and then, quite consistently, also do it myself.

That is what happened in the original preface to "Practice in Christianity." This original preface is in fact the right one; an outline of another on a scrap of paper together with "Practice in Christianity" is not to be used.

So it happened in that preface. It is also lenient. The pseudonym is rigorousness; he judges—whom? Me, the editor. But I acknowledge this myself in the preface.

Right! Here I acknowledge my nature again. There is a far off chord of the melancholy of irony. Ironically, the converse is also commonly characteristic of the convert, who judges everybody but himself, while here no one is judged but myself. It is a spiritual skirmish.

See 55, middle, in this journal [i.e., $x^2$ A 204].

$x^2$ A 199   *n.d.,*  1849

« **6535** *About "The Sickness unto Death"*

Perhaps there ought to have been, as first intended, a little postscript by the editor, for example:

The Editor's Postscript

This book seems to be written by a physician; I, the editor, am not the physician, I am one of those sick.

As mentioned, it was contemplated; in fact, in my desk, there are several outlines for such a postscript from that time, but the fact is that at the time I did not as yet have as deep an understanding as I do now of the significance of the new pseudonym. Furthermore (as is also noted in the journal [i.e., $x^1$ A 422] from the time *The Sickness unto Death* was printed), I feared that it would be misinterpreted in various ways, as if I myself were afraid and wanted to keep myself on the outside and so on.

Now I understand perfectly that an editor's preface must always accompany the new pseudonym, Anti-Climacus, in which I say: I am striving.

There must be some kind of judgment in Christendom—*aber*, in such a way that I myself am judged. [*In margin:* see p. 50 in this journal] [i.e., $x^2$ A 199].

This is, it may be said, a kind of heroism corresponding to my nature, a synthesis of rigorousness and gentleness.

$x^2$ A 204   *n.d.*, 1849

« **6536**

*Possibility and Actuality*, see p. 52 [i.e., $x^2$ A 202].

We all weep when the pastor preaches about being reconciled with our enemies. Actually to seek reconciliation is regarded as effrontery. Thus Councillor Olsen[2556] regarded it "as unheard of effrontery," was furiously incensed over it, or was when he came home.

$x^2$ A 205   *n.d.*, 1849

« **6537**

[2557]There is a time to be silent, and there is a time to be silent.

That I was cruel is true; that I, thinking myself committed to a higher relationship, not simply for the sake of my virtue, had to be so because of love is a certainty; that you[2558] have suffered indescribably I realize; but that I nevertheless have suffered more, I believe and know. Enough of this.

Your marriage with Schlegel[2559] has now presumably become so firmly established that finally, God be praised, I have the courage to dare that which I do dare. In the hour of our parting, oh, how much would I not have liked to do it—would indeed also have done it—had not your somewhat inconsiderate despair forced me to use cruelty. Awaiting only the moment from that time on, I have always wished for the courage to dare it, for I have always felt that I owed you a debt of gratitude and have honestly observed what you asked me when we parted, "to think of you now and then." For a long time I believed that I ought to remain silent until I died, but I have once again come to realize that perhaps it would be cruel in another way to withhold from you what might possibly give you happiness. —May God only grant that it is of use to you. Now I dare it.

Thank. . . . .

———

This move was occasioned by the impression made upon me by the death of *Etatsraad* Olsen.[2560] The letter was dated November 19, 1849.

The letter to Schlegel read as follows:

"Dear Sir,

The enclosed letter is from me (S. Kierkegaard) to—your wife. You yourself must now decide whether or not to give it to her. I cannot, after all, very well defend approaching her, least of all now when she is yours and for the reason I have never availed myself of the opportunity that has presented itself or perhaps has been presented for a number of years.

It is my belief that a small item of information about her relationship with me [*in S.K.'s draft:* concerning my relationship with her] might now be of use to her. If you disagree, may I ask you to return the letter to me unopened [*in draft:* but also inform her of this].

[*In draft:* I have wanted to take this step, to which I felt myself religiously obligated, and in writing, because I fear that my pronounced personality, which probably had too strong an effect at one time, might once again have too strong an effect and thus in either one way or another be disturbing.

I have the honor to remain etc.,

S.K."

———

I then received a moralizing and indignant epistle from the esteemed gentleman and the letter to her unopened.

———

Your father's death has changed and made up my mind for me. I had thought otherwise.

———

Cruel I was, that is true. Why? Indeed, *you* do not know that. Silent I have been, that is certain. Only God knows what I have suffered—may God grant that I do not, even now, speak too soon after all!

Marry I could not. Even if you were still free, I could not.

However, you have loved me, as I have you. I owe you much—and now you are married. All right, I offer you for the second time what I can and dare and ought to offer you: reconciliation [*in earlier drafts, first*: my love, that is to say my friendship; *later*: friendship, *and finally*: reconciliation. *One draft contains the following*: P.S. I had really expected you to have taken this step. When one is so absolutely in the right as was your late father, for example, with respect to me, then I know very well who ought to take the first step. It never occurred to me to doubt, and I took it once. With you the matter is somewhat different.]

I do this in writing in order not to surprise or overwhelm you. Perhaps my personality did once have too strong an effect; that must not happen again. But for the sake of God in Heaven, please give serious consideration to whether you dare become involved in this, and if so, whether you prefer to speak with me at once or would rather exchange some letters first.

If your answer is "No"—would you then please remember for the sake of a better world that I took this step as well.

In any case, as in the beginning so until now, sincerely and completely devoted, your

S.K.

[Address:
To
Mrs. Regine Schlegel.

I do not know the date on which I broke the engagement, but on this sheet of paper, which dates from November, 1849, I have written down the facts immediately surrounding it that I do remember; I have found these dates by reading through *Fædrelandet* for the period in question.

October 11 or 18
10/31

They performed *The White Lady*[2561] at the theater on the evening of the day it took place, and I was there to find somebody[2562] I had to meet. Sunday, October 17, Mynster[2563] preached. On Thursday the 21st, *Kean*[2564] was performed, and Printzlau was the guest actor. I was at the theater.

My first letter from Berlin[2565] is dated October 31.

───

*One last step concerning "Her."*
November 1849.

cf. Journal
$NB^{14}$ p. 65 [$x^2$ A 210]

It is my unalterable will that my writings, after my death, be dedicated to her and to my late father. She must belong to history.

*Letters*, no. 239  1849

### « 6538  *A Further Step with Respect to "Her"*[2566]

I wrote a letter to Schlegel with an enclosure for her and received his answer[2567] and the other letter unopened. Everything is found in a packet* in her tall cupboard[2568] in a white envelope labeled: About Her. It was November 19.

It was like this.

In view of the possibility that her father's death[†] may have led her to expect an approach[2569] on my part (something about which I perhaps have additional data), I once again took up the idea. For the second time I let a poet[2570] try his hand at the task and her situation and found that a sisterly relationship was a possibility, which probably would make her happy, and that would make me happy, always with the understanding that her marriage, and especially to Schlegel, was the highest benefaction toward me. Then, too, the whole matter may well come up again sometime if *qua* author I need to repeat it.[2571] My conflict was a religious one. To be deceived by a scoundrel was in her favor. Yet she was carried away in her desperate declaration of love, of wanting to die,[2572] her religious entreaties, etc.[‡]—she who now is married—and I unmarried. —I submitted to this view; notes with regard to this are found in journal $NB^{12}$ [i.e., $x^1$ A 542–682; $x^2$ A 1–68].[2573]

Then I acted[§] decisively, motivated by the following:

(1) A whole life is perhaps too great a criterion for a woman. It can give me satisfaction to preserve intact all my devotion to her and let my author-career glorify her name etc.—but how can it really help her if she or I must first be dead, and what does a woman really care about historical fame. Such faithfulness is almost cruel; it would be better for her if I were a bit less faithful and she got some good from it during her lifetime.

(2) I feared that it might be pride on my part that kept me from

action, that I was unwilling to expose myself to the unpleasantness involved. Well, then I dared not refrain from acting. As far as approaching her was concerned, I knew that refraining from doing so could not be due to my pride, for I am only all too confident in that relationship. No, the touchy element was really Schlegel. Consequently I made my approach to him, and he used the occasion for a moral lecture.

Now it is done. Praise God that I did it. At a later date I may have had such thoughts: you ought to have done it, and then it would have been too late. Now I can breathe. All lectures of that kind make the matter easier. Her prayer and pious entreaties—yes, that was a potent force.

———

In other ways it is impossible [*corrected from:* difficult] to do anything. I dare not be personal. To approach her personally—the minute she hears my voice I take the risk of her completely misinterpreting my approach before I get a chance to explain what I want.

———

Now the matter is finished. One thing is sure—without Schlegel's consent not one word. And he has declared himself as definitively as possible. It is in his hands now.

$x^2$ A 210    *n.d.,* 1849

« **6539**

*In margin of 6538* ($x^2$ A 210):
And of course not one word to her about winning Schlegel over to my idea.[2574] No, never! I know how to respect a marriage. I discovered this possibility for her and rejoiced to gladden her heart with it, enhancing her marriage—only God knows whether I demanded too much of myself by being so prodigal with myself—it was supposed to be a gift from Schlegel to her. If he had understood me, if he had believed in me, then I would have become practically a servant in his hands. —But now the affair is really ended. *And never have I felt so light and happy and free about this matter, so totally myself again, as just now after making this sacrificial step! For now I understand that I have God's consent to let her go and to take care of myself, complying only with her last plea: "to think of her sometimes," in this way keeping her for history and eternity.*

$x^2$ A 211    November 21, 1849

« **6540**

*Addition to 6538* ($x^2$ A 210):

*In the same packet there is also a quarto volume: "My Relationship to Her, August 24, 1849, somewhat poetic." And in a little packet in gray paper, labeled "to be burned after my death," lying in a little drawer in my desk, there is an older but similar interpretation of my relationship to her, about whom there are also various notes in the journals from two years ago (1848) and last year (1849), probably in older journals as well.

$x^2$ A 212    *n.d.,* 1849

« **6541**

*Addition to 6540* ($x^2$ A 212):

Since I have never known the date of the breaking of the engagement, I made an attempt to figure it out. This attempt is on a scrap of paper in the older packet, the one in gray paper lying in the little drawer in my desk, labeled: to be destroyed after my death.

$x^2$ A 213    *n.d.,* 1849

« **6542**

*Addition to 6540* ($x^2$ A 212):

A copy of my letter to Schlegel and the one enclosed to her[2575] is also in an envelope in one of the two small drawers in the high desk.[2576]

$x^2$ A 214    *n.d.,* 1849

« **6543**

[†] *In margin of 6538* ($x^2$ A 210):

To me it was also remarkable that Councillor Olsen's death[2577] coincided with my intention to make a turn away from the authorship and appear in the character of a religious author from the very beginning (see a scrap of paper[2578] in journal NB[13] [i.e., $x^2$ A 69–163]. And when I appear as such with the whole authorship as religious, a dedication would essentially be related to "her."[2579]

$x^2$ A 215    *n.d.*

« **6544**

[‡] *In margin of 6538* ($x^2$ A 210):

Yes, but she also has a great responsibility toward me because of her misuse of pious entreaties;[2580] in a certain sense she is to blame because by a desperate recklessness she forced the issue so high after it had been resolved in as humble a way for me as possible! A responsibility which first became really clear with her becoming engaged[2581] so soon afterwards.

$x^2$ A 216   n.d.

### « 6545

[§] *In margin of 6538* ($x^2$ A 210):
If it could have taken place, the reconciliation with "her" would have occurred simultaneously with the *Three Discourses* (The High Priest, The Publican, The Woman Who Was a Sinner), which contains in the preface—for sake of repetition[2582] of the entire authorship—a repetition of the preface to the *Two Upbuilding Discourses* of 1843, a book I knew she read at the time.

$x^2$ A 217   n.d., 1849

### « 6546

If there suddenly were to be a strong upsurge of interest in religion, I imagine that Goldschmidt,[2583] always the business man, would eventually initiate a devotional magazine for home use, Christian anthologies, and the like. I would bet four shillings on it. It would contribute to disclosing what a pastor is actually understood to be these days, for there is no doubt but that Goldschmidt would be able to do it just as well or better than many pastors. Of course, he reads a little in that field and uses his imagination for the rest—and thus we have an analogy to that temperance-preacher[2584] who gets four "schnaps" for every member he recruits for the society.

$x^2$ A 228   n.d., 1849

### « 6547

The expression "the authors' author," which I myself once used[2585] because it was unavoidable and later was appropriated by a few others—this expression actually is descriptive of the plus that I do have. I actually am an author for authors; I do not relate directly to a public; no, *qua* author I make others creative. That again accounts for my suffering, for as long as this is not understood, the more-than-ordinary in me becomes a minus instead of a plus.

Incidentally, there is something ridiculous about Martensen.[2586] With the aid of mediocrity it will finally turn out that he becomes classical—and I am labored. Thanks for that! Just note whether his work is related in the remotest way to making others creative!

$x^2$ A 242   n.d., 1849

## « 6548 *An Accounting of My Action Against* The Corsair[2587]

A. The consequences for those involved

(1) It was a matter of separating P. L. Møller and Goldschmidt and getting G. away from *The Corsair*—this was done.[2588]

(2) It was a relief for many of those who were being attacked to be placed in another situation when I jumped in—and from that very elevation to be immortalized and eulogized.

(3) With respect to presenting the religious, which is to be emphasized, things were prepared for an awakening of awareness, and if one is going to include the common man, the surest thing to do is first of all to let him make a mistake so that he himself gets to understand later that he has made a mistake, for the common man is always good-natured and is won over most positively when he is regretful; one must not struggle with him over power but give him the power and then get him to misuse it; it gives him satisfaction that he had the power and he is all the more willing to regret the misuse of it.

B. The Consequences for me

(1) The satisfaction that I was true to myself and my idea and did not shrink from any consequences but ventured farthest out. This satisfaction tallies with my historical significance; and the same action has extended the future of my name considerably.[*]

(2) When I gave up being an esthetic author and as a consequence lost this support in maintaining indirect communication: it once again was maintained although in another manner—namely, by creating this opposition to me.

(3) If I had not taken this action, I would have escaped completely the *double*-danger[2589] connected with the essentially Christian, I would have gone on thinking of the difficulties involved with Christianity as being purely interior to the self.

(4) It has become my own education[2590] and development.

(5) As author I have gotten a new string in my instrument, have been enabled to hit notes I never would have dreamed of otherwise.

(6) I have achieved "actuality"[2591] in a much stricter sense of the word.

$X^2$ A 251    *n.d.,* 1849

## « 6549

[*] *In margin of 6548* ($X^2$ A 251):

After all, I had set the tone of irony[2592]—what a satire on me, then, what a devastating judgment, if I had not done everything to prevent the opinion that *The Corsair* is the same kind of irony, that the two acknowledge each other, *The Corsair* immortalizes him[2593] as the master. And from the Christian point of view, what a judgment on me if I had been contemporary to such demoralization and was either too stupid to see it or too cowardly to act.

$x^2$ A 252   *n.d.*

« **6550**

[*In margin:* About Peter]
                    *About Peter*[2594]
Now Peter is going to have his say about the authorship.

How is one to react to that? I know very well that he has merely read here and there in some of the books—that is enough for him. (N.B. This is based on his own words.) Then he took it upon himself to give an address at the convention.[2595] But it so happened that the contemplated address could not be used—so he gets the idea the night before to say something about Martensen and Søren and R. Nielsen.

The lecture was given—and then printed.[2596] If one remonstrates that it lacks genuine knowledge, the answer is: Well, Good Lord, it was only a convention address. But why print it, then? Not only that, but the very fact that it is given as an address first, and then printed, falsely ascribes even more importance to it.

How tragic! In such a little country where I still have not yet had any reviews,[2597] everyone avails himself of my books to have an opportunity to say something. My cause thereby goes backward instead of forward. Of course it is "not the time and place" to enter into the whole more subtle concretion I have given the problem. I am flattened into a maundering mediocrity—I could just as well have not written anything.

And now the tragic delusion that it is my brother "who, after all, must know all about it in detail."

$x^2$ A 256   *n.d.,* 1849

« **6551**

Another consequence of living in a little country is that one's name may become so well known that the mere mention of it is taken by everyone or by many to be an allusion to the person. So also with my name: Søren.[2598] Yes, one's title, or whatever one wants to call it, can become that familiar. At one time the *Berlingske Tidende* published over a three- or six-month period a serial story from Swedish in which the character appeared under the name of Crazy Magister or Crazy

Preacher. There were many who were led by association of ideas to think that it alluded to me. (It was "A Night at Bullar Lake."[2599])

$x^2$ A 260   n.d., 1849

« 6552

[*In margin:* Martensen]

> An example of how not to preach, yes, of how it is far better to be silent and merely read Scripture aloud.

Martensen[2600] preaches on the self-chosen text:[2601] Let the dead bury their dead. And what does he do? Presto! He gets involved in the observation that whole epochs and generations simply buried their dead, spiritually speaking.

Well, thanks for that. Whole generations, epochs, millions, millions—what wonderful dissipation. Where does that leave me, the single individual, with my minuscule act; it is more or less the same whether I do it or not.

$x^2$ A 261   n.d., 1849

« 6553

[*In margin:* Peter's remarks at the convention]

> *Peter's Remarks at the Convention*[2602]

After all, there is some confusion-compounding to take a passage from Paul and then exhibit Martensen and me as the two positions.[2603] For if Martensen is to be compared with Paul, then Paul (and also his σωφροσύνη[2604]) becomes ecstasy pure and simple. The Martensenian-Petrian concept of composure is a partially irreligious concept of mediocrity and indolent comfortableness.

Moreover, Peter should also have pointed out that it is especially difficult these days to represent ecstasy. For mediocrity, worldly haggling, etc., are preponderant. It should also be pointed out that my ecstasy is characterized by equally great composure. The very fact that I use pseudonyms, invented characters (consequently not myself) to represent the ecstatic, while in the upbuilding discourses I myself speak gently and quietly. The difference between the category of the single individual as it is used by the pseudonyms and as I use it, etc.

But what does Peter care about all this. He self-complacently expounds to mediocrity (and of course to the jubilation of the rural clergy) that there are two trends (that is, the achievers)—and they are one-sided; but we, who achieve nothing, we are of the truth, and we are also the majority. Just believe me, I know; should I not know it—after all, I am eight years older than my brother.

$x^2$ A 273   n.d., 1849

« **6554**

[*In margin:* About Peter]

*About Peter*[2605]

During the long time I have been an author, Peter found no occasion to express his opinion. But scarcely does it appear that I am going to be treated as somewhat important than he promptly gets busy unloading (and presumably will also make an offer to me on behalf of the party), motivated especially by the fine chance to score a cheap point by ridiculing R. N.[2606] (a very rewarding business just now) and to punish him as a warning against being a follower—he who himself has been a follower and copier of Grundtvig to the point of ludicrous affectation.

The whole affair[2607] has been very painful to me. [*In margin:* See p. 158, bottom, in this journal (i.e., $x^2$ A 280).] Peter was completely devoid of sympathy all the time I was suffering rabble-persecution; literally not one word along that line was either spoken or written by him; we have never kept in close touch, but from that time on he pulled back completely. He knows that I have financial worries[2608]—never one word about it. He knows that I suffer from being disproportioned to the country—never a word about it.

But eventually he sees his chance. He assumes a standpoint superior to the two positions: Martensen—S. K. (for he declares quite properly that he is not mediating between us [*in margin:* His words are very singular: he does not wish to mediate between two sinful men; in ordinary human language this would be: I, a sinful man, do not want to take it upon myself to mediate between two men], but actually his presentation implies that he merely wants to avail himself of these two positions—*ergo,* he is supposedly on a higher plane). He lashes out in popular fashion with all the sloppy jargon and thus in half an hour is capable of judging seven years of work. He enthusiastically proclaims the supremacy of the rural clergy and the dominion of mediocrity. He takes the precaution of hiding behind the excuse that it was a rush job. He cashes in on the illusion: I, as the author's elder brother, am surely well informed (which is such a frightful lie that he certainly should have pointed it out); he ties my hands, for I cannot make a move without the world shouting: Scandalous! And he remains the nice fellow, for it is indeed favorable publicity for me, something I in another way have to suffer again, since it will be called partiality. He gets me into trouble with R. Nielsen, who possibly believes that I am jabbing at him from behind in this attack on him, and when R. N. attacks Peter, he no doubt will think that I am jabbing at him from behind R. N. —I do not think that all this was clear to Peter, but he should have been clear on part of it and would have been, too, if he had not been coddled into smug self-complacency by these rural preachers and convention-goers, so coddled that he even fell victim to a kind of stupid joviality and thought he was doing me a favor, although he should have understood that to do that he must apply a criterion and actually elucidate my work as an author, and least of all connive with illusions and numerical determination by men.

$x^2$ A 275    *n.d.*, 1849

« **6555**

As I have always said, only a dead man can rule the state of affairs in Denmark. Dissoluteness and envy and stupidity are preponderant everywhere. If I died now, my life would have an extraordinary influence; even much of what I have just roughly dashed off in the journals would acquire great significance and influence, for then men would accept me and could concede to me what was and is my due.

$x^2$ A 277    *n.d.*, 1849

« **6556**

If only I had physical energy now, just a little, I could do several things. It is burdensome and sad that much that is interpreted summarily as pride and the like is quite simply lack of physical energy. I am so weak that I practically have to use mental energy even in things of slightest importance.

$x^2$ A 278    *n.d.*, 1849

« **6557** *About Peter*[2609]

Peter came down in December. He told me that he had delivered an address at the last convention[2610] where he had talked about Martensen and me and was surprised that I had not heard it. He went on to say that in the same lecture he actually had directed his remarks against R. Nielsen[2611] and a certain H. H.[2612] At that point I told him that I myself am H. H. He was somewhat stunned by that, for he very likely had not read any farther in the little book, fully convinced that it was not by me. We discussed it a little, then Peter said: Well, there isn't much point in talking further about it, for I have to write up the address first. So he wrote up the address. He dealt very briefly with H. H. and also observed that he certainly had a remarkable similarity to S. K. God knows what he actually said at the convention.

It is an awkward situation, especially when one wants to be a man of conscience etc.

Lately, in a way that at least jars me, he has gotten hold of the Scriptural phrase: "All is yours."[2613] He also uses it in the address. Once in an earlier conversation I reproached him, saying that there was a certain integrity which requires one to give the source[2614] of certain thoughts and expositions, to which he answered: It is not at all necessary, for "All is yours" applies to the true believer.

$$x^2 \; A \; 280 \quad n.d., \; 1849$$

« **6558**

[*Penciled in margin:* Peter[2615]]
*Dr. Kierkegaard's Half-hour Address
at the Recent Convention*[2616]

---

When the proceedings were all over at the recent convention there happened to be a half-hour remaining. What is to be done with it; "What shall we do?" very likely was the question asked. I suggest that they should have made it a subject for discussion. In that event one probably would have read in the *Kirketidende*: The question of how the remaining half-hour should be used was the occasion for a lively and entertaining discussion, in which almost all the Brethren and all the Grundtvigians took part; it lasted two and one half hours.

But the chairman (F. Fenger,[2617] Grundtvigian), who always knows a way out and always has the chief spokesman (Dr. K., Grundtvigian) in reserve, knows a way out here as well. He requests Dr. K. to fill out the time with a little lecture.

Dr. K. steps forward. Just by chance he had had a half-hour the night before to prepare for such an event. It was in fact a happy coincidence. A half-hour's time, a half-hour's preparation—charming!

Strangely enough, the subject of his lecture is: two striking phenomena in the most recent period of Danish literature: Magister K.'s well-known books and Prof. M's *Dogmatik*[2618] and work done in dogmatics. This is striking enough; for these two striking phenomena, after all, are not from a distant historical past, already judged and rated (something like this is best suited to a half-hour lecture) but are contemporary phenomena which, if there is anything striking about them at all, are best suited for a bit more earnest and extended treatment.

"By gazing at the history of the Church" Dr. K. has discovered that there are two paths, the path of ecstasy and the path of composure.[2619]

We may add: by gazing at world-history ever since creation he would discover the same thing—and by gazing toward the end of the Church and the world he would discover the same thing. There are two paths: ecstasy and composure. Actually there is still a third: garrulousness, far and away the most traveled road, actually the main thoroughfare from beginning to end, through the history of the Church as well as the history of the world. In other words, the remark about the two paths is an extremely trivial remark: the only new thing is the pretentious form, that Dr. K. has discovered this by gazing at Church history. If he had discovered it by opening up a map, it would have been amusing.

From the standpoint of the two paths Dr. K. now considers the two striking phenomena. The lecture is delivered in a congenial, even conversational tone, is benevolently appreciative of both. Dr. K. knows Prof. M.'s work particularly from the time he was a tutor, but as far as Magister K.'s well-known books are concerned, Dr. K. seems to have only an extremely casual acquaintance with them, a deficiency that is scarcely remedied by the benevolent acknowledgment. For such an estimate of S. K. (who promptly is congenially confused with all the pseudonyms) only a bit of cursory reading is needed in just one of the pseudonyms, hardly that, just as the painters who fabricate the Nürnberg pictures portraying Wellington, Alexander, Roat, etc. do not need to have seen these gentlemen—and yet they get a likeness.

But the affair also has its more serious side. There is a party, a society, which speculates, so to speak, in Dr. K. The scheme is to consolidate the opinion that Dr. K. is an extraordinarily competent person; the speculating, then, consists in computing a certain percentage of profit for all the interested gentlemen who have a man like that in their party. And Dr. K. seems willing enough to go along with it. Now one may willingly and gladly make unusual concessions to Dr. K; but it nevertheless is dubious (just as it is unfair to the actual authors) that Dr. K. almost always avoids an actual criterion, and it is a question whether he has not actually suffered damage from the good fellowship at the convention and other places, along with being spoiled by preoccupation with the easy but rewarding little accomplishments especially loved and appreciated in our day, which has an appetite for bonbons and sweetmeats but is envious of actual competence and hates earnestness and rigorousness.

To deliver a lecture of that sort at a convention—well, there is no objection to that. But why should it be printed? And when it is printed, then the argument is reversed—it becomes more than an ordinary newspaper article. After all, it was delivered at a convention; some country pastors were interested in maintaining this in order, if possible, to become a force by virtue of the lecture, to which, as soon as the criterion is applied, one can only say: O, it was just a trifle, it was only intended to fill up a half-hour at a convention.

Johannes Climacus

S. K.

x⁶ B 130   *n.d.*, 1849

### « 6559 *Protest*²⁶²⁰

In the *Dansk Kirketidende*,²⁶²¹ no.——, Pastor Kierkegaard, B. D., a Grundtvigian known for his unusual competence, has contributed a review of sorts of my books, part of a lecture he delivered at the convention.²⁶²² For reasons too complicated to go into here, I must protest this review or discussion. No attention is paid even to what I so repeatedly have emphasized and so urgently have asked to be observed: that I should not be confused with my pseudonyms, something one would not even need to emphasize in a less busy world or urgently ask to be observed but would matter-of-factly assume would be observed.

What has moved me to take this step is the following. In the first place, in the review or written discussion there are many very appreciative expressions. In the second place, the reviewer, regrettably, is my brother—and for most people the illusion was all too natural: the reviewer is the author's brother, he knows him from his earliest childhood—*ergo**; furthermore he is the older brother, who was already a university student when the other was still going to school—*ergo*. *Ergo*, I must take this step.

S. K.

*his opinion is reliable.

x⁶ B 131   *n.d.*, 1849

### « 6560

Dear Peter,²⁶²³

I have now read your article in *Kirketidenden*.²⁶²⁴ To be honest, it has affected me painfully in more ways than one. But it would lead too far afield to go into detail here. However let me thank you for your article, inasmuch that it was well intended on your part.

If I am to be compared as an author with Martensen,²⁶²⁵ I do think in any case that it would be reasonable to say that only one aspect of me was considered, that I am really an author in a different way and by criteria by which Martensen is not. This, however, is of minor importance. But if I am to be compared with Martensen *qua* author, it does seem to me that the essential difference ought to have been indicated, namely this, that I have sacrificed to an extraordinary extent and that he has profited to an extraordinary extent. And perhaps it ought also to be remembered that Martensen really has no primitivity about him but permits himself to appropriate outright all of German scholarship as his own.

Finally, it seems to me that both for your own sake and for mine you should modify your statements about me. If what you have said is to fit reasonably well, then it must have been said about a few of my pseudonyms. For it really does not apply to me as the author of *Upbuilding Discourses* (my own acknowledged work, which is already sufficiently voluminous). I myself have asked in print that this distinction be observed.[2626] It is important to me, and the last thing I would have wished is that you of all people should in any way have joined in lending credence to a carelessness from which I must suffer often enough as it is.

*Letters,* no. 240 [December, 1849]

### « 6561

The words of John the Baptizer, "I am a voice,"[2627] could be applied to my work as an author. To prevent any mistaken identity and being taken for the extraordinary,[2628] I always withdraw myself, and the voice, that is, what I say, remains. But I always withdraw myself in such a way that I do own up to striving.[2629] Thus I am like a voice, but I always have one more auditor than speakers generally have: myself.[2630]

$X^2$ A 281    *n.d.,* 1849

### « 6562 *About H. H.*[2631]

Peter finds it inconsistent that when one says "Only the person who remains silent becomes a martyr,"[2632] he is in fact saying that. Quite true; *aber,* that happened because I wanted to take a new direction at just that point. You see, my dear Peter, here is a consistency of which you are not aware.

But the book[2633] does in fact hold out the possibility of a martyrdom nevertheless—namely, to be put to death because one has defended the thesis that a man does not have the right to let himself be put to death for the truth, since the contemporaries would regard this as enormous arrogance.

And finally it was and is my view that part of a step such as being put to death for the truth is that one's contemporaries are helped to share the guilt in an appropriate way, an invitation to participate is extended, for otherwise the responsibility is too great.

Incidentally, all this and much more is noted in the journal [i.e., $x^1$ A 281; *also* A 302, A 305] of the period when I published H. H.

But, after all, such things cannot be brought out without betraying the secret machinery; on the other hand I perceive that Peter is not a particularly resourceful *combinateur.*[2634]

$$x^2 \text{ A } 285 \quad n.d., \ 1849$$

« **6563**

[*In margin:* R. Nielsen]

The day before yesterday I took a walk with Nielsen.[2635] It was the last time this year. The conversation turned in such a way that he himself acknowledged that there was some personal reason, at least in part, for his changing his course. "He felt himself to be left out in the cold compared with Martensen; for several years now Martensen had been occupying the place in The Royal Society[2636] which belonged to him," and so on. Well, it is good that he himself says this. I am hoping both that actuality will properly shape him up and that through his relationship to me he will come to a completely different view of life, and then something good might come out of it. The fact that he himself now acknowledges it indicates that some change has already taken place in him.

$$x^2 \text{ A } 298 \quad n.d., \ 1849$$

« **6564**

The *Berlingske Tidende*[2637] trumpets Ørsted's book (*Aanden i Naturen*)[2638] as a work which will clear up the relations between faith and science, a work which "even when it is polemical always uses the finest phrases of the cultured urbanite." One is tempted to answer: The whole book from first to last is scientifically—that is, philosophically-scientifically—insignificant, and even when it tries to be most significant it always moves in the direction of the most insignificant phrases of triviality.

$$x^2 \text{ A } 302 \quad n.d., \ 1849$$

## « 6565

Just as a basso at times can carry the tune so deep that one cannot hear it at all but only by standing close to him and observing some convulsive movements of the mouth and throat is sure that something is happening—so also Grundtvig[2639] at times goes so deep into history that one sees nothing at all; but deep it is!

$X^2$ A 307   *n.d.*, 1849

## « 6566

When an author, in order to delineate more specifically the main point of his entire authorship viewed as a whole in its consecutive steps at various times, in order to point out particular factors and dialectical particularities, uses poetic writers (pseudonyms), "poetized thinkers," who pursue a conclusion unilaterally to its uttermost, when this author himself as emphatically as possible declares this to be the case (see my postscript to *Concluding P.*[2640]), when he urgently requests anyone who wants to make any comment on the matter to distinguish between the pseudonym and himself (see my postscript to *Conc. P.*[2641]), well, then the author has done everything to prevent misunderstanding—but of course by jumbling these together, me and the pseudonyms, there is a perhaps desired chance for every lightweight pate to find occasion to say that I am one-sided—which is not demonstrated—but he believes that the pseudonym is one-sided and thus it is I myself who said it.* In this vein a theological graduate, Hiorth by name, came leaping into Scharling and Engeltoft's *Tidsskrift.*[2642] Of course, a speeder like this has no time for such niggling distinctions.

Generally speaking anyone's judgment of me and my cause only leads to confusion if he is not honest enough toward the cause and himself and me to admit to himself that he has met an author from whom something can really be learned. If the situation is really such that any and every student, graduate, practically any and every professional and journalistic hack can judge the fruit of my consummate study and industry simply by paging a bit in one of my books, then I really am a fool, I who keep on working with unflagging perseverance year after year and yet get no farther than that which everyone else knows better.

*Note. Apart from what objections I may have to Prof. R. Nielsen's[2643] use of my pseudonym, Johannes Climacus,[2644] he does nevertheless have the merit of having refrained from confusing the pseudonym with me.

$X^6$ B 127   *n.d.*, 1849–50

« **6567**

*An Urgent Request*
by
S. K.

Once and for all I have solemnly asked[2645] that this be observed if someone wants to cite or quote any of my writings: if it is a pseudonymous work, cite or quote the pseudonym. As a concerned author I carry a great responsibility, and this is why I willingly do everything I can to insure that the communication is true. On the other hand, it is so easy to comply that I feel one should have no objection to indulging me in this. It is the fruit of long reflection, the why and how of my use of pseudonyms; I easily could write whole books about it. But if this distinction is not observed in citing and quoting, confusion and sometimes meaninglessness results.

To be sure, I have momentarily thought I could take on the responsibility of raising an objection every time it still happens, partly because Danish literature is so meager, and also because in a way I have stood (or been placed) outside of the literature. But for one thing it cannot help that I raise an objection afterward, for when it is done it is done, and for another I perceive that one cannot take such a responsibility on himself.

So I limit myself to a repeated urgent request. I feel very strongly about it, and I urgently ask that the request be heeded.

$X^6$ B 245   *n.d.*, 1849–51

« **6568**

In order to bear mental tension such as mine, I needed diversion, the diversion of chance contacts on the streets and alleys,[2646] because association with a few exclusive individuals is actually no diversion— now this has been made impossible, for diversion is impossible when one is recognized by all, who constantly, almost frenetically remind me of only one thing.

Formerly I had the consolation of taking to the country[2647] any time I wished, living in idyllic peace and quiet, keeping people somewhat at a distance by my reputation in the capital, and delighting in the easy way I could converse with everyone. Now this too is denied me.

A marked man, I can live only in a larger city where there are others who have an idea of what such things mean; already it is actually unfeasible to associate with the middle class in the city, since they have a quite different concept of such a thing, but the country folk do not know what is what.

And all this is the result of living in a country which is no country at all but a provincial market town.

$x^2$ A 315    n.d., 1849

« **6569**

[Letter to Henrik Lund[2648] about migratory birds.]

*Letters,* no. 262, April 12, 1850

« **6570**

Strictly speaking, the way Peter defended himself when efforts were made to remove him from office[2649] was not Christian but legal. His as well as the tacit claim of all Grundtvigians was that they are the only true Christians—*ergo,* they have to protest the whole concept of Christendom and the state church. Then the state church declares: You must either do it—or resign your office. He answers: Neither one; if you wish to dismiss me, that is your affair. But thereby he indirectly recognizes the state church and the concept of Christendom: that we all as such are Christians. That is, he hangs on to the concept of the state church just as hard as any one of its champions if he happens to disagree with it on a particular point.

$x^2$ A 338    n.d., 1850

« **6571**

> *The Title:*
> *A Contribution to the Introduction*
> *of Christianity into Christendom*[2650]

is categorically correct; nothing is said about Denmark or Germany or Sweden etc., nor about whether it is the present or the past—no, it is a purely dialectical definition: the relation between the two concepts: Christianity—and Christendom, with the purpose of introducing Christianity.

It is spiritual fencing.

$x^2$ A 345    n.d., 1850

« **6572**

*In margin of 6571* ($x^2$ A 345):

This observation was found on an old scrap of paper lying with the folder of writings.

But this title was not used; it if were used, it would, after all, be merely poetic, and that is too much. The original title was used, *Practice in Christianity, A Venture.*

x² A 346    n.d.

« **6573**

It is sad to have an eye such as mine. I saw R. Nielsen's[2651] ideal possibility—but do not dare say it to him directly, nor can it help to do so, for then it will turn into something else entirely and in the strictest sense not be the ideal. He did not see it. I see the possibility in Stilling,[2652] and here it is the same. So also with a number of others. I yearningly anticipate the moment when an existential identity will appear in our setting. Now if this were something reserved for only the exceptionally talented—but this is a possibility for anyone—and yet it is so rare!

x² A 352    n.d., 1950

« **6574  On Prof. Nielsen's Relationship to My Pseudonym Johannes Climacus**[2653]

### A.
### What I Cannot Approve

1. "There must be no direct teaching"—in the pseudonymous writers this has found adequate expression in the abeyance of direct teaching. A $\mu\epsilon\tau\acute{\alpha}\beta\alpha\sigma\iota\varsigma$ $\epsilon\acute{\iota}\varsigma$ $\mathring{\alpha}\lambda\lambda o$ $\gamma\acute{\epsilon}\nu o\varsigma$[2654] is made in relation to teaching directly; the idea is reduplicated in the form—everything is changed into a poet-communication by a poor individual human being like most people,[2655] an experimental humorist—everything is situated in existence.

It is different with Prof. Nielsen.[2656] His presentation, his address, are more or less direct teaching, especially if compared with the pseudonym's. The numerous scholarly allusions recalled by the professor are reminiscent of "the professor," and it becomes more or less a kind of doctrine that there must be no direct teaching.

From the standpoint of the idea, the cause has retrogressed, because it has acquired a less consistent form.

2. In the pseudonymous writings the content of Christianity has been compressed to its least possible minimum\* simply in order to give all the more powerful momentum toward becoming a Christian

---

\*Note. This has been found strange, naturally, by our industrious Prof. Scharling[2657] (who now tries to correct both Prof. N. and me, and also Stilling,[2658] without, it seems, having first tried to master the subject, or perhaps after having tried in vain).

and to keep the nervous energy all the more intensively concentrated so as to be able to master the confusion and prevent the intrusion of "the parenthetical."

It is different with Prof. N. With him the contents expand. He goes into an investigation of each particular miracle etc. etc.—in short, he goes into details. At the same time it is made difficult to provide momentum and to maintain the qualitative tension, because doubt and reflection are essentially related to this dispersive trend, to the details, and they get the upper hand as soon as one gets involved in them.

From the standpoint of the idea there has been a loss, and the tension of the issue has been weakened—and yet no doubt many have now become aware of the cause.

3. The new direction must be away from science and scholarship, away from theory. The pseudonym does not concentrate upon this thought; the pseudonym himself is continuously this new direction; the entire work is repulsion and the new direction is into existential inwardness.

It is quite different with Prof. N. Here this thought is dwelt upon, details are gone into, the same thought is followed through in relation to the particular theological disciplines—sheer lingering. But in the very second there is one second of lingering, science and scholarship are on the way to becoming the stronger, for science and scholarship are and consist in *lingering,* whereas faith is itself the impetus of the existential away from that from which one is to move. But in the very second of lingering, theory thrusts itself forward and begins to take shape, for theory is and consists in lingering. And with Prof. N. the new direction is not taken; it does not find its expression qualitatively different from all theorizing. A kind of concluding paragraph is formulated so one can always remember that a new direction is to be taken. N. is much too professionally serious to be able to take a new direction as that jesting Joh. Climacus can in all consistency, because "to turn," "to turn away," so one always takes himself back, is impossible without the unity of jest and earnestness.

From the standpoint of the idea, there is a loss—although no doubt more have now become aware of the cause.

4. The significance of the pseudonym, as of all the pseudonyms, is: the communication of interiority. In the infinite distance of the idea from actuality, yet in another sense so close to it, interiority becomes audible. But there is no finite relation to actuality, no one is attacked, no name is named; no one is under obligation to appropriate this

communication, no one is constrained, although it does not follow thereby that no one by himself has a truth-duty toward this communication.

In this context, Prof. N.'s attack on Prof. Martensen is not a forward step, especially the way it was done. Some individual theses were drawn out of the pseudonym and were transferred into subjects of dispute: whether Prof. M. is right or the pseudonym. In this way "that poor individual human being, a human being like most people," the pseudonym (as represented by these few propositions), is changed into a kind of assistant professor who is brought into a learned dispute with the eminent Professor M. The qualitative difference is thereby lost: that it is a communication of interiority which, as the pseudonym has done it, "without authority" must be made audible at the distance of the idea or be appealed to with authority. But it is not the subject of any discussion or dispute. To want to debate about interiority means that one does not really have interiority or has it only to a certain degree, i.e., not inwardly—which one can learn from Joh. Climacus.

The no less speculative Prof. N. cannot be in the right as opposed to Prof. Martensen, but in terms of the idea, there has been a loss for the pseudonym.

5. If I were to speak of Prof. N.'s relation to my entire work as an author or to the pseudonym on the whole, or if I were to go into the details of the professor's writings, I would have very many objections. But then this matter, which is already prolix enough, would become even more prolix. But there is, I think, one single observation that ought to be made. Even if Prof. N. himself was not immediately aware of his use of the pseudonyms, he gradually became aware of it; but to what extent will an ordinary reader of his works be able to see it, and I am probably the best reader. Essentially it is a matter of indifference. I mention it simply so it may not seem, if someone else raises the point, as if there were a definite solidarity between Prof. N. and me, inasmuch as I, who must have seen it very readily, had said nothing about it.

———

From the standpoint of the idea something has been lost; the matter is no longer at a point of intensity as with the pseudonym, the issue not in such qualitative tension, but instead Prof. Martensen has been attacked and a dispute about faith has been sought. But so it goes in the world. A view is always truest the first time; the next time it has already become less true, but then it extends itself, gains more and more attention and acceptability [*in penciled parentheses:* long since it has been completely victorious, is accepted, respected, esteemed by all, and now it has become utter nonsense.]

I had something else in mind that Prof. N. could have done, something simpler and commoner than what he has done—but it is just the simple and common that is great, but for that a very uncommon character is always needed, and that is why one is not justified in requiring it of anyone, and I may very well be under obligation to thank Prof. N. for what he has done. The simple and the common—that would have been something great. Prof. N. might have said in an altogether direct little explanation: These writings have convinced me: what the author's views are, whether he is attacking or defending Christianity, I am unable to determine—just that is their artistry. Here there is and must not be any question of imitating that artistry, for that would still be something halfway; it is impossible for anyone to do this more than half as well as he, the first. No, whether the author gets angry about it or not, I will convert everything into direct communication and myself into a serviceable interpreter. This intensive dialectical tension and coyness yield only to assault, but over against an assault it is defenseless, for its own point is simply: to have no position. Well, so I am the man who knows how to use the assault of "faith" quickly and well. This would have been the qualitative $\mu\epsilon\tau\acute{\alpha}\beta\alpha\sigma\iota\varsigma$ $\epsilon\acute{\iota}\varsigma$ $\ἄ\lambda\lambda o$ $\gamma\acute{\epsilon}\nu o\varsigma$ of "the second," whereby he himself again would become a first. If he had done that, had had the resignation and character for that, he would have been greater than the pseudonym. Prof. N. did something else. His performance bears the stamp of wanting "also" to be like the pseudonym, at times even wanting to "go beyond." That was a mistake, For it is a mistake for a second person to want "also" that which to such a degree is designed for singular genius, even if this second had even greater capacities than Prof. N. and even greater perseverance and industry than Prof. N.

### B.

What I must approve—no, this is not a suitable expression, for in no sense am I an authority. But to my mind it is rather unusual that an older person who long since has assured for himself the certain prospects of the well-traveled highway has the energy and the desire to want to begin working so industriously and intensely on something that previously had concerned him only as being utterly different. To

my mind it is rather unusual that a contemporary, in relation to another contemporary, although he also exposes himself to unpleasantness from various quarters, will use so much time and energy to be of
service, even though I consider the service, regarded from the standpoint of the idea, to have its dubious aspects. Youth, imagination,
possibility—rare enough in the young—just these qualities are even
more unusual in an older person. One service, and that not so small,
Prof. N. has given indisputably: he has called attention to my cause,
which others hereabout have in the politest ways of the world (by
making me into such an utterly curious, singular, and very *merkwürdigt*
genius and the like) tried to smuggle out of the way, far, far away into
the distant realms of the idiosyncratic and of *ausserdienstliche Merkwürdigheder,* [2659] which I have seen very clearly but have not troubled about
because of confidence in my cause.

Since this is the case, someone might expect me to express my
thanks to Prof. N. in much stronger terms. This I can very well understand, but I also understand that such a person does not have what I
have, my conception of the rightness and the victoriousness of the
cause that I have the honor to serve, even less my understanding that
the secret of the cause is that it will come again—indeed, the greater
the attempts to let it pass over, something I myself have cunningly
contributed to at times, the more earnestly and victoriously it will come
again.

## C.

Attempts have been made to explain Prof. Nielsen's intervention
against Prof. M. simply on the basis of personal antagonism. It seems
to me that another explanation comes just as close. To write a dogmatics in a limited setting like ours, one that even claims to "heed the signs
of the times," [2660] and then try to ignore completely my work as an
author or even try to sweep it away with a few casual words in a preface
to a dogmatics which, strangely enough, indirectly bears unmistakable
marks that there is considerable awareness of the existence of my work
as a writer—yes, this is strange. I do not know of anything better to do
than to smile, because I have nothing to say on this occasion. But
another person can look at this strange matter from another angle, and
it seems to me that it is quite understandable that Nielsen (who, paren-
thetically noted, is also a professor of the University of Copenhagen
and a better student of Hegel than Prof. Martensen) feels called upon
to protest against such strange conduct, he who has found these writ-

ings so significant that he has used two years to become acquainted with them. The point here is not that an objection can be made against Nielsen's attack upon Martensen from the standpoint of the idea and on behalf of the pseudonym; this was considered in its proper place anyway. Only this: it is a mistake, at times an offense, to want to ignore the corrective.[2661] But to want to change the corrective into doctrine is an alteration of the corrective and anything but imitating it, for the corrective should not be used by one who wants to be a corrective also, but by one whose greatness, yes, whose superiority to the corrective would be precisely that elevation by which he would say short and sweet: I have wanted to be corrected.

*Postscript*

To me it is of infinite importance that there be complete truth in all my public affairs. For the sake of the idea and of the cause it is of infinite importance to me to have it understood that I have stood alone, that there has been nothing that could resemble a coterie or a clique. And so it is also that I have not become involved privately with anyone concerning my cause.

With only one have I made an exception but conscientiously have kept the relationship such that I know there has been nothing in it that could resemble a coterie or clique.

That one is Prof. Nielsen. I was just about finished or expected soon to finish the writing I may regard as having been my task. The thought that I would not live long obtruded itself with unusual urgency. Then I considered it my duty at least to make an attempt to initiate another person into my cause. I chose Prof. Nielsen, who himself made an approach and with decided readiness accepted the invitation. So in the course of a year and three-quarters or a year and a half I spent much time and had many conversations for the purpose of initiating him into my whole way of thinking. With the most scrupulous conscientiousness I have kept myself out of his writing of the past year until the moment it became *publici juris*. I had not seen a single line of it previously, and except for the big book[2662] (containing in fact the lectures given at the University) I did not speak a single time with him about his writing, and there were not many words exchanged even about the big book. That this is the case Prof. N. will be able to testify; and in his own interests he, too, has seen to it that this did not happen. He will also be able to testify that he has never had a chance to see a single line of any of my manuscripts in advance or to learn the slightest word about them. And today he is just as unacquainted with the manuscripts, many of which were lying all ready at the time, as he was the first day I spoke with him. This arrangement was maintained most conscientiously, because to me it was extremely important not to get him to do something as I wanted it but to see how he, who was also a diligent reader of the writings, would do it independently, although as stated, I have spent much time in numerous conversations to initiate him into my way of thinking. As the various books by him appeared, I studied them and let him know my opinion. Prof. Nielsen will be able to testify that I did not approve of this writing, although I still expected more of "the next one."

This is the situation. As a general observation, it certainly seems that Prof. N's prospects are meager, he who indeed could have lived on in assured esteem if he had not, instead of ignoring, ventured—(and just this is what is commendable) to get involved in this matter, and no lynchean vision is required to see that it must be advanced. One of the pseudonyms[2663] in particular has indeed provided the corrective essentially, but this is an element within the whole cause, which essentially is completed and is only to be advanced. This cause is Christianity, traced through all the confusions of reflection back to the simplicity of faith, about which I have learned inexpressibly much, formally, from that noble "simple" wise man of old.[2664] Whether or not the conditions seem meager also to Prof. N. will depend upon his conception of the significance of the cause. Allow me to use myself for a moment. With my given capacities I have persevered as an author for seven years in almost sleepless tension. This is the flower of my life which has cost my best powers. Since I made nothing as an author, to be an author has cost me money[2665] year after year, money I otherwise could have used in some other way. Since I have amounted to nothing, it has also cost me labor, with half of which I could have filled amply a more complicated position with pay in another currency. Finally there has been the cost—the idea required this—of becoming a sacrifice to the derision of rabble barbarism, plus (something I myself have not prompted) being persecuted in various ways by the envy of a certain literary elite. Truly the conditions are meager! Yet there is one thing. Others cannot see it but I see it: my conception of the cause I have the honor to serve—and then everything is infinitely changed. Give me my youth again, that twenty-eighth year when I began, and I will bid again —but on the same cause. Make the conditions even poorer, the toil and sufferings more abundant, and I will bid again—but on the same cause.

Say to me: There are the seven years, but one minute before twelve on the last evening of the seventh year you will collapse exhausted, but you will not die, no, perhaps you will live a long time but exhausted by the prodigious exertion—I will bid again—but on the same cause.

$x^6$ B 121   *n.d.*, 1849–50

« **6575**

Could be used for a discourse.

The last two lines of every stanza in no. 45 of Brorson's *Svane-sang*[2666] for a discourse on "Faith" or on "Patience."

> (1) The greater the need, the more it looks fixedly
> toward the end. Therefore, it is not put off if
> the way is hard and steep.
> (3) Nor is it put off by the condition of the path,
> whether it is a swamp or is strewn with roses.
> Nothing really matters when our bent is toward
> heaven.
> (2) Nor the length of the path.
> The nearer to its home
> The more briskly it proceeds.

*In margin*: I have switched the stanzas; Brorson's stanza 3 is used as stanza 2, and stanza 2 as 3.

$x^2$ A 372   *n.d.*, 1850

« **6576**

There is a striking word-play in the words *fruit* and *fear* [*Frugt* and *Frygt*]. As they say: There is no fruit if a man has no fear.

$x^2$ A 374   *n.d.*, 1850

« **6577** *About My "Heterogeneity"*

No doubt in relation to what is generally prevalent I have had a heterogeneity, essentially rooted in early suffering, later redoubled by dialectical suffering, which made me in my silence even more dissimilar.

But for one thing I have never viewed my heterogeneity as a perfection, but rather as an imperfection on my part; for another, I have never been altogether satisfied with it but only relatively.

As a consequence, I can use direct communication to indicate to my contemporaries the indirect communication which is used.

Viewed in this way, any reflective person has a measure of heterogeneity. As long as he reflects on something and just uses indirect expressions, he is heterogeneous. I have a greater measure of it, because I have the whole published communication. But then I also view my whole literary activity as my own education.[2667]

Absolute heterogeneity continues in indirect communication to the end, since it refuses altogether to be in the context of the universal. But this heterogeneity, of course, is superhuman, demonic or divine.

All heterogeneity is based on the point of departure of particularity but seeks to get back again to the universal. In this way the forward impetus is provided. Absolute heterogeneity continues in the dissimilarity of the point of origin to the end. The effect then is qualitatively greater.

In consequence of this, the category I use is: I must make men aware. I have never assumed the character of heterogeneity simply because I have viewed it as an imperfection on my part (for this reason no "authority" either) and because the authorship is my own development.

But to make men aware is a category which still is in the context of the universal. Absolute heterogeneity includes nothing to make men aware; it is in character and denies the context. The difference is easily discernible. The fact that I poetically and pseudonymously communicate the latter is a concession. The situation is quite different when an individual communicates it under his own name and claims that his life expresses it.

Absolute heterogeneity would have to begin just about where I am now ending, with the developed consciousness, which I have arrived at by means of what has been traversed. But precisely because I have achieved it by means of what has been covered, I also have come to the realization that I cannot appear in the character of what has been presented but have a poetic relationship.[2668]

If I had not understood this and been helped to understand it, most likely I would have gone in the wrong direction and become a zealot.

But someone could say: "Yes, but the very presence of pseudonyms is itself indirect communication." The answer to that must be: You are overlooking something; in the "editor's preface" there is always the category: I am striving, together with my acknowledgement that this is the more ideal Christian requirement. The maximum of the indirect would be to deliver such a communication and leave it completely, altogether dialectically ambiguous as to whether it is an attack upon Christianity or a defense. Absolute heterogeneity would be to make it completely direct communication but then personally step forth in the character of the communication. For if this happened, the established order would be completely burst asunder because of this dissimilar individual.

But the category: to make men aware, developed in greater detail in my preface and safeguarded by my existential life, is intended for just the opposite, to let the established order continue, every stitch of it—and merely seek to breathe some interiority into it, leaving it up to each one whether he will use it.

For me to do more is unconditionally impossible, for then I would have to have authority, which I have denied having from the beginning, and why? Because I do not dare appeal to God in such a way that I in any manner dare suggest that he has chosen me for something special; what I can say again and again and never enough in the context of my need is simply how I feel he has helped me in what I myself had begun in a small way. I have not begun with boundless wisdom, which is implicit in being chosen by God and gives one authority; I began in just the opposite way with being an unfortunate, a sufferer—and thus I began. Then one thing followed another and I am the most surprised of all to see what has been granted to me.

But this situation cannot possibly give authority. This is why the indirect method always has been logical for me. The only departure is that since the writing is also for my own education and development, it ends with pseudonymous works[2669] which set forth the Christian requirement ideally and in relation to which I define myself as one who strives.

If I had been only a poet, I may well have ended up in the nonsense of merely poetizing Christianity without perceiving that it cannot be done, that one has to take himself along and either existentially express the ideal himself (which cannot be done) or define himself as one who is striving. Had I not been a poet I may well have gone ahead and confused myself with the ideal and have become a zealot. What, then, has helped me in addition to what is of greatest importance, that a Governance has helped me? The fact that I am a dialectician.

$X^2$ A 375    n.d., 1850

« 6578

Two scraps of paper lying with "From on High He Will Draw All to Himself."[2670]

This book cannot be made pseudonymous because it remonstrates against the transformation of preaching into observations,[2671] that is, the impersonal—and a pseudonym, after all, is also something impersonal.

> *N.B.* This objection is answered on an *accompanying sheet*, and the book is made pseudonymous.

That *paper*[2672] has the following content:

Oct. 9, 1849

In one way there is a dialectical heresy somewhere in this book—namely, where it is pointed out that preaching has become impersonal, that it is communicated by someone who is no one. The inconsistency is that this is done by a pseudonym, who is himself, after all, is no one. But here is my boundary: I can make men aware—no more. And on the other hand, I still am part of it as editor and will, in fact, take the responsibility, and everything will be understood as if I myself said it. Consequently there is nevertheless a very essential step forward, both in getting it said and in the actual attribution to me. The plus here is really this: that while the one who is speaking is indeed no one, a pseudonym, the editor is an actual person and one who acknowledges that he is judged by what this pseudonym is saying.

$x^2$ A 393   *n.d.*, 1850

« **6579**

[*In margin*: About Myself]

Yet it is a blessing, an indescribable benefit to me, that I was as mentally depressed as I was. If I had been a naturally happy person—and then experienced what I experienced as an author, I believe a man necessarily would have gone mad. But I knew still more frightful anguish within, where I actually suffer.

What happened then? An amazing thing, which is not all over yet, has occurred up to a certain point and will, I believe, go on happening, the amazing thing that precisely this external hullabaloo has lured my mental depression out of its hiding place, already has saved me from it to some extent, and will do it even more thoroughly! O depth of wisdom, how inscrutable are your ways. O God, but yet all fatherliness and grace!

$x^2$ A 411   *n.d.*, 1850

« **6580**

Another foolish objection to me and my life (and many of the persons involved are partly guilty inasmuch as they themselves understand that it is not true) is that I remain apart from life and that this precisely is not religiousness since true religiousness engages actively in life.

O, you fools or hypocrites; how do I remain apart from life? In such a way that literally not one single person here at home is so conspicuously at the front of the stage. No, to live apart from life is to run with the flock, to be in the "crowd," thereby gaining obscurity but also influence and power.

How do I remain apart from life? In such a way that I have created a body of writing hard to match. In such a way that when the rabble raged and domineered I was the only one who dared to act.[2673] I remain apart from life in such a way that I am recognized by every child, am a stock character in your plays, my name is a byword, my life is a daily sacrifice in order, if possible, religiously to tie a knot, and to get religiousness introduced again.

But why then this talk that I remain apart from life? Well, I will tell you. It comes from the fact that in spite of all my work I have no earthly reward, I am not applauded at public gatherings, which I do not attend, but am insulted in the streets, where I am active; it comes from not fashioning my life in a way appropriate to a cabinet appointment; it comes because people detect that I am a fool, a fool—who fears God!

O, you sanctimonious people with your love which does not set you apart from life—no, your love of self would prevent that! O, you sanctimonious people with your practicality that takes an active part in life—or hastily takes hold of the advantages! O, you sanctimonious people with your earnestness which does not have the imagination to withdraw from life—indeed, your cowardice would rather hurry you back into the herd, the animal herd, away from the place where earnestness lives: being the single individual. O, you sanctimonious people with your patriotism which forbids you to be callous to the woes and welfare of the country. Well, thanks for that, you have saved Denmark, saved it from being a country and made it a provincial market town, the promised land of pettiness and mediocrity, saved it from belonging to history in the future; for you no doubt are of the opinion that your two-bit exploits, your silly speeches at public gatherings, your names will go down in history—but before that happens everything, everything in life will have to be radically turned upside down so that "history" deals with what formerly was consigned to "oblivion." But maybe that is what you are working toward, to turn everything upside down, so that "history" becomes "oblivion," and the exceptional is forgotten; "oblivion" will become "history," and "oblivion" will carry historically all that along with it, all of you and your speeches and your seventeen amendments to the sixteenth section concerning nothing.

There is something dreadful about seeing individuals rushing into this mutual insuring, which does not, as does other insurance, cover shipwrecks, but which, the mutual insuring itself, is a *commune naufragium*.[2674] How many, many there are who already are devoid of all concepts, for whom all that counts is that there is a majority for something, to such a degree that they feel utterly unrepentant when this is the case! Let there be a majority for prostitution as a virtue and murder as right, and so it is.

And "strict Christians" as they are called, run to these meeting places and participate in the voting. Well, it is true that they sometimes have a little amendment, a little amendment to improve the monstrous evil which has gained complete victory—which is even more insane than trying to put out a fire with water from a sprinkling bottle! And when it is all done, when they have "saved their conscience" by improving and correcting the evil a little bit—that is, by making it even worse if they do anything at all—then they vote with the rest and worship—Christianly!—the majority! But they see through the whole odious practice. —Well, thanks for that. In private conversations they babble tirelessly about how wretched and low the whole thing is, but there where by energetic action—that is, by pulling out unconditionally, not to keep silent, no, but to stand as a tormenting reminder, mistreated, of course, that God is present—there they ballot and worship—Christianly!—the majority!

$X^2$ A 413   *n.d.*, 1850

« 6581

[*In margin*: the concept "complicity"]

In an age of moral disintegration such as ours, the concept of "complicity" must be very strongly accentuated. It is so easy to say that one participates out of zeal and earnestness and also tries in one's small way to counteract what is wrong; that is, one permits the total corruption to stay in power and at best promotes a little amendment. Thereby one profits by standing in well with the corruption, since on the whole one participates in it and also flatters himself by imagining that he is better than the age.

The matter is quite different. The totality in which I participate is, of course, far more important than my little amendment within the corruption.

Therefore the one who participates is responsible for the whole.

But this means acting decisively, means exposing oneself to danger, dedicating oneself to the patient suffering of seeming to achieve nothing at all (for at first the service of pure idea has the appearance of standing completely outside, whereas the tiniest amendment immediately "achieves" much), like a man drowned in the crowd.

In all critical times there is much villainy on the part of individuals who are somewhat aware of the real basis of the whole trouble, but instead of acting decisively and suffering, desisting completely from action, they convert their awareness into an amendment and as mentioned, by a blameworthy compounding of wrong and right, profit in two ways.

[*In margin*: Peter]

Unfortunately it is to be feared that Peter has become such a figure now. He has always been something of a nit-picker, lately quite devoid of ideas, but now it seems almost as if a light has dawned for him, that he wants to find success as the coryphaeus of mediocrity, triviality, and heartiness. He has needed diversion, it is true; I can understand that he is tired of living out there in the country with a sick wife[2675]—but such diversion! To run around to every meeting and speak everywhere —of course, heartily and earnestly "to counteract." In the assemblies of the Friends of the Peasants to maintain: I am not a member of the Peasant Party—instead of acting by staying away. —He is intelligent, is well informed, but he dissipates himself in inconsequential gadding about and taking part in everything. It is ominous that he stays with Christian Lund,[2676] for he no doubt will become Christian's ideal! Form-reduplication, which is character-consistency, is beyond his existential energy; he cannot pull himself out of a situation, thereby acting and expressing qualitative opposition and difference; he remains in it, maintaining that he does not agree, just as at a convention he delivered a criticism[2677] in which he maintained that it was no criticism.

$x^2$ A 415   *n.d.*, 1850

« 6582

If someone were to say: "Yes, it is very easy for you to be so altruistic, to serve the truth so purely, if you will, you who have independent means,"[2678] I would answer: Well, there is some truth to that. At the same time I have a particular view of existence. As soon as I do not have the means to do it in this way, I will unassumingly undertake an activity where I work for a living. If I need so much that I must work the whole day, well, then I will admit about myself: I regard it as my task to work for my living. If I do not need so much, then I will see to it I get a little extra time and a bit of spare money so that I can serve the truth, even if on a far smaller scale.

One thing I decidedly do not want: I will not have any confusion about whether I am working for my own advantage or for the truth.

In my opinion the tragedy of the world is simply this—human shortsightedness, many times well meaning, has thought somewhat along these lines: if on the whole you want the truth, then if once in a while a little consideration of your own advantage infiltrates, if at times a slightly tainted expedient sneaks in, it is of little consequence, and besides, that is how the world is, every practical man knows that, and I cannot remake the world.

O, you impatient, shortsighted one. No, remake the world, you certainly cannot. Well, then do what you can, live in quiet obscurity, working for your own living. Such a person at least does no harm. But if you want to work for the truth, then ponder before God exactly by what standard you are able to do it. Let it be according to a modest standard, in God's name, but promise God and yourself and hold to it that you will unconditionally use the purest means[2679] according to the standard.

The other is nothing but impatience and shortsightedness, and it has done irreparable harm.

$X^2$ A 425   *n.d.*, 1850

## « 6583 *The Shrewd and Sensible—The Good and True*

Take a fraction of the good or of the true—this is the shrewd and sensible way to be a success in the world. Take the good or true whole, and the exact opposite occurs and you run completely counter to the world.

I have an example of that.

I have considered inserting "her"[2680] [*in margin*: see enclosure[2681]] in an enigmatic dedication to the writings about my work as an author.[2682] It cannot be done now, for other reasons; for no matter how enigmatic it is, it nevertheless will be easily understood, and therefore I not only have no guarantee at all that it will be respected, but there is the strongest probability that a newspaper will pick it up and mention her name, and then everything is stirred up again and I perhaps will have done incalculable harm. But I would like very much to do it because I would also like to have it all in order, if possible, before my death.

Yet there is another matter[2683] I want to explain now. Assuming that I did do it, what then? Well, it would not have been shrewd and sensible. Why not? Because it aims too high. The story is now forgotten; I was a scoundrel, but now that is forgotten and everything is all right again in that respect; it should not be stirred up again. Yes, but I was not a thorough scoundrel; the whole affair has a far deeper meaning. It would be futile, that is precisely the trouble, and that is also why such a step would be unwise. That is, it would be so lofty that it would seem to be an attempt to rip people out of their cozy routines for a moment by explaining everything and having everything explained; and that would annoy them, and thus one would run counter to them.

$$X^2 \text{ A } 427 \quad n.d., \ 1850$$

## « 6584

If the period of writing esthetic literature were not long past, or if a recreation of that nature ever were to be allowed, I would like to write a book which would be entitled:

Conversations with My Wife.[2684]

In the preface the author will say that his wife was nineteen years old the day of their marriage, that the conversations, as we will see, stem from the first half year of their marriage.

They should be dialogues. I would portray the humorous side of this relationship, the husband is intellectually superior and yet genuinely in love, and the feminine figure charmingly naive—the humor which emerges when they talk together about their relationship. I would boldly risk a certain directness and yet would be so honorable and decent that our Lord himself could, if you please, listen to it.

$$X^5 \text{ A } 165 \quad n.d., \ 1850$$

## « 6585 *My Misfortune With My Contemporaries, Why I Am Misunderstood*

My trouble is that I have taken away illusions.

Instead of spending sundry thousands to support a life of writing[2685] like this, instead of exerting myself so strenuously, I should have gotten a professorial appointment at a good salary (then I would have been understood by all the job-holders—that is, by nearly all I would be understood, maybe not my *philosophemes*,[2686] but I would be understood to be a "serious" and reputable man) and accomplished little but promised much (thus I would have been understood by other professors and scholars). Then I also would have been assured of being understood by the students—since I would be examining them, which is very advantageous and helps in getting them to speak favorably about a person, since he is now, for better or for worse, the authorized teacher. (Instead, as a nobody, I have lived practically as one of their companions.)

I should have lived in professorial seclusion in "cliques"; then I would have had a great reputation and also would have had the security of belonging to the great aggregate of public officials who stick together according to the law that when one suffers, all suffer (instead I have lived as a single individual in whose fate not a single one participates).

$$X^2 \text{ A } 440 \quad n.d., \ 1850$$

« 6586

My need of Christianity is very great (because of my sufferings and my sins and my appalling inward turning)—and therefore I am not understood. And for that reason, too, I frequently have even been fearful of making another person's life too earnest; that is why I am so careful.

$$X^2 \text{ A } 459 \quad n.d., \ 1850$$

« 6587  *"Without Authority"*

The reason I have always spoken of myself as being without authority is that I personally have felt that there was too much of the poetic in me, furthermore that I feel aided by something higher, and also that I am put together backwards, but then, too, because I perceive that the profound suffering of my life and also my guilt make me need an enormous measure of Christianity, while at the same time I am fearful of making it too heavy for someone who may not need so great a measure. Of course, neither the God-man nor an apostle can have such a concern—but then I am just a poor human being.

$$X^2 \text{ A } 475 \quad n.d., \ 1850$$

« 6588

Someone less flawed than I, with just as deep an impression of Christianity as I have—well, I would put that down clearly in his favor. With me it is another matter, for it is (granted all sorts of other things connected with intellectual gifts and other qualifications) "not because of my virtue" that I have so deep an impression of Christianity. If someone had been the greatest of sinners—if one may put it that way —and was the best interpreter of Plato, the former factor is inconsequential, makes no difference at all. This is not the case with Christianity. Such a person ought to remember with humility that he has a qualification which very well may have helped him to a deeper understanding of Christianity, but a qualification which is not directly a plus but a plain minus.

$x^2$ A 476   *n.d.*, 1850

« **6589**

Just this alone, what suffering my inward turning creates in my life! Born for intrigue, with rare talents in this area—and then to be placed solely in the service of the idea. What a diversion if I had been turned outward; as it is now, I dissipate all my intrigue dissipating the intrigues of others, but with almost cunning cruelty keep myself from using even the slightest shrewd means.

$x^2$ A 488   *n.d.*, 1850

« **6590**

Stilling[2687] may be very close to creating an extremely calamitous confusion regarding Christianity.

What preoccupies him is really somewhat erotic, although this perhaps is minor; it is mainly a pride which *par tout*[2688] wants to realize the idea of remaining unmarried, loyal to his [deceased] wife.

He is suffering under this now, a kind of frightful self-tormenting, he says.

But for God in heaven's sake, what does that have to do with Christianity! Is it Christianity which forbids him to marry? It lets him do it seven times if he so wishes.

There is a confusion here. He now talks incessantly about Christianity striking him as being the most appalling self-torment etc. But this actually is devious talk. In a deeper sense he is not concerned with Christianity; he is tormenting himself with a fixed idea: I want to and I do not want to. He will not admit this—and so it is Christianity that is supposed to be causing all these sufferings, Christianity which in fact says: You are utterly, utterly free—get married!

Being unable at present to explain, at least openly, the true context, that it is his relation to his dead wife, his desire to marry, and his vacillating resolve not to, which cause the torment, there is a danger that in order to give vent to his feelings he will automatically transfer it all to Christianity, as if this were what preoccupied him and as if this were the most appalling self-torment.

I told him this most earnestly, showed him that he is turning everything upside down, told him that he should get married, that the whole conflict essentially has nothing at all to do with Christianity. I talk very seldom with him.

But it can get to be calamitous. For it is part of suffering of this nature to feel the urge for an outlet, even one contrived, and then, it is part of the cunningness of suffering of this nature to grab at something entirely different and to unload itself by talking about that, as if it were that which made one suffer.

This would be extremely unfair to Christianity.

His life otherwise is very confused. He does in fact concern himself somewhat with Christianity, but it must also be research, must yield a scholarly contribution, a historical view. Imagine oneself in such a situation—instead of keeping the most rigorous regimen, concentrated solely on himself, he devotes himself to the subject of atheists[2689] in order to describe them. Alas, first of all, silence! The only thing to do in a situation like that is to say to all reflections: Hold your tongue. But he does not have an authentic personal concern for himself; that always should be the reflective benefit of thinking. Thus he never actually begins to live personally, at least in a more profound sense.

But we will go on hoping. If the man really would, what potential he has! But he demonstrates precisely what it means not to be instructed and disciplined in Christianity any more, demonstrates the need for, if not the monastery, something similar to it. A Church institute would help him.

In my representation rigorousness is a dialectical factor in Christianity, but clemency is just as strongly represented; the former is represented poetically by pseudonyms, the other personally by myself. This is the need of the present age, which has taken Christianity in vain. But it is something entirely different if a despairing person has nothing to say about Christianity except that it is the cruelest self-torment. In order to put an end to playing fast and loose, I had to introduce rigorousness—and introduced it simply to provide movement into Christianity's clemency. This is my understanding of Christianity and my task. If I had understood only its frightful rigorousness

—I would have kept silent. This is what Johannes de Silentio[2690] has already called attention to, that in such circumstances one must be silent and at least demonstrate that he loves other men—by being silent, because merely negative outcomes, at least dreadfully negative outcomes, are not to be communicated. Such a thing is not communication, no, it is an assault, a betrayal, a character deficiency, which is determined at least to have the deplorable satisfaction of making others just as unhappy and confused as one is himself.

$X^2$ A 525    *n.d.*,  1850

« **6591**

My "misfortune" is really that I am naturally equipped with sheer intellectual elegance and that I presuppose others to have the same. For a time I actually did not notice anything; I buried myself in my work, practiced and developed dance steps, and did not perceive that in doing this I was getting too intellectual for this world, where everything centers on animal health, brazen straightforwardness, and meanness. Therefore, I had to miss out on all advantages.

Take a situation with Christian VIII, he "the King," and he, the King, who had such high pretensions of intellect and elegance.

Fine, the first time I spoke with him[2691] I said: "The situation here is far too cramped and limited; as a rule an author is told: If you want to earn more you should work harder. For a long time now I have been reduced to the situation: You must see to it that you work less, for you can no longer afford to work so hard." Elated, His Majesty smiled graciously.

Thanks for that. If I had been king, I would never have allowed anything like that to be said to me or promptly joined in the levity. I would first of all have answered earnestly: "My God, is that really so; do you not at least want to be publicly reimbursed out of public funds for your expenses." Only then would I have the advantage as King when I joined in the laughter. Otherwise the King, too, actually is satirized. It is an utterly satirical situation to be King of a country so small that an author (that is, not a man who makes a hobby of writing), a substantial author, can truthfully speak that way.

To be sure, Christian VIII was an extraordinarily cultured man, but in money matters he was demoralized both by his own financial straits and the hounding of foreign creditors.

Incidentally, the reply I imagined myself giving if I had been king would have been inconsequential, for I would have answered, "No." But it makes a devil of a difference to interpose this royal twist.

On the other hand, I would have liked that reply for another reason, because the King thereby would demonstrate that he was aware of such a situation and there would at least be a bit more serious tone about sacrifices I have made and am making.

But here again is my elegance—which will be the ruination of me. The rabble rage at me, bourgeois mediocrity and the job-mentality secretly smirk at my impracticality—I myself, religiously turned inward, perceive the meanness with sharper eyes than anyone else, deal with the matter in my inner being with an earnestness that far surpasses the clergy's understanding—but as soon as I speak of it I am transformed into a trenchant wit—and everybody laughs along with me.

Yes, as I have always said: the relationship to spirit is an examination. And here once again is an examination: I get a dreadful insight into the selfishness and worldliness of others, something I would not do if I were flatly earnest or even critical—whereas now I am sure to find out how they themselves judge a life which contains more than sufficient to make them aware of the presence or absence in them of any spirit and earnestness of a more profound nature. The facts of my life are sufficiently clear.

They say that one must not detect in a dancer that he is breathing heavily. I have followed this rule spiritually. And since I do not breathe heavily, do not look extremely earnest, am not given to lamentations —well, then the whole thing is a lark. The conclusion drawn is just as stupid as saying: The dancer is not breathing heavily—ergo, he has not made a leap at all; he has remained motionless on the ground. The difference is simply that in the one case any bartender can check directly and immediately on the physical facts; on the other—anyone who is not personally possessed of spirit and earnestness will not be able to see it either. Therein is the examination. "Spirit" always negates directness and immediacy—for this reason only "spirit" can become aware of "spirit."

$X^2$ A 534   *n.d.,* 1850

« 6592

[*In the margin:* About myself]

Proportions Involved in *Making Aware*

If I had had enough assets[2692] to continue being an author all my life, I would no doubt have become too sarcastic and light-headed and would have done wrong.

If I could have forced myself into a purely ascetic existence, then meritoriousness would surely have appeared and spoiled it.

Now the situation is as lenient as possible, and all this about founding a school and the like is prevented. Awareness has been prompted—and so I withdraw and go in under more ordinary rubrics.

In my opinion this also is fine, besides being the supporting truth in the whole situation. It certainly was not I who went out into the world with a fixed and finished theory about Christianity's collision with the world. On the contrary, with a rather complete idea of the inner collisions with respect to becoming and being a Christian, it was my idea to present this, to show that just as collision with the world was unavoidable in an earlier time, so now on the other hand the labor of inwardness with respect to becoming and being a Christian must be engaged in with greater intensity, so there would, after all, be some similarity. I was totally unaware of the collision of Christianity with the surrounding world.

What happens—the surrounding world helps me to discover it, yes, obliges me to discover it. What rigorousness I do stress is actually only the reduplication of what the contemporary age has done to me; the contemporary age punishes itself through me. It would be difficult to present Christianity more leniently than I, arrogating nothing to myself; a more altruistic disinterested author Denmark has hardly ever had—and then this treatment, and then that we are all Christians, 1,000 Christian pastors, all of whom keep silent, while rabble barbarism and jabbering were literally all that flourished in Denmark. The steadiness and the reassurance in the whole thing is that there is no exaggeration; yes, in connection with the way I have been treated in this Christian land, I from my side have truly kept the situation very moderate. I am really not a partisan, but I express the ratio between the contemporary age and a Christian striving. The rigorousness becomes greater in proportion to the way the striving is treated; it is the age which judges itself.

$x^2$ A 544   *n.d.*, 1850

« 6593 *Reduplication*

Every striving which does not apply one-fourth, one-third, two-thirds, etc. of its power to systematically *working against* itself is essentially secular striving, in any case unconditionally not a *reforming* effort.

Reduplication means to work against oneself while working; it is like the pressure on the plow-handles, which determines the depth of the furrow—whereas working which does not work against itself is merely a superficial smoothing over.

What does it mean to work against oneself? It is quite simple. If the established, the traditional, etc., in the context of which a beginning is to be made, is sound, thoroughly sound—well, then apply directly what has to be applied; in any case there can be no talk or thought of reforming, for if the established is sound, then there is nothing, after all, to reform.

Conversely, to the same degree that the established, consequently there where one's striving begins, is corrupt, to the same degree it will become increasingly necessary dialectically to work against oneself, lest the innovation resulting from direct action is itself corrupted the minute it succeeds, and thus is not maintained in its heterogeneity.

Again the difference between the direct and the inverted. Working or striving directly is to work and strive. The inverted method is this: while working also to work against oneself.

But who dreams that such a standard exists, and that I use it on such a large scale! Understood I will never be. People think I am involved in a direct striving—and now they believe that I have achieved a kind of break-through! O, such ignorance! The publication of *Either/Or* was a huge success; I had it in my power to continue. What is the origin of all the problems in my striving, I wonder if it is not in myself? It is public knowledge that not one single person has dared to oppose me. But I have done that myself. What a wrong turn on my part, if my striving was to be direct, to publish *Two Upbuilding Discourses* after *Either/Or*,[2693] instead of letting *Either/Or* stand with its glittering success, continuing in the direction which the age demanded, only in slightly reduced portions. What a counter-effort against myself that I, the public's darling, introduce the single individual, and finally, that I plunge myself into all the dangers of insults!

But such things can only be understood by someone who himself has risked something essentially similar. Someone else cannot conceive it or believe it.

R. Nielsen[2694] is actually confused about this, for he considers my striving to be direct striving.

$$X^2 \ A \ 560 \quad n.d., \ 1850$$

## « 6594 *About Myself*

When I think back on it now, it is wonderful to think back upon that stroke of a pen with which I hurled myself against rabble-barbarism![2695]

And this was my mood when I took that step. I thought of stopping writing with *Concluding Postscript*,[2696] and to that end the manuscript in its entirety was delivered to Luno.[2697] Grateful, unspeakably grateful for what had been granted to me, I decided—on the occasion of that article in *Gæa*[2698]—to take a magnanimous step for "the others." I was the only one who had the qualifications to do it emphatically, the qualifications along these lines: (1) Goldschmidt[2699] had immortalized me and saw in me an object of admiration, (2) I am a witty author, (3) I have not sided with the elite or with any party at all, (4) I have a personal virtuosity for associating with everybody, (5) a shining reputation which literally did not have one single speck of criticism or the like, (6) I altruistically used my own money to be an author, (7) I was unmarried, independent, etc.

So, religiously motivated, I did it. And look, this step was determinative for my continuing to write! And what significance it has had, how I have learned to know myself, learned to know "the world," and learned to understand Christianity—yes, a whole side of Christianity, and a crucial side, which very likely would not have occurred to me at all otherwise, and except for that the situation for coming into the proper relation to Christianity myself perhaps would not have been my fortune, either.

But what a range: an established consummate reputation as an author, and then suddenly almost beginning all over again!

$x^2$ A 586    *n.d.*, 1850

### « 6595 *My Curious Situation with Respect to Martensen*[2700]

There are certainly a few who see a bit more deeply into the matter; but according to the tradition of sorts being passed from mouth to mouth, the difference between Prof. Martensen and me is that he wants to vindicate reflection with respect to faith, reflecting on the faith, and I am against it.

Curious! Now look at what I have written. I began writing with just about the same level of scholarly education as the professor (perhaps with somewhat less German erudition but with a bit more Greek).

In many forms and under several pseudonyms, a whole pseudonymous literature is chiefly concerned with illuminating the question of faith, with discerning the sphere belonging to faith, with determining its distinction from other spheres of the intellect and spirit, etc. And how is all this done? By dialectic, by reflection.[2701] I venture to claim that it would be hard to find an author who has been so devoted to reflecting on faith—although certainly not speculating unceremoniously on particular dogmas; for I "reflected," yes, I thought (and that was, after all, reflection) that the first thing to be done was to clear up the whole question of faith. I venture to claim that in my writings the dialectical qualifications of specific points are set forth with an accuracy such as has not been known before. And then to be charged with this: not wanting to reflect about faith.

Take Prof. Martensen. He has written a dogmatics.[2702] Fine. In it he treats all the points and questions usually treated in dogmatics (about Scripture, the Trinity, creation, preservation, redemption, reconciliation, angels, devils, man, immortality, etc.). But there is one point he slides over quite easily, the point about the relation of faith to reflection.

This, you see, is calling men to reflection on the faith—in contrast to my striving.

But the point is: I have worked and accomplished something on this point—but no one has time to read such things. Martensen has maintained and protested—that is something for everyone to run around with. My full and detailed writings—well, they put people off, they run away from them; Prof. Martensen's winged assurances, they run around with them—*es gehet vom Munde zu Munde.*[2703]

*In margin:* I will not discuss other promoting factors that are in Prof. Martensen's favor: he is a professor, has an important office, has a velvet front- or stomach-piece, is a knight—while I am a nobody, have put out money on my own writing. Would that someone or other would spend just half an hour reflecting earnestly on this; then maybe he would arrive at some other thoughts about my striving.

$x^2$ A 596   *n.d.*, 1850

« **6596 *Occasioned by a Comment in Magnus Eiriksson's Latest Book* Spekulativ Rettroenhed *etc.*[2704]**

The comment[2705] states that in his book *Concluding Postscript* Magister Kierkegaard has ridiculed, yes, insulted Martensen's theology (the speculative professor etc.).

In reply it must be pointed out that *Concluding Postscript* is not by me but by a pseudonym, Johannes Climacus, and at the end of the book[2706] there is an adequate clarification of my relationship as editor. In the second place, Professor M. is mentioned nowhere in the book, and not only this, the scene is deliberately sustained in such a way that rather than being in Denmark it is in Germany, where, after all, the speculation that "goes beyond" originates. A comic type is created that is called "the assistant professor [*Privat-Docenten*]," a type I consider to be very valuable. Everything is kept as poetic as possible, because as the editor I am no friend of finite squabbles. And Germany is practically designated as the scene, because I, who otherwise am rather well informed on the speculative "scientific" accomplishments of Prof. Martensen and the Danish moderns, do not know whether either he or they have added anything at all new to what any fairly well-read student knows from Germany. I know very well that for a long time now here in Denmark certain ones have made themselves important by what they have learned from the Germans and rendered practically word for word (as if it were their own), that they have compiled various diverse German thinkers, professors, assistant professors, tutors, etc. But insofar as this is not the fraud one wishes to depict in a comic light, insofar as it is modern speculation (especially that of the post-Hegelian gang) one wishes to oppose from the side of "faith," it is poetically appropriate to keep the scene vague, roughly in Germany, recognizable by "the assistant-professor," of which there were myriads in Germany at that time, even though in various models, while in fact there was not one single assistant professor in Denmark the year *Concluding Postscript* came out. As the editor I was aware of this, yes, I regarded *Concluding Postscript* to be, among other things, a Danish protest against modern speculation; I understood, as time will surely bear me out, that when the tyrannical opinion by which "The System" maintained itself has vanished, my pseudonym will be acknowledged to have been right in his view that it was genuinely Danish to regard the exaggerations of this speculation as comic, yet without forgetting that it is also Danish to love and honor true scholarship, such as Greek scholarship at present, which actually is what the pseudonym uses, although he is also indebted very much to an earlier German scholarship as well as to Hegel.

$X^6$ B 128   *n.d.*, 1849–50

« **6597**

[*In margin:* About Theophilus Nicolaus]
*About Theophilus Nicolaus*[2707]

   This is what comes when bungling stupidity takes sides directly opposite to an artistic design.

Johannes Climacus himself declares that he does not have faith. Theophilus Nicolaus portrays the believer.

He does not perceive at all that to be consistent he has to assume that everything Johannes Climacus says proves nothing, since he himself says he does not have faith, is not a Christian.[2708]

But Theophilus Nicolaus has no inkling of this. He plunges in *bona fide.*[2709]

How tragic to live in such a limited setting that there is virtually no one who has an eye for a profoundly executed artistic design.

What daily toil, enormous effort, almost sleepless dialectical perseverance it costs me to keep the threads straight in this subtle construction—such is not for others at all. I am identified automatically with my pseudonyms, and some nonsense is concocted which—of course—many more understand—yes, of course!

$x^2$ A 601    *n.d.,* 1850

« **6598**

[*] Reply to Theophilus Nicolaus, author of a book entitled:[2710]

---

The reply is your own words on p. 178, as well as other portions. "If we categorically assume the dogmas of the *Church*, then we will readily believe that ultimately there is no other alternative left than to establish the principle of absurdity as the principle of *faith*, for to every thinking and also religious spirit these dogmas certainly must seem to contain very much that is absurd and paradoxical (at variance with the understanding as well as reason)."[†]

So, basically you are taking it upon yourself to defend my thesis of the paradox and in addition—what more could I ask—throughout the whole book to hit out very stalwartly and violently at speculative dogmatics and speculation, fatal if the blows make contact—one alone would be enough; I would appeal to you if there were not other difficulties involved in doing so.

N.B. [*In margin: To typesetter:* N.B. one line space between.]

[*] Note. Since there is no literary journal in Denmark, I have requested space for these lines in this paper[2711] and must therefore request—so much the worse for me—the pardon of the majority of subscribers, because in a way they get no paper tonight since my article will scarcely be of interest to them.

[†] Note. The italics in the quotation are the author's own italics, and this will be the case throughout this article wherever italics are used in quotations from the book.

The new and curious turn you give to the matter is this, then. You throw out all of Christianity and thereupon, with an exultant look, say something like this: Where now is Christianity? Incidentally, an amazing situation! I, Johannes Climacus, say that I "by no means make out that I am a Christian" (see *Concluding Postscript*[2712]), but I let Christianity stand. You throw out all of Christianity—and then continue to be Christian and, furthermore, in the capacity of a Christian make no petty distinctions between (see title page) "Jews, Christians, and Mohammedans."*

N.B. [*In margin:* To typesetter: N.B. one line space between.]

As far as Abraham's faith is concerned, which you maintain in particular, you do not entirely avoid the absurd here, for the absurd is also present in Abraham's faith. Abraham is called the father of faith because he has the formal qualifications of faith, believing against the understanding, although it has never occurred to the Christian Church that Abraham's faith had the content of Christian faith which relates essentially to a later historical event. This [I say] with respect to the difficulties you make for yourself in order to point out a contradiction between two different authors, one of whom is concerned "existentially" with the problem "of becoming a Christian," and the other "lyrically dialectically" with Abraham—Johannes de Silentio, who moreover does not claim to be a believer but himself says, "I do not have faith,"[2713] and the undersigned, who does not claim to be a Christian, and what he himself says he does not do.

N.B. [*In margin:* To typesetter: N.B. one line space between.]

And now for this oddity! You, a declared rationalist, who want to do away with everything called the absurd, the paradox, etc., you get rid of it in the following manner, among others, and for a rationalist this is a strange way: you assume—and this is quite clear in your book —that direct communications from God, higher intimations, visions, revelations, etc., that all these are entirely natural and in order, something the really religious person—thus very likely you yourself, in any case your brother—knows from experience, just as the rest of us know

---

*Note. You presumably are referring to yourself when you mention on p. 205 *"someone who, possibly motivated by pure piety, rejects all the distinctive doctrines of Christianity."* What is distinctive, then, about you is that you then go on being a Christian. Yet this is your distinctiveness, which I at least must deny to you. But you certainly have no right to hint darkly (pp. 204–5) that the world-famous Royal Councilor Ørsted secretly is in that situation: possibly out of pure piety rejecting all the characteristic doctrines of Christianity.

everyday things. Understand me correctly—what surprises me is that the writer is a rationalist who wants to get rid of the supernatural in this—well, certainly not rationalistic—way.

N.B. [*In margin: To typesetter:* N.B. one line space between.]

Finally a word about your scholarly essay, which stands approximately *au niveau* with Magnus Eiríksson's *Tro, Overtro, Vantro*.[2714] According to your interpretation, what we pseudonymous writers, who, please note, say of ourselves that "we do not claim to have faith," call the absurd, the paradox, is according to your explanation by no means the absurd but rather "the higher rationality," although not in the speculative sense. No, speculation, the speculatives (Prof. Martensen etc.) are scoffed down into the deepest abyss, so far down that Johannes de Silentio, according to your declaration, stands infinitely higher, and yet down lower with the speculatives, since you most likely stand infinitely higher than Johannes de Silentio. In truth this may be expected to be something rather high. Consequently "the higher rationality." But pay attention to the definition; if the absurd is not the negative sign and predicate which dialectically makes sure that the scope of "the purely human" is qualitatively terminated, then you actually have no sign of your higher reason; you are taking the chance that your "higher reason" does not lie on that side of "the human," in the heavenly regions of the divine, of revelation, but on this side, and somewhat farther down, in the underground territory of misunderstanding. The absurd is the negative sign. "I," says the believer, "I really cannot be satisfied with having only rhetorical predicates for determining where I have my life, where, from the spiritual point of view, I am, so to speak. But the absurd is a category, and a category that can exercise a restraining influence. When I believe, then assuredly neither faith nor the content of faith is absurd. O, no, no—but I understand very well that for the person who does not believe, faith and the content of faith are absurd, and I also understand that as soon as I myself am not in the faith, am weak, when doubt perhaps begins to stir, then faith and the content of faith gradually begin to become absurd for me. But this may have been the divine will: in order that faith—whether a man will have faith or not—could be the test, the examination, faith was bound up with the absurd, and the absurd formed and composed in such a way that only one force can prevail over it—the passion of faith—its humility sharpened by the pain of sin-consciousness."

N.B. [*In margin: To typesetter:* N.B. one line space between.]

You conclude with the invitation to Climacus to reconsider—as a consequence of your book—the subject of the paradox. The same invitation is directed to "the gentlemen who seem to agree most with me (Climacus)," and finally to "all thinking persons," but presumably only in these kingdoms and countries. What a frightful clamor! I for my part do not feel called upon by your book to reconsider the paradox. On the contrary, as I see it, if you are going to hold forth on Christianity in the future, whether you let your summons on that subject be sent out to "all thinking persons" or not, it is necessary for you first of all to take up Christianity, which, probably without even noticing it, you lost in your zeal to prove that there is no paradox in Christianity, which, as stated before, you did superbly well: both the paradox and Christianity, jointly and separately, vanished completely.

*Postscript*

Your endeavor is indeed well meant, honest, disinterested, of that I have no doubt; to that extent it may also be called religious in the ordinary sense, may actually have some moral value, especially compared to the orthodox gangrenous tissue in Christendom. It is this conception of you that made me decide to reply. But with respect to Christianity you are in basic error, and as a thinker you are not, as Johannes de Silentio is, in "fear and trembling," but very cavalier in your copious unclarity.

———

You have misinterpreted *Fear and Trembling* to such an extent that I do not recognize it at all. Johannes de Silentio's supreme concern (thus "the problems" which are the thought-categories of the book read: "Is there a teleological suspension of the ethical?"[2715] "Is there an absolute duty to God?"[2716]), all this, that is to say, the heart of the matter, also the subject of Abraham and Isaac, you have completely overlooked or forgotten, but on the other hand, with an almost infatuated prejudice, you have devoted yourself solely (making it the chief substance of your book) to the story of the princess, a minor illustration, an approximation, used by Johannes de Silentio merely to illuminate Abraham, not to explain Abraham directly, for after all he cannot understand Abraham. [*Addition with reference markings on the back of the sheet:* while you so forget the point, which is to illuminate Abraham, and so forget Abraham, that you create for yourself a new prototype for the knight of faith: Captain Jessen of the navy. See p. 94, note.]

And even the instance of the princess you have made unrecognizable. Johannes de Silentio proceeds on the assumption that, humanly speaking, it is *impossible* for the lover to get the princess. This is the assumption. And for reasonable people, especially for thinking persons, it is a rule that the assumption must remain fixed. It is the same with Johannes de Silentio; if it were not, it would not be feasible to point out the slightest difference between resignation and faith. Now read your version of the story. To you the "knight of faith" is preoccupied with understanding that it is not *impossible* to get the princess,[2717] yes, that for many reasons it is *"possible,"* which becomes especially clear to "the knight of faith" when he—and this possibility certainly is what we call, humanly speaking, the possible—*"contemplates himself, his own personality"* (see p. 92), "since with respect to his own inner worth the knight of faith does not stand on a *lower* level than the nobility," and therefore the union is by no means a misalliance. Ye gods, what is this! The story does not resemble in the least that little illustration in *Fear and Trembling*. With you it actually is a kind of defense for falling in love with a princess, showing that, humanly speaking, it is very well possible (the assumption was that, humanly speaking, this was impossible) to get the princess, which demonstrates that it is by no means *absurd* when a man, perhaps of lowly extraction, if only he is a knight of faith, falls in love with a princess: humanly speaking, the two may very well get each other. And just as the nobility usually send their portraits to the beloved, so you provide a kind of portrait of the knight of faith (somewhat more plump but otherwise much like the pagans' description of "the wise"), presumably intended for the princess. Consequently, to repeat, with you it is *possible*, humanly speaking, for the lover to get the princess, something he is very sure of, especially when he "contemplates himself, his own personality," its high inner value which makes him perfectly equal in rank to the nobility, yes, even places him above *"kings and princes"* (p. 105). With Johannes de Silentio the assumption was that, humanly speaking, it was *impossible*; and least of all did he think that her being a princess would be taken so seriously. Johannes de Silentio is by no means that aristocratic; he could just as well, absolutely just as well, have used a commoner, a maidservant. The only important thing to him was the assumption that the lover is totally in love and, humanly speaking, cannot possibly get her. On the basis of this assumption, if it is firmly

maintained, the difference between resignation and faith can be eluci-
dated, as is done in *Fear and Trembling*—and is made of no consequence
with the help of your princess.

Respectfully,
Johannes Climacus

$X^6$ B 68    *n.d.*, 1850

« **6599**

Reply to Theophilus Nicolaus, author of a book entitled: *Er Troen
et Paradox og "i Kraft af det Absurde" et Spørgsmaal foranledigt ved "Frygt og
Bæven af Johannes de Silentio," besvaret ved Hjælp af en Troes-Ridders fortrolige
Meddelelser, til fælles Opbyggelse for J ø d e r, C h r i s t n e    o g
M u h a m e d a n e r e, af bemeldte Troes-Ridders Broder Theophilus Nico-
laus.*[2718]

$X^6$ B 69    *n.d.*, 1850

« **6600**

Regarding Theophilus Nicolaus.[2719]

> If there is to be a reply, it might be a few words by me,
> and then the remainder a little information by Anti-
> Climacus, but personally I must give no information. The
> few words by me are found in this packet, together with
> the basic material for Anti-Climacus's reply.

$X^6$ B 77    *n.d.*, 1850

« **6601**

*Addition to 6600* ($X^6$ B 77):
If there is to be any explanation, perhaps it is right to use a
pseudonym: Anti-Climacus.

With reference to Theophilus Nicolaus[2720]

———

If I were to congratulate myself on any one thing, it would be the
deliberateness with which I—while the poetic characters, the pseudonyms, were doing their utmost to present the ideal or the idealities—
the deliberateness throughout a whole authorship with which I soberly
and unreservedly have taken care and have employed safeguards lest
confusion arise and I be mistaken for the ideal.

From the book at hand[2721] it has become clear—as some other
books bearing the author's name already have made clear—that there

lives a man among us who is very willing (if only we are willing) to be the ideal himself: "the apostle" who reforms all the established, "God's friend and confidante," whose life is guided and led by "special orders." On that I can have no opinion.

Just one thing. If Theophilus Nicolaus is the person I think the author to be,[2722] it strikes me that he writes far better now than before. [*In penciled parentheses:* But the misunderstanding is so great that neither Johannes de Silentio nor I can get involved with him. If Johannes de Silentio gets involved with him it would have to be in jest, but I do not feel I ought to give my consent to that.] But the misunderstanding is so great that there is scarcely any hope of an understanding.

Incidentally, I would be glad to have another pseudonym, one who does not like Johannes de Silentio say he does not have faith,[2723] but plainly, positively says he has faith—Anti-Climacus—repeat what, as a matter of fact, is stated in the pseudonymous writings.

$X^6$ B 82   *n.d.*, 1850

## « 6602 *Goldschmidt*[2724]

Apart from the fact (1) that it really is nothing but brashness (except that he perhaps realizes this himself) and (2) that it is a silly imitation of what he has heard about metamorphoses and stages in the development of a life, he has gotten the bright idea that *The Corsair* is the first stage[2725]—apart from this, there is still the psychological oddity that he manifests the *Merkwürdighed*[2726] of the comic as the first stage. As a rule the comic is at the end—comedy quite properly concludes Hegel's *Esthetics*, and an Aristophanes certainly would feel strange if he were advised to make his life as comic poet the first part —and then become "earnest." Generally speaking, the gibberish which G. introduces into the world with his personal life is of interest in the clinical task assigned to me: Copenhagen in moral disintegration.

As a writer, I have never banned the comic; it was utilized in an auxiliary way by the pseudonyms, who, of course, quite consistently would find it ridiculous to be allowed to reach a new stage, inasmuch as the comic is a territorial designation for the highest. From the beginning I myself was an upbuilding author. In the pseudonyms the comic is, if anything, too high a stage, since it is something demonic.

$X^2$ A 605   *n.d.*, 1850

## « 6603 *Personal Remarks about Myself*

Humanly speaking, it could be said that my trouble is that I have been brought up so rigorously in Christianity.

From the very beginning I have been in the power of a congenital mental depression. If I had been brought up in a more ordinary way —well, it stands to reason that I then would hardly have become so melancholy—then I probably would have undertaken earlier to do everything to shake off this depression which almost prevented me from being human, to do everything to break it or be broken myself.

But familiar as I was in the very beginning with the Christian concept of the thorn in the flesh, that such things are part and parcel of being Christian—I discovered that there was nothing to be done, and in any case my depression found acceptance in this entire outlook.

So I reconciled myself religiously to it—humanly speaking, it has made me as unhappy as possible: but on the foundation of this pain developed an outstanding intellectual life as an author.

I accepted this life, the torment was frightful—but the satisfaction was all the greater: I can never adequately thank God for what has been granted me.

But then—then it was my fate to be an author—in Denmark. Such an author-existence in any other country would have been the path to wealth—in Denmark it cost me money. Insults were poured on me, almost everything was done to make my life unbearable to me, make me do nothing—but this author-existence which was and is my possibility was a satisfaction to me, and I could never thank Governance sufficiently, for the more opposition there was, the richer the productivity.

But—it costs money (yes, the situation is practically insane, to the hilarity of the market town where I live, exposed to insults, pursued by envy) and I can no longer afford it.[2727]

I would gladly accept an appointment—but there comes my depression again to create problems. No one has any idea of how I suffer and the scale on which I am placed outside the universally human. This has to be rescinded if I am to be able to live together with people as one holding a position.

Yet one thing remains: that I can never adequately thank God for the indescribable good he has done for me, far more than I expected.

$x^2$ A 619   n.d., 1850

## « 6604 *The Turn the World Is Taking*

As I demonstrated in the last section of the review of *Two Ages*,[2728] the punishment will conform to the guilt, and for this very reason [the punishment will be] to have no government, so that the tension but also the forward step will necessarily be that everyone must himself learn in earnest to be master, to guide himself without the supportive indulgence of having leaders and rulers (which was an amelioration, but rejected by the generation). Thus the step forward will be religious,[2729] and the tension will be that everyone must carry within himself the ambivalence of realizing that Christianity conflicts with the understanding and then still believe it. This is the signal that the age of immediacy is over. Just as in the "Psychological Experiment"[2730] Quidam is no spontaneously unhappy lover (he himself perceives that the matter is comic and yet tragically clings to it by virtue of something else, but therefore with a constant split, which is the sign that immediacy is over), so also with the religious.

$X^2$ A 622   *n.d.*, 1850

« **6605**

In my association with others maybe I was wrong in always turning the ill-treatment I suffered into witty conversation; duping them that way (this easily could hide a profound contempt for men as well) may also lead them astray.

$X^2$ A 627   *n.d.*, 1850

« **6606**

Dear friend,[2731]

During the years I have conversed with you, our relationship has been approximately this: with regard to every single one of your public performances[2732] (your writings), I have most firmly told you that from my point of view I could not approve of them. Furthermore, I have explained why not, and you yourself have also spoken in such a manner that I must consider myself as having been understood. Moreover, in private you have always expressed yourself very differently from the way you have in public. But you always said that I would find that your next book would be different. Therefore I have continued to wait.

But now this will have to come to an end. I must hereby—completely without anger—break off a relationship that was indeed begun with a certain hope and that I do not give up as hopeless at this moment either.

That is to say, I am no longer able to go walking with you according to a set agreement. It is another matter if our paths meet by fate or by chance; then it would be a pleasure for me to speak with you as with so many others.

Please do not misunderstand this, as if it were my intention to prompt you to make a public statement or in any other way to influence its nature [*in margin:* or hereby to let you understand what my judgment would be of such a possible statement]. Not at all! As you have your unconditional freedom, so I reserve my unconditional freedom to myself. I cannot do otherwise.

But do not make the mistake, either, of interpreting this as a complaint about something, as though I were reproaching you. No, I am unalterably the same as in the beginning, but I dare not let any more time pass in this manner.

Yours,

S.K.

*Letters,* no. 257 [1850]

« **6607**

[*In margin:* R. Nielsen]

With the thought of death as imminent and feeling it my duty to initiate, if possible, another person into the cause I have the honor to represent so that he could represent it in the same character, I drew him[2733] to me after he himself had made overtures. I did not permit myself the slightest direct influence on his writing, regarding it as my duty to have it happen, if it was supposed to happen, by unfolding independently in him; but I put a great store of communication at his disposal.

My hope is disappointed—I say no more, add no adverb to describe the extent of it; no adverb would be satisfactory.

One who could understand me—imagine what it means to me to keep myself inactive this way, only tensely expectant with regard to him, keeping it up a year and a half or two years, and with such an intensive life as mine, time and time again disappointed by every one of his performances, disappointed, and yet feeling obligated to hope, since I had approached the matter religiously.

Imagine what I have suffered! But perhaps it is not his fault at all but mine because I had such a hope, alas, perhaps my fault because I was responsible for permitting the kind of ideas appropriate only to my personality with its character to take another direction.

The criterion established is perhaps far, far too high. In private conversation he was well able to understand and understand, understand that what he had done was wrong, that the right thing would have been this—and then he still did the wrong thing again, or even used the observation as a productive ingredient.

To repeat, perhaps the criterion has been far, far too high. That is the trouble. As soon as I judge by this criterion, it seems to be an enormous injustice to him.

If I take the criterion away, I will have no more difficulty with him than with Stilling, who certainly has never complained of injustice. But the point is that I never invested in Stilling[2734] this way. But Nielsen certainly ought to understand this fairly well. But I perhaps did to him an injustice in what I said to him last time.

$X^3$ A 3  *n.d.,* 1850

« **6608**

..... I believed that it was part of self-renunciation to keep silent about what good, humanly speaking, I have done, and God has helped me to do so.

But my life will call out after my death. And what is a living person who uses these few moments to talk compared to one dead who continues to call out. Of every living person it is certain that his talking must come to an end—but as soon as one dead (instead of observing custom and keeping silent) begins this strange business of calling out, how is his mouth to be stopped?

$X^3$ A 4  *n.d.,* 1850

« **6609**

It is so true, so true—what Denmark needs is a dead man.

That very instant I will have been victorious as few men have ever been. That very instant all that about my thin legs and my trousers[2735] and my nickname "Søren"[2736] will be forgotten—no, it will not be forgotten, it will be understood in a quite different way and will give considerable impetus to the cause. That very instant the envy will be quieted. That same instant those who are to witness for me will speak a language different from the present one, for then no self-denial will be necessary. Then even my most trivial utterance will gain significance and access—whereas now the immense achievement is pushed aside so that insult and envy can get at me.

Only the voice of one who has died can penetrate the moral disintegration which prevails in Denmark—a dead man whose whole life was a study directed toward preparing this situation—the possibility of speaking about one who is dead.

$X^3$ A 8  *n.d.,* 1850

### « 6610  *R. Nielsen*[2737]

I wrote N. a note[2738] (so that in no way I would be the one who had done him an injustice, even the slightest). We talked together Wednesday, April 30. I told him that I wanted a freer relationship.

To hope is my element, especially when it has a touch of implausibility. I hope for him. It is still possible that he will finish properly even though he began in a wrong way. Would that he had never written the big book. His conduct after what happened between us, the way he has behaved for a year—O, that forced me to keep a detective's eye on him, something so alien to me, something I never desired, even though I always have this penetrating eye but never use it. Yes, if the relationship were such that the problem was whether to do something very contrived and that he perhaps was not sufficiently ingenious—O, something like that does not prompt me to use this penetrating eye. But the nub was that what he should have done was very simple and uncomplicated (something he himself frequently admitted he understood) and that he nevertheless continues to do something contrived instead.

The difficulty, the danger for him (which he frequently admits he understood very well and understood it from the beginning), was to slip past me as he steered, as he sought to move ahead and at the same time, using Martensen, sought to win the victory, without my attacking his flank, a battle he did not wish to risk in any way. This accounts for his personal overtures. Now he probably thinks he has achieved this, and I have not stopped him. So he tried to sneak away with a kind of independence without once signaling to me, whom he privately put off by saying that it depended particularly on "the next one." He no doubt believes that he has been successful in this, yes, that I could not ever stop him now, whereas he originally wanted to play the independent who not only had everything I wrote at his disposal but also the wealth of my conversations, completely unknown to others, and finally the incalculable capital, that a contemporaneous life guarantees the teaching, but the contemporaries are unaware of this; he, however, has communications. Little by little, he began wanting to approach closer to the truth and to take me along. But he seems to be continually reluctant to do what he well understands is the simple, uncomplicated, and true thing to do, but postpones it as something he will do in an emergency, while he goes ahead and does something else, even though this something else scarcely becomes any truer. But precisely this was the error. Air was what was needed and to that end a primitively simple, uncomplicated step was needed; instead, he shuts up everything more than ever with his big book,[2739] contrived as it is.

But I do not want to do him an injustice; he perhaps means well, but it is so hard to do the simple thing.

And that is why I hope.

« 6611 *Stoicism—and My Life*

When I read a Stoic I see correctly how essentially I am related to Christianity. What he says may be absolutely true and frequently is vigorously and expertly expressed—but he does not understand me. With the Stoic everything is pride—there is no place for sadness. He despises all the general run of men, the ignorant rabble; he treats them as children, they do not exist for him. Everything they do means nothing to the wise man; they are unable to offend him; he not only forgives them their offenses but proudly thinks: Little children, you simply cannot offend me.

O, but this is not my life at all. Of course, I can be tempted to use this tactic, arm myself in this way, against the upper class and the elite. That is why their behavior[2740] toward me never really distressed me; I revenge myself a bit stoically.

But the common man whom I loved! It was my greatest joy to express some measure of love to the neighbor; when I saw this loathsome condescension toward less important people, I dared say to myself, "I do not live like that." It was my consolation to alleviate this when possible; it was my pleasure, my blessed diversion. My life was made for that. So when I have to bear the derision[2741] of the common man it saddens me indescribably. There was in fact hardly anyone around here who loved the common man this way—and now to see him turned against me in hostility. A journalist who tricks the common man out of his money and in return gives him confused concepts is regarded as a benefactor—and the person who sacrificed so much, every advantage of solidarity with the upper class, is represented as an enemy of the common man, as someone to insult.

See, life never takes this form for the Stoic.

« 6612

At vespers in Frelsers Kirke the other Sunday (it was my birthday) I heard a theological graduate, Clemmensen, preach. It was a simple sermon, but the kind I like.

In his sermon, probably without knowing it, he slipped in a bit of highly poetic beauty; following the Gospel text,[2742] he had preached about life as a coming from the Father and a returning to the Father. Then came the usual part about life as a path. After that he quite effectively drew a picture of a father who sends his son into the world. Then he abandoned the metaphor for actuality, and it became our relation to God. And then he said: And when at last, in the hour of death, the traveler's cloak is discarded and the staff laid down—*the child goes in to the father*. Superb! I wager that Clemmensen said that quite unwittingly; if he had thought about it he perhaps might even have preferred to say: the soul or the transfigured one or something similar. But no, "the child"—that is superb.

$X^3$ A 30    *n.d.*, 1850

### « 6613  *About Myself*

How much I could do to ease my situation!

Is it pride, then, which deters me? To be sure, but there is also something else that restrains me. I realize that the longer I can sweat it out, the deeper I will wound. So it seems as if God wanted to test me. Now if I had contrived or sought relief—and the help came as I needed it, and I had to understand that if I had stuck it out a bit longer I would not have needed to seek relief, and I would have benefited the cause more—I think God might then say: You of little faith, why did you not hold out longer?

The spiritual sufferings in maintaining this tension are terrible, and suppose it is self-torment or pride—but suppose on the other hand that the task is simply to stick it out in complete silence.

$X^3$ A 41 *n.d.*, 1850

### « 6614  *Rigorousness—R. Nielsen*[2743]

My task was to introduce rigorousness. This I have done and have formulated it consistently.

Then Nielsen came along; he wanted to make improvements. He goes ahead and changes it to discussion. Nothing is more foolish and there is no more certain way of losing. If it is left to men to discuss whether they want leniency or rigorousness, the decision is easily made.

No, rigorousness is introduced either with authority or without authority; but *mir nichts* and *dir nichts*, it is above and beyond discussion.

The tragedy is that we have brought Christianity down to our level and imagine that it is up to us to discuss whether or not we want rigorousness, while we go around thinking we still have Christianity if we do not want it so rigorous. But then I surely am mad to want to have it rigorous. Eulenspiegel[2744] never did find the tree he wanted for his hanging (he had bargained for permission to choose the tree himself) —so it is with rigorousness.

X³ A 67   n.d., 1850

« 6615  *Perfect love*

Perfect love is to love the one who made you unhappy. No man has the right to demand to be loved in this way.

God can demand it; it is his infinite majesty. It is true of the religious person in the most rigorous sense that in loving God he loves the one who made him, humanly speaking, unhappy in this life—even though blessed.

I do not have the strength to understand it this way. I am also so very afraid that I might get trapped in the most dangerous of all snares —becoming self-righteous. The religious man in the most rigorous sense has, however, vanquished this danger also.

X³ A 68   n.d., 1850

« 6616  *Christianity*

Yes, of course there is a conflict between God and men. And if Christianity is to be introduced in all its truth (something only Scripture succeeded in doing) or be introduced by an apostle, then it sets up a life-and-death enmity.

It is appalling just to think of how the person who actually presents Christianity must die to the world, die to being human in the ordinary sense.

For my part, I feel infinitely far from it. I love being human, do not have the courage to be spirit to that extent. And yet in our setting I probably am one of the most advanced.

Therefore my life manifests at least something of Christianity. It certainly was not my original intention to occupy myself this way with the religious. No, miserable from early times, so miserable that I realized that for me there was no help, no recourse to be found among men, placed outside of human society, assigned to myself, daily reminded of my wretchedness—in the days of youth when the blood was warm and I so wanted to be like the others, in the days of romantic love when the heart beat rapidly and I so wanted to be like the others—I learned to cling to the religious as my only consolation.

Nevertheless I have always presented it in mitigated form, even in relation merely to my own understanding of it; I have presented it mitigated both to spare others and myself.

Without authority, that was my category; on the other hand, I have never declared that love to God is hatred of the world, and the reverse, as Christianity does.

I am not a happy man who by virtue of a spiritual impact has voluntarily decided to become involved with Christianity (and God knows if it actually can be done, if suffering is lacking at first); I am first of all an unhappy man placed outside of the universally human. This is not such a happy thing—and that is why I never dare directly charge others, for it seems that the first thing I have to do is to make them unhappy, and I cannot do that, I who—all the worse, as the rigorous Christian would say—still so love to see others have a purely human joy in life, something for which I have a more than ordinary eye, because I have a poet's eye for it. Moreover, I am a penitent—and again I cannot take it upon myself to compel others to be that, but certainly I am that myself.

In short, I have the prerequisites assumed by Christianity (suffering in a more than ordinary sense and guilt in a more particular sense), and I find my stronghold in Christianity. But authority or direct proclamation is not really in my range, for I cannot, after all, fulfil the prerequisites. I can very well assume a pastoral appointment, for it does not involve the rigorous concept of Christian proclamation; and least of all do I have any place there as a missionary.

$X^3$ A 77    *n.d.*, 1850

## « 6617 *A Trait of My Father's Which Deserves To Be Preserved*

At lunch one day I overturned a salt-shaker. Passionate as he was and intense as he easily could become, he began to scold so severely that he even said that I was a prodigal and things like that. Then I made an objection, reminding him of an old episode in the family when my sister Nicoline had dropped a very expensive tureen and Father had not said a word but pretended it was nothing at all. He replied: Well, you see, it was such an expensive thing that no scolding was needed; she realized quite well that it was wrong, but precisely when it is a trifle there must be a scolding.

There is something of the greatness of antiquity in this little story. This objectivity which does not scold on the basis of what has been done to the reprimander but purely objectively on the basis of the need for a scolding.

« **6618  *About Myself***

Never have I made the slightest attempt or move to oblige or force anyone else to serve Christianity on the terms I use or to judge anyone for not doing it. On the contrary, I have supported those who proclaimed Christianity on completely different terms, have supported people of esteem, since I discerned the present chaotic insurrection from below.

This has to be maintained, for otherwise I would bear some guilt toward them in this respect.

But now their own guilt is completely exposed, namely, that they not only do not proclaim Christianity themselves on those terms but will not even allow me to do it, but declare me a fanatic, an eccentric, who rightfully is a sacrifice to the rabble.

« **6619  *Fædrelandet***

Anyone who knew something of the situation knew how *Fædrelandet* winced under the journalism of rabble barbarism,[2745] which completely outstripped it.

I acted; Gjødwad[2746] stood impatiently at my side and waited for the article in which I demanded that I be abused.

One of two alternatives: *either* they had to insist that that press should be ignored—and then not even accept my article,[2747] even though I had requested it, *or* (and this was the case) they perceived that their position was so desperate and general conditions so perverse that there had to be some action—and then they would have to support my intervention, which would require merely an acknowledging word.

They did not do it, they betrayed me. At long last they canceled their subscription to *The Corsair*, as if that were doing something. When in the course of conversations they seemed to be asking me if they should do something (without directly raising the question), I always said: Just do nothing. If there is no more feeling than that for a just cause, I am not one to solicit.

*Fædrelandet* perhaps bears more guilt toward me than even

Goldschmidt.[2748] In any case, there is the continuing guilt of not trying to give even a little bit of orientation with one single word on my behalf. To tell me privately that my works are so extraordinary that no one can take it upon himself to review them is, in fact, just a joke. After all, they could say it publicly—and not remain silent while the rabble alone hold forth.

I write this down specifically for the following reason. My day will surely come. Then it will be convenient for *Fædrelandet* to throw some blame on Heiberg,*[2749] and especially on Mynster,[2750] for not having spoken up on my behalf—and thus *Fædrelandet* will undoubtedly pretend to be so innocent. But I do not intend to put up with that.

I regard Gjødwad as a personal friend, and in the last three or four years I have spoken with him every blessed evening and, as I knew I would, found him to be a likable man. If he had not been a journalist, he no doubt would have been the one who could have been my closest friend. But the paper *Fædrelandet* changes things completely. I willingly acknowledge that they were in a difficult position to act at that time, but that was also the real test.

$$x^3 \ A \ 88 \quad n.d., \ 1850$$

### « 6620

*Addition to 6619* (x³ A 88):
*Note. He also thanked me *privately* in the strongest terms for the article[2751] against P. L. Møller, and added: I should have done it myself long ago. So *privately* he talked that way, but *publicly* he remained silent.

$$x^3 \ A \ 89 \quad n.d.$$

### « 6621

*In margin of 6619* (x³ A 88):
The situation prior to my action was this. Officially they tried their best to maintain the view that this rabble barbarism was nothing, something to be ignored. Privately they long ago had mutually agreed that the whole situation was intolerable. Subscriptions to *The Corsair* increased; subscriptions to the other papers decreased; it was read by the higher and the lower classes and with enormous curiosity; it was a power, sheer tyranny. People looked to each other to do something; they looked to me. So I acted. That is, I changed the method. They knew very well that all by myself I had ten times the polemical power that was necessary. The only trouble was that few understood that it

was proper to change the method. For that *Fædrelandet* should have taken a step, made note of it—otherwise why did it accept the article. But no. They found it most prudent to retreat to the old tactics: that such a paper is nothing, something to be ignored—and let me stand like a semi-lunatic—and this was the country's greatest young luminary, hitherto without a single blot on his name.

There was some truth (as I acknowledged then but for other reasons) in what Goldschmidt[2752] told me immediately after the first article[2753] came out, thus prior to the beginning of his attack: that he could not understand why I would do so much for *Fædrelandet;* after all Ploug[2754] was not much better than he. He said the same of Gjødwad,[2755] but to that I rebutted: Gjødwad is my friend.

But what an indirect concession Goldschmidt made after the publication of the first article when he asked me privately: "Have you read the article; it completely annihilates P. L. Møller." Presumably he secretly wanted to prevent *The Corsair*'s attack, which I of course did not wish to do. And, furthermore, *Fædrelandet* actually credited me with being the only man able to take on the whole rabble.

And all this is suppressed, while a class of people which has no conception of me and no intimation of the true situation is incited against me.

$x^3$ A 90   *n.d.*

### « 6622  *A Lodger*

Upstairs in the house where I am now living on Nørregade[2756] there is a lodger who can be called a quiet and orderly lodger—in fact, he is out all day. Unfortunately he keeps a dog that is at home all day. It lies in the open window and takes an interest in everything. If a man goes by and sneezes louder than usual, it immediately barks and can go on barking for a long time. If a coachman drives by and snaps his whip, it barks and another dog starts barking—thus the least incident cannot take place on the street without my getting a second edition of it, thanks to this dog.

$x^3$ A 94   *n.d.,* 1850

### « 6623  *About Myself Personally*

If I had had no financial assets at all, I believe it would have helped me, for then I would have been compelled to do all I could about my livelihood and would have had no scruples of conscience about being allowed to do so.

But now when I am able to understand how extraordinarily much has been entrusted to me and of what benefit I am—it seems to me, since I do in fact still have money—that I ought to stay put. The hard thing about this conflict is that on the one side I fear "grieving the spirit" and, on the other, "tempting God."

The financial crisis of 1848[2757] suddenly saddled me with this whole matter. And now a general property tax is very imminent, which will put me in financial straits. And no one will understand me. Even if I have been prodigal, it nevertheless also had a purely ideal significance for me, simply because I comprehended how much had been entrusted to me. If I had allowed a worldly, commonsensical outlook to rule, I never would have achieved what I have achieved; I would have become a completely different man. Before God I readily confess my improvidence, that before him I am in the wrong[2758] here as everywhere. He has it in his power to say to me: "You ought to have been economical." And yet he above all knows what gives another interpretation to the matter from another side. But one can never have anything to do with God in any other way—he always turns out to be right. A person who actually ventures something—after all, it is not determined in advance that he can bear it every moment (that is what it means to venture)—consequently, if the one who ventures becomes afraid, God can say: Yes, you are to blame yourself for that. But on the other hand, one who trusts in God rests in the faith that God will surely help him. But one is always in the wrong in relation to God. For if there is success—the credit goes not to me but to the help of God, who at any moment could have let me go; if it does not succeed, the mistake is mine, that I ventured.

Thus it is actually frightful to become involved with God, who cannot and will not provide positive assurance or a contractual relation —and yet it is blessed, blessed to be as nothing in his hands, he who nevertheless eternally is and continues to be love, however things turn out. Only this do I have for sure, this blessed assurance that God is love. Even if I have made a mistake at this or that point: God is still love—this I believe, and he who believes this has not made a mistake. If I have made a mistake, it will surely become clear to me; then I repent—and God *is* love. He *is* that; not he *was* that nor he *will be* that —O, no, even this future would be too slow for me, he *is* that. How wonderful. Sometimes, perhaps, there may be a long time of waiting for my repentance and then there is a future—but God does not allow any waiting for him, he is love. Just as the water of a spring has the same coolness summer and winter, unchanged—so is God's love. But just as it sometimes happens that a spring runs dry—no, no—well, how shall I give praise, I have no other cry than the one which refers specifically to him who is the subject here: "God be praised!" —Therefore, no, God be praised, God is not love such as that. His love is a spring, but it never runs dry.

$X^3$ A 98   *n.d.*, 1850

« **6624 *About Myself***

In Denmark I have been offered an enormous fee to write in the papers (when Carstensen[2759] had *Figaro* or *Portefeuillen* he once offered me 100 rix-dollars a printed sheet for an article against Heiberg[2760]) —I have paid out rather much for the publication of one or another of my big books, the fruit of hard work for a year or a year and a half.[2761]

$X^3$ A 99   *n.d.*, 1850

« **6625 *From My Life***

Just once in my life have I been present at a public general meeting (my very infrequent attendance at a student assembly or an insurance company meeting is something else again), and I was chairman[2762] that time.

It was the second general student assembly immediately after Christian VIII took the throne.

After a few introductory words about how deeply flattered I felt at being elected, I turned to the business.

This began with and practically consisted of a Levin's (not Israel,[2763] but another) requesting and receiving permission to speak. He said: Gentlemen, what is a petition? Here he was interrupted. The uproar lasted for some time; finally I managed to get order and said: Mr. Levin has the floor. The scene was repeated and once again. Mr. Levin gradually worked his way up to the podium and wanted a private discussion with me to explain what he actually meant, probably thinking it was out of a private interest in him that I had made so many attempts to let him be heard.

Then French Bjerring[2764] asked for the floor and began like an orator with a question: Is there anyone who ventures to oppose me on this? Here he was stopped by the whole assembly beginning to shout: Yes, yes. The scene lasted a long time.

Then my brother came up to me and asked that the appeal be

returned, since that was what really was supposed to be discussed at the meeting; he also asked me to say as he himself said that the appeal would be placed in his apartment for signatures. That, of course, was against all the rules. And to make it complete, I finally got the floor and said: the general assembly is adjourned. This was done instead of discharging the chairman.

Incidentally, strange to say, although a long time had elapsed since this event, the second time I spoke with Christian VIII[2765] he indicated that he was informed about this general assembly and that I had presided.

$$X^3 A 112 \quad n.d., 1850$$

### « 6626 *About Myself*

What I have achieved will be admired for a long time; I *have had* extraordinary capabilities (alas, how I do recognize myself in this past tense which I always use; even when I feel my strongest I say: I have had—this is a composite of melancholy, reflection, and piety, and this compound is my essential nature): with respect to being human, what I lack is the animal-attribute.

People make use of that against me. They feel physically stronger, can take part in everything, something I cannot do—then they regard it as eccentric, affected, ridiculous, proud, and God knows what else that I am not just the same; they take brutish joy in demanding of me what has been denied me and deriding what has been given me. And this is easy to do, since in our limited setting I am such a rarity that I presumably am the only one of my kind, and with whom, therefore, no one feels a bond of affinity.

Even those who have some spirit enviously make use of this. They, too, find it farfetched, eccentric, and ridiculous of me, although, it is by no means ridiculous, whether one looks at the suffering or the product of the suffering. Suffering frightful anguish, frequently to the point of the impotence of death—my spirit at such a time is strong and I forget all that in the world of ideas. But then I am upbraided for only wanting to be a thinker and for not being like other men; they grant me every possible suffering and abuse as well-deserved punishment. O, how false and foolish you are! Give me a body, or if you had given me that when I was twenty years old, I would not have been this way. But you are envious, and this is the suffering the more highly endowed person, spiritually-intellectually, has to suffer in his generation. It is so easy to say of the past: Whatever is going to be immortalized in song must die—but in actual life one prefers to be exempt from this himself —yes, one resents the person whose life bears all the marks of being that kind.

Moreover, it is entirely certain that direct and immediate sufferings at least have the mitigation of not being identified with a person's character. If a person is a cripple, at least no one says it is eccentric, affected, and ridiculous of him to be that. But of course all direct, immediate, identifiable sufferings are also subject to that painfulness called sympathy.

$X^3$ A 115   n.d., 1850

## « 6627 *Mynster's Sermons—and I*

I was brought up on Mynster's sermons—*aber* [read aloud[2766]] by my father, a simple, unassuming, earnest, and rigorous man to whom it never in the world occurred that one should not imitate what was read.

If I had been brought up by Mynster, I of course would have found out on Monday, Tuesday, etc., the weekdays, that one is not to be a fanatic who goes and promptly imitates in that way.

What a difference! And, alas, what a satire on Mynster I have actually become. This is not perceived; I have kept the reverence for him that I inherited and it no doubt has served me well and kept me from being guilty of exaggeration, which as a matter of fact is totally foreign to my nature, for discretion characterizes the way I operate where another, *ein, zwei, drei,* would get too excited. Incidentally, this is also a result of my having understood so early and so profoundly that I was an exception.

$X^3$ A 128   n.d., 1850

## « 6628 *About Myself*

What confounded consequences now that thousands and thousands who understand nothing presume to judge, led by persons who do not understand anything either, since with regard to my cause I actually am the only one with the catagories.

They are always twisting my relationship around, explaining my break with rabble barbarism[2767] as the result of my being an aristocrat and wanting to show my contempt for men.

What nonsense. It could never occur to an aristocrat to take a step such as that, such conduct is utterly unaristocratic.

I acted precisely because I was conscious of being anything but an aristocrat, conscious that this was what my daily life expressed, conscious that in my sadness and religiousness I at least had been attentive to loving "the neighbor."

Having assumed that I acted as an aristocrat, they expected that I would go on being the aristocrat—that is, travel or withdraw in patrician pride.

Here it comes again: my whole preoccupation is Christianity; and the common man has hardly anyone who loves him more truly.

But this, which is so plainly Christian, has become completely foreign in Christendom!—where we are all Christians.

$x^3$ A 142   *n.d., 1850*

### « 6629 *My Home*

When a person lives alone the way I do, he resorts all the more to his home, where if anywhere he can feel comfortable.

And what is my home like now! Last summer at the tanner's[2768] I suffered inexpressibly from the odors. I dared not risk remaining there another summer, and furthermore it was too expensive. Where I live now,[2769] I suffer so intensely from the reflection of the sun in the afternoon that at first I was afraid of going blind.

And now the trouble with Strube.[2770] That the man I depended upon as on no one else, the man I inherited from father, knew for twenty years, whom I have regarded as one of these healthy, strong, energetic workers—that of all times just when he is with me he becomes unbalanced, has to go to the hospital, wants to reform the world, and all that. When one himself works intellectually as hard as I do, he desires his surroundings to be just what I imagined I had with Strube. And now all that is involved in taking care of him, the sight of him still suffering, although they have managed to control him fairly well, the concern that it may recur and then, since it is in my house, become a spectacular event which the papers seize upon, while on the other hand I am afraid that if I let him go now it would affect him too powerfully, and God knows he is the same, the most good-natured soul I have known, or one of the most good-natured, and solicitude for me personified, but I did see in the past how vehement he could be and how obstinate.

And now from another quarter. Not long ago (while still living at the tanner's) I came home one day and saw that someone must have been in my desk and in my only chest, the mahogany one. I may have forgotten to lock them when I went out, although that is practically unthinkable, but nevertheless most unpleasant. Such things can make a home unpleasant, even if one has, as I do, the most loyal people around me. It was very unpleasant for me for Anders's sake—Anders,[2771] with whom I have been especially happy, for[2772]

And when tired out, to come home to all this, often disagreeably disturbed by the brutality to which I am daily exposed—O, to proclaim Christianity in that way is entirely different from being a pastor.

And then not to be able to afford going on writing,[2773] for when I write I forget everything.

x³ A 144   n.d., 1850

### « 6630  *R. Nielsen*[2774]—*and I*

I certainly am no Socrates and Nielsen no Plato, but the relation may still be analogous.

Take Plato, now! Indubitably Plato had a great preponderance of ideas that were his own, but he, in order to keep the point of departure clear, never hesitated to attribute everything to Socrates, he never wearied of what the people perhaps got tired of—that it was always Socrates, Socrates.

But Nielsen took the ideas and concealed where they came from; finally he gave his source but concealed the extent of his borrowing, also that I had gone out of my way to initiate him into my cause.

I have done nothing but have put everything into the hands of Governance.

x³ A 146   n.d., 1850

### « 6631  *About Myself*

Imagine a nymph with only a spectral voice, living alongside one of the concessions at the amusement park in Dyrehave,[2775] where the shouting and trumpet blasts of the barkers are incessant: that is how I live.

But heard it will be, long after they have become silent, all these sensately powerful fellows in their clerical gowns who sensately satisfy the congregation by getting married seven times and are busy with secular enterprises while they also declaim or shout Christianity once a week.

x³ A 147   n.d., 1850

### « 6632  *About Myself*

Actually Christianity is just about abolished. But first of all a poet-heart must break, or a poet must so upset the apple cart that he blocks the way for all illusions.

This is the halting, and in the narrow confines of our little country this is my task.

This poet loves the ideal; he differs from the usual poet to the extent that he is ethically aware that the task is not to poetize the ideal but to be like it. But it is just this that he despairs over; also the pain he must bring upon men when the ideal is to be brought into actuality. But no one is more scrupulous than he with respect to all the illusions he discovers and dispatches on an incredible scale; in fact, it is like an unhappy love affair (and, indeed, his life is an unhappy love affair with the ideal).

x³ A 152   n.d., 1850

### « 6633  *Light—To Lighten*

Rigorousness lightens decision (as is said: I will lighten your load); decision is lightest out of rigorousness, light as the bird that takes off from the wind-tossed branch, assisted by the rocking.

(This thought is the original draft of the three discourses on "The Lily of the Field and the Bird of the Air," in the opening of the first discourse, I believe, or it may be jotted down some place else;[2776] I know not where—so I record it again.)

x³ A 161   n.d., 1850

### « 6634

[*In margin*: Martensen]
What infinite self-assurance Martensen[2777] has! He always talks so broadly about the whole Church, the apostolic age, the dogmatics of the first three centuries, the dogmatics of the Middle Ages, of the Reformation period, of the whole succession of famous Church Fathers—and Christ says: I wonder if faith will be found on earth when I come again.[2778]

Such things do not concern Martensen—he is objective

x³ A 163   n.d., 1850

### « 6635

[*In margin*: Martensen's *Dogmatiske Oplysninger*]
In *Dogmatiske Oplysninger*[2779] Martensen complains that Stilling[2780] mixes in things with "unwashed hands,"[2781] and therefore one cannot get involved with him.

From the essentially Christian point of view, this should not be disturbing, because, after all Christ (who, by the way, was no elegant court preacher who continually brings Christianity back to external elegance) himself declares that whether or not one eats with unwashed hands is of no consequence. How natural for Christ to make this appraisal, he who was more concerned with the very opposite, that a Lady Macbeth, for example, can wash her hands from morning until night, use the ocean to wash them—and they still do not get clean, or that Pilate also washed his hands, presumably not to crucify the truth with "unwashed hands." [*In margin*: for to crucify the truth presumably is of no consequence, the important thing is whether one does it with washed or—horrors!—with unwashed hands.]

$x^3$ A 164   *n.d.*, 1850

« **6636**

*Recollections from the Lives of the Pseudonyms*
*A Contribution to the Current Theological Controversy*[2782]
by
S.K.

_____

### Preface

The defense for the tone of this little essay is very briefly as follows. In his *Dogmatiske Oplysninger*[2783] Prof. Martensen bluntly declares that the pseudonyms are nothing but modes of expression. That does not bother me at all, for such conceit, in part stupid, warrants any tone whatsoever.

The reader perhaps will not wonder at my finding it necessary to say this in advance before he has read what follows. For the tone actually used is most mild and inoffensive; in a way it is idyllic, recollections: "Do you recall that time in the Royal Gardens" etc.

### Introduction

*Dogmatiske Oplysninger* is published! Now this is what can be called clarification. If there is anything it does not clarify, then it must be because it does not appear in the book, and thus the clarification cannot be required to clarify it, at most one could ask that it be included in the clarification. It clarifies not only for us, but I am convinced that Fredrikke Bremer[2784] (who is linked by so many sympathetic bonds to Martensen's *Dogmatik*), as soon as she sees this light, will suspect, without any previous knowledge of it, that it is Martensen's clarification, unless she (who both read the book in advance in proof sheets, reviewed it in advance, declaring that M. would reform scholarship in the whole North, finally rushed off to N. America, presumably to prepare the way for the *Dogmatik*), unless she also knew in advance that Martensen had in mind the tactic, if attacks should come, of waiting until they were forgotten—and then to publish clarification.

## To the Subject

While Prof. Martensen, as mentioned, brushes aside "this whole prolix literature"[2785] (the pseudonyms and presumably me, Magister K., with them) as modes of expression, he declares repeatedly in other places that he really has no acquaintance with this whole literature. That is more or less wanting to have one's cake and eating it, too: wanting to put on airs in two diametrically opposite ways, for one thing to ignore, not to have read—and also to make an Olympian judgment, which instead implies an admission to having read—but presumably mediation is his existence-category, by virtue of which he can be heard once or twice every sixth Sunday on the text: No man can serve two masters. —But enough of that.

So he himself admits to a very slight acquaintance with this whole literature. Possibly there is some truth to this, but when it is said in just this way, the effect it produces can be less true. To the ordinary reader who does not know the situation, the impression may be given that these pseudonymous writings are a literature in a class by itself, having nothing at all to do with Prof. M., and therefore it is quite natural for Prof. M. to have only a very slight acquaintance with it.

But this is as far as possible from being the case. However much or little he knows this literature in the sense of having studied it, there is absolutely no contemporary literature of whose existence he has been so much and so long aware.

But you will not deny it, will you, Prof. M. You do not want the embarrassment of being the only one in the kingdom to deny that from the very beginning these pseudonyms, in a highly disturbing and annoying manner, have had a bearing on the system. And this whole matter of the system, again, was chiefly linked to your name. That this is so not even your zealous apologist, Prof. Scharling,[2786] has dared deny but has spoken quite *bona fide* about it as a matter of general knowledge. If it had been suggested to him to speak differently, he no doubt would have taken this as suggesting that he be shameless—and Prof. S. is much too respectable and upright a man for that.

"The system" in Denmark and the pseudonyms essentially belong together.

Do you recall . . . . . it was "the system." Yes, there was a matchless movement and excitement over the system then, and Prof. M., the profound genius, who praised it, and Prof. Heiberg,[2787] who also praised it, and Stilling[2788] and Nielsen[2789] and Tryde[2790] and God knows who else—yes, there was hardly anyone in the whole kingdom, or at least in the whole capital, who in one way or another was not related to the system in suspenseful expectation. It was the system. If anyone desires a true picture of the situation at that time, pictures from life, then read one or two of the pseudonyms,[2791] who have preserved this for history. As stated: it was the system.

*And then there were the pseudonyms.* Yes, it is true, there was one man who, if he somehow were not what he is, "the headman,"[2792] would nevertheless be headman, for he ranks a head above all the rest. He was no friend of the "system" either, which originally was out to diminish him by saying that he had gotten old etc., could not comprehend the system etc., all of which one can reread in the pseudonyms, for example, in Nicolaus Notabene.[2793] He, this headman, put on pressure from above—but otherwise it was the pseudonyms. —Consequently, and then there were the pseudonyms.

And *then*—well, God knows how it actually happened—then it was all over with the system. It was scarcely mentioned any more; many even began involuntarily to smile when the word "system" was mentioned. The whole thing disappeared quietly, in part perhaps because the pseudonyms always made only an indirect attack.

———

Here are a few recollections of the pseudonyms.

At midsummer, when the manuscript for *Either/Or* was just about ready, I wrote a little article in *Fædrelandet* under my own name: "Public Confession."[2794] It began with my disavowing, entirely on my own initiative, the authorship of everything possible that had been written in the papers etc. up until then—and I also used the opportunity to ask the readers never in the future to regard me as the author of anything to which my name was not signed. —This article also contained a hint that it was Bishop M. and Prof. Heiberg, for example, who I thought should be supported. —And primarily, already here it was apparent that I was aiming at the system. "It is the system," etc.

Now some quotations from the preface to *Fear and Trembling,* from the prefaces, and from *Concluding Postscript.*

——

In 1850 Martensen's *Dogmatik* came out. It does not call itself a system. What has been considered speculation over the last forty years or so—and it is the only concept of speculation which has been maintained—M. has given up.

So there was nothing to say here. The pseudonyms have unselfishly served in the interest of religion, have never asked for recognition; they have never made a move to affirm their claims, if only this business with the system would pass.

But in the preface to his *Dogmatik*[2795] Prof. M. writes about certain others "who are able to think only by fits and starts, in flashes, in aphorisms." He had the pseudonyms in mind, whom he himself says he has read only by glimpses. This was a falsehood; so at any rate Prof. M. has a right to talk about the pseudonyms.

Meanwhile both the pseudonyms and I kept silent.

But what happens? A pair of the most zealous systematizers in the past underwent a change, Prof. Martensen's literary friends for a number of years, whose speculative eye I daresay he recognized since he chose them and stood with them so many years—while now he seems to have discovered quite *en passant* that the two are nonentities, which is either in one way or the other all the worse for Prof M., either that he has been *Busenfreund*[2796] of two nonentities for so many years or that they actually are important people, in which case their judgment of M. is important.

So these two systematizers (Prof. Nielsen and Magister Stilling) had changed, but in such a way that they gave greater emphasis to what they owed the pseudonyms, with whom they now agreed.

They criticized among other things the impropriety of that preface. Both the pseudonyms and I kept silent.

Then came *Dogmatiske Oplysninger,* and the whole pseudonymous literature was declared to be nothing more than modes of expression —and now I speak up.

——

Prof. Martensen certainly enjoys a good deal of prestige here at home. I could continue what I have been doing up until now: mind my own business, make sacrifices, keep quiet, otherwise secretly smile a little at all this prestige, gained by means of so much—and this I will

repeat on judgment day—so much downright shabbiness and characterlessness. It [what I have been doing] comes naturally to me and that
is why I have deported myself this way for a number of years. But I have
discovered that what is partly my intellectual-spiritual endowment,
partly Christian self-renunciation, is used in a shabby way.

Humble before God, submissive to the cause I have the honor of
serving, I have honestly tried in my serving the truth to remove illusions. I did hope possibly to move one or another of those who are
disinclined to serve the truth on those conditions. But it did not happen. And the fact that I did not directly attack the others, that I
remained silent, was so willing to let my life be the butt of jest, with
only one reservation: in my interior self, in my work, in my conduct,
there to know about earnestness according to a somewhat different
criterion than the so-called earnest people use—this has even been
used to make me out an eccentric and to confirm themselves in the idea
that to serve the truth with illusions is true earnestness.

Thus I have understood it to be my duty to speak somewhat
differently.[2797]

$X^6$ B 137   *n.d.*, 1850

« **6637**

The dedication to Mynster[2798] perhaps could be used. (1) I have
always wanted to do it. (2) The moment is propitious, since Martensen
is polemically isolated in another quarter.[2799] (3) Mynster can use it at
this moment.

But no, I cannot very well do it (1) for the sake of the one who
comes next; (2) and I will weaken the impact of the whole authorship
if he is the only living person who gets a dedication, he with whom I
am so at variance. (3) It might be hard on R. Nielsen,[2800] even if I could
give the affair a turn that would benefit him, so that he has only
Martensen. (4) There is a person living who has a much greater claim
and who has nothing to do with literature, where as a consequence the
stress can fall where it should, on the purely personal, and my life's
God-relationship.

$X^6$ B 162   *n.d.*, 1850

« **6638**

If possible it could be used[2801] but altered in one place,
thus: an old man in discretion very early in his life, now
—O, beautiful earnestness!—an old man in years and discretion—etc.

What most younger people presumably have received handed down from their elders but I very particularly from my deceased father, what I in honesty and filial piety have preserved to the best of my ability, I have wished to express in a more public way in this dedication, which in all its insignificance perhaps still has one importance, that in a certain sense it is just as old and—alas, but only through a successor! —just as young as its subject, the venerable old man who still young outlives the generations—O earnestness of life!—an old man in wisdom, now—O, beautiful earnestness!—an old man in years and wisdom, but as mentally vigorous as a young man. What does it really mean to preserve oneself? It is in the days of one's youth, when the blood is warm and the heart beats strongly, to be able to cool oneself down with almost an old man's discretion; and when the day is waning and dusk is falling, it is to be able to be aflame with almost the fire of youth. But in preserving himself this way he has also preserved the established; he has never shaken the pillars of the established, but on the contrary he stood and stands unshaken as its firmest pillar. He has never had anything new to bring, it was always the old; when he edits the new edition of his first published sermons he will find "essentially nothing to change."[2802] No, it was the old confession which in him found such a rich, strong, powerful, eloquent, and penetrating expression that through a long lifetime he moves many with this old confession, and when he is dead many will long for this old confession and this old man, just as in the summer heat one longs for the coolness of a spring.

May it please Your Grace to accept this dedication, for which I have sought a place from the very beginning and decided that it was most appropriate here at the conclusion to be able to get expressed as forcefully as possible what I have wished to express: that at the conclusion I have not moved away from my position but stand at the beginning.

Just one word more, an appeal to you, Your Grace, that you will not take exception to what I now add. I have never concealed it, but precisely because I as an author always have singled you out for my admiration, perhaps you also will be sure to appreciate that I publicly say it here and now, if I for one moment dare think of myself as a religious author together with you: We are extremely different, just about opposites within the essentially Christian. Just this—it cannot possibly weaken the impression of my devotedness and veneration; to me it seems that it must rather heighten it.

$X^6$ B 163   *n.d.*, 1850

« **6639**

*Addition to 6638* (x⁶ B 163):

To His Excellency

   The Right Reverend Bishop Dr. Mynster

   Grand Cross of *Dannebrog* and Member of *Dannebrog* a.o.

      is dedicated

         this little book

            in

               profound veneration.[2803]

x⁶ B 164   *n.d.*, 1850

« **6640**

*In margin of later draft* (x⁶ B 165) *of 6638* (x⁶ B 163):

If this is used, a notation should be made on the cover of "Three Minor Ethical-Religious Essays by F. F."[2804] (lying in the tin box), in which it was originally.

x⁶ B 167   *n.d.*, 1850

« **6641**

*From later draft of 6638* (x⁶ B 163):

. . . This has been for me a need, because I have felt indebted to you, indebted to one now dead,[2805] indebted to myself, indebted to my contemporaries, in short, indebted in every way. Of course one does not get out of such indebtedness all at once, that I well know—but on the other hand I also desire, and with the same fervency, to be bound in debt always.

In profound veneration
S. Kierkegaard
x⁶ B 169   *n.d.*, 1850

« **6642** *My Category*

What I actually represent is: the roadblock which puts an end to the reflections continuing from generation to generation and posits the essentially Christian qualities. I have assistance which enables me to do this, for very early in life I was "halted" myself by being set outside the universally human in unspeakable sufferings and thrust solely upon the relationship to God.

Although standing in the middle of actuality on a scale unknown to anyone else here at home (for I have more or less reached "actuality"); in another sense I have lived as though in a world of my own.

Of the rightness of my cause and its significance I have never doubted—doubted, no, I am as far as possible from that; I have had but one expression: that I can never thank God sufficiently for what has been granted me, so infinitely much more than I expected or could or dared expect, and I have longed for eternity to thank God unceasingly.

A young girl,[2806] my beloved—her name will go down in history with mine—in a way was squandered on me so that in new pain and suffering (alas, it was a religious conflict of an unusual kind) I might become what I became. In a certain sense I, again, was squandered in the cause of Christianity; in a certain sense, for, humanly speaking, I indeed have not been happy—O, but still I can never adequately thank God for the indescribable good he has done for me, so infinitely more than I expected.

Does anyone ask if I feel that something could have happened differently and thus have been better? Foolish question: No. There are some things I feel could have happened differently so that I could have been, humanly speaking, happier—but that it would have been better, no, no. And in retrospect I more and more perceive with indescribably blissful amazement how that which happened was the only thing, the only right thing.

$x^3$ A 168    *n.d.*, 1850

« **6643** *The Difference Between My Struggle and Those Earlier*

Previously there have been controversies over doctrine, one party would not accept a doctrine etc. This is the struggle between orthodoxy and heterodoxy.

My struggle, much more inward, is about the *how* of the doctrine. I say that someone can accept the whole doctrine, but in presenting it he destroys it. The contention here is not over the unwillingness of others to have Christianity but their wanting to have it in the wrong way. For example, they want to have the whole of Christianity—but by virtue of reasons—so it is not Christianity. They want to have the whole of Christianity, but by way of speculation—so it is not Christianity. They want to have the whole of Christianity, but as a doctrine. So it is not Christianity.

This struggle is much more inward and is not likely to become popular.

x³ A 174   n.d., 1850

## « 6644  *Christ's Tunic*

In a devotional writer (Scriver[2807]) I read that there is a legend which says that the Virgin Mary had knit this tunic for him when he was a child and that it grew with him as he grew.

x³ A 183   n.d., 1850

## « 6645  *Genuine Self-Denial—The Important*

Christianly, it is more important that I deny myself in one respect or another, renounce one pleasure or another, than that I, condoning it, bring forth the most perfect masterpiece of pure thought, art, etc., or that I accomplish something most amazing, even if this is beneficial.

This, you see, is genuine Christianity. But my life is not that elevated. I have had a childish delight in many, many pleasures, and have rejoiced and thanked God when they have helped give me new strength to do something that I could consider true and right.

But this thorough-going sobriety, which the rigorously Christian is, is too elevated for me; I can only laud and praise it, this sobriety! Because I and my kind, we are more or less intoxicated by imagination and involuntarily create God somewhat akin to it. Whereas he, the only beatific one, with beatific sobriety, if I dare say so, looks simply and solely at the ethical, and all this business of achievement, getting things done, etc., means nothing at all to him, has no impact on him whatsoever.

How many a man is there who calmly could maintain this so that it convinced him to act accordingly: if, for example, by living in abundance he actually was able to achieve such a masterwork that from generation to generation it would convince thousands of the truth, and would be unable to do so were he not allowed to live in abundance— how many would there be who are so sober as to perceive that the latter is what is important, that it is more important to live impoverished and let all the masterworks go. But so it is before God. But, on the other hand, it would be the ruination of me and, I am sure, most men, if I were to breathe only the pure air of the ethical.

I do not say more; I merely continue to call attention to it and place myself much lower. If only I would not be forced into being perfect, which I am not at all.

In quiet thought I am able to maintain the thoroughgoing sobriety of the ethical, but when it comes to acting on my own I cannot force myself to it. Then I become anxious and afraid of it as of the most dreadful pedantry that would strangle me inhumanly. Yes, it seems to me that God is opposed to my deluding myself into attempting anything so elevated. But I extol it just the same. And one thing is sure, at peace with God, as I always seek to be, I can be serene and childishly happy in the way I live. In a completely childlike way I can say to God as I would say to my father (and this comes so naturally to me): May I have a little free time to enjoy myself?—and then I enjoy myself. At other times it occurs to me that since sobriety is the ethical, it is my obligation, and therefore I am supposed to be able to be like that. So at times I make a strenuous effort—but I am brought practically to despair and must revert to my lower approach. But I continue to insist that the other is the higher, and I determine my life in relation to it by making an admission about myself.

$X^3$ A 189   n.d., 1850

## « 6646  *My Concern Over Publishing Writings Already Completed*[2808]

Although I realize that with almost exaggerated care it takes the direction of a movement of inwardness and never the direction of a pietistic or ascetic awakening, which wants to actualize it externally, I nevertheless constantly fear that communication of this sort somehow obligates me promptly to express it existentially, which is beyond my capability to do, nor is that what I mean. My intention is that it be used to intensify the need for grace; but, even if I were more spiritual than I am, I have an indescribable anxiety about venturing so far out and so high up.

But as long as I am leading the life I now lead, it easily could be misinterpreted, as if I thought I already realize such a thing.

That is why I was thinking of first of all getting a pastoral appointment or something like that, to show that I did not make myself out to be better than others.

But that again has its own special difficulties and that is why the time has passed and I have suffered exceedingly.

$X^3$ A 190   n.d., 1850

## « 6647  *My Boundary Line*

(1) There is a predominant poetic strain[2809] in me, and I am not spiritual enough to be able to slay it or ever really to understand (simply because the poetic strain is there) that it is contrary to God's will for me; neither am I spiritual enough to live as an ascetic.

(2) On the other hand I am exceptionally informed as to the nature of Christianity, know how to present it, and in that respect have rare aptitudes.

(3) So, with the help of God, I use these gifts to present it to men so that they at least get an impression, become aware.

(4) Thus I believe there is one thing I still will be empowered to do, to provide a constant reminder: just when I get people to accept it, then to remind them gently, kindly, but in loving truth, that the reason they are now accepting it is simply that I myself am not a true religious on any great scale but something of a poet who has used more lenient means, consequently less authentic means in the highest sense; whereas the authentic religious would be badly treated and persecuted because he used absolutely authentic means, was truly earnest, actualized everything ethically, instead of conceding to himself and to others a somewhat poetic relation to it.

$X^3$ A 191   *n.d.,*  1850

« **6648**  *The Deceitfulness of the Human Heart*

O, how deceitful is the heart of man, mine as well as others.

An orator steps forth and—as we are accustomed to hear, and in fact I speak the same way—prays: Lord Jesus Christ, draw me completely to yourself.

God in heaven! That the one who suffered soul-anguish all his life and finally ignominious death in order to save everyman: that there should be on his side an hindrance to drawing me to himself with the greatest joy—that would be charging him with an almost insane kind of self-contradiction.

But then do I speak backwards? Ah, that is the deceit of it. It is I who know that to die to the world is so painful that I shrink from it. Instead of self-accusingly saying: Lord Jesus Christ, forgive me for still being so far behind—instead of that I speak backwards and pretend that I am willing enough to do it but the trouble lies somewhere else, probably that Christ in his holy sublimity does not have the time or opportunity to help me.

"Strip me of everything that holds me back." But, my Lord and God, what is it then that holds me back? It is just myself; if I had not craftily been in secret collusion with that which holds me back, then it would be assumed *eo ipso*[2810] that Christ would draw me completely to himself, for his only concern is to draw every man to himself.

So once again I speak backwards. Instead of accusing myself and praying for forgiveness because I am so far behind because I allow so many things to hold me back, I pretend that I am willing enough but something else is holding me back. Thus my prayer becomes almost a reprimand to Christ, for if it is really true that I am unconditionally willing but something else is holding me back completely against my will, then it does seem that Christ does not will to be the Savior.

But such is the deceitful human heart: we actually get no farther than desiring, and when our desire is expressed fervently, we believe we are extraordinarily far ahead.

x³ A 194   n.d., 1850

### « 6649  *Another Dimension to Being a Christian*

What is called humanity today is not purely and simply humanity but a diffused form of the essentially Christian.

Originally the procedure was this: with "the universally human consciousness" as the point of departure, to accept the essentially Christian.[2811] Now the procedure is this: from a point of origin which already is a diffused form of the essentially Christian, to become Christian.

*Ergo,* there is another dimension to being a Christian.

Here, as I have developed in "Armed Neutrality,"[2812] it is apparent that the procedure turns out to be one of instituting reflection on a full level deeper and more inward, something like the change from σοφοὶ to φιλόσοφοι, simply because the task has become enormously greater.

x³ A 204   n.d., 1850

### « 6650

Usually a man begins by first of all seeing how far he may moderately dare get involved with Christianity. If he finds something which does not demand all too much from him, he calls that Christianity and now proclaims Christianity.

The problem of ideality has occupied me first and foremost—what is Christianity; whether I myself might possibly collapse under it has not occupied me.

This interest in pure ideality is the *more* that I have, and this is why it has been natural and necessary for me to use pseudonyms.

x³ A 210   n.d., 1850

### « 6651  *Luther—Mynster*[2813]

Imagine Mynster as Luther's contemporary. Now say everything remarkable about Mynster that can truthfully be said and a little more.

If anyone denies that what I now say about Mynster is true, I will call him a liar: Mynster is an intelligent, circumspect man who shrinks from nothing, nothing, more than he shrinks from scandal. In this respect he has the kind of sensitivity such as one can have to saw-sharpening and the like.

But what is essential Christianity! From first to last it is scandal, the divine scandal (σκάνδαλον). Every time someone risks scandal of high order there is joy in heaven, for only the divinely chosen instrument achieves a scandal of high order.

What is Luther's greatness? His writings will perhaps be forgotten, even his opposition to the pope (although that was indeed scandal enough) will very likely vanish—but at the peak of the mentality of the middle ages to dare to marry, himself a monk, and with a nun! O, God's chosen instrument! By this act the biggest scandal ever raised in Christendom is reserved for you! First of all comes the introduction of Christianity into the world, when Christ and the apostles proclaimed it: this in itself was the divine scandal. But next, and in Christendom, Luther takes the prize for having raised the biggest scandal.

And now Mynster with his—Christian—dread of even the slightest scandal! And he and others are inspired by Luther! All is vanity, declares the Preacher.

$x^3$ A 219    n.d., 1850

« 6652  *Wilhelm Lund*[2814]

The similarity between his life and mine occurred to me today. Just as he lives over there in Brazil, lost to the world, absorbed in excavating antediluvian fossils, so I live as if outside the world, absorbed in excavating Christian concepts—alas, and yet I am living in Christendom, where Christianity flourishes, stands in luxuriant growth with 1,000 clergymen, and where we are all Christians.

$x^3$ A 239    n.d., 1850

« 6653  *Mynster*[2815]*—Luther*

Somewhere in his sermons Luther[2816] declares that three things belong to a Christian life: (1) faith, (2) works of love, (3) persecution for this faith and for these works of love.

Take Mynster now. He has reduced faith oriented toward tension and inwardness. He has set legality in the place of works of love. And persecution he has completely abolished.

$x^3$ A 249    n.d., 1850

« 6654

*Regarding a Statement in the postscript to "Concluding Post-script" with respect to publishing the books about my work as an author*

The statement is: "So in the pseudonymous works there is not a single word by myself; I have no opinion about them except as a third party, no knowledge of their significance except as a reader, not the remotest private relation to them, since it is impossible to have such a relation to a doubly reflected communication. A single word by me personally, in my own name, would be presumptuous self-forgetful-ness, which, regarded dialectically, would have been guilty of essen-tially destroying the pseudonyms with this one word."[2817]

Now it could be said that in "The Accounting,"[2818] for example, there is indeed direct discussion of the pseudonyms, pointing out the principal idea that runs through the whole.

With regard to that, it may be observed *both* that what I wrote then can be altogether true and what I wrote later just as true, simply because at that time I was not as advanced in my development, still had not come to an understanding of the definitive idea for all my writing, still did not even dare to declare definitely whether or not it would possibly end with my finding something that would thrust me away from Christianity, although I still continued with religious enthusiasm and to the best of my ability to work out the task of presenting what Christianity is. *And* it may also be noted that I do not discuss the pseudonyms directly in the books about my authorship or identify with them, but merely show their significance as maieutic method. Finally, I must add: This is how I understand the totality *now;* by no means did I have this overview of the whole from the beginning, no more than I dare say that I immediately perceived that the *telos* of the pseudonyms was maieutic, since this, too, was like a phase of poetic-emptying in my own life-development.

$x^3$ A 258   *n.d.,* 1850

« 6655  *Martensen*[2819]*—and I*

It never crossed my mind that it was supposed to be a conflict over concepts;[2820] I knew better where the difficulty lies.

In no way do I conceal the fact that I regard him at present as the much, much stronger one. For it could scarcely cross my mind that besides me there could be found such a fool as I who would enter into the kind of proclamation of Christianity that I represent. however true it is.

Martensen expresses that proclaiming Christianity is the way to make a brilliant career, the way to all secular advantages, the way that certainly leads farther and farther away from the truth, more and more enchantingly, deeper and ever deeper into the flower-strewn, smiling jargon of illusions—and Martensen assures us that what he preaches is Christianity. And the majority are all too eager to believe that this must be true. No wonder that they throng to him in crowds.

But everyone is reluctant to believe that my proclamation of Christianity is the truly Christian one and what I proclaim is Christianity. And I have no enticements, for the enticing is precisely what they miss in my proclamation. Neither do I have anything compelling, since I am without authority. No wonder, then, that I stand alone.

This is the difference between Professor Martensen and me. It never crossed my mind that it was supposed to be a scholarly conflict; in daily suffering and sacrifice I am prevented from forgetting what the battle actually is about.

$x^3$ A 161    *n.d.,* 1850

« **6656 How the New Pseudonym Anti-Climacus Came Into Being**

This is recorded in the journals[2821] of that period.

My intention was to set aside what I had written and see about getting an appointment to a seminary in order to work more extensively and slacken up a bit on the intensive work.

It was a soothing thought. But then the counter-thought awakened so strongly (it is all recorded in the journals[2822]) that it seemed to me that I had to act.

I wrote to Luno about beginning the printing. The thought of a reconciliation with "her"[2823] was joined to the idea of an appointment at the seminary; for if there was to be mitigation for me, there should also be mitigation for her, if she so desired.

Strangely enough, the same day or the day after I wrote to Luno and was informed that he expected the manuscript as soon as possible, I learned that Councillor Olsen was dead. If I had known that before I wrote to Luno, I could have waited longer. But now it seemed that the whole thing would raise a commotion that would suffocate me if I cancelled again and wrote about it again to Luno.

So the printing began, and in the tension of actuality (which I had

wanted in order to teach myself to be discerning) it became clear that
I ought to introduce a pseudonym.

$x^3$ A 265   n.d., 1850

### « 6657

The Grundtvigian talk about the *dead* letter he himself has spun
into a *deadening* epigram.[2824]

$x^3$ A 304   n.d., 1850

### « 6658 *About Myself*

Formerly I took pride in my ability to see everything, that nothing
escaped me. Now I take pride in seeing nothing, in being calmly oblivious to all the crudeness and ridicule etc. round about me.

$x^3$ A 309   n.d., 1850

### « 6659 *About Myself*

I have been used this way as well. The category which was to be
advanced was "the single individual"—and then a life that measured up
to it fairly well.

This has been done. But who am I, then? Am I some devil of a
fellow who has understood this from the beginning and has had the
personal capacity to maintain it in my daily life? Far from it. I have been
helped. By what? By a frightful mental depression, a thorn in the flesh.
I am a severe melancholic who has the good fortune and the virtuosity
to be able to conceal it, and for that I have struggled. But Governance
holds me in my depression. Meanwhile I come to a greater and greater
understanding of the idea and know indescribable contentment and
sheer joy—but always with the aid of the torment which keeps me
within bounds.

Thus in a way I have been successful in something Governance
perhaps would hardly risk assigning to any other man, almost categorically to express what it means to be the single individual, that he
should neither become fanatically arrogant nor ever get trapped in
associations. Governance, however, has provided itself with an utterly
different explanation—but the achievement is there, the category of the
single individual has become visible.

$x^3$ A 310   n.d., 1850

### « 6660

When I had published *Concluding Postscript* I intended to withdraw[2825] and devote myself more to my own relationship to Christianity.

But in the meantime external situations involved my public life in such a way that I existentially discovered the Christian collisions. This is an essential element in my own education.

x³ A 318   *n.d.,* 1850

« **6661**

In his sermon on "Christian Sagacity"²⁸²⁶ Mynster has an excellent passage on how worldly sagacity hastily engages in declaring that anyone who actually risks something for truth etc. is a fool. Mynster goes on to show how this has always been the case, how this happened not only to Christ and the apostles but to all zealous servants of the truth, how it is still true that worldly sagacity calls them fools—

Alas, it never occurs to Mynster that worldly sagacity certainly has never called him a fool.

x³ A 321   *n.d.,* 1850

« **6662**  *The Old Approach—and Mine*

The old approach was: to be so zealous and busy getting men²⁸²⁷ by droves (if possible, all) to accept Christianity that they forgot or were not so scrupulous about whether what was accepted was Christianity or not.

My approach is: to take the greatest care that clarity be achieved about what Christianity is—even if no one at all, not even I myself, could accept it.

x³ A 367   *n.d.,* 1850

« **6663**  *Concerning Professor Nielsen's*²⁸²⁸ *Relation to My Literary Activity*

1

No doubt most people will consider making an explanation such as this extremely overscrupulous. But I owe it to myself to make it.

Through conversations the last two years I have tried to initiate Prof. Nielsen into my cause.²⁸²⁹ With regard to what he has written during that period, I have kept out of it completely, as he can testify, until this one book,²⁸³⁰ by being printed, came to be *publici juris.*²⁸³¹ I have read it through, expressed my opinion of it, and, as Professor Nielsen can also testify, have had many objections to the whole production, but no doubt my objections are made from a completely different viewpoint than the ones usually made against this book.

My decision to give a detailed explanation of my cause in private conversation has the following background. It was the summer of

1848. I was essentially through with what up to that time I had considered my task. Partly because of my physical weakness, I had stronger than usual intimations of death, so strong that I considered it my duty to bring another person into the cause, at least attempt to do so through private conversations. I selected Professor Nielsen, who sometime before had himself made approaches.

2

From the standpoint of the idea, also ethically, I have, as suggested, many objections to the new direction the cause has taken through Prof. Nielsen's intervention. But this does not seem the time to make this protest in print, for one thing because it would be about such a relativity that few would really understand it, whereas it swiftly and easily could be used to confuse even more people.

Indisputably Prof. Nielsen has done one service: has drawn attention to a cause which certain others hereabouts in the most polite way of the world (by making me into a kind of curious, odd, and singularly *merkwürdigt*[2832] genius, etc.) have tried to smuggle away, far, far away into the distant realm of eccentricities and *ausserdienstliche Merkwürdigheder,* or to transform into an exaggeration one lets blow over.

Perhaps someone may expect that if this is the case, then I should thank Prof. N. in much stronger terms. This I can well understand; but I also understand that such a person does not have what I have, my conception of the rightness of the cause I have the honor to serve, its ultimate victory, still less, my understanding that the secret of the cause is that it will come again, that the more they try to get it to blow over—something I myself at times have cunningly encouraged in the interest of the idea—all the more earnestly and victoriously it will come back again, if not through one, then through someone else. For my task has been essentially to introduce it, if possible to divert attention from it until it stood there, just as a commander carefully conceals the dispatch of one company after the other—until the army stands there, but my task was not to fight the battle, it was a position that should be taken and made impregnable. But next to me Prof. Nielsen is the one or one of those who in all probability best understands this.

S.K.

Summer, 1850

X[6] B 94   Summer, 1850

« **6664**

*In margin: Concerning the Publication of the Completed Writings*
For a long time I believed that I had not long to live; I was convinced, according to what I could understand, that if I died now my life would have great influence because what Denmark needed was a dead man.

I have also delayed in order to give R. Nielsen[2833] room to get under way.

But if I am to go on living, there is not a moment to waste—and therefore I have sent a manuscript[2834] to the printer.

There is no doubt in my mind at all that it probably will turn out as it always does, that the thoughts of Governance are far superior to my thoughts, and that it was right for me not to publish the writings previously.

Infinite love, which I can never sufficiently thank for what has been done for me.

$$x^3 \text{ A } 381 \quad n.d., \ 1850$$

« **6665** *About Myself*

To depict the story of Christ's suffering was a task I once thought of doing;[2835] I had already made quite a few preparations with that in view. I do not doubt that in respect to inwardness, imagination, heart-rending and gripping description, it would have become a master-piece, yes, it would have enthralled as those works of visual art which present Christ.

I would have differed from those artists,[2836] however, in that I would still have had enough Christianity to thank God in a childlike way for the permission, like an indulgence, to sit way off here enjoying this life and working on such things.

Ah, but I still would have become a Sophist for all that, even if the saving factor remained—namely, that in all humility I myself understood that I was a Sophist.

Truly, if God does not constrain man, if God does not sit and watch over him, even the most honest of men becomes a Sophist.

At the same time an honest Sophist is not to be scorned. What I say never goes farther than to ask that a person at least confess that being excused from actual imitation or discipleship is an indulgence. More I have never demanded of anyone; I have not once demanded this but only, without authority, called attention to the fact that this is the way it ought to be.

Therefore, if God does not constrain me, I myself do not get any farther either.

x³ A 389   *n.d.,*  1850

### « 6666 *Jottings*

This year, August 9 (the date of Father's death[2837]) happened to fall on a Friday. I went to communion that day.

And, strangely enough, the sermon in Luther[2838] I read according to plan that day was on the verse "All good and perfect gifts etc." from the Epistle of James.[2839]

The day I sent the manuscript[2840] to the printer, the Luther sermon I read according to plan was on Paul's verse[2841] on the tribulations of the day etc.

This strikes me as very curious; I myself also find it curiously impressive since I do not remember beforehand which sermon is to be read according to the schedule.

September 8 (which I really call my engagement day[2842]) is on a Sunday this year, and the Gospel[2843] is: No man can serve two masters.

x³ A 391   *n.d.,*  1850

### « 6667

... If I saw a frail, delicate young girl who said, on seeing a woodcutter swinging over his head an enormous chunk on an axe: "It is a shame that my parents will not let me chop wood; if they just let me I could do it," I would smile.

So it is, too, when I hear a sophisticated, cultured, Goethean kind of person who in a romantic moment in the pulpit tearfully maintains that he often has longed to be contemporary with Christ.

Of course he does not say it in precisely this way; he says he wishes he could have seen Christ—aha! perhaps a private diversion in a remote place in a "quiet hour."

There is hardly anything as offensive to me as this rubbish about the quiet hours—as if Christianity had the remotest connection with that kind of proclamation. The most horrible episode in all history, and it is supposed to be presented in its truth "in a quiet hour." In the most obvious way possible this makes the whole thing a comedy or a game, such as when children in the parlor play Napoleon's journey over the Alps etc.

x³ A 399   *n.d.,*  1850

« **6668** *Bishop Mynster*[2844]

This is perhaps the way he once took the direction he did in his life. He said to himself—and with complete justification, which is still valid: I am the most competent; if I do not take the no. 1 place, a less competent, less honest person very likely will take it—ergo, I will take it. Here he turned away from the ideal. The ideal would have beckoned him on further, saying: Never mind your being the most competent by way of comparison; if you want to get involved in the comparative, follow me further—to be sure, then you will end up being a nobody in this world.

$x^3$ A 402    *n.d.,* 1850

« **6669** *My Relation to My Contemporaries,*
*One of Misunderstanding*

It is not my fault; the thing is quite simple.

As long as I am considered to be lacking earnestness but all the others are earnest men,[2845] there can only be confusion.

So my life is and always has been said to lack earnestness and people wished I would settle down and get serious about something etc. Upon closer inspection the basic reason, they discover, is that I have no job, no career; I have amounted to nothing, have even put myself in the position of becoming the plunder of ridicule—for the sake of the idea, I would say, but such things are nonsense in the eyes of the world.

So, jobless, without a career—that is, without any earthly reward —ridiculed, consequently paid with insults, because I work—and this I dare say—more than any career man and jobholder: my life is lacking in earnestness.

Yes, in this manner only confusion can be drawn out of me and my life. The worldly secular mentality has clean forgotten what earnestness really is, and I, who, even if slightly, do have a little of it—I am the only one who completely lacks earnestness.

$x^3$ A 403    *n.d.,* 1850

« **6670** *The New Form of the Sermon*

must in the first place be a monologue.[2846] For one thing, there is a unique difficulty regarding the extent to which one man has the right to speak this way to another, saying "you must," and for another, men as yet cannot tolerate being spoken to this way, and the relevance of ordination here is not clear to me.

So the monologue is used—I do not address you, but I listen and hear how Christianity is speaking to me. Then I may use this *you must* to some purpose.

$X^3$ A 404   *n.d.*, 1850

### « 6671 *The Established Church—My Position*

From the highest Christian point of view, there is no established Church, only a Church Militant.

This is the first point.

The second, then, is that factually there is such a one. We must in no way want to overthrow it, no, but above it the higher ideality must hover as a vivifying possibility—so that in the strictest sense there actually is no established Church.[*]

This has now taken place through me, with the aid of a pseudonym, in order that it all might be a purely spiritual movement. There is not a shred of a proposal pertaining to the external.

And while the pseudonym[2847] lifts his hand for the big blow, I stand in between parrying; the whole thing recoils on me for being such a poor Christian, I who still remain in the established Church. In this way the whole thing is a spiritual movement.

O, my God, I am almost tempted to admire myself for what I have done—but God be praised that you help me to trace everything back to you in adoration, I who never can thank you sufficiently for the good that has been done for me, far more than I ever expected, could have expected, dared to expect.

$X^3$ A 415   *n.d.*, 1850

### « 6672

[*] *In margin of 6671* ($X^3$ A 415):

Even an established Church composed of earnest Christians in the more rigorous sense would need to be reminded of this essentially Christian point: that in the highest Christian sense there is no established Church, only a Church Militant. But this may be said only at the distance of ideality from the established Church. Then if an established Church will not put up with this being said, not even on that condition, it signifies that such a Church is in error and must be attacked directly.

$X^3$ A 416   *n.d.*

### « 6673

The eighth of September![2848] The Gospel: no man can serve two masters (my favorite Gospel[2849])! my favorite hymn:[2850] "Commit Thy Ways Confiding," which Kofoed-Hansen[2851] selected today.

How festive, and how relevant to me who have been occupied these days with publishing "On My Work as an Author"[2852] and the dedication[2853] in it.

$x^3$ A 422    September 8, 1850

### « 6674  *The Publication of the Book:* *"On My Work as an Author"*[2854]

"On My Work as an Author" still must be kept back. I feel that it would come disturbingly close to "Practice in Christianity,"[2855] so that they would mutually diminish each other, even if in another sense I feel it could be more impressive.

But the main point is that the spirit has not moved me to a firm and fixed conviction that now is the time, something I did feel about the timing of the publication of "Practice in Christianity."

The difference between being moved by the spirit or not, between being completely at one with myself or not, I know at once, because in the latter case I cannot stop thinking about details, changing something, this detail or that. In the other case this never occurs to me, because the whole attention of my mind is solely and unanimously concentrated on the fact that the whole matter has now been commended into God's hand, I have relinquished it.

God knows that I in one sense would gladly publish "On My Work as an Author" now and then be completely free, but since I cannot find the unqualified sanction within me, I dare not do it. It may be a mistake on my part not to find this sanction; perhaps without quite detecting it I am seeking to spare myself. Or the right thing for me to do may be not to give in to an impatience which in another sense nags me to publish it now. This I do not know, but I commend myself to God; surely he will see to it that when the time has come I will find in myself complete oneness about publishing it.

$x^3$ A 423    *n.d.,* 1850

### « 6675

The Dedication to Regine Schlegel,[2856] if there can be such a thing during my lifetime, could very well be used in the front of a small collection of Friday-discourses but properly belongs to the writings on my work as an author. Inasmuch as I appear so decisively in the character of the religious, which I have wanted from the very beginning, at this moment *she* is the only important one, since my relationship to her is a *God*-relationship.

The dedication could read:

To R. S.—with this little book is dedicated an authorship, which to some extent belongs to her, by one who belongs completely to her.

Or with a collection of Friday-discourses: this little book is dedicated to R. S.

$x^5$ B 263   *n.d.,* 1849–50

« **6676**

To a contemporary,

whose name must still be
concealed, but history will
name—for a short time or long—
as long as it names my name
is dedicated
with this little book
the whole of the authorship, as it
was from the very beginning.[2857]

$x^5$ B 264   *n.d.,* 1849–50

« **6677** *My Presentation*

is supposed to be an exaggeration. All right—show me then how the New Testament cuts prices and bargains—and we have nothing else to go by than the New Testament. But Christendom has invented the following nonsense—there is a clearly revealed Word of God—but then there is among us men a tradition according to which it is agreed that it is not readily self-evident, we should not take it so literally, God's Word is really not for us.

Or show me how the Church Fathers cut the price. Or is Luther also an exaggeration!

On Sunday the minister stirs up his own and the congregation's imagination—in a quiet hour, and on Monday he is the first to shout "Crucify" against anyone who dares to act accordingly, or if he does not shout "Crucify," he would still find it just as ridiculous as if someone were to act according to what he sees or hears in the theater.

This quiet hour—abominable invention! What was presented in the market place and on the street and in actuality became catastrophe can now be presented only in a quiet hour—the other would be profane. So Jesus Christ was also profane.

And so they censure the monastery, say it is escapism, but to have all one's religiousness in one quiet hour once a week and otherwise be conformed to the secular mentality, this is an even greater escape from actuality than that of the religious, for it cannot be denied that in other respects we are all too deeply immersed in actuality.

$x^3$ A 43　n.d., 1850

« **6678**

But Mynster[2858] originally had the idea that they certainly have relaxed somewhat into secular self-satisfaction. And then that is where Martensen[2859] begins. Yes, it gets better and better.

$x^3$ A 435　n.d., 1850

« **6679** *Mynster's*[2860] *Administrative Skills*

If from a political point of view they are commendable, but from the essentially Christian point of view they are indefensible, then in principle they are diametrically opposite to Christianity.

The most important concern to Mynster has been and still is to see to it that on no account is anyone's life to be allowed to express that there is something in and for itself. For secular and temporal government this being in and for itself, together with the fact that it exists [*er til*], is upsetting and most dangerous; thus if anyone wants to do something gratis, this is a crime in Mynster's eyes, for then he and his own life become incommensurable. No, if someone, for example, has an urge to preach, then it must be expressed by his getting himself a position, and so it is in everything. There must be no infinite as such —no, it must cancel out; everything must be explainable by the relative and must cancel out in the relative. Then it is a pleasure to administer, yes, almost a voluptuous pleasure. One permits (and does it himself) the infinite to be talked about in lofty tones, the noble enthusiasm that simply and solely wills the good—but also makes sure that this is only a manner of speaking by always appending a note to actuality which interprets it in and by the relative.

According to this view, religiousness has a place but great pains are taken to keep it from coming out into actuality, to keep it limited to certain quiet hours. In a quiet hour the speaker (and one does it himself) may gesticulate vehemently in the pulpit—but no more than that; this sublimity is out of place in actuality.

So it is in everything Mynsterian. It is political pedagogy but diametrically opposite to Christianity.

$x^3$ A 448　n.d., 1850

### « 6680  *Illusions. Mundus* vult *decipi*[2861]

Let me use myself, and at least do me the favor of being willing to understand.

When I was reduplicating most resolutely, was concentrating most of my energy on abolishing illusions, my standing was lower.

Then I took the plunge, hurled myself at the rabble.[2862] Then I saw that the task was too big for me; I almost feared mob violence against me in the streets.

So I pulled back somewhat, I was seen less frequently on the street,[2863] I turned somewhat toward maintaining associations with the elite, my behaviour altered, I did not involve myself with people so much, isolated myself—and my standing increased—alas, for now a little illusion was involved.

Why has Mynster's[2864] standing been so high? Because he has been supported so very powerfully by illusions. But does not his reputation rest on his talents etc.? Out with talents and genius; no genius has ever been born so powerful that it could assure itself of the esteem of the crowd—without using illusions.

It is easy to perceive that this is the way it has to be. If the crowd were to recognize the truth without illusions, then the crowd itself would have to be in the truth. Take this for granted: it is an extremely rare person who is able to recognize truth without illusions. But if the crowd cannot recognize the truth without illusions, then, after all, it is also impossible for them to be able to honor and esteem it. Ergo, there must be illusions if one is to achieve honor and esteem.

Geniuses, therefore, are ranked according to their ability to abolish illusions or remove them—but their esteem among their contemporaries is correspondingly less.

If naked truth just by itself could be recognized by the crowd and esteemed as such, God would have benefited when he wanted to reveal himself. But the very opposite happened; he was mistreated and put to death. Why? Precisely because he has the divine power to abolish illusions. What helps us human beings is that we do not have such powers and the kind of purity which remove illusions—in our presentation of truth there is always a portion of illusion and thus, too, a little esteem for us.

This, among other things, is what I want to make men aware of, and to that purpose I intend to use my own life. With God's help I will not be tricked into the illusion that my increasing esteem has any other ground than that I have been forced to set up a little illusion—alas, I am just a poor wretch of a man, but I can be an occasion for awareness.

x³ A 450   n.d., 1850

### « 6681  *Mynster*²⁸⁶⁵*—and I*

Mynster has preached Christianity into and established it in an illusion (not that what he said was not Christianity, no, but by virtue of the proclamation it has not been Christianity)—that is why I have had to operate dialectically as I have done.

Mynster resembles Louis Philippe:²⁸⁶⁶ lacking the impetus of the idea and lacking existential pathos, but shrewdly using petty means, and with the understanding that the job mentality actually rules the world and that the person who has jobs to give away rules fairly securely.

x³ A 453   n.d., 1850

### « 6682  *Mynster's Preaching*

Who would ever think on reading Mynster's sermons²⁸⁶⁷ that becoming a Christian is a life-and-death battle, a protracted life-and-death struggle, full of the most dreadful episodes (which dying to the world,²⁸⁶⁸ corresponding to dying, naturally must be).

x³ A 472   n.d., 1850

### « 6683  *About Myself and My Operation*

The level-headedness with which I indisputably manage has, incidentally, a very good guarantee: that I, who surely best understand how earnest things are and can become, would gladly have the most reasonable terms possible.

Also, I have a human fondness for being human, as yet have not been burned into pure spirit—but of course I can be pressured out farther and farther. At all times I proceed as cautiously as possible.

Regarding my presentation of essential Christianity (which at various points is closer to the Gospel than the official presentation), it actually cannot be said to be an exaggeration, but the truth is that the official proclamation has diminished it outrageously.

But of course I am but one man, the others have the power, and I feel compelled to follow my cause to the limit. For every time it is declared that my presentation is an exaggeration, the price is marked up, but yet always as cautiously as can be in this situation, for I, too, would gladly spare myself.

Thus I am as far as possible from being a muddlehead or a misanthrope, who plunges ahead and blindly attacks. Alas, no, I even have furnished proof all along that I am right. I did not begin by summarily attacking—I have supported the established order, have made my presentation (which compared to the Gospel is all too far from being an exaggeration), and they shouted: What exaggeration. But precisely this is the guilt and the proof that I am right. One can say, as I do: "It is too lofty for us, we take comfort in grace," but one truly has no right to say it is an exaggeration in the sense that it is not Christianity, for then Christianity itself becomes an altogether dreadful exaggeration. And right here is the basic guilt, that men arrogantly want to decide for themselves and according to their own convenience what Christianity is to be.

$x^3$ A 483   *n.d.*, 1850

« **6684** *The Official Proclamation of Christianity—and Mine*

This is how the official proclaimers of Christianity ought to have received mine. They should have been said: "This proclamation is completely true, but it is too lofty for us, which in fact the author himself admits about himself. But even if it has no other use, it is useful in that it could make us aware of how lukewarm our Christianity is, we who scarcely want to get involved in the mild Christianity which is being proclaimed at present." And to that I would say: This is absolutely true, except for the last statement, for I believe that people will more readily become involved in Christianity if it is somewhat more rigorous.

But at the beginning I will scarcely get many to believe this. The immediate reaction is against it and not many will be persuaded to believe it. Let me give an illustration. There are times in the year (this may also be the case in apartments when, for example, there is only a little sun) when one opens the windows and gets warmer air—but no maid can be made to understand the idea of opening windows to let warmer air in or of keeping windows shut in order not to let warm air in. She sticks to the old routine: shutting windows so that it will not get cold—even if she is told ten times to open the windows to let warm air in. On the other hand in the heat of summer she opens all the windows, thinking to make it cool—even if she is asked ten times to keep the windows shut, especially in the living room, in order not to let in too much warm air.

$x^3$ A 487   *n.d.*, 1850

## « 6685 *What I Have Wanted and Want*

I have never, not in the remotest manner, suggested or attempted trying to extend the matter into pietism, into pietistic strictness and the like.

No, what I do want is truth in our speaking and above all in our preaching, and not, as now, almost pure falsehood with respect to the existential, so that not only is the higher abolished but the lower is even put in its place, the prototypes are misused, nothing is made relevant to the present, and possibility and actuality and their existential relations are handled quite wrongly.

One simple example. If someone wants to spare himself and does not dare to witness either for the truth or against untruth—fine, I do not coerce him. But he must not have the right to turn things around, so that excusing himself also becomes laudable wisdom and venturing becomes fantasy and foolishness. —So it is throughout.

Why did I become a sacrifice to Denmark? Was it only because the rabble were able to do it? No, it was because those who should have ventured what I ventured not only spared themselves but even turned things around so that it became laudable wisdom to spare themselves, and my venturing was foolishness.

This is the kind of untruth I want to root out of our speaking and preaching—everywhere almost, where conditions Christianly call for a little admission, even these are usually made into a virtue which is honored and glorified.

$$\text{x}^3 \text{ A } 519 \quad n.d., \ 1850$$

## « 6686

[*In margin:* Anti-Climacus.]
*A Passage in Anti-Climacus (Practice in Christianity,* [2869] *no. 2)*
*Pertaining to the Angel's Song of Praise at the Time of*
*Christ's Birth*

Anti-Climacus declares that when Christ resolves to become the Savior of the world, a lament goes through all humanity like a sigh: Why do you do this, you will make us all unhappy—simply because to become a Christian in truth is the greatest human suffering, because Christ as the absolute explodes all the relativity in which we human beings live—in order to make us spirit. But in order to become spirit one must go through crises which make us, from a human point of view, as unhappy as possible.

But an objection could be made here that, on the contrary, the angels sang a song of joy at the birth of Christ. To this must be replied: It is the angels who are singing. Furthermore, if the word "Savior" is taken summarily and men are permitted to decide for themselves what it means—well, no wonder that man also jubilates spontaneously.

But this is taking Christianity in vain. When the meaning of the word "Savior" is defined more explicitly, God's conception of it emerges, and Christ fulfills it absolutely. Here it is again—humanly speaking, it is the greatest suffering to become a Christian, to be saved in this sense.

Luther[2870] is right in saying in his sermon on the Gospel for Christmas Day that there is nothing else to say about Christ than that he is "a great joy"————but, but "for sin-crushed consciences"—otherwise not, otherwise he is taken in vain. The part about joy is promptly seized upon—the part about "a sin-crushed conscience" meets with extreme resistance.

But it is all taken in vain. We take the word "a Savior," run away with it, and understand something else by it than Christianity does. We take the words " a great joy"—and then, scram, we want nothing to do with a more explicit understanding of it.

It is this shameful, frivolous use of the essentially Christian which has abolished Christianity under the guise of preserving it, for, as it goes, "After all, we are saying the same thing; we call Christ a Savior, say his birth is a great joy"—rubbish, what good does that do if you understand something different and exclude the more specific understanding by which the words first became Christianly true.

$$X^3 \text{ A } 526 \quad n.d., \ 1850$$

« **6687**

[*In margin:* Anti-Climacus.]
*Concerning the Impression Anti-Climacus's Latest Book*
(Practice in Christianity) *Will Make*

Today I talked with Tryde.[2871] He told me that it was too strong to say that Christianity had been abolished through "observation."[2872] He himself had stressed the subjective, and that was true also of all the more competent preachers.

O, my God, how I have had to bear down on this and maintain that I was purely subjective, not objective, etc.—and now the same people claim that they also emphasize the subjective.

Moreover, the point is that in defining the concept "preaching," the sermon never amounts to more than a speech, talking about something, consequently does not pay attention to existence at all. An officeholder, shackled in seventeen ways to finitude and objectivity—achieves nothing, no matter how subjective he makes his talk. A nobody who preaches *gratis* on the street—even if he makes observations that are ever so objective—remains a subjective and vivifying person; and one who is ever so subjective but is trapped by his position and the like in all possible secular considerations, his preaching remains essentially nothing but observation, for it is easy to see that he has made it impossible for himself to actualize even moderately that which he preaches about.

But I have to say one thing about Tryde, something splendid about him: that he said, that he did not deny, that he had been predisposed to be objective.

$x^3$ A 530   *n.d.,* 1850

### « 6688  *What I Want*

My position is that the whole prevailing official proclamation of Christianity is a conspiracy against the Bible—we suppress what does not suit us.

I will not be a party to that. I will include the requirement and then make an admission.

$x^3$ A 550   *n.d.,* 1850

### « 6689  *Sins of Omission*

In a book by F. W. Newmann, *Die Seele ihr Leiden und ihr Sehnen,*[2873] Leipzig, 1850, I find somewhere in the section on sin that the sins of omission are the most dangerous and the ones that most pain the devout.

This is entirely correct and reminds me of Anti-Climacus's *Sickness unto Death.*[2874]

$x^3$ A 551   *n.d.,* 1850

### « 6690  *Johannes Climacus–Anti-Climacus*[2875]

Just as Johannes Climacus dialectically formulated the issue so sharply that no one could directly see whether it was an attack on Christianity or a defense, but it depended on the state of the reader and what he got out of the book, so also Anti-Climacus has carried the issue to such an extreme that no one can see directly whether it is primarily radical or primarily conservative, whether it is an attack on the established or in fact a defense.

$x^3$ A 555   *n.d.,* 1850

« **6691** *My Conversation with Bishop Mynster*
*October 22, 1850, after he had read*
*"Practice in Christianity"*

The day before I had spoken with Paulli,[2876] who told me the following: The Bishop is very angry, the minute he came into the living room that first day he said, "The book has made me furious; it is playing a profane game with holy things." And when Paulli obligingly asked him if he should report that to me since he probably would be talking with me, Mynster answered: "Yes, and he no doubt will come to see me sometime and I will tell him myself."*

Perhaps, who knows, those last words were fabricated by Paulli to keep me, if possible, from going to the Bishop.

But in any case I interpreted the matter another way. When Mynster talks like that: "The next time he visits me I shall tell him so myself," he has essentially given the book a permit and me along with it.

My decision was made at once.

The following morning I went to him. Acquainted as I am with his virtuosity in stateliness (recalling the time I visited him and as I made my entrance he asked most formally and ceremoniously: Is there something in particular? —To which I answered: No, I see you have no time today, so I would just as soon go. And then when he said he did have time, I stuck to what I had said and parted from him *in bona caritate*[2877] etc.), I began at once: "Today I do have an errand of sorts. Pastor Paulli told me yesterday that you intend as soon as you see me to reprimand me for my latest book. I beg you to regard it as a new expression of the respect I always have shown you that, immediately upon hearing of it, I come at once."

In my opinion this was a happy notion. The situation was all in order; there could be no vehemence or stiff sarcasm, both of which I deemed unworthy in this case. No, his role was delineated for him as one of venerableness and mine of piety.

He answered: "No, I have no right to reprimand. That is, as I have said to you before, I do not mind at all that each bird must sing with its own beak." Then he added: "Indeed, people may also say what they want to about me." This he said mildly and with a smile. But his added remark led me to fear a little sarcasm, and I tried at once to save the situation. I answered that such was not my intention and I would beseech him to tell me if I had distressed him in any way by publishing such a book. Then he replied: Well, I do believe that it will not prove useful. I was pleased with this answer; it was friendly and personal.

Then we went on talking just as we are accustomed to doing. He pointed out that wherever one went or turned, there had to be observation.[2878] I did not pursue this further, fearing to get into the existential, but I explained what I meant with a few ordinary examples.

The rest of the conversation was not noteworthy. Except that in the very beginning he said: Yes, half of the book is an attack on Martensen,[2879] the other half on me. And later we discussed the passage on "observations," which he thought was directed at him.

Otherwise the conversation was just as usual.

I explained this and that about my method, also informed him that now we were over the worst, at least this was the way it looked to me at the moment—but I was a young man and therefore dared say no more than that this was the way it seemed to me at the moment: that now we were over the worst.

As I stated, the rest of the conversation was just as usual.

God be praised. O, what have I not suffered. I considered it my duty to maintain the cause in such a manner that I might let the established order determine to what extent it would force me to go farther, by taking steps against me.

Nothing has happened yet, all are silent—and Mynster talked this way.

Perhaps what Paulli said is true—but that, after all, was the first day. Maybe Mynster, having given up the intention of doing something officially, actually thought of doing something privately but later gave that up.

Still, a little nip may well come out in a sermon.

$x^3$ A 563   *n.d.,* 1850

« **6692**

[*]*In margin of 6691* ($x^3$ A 563):

It must be remembered that before my conversation with Paulli[2880] the book[2881] had already been out for, I believe, three weeks; from the establishment side not the slightest thing had been done or the slightest move made toward any government measure; there was not the slightest mention in any newspaper about government disapproval. Finally, Mynster[2882] preached a Sunday sermon after the book had been published and far from arguing against it he even put up a strong argument against something I also take issue with—naturalism!

"Unfortunately we know far too well what people in our day think of miracles." All this, plus Mynster's words, "the next time I visit him," made me feel it my duty to take the hint, made me feel fortunate that the opportunity presented itself in that way, for I was obliged to go see Mynster and it might otherwise have proved difficult to find an occasion.

$X^3$ A 564   *n.d.*

### « 6693  *Mynster's*[2883] *Significance for My Writing*

My task has been to apply a corrective to the established order, not to introduce something new which might nullify or supplant it.

Now if I had envisioned this completely from the beginning and there had been no Mynster, then first of all I would have had to create someone to represent the established order and firmly bolster him up.

But since I did not understand my task that clearly in the beginning, I very well could have failed to notice this and the whole thing would have turned out differently, perhaps gone wrong.

But, as it was, Mynster stood there as a representative of the established order; this came as a free gift, and it was inevitable that I venerated Mynster and did everything to express it.

That is how I found my proper position. Here again my good fortune is apparent. Purely personally my veneration for Mynster was indispensable to me—and not until later did I see that this was very important for my task and for enabling me to get positioned properly.

$X^3$ A 565   *n.d.*, 1850

### « 6694  *About the Inserted Lines in Practice in Christianity,*[2884] *No. 1*

There inevitably will be someone who will get the idea of reading them simply for a lark, comically.*

Paulli said this to me—and looked exceedingly grave. Paulli[2885] with the whole gang is a gossip who unctuously spreads stuff like this as if it were true and not something they themselves have concocted.

Well, even if it were true—what then? Anything new or beneficial can give rise to misuse.

But in other respects I have this to say about the use made of the comic and the humorous in these lines.

Take an esthetic situation. The one who first began to use comic roles in tragedy, believe me, he had to take the rap; people found it objectionable, still have not understood that using the comic in tragedy intensifies the tragedy.

But forget the esthetic.

But why is it extremely important to use the comic in religious discourse?

Quite simple. Our age is very far from any childlike naïveté about wanting to strive toward likeness to the idea. Christianity has halted in secular prudence which says goodbye to ideals and regards striving after them as fanaticism.

What we are living in is this secular prudence. But this secular prudence finds it very advantageous to have the religious represented solely by the Sunday ceremony.

This Sunday ceremony has become the category of the sermon-lecture—and secular prudence fills up the rest of life and tolerates the Sunday ceremony because it has the least likelihood of becoming actuality.

That is why the comic has to be used to show the incongruity between this Sunday ceremony and daily life, and that is why secular prudence, which arranges the Sunday ceremony, becomes angry at this use of the comic, but if this secular prudence circumspectly takes on the form of religiousness, it is neither more nor less than Sunday ceremony.

$$\text{x}^3 \text{ A } 568 \quad n.d., \text{ } 1850$$

« **6695**

[*]*In margin of 6694* (x³ A 568):

Peter[2886] thought that these lines were too extended, that it would have been sufficient to indicate them. Ye gods, and that is supposed to be so wise! No, to indicate is not sufficient, I saw that in *Works of Love*, where I did it. The point is that people prefer to get away from such things as fast as possible—and instead of admitting it, there comes this wise critique about their being too extended. But Peter always fraternizes with triviality, in which he also has frittered away his life. And so it always goes, that writing substantial books such as I write is no art; we can all do that—and much more: with one single hint and clue teach the author how it ought to have been done. It is really fun and games for mediocrity not to have any criterion at all in Denmark.

All of No. 1 in *Practice in Christianity* is actually a tremendous break-out from Sunday ceremoniousness (a break-out in the sense used in speaking of a prisoner breaking out)—and then along comes

Sunday ceremoniousness, and says with great self-importance: "Yes, a little of it might have been good"—that is: Sunday ceremoniousness is really the good. We want to have the old and then four shillings worth of the new.

$x^3$ A 569  *n.d.*

### « 6696  *Curiosum*

The other day Sibbern[2887] told me that someone had read the inserted lines in No. 1 of *Practice in Christianity*[2888] as purely comic—and thought that the clergy ought to intervene, so grave was the matter.

Sibbern burst out laughing when he told me this. It would in fact be a splendid satire on the present-day clergy, however little my desire for such troubles.

$x^3$ A 577  *n.d., 1850*

### « 6697

..... Basically everyone knows I am right—also Bishop Mynster. That I do not get my rights, we all know—I, too.

$x^3$ A 578  *n.d., 1850*

### « 6698  *Faith*

It is clear that in my writings I have supplied a more radical characterization of the concept "faith" than there has been up until this time.

$x^3$ A 591  *n.d., 1850*

### « 6699  *Practice in Christianity—the Established Order*

It is tragic that the established order (the majority of those in it, at least) know so little about governing that they promptly mistake *Practice in Christianity* for the opposition, although it is as different as possible from that, indeed, is diametrically opposed to that.

"The opposition" wants to do away with *government*—what does Anti-Climacus want? He is a single individual (in no way a party-man, indeed, hates parties, yes, takes a polemic aim at the crowd, the public, etc., indeed, is stamped by the kind of danger with which every authentic government official ought to be stamped). He addresses the established order something like this: "For God's sake, what kind of government are you; as a matter of fact you do not know how to govern. Go ahead and govern!" Is this opposition to the government? But those who govern have lost the high conception of what it is to govern and on the other hand have hung on to the idea of having a little power—therefore Anti-Climacus can be confused with the opposition.

The matter is simple. In the area of Church affairs, the established order, with its fear of men, has compromised, bargained, and dickered to such an extent that it veritably has lost the reins. In order that it may be able to govern again, new admissions must be made. "A new admission," I hear the establishment say—and then considers that it is to the opposition to whom a new admission has to be made, as if it had not been conceded enough. O, no, no! You who govern must make an admission to God and Christianity—a kind of penalty—and then see to it that you grasp the reins again.

Only this way can the established order be guided through.

Yet the whole matter also must in God-fearing artfulness be maintained in such a way that the established order would also be investigated if it now officially wanted to transform Anti-Climacus into the opposition and thereby force me out into more rigorous forms.

God knows that I anticipated it in fear and trembling, for my own sake as well, lest the task become too hard for me. But, just the same, I have ventured.

As is always the case, here too I did not understand things in the beginning as clearly as I do now.

$X^3$ A 599   *n.d.,* 1850

« **6700  About Indirect Communication and Myself**

It must above all be pointed out that I am not a teacher who originally envisioned everything and now, self-confident on all points, uses indirect communication, but that I myself have developed during the writing. This explains why my indirect communication is on a lower level than the direct, for the indirectness was due also to my not being clear myself at the beginning and therefore did not dare speak directly at the beginning. Therefore I myself am the one who has been formed and developed by and through the indirect communication.

$X^3$ A 628   *n.d.,* 1850

« **6701  Concerning a Statement in the "Postscript" to The Accounting[2889] About My Direct Communication**

It must be pointed out that here it is not a question of direct communication, pure and simple, for this is not really the first instance of that, since all the upbuilding writing has been direct communication.

No, it is direct communication about the authorship, about the total authorship, an authorship which has consisted of indirect communication through the pseudonyms and then of direct communication in the upbuilding writings, but consequently even the direct becomes indirect as long as I have not given a direct explanation of the whole, for in that case there would always be the possibility that I actually adhered to the pseudonymous writings and did not consider them to be maieutic.

x³ A 629   n.d., 1850

### « 6702  *The Unrecognizability of That for Which I Am Really Contending*

When conflict is over a doctrine, it is easy to stick to the point.

The difficulty of my task[*] is that I do indeed say: On the whole, the doctrine as it is taught is entirely sound. Consequently that is not what I am contending for. My contention is that something should be done with it. But an attempt is continually made to drum this out by saying: After all, we are saying the same thing he is, we are teaching the same thing.

And since I by no means intend to lead the matter out into external work-righteousness (for then easy recognizability comes again), and since I constantly stress that every one must resort to grace, then it seems as if I am contending for nothing at all.

And yet what I am contending for is perhaps the greatest possible distinction: the kind of daily existence led by one who proclaims the doctrine, whether he has all sorts of losses from it, or all sorts of advantages.

x³ A 635   n.d., 1850

### « 6703

[*] *In margin of 6702* (x³ A 635):

I have read a similar observation somewhere in Neander's *Bernhard of Clairvaux,* [2890] undoubtedly in connection with Arnold of Brescia or a reformation of an ethical nature, which, however, concedes the doctrine to be correct and does not dispute about it.

x³ A 636   n.d.

### « 6704  *Concerning the First of H.H.'s Two Essays*

It is stated there that a person has power to act only as long as he is silent. If one is actually to be a martyr, he must not say so.

In his convention address Peter[2891] observed that there was an inconsistency here: here it was spoken. —Yes, quite right, for it was precisely because there had to be a halt along that line. Furthermore, by taking such a step one ought to motivate men to act accordingly. And it is one thing to say: I will let myself be put to death, and another thing to introduce these thoughts anonymously, that is poetically, and still open the possibility of martyrdom so that men would become so furious because he defended the principle that a man does not have the right to let himself be put to death for the truth that they would put him to death for that reason.

All this is recorded in the journals of that period [i.e., for example, $x^1$ A 336, 338], and it actually is redundant to make this entry, but I do it only to save rummaging around in the old journals in order to make sure.

$x^3$ A 637    *n.d.*, 1850

## « 6705 *An Either-Or for an Established Order*

Either the established order—or the single individual, unconditionally the single individual, but with nothing in between, for that is half-and-half, parties, sects, etc.

That is how I support the established order, for there is scarcely one in any generation who manages to be unconditionally the single individual; they all want to dabble around in parties etc.

$x^3$ A 647    *n.d.*, 1850

## « 6706 *Dabbling Performances*

The characteristic performance of our day is to dabble away one's time in trifles. This is what Peter[2892] is doing under the name of conviviality and cordiality, but this is the way to make a big hit in our age of envy and leveling.

An authentic performance, the fruit of perhaps years of strenuous work, always calls for a certain silence—which irks, yes, rouses the age to indignation, because it has something of an aristocratic smell. It would scarcely occur to the author of such a performance to include in his preface a request for a lenient critique or to get involved with people in that way at all, for he himself knows that the performance has been thought through and calmly asks for a thoughtful evaluation. But how different it is with dabbling! A man is very conscious of not having carefully worked through and advanced the subject—no wonder then that there is this rapid succession of "I ask a lenient critique" etc., all of which titillates the power-hungry crowd. Thus what is communicated actually is in essence no higher than the public, the average listener: this again is pleasing to the power-hungry. The author protects himself with all sorts of remarks about not really having had sufficient time to work through the subject carefully, that it is merely a trial-attempt, etc., thereby protecting himself against every genuine criterion and acquiring a favorable image in the eyes of triflers who love nothing but mediocrity.

In short, the whole age from one end to the other is a conspiracy against authentic performance, just as it is a conspiracy against property etc.

But I too have a heart, and I have tried to continue to have a heart, and therefore I have tried to keep it in its proper place, not having it on my lips at one moment, down in my boots the next, but never in the proper place, and I have tried not to confuse cordiality with gossip and gabbling.

$x^3$ A 650    n.d., 1850

### « 6707  *Practice in Christianity*

It will be called unfair to introduce something like this at the very moment when the clergy are sufficiently hard-pressed. But the intention in fact is to get them to work more intensively at their task so that they do not mistakenly yield: so it is that the coachman lays on the whip just when things are most difficult.

It will be said: After all, the clergy are up and moving at this very time. Well, thanks, and how? In a purely secular struggle for positions and livings. For that very reason it would be important that right now the requirement be heard from an entirely different quarter, that it not be the secular mentality pure and simple: a secular struggle for secular goods—by the clergy, to be sure, but does that make it a spiritual struggle.

$x^3$ A 661    n.d., 1850

### « 6708  *Apologetics in Ancient or Original Christianity—and Now*

As a matter of fact, Christians used apologetics in the beginning too—but, please note, directly to people who by no means had admitted that they too were Christians and who did not want to be either.

Now the scene is "Christendom," where all are Christians.

The basic lie is in the dastardly irresponsibility with which we have seen to it that all become Christians—all the time conscious that this is a lie, and now approach it as if they were pagans but without first and foremost demanding that they give up the name Christian.

To "defend" Christianity to *Christians* is abysmal nonsense.

$x^3$ A 663    *n.d.,* 1850

« **6709** *"Clara Raphael"*[2893]

### A Review

A young girl. Full name: Clara Raphael. Age: 20. Appearance: good-looking. Religion: freethinker. Occupation: governess in the household of a business manager. Character: original, a characteristic affirmed by her, by her friend Mathilde, by many respectable men and women in the neighborhood where she is governess—she gets the no less original idea: I will also be original. Very original!

Then it perhaps occurs to her that this is a much too inadequate category, so she looks around for an idea for which she can live unmarried, for she does not wish to get married.

And this is the idea: the emancipation of women. This is the whole thing; her letters offer nothing more concrete about this idea of hers; it is original enough. If the idea were more concrete, she might possibly have shared it with another, but she has protected her originality.

Although the idea she has chosen is so exceedingly abstract that it cannot be considered the slightest hindrance to her marrying, even to a widower with ten children—yet Clara Raphael is determined not to marry, she will live for her idea. Almost incomprehensible originality! For the less the idea stands in her way, the more original it is to stick to it—but of course when the idea is not so abstract, that is, empty, that is, no idea at all, less resolution is required. Basically the idea makes its own decision, and it is not so much a question of resolving and again resolving not to marry, as it is of not getting time to marry, because the idea completely fills up one's life and one's time.

One day she goes to communion, which again is something very original for a freethinker like her. For a young girl she apparently has had a most unusual religious education, which the reader, as well as the editor, cannot admire enough—having read a few pages in Magnus Eiríksson's book[2894] on the Baptists and the Trinity.

She goes to communion and promises God that she will live for her idea—a vow which no doubt embarrassed God because of the originality of her idea—namely, that she actually has no idea.

She makes her vow, then she goes home—and falls in love.

But Clara Raphael is not merely virtuous like Charles,[2895] but she is a heroine—she will not marry.

The suffering caused by this decision makes her ill; nobody knows how she suffers, says her closest friend; and since there is no one in a better position to know it and she does not know it, it is quite true that no one knows it.

No, she wants to enter a convent, she wants to live for her idea —and proceeds to found a completely new order: that is, she marries her beloved—but as brother and sister.

Truly an original kind of convent!

Just one more observation on the original thought: a marriage between a brother and a sister. From novels one is acquainted with the phrase: "I esteem him highly, but I cannot love him" and also "I can only love him as a sister." This usually means that the two do not get married. That is not so original that it cannot be understood. But that it becomes a signal for them to be married is a most original turn, an almost indecent turn, as everyone will no doubt agree, no matter how far he otherwise is, as I am, from being as potentially severe as Herr Zierlich,[2896] who considers it indecent for men's and women's clothes to hang together in the same closet. If this goes much farther, it will not be long before a couple of men will want to be married, which is almost as indecent as a brother and a sister getting married.

———

This book has an unusual feature: a lengthy and detailed introduction by the editor (a one-time obedient servant of the system,[2897] the unforgettable author of promises,[2898] later the if-not-incarnate nevertheless astronomical heaven-ascending professor,[2899] at present the champion and promoter for the convent, the Clara Convent, or the Clara-Raphael Convent), theater director, Councillor Heiberg, Knight of Denmark. In this introduction he does his best to show that this book is an extraordinary production—which is perhaps the worst thing he could do for himself and for the book. He shows that it is the idea of the Protestant monastery—which idea? To marry? No, not to marry, but not to marry as man and wife but rather as brother and sister. In short, a theatrical marriage—that is what Protestantism understands by the monastery and by living celibate for an idea.

The editor unreservedly gives all the credit for this discovery and for having introduced this idea to the world to his client Raphael, even keeping to himself a few possible objections, such as to Clara Raphael's doctrine of the Trinity, perhaps also counting on Professor Martensen's being provoked by this extremely important contribution to the dogma of the Trinity to take up the matter. For he cannot possibly agree with her any more on this than on her intended mixed monastery (to say nothing of paired-monastery), since according to his *Dogmatics*[2900] Professor Martensen transfers the monastery to the next world, where all we dead will be scrupulously careful to refrain from marriage, even more scrupulously than Adam before Eve was created.

———

If no one else will take it upon himself to oppose the intrusion of this esthetic invasion into the religious realm, I at least do not wish to have kept silent about it.

$x^3$ A 678   *n.d.*, 1850

« **6709a**

[*In margin:* About myself.]
Frequently I find something sad in the fact that I, with all my capabilities, must always stand outside as a superfluity and impractical exaggeration.

But the whole thing is very simple. Conditions are still far from being confused enough for proper use to be made of me. Each one of those who take it upon themselves to govern flatters himself that he no doubt will succeed in maintaining the majority. They do not risk grasping what is decisive, the truth is in the minority, but that nevertheless it is the only ruling power.

Since such is the case, they quite naturally do not want to have anything to do with me. They fear that I will begin by engaging such a strong minority in affairs and by acting so decisively that what they really live for will be lost.

But it will all end, as they shall see, with conditions getting so desperate that they must make use of desperate people like me and my kind.

$x^3$ A 680   *n.d.*, 1850

« **6710** *Leniency*

I believe that I dare say of myself that in the proclaiming of Christianity's leniency I seem to have at my disposal—although of course this gift can be taken from me at any time—a pathos possessed by none of those proclaiming Christianity among us.

This is something which a more profound psychologist might become aware of, because the very anxiety with which I describe the terrifying aspects reveal that I fear the capacities of an opposite nature which are entrusted to me, fear that I shall come to have a purely infatuating influence.

Leniency is so much a part of me that I seem unable to get it out, as it were; it seems to me that if it once burst forth I would expire in it and preach men into a security which almost could become light-headedness or sheer unconcern.

Having leniency in this way is like having an emotion. The deeper the emotion, the greater the anxiety about showing signs of it, because one knows very well the scale on which it will break forth.

$x^3$ A 716   *n.d.*, 1851

### « 6711

Brorson's Hymn no. 209[2901]
(the secret of the cross):
Surrender yourself to it
And then you will be free.

$x^3$ A 730   *n.d.*, 1851

### « 6712 *Mynster—and I*

Often I can become very sad at the thought that Mynster and I have been contemporaries! I who so inexpressibly desire to do everything to please him—if the truth does not suffer in the process; I who feel bound by filial piety to one dead to do everything possible to please him[2902]—and then that I am probably the most dangerous illumination Mynster can come under! The dubiousness about Mynster concerns just one certain aspect of the existential; it helps then, that I fortunately consider that my only task is poetically to make aware.[2903] Mynster's virtuosity also helps, for he is as great in his prudence and circumspection as he is also greatly gifted in many other respects.

$x^3$ A 742   *n.d.*, 1851

### « 6713

[*In margin:* About "Her"]
*About "Her"*[2904]

At the time of her father's death I wrote to Schlegel.[2905] He was furious and would in no way "tolerate any intervention by another in the relationship between himself and his wife."

That actually settled the matter. I really cannot ask for more.

But the point is that she perhaps never learned about my overture, Schlegel has not told her.

To that extent she has not had justice done to her.

Later she herself seems to be more attentive. We see each other more often.[*]

The main point is that in the course of a month to a month and a half we have seen each other almost every single day or twice every other day.

I take my usual walk along the ramparts. She also goes for walks there now. She comes either with Cordelia[2906] or alone and always goes back the same way alone; consequently we meet both times.

This surely is not purely accidental.

If she wanted to speak with me, she has had ample opportunity. I cannot make myself believe that she dares not, since in the past, after our engagement was broken as well as at the time she became engaged to Schlegel, she sought by way of mimetic telegraphy a little intimation from me, and in fact received it, signifying to her that she must give me up but that otherwise she was dear to me and she had my devotion.

But I cannot speak to her. No.

There is an utterly unique difficulty about this matter. It is not the usual case of a man perhaps feeling disinclined to lay himself open to the possibility of being thought a scoundrel and the like. No, if nothing else were possible, I would gladly, very gladly, speak to her.

The difficulty is just the opposite: that I might find out too much. Perhaps she has put me out of her thoughts—and then by talking to her I perhaps would disturb everything. Perhaps her whole marriage is a mask and she is more passionately attached to me than before. In that case all would be lost. I know so well what she can get into her head if she gets hold of me.

And then there is Schlegel, to whom I owe being on guard as conscientiously as possible![†]

Consequently, no. After all, it is not I who publicly express that I have given her up; she has in fact married another.

The whole thing moves me painfully inasmuch as it coincides with my own thoughts about giving up being an author, and it has been somewhat of a strain to introduce the last pseudonym.[2907]

X³ A 769   n.d., 1851

« 6714

[*]In margin of 6713 (x³ A 769):

In church, especially Slotskirken, we have seen each other regularly over the years, and lately more often than usual. I have my particular place where I invariably sit. She often sits nearby. She often seems to be suffering considerably. Three weeks ago she sat right ahead of me. Usually she sings the hymn after the sermon, which I never do. That day she did not do it. Consequently we left at the same time. Outside the church door she turned and saw me. She stood at the corner leading left from the church. I turned as I always do to the right, because I like to go through the arcade. My head tends to incline somewhat to the right. As I turned I perhaps tilted my head a bit more pronouncedly than usual. Thereupon I continued my pace, and she went her way. Later I reproached myself severely, or more correctly, became concerned that this movement could have been noticed by her and been interpreted as beckoning her to go my way. Probably she did not notice it at all, and in any case I would have had to leave it up to her whether she would speak to me, and in that even my first question would have been whether she had Schlegel's permission.

$x^3$ A 770    n.d.

« 6715

*In margin of 6713* ($x^3$ A *769*):

†And he can truthfully say that his cause is in good hands with me, for only with his approval does it interest me. A relationship to her with even the slightest trace of the clandestine—Good Lord, no, then no one knows me. It is the idea which preoccupies me, wherever I am; I cannot be without the idea. But for an expression of the idea it is required (1) that she be essentially content with her marriage to Schlegel, (2) that Schlegel is happy to consent that I speak with her:[2908] then I am very willing to do everything to let my life express both her worth and how important she has been to me. But if there is anything dubious about getting the idea expressed, then my idea demands not merely that I do not get involved in such a matter but that I even oppose it.

$x^3$ A 771    n.d.

« 6716  *Chrysostom—Mynster*[2909]

Mynster has made being a religious speaker into an artistic performance and studiously guards against becoming personally involved. Right there is the mistake.

Chrysostom is also very eloquent—but he gesticulates with his whole life. He initiates some action in public life—and the next Sunday preaches about it. He uses the pulpit for action; his speaking is not an artistic performance theatrically removed from life's actuality. No, it is an act which intervenes right in the middle of the actuality of life.

X³ A 780    n.d., 1851

### « 6717 Mynster's sermon today

Today Mynster preached about the beauty of the Christian life[2910] —and very beautifully.

But to penetrate, give impetus to action, etc.—no, that is foreign to Mynster's nature as he is now. Instead of Christian restlessness,[2911] always artistic serenity. Inasmuch as he chose hymn no. 588 I momentarily expected something different today, but it did not happen.

X³ A 782    n.d., 1851

### « 6718 The Poetic—and Myself

Here it is again. The idea-struggle which I represent, yet also moderately actualizing it and therefore incurring various worries—if I were to transform this struggle into literary works, even present it on the stage as straight drama—well, there is no one, no living person who could make such a hit and become the hero of the moment.

But since I resist and still actualize it somewhat, I create nothing but opposition and cause many spiritual trials for myself.

But these are the frontier disputes inherent in my nature. I am a poet. But long before I became a poet I was intended for the life of religious individuality. And the event whereby I became a poet was an ethical break or a teleological suspension of the ethical. And both of these things make me to want to be something more than "the poet," while I also am learning ever more anxiously to guard against any presumptuous arrogance in this, something God also will surely watch over.

And every time a phase of this inner frontier struggle is behind me, there comes back to me all the more emphatically—it is, in fact, the refrain in the battle: that I can never adequately thank God who in infinite love has done and is doing for me far more than I ever could have expected, could or dared expect. What blessedness!

The source of my strength and bold confidence for reaching such a heterogeneity with the universally human is that my strength is my weakness. Practically from childhood I was set outside of the universally human by reason of distinctive sufferings. I am not a capricious experimenter or even perhaps a rash venturer—no, I am a sufferer, constrained in suffering. Without these sufferings I of course would have married long ago, perhaps also have had an appointive position. But my sufferings had a dialectical quality so that it was still possible that they could be relieved. Perhaps it will still turn out that way, and at the time, I hope, when I can no longer afford to maintain an author-existence at my own expense; if not, I will surely get my orders. Meanwhile I take my time, lest I prematurely, out of fretful anxiety for my earthly welfare, plunge ahead and disturb what goals Governance might have for me.

$x^3$ A 789   *n.d.*, 1851

### « 6719  *The Age—and My Task*

(1) It is not an age which needs a reformer, but it is a conceited, pompous, confused age in which each and every person wants to dabble at being a reformer and which therefore needs just the opposite of a reformer, a servant who can devour all these reformers the way Socrates ate up the Sophists. It is not an age in which malfeasance by government makes a reformation necessary, but it is an age which must learn to need government or learn to be governed.

(2) As I have so often said, the highest and the lowest have a certain resemblance to each other. I shall explain this further.

The highest is not the conventional human normalcy. On the contrary the highest is abnormal. All the religious paradigms are recognizable by being offensive to the ethical. As an example: to cause offense—yes, nothing is easier, any lout and any lubber can do that; and yet, yet it is precisely the highest that also causes offense.

The order is as follows:

A. First of all comes the highest, which is the abnormal.

B. Then come the upright honest humanness, which is a kind of relativity.

C. Then come the louts, the fake reformers, etc.

B is obviously more legitimate than C, but B again is untruth when it wants to ignore A completely.

Take our present situation. Mynster[2912] represents B. He has detested C and has fought it to the best of his ability. There I agree with him. But he has forgotten to stress or even to suggest A, and there I disagree with him.

In fair weather only the Mynsterian principle prevails.

But when trouble comes, A must be applied simply in order to be able to govern.

The confusion in our age is simply this dabbling at reforming.

This is C. How can this C acquire a certain legitimacy, even though simulated? Precisely by making capital of A, but unfortunately, A is not suggested in the Mynsterian approach.

Under such circumstances, what must be done to get control of C? Cut off communication between C and A, or make any confusion of C and A impossible.

This does not really happen by silencing A in the Mynsterian way, since just because A has been silenced, C has been able to make capital of it and put forth the theory which in the highest sense is the truth: that the highest is abnormal.

What is to be done then? Here is my tactic.

I apply A poetically, suggesting that this is too high for us, it is only for the chosen ones, the highly entrusted ones. So I adhere to B, and in this way I am able to scuttle C.

If the most clever statesmen, if the most experienced leaders of the Church were to pass judgment, they would say: He has hit the nail on the head. And then I have to put up with living here in Copenhagen as a ridiculous exaggeration, have to steer the whole thing on my own —while Mynster sits in state and rules—*in absurdum;* and the officials regard me doubtfully.

Yet Mynster understands me somewhat. I have also done various things privately to explain my approach. But the point is this—he also understands that this implies indirect criticism of his whole approach. But that is what it does.

What makes my position more difficult is that what I want I cannot communicate as such, perhaps advertise in print to the public. No thanks, all I want is that there be governing. But this, again, is the confusion of the times—that everything has to be communicated to the public, also the fact that there must be governing—but that is impossible, after all, if it is communicated to the public. Consequently, I must put up with governmental officials who actually do not govern; and I give strong support so that there may be governing, and as a reward the state officials become enraged with me.

$X^3$ A 799    *n.d.,* 1851

« **6720**

*In margin of 6719* ($X^3$ A 799):

Our age imagines itself to be a reforming age. On closer inspection it is obvious that those who want to reform the Church are not religious individualities at all but politicians. This being the case, the established order has more religiousness. If these reformers get a footing, a *reformation* would occur which, with less religiousness, yes, with minus religiousness—reforms what does still have some religiousness.

No, stop, says Governance; nothing will come of this. You will not have a reformation, but you reformers are going to be cashiered, turned out, shown up for what you are.

Imagine Luther alive today[2913]—he would say: everything must be done to put down such an ungodly and blasphemous rebellion, which in addition wants to call itself a *reformation*.

What a difference. When Luther stepped forth, a reformation was needed; and Luther had essentially more religiousness than the established order. It became the Reformation.

Nowadays the evil, the sickness, is simply this conceitedness that a purely secularized generation wants—to reform—the Church. Religiously understood, the task is simply that of thrusting back this abuse, which is the profanest aping of and taking-in-vain of Luther's Reformation, so far from being reformation that it is the downfall of all religion —by means of—horrible nonsense!—a reformation.

$X^3$ A 800    *n.d.*

### « 6721 *My Task*

Precisely in order to be able to fall repressively like a lead weight on this whole political and profane reforming of the religious, I must be led so far out that when it comes to representing the movement I can outbid any of its representatives.

And then the turn, such as was made in the preface to *Practice in Christianity*,[2914] a kind of symbolic act—that I was the only one judged to be a mediocre Christian.

The tragedy of the times, especially now after 1848, is precisely this misconceived movement that wants to reform *en masse*.

But if I had not released *Practice in Christianity*, if I had withheld it until later in order not to trouble myself with possible misunderstandings with the established order, I would have been preyed upon continually by the question of whether or not I had spared myself. [*In margin:* And it perhaps could have consumed my whole life, since it was indeed possible that I would never have been able to decide to publish these writings.] Furthermore, if I had released the three treatises in *Practice in Christianity* separately, one after the other, I would have done it with the idea that it was my task to incite a movement—instead of its being my task to dispatch the reformers.

When everything in Copenhagen became ironical, I, the master of the art of irony, converted the relation and became the object of irony. When chaos won in 1848, then it became very clearly my task—I who had been a stimulus toward movement—to oppose the reformers. I have always understood this, but I simply had to understand it even more fully.

Thus everything was guided for the best. And the blessed consolation in which I have always found rest is this: either I am going about this the right way—and I thank God, or I am going at it the wrong way, and then his infinite love makes it right just the same—but far more right than it would otherwise have been, O infinite love!

$x^4$ A 6   *n.d.,* 1851

### « 6722 *The Old—the New*

Yes, of course, what I say is somewhat out of fashion,[2915] but wait and see—with the help of the year 1848 it will soon be the newest of the new.

$x^4$ A 8   *n.d.,* 1851

### « 6723 *My Later Conversations with Bishop Mynster*[2916] *after the One about* Practice in Christianity

The various times I have spoken with him I have also taken the opportunity to touch upon these points. That the mistake from above has been that there has actually been no governing. That above all it was a matter of properly grasping the reins. That one ought to make a little admission to God about the past—in order to take up the reins properly. That eloquence had one of the most fortuitous situations imaginable when the shout went up from below for freedom, freedom, and more freedom—and then the one at the head stepped forward, drew himself up in all his dignity and said: We also have felt called to self-examination by the revolutions of the day and have acknowledged before God that until now we perhaps have been unduly slack—it now is our intention to govern. I said to him: You are gifted, eloquent, a man of character, dignity, years, and tradition. You are the only one in sight who can do it.

Mynster listens to me. He then usually answers that it is futile to want to tyrannize.

$x^4$ A 9   *n.d.,* 1851

### « 6724  *Grundtvig*[2917]

In his younger days he represented the old, the old-fashioned, the hoary past, primitive, primeval Christianity; now in his old age he has spruced up to be the latest thing out, a regular fashion-setter.

$x^4$ A 14   *n.d.*, 1851

### « 6725  *Dr. Rudelbach*[2918] *and I*

We shall never understand one another.

For him it has long since been definitely settled that he is a Christian. And now he busies himself with history and the external forms of the Church. He has never felt the disquietude of the idea, wondering every single day whether he is now a Christian or not. "Never"—no, because anyone who has felt this once, one day, one hour, does not let go of it during his entire life, or it never lets go of him.

The idea has involved me in personal self-concern, and therefore I can never find time for projects, for I must begin every day with this concern: Are you a Christian now? Indeed, perhaps this very day there will be an existential collision which will make it clear that you are not a Christian at all.

$x^4$ A 20   *n.d.*, 1851

### « 6726  *My Psychological Tactic*

I never deny directly what a man says about himself.

The usual thing is for someone to make some inflated statement about himself and then to be told that it is a lie, a delusion—and there is a quarrel.

I do not do things that way. No, when a man says something like that, I answer: If you yourself say so, then I believe it.

Then I take his statement and think it through to all its existential consequences. I confront him with them. One of two things happens —either he more or less accepts them and then there is more or less truth in him, or he does not accept them—and then he has judged himself. I judge no one, but this brings things into the open.

$x^4$ A 23   *n.d.*, 1851

### « 6727  *The Significance of My Life at Present*

The Church does not have to be reformed, nor does the doctrine.[2919] If anything has to be done—then it is penance on the part of all of us. That is what my life expresses.

Humanly speaking, I am the most precocious person among us.

And what have I learned? That I hardly dare call myself a Christian—how, then, should I dare want to reform the Church or occupy myself with such things.

Just as other young men go abroad and bring back reports about foreign customs and manners, so I also have lived for many years as if in a foreign country—in the company of ideals, where it is so wonderful to be, all gentleness and mildness, if one is only humble and modest.

Then I was parted from them. In farewell they said something like this: Go with God. Tell others what you have learned. And that you may remember us, take the ideals along *poetically*. Make the best use of them you can but remember that you are still responsible.

What did I learn? I learned that to be a Christian is something so infinitely elevated that I scarcely dare call myself one. But I received permission to use the ideals *poetically*.[2920]

The doctrine in the established Church and its organization are very good. But the lives, our lives—believe me, they are mediocre. [*In margin:* The proclamation of the doctrine is done at too great a distance,[2921] Christianity is not a power in actuality, our lives are only slightly touched by the doctrine.] But this can be forgiven if it only is acknowledged.[2922] But do not incur new guilt by wanting to reform the Church when Christianity is no more.

Just as Luther stepped forward with only the Bible at the Diet of Worms, so I would like to step forward with only the New Testament, take the simplest Christian maxim, and ask each individual: Have you fulfilled this even approximately—if not, do you then want to reform the Church? [*In margin:* And no one says: I am just as good as the others, for anyone who says that is most unworthy.]

They just laugh! But even that I have put in its right place in advance. In the past they were allowed to get their fill of ridiculing me —something I asked for myself.[2923] Now presumably they are tired of it.

Stop, stop. At least be satisfied for the time with what I can offer.

And what can I offer? I am a poet—alas, only a poet. But I can present Christianity in the glory of its ideality; and that I have done. Listen to me—at least before you begin reforming and voting.[2924] First see how ideal Christianity really is and then take some time for yourselves—before you reform.

I am only a poet, alas, only a poet. Do not look at my life—and yet, do look at my life only to see what a mediocre Christian I am, something you will see best when you listen to what I say about the ideal. Listen to that and never mind about my trifling person.

I am only a poet. I love this earthly life all too much, would like to have a comfortable life, humanly speaking, to have diversion, to enjoy life, etc. Ah, but I perceive that in the strictest sense Christianity demands something altogether different. But precisely because, deeply humbled, I confess my inferiority, I have realized that Christianity permits me, at least for the time being, to live in this manner (for I am indeed under obligation to inquire, as a child asks his father or his teacher).

And this is what I offer; on this condition I dare to offer Christianity—O, listen to me, at least before you reform it.

I am only a poet. And what, then, is my task (if I could carry it out, for I cannot know definitely today whether I can do it even tomorrow; at all times I only dare be assured that yesterday I was able to do it approximately).

Wherever there is a movement that I feel is dangerous to Christianity, there I go. I do not say a word to those present, God forbid, not a word about myself—that would be disrespectful. What do I do then? I take my stand, so to speak, in a corner or in the middle of some gathering, according to the circumstances. I then begin to talk out loud to myself, just like an absent-minded person, talk out loud to myself about the ideals. If only you clamorous ones would talk this way, you whose speeches, except for the many brilliant parts in the middle, all end with the brilliant conclusion: Now let us take a vote. Something else will happen. Now one, now another will go aside, saying to himself: That was strange talk, that about the ideal—believe me, he will not vote.

And so it goes. For just as little as any woman, regarded in the sphere of the idea, can resist the poet's Don Juan, so no man or woman, regarded in the sphere of the idea, can in the long run resist this speaking about the ideal—how unfortunate the man who could do so. But he cannot. It creeps in, no one knows through what pores and openings, creeps into the heart. A long time may elapse; one day he begins to act strangely. He shuts himself in, or he goes out for a solitary walk. He says to himself: That was strange talk, that about the ideal; I want to think it over. And when he opens the door again or comes home, he is a changed man—believe me, he will not vote on Christianity.

In a certain external, godless way we men also have it in our power at all times to vote on Christianity. We can in fact say: This is the way we want to have it, and this we will call Christianity. Let us beware!

Listen to me! O, my friends, I have never before pleaded for anything like this, but now I plead for this in the name of Christianity! Listen to me! And you, O you women, you have always been receptive to what the poets say, O be receptive now and stop the men! You cannot and will not hear more gentle talk than this from a wretched poet. But just look at Christianity once. Just examine my characterization of a witness to the truth, to say nothing of an "apostle" (and one must be at least a witness to the truth to dare want to "reform"). Consider what I am saying here, and then look, for example, at me and see what a spineless fellow I am by comparison—ah, but humanly speaking I am in the vanguard here on the mountain.

I am only a poet, and for this very reason I want to have, humanly speaking, a good understanding with you, for in this respect a poet is always weak. If you want to understand me, if in recompense you want to provide my life with earthly embellishments—I will accept it with gratitude. And I dare do that precisely because I call myself only a poet; like a child I dare take pleasure in these earthly things. O, but if the matter goes to the next higher court, if a witness to the truth is required to stop this—no, he will not accept such things. Frightfully tough and hardy as one who has died to the world, unmoved and immovable, he quotes the price of being a Christian to you and me, to all of us, a price as high as "spirit" is high; he abolishes all boundaries; he hastens with longing after his own martyrdom, and therefore he cannot save the rest of us. Thus many weak and frail ones topple who could go along under a bit more lenient conditions, if there were some concession, and many vacillating ones become hard of heart, etc.

$x^4$ A 33   n.d., 1851

« 6728 *The Old Orthodox*

who claimed that they were the only true Christians in Denmark.

I have nothing against their separating from us—but it is indefensible that they should achieve this by balloting[2925] and without giving up the claim that they are the true Church.

But this is supposed to be the tactic—and then judgment is supposed to fall upon Mynster[2926] and his party.

In what frame of mind could honest Spandet[2927] make his proposal? Did he look upon it as similar to a motion about gas streetlighting and the like—if so, then of course a vote may be taken, but it was certainly improper to make his proposal in this vein. Or if he insists that he has regarded it as a matter of conscience, how in the world can he then be satisfied with serving a matter of conscience (which as a "royal service" not only must be promoted quickly and be put through —but must be put through or the one commissioned falls)—by making a motion for balloting and then seeing how many votes it will get.

Even if it did go through, the cause would still be wrongly served, and an *indirect* proof would be given that it is not a matter of conscience for him and that he has bitten off too much.

And if it fails to pass, then perhaps he will step forth in character.

$x^4$ A 36    *n.d.*, 1851

« **6729**

*In margin of 6728* ($x^4$ A 36):

The Old Orthodox would like to withdraw from the whole Church and yet reserve for themselves the status of being the true Church, and perhaps also (as Rudelbach seems to indicate in his book[2928] on the constitution of the Church), keep all the Church property for themselves, which per capita is not so insignificant, since the Church property is rather considerable and, according to Rudelbach, the true Christians are very few.

$x^4$ A 37    *n.d.*

« **6730** *Christian VIII*

In my first conversation with him (which is noted somewhere else [i.e., $x^1$ A 41], I said (and I do not remember if I made a note of this) when he hinted at drawing me into a closer relationship to himself:

No, Your Majesty, the very point of my life is that I lead a private life, that I am a private man able and willing to defend absolute monarchy in our day. If I am drawn into closer relationship to you, I am immediately weakened. Everything is weakened when explained by mixed motives. The only way to remain unimpaired is to be a private citizen.

I could have added that people diminish a private person by calling him an eccentric.

How sound that answer was. As a matter of fact, everything has so disintegrated that a monarch himself must admit it—and he did. A private citizen is a power, and he must have sufficient resignation to refrain from accepting even the smallest favor—otherwise he is weakened.

At one time the king's favor meant power—how changed things are now when the king must refrain from showing his favor precisely in order not to weaken. How impotent.

$$x^4 \text{ A } 52 \quad n.d., 1851$$

« 6731 *My Relationship to the Movement*[2929]

In one sense no one, no one, no one here on the mountain is as close to the movement as I am; yes, I am its ultimate point.

But the very moment one of our agitators would say: Splendid, let us organize and get this or that external change—then no one, no one, no one here on the mountain is as far away from the movement as I am, separated and distinguished from it by a whole world of difference.

Even that venerable old gentleman, the Very Reverend Bishop of Sjælland,[2930] whom I have admired and respected from the beginning and still do, even he can get involved. He can say: If necessary, I can join with you at many points if you will use common sense. But I cannot. It is much like a dance attended by a dignified elderly matron. Of course she did not come to dance; no, she came along with her children and grandchildren. She sits in an inner room where the older ones are gathered, also in a festive mood, but not to dance. Then the young people get the idea: We must get old Mrs. H. to dance once— she outshines us all in her matriarchial beauty. She demurs, saying: No, my little children. But finally she concedes and says: On one condition, no waltz; I absolutely will not waltz. But if it will make you happy, I will dance a polonaise around the hall. That evening at the ballet a dispute may arise and continue later at social gatherings concerning to what extent it can be maintained that old Mrs. H. danced that evening. I do not enter into such disputes with the dancers and conversers. In my opinion it can be said: She was involved, something she could very well do and still preserve her dignity. It is different with me. Even if both youth and madness joined together to invite me, I literally will not dance[2931] any more than, if you please, an invalid dances. If people wish to put this interpretation on it, I do not object, but it is literally true: I will not dance.

———

It is one of my pseudonyms (Anti-Climacus) who says: Christianity does not exist at all.[2932] It almost sounds as if an apostle were speaking, and thus all relations must be affected appropriately. Just as the movement of a huge fish, almost just by breathing, stirs the sea to its depths, so the movement of an apostle, almost just by breathing, affects everything. Thus no one, no one, no one of the agitators, dares make an offer. Even the person who offered the most and risked the most would qualify it and say: One is *almost*, almost tempted to say that it seems as if Christianity did not exist.

So it is the pseudonym who says these words. But prior to these words there is the preface[2933] to this little book. There it says: I understand this as being spoken to me, solely to me (not to any other man) —so that I might learn to flee to grace. No one, no one, no one of our agitators would characterize the turn this way. He would say: I and a few others, we are Christians, or at least I am—that is, on that first point he will not make a great flourish, but on the second point he will decisively establish his character, the certainty that he is a Christian.

But precisely because I poetically (through the pseudonym) gave the momentum of the infinite and then again, with the aid of the preface, Christianly let the whole thing fall on me, me alone, the movement necessarily is just the opposite of what it must seem to inexperienced and ordinary seamen, to say nothing of the passengers.

The sailor speaks of tacking. When this is to be done, he is not satisfied to have a couple of sails up. No, every stitch is stretched to capture every breeze and give the greatest possible speed. Now the ship sails at a speed—let us say it although presumably impossible—of sixteen knots. The orders are given: All men to the sails. The captain himself stands at the helm. The passengers say: We are heading over there and at the tremendous speed we are going we will be there right away. The time has come. The signal sounds. He lets the ship tack—and we do not arrive there at all, not even in the vicinity; no, it is the place directly opposite. Thereupon he hands the rudder over to the first mate. He takes a cigar case out of his pocket, while all the time his thoughts still seem to be elsewhere, for his face expresses the solemn joy discernible in experienced sailors when a difficult maneuver has been executed with God's help—and this the experienced sailor never forgets! Then he takes a cigar out of the case as a roguish smile, characteristic of the experienced sailor, plays on his lips. Then without saying a word he goes into his cabin to work on his report to the admiralty. —Let me just add a novelistic touch to that incident. There was a passenger on board with binoculars; standing toward the front of the cluster of passengers, he put the binoculars up to his eyes and signaled with his hand. It was obvious that the passengers practically took him to be the captain, and it was obvious that this did not displease him. He announced: We are heading over there, and at the speed we are going now we will be there immediately. By nature he had a long nose (see Claudius[2934])—when the tack was made, I had never seen such a long nose. For one moment he stood as if paralysed, but then he became furious. He threw the binoculars to the floor and tried to incite the passengers against the captain. But this evoked no response among the passengers and passed off so quietly that the captain did not hear a thing of it in the cabin where he sat fully occupied with making his report to the admiralty.

To the admiralty. Yes, for the admiralty and the general staff—those are two major powers.

But there is a greater one: God in heaven. But to be obliged to steer on the condition of having to make a report there and consequently with the responsibility of eternity—that is sheer fear and trembling. I would rather cut peat every day for seventy years than have to steer just one hour on that condition. Good Lord, after all one is just a poor wretch of a man, and even the greatest man can easily miss the mark, albeit only 1/999 of a point—but when it is with the responsibility of eternity, it does not help to come that close to the mark. And yet in another sense it is so blessed to steer on the condition that all the glory of the world, and offered for 70,000 years—yes, well-advised—but, no, that is not even something to be considered—I will exchange it for this bliss for just one hour.

Now, then, this is granted to every man, yes, he must do it. A servant girl, a professor, an infantry soldier, Councilor Deichman (O, excuse me!), a bishop, a mailman, you [in margin: O, away with all emancipation!—you] my dear girl, and I: everyone is to be the single individual who with eternal responsibility steers his own ship. In one sense this is frightful. But if it is properly understood in fear and trembling and not fatuously forgotten again—then, in Christ's name and for his sake, it is even gentler than simply being responsible to the admiralty, for the admiralty, if I may jest, is not as terrifying as God in heaven can be—in fact, and here is the earnestness, even less can it be love and compassion such as God in heaven is—yes, for that matter it does not even have the right to be that, for the admiralty does not have the divine royal prerogative to be love and compassion as God in heaven is! And this is Christianity and God's own doing. Do you want to delete some of it—and by balloting! Or do you think that now is the time to make some external changes instead of pondering how blessed Christianity really is and, alas, how little all of us—or at least I—have appreciated this blessing. Period!

x⁴ A 53   n.d., 1851

### « 6732  *Poetic Humor Verging on a Higher Madness*

..... My opinion is that Christianity does not exist at all.[2935] Moreover, I am all for Bishop Mynster,[2936] who I hope is of the same opinion. —It would be in the vein of Hamlet; thus pathos is brought to the bursting point and the individual is split.

x⁴ A 55   n.d., 1851

### « 6733  *Grundtvig[2937]—and I*

Grundtvig stepped into the world with his trial sermon: Why has God's Word departed from God's house.[2938]

I could never make such a remark. I would have to say: Why has power departed from the proclamation of God's Word.

For I do believe that it is still God's Word which is heard round about the country—the trouble is that we simply do not act according to it. I can be satisfied with little, a little verse from the Bible is sufficient—and I promptly ask myself: Have you done it?[2939]

This explains why I can listen to any pastor, any student, theological candidate. Almost from the beginning Grundtvig was limited to listening only to himself. And always this insistence on Christianity as doctrine, propositions—and then the world-historical.

x⁴ A 56   n.d., 1851

### « 6734  *Grundtvig[2940]—and I*

There can be no greater difference between us than in our tactics.

An unknown theological candidate wants to raise a big tempest and with a fourteen-page sermon,[2941] a trial sermon at that, consequently a sample sermon for which he should even have received a grade.

And I have worked prodigiously for seven years consecutively. As an esthetic author I captivated men, reached a culminating point—and then have a pseudonym declare: Christianity does not exist.[2942]

x⁴ A 57   n.d., 1851

### « 6735  *Grundtvigians[2943]—The Peasant Party*

Do the Grundtvigians dare deny that they are cognizant of the fact that the Peasant Party wants freedom in a purely secular way on purely secular grounds (consequently in opposition to Christianity), while the Grundtvigians want freedom on super-Christian grounds? And how,

then, do they dare vote together? I do not question the Peasant Party
—they do not pretend to be anything but politicians—but I question the
Grundtvigians, who even have posed as the only true Christians in the
land. Is such a thing Jesuitic concealment, is it Christianity?

x⁴ A 58   n.d., 1851

### « 6736 *About Myself*

I am a kind of existential master of ceremonies. That is, with
regard to what anyone claims himself to be in the sphere of religion,
I am promptly his existential implications, forcing him either into
character to become manifest as a deceiver or one self-deceived.

Ideally seen, this is my task, although this does not mean that
empirically I have dealings with every individual.

But we must move back—this I constantly express by constantly
saying of myself: I am only a poet,[2944] which is the truth, but a truth
which can still be considerably embarrassing to muddleheads who
would rather be the ideal themselves or close to or somewhat close to
the ideal.

x⁴ A 64   n.d., 1851

### « 6737

For "The Accounting."[2945] Something, however, which
is not to be included.

*Concerning Myself*

Inasmuch as before God I regard my entire work as an author as
my own upbringing or education, I could say: But I have remained
silent so long lest, in relation to what I understand before God to be
my own education, I become guilty of talking out of school by speaking
prematurely. This could then be added to the passage in the final draft
of "The Accounting":[2946] Before God I call this my upbringing or
education etc.

I would have liked very much to have made that statement; lyrically it would have gratified me to use this expression. But there is
something else that holds me back. As is frequently the case, the most
humble expression seen from another angle is the very one that is
likely to say too much, and so it is here. Precisely this humble expression would accentuate the fact that it is my education, almost in the
sense of my being an authority. It is simpler as it stands in "The
Accounting," with the addition that I need further education, and the
tone is such that it can be said of every man.

x⁴ A 85   n.d., 1851

« **6738** *Copenhagen and Denmark*
*Are a Provincial Market Town*

to such an extent that the fact that I received the poor and unfortunate name "Søren"[2947] has been a downright hindrance to my becoming regarded as being somebody. No, in order for it to be conceivable in Copenhagen that I am a thinker, I really would have to have a nicer name.

This may be denied. But nevertheless it is the case. For one thing, people are so provincial-minded, and for another, if anyone says this, they deny it.

$x^4$ A 87   *n.d.*, 1851

« **6739** *My Tactic,*

always to *disputere* only *e concessis*[2948] (to take a man's words when he says something great about himself and then to press the existential consequences upon him), might seem to be "villainous malice and envy." By no means, it is admiration. But it is the admiration of reflection which looks where it is going, and ethically it is irony, which the lack of character in our age needs.

$x^4$ A 101   *n.d.*, 1851

« **6740** *About Myself*

I believe I might have the courage to lose my life in order to make room for the extraordinary—but to be regarded as the extraordinary myself—no, that cannot be;[2949] to me that would be the same as defiling what has been entrusted to me. In a pinch I could better try to find a man who is perhaps not as advanced as I am myself and get him proclaimed as the extraordinary and then perhaps risk everything to put him through. But I myself may only say incessantly: It is not I who am the extraordinary; I only bow to it. Only then am I happy and have a zest for life and for conflict. Incognito[2950] is my element; and there, too, is the stimulating incommensurability in which I am able to move. Not to be more than one is considered and assumed to be is frightfully crippling, as pinching as tight boots, to me deadly. Perhaps for most people being regarded as more than they are is stimulating bait so that they still make some effort. For me it is just the opposite—being regarded as less than I am is my *working capital* (the propelling agent). But I am also by nature polemical.

$x^4$ A 130   *n.d.*, 1851

« **6741** *Nonna*

The mother of Gregory of Nazianz. He had a brother Caesarius who was a physician. When he was buried, his mother followed, not in mourning apparel but clad in white: "She mastered her tears with philosophy, her sorrow with hymns."

See Böhringer, I, 2, p. 386.[2951]

x⁴ A 154   *n.d.*, 1851

« **6742**

Somewhere in an earlier journal [i.e., x¹ A 131] where I mentioned my willingness to take it upon my conscience to let the journalists shoot, there is added:

But no, no! I prefer to do battle in such a way that I take personal command at the execution[2952] where I am to fall before the journalists.

x⁴ A 166   *n.d.*, 1851

« **6743** *Goldschmidt*[2953]

Once an instrument of contemptibleness—now the respectable, the virtuous one! Once the grinning buffoon—now the ethicist! Once hiding behind street loafers, the rabble-hero—now the aristocrat, the fine, fine aristocrat who converses during dinner with barons and counts. —And yet, despite all these changes, essentially the same—the only striking thing in these changes!

x⁴ A 167   *n.d.*, 1851

« **6744**

*In margin of 6743* (x⁴ A 167):

Now that Bishop Mynster has honored him,[2954] the designation "the virtuous" would acquire new point. It could be introduced as follows.

Since the designation "the instrument of literary contemptibleness" is too long, I deem it best to use a new one as an epithet for Goldschmidt: the virtuous. It says exactly the same. It suggests a passage in *Det lykkelige Skibbrud*:[2955] a prostitute about to be married comes to Rosiflengius—not in order to be married by him, for R., after all, was not a priest—but in order to get a wedding song, which she gets, and the title reads: The Lily United to the Rose, or Thoughts by the Virtuous Virgin-Bride.

June, 1852

x⁴ A 168   June, 1852

« **6745** *Personal*

Today I read my usual portion in the Old Testament. And the sequence came to David's Psalms (24, 25, 26, 27, 28).

It made an especially strong impact because last evening I got the little book[2956] by Bishop Mynster in which he has blurred the impression of Goldschmidt by bringing us two together[2957] just where we should be separated.

Psalms 26:4 and 27:10 made a special impression on me.

$x^4$ A 195   *n.d.*, 1851

« **6746**

[*Diagonally in upper left corner:* On the Impossibility of Doing Anything about Mynster's Latest Book: *Yderlige Bedrag* etc.]

Early in April, 1851

For the journal. Page given on the front cover.

*On the Impossibility of Doing Anything about*
*Mynster's Latest Book (Yderlige Bidrag,* [2958] *etc.)*

(1) Quotations are altogether properly used—nothing to object to here.

(2) I would unqualifiedly esteem recognition by Bishop Mynster. But the way he has brought in Goldschmidt[2959] makes the whole thing an insult (formally, for actually the quotation is perfectly correct). But I usually do not pay any attention to insults; to defend oneself against insults is not fighting devoutly; one defends oneself devoutly only against honor, distinction, etc.—especially when it is misunderstood.

(3) My existential category is "without authority." But in this case authority actually would have to be used, and to attack Mynster would tend in that direction. But I continually stick to the poetic approach.[2960]

(4) More than for anyone else, Mynster of course was the one for whom I would risk almost everything. But here he has impaired himself. As far as that goes, he also has placed me with my profound veneration[2961] for him in an almost ridiculous predicament, for that is really not a category for a man who acts in such a way. But I could derive some satisfaction from being the one who would jolt him. But for the reasons mentioned I cannot bring myself to that, and furthermore *Practice in Christianity* will certainly be interpreted by many to be aimed at Mynster, notwithstanding my keeping the whole book poetic and wishing to be able to go on without deviation "in profound veneration."

$x^5$ A 166   *n.d.*, 1851

## « 6747 *Regarding My Relationship to Bishop Mynster*[2962]

Perhaps it is best that I explain in a few words how I regard my relationship to Bishop Mynster at present; it will always be of interest to my reader. And since something is being done publicly—and perhaps much more is being done secretly—to frustrate my work, an explanation such as this is always helpful.

As I see the relationship now, Bishop M. must be regarded as my most dangerous and zealous opponent.

"But how did that happen? What outrageous wrong have you done him to bring this about?" No, not so, for even if I had wronged Bishop M. scandalously, I still would not regard him as my most zealous opponent. O, no, Bishop M. is a proud man, and a proud man can forgive even an outrageous wrong.

Only one thing, only in one case can he not forgive. The remark I am about to make is not my own but one of the most distinguished, most experienced and tested, as well as one of the most noble observers the French nation has to boast of, Duc de La Rochefoucauld.[2963] He says: One forgives the person who has done him wrong but one never forgives—and in proportion to his pride—never forgives the person he himself has wronged. No, one does not forgive him; he in fact is also far more dangerous than one's worst enemy. For at most what can the worst enemy do? He can do me wrong, but no, more than that—indeed, the prouder a person is, the less it bothers him. No, but the one who is a plaguing reminder that I did him wrong—him I never forgive. Yes, there no doubt have been cases of a proud man who, having wronged somebody, became so furious with the person he wronged that he then did everything possible to plunge this man into vice and crime and thereby managed to feel justified in the wrong he originally did him—as if something later had retroactive power! No, one never forgives the man he himself has wronged.

Alas, poor me, so in Bishop Mynster I have my most zealous opponent—for I am in the situation that Bishop Mynster has wronged me, poor me, and once again poor me with my steadfast devotion to Bishop M.

To place *The Corsair*'s Goldschmidt and me on a par as authors (and this is what Bishop M. did in his latest book[2964]) was a wrong; Bishop Mynster knows it himself, and he will never forgive me. There is only one condition on which Bishop M. perhaps would forgive me for his having wronged me: if the whole affair would pass off unnoticed. But if that cannot be, if it is touched upon—each time Bishop M. will become more and more inimical toward me; he will never forgive me, for he undoubteedly feels: basically it was an enormous wrong I did Magister K., and I hereby have exposed myself frightfully—*ergo*, I will never forgive him.

*Note. In his most recent book: *Yderligere Bidrag til Forhandlingerne om de kirkelige Forhold. i Danmark.* 1851.

x⁵ A 167   *n.d.*, 1851–53

« **6748** *A Statement by Bishop Mynster*\*²⁹⁶⁵

[*In margin in penciled parentheses:* and prompted by that, something about our literary situation.]

———

*Tone*

(This is to be set in the smallest possible brevier.)

This matter may at first seem insignificant, it is possible, but on the other hand it is also possible that it is of extremely serious importance for both our literary and moral situation.

———

The statement is on p. 44.²⁹⁶⁶ "Among the gratifying *phonomena*²⁹⁶⁷—we borrow this word from one of our most talented authors —to appear during these discussions is the resonance accorded a voice recently raised against 'the belief, etc.' "²⁹⁶⁸ (see *Fædrelandet*, no. 26).

The speaker is His Excellency, the Right Reverend Bishop of Sjælland. The talented author, "one of our most talented," who is the inventor of the word *phonomenon,* which the Bishop is now adopting out of linguistic interest, is *The Corsair*'s Goldschmidt, at present ethicist, aristocrat, the elegant, gallant, piquant editor of *Nord og Syd,*²⁹⁶⁹ although until now he has not seen fit to retract, not even with one word, his six-year public past (which pertains in no way to "elegance" but certainly pertains to teachers of Christianity, the highest ecclesiastic, the appointed guardians of morals. The "gifted"—for Bishop Mynster seems to care simply and solely about talent!—the "gifted" author in *Fædrelandet,* whose words are quoted, is I, S. Kierkegaard.

(1) With my "profound veneration"²⁹⁷⁰ for Bishop M.—which surely is commonly recognized as the unaltered, continuing expres-

sion of my relationship to this man from the beginning—can I be anything but disturbed in this company?

(2) Has not Bishop M. weakened his own position here? M. and G. are opposites. For G. it is most dangerous of all to be placed in proximity to Bishop M. this way. In any other company his public past would not be so glaringly conspicuous as it is here, unless he repentantly revokes it. M. and G. can only diminish each other by proximity; that is, M. is actually the one who will be diminished, for G. is secure in another way. Every recommendation by M. is for G. a minus, is a loss for M.; every recommendation by G. for M. is a minus for M. An example of the former comes right away in Bishop M.'s most recent book, p. 5, where Bishop M. thanks G. for acquainting him with a French author who says, "There is nothing more estimable than" " 'a nation that defends its morals.' " It is G. who told him about this, the Goldschmidt of *The Corsair,* who for six years, hidden behind scoundrels, presumably "defended" "morals"—by subverting them, and by introducing the new morals of foreign demoralization—with tragically mounting success! And it is Bishop M. who thanks—G.—for this information! And this is not chilling irony, no, this is a distinguished man's affable, patronizing compliment to a supposedly deserving inferior!!! But it does not help; it is irony just the same, irony upon both of them, or, more correctly, it is irony—chilling or burning as you will, upon Bishop M., for G. is safeguarded in another way.

(3) In the no. 26 issue of *Fædrelandet* referred to, I have very sharply taken issue with what Bishop M. in his recent book mildly took issue with—the dubiousness of a possible coalition between the so-called Old Orthodox and radical politicians, the possible purely political alliance between the qualitatively heterogeneous[2971]—the combination of M. and G. is actually an even more contentious union of the heterogeneous, is it not?

(4) In the enterprising busyness of busy secular life only talent is clamored for, there is concern only about talent and talent. The Christian has another view, which is almost unconcerned about talents, or at least not first of all or not solely, but essentially about what use is made of the talent. Every Christian is under obligation most sacredly and solemnly to maintain this view in his life, especially every clergyman, the highest ecclesiastic most of all—is this not true?

(5) To maintain this view, I have worked—if not in human wretchedness—yet to the best of my ability and with many sacrifices. Bishop M. knows this. To make this view known, I also exposed myself

to ridicule and abuse from Goldschmidt of *The Corsair,* who expressed
the opposite view, even disdainfully; strangely enough, it happened,
among other reasons, once again simply because I (in *Concluding Postscript*) thanked Kts[2972] in "profound veneration." So it actually is for
me a strange abracadabra: this equality before the Christian authority,
the Right Reverend Bishop, that—equally, in one breath, without even
the least mention or hint of the author-character, so that either there
is homogeneity here, and consequently it is not a matter of indifference
or homogeneity, which is an unchristian view of life—there are, according to Bishop M., two talented or gifted authors, Goldschmidt of *The
Corsair* and S.K.—it almost seems as if we two, under our own or the
Right Reverend's auspices, should form an alliance, something I shall
guard against; but is not all this true?

(6) Christianity is a unity of gentleness and rigorousness, in one
sense infinitely rigorous, and the Christian shudders at this confounded confusion of magnanimous Christian leniency and cowardly,
secularly-shrewd weakness. First of all an eternity of memory, until the
ethical demand is honored (through suffering the penalty, through
*restitutio in integrum* where this is possible, through retraction or the like
—and *in casu*[2973] the issue is not in the remotest way a man's private
life but a six-year public past), and then an almost miraculous forgetfulness: this is Christianity. This is also Christianity according to Mynster's most remarkable and to me unforgettable preaching, which I
have read, do read, and will read again and again to my upbuilding.
But then is it not also Christianity to act accordingly? I do not think
that it is Christianity to have a new sermon **about** the obligation to act
according to the sermon, and then a new one **about** the danger in
merely preaching **about** the obligation to act according to the sermon
about, and then to the nth power a sermon **about**. In my opinion this
constitutes a moving away from Christianity. And that simple middle-
class man, "the former clothier here in the city," my deceased father,
who brought me up in Christianity on Mynster's sermons, was also of
this opinion—is this not so?

(7) If the word *phonomenon*[2974] must be introduced, it would be
easy to find room and occasion on practically every page. But the line
chosen to introduce it is the very one where the inventor's qualitative
literary opposite is *also* (thus very plainly) given prominence as a gifted
author—almost as if this juxtaposition were calculated to stand, and
very conspicuously, as a kind of ἀπομνημόνευμα,[2975] as a transmis-
sion to the next generation from the previous one, here represented,

and on behalf of Christianity, represented by the rigorous old man of earnestness: that there were two absolutely identical bees, two talents (something that when M. is long dead G. can spread around for a long time, even if it is wrong, and use against me if I remain quiet now)— that is the line chosen, precisely that one—does this seem intentional or to betray an intention—am I right or am I wrong?

(8) Linguistically, Bishop M. is practically the absolute authority here in the north, something G. perhaps has not managed to achieve either in the north or in the south.[2976] So now this word *phonomenon* has been taken up into the language; Bishop M. has "taken it up." Dictionaries will come to refer to M., or their name will be joined, forever joined—also a ἀπομνημόνευμα. In strict accuracy perhaps their relation to this word can be designated correctly this way (just as a woman is called, for example, Madame Hansen, née Jensen): Mynster, née G.—is this going too far, or is it Bishop M. who has gone too far?

(9) This passage may be an appreciative acknowledgment falling to my lot from the Right Reverend old gentleman; it may also be an affront to me; it may be a mistake of ignorance, a distraction; it could also be an intrigue—it can be any one of many things.

If it were definitely an *appreciative acknowledgment* it would be unspeakably precious to me to thank him in the old-fashioned way, "in profound" veneration.[2977] With respect to this man it was my wish, and a very precious wish to me, that at the end of my literary activity I would not have changed with age or my more independent standing my esteem for him in such a way that I could not end as I began, with this almost childlike, yet therefore more valuable, perhaps: in profound veneration.

It was an outright affront: I shall remain silent; at least until now I have not been in the habit of paying attention to insults.

But there is an ambiguous something here; and even though it makes me sad I must call attention to this ambiguous something— unless perhaps Bishop M. is utterly ignorant of certain things or, certainly from a Christian point of view, has a scarcely tenable opinion about it.

But it is true that it also could have been an *intrigue*—it was possible, and a more suspicious person could get that idea—an intrigue based on the idea that if I did not remain silent, whereby perhaps the purpose would be achieved in another sense, certain things would be raked up again and I would get into a ruckus (which would bore people and thus harm me) at least with G., and I (usually both taciturn and forbearing) would be depicted as terribly irritable and pathologically vain, also suffering delusions of self-righteousness, almost (*risum teneatis!*[2978]) a pietistic prude and dullard, especially alongside the humane, cultured, gentle Christian love in relation to an ill-spent past public life (the intellectual liberty of the genius), which was Mynster's grateful role. Was this possible—of course from a Christian point of view I cannot sanction it, and intellectually I cannot understand it. When one is the stronger antagonist, why intrigue?—the weapon of the weaker! When one is Bishop M., *per deos obsecro*—why *per* G.![2979] When one is Bishop M., if one wishes to stamp me out, religiously understood, demolish my life, the significance of which is specifically in the religious sphere, and not along the lines of being a talent à la *The Corsair* —if that is the purpose, why then begin by diminishing oneself by summoning G. *in this way,* who in order to be used by Bishop M. must first *éclatant*[2980] make a retraction or he must be used in secret. When one is His Right Reverend Excellency and wants, for example, to go to Nyhavn,[2981] why and for what purpose go through Peder Madsens Gang,[2982] where something could so easily happen, while along the main streets all would take off their hats in deepest reverence and make way for His Right Reverend Excellency.

For me it has meant a great deal, this "in profound veneration"; to those who have regard for me, the religious author, I know this phrase "in profound veneration" has significance: therefore I ought to be a bit careful. If Bishop M. wants to fritter away his reputation, then I at least ought to see to it that I do not fritter away my "profound reverence." I ought to be careful, but I do not mean of myself, and I do not believe that they who have regard for me, for whom this "in deep veneration" has had significance," will find that I have been too careful; on the contrary some of them no doubt would readily consider it a worldly-shrewd weakness on my part if I remained silent. Alas, and if I remained silent, others would talk!

————

In a certain sense curiously unnoticed (hardly once have I been able to get reviewed properly[2983]) but also almost fatefully I have gone my thankless way through literature.

Since I began I have really asked nothing of the world; why not and by what criterion I cannot further explain, because it is all connected with the most intimate and sensitive story of my life and its anguish. But while I asked nothing for myself, I was very devoted to the more distinguished names in literature. It was my wish that when I had traversed my path, which I never thought would take many years, it would be a kind of passageway and that all the elder literary figures would be standing in the very same place as when I began. My devotion and respect for the elder literary men was provisionally expressed in an article in *Fædrelandet*[2984] in 1842: "Public Confession," which was a kind of signaling, and in which I very specifically singled out as objects of my veneration: Professor Heiberg[2985] [*in margin, underlined with pencil, a question mark*: Professor, now Minister, Madvig], and Bishop Mynster, which I also did later in *Fædrelandet*[2986] after my literary activity had begun and was going full speed, and which eventually was indicated in a very formal way in the postscript to *Concluding Postscript.*[2987]

Then in the spring of 1843 came *Either/Or.* I had steadfastly expressed nothing but respectful devotion to Prof. Heiberg,[2988] had also received proofs of his favor; there is surely not one single syllable in the whole book *Either/Or* which can affront him, but there certainly are good words expressed for him, and yet Prof. H. could not resist a compulsion to make himself (falsely) important (in *Intelligentsbladet*[2989]), trying to make it ridiculous, saying it was such a big book, etc.; the whole thing was only a tap, but one for which he perhaps has paid and will continue to pay dearly.

Then it became more and more clear that I actually am a religious author. There is another man here, Prof. Martensen,[2990] not one of the old names but a younger man, and not regarding myself as an authority in literature, I fully affirm Bishop M.'s judgment of him: this is a man of talent—of course not in the same sense as Goldschmidt, which must be mentioned since that is Bishop M.'s judgment. Home from abroad at the opportune moment with Hegel's philosophy, he made a big sensation, had extraordinary success, won over the whole student generation to "the system," which even threatened, alas, to render him, my venerated Bishop Mynster, superfluous. Then he entered upon an official career, took a high position, used his powerful (compared with our conditions) connections to make his life secure in every possible way, and later as a distinguished ecclesiastic enjoyed new rapport with the whole cultured world. I was a nobody and remained a nobody, but I devoted myself to what for me was the costly—financially as well—pleasure of being an author in Denmark. Then I became even less than a nobody, was ridiculed and insulted, which again the envious elite used against me, for they refused to understand that I was religiously motivated, but admittedly they could not know that, but they also refused to see that on my part it was indeed an estimable act with regard to our demoralized literary situation. Since he represented the "system," I disagreed with Prof. Martensen and he with me, I suppose, since the general tenor of the opinion he and his "circles" controlled was that what I was doing was somewhat antiquated. For my part I let the pseudonyms express the disagreement, but so softened and blurred that the scene could just as well be in Germany, where at that time the *Privat-Docent*[2991] was a stock character, whereas we did not have a single one. Martensen was never named: the whole context was poetically maintained, which both poetically satisfied me and gave me joy, for I knew what a great friend of peace he is, the Old One among us, Sjælland's venerable Bishop. But M. could not resist. In the preface to his *Dogmatik*[2992] there came a tap. Why just a tap: strike in earnest or keep completely quiet! [*In penciled parentheses:* Incidentally, he perhaps will pay dearly for that tap.]

And now Bishop M. comes along—O, my God!—he also with perhaps a tap! If it really is that, then would to God it had been a devastating blow! For I perhaps will not succumb to a devastating blow, not even from Bishop M., nor to a tap. But if it is a tap, then there is another one who may easily fall. For when a little bit of a man is beside himself and wants to strike a devastating blow, he easily goes down. But when a big man administers a tap, in that moment he is beside himself, and to be beside oneself is like stumbling, and to stumble when one is a big man is close to falling (for a very little man can stumble seventeen times without falling. Maybe Bishop M. is able to slay me with a devastating blow; it is possible* but it is not certain. However it is certain that he can slay himself by tapping. This has grieved me; I bow, but not my head, which I proudly have held high above all the insults and injustice shown me, but am not therefore brusque with the good will and sympathy shown to me, but my heart is bowed down when it is Bishop M.! —When I began as an author I asked nothing; I asked nothing later.† I had only one wish, a childlike

---

*Note. And afterward Bishop Mynster perhaps will regret it. For when the sea is as rough as it is now—if my proposed tactic of using ideals cannot steer the established through, then it is impossible. M.'s tactic of administering is based on fair weather. But on the other hand M. is completely indispensable as the representative.

†Note. For the fact that it had been my desire, my idea, to end as a rural pastor,[2993] that I later thought of an appointment to a theological seminary,[2994] is not related to my work as an author but to my being a theological candidate who in using the past years as an author nevertheless has used them just as well as another candidate may use them for teaching.

wish that when I did lay down my pen Mynster's reputation might shine, if possible, even more brightly than it did in the beginning. When I was fighting down in the lower regions against the "system," spurned by the elite for my antiquated notions, on my own initiative and at my own cost ridiculed by the crowd, then it was Mynster's cause which was fought through—then it was M. who won. As a reward he complimented Martensen. But not a word, not a look from me; just as pleased, unspeakably pleased, I bowed "in profound veneration" because Mynster's reputation shone more gloriously—and I do not matter—yet Martensen is a man of really great ability. Now he draws Goldschmidt to the fore.* I could say that it was ungrateful, unfair. No., no! But in vain have I pondered, almost without sleep, how this could be explained to M.'s advantage. But it cannot possibly be done—his reputation does not shine as before; and in one sense I am tired of life. For myself I fear nothing. But just as I stood there and was ready to thrust the sword into its sheath, something happened to prevent it. It seemed to me that my dead father put this demand to me: You must present Christianity in its utmost rigorousness, but you must keep it poetic,[2997] you may attack no one, and on no account may you make yourself out to be better than the most insignificant person, for you know very well that you are not better.[2998] In that light M., just as everyone else, will appear to have weak sides; yet you must not make any compromise in presenting Christianity. But you must use all your ability in such a way that M.'s reputation shines more gloriously when you are finished than at the beginning. This is not the case. The Christian Bishop, His very distinguished, illustrious Excellency, has wounded himself on G. If it were possible that it was done to wound me—truly, when so much is at stake, it makes no difference to me! But something has happened that cannot be concealed, something that cannot be made good again, something that every second lieutenant

*Note. And Goldschmidt has done us incalculable harm in both the moral and literary spheres. It was indeed necessary at the time for that Christian Bishop, that chief literary figure, M., personally to enter in and sternly call for order. But no one would; so I, a subaltern, had to take the job,[2995] which also for that reason was undertaken with suffering. So while G., with the largest circulation in Denmark and with privileged, free-reined unconstraint raged against me with all his talent (and he is, indeed, "one of our most talented authors"; see Mynster, by whom he is now accredited in exactly the same sense as, for example, our talented Martensen, Paludan-Müller,[2996] myself, and such others among us), I was too pleased for words to bow "in profound veneration" to the old gentleman, for whatever dubiousness there was in M.'s silence, or ignorance, could be concealed—and I do not matter—if I only manage to maintain M.'s reputation shining the same as before.

in literature who knows what Christianity is can see, and in the face of which I am powerless to explain—and this is what I have pondered to the point of sleeplessness—to the Bishop's advantage as higher statesmanship, or as level-headedness and wisdom, or as intellectual freedom, or as Christian love and forbearance, etc.—in short, powerless to explain it as something great by the great man in any of the ways which could let the Bishop's reputation shine the same as before. And, alas, with an inevitability almost inconceivable to myself, there is—also what a source of anguish even though the well-spring of great joy—always an either/or in my being.

———

A word about Goldschmidt. That I never have wished him harm he knows very well himself; that I have wished him well and do still I know. When he got me into *The Corsair*[2999] it was a kind of triumph which—and this I am positively sure of—he never even remotely desired; his admiration for my work as an author surely was genuine.[3000] But perhaps the same thing happened to him as to a fisherman fishing for a big fish. But I never in the remotest way wished him any harm. No, I wished to get him away from *The Corsair*. At the time he would not do it; a little later he left. Personally he does not concern me, except insofar as I wish his talents might find a good use. What concerned me was something else. *The Corsair*, especially with its altogether abnormal circulation (for now the situation with circulation is quite different; life in Denmark has also taken a tremendous upward swing in pathos) was a symptom of disintegration in Denmark. [*Penciled in brackets*: This is to be a note. And to emphasize a curious thing, yet we were all Christians and we had a well-manned clergy, who of course *ex officio* had watched and watched over the morals, which is why they were salaried by the state, a clergy with Bishop M. at the head, who, strict about morals, strictly insists (in his recent book) that civil marriage is responsible for a stain in the public mind that "we should not in the least seek to obliterate" (p. 20).[3001]] And in historical retrospect, this will be noted, whether through me or not. But I am not so childish as to think it was G., almost as when one says to children: It was just the cat—to quote a book of the time, my review of *Two Ages*. No, if G. is successful, I will be pleased. When he started *Nord og Syd*,[3002] I also believed that he himself (if not exactly in the capacity of an ethicist, for his attempts in that direction were not felicitous), as an intelligent man with presence of mind and a quick eye and sometimes with a readily decisive passion, should have made a retraction of his public past, because his attempt to make the six-year financial venture, *The Corsair*, into an ironic transitional element in his life development only made matters worse, inasmuch as his public past relates inversely to "history"—that is, it must, if possible, be forgotten—otherwise it is a bad history. This he did not do; I have not made a move to demand it, not even with a word. Now Bishop M. wants to help him: so Bishop M. must demand it, as we others again must demand it of Bishop M. on behalf of the situation in the moral and literary spheres. He cannot reproach me for that; it actually pains me that the matter has taken this turn for G., who incidentally is one of those who best see the dubiousness of the Bishop's allusion to me and how dangerous it can be for the Bishop.[3003]

S. Kierkegaard

$x^6$ B 171   *n.d.*, 1851

« **6749**

. . . Perhaps I may take the opportunity here to say something else.

From the beginning it has been my wish and my idea (as I also have said to Bishop M.) to end as a rural pastor.[3004] I have now essentially finished as a writer, as one can also see in the new direction I take in the preface to the last pseudonymous work.[3005] A little piece "On My Work as an Author" has been ready for about two years and perhaps will be published.[3006]

But for the last four or five years I have also had another idea. Recognizing the special nature of my capacities, but also because I believe it could be advantageous to the established order and Bishop M., and also for my own sake, I have wanted an appointment to a pastoral seminary.[3007] Over the years I have urgently expressed this to the bishop. But no! Perhaps I went about achieving this goal in the wrong way; perhaps I have other means at my disposal to achieve it sooner. But I did want it only on the condition of a filial understanding with Bishop M. And, if not from the venerable old gentleman's hand —for he does not give away appointments, after all—yet in such a way that I could say that I owed it to Bishop M., thanked him for it. This wish has been given up.

———

Just one word in closing. I dare not say that I had the honor of knowing Bishop M. from my father's house; that would have been an almost unnatural relationship since there was, in fact, the greatest possible and most distancing difference in the circumstances of life: the honorable conspicuousness of loftiness and the inconspicuousness, yet honorable in its own way, of lowliness.

But from my father's house I do know Bishop M.'s sermons; I inherited many good things from him, among them Bishop M.'s sermons, which for my own upbuilding I have read and do read and will go on reading again and again. I have consulted them—also when I took the step of opposing that literary contemptibleness[3008]—and intend to consult them every time I am to act. I have but one thing to say about this man's sermons to everyone who pays any attention to my voice: Listen to him, read him, and again I say: Listen to him, read him. As for myself I wish that I may feel even more strongly, every time I pick up Bishop M.'s sermons for my upbuilding, the presence of the one who is dead, that departed one who brought me up on Bishop M.'s sermons. Thus I am well provided for religiously, because Bishop M. tells me exceptionally well what to do and the departed one says: Will you do it immediately now.

But with respect to doing it and doing it immediately, I no doubt am way behind, probably will never do it perfectly. That I have known how to present ideals and accentuate ideality poetically[3009]—yet for God in heaven's sake and with honest fear and trembling guarding against being confused with what I have presented[3010]—is something quite different, but then I have never pretended to be essentially more than a singular kind of poet. Therefore it is not true, as Dr. Rudelbach says in concluding his reply to me in *Fædrelandet*, no.———:[3011] "that I have made the one great sacrifice the world does not recognize, my time, my diligence, my life." This is a misunderstanding, although uncommonly sympathetic, especially after my article in the same newspaper.[3012] But it is a misunderstanding; *essentially* I am only a poet. I have not "sacrificed," not "my time," not "my diligence"—the most that can be said is that I have dedicated or devoted my time and my diligence in a part of my life to the service of an idea; and least of all have I sacrificed—"my life." No! *Essentially* I am only a poet who loves what wounds: ideals, what infinitely detains: ideals, what makes a man, humanly speaking, unhappy: ideals, what "teaches to take refuge in grace":* ideals, what in a higher sense makes a man indescribably

---

*Note. See my thrice-repeated preface to the pseudonymous *Practice in Christianity*,[3013] the latest book I published.

happy: ideals—if he could learn to hate himself properly in the self-concern of infinity. Indescribably happy, although humbled, deeply, profoundly humbled, before the ideals, he has had to confess and must confess to himself and to others that there is the infinitely higher that he has not reached, yet unspeakably happy to have seen it, although it is precisely this [having seen] and that [ideals] which cast him to the earth, him, consequently the unhappy one. [*Crossed out*: –Well, perhaps for time, but not for eternity: what unspeakable happiness, what bliss! *Underneath here:* S. Kierkegaard.] No, no, the eternally happy one. For eternity! For one can grow weary of all temporal and earthly things, and so it would be tormenting if they were to continue eternally. But the person who gets a vision of ideals instantaneously has but one prayer to God: an eternity! And this prayer is instantaneously heard, for ideals and eternity are eternally inseparable. Thus he, the happy one, has an eternity for contemplation. And should he finish, then he has—what good fortune!—an eternity in which to begin from the beginning. And there is no hurry, there is time enough, plenty of time, still an eternity left . . . . . what ineffable happiness, what bliss!

And in calm weather, when life seems to be tranquilized in illusions, one may think he can do without all this fantasy about ideals, think that all they do is disturb everything, and quite right—they will disturb all the illusions. But when everything is tottering, when everything is splitting up into parties, small societies, sects, etc., when, just because everyone wants to rule, ruling is practically impossible: then there is still one force left which can control men: the ideals, properly applied. For in the first place, the ideals, properly applied, do not come too close to anyone, do not give offense to the ambitions of all, to the ambitions of anyone, which can so easily happen to someone who wants to rule; and in the next place ideals split up every crowd, seize the individual and keep control of him. I point to my own life. Through my considerable association with the ideals I dare say I have become a good subject—which perhaps is quite a rarity these days when everybody wants to rule.

S. Kierkegaard<br>X⁶ B 173   n.d., 1851

« **6750**

. . . The word *phonomenon*[3014] [*Fremtoning*], it seems to me is not a felicitous word. There is somewhat too much of precocity, pretentiousness, and pomposity about it, which to the ordinary person will always sound as if he is supposed to use two senses in order to "see" the appearance of a "tone." In short, it seems to me that there is something contrived in the word. And, to be honest, I think there is something contrived in the entire passage of your book[3015] in which the word is used. To be honest, the association is contrived, and even though chosen (which I do not doubt but rather fear) it is still not a choice association; the word is contrived, and the place in which it is used is contrived, and the joining, whereby I am brought in, is also contrived. There is something strangely contrived in the whole thing.

Are you really serious about adopting this word? Is it "purely" out of unalloyed linguistic interest that you have adopted it this way? . . .[3016]

x[6] B 188   n.d., 1851

### « 6751

And how contrived the quotations are. A line by a French author,[3017] one which Goldschmidt had translated! And then such an unfelicitous word as *phonomenon*.[3018] It is quite obvious that the Bishop's intention is to draw him to the fore. He almost has to use violence to find an occasion.

x[6] B 194   n.d., 1851

### « 6752  My "Character"

There is some truth to the notion that I am more or less incognito.[3019] One is right in character by being incognito; I do not step into character by stepping out of my incognito. It is the same with a secret police agent[3020]—he is right in character by being disguised and by seeing to it that no one finds out that he is in the police. One cannot say to him (except meaninglessly): Step into character by throwing off your disguise and reveal yourself as a policeman—no, just that would be stepping out of character.

x[4] A 201   n.d., 1851

### « 6753  My Relationship to the Established and the Intrigue against Me

(1) My position has never been an emphasis on "doctrine"; my view is that the doctrine is very sound.[3021]

Note. This alone shows that it could not be to my interest to form a party, a sect, and the like, for the question is not a matter of doctrinal differences.

(2) My position (which, however, I never assert directly or authoritatively) emphasizes the existential: that the lives men live demonstrate that there is really no Christianity—or very little. The proclamation as far as it goes is ambiguous (as Mynster[3022] splendidly illustrates): in "quiet hours"[3023] they indulge in high concepts—then go home and say to themselves: Such things of course do not apply to practical life—but instead Christianity is precisely this: it must be done in *actuality*.

Note. This explains why I take the poetic approach[3024] so much. If I did not, I either would have to be the absolute, the ideal, myself (which I am far from being[3025]) and use absolute authority, or I would have to make my existential life the maximum and then judge others, forgetting to strive myself. This is fanaticism and arrogance. Instead, I affirm the ideals poetically. But I do affirm them and they are heard. Mynster, on the other hand, wants them suppressed, wants a deliberate separation between the quiet hours and daily life, whereas I want the religious to be heard right in the midst of daily life, in its ideality, which pronounces judgment on me also and finds me imperfect and second-rate.

(3) In order to do everything in my power neither to clash with the established order nor to do it the slightest harm but only good, I constantly have remained an individual, have resisted intimate relationships, and thereby have angered many people—alas, it was due to my zeal for the established, for which an effort such as mine can be dangerous as soon as it becomes a party.

(4) The danger which threatens the established these days is the crowd, the numerical, parties and sects. To protect the established all the forms of the numerical have to be split up. That is how the religious establishment should use its officials. But it is a thankless job; one takes the risk of being badly treated, regarded as proud, etc. No one wants to do it; regardless of the party the established order courts popularity and the numerical. That is to say, there actually is no governing and Mynster himself exemplifies that.

Thus again in self-denial serving the established, I have taken on this whole affair, have doubly exposed myself to ill-treatment since it can never be said that I do it in the capacity of an appointed official

—and on the other hand, without enjoying the basis and security of being a state-appointed official.

### The Intrigue

It is easy to see now how it can be shaped. Just as I have no basis in the established order, I have also had none of the benefits of office or the recognition thereof. On the other hand, in serving the established I have run afoul of the crowd. Now the established is pushing me, so I am as good as abandoned.

I merely want to point this out, for with the help of God I will surely make my way.

But that this could be intrigue may be surmised from seeing how Mynster in his latest book[3026] accentuates Goldschmidt at my expense.

$x^4$ A 204    n.d., 1851

### « 6754  *The Established—and I*

If I clash with the established, it will be possible simply and solely through a blunder on Mynster's[3027] part. Everything I do is for the defense of the established; it is the only thing that can be done with truth. Everything has been done to make things as easy as possible for Mynster. But if in the end he solidifies his idea that his whole dubious proclamation of Christianity, which has made Christianity into a theatrical performance, is wisdom, is Christianity, well, then he is the one who makes my cause into something else.

But in that case he will not be able to see it through. His time will come, and whatever happens to me, Mynster will have an auditing in his lifetime, if not by me then by others, which will be very costly to him.

Mynster's whole secular-prudent traffic is transformed to something even worse when he insists that precisely this is Christianity and that a description of Christianity such as mine is fanaticism.

$x^4$ A 228    n.d., 1851

### « 6755  *Ridiculous!*

I am reading Petersen's *Die Idee der Kirche*.[3028]
It is rather a well-written book.

But I can only laugh when reading such a book. There sits a *theologus* holding forth on the future task of the whole Church, making himself important by interpreting Luther and the Reformation, taking the credit almost as if it were his own personal property and personal achievement. —And Mr. Petersen, there is a man whose life is lived to

the refrain: What appointment should I look for now, are the surroundings beautiful, etc. Also: It was really fine of the University of
Erlangen to send me a doctoral diploma.

And this is the way it is with everything in our day: sheer and utter
dissipation in doctrine, imagination, observations, attitudes, etc.—but
not a trace of, not a thought of, not a hint of action.

$x^4$ A 231    *n.d.*, 1851

## « 6756 *"The Church" Exists Only for the Sake of Our Imperfection*

This is Calvin's teaching. See Petersen, *Die Idee der Kirche*,[3029] III,
p. 405, note. Petersen, of course, is of a different opinion.

$x^4$ A 233    *n.d.*, 1851

## « 6757 *Conversation with Bishop Mynster, May 2*

As I entered, I said that this was just about the time he usually
traveled on his visitations and I usually liked to call upon him some
time before.

So we talked together about the minister and the department,
which I do not note down since it does not concern my cause.

Then the conversation was drawn to more recent events. I mentioned again the tactic with my latest pseudonym[3030] and pointed out
how without it I could not have taken the position against Rudelbach,[3031] which he admitted. I then repeated that even if he had something against this book of mine, which was possible, it was nevertheless
a defense of the established order.

Then I turned suddenly to his book[3032] and said outright that I
had not come to thank him for my copy because there was something
in it which I could not approve, and this was why I had been delinquent
about visiting him.

We talked about this; yet he was momentarily startled when I
turned the conversation this way. So we talked about this. He maintained essentially, as I could well understand, that he had merely said
that Goldschmidt was talented;[3033] whereupon I pointed out that this
could be understood as an understatement. I reminded him that he,
too, had enemies and how an enemy might construe his behavior. I
repeated again and again that what concerned me was whether his
reputation had not suffered too much by directing attention to
Goldschmidt in this way.[*] I pointed out to him that he ought to have
demanded a revocation by G.; I told him that with his permission I

would show how he should have done it—that is, demanded a revocation. The precariousness of it all lay, I told him, in this, that he should keep in mind that he has to represent prestige—and that it was impossible for me to defend his conduct. I pointed out to him how he now had G. in his power, that he could give a turn to the affair—one usually brings out the good in a man by means of the good; the fact that M. had directed attention to G. in this way ought to have made G. aware that a revocation was necessary; since it was lacking, what had been done was also of a different character. But M. was of the opinion that there was still something in the fact that G. had remained silent. I explained again how insidious G. was and that it probably would appear some time.

Then I said to him: It may seem strange that youth speaks to age in this manner, but for the present will you permit me to do so and allow me to give you some advice. If there is anything about me of which you disapprove, if you would like to give me a whack, do it, do it; I can take it and shall see to it that you do not suffer for it; but above all do not do it in such a way that your own prestige comes to suffer thereby. It is your prestige that concerns me.

Again and again I repeated: "I want it said plainly and bluntly," "I want my conscience to be clear," "It must be noted that I have said that I cannot approve of it" (and as I said it I bent over the table and wrote, as it were, with my hand). To this he replied: "Well, it is very explicit." And I saw to it that every time I said this he replied and indicated that he had heard it.

In other respects my conversation was permeated by all the affection for him I received from my father and still have. I talked much longer than usual. Incidentally, he was more friendly and attentive than usual today. I did something which I otherwise do not do—I spoke a little with him about his family, a subject he brought up himself by saying that his daughter was to be married. And I spoke a little with him about himself, about the joy of his old age, and how grateful he must be. And then again—that he must be sure to watch out for his prestige.

Usually he has to be pressed when I speak of paying him a visit, and generally he is in the habit of saying that I might better come some other time, without saying when. This he did not do today. On the contrary, he said that I would be welcome. And when I said: Is another time perhaps more convenient to you, he replied: Come at the specified time. To which I answered: I would certainly prefer to come at that time; it is very special to me, I am accustomed to it, and "tradition is still a great force." (This was an allusion to something in the conversation.)

And so it went—Thanks, good friend, etc.

I parted from him on the most friendly terms possible.

Incidentally, when we spoke together of Goldschmidt he made an attempt to point out that he had used "talented" for Goldschmidt and "gifted"[3034] for me and that the latter meant much more. To which I answered: That is of no consequence, the question here is your prestige. Thereupon he abandoned this attempt.[†]

On the whole I was happy to have spoken with him. My affection for him belongs to him,[3035] after all, and it does not help much to put in print how devoted to him I am—it would never be understood anyway.

$x^4$ A 270   *n.d.*, 1851

### « 6758

[*]*In margin of 6757* ($x^4$ A 270):
He said that G. was a useful man and that one ought to utilize such people. I replied that there is an impatience which sees only what appears advantageous at the moment but which is dangerous, and that it was a question of whether or not he had not bought too dearly by paying with his prestige.

$x^4$ A 271   *n.d.*

### « 6759

[†]*In margin of 6757* ($x^4$ A 270):
The dubious aspect (of the extent to which Mynster nevertheless did not want to affront me by this grouping of me with Goldschmidt[3036]) was something which up until now I had not wanted to note down although I hid it in my memory. When I said that he at least ought to have let G. first disavow his past, M. answered: Then I would have to have read through all of his numerous books. Thus I was supposed to believe that M. was actually ignorant of the fact that there was a paper called *The Corsair,* that G. had edited it for six years, and that M. did not understand that this was what I was aiming at!

$x^4$ A 272   *n.d.*

### « 6760 *Mynster*[3037]*—and I*

Think of a knot. There are some who want it untied. This of all things Mynster does not want. Then I come along and say: Let me tie the knot just a little tighter. No, he is afraid of that, too, for no one must touch it, and that despite the fact that it is so loose that it cannot hold without being tied more securely.

$x^4$ A 285    *n.d.*, 1851

« 6761  *My Reckoning*

There is hardly a person hereabouts who is as cognizant as I of all the objections that can be leveled from a Christian point of view against a state Church, a folk Church, an established Christian Church, and the like, also that in the strictly Christian sense the demand is: separation—this is ideality's maximum requirement.

But I maintain that undertaking this separation requires such a qualitatively religious operation that only a qualitatively distinguished religious character can accomplish it. Strictly speaking, it requires an apostle, at least a witness to the truth. And it has to be done in character. There must be no characterless confabulating about this. Getting a characterless rattle-brain to venture such a thing is far more insane than to put a butcher in command of a brigade, or have an apprentice barber do a difficult surgical operation.

Now, I have not found one single person on our scene who bears any likeness to such a distinguished religious character. However there are a few who want to dabble blindly in trying to organize this operation in a characterless manner and inadmissible form.

This is absolute corruption [*In margin:* from the phrase: *corruptio optimi pessima*[3038]]. A mismanaged established order—well, there is nothing commendable about that, but it is far preferable to a reformation devoid of character.

This is how I go about it. If I were to pass myself off as a witness to the truth or something similar, I would be a nonentity. But I do not do that. For that very reason I am sufficiently authentic to be able to cope with these characterless, unmoral reformers.

In this way I safeguard the established.

But to do this, I demand what I demand of myself: admissions. Just as when a regiment has disgraced itself and has been totally reduced in rank, so I believe that we—if we will not and dare not venture out any farther than the folk Church and the like—must tolerate being totally reduced in rank, and we must confess that in the more rigorous sense we are not Christians.

And how do I operate in this respect? Do I step forward as one who in God's behalf, so to speak, has orders to reduce Christendom in rank? O, no, I am without authority. Stirred by the ideal myself, I find a joy in being reduced in rank myself, and I strive "without authority" to stir others to the same.

The mistake in the Mynsterian approach is: (1) he has subscribed to the notion, as if there were truth and meaning in it, that all of us thousands and millions are true Christians, (2) second, he has become set in opposition to me.

Thus the whole established order can continue. For a Christian in the rigorous sense is so rare that there hardly is one to be found in each generation.

A Christian in the volatilized sense, a Christian such as we are, is one who accepts the doctrines, rests in grace, but does not in the more rigorous sense enter into "imitation." To such a Christian Christ is the Savior, the Redeemer, but not in the stricter sense "the prototype," except in the form of humiliation unto inward deepening.

You see, "imitation" in the more rigorous sense is precisely what Mynster has abolished, completely omitted. His malpractice consists precisely in pretending that nothing is wrong, for it has to be said, the truth about where we are has to come out—otherwise everything is secularized.

$x^4$ A 296 *n.d.,* 1851

« **6762 How the Publication of the Last Pseudonym Took Place: Anti-Climacus,**[3039] *The Sickness unto Death*

(This no doubt is noted in the journals of that period, but I never read such things afterward and always carry around a general summary in my head.)

It was in the summer of 1849. I was under severe strain from the previous year. The financial crisis[3040] had affected me very much and made it clear that in the future I would have to think about my finances. The whole R. Nielsen affair[3041] had distressed me. Strube[3042] had caused me concern.

I had struggled for some time about whether I should publish these books. If it were done, it was my intention then to travel a while for recreation and then after that be obliged to make a living. I realized, too, that if they were to be published there was not much time to lose, for one thing because it was important to the whole maieutic foreground of the structure of the authorship that they come as quickly as possible, and for another external reason, an income tax was threatened any minute. But throughout all this I continually prayed to God to prompt me in every way if I was supposed to go ahead and publish them, but that he would check me in every way if it was at all presumptuous.

The decision not to publish prevailed. It seemed to me that I had the prospect of a happier life if I could manage to resolve the problem in my personality which had made it impossible for me to take on any official position. It seemed to me that I had to have the help of a Savior to do this, whereas formerly I had looked upon this suffering as a limitation which I could not exceed but by the help of God must accept, since in another sense I had been so extraordinarily endowed. So I prayed God that I might be appointed to the pastoral seminary*[3043]—and also to be reconciled with her, something she, the married one, would have to request herself.

Earlier, of course, I had had misgivings, and they promptly returned: what should I do with all the writing that now lay completed. If I got an appointment first, then it could hardly be published—and I would risk making a mess of my own life. I then decided that I could use them as a kind of esoteric communication at the seminary. But the problem there was that it seemed to me to be a far too easy way to set forth such earnest thoughts, and that it was, after all, an awkward matter to have such thoughts communicated to me and to avoid the responsibility of setting them forth. Also with respect to her, if a reconciliation with her[3044] was at all possible, I was concerned lest I assume the enormous responsibility of suddenly disturbing her whole marriage, inasmuch as either I would have to explain the whole truth of the matter (and then perhaps everything would be disturbed) or I would have to use a new form of deception.

Meanwhile I went to Madvig.[3045] I did not see him. I went to Mynster[3046] and did not see him. I went to Mynster once again and was told as politely as possible that he had no time today.

During the same period I had been reading Fenelon and Tersteegen.[3047] Both had made a powerful impact on me. A line by Fenelon struck me especially: that it must be dreadful for a man if God had expected something more from him. Misgivings awakened full force as to whether such a change in my personal life could even take place. On the other hand, I was qualified to be an author, and I still had money. It seemed to me that I allowed myself to panic too soon and to hope for what I desired but perhaps could not attain and thus perhaps would make a complete mess of things.

So I wrote to the printer.[3048] I was informed that their services were available and could they receive the manuscript the next day; decisions are seldom made that fast.

Then the evening before the printers were to receive the manuscript, as arranged, I learned that Councillor Olsen had died.[3049]

That affected me powerfully. Strangely enough, he had died one or two days before and I had not heard of it, and I learned of it only after my arrangement with the printer. I said to myself: If you had found out about it before you wrote to the printer, you perhaps would have held back in order to see if this could have some significance, however firmly I was convinced that it was extremely dubious to speak to her precisely because I deceived her by pretending I was a deceiver.

As mentioned, this had an unsettling effect upon me. I did not sleep well that night. Furthermore, it seemed as if someone were talking to me or I talked with myself. As I view it now,[†] I well recall the words but cannot say definitely which words were mine and which were mine in the other person. I remember the words: See, now he intends his own destruction. But I cannot say for sure whether it was because it was I who wanted to call off sending the manuscript to the printer and make an overture to her or the reverse, that it was I who stood firm on sending the manuscript to the printer. I can also remember the words: After all, it is no concern of ——— (but I cannot remember exactly whether the word was *yours* or *mine*) that Councillor Olsen is dead. I can remember the words but not the particular pronoun: you—or I—could, in fact, wait a week. I can remember the reply: Who does he think he is. N.B. [*Addition on back of sheet:* N.B. See Journal NB²⁶, p. 92 (i.e., x⁴ A 587)].

In the morning I was utterly confused. The arrangement with Luno had been made. It seemed to me that after having grappled with the problem of publishing for such a long time and worn myself out in the process, and after having come so near to it, I would be an utter fool to make a reversal, something I had never done—I feared losing hold of myself completely, and on the other hand, as far as she was concerned, I had nothing to hold on to; even though the Councillor was dead, the responsibility for becoming involved with her was just as great.

I was at my wit's end. But yet it seemed to me as if something had happened to scare me off, even though I also was aware of the possibility that I myself wanted to be excused from publishing, and still at the same time I perceived that it was as it should be if I was confronted with something terrifying in connection with publishing such books. I remember clearly thinking that God's terrifying a man does not always signify that this is the thing he should refrain from but that it is the very thing he should do, but he has to be shocked in order to learn to do it in fear and trembling.

So I sent the manuscript to the printer. I prayed God to educate me so that in the tension of actuality I might learn how far I should go. I desperately needed a decision; it had been a frightful strain to have those manuscripts lying there and every single day to think of publishing them, while correcting a word here and a word there.

Then the book was made pseudonymous. That much was dismissed.

As for the other books[3050] by Anti-Climacus (*Practice in Christianity*), the original title page already had the inscription: poetic. And it was only to emphasize this even more that I used the pseudonym, and then by means of the preface under my own name I put all the more pressure on myself. Of course the passages referring to me and actual circumstances in the authorship were deleted from the works, things that a poet (a pseudonym) cannot, after all, say, and only a few lines were left that were appropriate to a poetic individual, and if they were inappropriate they were changed.

When *The Sickness unto Death* was made pseudonymous and the decision was reached to make the other books pseudonymous as well, I was of a mind to travel, for now it did not seem so urgent to publish the other books, and there was the constant threat of an income tax.

Then I made an overture to her by writing to Schlegel.[3051] He was extremely offended etc. Everything related to that is in her tall cupboard.[3052]

Then I moved from the tanner's.[3053] I had been thinking of traveling and therefore had not even looked at the rooms myself but let Strube do it, and when things turn out miserably they always go whole hog. He was afraid of offending me by saying the apartment actually was unsuitable (he believed that I was eager to live there, although I had told him that I had not seen the apartment at all)—and so the apartment was as might be expected.

I was so overwhelmed that I got something else to think of than traveling. I suffered considerably.

Then it became clear to me that there was no time to waste and that I ought to publish the other manuscripts by Anti-Climacus.

This I did, and then my mind was uncommonly at ease. I remember being afraid that the tension and unrest of 1849 would recur, but no.

So this is the way it was. In one sense I have suffered much, purely externally as well by reason of my living quarters and my financial troubles.

What made this publication (in 1849) a strain on me was that I had begun to consider another alternative. When a bit of pressure comes, I so easily think: You could, after all, have done it differently.

But suppose that I had refrained from sending the manuscript to the printer, suppose I myself had not made any advance in "her"‡ direction but had waited to see if she would do something herself, or suppose I had taken a step and nothing had come of it (not the worst thing to happen) or it had hung as an enormous responsibility upon me, had disturbed her marriage—and meanwhile I had all those manuscripts lying there and was plagued with the thought that I had been so close to a decision!

That a publication such as the latest one, involving a turning point, should be a strain on one is natural.

However, it actually turned out as I had prayed God it would: I have been both scared off and urged on. Urged on, among other things, by those words of Fenelon that had made such a strong impact on me, urged on by the circumstance of futile visits to both Madvig and Mynster, twice to Mynster; scared off by the fact of that death. The unity became that stated in my preface:[3054] Everything is said to me that I might learn to resort to grace. For me the publishing of these books has been an education in Christianity. I have come to a personal involvement so that I am not occupied with depicting Christianity just intellectually and poetically.

$x^4$ A 299    n.d., 1851

« **6763**

*In margin of 6762* ($x^4$ A 299):
*Note. It was my intention to direct my efforts toward the extensive, whereas my earlier efforts had been directed toward the intensive. I would then have to consider myself as having won out in such a way that the established order would gladly agree with me. So I hoped for an appointment to the seminary.[3055]

If this had happened, the pressures on my life would have been lessened. Drawing her to the foreground was also connected with this[3056] and was something I had quite varied reasons for doing (see the journals of the time [i.e., $x^1$ A 568–70, 659, 661, 663, 667–68]); also because it would gratify my pride to give her the greatest compensation possible, would give me the joy of expressing my loyalty, religiously would benefit my cause, and my life would be touched with pathos. —But then she herself had to ask for it.

The thought of the seminary, however, I had to give up, for in the first place Mynster obviously would oppose it. Then there were other influences—and I sent the message to the printer,[3057] received the answer: Could they receive the manuscript the next day.

Then that same evening I learn that Councillor Olsen is dead.[3058] That really played havoc with me: should I wait a while to see if something would happen on her side—and these two thoughts now united: the seminary—her.

Meanwhile I actually went ahead with it. I dared not make a reversal. Besides, if anything happened from her side, I could let the book be printed (as I intended) and then hold the copies.

But if there was no possibility of triumphantly bearing down on the established order, then I would have to keep her out of it; otherwise the step intended to benefit her could easily turn out to mean something entirely different.

But this death was so singularly fateful that it of course had to have a powerful effect on me.

$x^4$ A 300    *n.d.*

### « 6764

[†]*In margin of 6762* ($x^4$ A 299):

It must be noted here that my mood the next morning was one of vague consternation. It actually was much later that I began to remember any details, mainly after coming to live on Nørregade[3059] in the miserable apartment Strube[3060] had rented for me. There are few externals that have depressed me as much as that apartment, where I sat for a long time unable to do anything because of the glare of the sunlight that troubled my eyes.

$x^4$ A 301    *n.d.*

### « 6765

*In margin of 6762* ($x^4$ A 299):

**N.B.** During the last week or two the implication of the conversation[3061] that night suddenly dawned on me, that it was my common sense wanting me to refrain from publishing the manuscripts. A line that always comes to mind but whose meaning was not at all clear suddenly has become clear to me. The words went like this: "Is this what is required of me," and then came the answer cited: Who does he think he is. Consequently this is what is required of me. Previously I had been unable to figure out what I may have meant or intended by that. Up until now I interpreted it to mean that I was willing to sacrifice my life etc., something I have not been able to comprehend anyway, since it has never occurred to me to talk in such elevated tones. In the meantime I more or less took it to mean that and interpreted "Who does he think he is" as a reprimand for an almost arrogant remark. —But now it has become clear to me. Prior to that night I frequently had said in quietness of mind before God that although it seemed to me that she had to be the one who asked for an understanding with me, I would be willing to be the one to take the first step[3062] if it were asked of me, so that my misgivings would not be grounded in my pride. And see, here I have the reply: Is this what is required of me.

$x^4$ A 302   August 5, 1852

« **6766**

‡*In margin of 6762* ($x^4$ A 299):
This is why I actually have always believed that she herself had to be the one to ask for it.[3063] Not to mention about seventeen other considerations (see the journals of that period [i.e., $x^1$ A 568–70, 659, 661, 663, 667–68]) but only this, that maybe she had given me up completely, had completely changed, and on her account I did not have the heart 'to find out.

$x^4$ A 303   *n.d.*

« **6767**

. . . . . I hear that they were not able to hear me when I preached on Sunday.[3064] No doubt it is people who were not in church who want to let me know this, and perhaps by way of the daily newspaper it finally will be known all over the country that they were not able to hear me —after all, that is still something.

Yet, as I had expected, the crowd was not especially large. Thus I did not experience what I imagine could happen to an orator or barker who was really in voice, that the crowd was so large when he preached in the morning that even in the afternoon there were many citizens with their families who went to listen to the church for whatever might still be heard, and the next day the crowd was so large that pastry-women were out there with their stands.

$x^4$ A 318   *n.d.,* 1851

### « 6768 *An Entry Concerning Me Personally*

If *ex tempore*[3065] preaching were possible on occasion, I would have considered doing it a few times, and then next Sunday,[3066] instead of preaching myself, taking one of Mynster's sermons and reading it aloud to show that upbuilding is something quite different from a possible curious interest. In the introduction I would have said a few words about the rewarding practice in England of requiring sermons to be read aloud (for a speaker's spoken words can easily have an intoxicating effect and may intoxicate him as well), and it is also rewarding to read another's sermon aloud so that the one speaking is reminded that he also is being addressed.[3067] I would also have said a few encouraging words about the significance of Mynster's sermons for me personally, something I inherited from my father.

$x^4$ A 322   *n.d.*, 1851

### « 6769 *About Myself*

*In margin*: See p. 118 in this journal [i.e., $x^4$ A 339].

On Sunday, May 18, I preached in Citadelskirken. It was on my first, my favorite, text: James 1. Also, I confess, with the thought of "her,"[3068] also whether it would give her pleasure to hear me.

I suffered very much in advance from every possible strain, as I always do when I must make use of my physical being.

I delivered the sermon. It went fairly well, but I spoke so faintly that people complained about not being able to hear me.[3069]

When I went home I even felt well, animated. My intention had been to deliver a few such sermons during the summer—of course, after preparing them in detail.

But in the meantime it became clear to me that this was going to take an abnormal amount of time and would take a lot out of me.

Then the thought occurred to me: You can, after all, preach *ex tempore*.[3070]

It struck me that I would then be taking a desperate risk.

But what happens? On Monday I was so weak and faint that it was terrible.

Several days went by. I did not relinquish the idea of preaching *ex tempore* and thus accentuating Christianity existentially as far out as possible.

Yet I felt that it went against my whole nature.

I became more and more listless. But I did not give up the idea entirely.

But eventually I had to give it up for the next time.

Then I really got sick. I began to feel terribly the dismaying, agonizing pain which constitutes my personal limits, something which had not happened to me for a long, long time.

At the moment I took this as punishment for not having proceeded swiftly enough.

I became more miserable.

On Sunday, the one following May 18, I read one of Mynster's sermons[3071] as usual, and the text for the day was about the thorn in the flesh: Let my grace be sufficient for you.

That struck me.

Meanwhile I was still reluctant to give up my idea, even contemplated forcing myself to do it. Now my torment increased.

So I changed my mind, saw that once again I had wanted to go beyond my limits, and now I rest in the thought: Let my grace be sufficient for you. Inward deepening is my task, and there is much of the poetic in me.

On the morning of Sunday the eighteenth I had prayed God that something new might be born in me (I do not know myself how it occurred to me); even then the thought pressed in on me that just as parents bring up their children and finally bring them to confirmation, in the same way this was the confirmation to which God was bringing me.

And in a way that has happened. Something new has been born in me, for I see my task as an author in a different way—it is now dedicated in a quite different way to advancing religion directly. And I have been confirmed in this, and this is how it is with me.

The special reason I had such misgivings about venturing so far out was grounded in a very different concern that vexes me: the problem of my livelihood,[3072] and I was so afraid of this turning out to be a drastic delusion that instead of doing something about it I ventured farther out ideally.

God surely will keep on doing all that is good for me, he whom I can never sufficiently thank for what has been done for me.

$X^4$ A 323   *n.d.*, 1851

« **6770** *Preface*[3073]

What I have understood as the task of the authorship has been done.

It is one idea, this continuity from *Either/Or* to Anti-Climacus, the idea of religiousness in reflection.[3074]

The task has occupied me totally, for it has occupied me religiously; I have understood the completion of this authorship as my duty, as a responsibility resting upon me. Whether anyone has wanted to buy or to read has concerned me very little.

At times I have considered laying down my pen and, if anything should be done, to use my voice.

Meanwhile I came by way of further reflection to the realization that it perhaps is more appropriate for me to make at least an attempt once again to use my pen but in a different way, as I would use my voice, consequently in direct address to my contemporaries, winning men, if possible.

The first condition for winning men is that the communication reaches them. Therefore I must naturally want this little book to come to the knowledge of as many as possible.

If anyone out of interest for the cause—I repeat, out of interest for the cause—wants to work for its dissemination, this is fine with me. It would be still better if he would contribute to its well-comprehended dissemination.*

A request, an urgent request to the reader: I beg you to read aloud, if possible; I will thank everyone who does so; and I will thank again and again everyone who in addition to doing it himself influences others to do it.

Just one thing more. *I hardly need say that by wanting to win men it is not my intention to form a party, to create secular, sensate togetherness; no, my wish is only to win men, if possible all men (each individual), for Christianity.

June 1, 1851   S.K.

$x^6$ B 4:3 June 1, 1851

### « 6771 *About Myself*

*In margin*: See p. 92 etc. in this journal [i.e., $x^4$ A 323].

The matter is quite simple. I can truthfully say of myself along the line of talents and spiritual-mental gifts that what has been entrusted to me is extraordinary.

But as for the next—the extraordinary in terms of character, the capacity to live in poverty etc—that I do not have.

As I have always acknowledged, I have the advantage of private means.[3075] This changes everything.

It may well be that my imagination visualizes the troubles and dangers as much too huge, but in any event I do not feel my powers, and furthermore I fear that if I could in fact live in poverty, totally in character, I perhaps would become proud and arrogant; and then, too, I have a sympathy with the purely human which makes it unnecessary for me to venture so far out, even if I could. Yes, even with respect to "her"[3076] it would almost pain me; I feel (if I could venture so far out) that I would be alienated from her.

So it seems that I ought to stay within my limits and try to safeguard myself somewhat in finite respects.

O infinite love that continues, always in love, to put up with me. While I sleep you stay awake, and when I am wide awake and make a mistake, you turn my mistake into something even better than the right thing would have been—and I, all I can do is be amazed at you, infinite love!

$x^4$ A 339    *n.d.,* 1851

### « 6772 *About Myself*

Now they[3077] are being printed. I feel inexplicably, unspeakably happy, calm and content, and overwhelmed.

Infinite love! I have suffered much during the past days, very much, but then it comes again. Once again my understanding of my task is clear to me but with greater vividness, and even though I have blundered seventeen times—nevertheless an infinite love in its grace has made it all completely right.

Infinite love! It is blessed to give thanks, but one perhaps never feels his wretchedness and sin more than when he is overwhelmed in this way, just as Peter[3078] said: Depart from me, for I am a sinful man —on the very occasion of the great catch of fish.

$x^4$ A 351    *n.d.,* 1851

### « 6773 *Mynster*[3079]

has never had a conception that there is an unconditioned. Everything for him is the conditioned. Therefore his proclamation of Christianity is essentially "reasons."

Furthermore, since Christianity had the support of the government (state church), since he governed with the help of sensate power, I perhaps have let myself be duped and believed that he actually was one who governs.

Now this relationship is broken—and Mynster seeks to become democratic (as in his latest book) and embraces the journalists, the public's time-servers, now even embraces Goldschmidt.

Mynster should have done one of two things in 1848–either he should have resigned his office and said: What I represent has done an about-face, or he should have stood his ground and fought and suffered for the unconditioned.

He chooses a third alternative–to manage, if possible, to stand in well with the powers that be: the public and the like.

X⁴ A 353    n.d., 1851

### « 6774  *The Established—and I*

It is as far as possible from being true that I am attacking the established–I am defending it against the party of agitation, against the age's evil lust to reform.

But I do think that Bishop Mynster,[3080] for example, who is also defending the established, is not defending it properly.[*] Admissions have to be made to Christianity; we must confess that we actually are only an approximation of what it is to be Christian. This is the result of affirming the ideals, and if the ideals are not affirmed, the agitation cannot be guided.

But I am scarcely ever understood, for I lack the finite and illusions. People simply cannot understand that a private citizen could ever think of defending the established–and the fact that public officials do it they explain by saying it is their livelihood, their career.

So it is everywhere–the whole thing is shabby and paltry, utterly devoid of ideality.

X⁴ A 358    n.d., 1851

### « 6775

[*]*In margin of 6774* (X⁴ A 358):

The trouble with Mynster is that in the back of his head he thinks something like this: Most likely it will last the few years I have to live.

X⁴ A 359    n.d.

### « 6776  *The Mynsterian Approach—Mine*

On the whole Mynster[3081] must still agree with me that in the more rigorous sense this whole established order is not Christian. He perhaps has made his own personal admission to God regarding this but believes such things must above all be suppressed in order to get men to accept Christianity. This is shrewdness and extremely dubious, especially when continued from generation to generation, for then it becomes utterly corrupting. And I wonder if Mynster has not partially forgotten what he once understood and now, pluming himself on the fruits of his prudence, that he got some to accept Christianity, really believes that this is Christianity and that the more rigorous Christianity is fanaticism.

My proposal is: let us rather be honest and admit that, strictly speaking, all this is not Christianity. This is at least being truthful and is the condition for going further.

x⁴ A 367   n.d., 1851

« 6777 *Conversation with Mynster*[3082]

August 9, 1851

As I entered I said, "Welcome home from your visitation; I dare say Your Reverence has already visited me as well through the two little books[3083] I sent you." He had read only the one (and, to be honest, for a moment I thought how strange if it had been the two discourses), but no, sure enough, he had read the book on my work as an author. "Yes, it is a clue to the whole," he said, "but spun later, but, after all, you do not say more than that yourself." I answered that the point to bear in mind was the continuity over so many years and in so much writing, that my pen had not made one single deviation. To which he said he thought the little review of *Two Ages* was an exception. I did not say any more to this, for it is in fact discussed in the little book about my work as an author, but I did make the remark that this review is essentially part of the whole authorship and that I attributed it to another because there were certain things I wanted to have said[3084] and at the time felt unable to say them as well myself. —I got the impression from Mynster that basically he was impressed by the little book, and therefore he was not saying much.

We went on talking. He was in agreement with me, and what I said about the government was fully his opinion. We spoke a little about that. I said it was not so very pleasant to have to say such things and therefore no one was willing to do it, but they had to be said, and so I had done it.

He was pleased and gratified and agreed with me.

Then I told him that I really was happy to talk with him today because today was the anniversary of my father's death and I wanted everything to be as it should be on this day.

Then a few words were dropped about the pastoral seminary,[3085] but he avoided the subject and thought it was best for me to begin at once to establish a pastoral seminary myself.

The conversation was very friendly and not without emotion.

Then I once again said a word disapproving of what he said about Goldschmidt in his latest book,[3086] something I felt I had to say, especially when I expressed such high regard for him.

Then we parted with his customary "Goodbye, my dear friend."

X⁴ A 373   n.d., 1851

### « 6778  *My Present Relationship to Mynster*[3087]— *Practice in Christianity*— *The Goldschmidt Matter*[3088]

My category is the single individual. With this category in a dialectical unity my task has been to be a vivifying stimulus in an established order and to defend an established against the numerical, parties, etc. by means of ideals.

Consequently I am defending the established.

For some time I had continued to serve my idea solely in the sphere of ideas. Then for several reasons the question arose as to whether or not I could align myself directly with the established.

But the fact that I defend the established ideally does not necessarily mean that I out and out agree with the established.

This has to be looked into, and as earnestly as possible. To speak with Mynster or anyone like that would be childish.

What do I do then? I develop unconditionally and ideally the whole dialetic of the Christian movement, the communication of which turns the established upside down. I make this communication pseudonymous and repeat a preface[3089] three times, stating that I understand it as being addressed to me alone so that I may learn to resort to "grace."

This is the formula for Christianity as the established. It is an indulgence; "grace" must be applied here. If the established does not see itself this way, if it does not apply grace here, then we are in disagreement. But the communication was ideal; no one was being attacked.

This I set forth. If there is anything qualified to agitate Mynster, it is this. But that is just as it should be in order to bring out the truth and not to spare myself, and I do suffer very much both on my own behalf and also in my veneration for Mynster.[3090]

I now must see to the results of this. *Either* Mynster has to rise up in all his power—perhaps crush me: well, then the true state of affairs would be revealed. Or no one will be the complete victor: well, everything was done on my side so that no irregularities would be concealed. *Or* perhaps Mynster will have the spiritual-intellectual freedom to say: This is the truth; I rejoice in the very thought of it. Or he will do nothing at all: well, my intention in that case was to end with a eulogy upon Mynster,[3091] for I would be satisfied if he remained silent.

Then I learned that he was furious. So I spoke with him. All this is found in the journal of that period [i.e., x³ A 563, 564].

Then I spoke with Nielsen.[3092] In my joy I told him that I had talked with Mynster and I praised his spiritual-intellectual freedom. I forgot that this would incense Nielsen, who hates Mynster. I saw at once that if I now introduced the eulogy upon Mynster, Nielsen would hazard the uttermost. And the matter was also dubious because I did not know what Mynster might have been hiding from me. If I introduced the eulogy too soon, I risked his using it against me.

So I had to wait.

Then from several sources I heard about Mynster's disfavor. Madvig[3093] began to act very strangely toward me, and I could only conjecture that it came from Mynster, who consequently was hiding something. So I had to bide my time. All the time I was longing to do it only for Mynster's sake. But as stated, it was impossible to know what he was hiding and whether he might not take advantage of the eulogy just when it appeared, use it against me, and break with me officially.

Then came the article against Rudelbach.[3094] Mynster was pleased, and I was happy.

Now just one word from Mynster—and then the eulogy will come.

The word came—but it introduced Goldschmidt[3095]—and in such a way!

Now the eulogy is impossible; even though I wanted to do it ever so much, it is impossible, for I will incite Nielsen etc., and then the last will be worse than the first. There can be no eulogy. I must be content with the earlier tradition of my reverence and affection for Mynster. The eulogy cannot be introduced. My whole authorship cannot be transformed into a triumph for Mynster; it would make me ridiculous, since Mynster has brought Goldschmidt into the picture this way, and, as mentioned, it is impossible because Nielsen etc. would be goaded to the extreme and rush at him and do incalculable harm.

In a way Mynster has his deserts, for he has never acted generously toward me. Basically he has wanted to use me to satisfy his egotism, and in any case he long ago ought to have offered me a position at a seminary,[3096] to say nothing of helping me if I wanted it.

But this hurts, for I have wanted to do infinitely more for Mynster than was called for. But he himself has made this impossible.

But my relationship to the established is all in order. Essentially Mynster has been silent; this Goldschmidt matter is more a personal insult to me, for Mynster, after all, has simply wanted to advance Goldschmidt because he defends the established. What is dubious about it is Goldschmidt's *vita ante acta*[3097] and, personally for me, his history with me; I just ask that Goldschmidt repudiate his past six years.

$$x^4 \text{ A } 377 \quad n.d., \quad 1851$$

## « 6779 *The Review of My Two Latest Books*[3098]

August 13

In *Flyveposten*[3099] there is one which states, "It appears from this that the author now considers his literary activity virtually at an end."

This is really odd. Imagine an author declaring explicitly that he intends to lay down his pen, and let us assume that this author is still a young man, what will the "journal," the critical intermediate authority ordinarily do? It will say: Well, it must not be taken altogether literally; it may mean for a time, or perhaps he will begin again in another manner etc., etc.—in short, the journal will write it up to mean that the author will continue.

But the situation is this. I have in no way said that I am ceasing to be an author, as the journal adequately demonstrates by having to confine itself to saying: It appears—and then what does the journal do? It takes it upon itself to circulate the news that I am going to stop, it takes it upon itself to be instrumental in getting me to stop.

This is very amusing! I must have a friend, a patron, who is interested in this and perhaps for some time has been interested in my quitting as an author damn soon. [*In margin:* Perhaps he would even be glad to see me leave the country—but it would be ungrateful of me, who must say as did Peer Degn:[3100] Shall I leave a congregation that loves and esteems me and which I love and esteem.]

Strangely enough, quite accidentally today I saw the same article in *Fyens Avis*[3101] and with no indication that it was from *Flyveposten* but otherwise the identical article, except that the word "brilliant" was left out.

Thus it seems that my friend and patron must have sent it to *Fyens Avis* himself. Perhaps he has sent it to several provincial newspapers —all for the purpose of getting me to stop writing.

This could be one interpretation. Maybe the whole thing is nothing but journalistic clumsiness, hurrying to get something put in circulation, such as: Am I actually going to stop etc.–for then the content of the books is of no consequence.

« 6780  *On My Work as an Author*³¹⁰²
*The Significance of This Little Book*

The state of "Christendom" is as follows: the point of view of Christianity and of what Christianity is has been completely shifted, has been cast in terms of the objective, the scholarly, and differences such as genius and talent have been made crucial. This little book reverses the whole thing. It says (precisely because this enormous productivity preceded it): Forget genius, talent, scholarship, and all that–Christianity is the existential, a character-task. And now it is turned that way.

For that reason this little book is not a literary work, a new literary work, but an act, and therefore it was important that it be as short as possible, that it not mark a new productivity which people could then discuss. This little book is μετάβασις εἰς ἄλλο γένος³¹⁰³ and illuminates to what extent it was already present in my total work as an author.

Even if I had fathomed or foreseen in advance my total work as an author down to the smallest detail, what I say in this book about my authorship never could have been said at the beginning, for it would have shifted the point of view, and the interest of the reading would have shifted to curiosity as to whether I actually took the direction and fulfilled what I predicted.

No, it has to come at the conclusion, with one single stroke doing what the sailor calls tacking, the turn.

The little book is not a literary work but an act. It is an intensive act which will not readily be understood, no more than the action I took in the past against *The Corsair*.³¹⁰⁴ It may even be found that I have made too little of myself, I who could preen myself on being a genius, a man of talent–and instead I say it is "my own personal development and education." But precisely this is the turn in the direction of Christianity and in the direction of "personality."

Consequently, here is a single individual who relates to Christianity and not in such a way that he is now going to proceed to be a genius and a man of talent and do something big–no, just the reverse.

Here the listed price of Christianity is so low, so lenient, that it is dreadful—but nevertheless it is an authentic relationship to Christianity; here there is no trick, no illusion. The Mynsterian approach[3105] is *in toto* illusion and, from a Christian point of view, is tenable only by means of what I propose: admissions. I resort to grace; it is not Christianity in the more rigorous sense—something Mynster is silent about and wants to have suppressed. In my approach, however, Christianity truly is turned as the unconditional, and the whole viewpoint is utterly different: that we come to admit that in the most rigorous sense we are not Christians. In short, the cast of the whole thing is as different as possible from the official delineation, and yet it is even milder. But what is there is truth; it is not appearance and illusion.

Without this little book the whole authorship would be turned into new doctrine.

$$x^4 \text{ A } 383 \quad n.d., \quad 1851$$

## « 6781 Mundus Vult Decipi[3106]—*Illusion*

Without "persons" the human race is immoral rubbish.

That is what it is. Everything is designed to make persons impossible; the daily press is especially guilty of this.

My best time was when I lived on the streets, for it bore down hardest on illusions.

At present I have pulled myself back somewhat: this is inferior, it is an accommodation. Meanwhile the people want to read it this way: that now I am on a higher level. Yes, *mundus vult decipi*.

No, if without financial means I could have kept on living on the streets,[3107] then I would have been made mad—that is, declared to be mad, perhaps put to death: but it would have been the great thing to do.

But while accommodating myself a bit this way, also recognizing my physical limitations, I am doing two things. (1) I do not let myself be fooled into believing that I am on a higher level now inasmuch as my being seen infrequently contributes—by means of illusion—to a mounting esteem. (2) Nor do I forget the accounting, that someday we will be up for review and then light no doubt will be shed on what went before.

But while I am accommodating myself a little in this way and letting down, I am nevertheless making some progress. For the point was that my having had financial means made me uncertain as to whether or not some pride had entered into my earlier pattern. I am harder pressed by financial troubles[3108] as well, and to that extent perhaps there is progress in enduring what I am now enduring.*

$x^4$ A 389   n.d., 1851

« 6782

*In margin of 6781* ($x^4$ A 389):
*Furthermore, in the beginning I was not so mature that my extensive walking the streets and talking with each and all[3109] were not a diversion, a pleasure, that I needed; thus in another sense my more withdrawn life is a character-task, a step forward in that direction. In order that living on the streets may have in the most rigorous sense the character of simply and solely doing it for the sake of the idea, one must be a man who first of all has become convinced that he could live in the solitude of a desert.

$x^4$ A 390   n.d.

« 6783 *About Myself*

Introducing the ideals that way—and letting it seem as if I remained on the outside personally (indirect communication)—had the dubious result of another possible interpretation, that I actually was keeping myself out of it personally, as if I did not feel my life bound to the ideal, thereby avoiding the humiliation of actually feeling—I, myself, involved and striving—my own imperfection.

Now it is certainly true that in my inner being and before God that was not the way it was; there I realized precisely my own imperfection. But avoiding this humiliation before men could very well be a trick on the part of my heart.

Furthermore, in connection with Christianity the indirect method is only transitional, for Christianity, after all, has grace to proclaim. Then, too, Christianity tends toward making things manifest. If it is said that Christ, after all, was incognito, the answer must be, *for one thing* it was impossible for him to be otherwise, for the God-man, this synthesis, is possible only in an incognito, while he in fact himself directly states that he is God; *for another*, the Christian is not to imitate this, he is not supposed to be the God-man but is to proclaim the God-man and to proclaim grace.

Finally, as I also have frequently pointed out, the dubiousness of the indirect method in the proclamation of Christianity is that it could be an attempt to avoid suffering for the doctrine.

The indirect method in the proclamation of Christianity is a maieutic approach. A beginning can be made with it in order to shake up the illusions, and at times it also may be used to keep "grace" from being taken in vain.

$x^4$ A 395    *n.d.*, 1851

« **6784** *Everything Depends on "How"*[3110]

Suppose I confine myself to introducing by way of a witty novel the idea that Christianity actually does not exist at all. Then no one will raise an outcry, no, I will be a brilliant success, and the clergy will read it, yes, perhaps next Sunday preach on the interesting fact that Christianity actually does not exist at all.[3111]

But if I do it in the interest of religion, people become angry—then the matter becomes too serious.

And still worse: if I did it in a way that disturbed the regular operation of the hurdy-gurdy of the established with its 1,000 livings —well, by Jove, the preachers, bishops, and assistant sextons—all of them—would fight for Christianity with religious zeal.

$x^4$ A 404    *n.d.*, 1851

« **6785** *4651*

In *Flyveposten*[3112] for September 16 or 17 someone using 4651 as his signature—no doubt to be striking—took it upon himself to orient (the passion of the disoriented whereby they are identified) my readers or even to warn them against being confused by my little book *On My Work as an Author*. The only thing I find meriting attention, and especially as the orientating factor, is the signature: 4651. It is striking, persuasive, and overpowering. If the dreadful thing happens (and how easy) that someone now comes along who signs himself 789,691, I will be shattered.

$x^4$ A 408    *n.d.*, 1851

« **6786**

. . . As is well-known, my authorship has two parts: one pseudonymous and the other signed. The pseudonymous writers are poetic creations, poetically maintained so that everything they say is in character with their poetized individualized personalities; sometimes I have carefully explained in a signed preface my own interpretation of what the pseudonym said. Anyone with just a fragment of common sense will perceive that it would be ludicrously confusing to attribute to me everything the poetized characters say. Nevertheless, to be on the safe side, I have expressly urged that anyone who quotes something from the pseudonyms will not attribute the quotation to me (see my postscript to *Concluding Postscript*[3113]). It is easy to see that anyone wanting to have a literary lark merely needs to take some verbatim quotations from "The Seducer," then from Johannes Climacus, then from me, etc., print them together as if they were all my words, show how they contradict each other, and create a very chaotic impression, as if the author were a kind of lunatic. Hurrah! That can be done. In my opinion anyone who exploits the poetic in me by quoting the writings in a confusing way is more or less a charlatan or a literary toper.

The little book *On My Work as an Author*[3114] declares: "It must end with direct communication," that is, I began with pseudonyms representing the indirect communication I have not used under my signature. And somewhat earlier (in my preface to *Practice in Christianity*,[3115] whose author, the last pseudonymous writer, Anti-Climacus, again discourses indirect communication) there is the statement: I understand the whole (whole book) as addressed to me so that I may learn to resort to "grace." Consequently, it ends with direct communication.

$X^6$ B 145   *n.d.*, 1851

« 6787

[*In penciled brackets:*
    Ein, Zwei, Drei
            or                                    [*In pencil:* Reflections.]
    Three Aphorisms.]

        respectfully dedicated to a most esteemed public by the author, who requests a lenient judgment of this his first attempt, the imperfection of which no one—except, of course, a highly-esteemed public, which knows everything—knows better than the author.

                            1.

Geniuses are like a thunder storm: they go against the wind, terrify people, clear the air.[3116]

The "established" has invented various lightning rods to counteract or divert geniuses: they are successful—so much the worse for the established, for if they are successful once, twice, thrice—"the next thunder storm" will be all the more dreadful.

There are two kinds of geniuses. The first is characterized by a lot of thunder, whereas the lightning is slight and rarely strikes. The other kind has a quality of reflection by which they constrain themselves or hold back the thunder. But the lightning is all the more intense; with the speed and sureness of lightning certain selected points are hit—and lethally.

### 2.

"Did the apostle Paul have an official position?" No, Paul did not have any official position. "Did he earn a lot of money some other way?" No, he did not earn money in any way. "Was he not at least married?" No, he was not married. "But then Paul certainly was not an earnest man!" No, Paul was not an earnest man.[3117]

### 3.

When a man has a toothache, the world says: Poor man! When a man is financially embarrassed, the world says: Poor man! When a man's wife is unfaithful to him, the world says: Poor man! —When God lets himself be born, becomes man and suffers, the world says: Poor man! When an apostle with a divine commission has the honor to suffer for the truth, the world says: Poor man! — —Poor world!!![3118]

### 4.

In the splendid cathedral a handsome Royal Chaplain,[3119] the cultured public's chosen one, appears before a select constituency of the select, and preaches movingly—I say "movingly," I do not say "dryly"[3120]—no, he preaches movingly on the apostle's words:[3121] God has chosen the poor and the despised of the world—and no one laughs!

### 5.

It is one thing to profit (*profiteri*) an art, a science, a faith—it is another thing to profit from it.

### 6.

When someone asks a man "Do you know this and that" and he promptly answers "Yes" or "No," then this answer is a *popular* answer and shows that he is a simpleton, a seminarist, etc. But if it takes ten years before the answer comes, if it comes in the form of a detailed dissertation which scrupulously, as Holophernes[3122] says, maintains the strict tempo of *"Ein, Zwei, Drei,"* and at the end of the detailed dissertation it is *not exactly clear* whether he knows it or not—this is an authentic speculative answer and proves that the one who was asked is a professor in speculation, or at least so artful that he ought to be.

7.

The reflection found under no. 1 of the reflections on a loose sheet in the high desk is about a poet who wants to be mistaken for a witness to the truth.

———

Respectfully,
Victorin Victorius Victor

[*In brackets:*
Respectfully,
Johannes de Silentio]
x⁶ B 253    *n.d.,* 1849–51

## « 6788  *Ein, Zwei, Drei*
### *or*
### *Three and a Half Aphorisms*[3123]

No. 1. The one about geniuses and thunderstorms
perhaps under the title: A Meteorological Observation.
No. 2. The one which ends: *ergo,* Paul was not an earnest man
perhaps under the title: A Flower Respectfully Planted
on the Grave of "Established Christendom."
No. 3. The one ending with: Poor world.
perhaps under the title: For the Jaw–harp.[3124]
No. 4. The most dreadful punishment, according to their own view, with which the prophets threatened the Jewish people is this: Children shall rule over you[3125]———this is only half an aphorism; the clause with consequences is lacking.

x⁶ B 254    *n.d.,* 1849–51

## « 6789  **Night and Day** *or* **Nicodemus and Stephen**
### *or*
### **Established Christendom** *and* **the Militant Church**

For Self-Examination    Recommended to the Present Age

*The draft on Nicodemus* is on quarto sheets and, together with the draft of the sermon, is in an envelope in the corner of one of the shelves in the tall cupboard.[3126] *Nicodemus* perhaps is not written on the envelope but rather *Trinity Sunday* ("the long Trinity," as it is called, begins quite characteristically with "Nicodemus").

*The draft on Stephen* is found right at the beginning of this year's journal [i.e., x⁴ A 434–36]. It no doubt is NB²⁵.

x⁶ B 259    *n.d.,* 1851

« 6790

*On the cover:*

Draft of two sermons: Trinity Sunday and the second Sunday after Trinity.

Draft or suggestions for a discourse: The Kingdom of Heaven is like— —

$x^6$ B 260   *n.d.*, 1851

# VIII. THE GATHERING STORM
## 1852–NOVEMBER 1854

« **6791** *Abraham*
   *New* **Fear and Trembling**

[*In margin:* In journal NB²⁴ or NB²³ (from the summer or spring of 1851) there is a draft³¹²⁷ relating to this.]

The mood here should more decidedly border on madness. The point should be that Abraham had not been able to keep himself *in suspenso* at the apex of faith until the end—and therefore had sacrificed Isaac.

### The Mood

There was once a man who as a child had learned the story of Abraham, and, as usual, knew his lesson brilliantly, inside and out.

The years went by, and as happens to much of what is learned in childhood, so also here, he found no use for it—and it faded into oblivion.

In the meantime his life underwent a change; he had severe trials and was involved in a singular conflict that all at once or with one blow placed his life in abeyance, and just that alone gave him plenty to think about.

This preoccupied him from morning until night, awake and in his dreams, and he became old before his time.

Fifteen years went by. Then one morning as he woke up the thought suddenly struck him: What you are experiencing is similar to the story of Abraham.

And now he began to read. He read and read, he read aloud, he delineated the whole story, he cut it out in paper silhouettes,³¹²⁸ he did nothing else—but he did not understand Abraham or himself.

X⁴ A 458   *n.d.*, 1852

« **6792** *Modern Sophistry*

When I underscore the existential in the essentially Christian (alas, not nearly as strongly as the N. T.!) the cry goes up: This is exaggeration, this is law, not gospel. They say: You forget to talk about the Holy Spirit and his aid, for thereby what is heavy becomes light.

Fine. So the others have the aid of a Holy Spirit who makes everything light and helps them to—to what? What do their lives ex-

433

press? Do their lives express self-denial, renunciation—so that the difference between them and me is that when it comes to self-denial and renunciation we agree that they must be included, yet they are hard for me but easy for them with the help of the Holy Spirit? No, their lives express a pure and simple secular mentality. Aha! So it is for this that the Holy Spirit helps them. Double nonsense—that the secular mentality is supposed to be Christianity—and the help of the Holy Spirit is for being secular, which certainly is not Christianity and which one achieves best without the aid of a Holy Spirit.

But the whole thing about the Holy Spirit is rubbish, an escapism by means of which one evades the tasks—whereas I have so much respect for the Holy Spirit that I have not dared speak of him because I understand that as soon as I begin doing so I must present the existential even more strongly.

x⁴ A 472   n.d., 1852

### « 6793 *Bishop Mynster*[3129]*—Christianity*

Apart from all the other glossing over in the Mynsterian proclamation of Christianity, Mynster has also perverted Christianity, dislocated Christianity or its point of view. Christianity is the unconditioned, being-in-and-for-itself, and at most Mynster has a finite teleology. (I am tempted to remind him of that old distinction between Stoicism and Epicureanism: Epicurus also praises but he provides a "why"—that is, to him virtue is not being-in-and-for-itself, it is *in order to* live pleasantly, for one cannot live pleasantly otherwise.)

As is clearly shown in one of his Spjellerup sermons[3130] on John the Baptist, where he speaks of the kingdom of God, he obviously has the following conception of Christianity: in order that Christianity may prevail there is suffering and sacrifices are made—but no doubt it is not always supposed to be that way; at some time there must indeed come a period, a generation, after all, that is to have the benefit of all these sacrifices, that is, enjoy them and thereby enjoy life. Well now, that would be a fine kind of Christianity. No doubt that age and that generation are presumably the very ones that have been contemporary with Bishop Mynster. A complete dislocation of Christianity, as if it were something historical in the finite sense instead of being the unconditioned in the infinite sense.

It always comes back to the confusion that God has a cause in the finite, the historical, sense, something which has to be fought through to the end—for that reason the conditions are changed, and on the other hand God (completely *à la* a worldly monarch) for the same reason cannot be too scrupulous about anyone wishing to serve his cause if he is to be useful at all.

No, Christianity is the unconditioned; not something for which there at times has to be suffering and a later generation then enjoys the benefit of that suffering. No, Christianity is the unconditioned, for which there has to be suffering in this world as long as the world stands, but then again in the next world this suffering becomes bliss. (But Mynster abolishes eternity and puts Christianity completely into the historical as commensurable with the historical.) And God is the infinite supervisor who is not having trouble over a cause but has won infinitely and therefore regards only the ethical. On the other hand, we human beings, each one of us, have a great cunning in and a great desire for shoving this aside, saying: It is my task to proclaim Christianity objectively—of course, there are millions who are supposed to act accordingly. No, thank you, says God, I am checking on you.

Every conception of Christianity which makes it into history is confusing, not to speak of the conception which makes Christianity perfectible. It is just the reverse: the unconditioned truly existed only once, when Christ lived, suffered, and died. Its history is regrettably a steady retrogression. With a historical phenomenon this is not the case—it progresses (but for that very reason Christianity is not something historical). This is what Mynster, confusing everything, has transferred over into Christianity.

$x^4$ A 474   *n.d.*, 1852

« **6794** *Suffering*

The purely human, as stated, never gets any farther than to define suffering teleologically and within this life: a person suffers a few years, for a time, and then through it has achieved or achieves this and that.

But sometimes suffering does last a man's lifetime—so we human beings have hit upon an explanation which is the generation's most egotistical cruelty toward the individual. We define this individual (whose suffering lasted his whole life) and we define his suffering teleologically for the rest of us, those of us who come after him: he suffered—in order that we should be better off. What a dreadful Phalaris-invention.[3131] The good men, precisely the good men (therefore the ones who ought to be better off in this life if anybody is), must suffer in order that we (scoundrels) can be better off—truly an additional proof that we are scoundrels.

But we, however, think this is all in order. We honor and praise such a martyr and celebrate his name-day—for example, in memory of what Luther suffered we eat goose on St. Martin's Day. The only thing lacking was that Luther actually had been martyred and that it had been that dreadful martyrdom of being roasted on a grill—how lovely of us that we who survived, we later ones, roast and eat goose in his honor and memory! What human brutality and bestiality!

And what has been the result of this for Christianity? Well, to put it simply—those first Christians suffered; now we are supposed to enjoy. They suffered—we honor and praise them, "build their tombs,"[3132] eat a certain kind of pastry on that day, go on a picnic in their honor —O what human brutality and bestiality! To be capable of being happy in that way, that is, by altogether denying kinship with those glorious ones of mankind.

What then is Christianity's view (Christianity, which is suffering, so that if it becomes enjoyment it is abolished, as it is now in "Christendom")? The view of Christianity is that suffering has a completely different context, infinitely higher than every teleology. To suffer in this world for truth, for the good, for Christianity, is blessedness. Thus suffering is not an evil so that the teleological approach first converts it into something else (which in the relation between the generation and the individual would indeed perpetrate the most outrageous wrong against the one who is sacrificed)—no, it is blessed to suffer. Because to suffer expresses the deepest inwardness of a God-relationship, to suffer is to have a secret with God! What bliss! Behind this world of actuality, phenomena (in which it appears as if God, too, were against the sufferer, since he does not help him out of it but lets him suffer), lies another world, a world of spirit, and here the sufferer has a blessed secret with God—what bliss to have a secret with God!—that this phenomenal event really means just the opposite, that it is precisely out of love that God lets the sufferer suffer.

It is God who has to be a little severe with such a person who is to suffer in this way, although he forces him out sometimes with the good, sometimes with stringency. It is Christianity which, by requiring "imitation" of the Christian, seeks to lead him so far out—alas, at first it is dreadful for a man. And yet there comes a moment when he himself understands that this, precisely this, is the only thing a person who thinks earnestly about life could desire. Or if I could want to have lived out my life in such a way that it expressed (although I would still be a human being) that I had no kinship whatsoever with the glorious ones of the race, then either they must be gods, if I am supposed to be human, or I am an animal, if they are supposed to be human beings.

O, my God, my God, how unhappy my childhood was and how tortured my youth—I have groaned, sighed, and cried out—yet I thank you, not you the all-wise, no, no, I thank you, infinite love, you who are indeed infinite love, for doing it that way! A man has thirty, forty, perhaps seventy years ahead of him—you prevented me (in love) from spending the sum of my years merely in buying cakes and sweets and thus having nothing to remember in eternity or being compelled to remember in eternal torment that what I bought was despicable. You compelled (there were also many times when you, as it were, talked graciously to me, but about the same thing, not about my getting out of suffering, but that it was your love that made you keep me out there), you compelled me to buy sufferings. How blessed—for every suffering of that kind means community of suffering with you, and every suffering of that kind is an eternal gain for eternity. For only sufferings can be remembered.

A pagan (Cicero, in *De finibus*[3133]) relates that the greatest sensualist in the Orient (Sardanapalus) put on his tombstone: I took all the pleasures of the world with me to the grave—to which another pagan (Aristotle) is supposed to have said: How so? You could not even hold on to a single one of them while you were living. No, pleasures cannot be remembered—least of all in eternity. If a person avoided all suffering in this world—how frightful, perhaps dressed in purple and velvet, a pasha with seventeen tails, with a ring in his nose, which he alone dared wear, and before whom every one kneeled—how frightful that as a consequence he has no kinship whatsoever with the glorious ones of the race but in relation to them is a flesh-eating mammal—how frightful to have nothing at all to remember in eternity!

————

But if suffering in this way is a blessing, is not suffering actually a pleasure?

Let us be cautious here, for those with the most varied views come up with this same false position.

There is a wretched ingenuity which, wanting only to be free of suffering, reasons like this: Doing good has its own reward, ergo, if the good man finds satisfaction in it, just as I do in sensuous enjoyment, ergo, there is no essential difference between us! This is hypocrisy aimed at an escape from suffering.

Next there are the pagan Stoics who demonically intensified this to the point where doing good is supposed to be so satisfying—that it is pleasure. Yet the Stoic believed suicide to be expedient—but why put an end to pleasure with suicide? Consequently this is untrue.

Then there are those muddleheads like Rousseau,[3134] who use the strongest expressions in declaring that suffering is nothing, suffering —it is a pleasure—that is, theoretically, for in practice he was extremely thin-skinned. Consequently this is a self-contradiction.

No, I hold with Christianity, which precisely because it takes seriously the fact that one actually does come to suffer (while the others really evaded suffering and decked themselves out in figures of speech, which of course can be a form of enjoyment) puts it like this: it is suffering—but it is a blessing. Here it is not only a matter of suffering for the good but of the sufferings that are indigenous if one is going to be capable of being an instrument for God. This is such blessedness that, although the suffering hurts, he dares believe with God that it is precisely this way so that God can better use him. The blessedness is in knowing that while the world of phenomena witnesses against him by way of misfortune, adversity, and opposition, he dares know with God that this is simply because he relates himself to God.

———

Yet suffering does not enter in as a blessing in and for itself—then Christianity would be nonsense, would not exist at all, which is just about the case in our time, too, when the sufferings of the past ages as unchristianly as possible have been defined teleologically along the line that we are supposed to derive pleasure from them.

———

Here is an end to all sophistry; let them all be united in one head[3135] and let Satan himself be along—no Sophist can take that.

x⁴ A 488   n.d., 1852

## « 6795 The Possible Collision with Mynster[3136]

From the very beginning what Mynster has fought for in opposition to me—often in rather ordinary ways—has been to maintain this view: My proclamation, the Mynsterian approach, is earnestness and wisdom; the Kierkegaardian an odd, perhaps remarkable, but an odd exaggeration.

My position is: I represent a more authentic conception of Christianity than does Mynster.

But I desire nothing less than to attack Mynster, to weaken him. No, just the opposite. A little admission from his side, and everything will be as advantageous as possible for him, no one will see how it all hangs together, something I always have concealed by bowing so deeply to him.

From the very beginning I actually have been an alien figure to Mynster (in fact, he said so himself the first day: We are completely at variance, something he no doubt instinctively perceived even better than I). I have a kind of passion for the truth and ideas which is utterly foreign to him. In this way I am opposed to him. —Things were still all right with *Concluding Unscientific Postscript,* partly because in the conclusion[3137] I personally emphasized him so strongly, partly because Johannes Climacus is a humorist, and thus it was easier for Mynster to maintain that this was only poetic exaggeration, humor, but his own approach was authentic earnestness and wisdom.

The first part of *Upbuilding Discourses in Various Spirits,* [3138] Part I, irritated him; but perhaps in appreciation of the postscript to *Concluding Postscript* he let the judgment be: This is an excellent book—especially the last two parts. *Works of Love* offended him. —*Christian Discourses* even more. —And so it mounts. *Practice in Christianity* distressed him painfully.

Am I out to get Mynster? No, no, I am attached to him with a hypochondriacal passion, the extent of which he has never suspected. [*] But here there is something else which puts pressure on me. I can no longer afford to maintain the battle for the idea which I have represented. Therefore I must make haste. If my future were economically secure[3139] so that I knew I was completely able to give myself to the idea, I certainly would bide my time and let Mynster live out his life—O, it pains me so deeply to have to draw my sword on him. But the economic situation forces me to hurry. Only when I accept an official position can Mynster more easily make his interpretation prevail. He knows that I have financial worries, has known it for several years; I myself told him. Now he is waiting and watching for this to force me to cut back, perhaps even to throw myself into his arms so that he can exploit me and have further proof that his way is the way of wisdom and earnestness.

The line about Goldschmidt[3140] was fateful. (1) It gives a sad insight into the bad side of Mynster. (2) It provides me with the circumstantial datum against Mynster that I had to have if I were to attack. That everything about him is rather close to the secular mentality I have perceived for a long time, and therefore I made a division and took his *Sermons*.[3141] But this plain fact betrays everything. And it has happened here as generally happens, that I first of all induce someone to provide me with the circumstantial datum I need. (3) It shows that in the sphere of the idea Mynster considers himself impotent. But he has been in an emotional state.

For me the possibility of this conflict means that in order to survive I must take a still higher view of Christianity. This is a very serious matter; I have very much to learn and to suffer. —But on the other hand the possibility of this conflict signifies that there is a power that works against Mynster. For the collision, if it occurs, will occur against my will; it is my economic situation which pressures me to hurry, and Mynster has had it in his power to buy at the most advantageous price what can become extremely dangerous to him if there must be a collision.[†]

He was an old man. Something truer was offered by someone who "in profound veneration"[3142] was willing to introduce it in such a way that it appeared to be Mynsterian. He would not have it. True enough, after having enjoyed life as he has, it could be a bitter experience to find out at the end of his life what kind of a Christianity it actually was.

$X^4$ A 511   *n.d.,* 1852

« 6796

[*]*In margin of 6795* ($X^4$ A 511):

Moreover, I remember that the following observations also pressed in on me. (1) If I were completely free of economic concerns, I would have confidence in myself, would know for sure that it was not to spare myself that I kept on avoiding a collision with Mynster.[3143] But when I have finite concerns—and in this respect Mynster could in fact be helpful to me—then I would have to suspect myself of possibly sparing myself in order to avoid conflict. (2) I shrink from having Mynster actually help me in a finite way, for in my opinion he has far too much of the secular mentality which finds it completely all right to secure earthly advantages. (3) If I were to let things go on and did not publish while Mynster is still living what I have written most recently, there would hardly be a person later who would be capable of forming any opposition to me—but then would I not avoid making possible the inspection that could be made if I published it while Mynster is still living.

X⁴ A 512   *n.d.*

« **6797**

†*In margin of 6795* (X⁴ A 511):
It is also strange that for a long time I was opposed to publishing, reluctant to publish, what I had written recently. Finally it happened —and it was done pseudonymously. (It was *The Sickness unto Death.*) Then I said to myself: Now there is no hurry with the rest since it is to be pseudonymous. Then I moved from the tanner's:[3144] my idea had been to travel. For that reason I did not look at the rooms myself. So I got a miserable apartment. I was very unhappy there, very. Then the remainder of the literature by Anti-Climacus[3145] was published. It seems as if a Governance wants Mynster to have this experience.

X⁴ A 513   *n.d.*

« **6798** *That We Are Brought Up in Christianity from Childhood*

still has its good side in that we, if we actually want to become Christians, come to experience a parallel to what Christ's contemporaries experienced. They first of all entertained earthly expectations—and then everything was turned upside down and becoming a Christian in spirit and in truth became an earnest matter. So also when a child is brought up in Christianity from childhood. The child appropriates Christianity as a worldly gospel—and then at a later age the man experiences the terror if he is to have the spiritual impact of Christianity.

X⁴ A 539   *n.d.*, 1852

« **6799**

Dear Henrich,[3146]
Can you meet me this evening at the usual time and place? If not, then please call on me tomorrow morning between 11 and 12 A.M.

Your Uncle,
S.K.

[Address:]
Mr. H. Lund, M.B.
Fredrik's Hospital.

*Letters*, no. 276 [1851–52?]

« **6800**  *"About Her"*[3147]

May, 1852

During the latter part of 1851 she encountered me every day. It happened each morning at ten o'clock when I went home along Langelinie. It was precisely on the hour, and the place we met merely moved farther and farther along the road to the lime kiln. She came walking as if from the lime kiln.

I have never gone a step out of my way and always turned off on the Citadel road, even when one day it so happened that she was farther along the lime-kiln road and consequently I would have met her if I had not turned off.

So it went day after day. The trouble is that I am so appallingly well known, and it is seldom that a woman walks along those roads alone at that time. Nor did it escape me that a couple of the habitual walkers who met regularly about this time and recognized both of us were taking notice.

So I was obliged to make a change. I also believed that it would be best for her, for this constant dailiness is trying, especially if she is thinking of reconciliation with me, for which I of course would have to ask her husband's consent.

So I decided to walk along that street for the last time on December 31.

I kept my resolve, and on January 1, 1852, I changed my route and walked home by way of Nørreport.

So for a time we did not see each other. One morning she met me on the lake path which I now was in the habit of walking. I walked my usual route the next day also. She was not there. As a precaution I nevertheless changed my route in the future, walking along Farimags-Veien and finally went home by different routes. Later I did not meet her at this time on the streets; it had now been made difficult because my way home was indefinite; it was difficult if she normally took the path along the lake.

But what happens? Some time passed and then I meet her at eight o'clock in the morning on the avenue outside of Østerport, on the way I take every morning into Copenhagen.

But the next day she was not there. Since I could not very well change my route, I continued to walk this way into the city. Here she has often met me, sometimes on the ramparts along which I walk to the city. Perhaps it was coincidental, perhaps not. I could not understand why she should be walking that way at that time, but, just as I notice everything, I noticed that she walked this route especially if the wind was from the east. So it could be because she could not bear the east wind on Langelinie. However—she did come also when there was a west wind.

Time passed in this way—she saw me now and then, precisely at the same time in the morning, and then Sundays in church.

Then came my birthday. As a rule I always go out on my birthday, but I did not feel quite well. Consequently I stayed home, went to the city as usual in the morning to speak with the physician, since I had contemplated celebrating my birthday with something new, having never tasted castor oil before. Right outside my door on the sidewalk just before the avenue she meets me. As so frequently happens of late, I cannot refrain from smiling when I see her—ah, how much she has come to mean to me! —She smiled back and nodded. I went a step past her, then took off my hat, and walked on.

The following Sunday I was in church and heard Paulli,[3148] she too was there. She sat near the place where I stand. What happens? Paulli preaches on the Epistle lesson, not on the Gospel, and it is: Every good gift and every perfect gift is from above etc.

Upon hearing these words she turns her head, hidden by the one sitting next to her, and looks toward me very fervently. I looked vaguely straight ahead.

The first religious impression she had of me is connected with this text, and it is one I have strongly emphasized. I actually did not believe that she would remember it, although I do know (from Sibbern[3149]) that she has read the *Two Discourses* of 1843, where this text is used.

So on Wednesday she nodded to me—and today the text—and she is aware. I confess that for me too it was somewhat jolting. Paulli finished reading the text aloud. She sank down rather than sat down, and I actually was somewhat worried as I was once previously, for her movement is so vehement.

Now to go on. Paulli begins to preach. I believe I know Paulli fairly well; it is inexplicable how he came to think of such an introduction. It may have been intended for her. He begins: These words, all good gifts, etc., "are implanted in our hearts." Yes, my listeners, if these words should be torn from your hearts, life would lose all its value for you etc. I seemed to be standing on thorns.

For her it must have been overwhelming. I had never exchanged a word with her, had walked my way, not hers—but here it seemed as if a higher power were saying to her what I had been unable to say.

Only God knows how eagerly I would promptly make a place for her, a place for her among her contemporaries, just as with God's help a place will be made for her memory. O, it would gratify my pride so very much. All the admiration I have acquired—to transfer this to her, to have her become the one who is admired: yes, truly that would suit me fine.

But there are seventeen reasons why it cannot be done.

But I do think that this impact was so inwardly fortifying that she certainly will carry on.

A few mornings later she met me again, but there was nothing to detect. Ah, if she thought that it was my turn now to greet her: I cannot do it. I am ready for anything, but if anything is to be done, I must have her husband in the middle. Either—Or! If I am going to become involved with her, then it must be on a large scale; then I want everyone to know it, I want her transformed into a triumphant figure who will get the fullest reparation for the detraction she suffered because I broke our engagement, while I still reserve my right to give her a good scolding for her vehemence at the time.

$x^4$ A 540    May, 1852

« 6801  *The Movement of My Life*

In frightful inner suffering I became an author.

Year after year I was an author, suffered for the idea in addition to the inner sufferings I endured.

Then came 1848;[3150] that helped. There came a moment when, overwhelmed by blessedness, I dared say to myself: I have understood the highest. Truly this is not granted to many in each generation.

But almost simultaneously something new struck me: After all, the highest is not to understand the highest but to do it.

Of course I had been aware of this from the beginning and therefore am different from an author in the usual sense. But I had not so clearly perceived that by having private means and being independent I could more easily express existentially what was understood.

When I perceived this, I was willing to declare myself a poet, that is, my having private means made action easier for me than for others.

But here it comes again: the highest is not to understand the highest but to do it and, please note, with all the weights laid on.

Only then did I properly understand that "grace" had to be introduced; otherwise a person is shattered the minute he is supposed to begin.

But, but "grace" is not to be introduced in order to prevent striving, no, here it comes again: the highest is not to understand the highest but to do it.

$$x^4 \text{ A } 545 \quad n.d., 1852$$

## « 6802  *The Established Christendom*

Given Mynster's[3151] and Paulli's[3152] kind of preaching, preaching could continue by the same and to the same for 170,000 years, if possible, and they would not come one single step farther in the Christian life; on the contrary, it would retrogress for them.

It is one thing to shut a door; it is something quite different to jam the lock. But this kind of preaching jams the lock on "imitation."

An established Christendom is a toning down; therefore it must be officially admitted that it actually is not Christianity. When the relation of the established to true Christianity is depicted in proper perspective, there is possibility. But if "established Christendom" is supposed to be true Christianity, then the lock has been jammed on Christianity. Throughout the 170,000 years it remains exactly the same: a little lyric poetry in a quiet hour once a week—but there must be no breakthrough, it must not come to the point of actuality (in action, in self-renunciation). But in the course of time this lyric poetry once a week will have a weaker and weaker influence compared to the corresponding weeks and weeks of the secular mentality.

$$x^4 \text{ A } 554 \quad n.d., 1852$$

## « 6803  *About Myself*

Have you ever seen a hunting dog: bloody, exhausted by his struggles and loss of blood in the battle inside the foxes' burrow—it still does not let go; it has clamped its teeth shut and dies that way.

I, too, am exhausted, but I have not let go of my idea, I have not made my life more comfortable, thereby making it less obvious what my goal has been.

As I have so frequently said: The end must be tied,[3153] otherwise we still remain in reflection, and in a short time I will be consumed. And to tie the end, a life, an existence, is required.

The didactic approach cannot be stopped by a new doctrine but only by personality. True, it was easier for me when I was free of financial concerns.[3154] And not only that, but when it was easier for me the cause was almost easier also for others. For I did not exert so much pressure. But the more earnest things became for me, the more pressure I exerted—and it became all the more important for the others to defend themselves against the truth.

x⁴ A 557   n.d.,  1852

### « 6804  *Unrecognizability—Recognizability*

Particularly toward the end of *A Literary Review*[3155] I said that none of the "unrecognizable ones" dares at any price to communicate directly or to become recognized—and yet in *On My Work as an Author*[3156] I made myself responsible for the esthetic foreground of my authorship and said: "The whole thing is my own education." How is this to be understood?

In this way: assume that the illusion "Christendom" is truth, that it must be left standing: then unrecognizability is the maximum. If, however, the illusion must go, then it gets down to this: you actually are not Christians—then there must be recognizability. And here I have suggested the lowest: that it is I who am being brought up in Christianity.

If the illusion "Christendom" is truth, if the preaching prevalent in Christendom is as it should be, then we are all Christians and we can only speak of becoming more inward: then the maieutic and unrecognizability are the maximum.

But suppose now (something I was not aware of at first) that the preaching prevalent in Christendom leaves out something essential to the proclamation of Christianity—"imitation, dying away to the world, being born again, etc."—then we in Christendom are not Christians, and here the emphasis must be on recognizability. As stated, my place is on the lowest level of direct recognizability—namely, that the whole authorship is my own upbringing.

O my God, I am grateful—how clear you have made everything to me!

x⁴ A 558   n.d.,  1852

### « 6805 *About Myself*

The fact that I do not make my life more comfortable and am not looking for financial security[3157] could be called pride, arrogance.

Is it that? Well, who knows himself completely; but if it were that or if there were something of that, I believe that keeping on that way would soon make it clear and eventually I would suffer my punishment. Incidentally, this is how I feel about it. It seems to me that I am indebted for what I have understood, that the higher can require me to hold out as long as there is even the slightest possibility. As soon as I begin to make my life secure in finite ways (while there is still a possibility of keeping on longer), I am done for and the whole secular-minded world will promptly understand that there is no more danger. It seems to me that something higher is constantly moving within me; I believe that I cannot justify anything else but continuing to serve it as long as possible. If I am in error, in God's name the sin can be forgiven and its punishment will come in this life, but if I arbitrarily stop before I am obliged to do something for my living, if I stop now —and something higher was moving within me wanting to come forth in and through me—this will be disclosed only in eternity, when it is too late.

$x^4$ A 559    *n.d.,* 1852

### « 6806 *Remarks by Bishop Mynster*

In one of his "observations" (probably the one on God's Word or on hearing the Word or one similar, anyway it is in his *Betragt-ninger*[3158]), he has some moving words to say about the futility of tears. He says that he will collect all those hypocritical tears wept by people listening to his sermons; afterwards, however, it has become evident that they have not acted accordingly at all. He will step forward on Judgment Day with these tears and say, "I have done my part." —Strange to say, I have just been thinking of collecting the tears Mynster has shed in the pulpit; afterwards, however, it has become evident that he does not act accordingly at all. This hangs together with something Mynster said to me the first time we talked together—"We complement each other"—I complete his collection of hypocritical tears with the collection of his tears.

$x^4$ A 566    *n.d.,* 1852

### « 6807 *On Being a Pastor*

When being a pastor means to have every possible earthly and secular security, to be along in all the pleasures of life, plus the enjoyment of honor and esteem—in return for orating eloquently, beautifully, and soulfully once a week in a quiet hour (in that splendid edifice called a church where everything is arranged esthetically)—then I maintain that this is as far as possible from Christianity, is the most refined life-enjoyment, a titillation of the senses, so subtly intensified that paganism could not have thought of anything so refined.

Ask any actor whether it is not enormously gratifying to feel sensuously the surrendering to passions, to sense his power over the audience. That is why actors cannot live without acting; in one sense vacations are a deprivation, because he misses that intensification.

How far more gratifying it is to play the priest, to take men's highest moments, their moods and feelings, and to feel life-emotions swell within one, reflected back from the listeners. And now that transfiguring splendor over the whole thing, that this is supposed to be earnestness, so there is no question of applauding or booing, no, but there is the adoration of the women and the young.

Paulli[3159] told me with visible emotion that when Bishop Mynster was sick he longed very much to preach. How moving! If Phister[3160] were sick a few months, how he would long for the intensification of the stage!

There is a depth of confusion here and also a bit of hypocrisy which is quite terrible. An adulterer, a robber, a thief in the moment of his misdeed is not as far from Christianity as such a minister at the very moment he is most transported by his own eloquence in the pulpit, for the robber and the others do not think that this is Christianity.

$$X^4 \text{ A } 568 \quad n.d., 1852$$

### « 6808 *The Human—The Christian*

One thousand pastors orate on Sunday—and if anyone dared to act accordingly on Monday, he would be ridiculed as a fool, an eccentric, or, if he has more energy, stigmatized as a fanatic against whom society must earnestly defend itself to the utmost, which it does with much greater zeal than against cholera—and next Sunday the pastors orate again, and we are all Christians.

To want to imitate Christ, consequently, to be willing to make oneself unhappy, to be willing to suffer, is called "frightful arrogance," and in the moment of spiritual trial [*Anfægtelse*] I myself am not far from regarding it as arrogance—and yet in the New Testament[3161] Jesus says again and again: He who does not follow me is not worthy of me (consequently humility may mean, among other things, that it takes humility to bear all the accusations of arrogance). And then we are all Christians, we who would condemn to death, if possible, the one who dares to imitate Christ, probably to fulfill what Christ prophesies will happen to one who "imitates."

If, then, with God's help I faithfully hold out—well, then my writings will be read, perhaps read widely, but if I write on every single page: Take care that this does not become doctrine, it will become doctrine nevertheless.

$x^4$ A 584   *n.d.*, 1852

## « 6809  *About Myself*

"Christianity does not exist here at all,[3162] but before there can be any possibility of getting it back again, a poet's heart must break,[3163] and I am that poet"—these words by myself about myself will still come true.

$x^4$ A 586   *n.d.*, 1852

## « 6810  *About Myself*

*See Journal NB24 p. 68* [i.e., $x^4$ A 299].

August 7

It is now becoming clear to me these days that the nocturnal conversation[3164] I had with myself prior to publication of the last pseudonym, Anti-Climacus, was my common sense wanting to hold me back and not my better self. It ended with: "I (or you) could in fact wait a week," "See, now he intends his own destruction." If I assumed that the first lines are: You could in fact wait a week, then it is no longer conversation, then it is the other voice which says both this and the reply, "See, now he intends his own destruction," and it is so clear to me that these two statements relate to each other as reply and counter-reply. But as a consequence the reply must be: I could in fact wait a week.

Allow me once again to take up the matter which has been of such vital importance to me, the publication of the last pseudonym and then the later things.

This was the situation. For a long time I had realized that by stopping my writing, ceasing to be an author, by using my talents for my own gain, I easily could secure for myself a very comfortable life. But there was always something in me which held me back, for it seemed as if more was being demanded of me.

Meanwhile conditions became more and more strenuous for me; then the whole economic situation[3165] became critical, and many, many other sufferings entered in—I began to wonder more and more whether God did not really want me to enjoy life. The thought that I would help her[3166] by stopping my writing appealed to me very much. But I could not make up my mind to take this step; it seemed as if more were demanded of me, while I was also troubled that not wanting to do it might be pride on my part.

So I wrote to the printer. That was when I learned about Councillor Olsen's death.

Then came the nocturnal conversation with myself.

I did not know what to do but resolved to venture out.

Of course my life now was bound to become more and more exhausting. And that is what happened. Yet all this would not have been so hard on me; what was frightfully hard on me, even if it has matured me considerably, was my inability to determine whether it was my pride that had wanted to venture out despite the warning voice ("See, now he desires his own destruction") or just the opposite, that it was my common sense which wanted to hold me back and have me wait a week, in which case everything would have fizzled out again, and that this would have been my own destruction ("See, now he desires his own destruction").

O, these have been harsh and stringent days—unto death. And excruciatingly painful as a death blow was the possibility that it was my pride which insisted on venturing out despite my common sense, which had adequately anticipated the dangers ahead, and even despite a warning voice. It is dreadful, I have suffered something akin to death pangs.

But Governance knew well enough what it was doing. For if on top of all the sufferings there had not been added this one: whether or not it was my own fault, whether or not it was because of God's disfavor that this happened to me, my suffering would never have been unto death—and that no doubt was the determining factor.

That was why Governance let me go on being uncertain about my nocturnal conversation, in order that with this uncertainty I would inflict a wound unto death.

That, too, I have done. O, what I have learned! Wearied by this internal torment, I lost the urge to enjoy life, even if the conditions were offered—but in the profoundest sense I became aware of Christianity.

x⁴ A 587   August 7, 1852

### « 6811 *Youth—Old Age*

Up leaps a young man and delivers an enthusiastic speech, applying the criterion to an old man whose life can by no means be said to correspond to this high and inspired ideal. And the world (which always wants to be deceived) believes that if only the young man gets control everything will be all right.

How stupid! Let's get a look at the young man when he has grown old and see what his life is like.

But this is the cruelty perpetrated against the old again and again.

I am aware of having made an exception, for basically I have spent the advantage of my youth on Mynster.[3167]

But just as youth can do old age an injustice so also, just the opposite, old age can do an injustice to youth by rubbing it out. This is really what Mynster has done to me.

I am deeply pained by this relationship to Mynster, for I did so much want to do everything that would be good for him.

x⁴ A 592   *n.d.*, 1852

### « 6812 *About Myself*

With all my sufferings, with more and more opposition from the outside since I must push ahead more decisively, and finally, with my financial insecurity[3168]—then to have to venture out: that is why I said: No, I dare not do it, it is too high for me, to me it is the same as tempting God.

And yet this was what was required of me.

That I perhaps would eventually suffer want was not certain, but I had to venture ahead under the pressure of that possibility.

There have been hours when I wished there were someone with whom I could talk, an ascetic. But wherever I look I see this nauseating spectacle: the professor who lectures and otherwise existentially knows only about a job and a career. It would never occur to me to speak with anyone like that; indeed, I could not even justify it, for of course he would try to help me get rid of all modesty so that in utterly shameless security I promptly would make a livelihood the earnestness of life.

But no doubt it has been good for me that there is no such person; conferring with another person might have weakened me instead of keeping me close to God.

O God, O infinite love, I do desire to be involved with you! If I make a mistake, O, you who are love, strike me so that I get on the right path again.

x[4] A 603   *n.d.*, 1852

### « 6813 *Mynster*[3169]

When I spoke with Mynster the first time after the publication of *Practice in Christianity,* he said among other things that it was plain to see that I was out after him, that two-thirds of the book was against him and one-third against Martensen; he referred specifically to what was said in Part III about "observations."[3170]

But this is a misunderstanding. When I brought the book to him I expressly told him that I wished that one of us two were dead before it was published. But if one is out after a man, he certainly does not desire him to be prematurely dead.

Moreover, when I read proof there was a point in the part on observations which offended me also. But I was under such a strain that I was afraid that if I made the slightest change then it could end with my not publishing the book at all. I told Bishop Mynster this, too, the day we talked about it. What offended me was the point: Observations! One sees it on him, the eyes recede, etc. N.B.

But my relationship to Mynster is a curious thing; after all, it is he himself who goads me farther out.

There is nothing to which Mynster is so opposed as genuine altruistic enthusiasm. Like that Sophist (in Wieland's *Agathon*[3171]), he will risk everything to prevent it.

The reason it takes so long is that Mynster cannot quite make out whether I actually represent an especially subtle sagacity and by an ingenious turn will end up grasping earthly advantages. In that case he would not be so at odds with me.

But he is constantly putting me off. As early as several years ago I spoke with him about an appointment to the pastoral seminary. Incidentally, I am not saying that I therefore would have accepted it, but I wanted very much to have the possibility at hand so that I could more freely see whether that was the way I should take or not. But Mynster, after all, cannot know anything about this. But he has not wanted to do the least thing and merely procrastinates. Probably he is counting on my not being able to hold out for economic reasons (and as early as several years ago I told him that I had some worries about that: I mentioned it to him as early as 1846).

Well, what shall I do? If I were to compromise, I might manage to work extensively—and that would fit in with an appointment to the seminary. But Mynster will not have it. But then I must continue intensively and thus must raise the price—this in fact is Mynster's own fault.

So it cannot be said that I am out after him.

x⁴ A 604   n.d., 1852

### « 6814

*In margin of 6813* (x⁴ A 604):

N.B.  Incidentally, I remember very well that when the manuscript of *The Sickness unto Death* was sent to the printer I was impatient with Bishop Mynster and the amicable way he actually had worked against me. I remember my remark on the occasion of the publication of the book: Now let him (namely, Mynster) have it. But between *The Sickness unto Death* and *Practice in Christianity* a great change has taken place in me. I have suffered much. On the other hand I essentially had forgotten the particulars in that manuscript (*Practice in Christianity*), which was almost two years old. My main concern was whether or not to publish the book at all. As I said before, I did not become aware of that point [3172] until I read the proofs. Anyone who knows how loath I am to make changes in the proofs, because I am so flexible that I easily could rewrite the whole thing, understands that I did not dare decide to make changes no matter how much I wanted to do so, and I did not dare do it even for my own sake lest I dodge the responsibility of having exposed myself to Mynster's bitterness. That point perhaps could be deleted (and yet it is a question whether just such a point did not belong in the book, a point which would be noticed and actually was noticed only by Bishop Mynster, a point which, although in one sense it amounts to nothing, nevertheless may have disturbed Mynster inexplicably), but for fear of getting into trouble with myself I did not dare delete it in the proof, that is, after it was written.

x⁴ A 605   n.d.

### « 6815  *The Relationship to God*

The more tender and sensitive I am, the more I can be said to need God—moreover, it would seem as if an ascetic toughness could lead to wanting to do without God and to that extent would be dubious.

Rubbish, rubbish, rubbish. This sentimentalism is not at all the kind of worship God desires.

$x^4$ A 610   n.d., 1852

### « 6816 *The Present Generation*

cannot be bearers of Christianity. People as they now are can be called carriers of Christianity only insofar as they (to use an expression[3173] a modern author used in another context) are carrying it to its grave.

$x^4$ A 625   n.d., 1852

### « 6817 *Sadness*

Somewhere in a psalm[3174] it tells of the rich man who painstakingly amasses a fortune and "knows not who will inherit it from him."

In the same way I will leave behind me, intellectually speaking, a not-so-little capital. Alas, but I know who is going to inherit from me, that character I find so repulsive, he who will keep on inheriting all that is best just as he has done in the past—namely, the assistant professor, the professor.*

But it is part of my suffering to know this and then quite steadily go ahead with the project which will bring me toil and trouble and the yield the professor in one sense will inherit—in one sense, for in another sense I will take it with me.

$x^4$ A 628   n.d., 1852

### « 6818

*Addition to 6817* ($x^4$ A 628):

*And even if "the professor" happened to read this, it would not stop him, it would not prick his conscience—no, he would lecture on this, too. And even if the professor happened to read this remark, it would not stop him either—no, he would lecture on this, too. For the professor is even longer than the tapeworm which a woman was delivered of recently (200 feet according to her husband, who expressed his gratitude in *Addresseavisen*[3175] recently)—a professor is even longer than that—and if a man has this tapeworm "the professor" in him, no human being can deliver him of it; only God can do it if the man himself is willing.

$x^4$ A 629   n.d., 1852

### « 6819

. . . . . During that time and later this one or that probably wondered why Kierkegaard does not go abroad. I am tempted to answer by combining two replies. One is by Socrates, or it is the laws speaking to him (in the *Crito*[3176]) of how he had loved this city and had never felt the urge to see other cities or learn to know their laws—so much has he loved the ones at home. The other is by Peer Degn:[3177] Why should I forsake a congregation that I love and esteem and that loves and esteems me in return.

$$x^4 \text{ A } 646 \quad n.d., \; 1852$$

### « 6820 *About Myself*

Yes, no doubt I have been gifted with the extraordinary. But Governance is completely the judge of what the extraordinary is. It was too good a bargain for me to understand this and to have financial independence to boot—that simply would not have been the extraordinary.

For that very reason the minute I more deeply understood my life—at that very moment financial worries[3178] entered the picture and Governance said: Come now, my little friend, now it can be in earnest.

There I stopped and realized the earnestness of the situation.

For a moment I was completely confused.

In this agony I cried out to God (it was at the time a work by the new pseudonym was published, *The Sickness unto Death*): Educate me. And that was right, it seemed as if Governance itself inspired me.

If I had had sufficient capital, I eventually would have taken the extraordinary in vain—and then that deepened understanding of my life probably would not have been granted to me either. On the other hand, if I had had no capital at all at the time when I understood myself or my past, then I would have hurled myself passionately into becoming a success in the world and would have despaired over the extraordinary.

But such was not to be—Governance always reckons correctly. I had enough capital so that year after year could pass in which many a time I was almost distressed to have that little nest egg, for otherwise I would have thrown myself into earning and making sure of a living. But I could not make up my mind to throw away my small assets (I dared not assume that responsibility); on the other hand I could not make up my mind to apply myself to finite affairs and take steps to make sure of a living, either (to me that would be breaking with God), for as long as I had a bit of capital it was possible to persevere with the idea.

This among other things has been my education (and truly it is very strenuous). I have been made aware of dying to the world.

This was real education, and it is still by no means finished.

x⁴ A 647    *n.d.*, 1852

### « 6821 *The Deceitful Heart*

How often I have caught myself really understanding something, seeing it in all its persuasive, clear, and also eloquent form—and then devoting myself to getting it in writing because I was afraid that I might not be able to do it so well next time—alas, the important thing was something entirely different, namely, that I would come to act according to it.

But I also remember that frequently a thought has become clear to me and in a particular form—and yet in such a way that I could not bring myself to put it in writing because I perceived that I myself should use it.

Then at long last such a thought is put in writing after it has been consumed, so to speak, for in the meantime a new thought would have entered my mind, a new thought which should not be put in writing but should be consumed. For the soul, too, needs nourishment, and the very thoughts which actually nourish my soul are just the ones I am unable to put in writing at once.

x⁴ A 651    *n.d.*, 1852

### « 6822 *The Provisional Movement*

The official position that pretends that something is Christianity which is not Christianity at all and wipes God's mouth with trumpet calls and by binding the Bible in velvet and gilding the apostles—this is utterly intolerable.

The next thing is to declare quite openly: I am toning down Christianity.

But this cannot be maintained, for how could a person go on day after day announcing to God: I am toning down Christianity—forgive me. It must end with God being the stronger and making his will prevail.

But the main point above all is quite flatly to get out of the mendacity and lying which the established is.

x⁴ A 661    *n.d.*, 1852

### « 6823 *Either—Or*

That is what I was called at the time. What a succession of interpretations of my *Or* I have already gone through!

I eliminated marriage as an *Or*. But marriage, after all, was not the *Or* of my life; I am much farther distant from the prior *Either*.

To be specific, the prior *Either* signifies the licentious enjoyment of life. Then come all the intermediate stages: the enjoyment of life with an admixture of the ethical. But my *Or* is not here. Then follows: the enjoyment of life with an ethical-religious admixture, but this is still not my *Or*.

So there is only one *Or* left: suffering, renunciation, the religious —to become less than nothing in this world.

If I am an original dialectician, if I am dialectical by nature, then I can find rest only in the last *Or*, not in any intermediate *Or*; for *Either* —*Or* is not exhausted until one comes to rest in the final *Or*.

$x^4$ A 663   *n.d.*, 1852

« **6824**

*It is more blessed to give than to receive, but then it is also more blessed to be able to do without than to have to have.*

Meanwhile people have managed to get God completely transformed, and also have made God into a sovereign who rules with the help of this dreadful, demoralizing political shrewdness (which has also come to be used in the Church) which gets men to have more and more needs—in order the better to coerce and manage them.

Abominable! No, in his love God wants to bring up and develop a man to be able, if possible, to do without—with the exception of God —so that the only thing he unconditionally cannot do without is God; for as ruler God has no fear that he might not be able to rule mankind, and as love he wishes to be loved by them, to be in kinship with them, which on man's part can only be expressed by renunciation.

For a good many years a man can be related to God as a very young child to its parents—as, for example, a little girl who picks up her skirts and dances to honor her parents, laughs and leaps, etc., and this is her expression of thanks. It is the same in the relationship to God. There is a time when a man cannot understand it in any other way but that God is the kind of love that gives what corresponds to apples and pears—and divine worship consists properly of being childishly happy.

As long as this is truth in a man, God is also very well satisfied with it. And it can be truth in a man for a long time. Yes, I really am inclined to think that the change that has come over the whole race is that God has become so elevated for us that we cannot really attain any other kind of worship.

But this is not the way it is. There comes a time of maturity when God no longer wants man to worship him in this way. It is not a miserable something which God desires—O, no, it is a higher form of love. It will fill you with wonder; he says to such a man, as to everyman, it will fill you with wonder to love me and in such a way that you are actually aware of your relationship with me—therefore you must die to the world.

The way renunciation has usually been presented has appeared to me to be an attempt to make God into a foolish pedant and the God-relationship into an eternal parsimoniousness and a nagging paltriness. This is why it has not appealed to me at all. But the relation is entirely different, for renunciation, yes, the delight of renunciation is nothing other than a love-understanding with God. And as far as I am concerned I am obliged in truth to confess that it was God who intimated it to me. I would not have dreamed of this nor believed myself capable of it. But it was as if God whispered to me this secret: renunciation is a higher relationship to God, is actually the love-relationship. And thereby renunciation became fascinating—at least to me. I have never before been so fascinated.

I have loved this thought as I love my life. Yet I have been ready to be reconciled to having to let go of the thought, to the fact that it was my task to humble myself under having to let go of it since I no longer have the means[3179] to live for it.

Now I am again—happily—restored to this thought and in a far higher sense. Yes, it is as if God said to me: "My little friend, I who am love, I could with utmost joy make a way out for you and once again render you independent; but then your cause does not advance, then you come to have actually nothing to do with me, at least you do not come to love me in a higher sense. You are now so developed that if I now made you wealthy I would have to be almost angry with you if you did not immediately give it back, saying: No, under the circumstances, I dare not. Is it not true that you are too developed* not to feel for yourself the impropriety of proclaiming in your abundance that it is blessed to do without, too developed to be able to help yourself by declaring that you are only a poet,[3180] although it will always be to your credit that you had the honesty to say it." And this is the way it is, even if I, humanly speaking, can be said to have been something more than a poet.

$x^4$ A 673   n.d., 1852

« **6825**

*Addition to 6824* (x⁴ A 673):

*N.B. Here stood: "You are now too developed not to perceive for yourself the impropriety of living in abundance and proclaiming that it is blessed to do without." It seemed to me that these words put it too strongly, for I have not really occupied myself with this aspect of proclamation, and as for the theme I have used, the suffering of mockery, there I have in fact been in character. But the words can very well remain; after all, they were said primarily about a future time, if I imagined myself to be wealthy and then wanted to proclaim that it is blessed to do without, a proclamation which, however, is always more forgivable than earning wealth by proclaiming that it is blessed to do without.

$$x^4 \text{ A } 674 \quad n.d., \; 1852$$

« **6826** *September 10*[3181]

Today it is twelve years since I became engaged.

"She" of course did not fail to be on the spot and meet me, and although in the summer I take my walk earlier than usual (thus the one time this summer that I met her—less frequently, perhaps, because she has been on holiday in the country—we met on the embankment near Nørreport) she met me both today and yesterday morning on the avenue near Østerport. When she approached me yesterday she suddenly averted her eyes, which made me wonder. But the explanation was immediately at hand. A man on horseback shouted to me that my brother-in-law[3182] was right behind me and wanted to talk with me. She had seen him. Today she looked at me but did not nod, neither did she speak to me. O, perhaps she expected me to do so. My God, how gladly I would do that and everything for her. But I dare not assume the responsibility; she herself must ask for it.

But I have so wanted it to happen this year; furthermore, it is tormenting to keep a situation on tenterhooks this way year after year.

But no doubt it was good that nothing did happen. For it may have had the effect of tempting me to set something in motion to win out in a worldly way and make a sort of success in the world in order to make a celebrity of her.

This is why it made a strong impact on me that today, too, went off smoothly. It reminded me deeply and vividly that she does not have first priority in my life. No, No—yet humanly speaking it is true, and how gladly I would express it, that she has and will have the first and only priority in my life—but God has the first priority. My engagement to her and breaking the engagement are actually my relationship to God, are, if I dare say so, in all devoutness, my engagement to God.

And so September 10, the anniversary of my engagement, is understood in such a way that I commemorate it in loneliness—and perhaps I needed to be reminded of this once again so that I do not go out and become a Sophist who makes a hit in the world by proclaiming that it is blessed to suffer, a Sophist who even though he himself does not really enjoy life still could relish enjoying a woman's delight over becoming a celebrity.

Perhaps she will meet me tomorrow and ask it herself, perhaps the day after tomorrow, perhaps in a year—I shall be willing enough. But it certainly was a valuable lesson to me that today, of all days, nothing happened. I may have misinterpreted it as a hint from God with regard to wanting to enjoy life, to be temporally successful—and thus I eventually would have grieved the spirit, but perhaps I would not have realized that I had taken a wrong direction until the hour of my death.

$x^5$ A 21 September 10, 1852

« **6827  Excerpts, Book Titles, etc.**

October 24, 1852

$x^6$ C 4 October 24, 1852

« **6828**

*Addition to 6827* ($x^6$ C 4):
N.B. In the back[3183] there are book titles from an earlier time.

$x^6$ C 5   *n.d.,* 1852

« **6829**

*Addition to 6827* ($x^6$ C 4):
Zeller, *Die Philosophie der Griechen.*[3184] Tübingen, 1844. . . .
*Rheinisches Musæum für Philologie,* by Welker and A. F. Näke, vol. I, 1833. . . .
*Rheinisches Musæum für Philologie,* 1834. . . .
Zumpt, *Über den Bestand der philosophischen Schulen in Athen.* Abhdl. der Berliner Academie, 1842. . . .
    A. Planck, *Lucian und das Christenthum,* in *Studien und Kritiken,* 1851, p. 882 etc.
Waitz, *Aristoteles Organum,* is presumably more than one volume, since volume I is quoted in Zeller, *Die Philosophie der Griechen,* II, p. 405 note.

In the same place, Heyder, *Kritische Darstellung und Vergleichung der Aristotelischen und der Hegelschen Dialectik*, is also quoted.

Trendelenburg on the Aristotelian τί ἦν εἶναι in *Rheinisches Musæum—Rheinisches M. für Philologie, Geschichte und griechische Philosophie*, v. Niebuhr und Brandis. Available at the Athenæum. 1828, II, p. 457 etc.

Spengel, *Ueber die unter dem Namen des Aristoteles erhaltenen Schriften. Abhandl. der Münchner Academie*, III, 2, 1841, pp. 439–551.

Heinroth in his *Lebens-Studien* (which I have home from the Athenæum) cites also some other writings by himself: *Gesammelte Blätter, Über die Wahrheit, Pisteodicee, Orthobiotik, Lehrbuch der Seelenstörung*.

St. Vincens (director of the *College des bons enfants*, which was elevated to a congregation by the Pope in 1632), d. 1660. A number of biographies have been written, by Abelly and Gossen, by Stolberg in German (see Reuchlin, *Das Christenthum in Frankreich*, Hamburg, 1837, p. 215).

In the same book by Reuchlin, p. 230, a work is quoted: *Die barmherzigen Schwestern in Bezug auf Armen- und Kranken-Wesen und das Bürgerhospital zu Coblenz in ihrer Pflege. Ein Almosen für die Arme-Kinder-Schule des milden Frauen-Vereins*, which work he attributes to Clemens Brentano.

Vincent, *Vues sur le protestantisme en France*, 1829. Quoted in the same book by Reuchlin mentioned above, p. 362.

*Sinai und Golgatha. Reise in das Morgenland*, v. F. A. Strauss. 4 edition, 1852.

Gerhard Joh. Vossius. *Oratoriæ Institutiones*.

Heinrich, *Epimenides von Kreta*. This treatise is quoted in *Aristoteles Rhetorik*, übers. v. Knebel, Stuttgart, 1840, bk. III, ch. 17, note 3, p. 207.

This is the passage in which Aristotle says of this Epimenides that he concerned himself with prophesying not things to come but things past; he prophesied (ἐμαντεύετο) not about things to come but about the dim past (περὶ τῶν γεγονότων μέν, ἀδήλων δέ).

Ernesti, *Lexicon Technologiæ*. Ernesti, *Lexicon Rhetor* is quoted in another passage.

It is in Knebel's translation of Aristotle's *Rhetoric to Alexander*, in the notes to ch. 3 and ch. 15.

*Alcibiades, der Statsmann und Feldherr, nach der Qvellen dargestellt*, v. Dr. Hertzberg. Halle, 1853.

x⁶ c 6   *n.d.*, 1852

« **6830**

The following reply was given by the University Library to an inquiry about a monograph by **Abælard**:

The Library has only Frerichs, *de Petri Abælardi doctrina dogmatica et morali,* Jena, 1826, quarto, and Rheinwald, *P. Abæl. epitome theol. Christi;* also *Ouvrages inédits d'Abæl.,* by Cousin, Paris, 1836, quarto, and Petri Abæl., *Opera,* ed. Cousin, I, Paris, 1849, quarto.

Spener, *Theologische Bedenken.*[3185]

Erhard Schmidt, *Adiaphora wissensch. und historisch untersucht.*

Herzog, *Charakteristik,* v. Calvin.

Gottfried Arnold (author of *Unpartheiischen Kirchen und Ketzerges.*[3186]), *Das erste Marterthum,* 1695; *Die erste Liebe,* 1696; *Historie und Beschreibung der mystischen Theol.,* 1703.

Stobæus, *Eclogæ physicæ et morales,* ed. Heeren, Goett., 1792–1801, I–II, octavo.

Philostratus, βίοι σοφιστῶν, ed. Kayser, Heidelberg, 1838.

Bonnell, *De mutata sub primis Cæsaribus eloquentiæ, Romanæ condicione inprimis de Rhetorum scholis.* Berlin, 1836. School prospectus.

Delprat, *Die Brüderschaft des gemeinsamen Lebens,* übers. v. Mohnike. Leipzig, 1840.

Macarii, *Sämtlich. Sch.,* übers. v. Casseder, I–II, Bamberg, 1819–20.

*Franz. v. Assis kleine Werke oder dessen Leben und Regel aus dem Lateinischen,* v. H. Haid, I–II, München, 1828–29.

Lassaulx, *Die Gebete der Griechen und Römer.* Wurzburg, 1844.

Rossweid, *vitæ Patrum.*

Wigger, *Versuch einer Charakteristik des Socrates als Mensch, Bürger und Philosoph.* Neustrelitz, 1811.

Zitte, *Lebensbeschreibung des Joh. Huss.*

Zachar. Theobald, *Hussitenkrieg oder Leben, Lehre und Tod des Joh. Huss.* Nürnberg, 1621.

(I. F. Fischer) *Joh. Hussens Leben.* Leipzig, 1804.

Theiner, *Die Einführung der erzwungenen Ehelosigkeit bei den christl. Geistlichen.* Altenburg, 1828.

Voigt, *Hildebrand als Gregor VII und seine Zeit.*

Frank, *Arnold v. Brescia und seine Zeit.* Zürich, 1829.

X[6] C 7   *n.d.,* 1852

« **6831**

*He who does not hate father and mother for my sake etc. is not worthy of me.*[3187]

How does this conflict appear in "Christendom," for surely it cannot mean that we should begin right off by hating them?

Very simple. "Christendom," or that all as such are Christians, has only been made possible by making Christianity into something totally different from what it is in the N. T.

But outside of the N. T. there is no official definition of what Christianity is.

Consequently everyone is under obligation to do his utmost to acknowledge, confess, depict what Christianity is according to the N. T. And then the collisions will appear—that is, will be able to appear. Something as deadened as what in Christendom is called Christianity of course cannot produce conflicts of this nature.

Is a possible collision with Bishop Mynster[3188] related to this? He dare not deny that what I have depicted is N. T. Christianity. But he says: If we two are to be friends, you must not go so far out; you must suppress this last emphasis and stick with what I have proclaimed—this is true Christianity.

Just think of the emotional conflict. There is a man I love with all my heart—but I know that if I present what Christianity is essentially he will be furious, will become my enemy. And Christianity commits me to it.

$$X^5 \text{ A } 33 \quad n.d., 1852$$

« 6832 *"The Spirit"*

It is not as the mockers and freethinkers boldly maintain, or as the half-experienced despairingly or rebelliously sigh or fume—that such a Spirit does not exist, a Spirit who, when one calls upon him, transforms a man, renews him, gives him strength for renunciation, all possible renunciation.

No, it is not so. Such a Spirit actually does exist. But the point is that for the person who understands this it is so frightful to call upon this Spirit that he does not dare to do it, especially one who has been spoiled from childhood by grace, spoiled by wholesale, unmitigated leniency. To do it requires that he get a completely different conception of God, and he must learn to pray quite differently than he has been accustomed to pray from childhood, a way which has been to him a blessing.

Take an illustration. There is a winged horse, for example, more than winged—of a boundless speed—you have but to mount it and in one second you are more than a world's distance away from this world and its way of thinking and its life and its ideas and the understanding of one's contemporaries. The freethinkers, the mockers, the half-experienced now concentrate their attention on denying that such a horse exists—all under the hypocritical pretense that if such a horse did exist they would surely be ready to mount it. I speak differently, I assume that such a horse does exist (continuing the illustration) but I–I dare not mount it.

Here is the difficulty for all of us in Christendom who still have some Christianity. We are unable to deny that such a Spirit exists, that he only waits for us to surrender ourselves completely, and then he will surely take care of the rest.

Alas, but we dare not. And then comes the hitch that God wants to have something to do with us just the same. And this is what I mean by saying that in Christendom "grace" is applied in the first place, not only "grace" with respect to the past but grace with respect to the venturing that is required.

But, as stated, it is infinitely hard for a person brought up in Christianity from childhood to come out of this, for he is spoiled by "grace"—and yet "grace" is and remains this—that a person is saved, even the apostle.

$X^5$ A 43   *n.d.*, 1852

« **6833  *A Deceiver's "Hidden Inwardness"***[3189]
       ***and***
       ***How the Case Was Cracked***

A kind of religious [*In penciled parentheses:* short story]
                    [*In margin:* detective story]

----

There was once a teacher of Christianity, a clergyman, possessing unusual gifts and great worldly wisdom; he enjoyed considerable honor and esteem, and enjoyed this once again in self-complacent consciousness of his sagacity.

He was also conscious of something else: he was secretly aware that he was a deceiver who had made himself out to be more than he was by talking about a hidden inwardness. But in his closet with the door shut and certain that no one was around to hear he said to himself: "By means of the idea that Christianity is an objective teaching which is so firmly established that no one dares contradict it, and by means of all this about the hidden inwardness, I am so secure in my deception that even if our Lord sent ten witnesses to the truth, not one of them would succeed in exposing me." And this was not untrue, for "the witness to the truth," at least previously, was a direct and immediate category, and since the deceiver in his deception was above him because of reflection, the witness to the truth could not trap him.

I assume now that this secret conversation he had with himself in his closet, after making sure that no one could hear him, was heard in heaven—truly existence is wonderfully constructed acoustically: the most secret conversation with oneself is heard—in heaven—what a blessed comfort for all who suffer.

So the conversation is heard in heaven. Then I imagine that God (as it says in Holy Scripture, where in fact there is no mention of a conversation) replied and said: Yes, yes, my good man, if you are smart enough to change the method—I can too. You are going to be exposed, but it will happen slowly, for divine punishment is slow, yet inevitable, and it will happen in a way you will least expect, for God's thoughts are not man's thoughts, but you will be trapped in your foolishness by your own shrewdness—as I am in the habit of doing it—I, the Lord God, who catches up the wise in their foolishness. For this purpose I will use a man whom I shall send to plague you. Do not be afraid, be calm, I will not choose someone who is ten times as clever as you; no, clever folk are the last ones to whom I entrust anything, and moreover I seldom become involved with a man in such a way that I use him directly, entrust to him directly the what and the why and the wherefore. No, I use men in such a way that they do not notice it; they follow their ideas, and then I bring something entirely different out of it. Do not get excited about it. The one I will use—just imagine it!—is a young man, yes, what is more, a young man who will be admiringly attached to you with the most ardent enthusiasm. And since the young man's unselfish and honest devotion will conceal from him that he, precisely he, is the one who—yes, if he suspected it, I would never get him to do it except by force!—will expose you. And just so it will be completely hidden from you in the beginning how dangerous this young man is going to be for you, you will—and justifiably so—see in him your most fervent admirer.

This young man will be well instructed in Christianity. He will admire your great gifts and he will believe everything you say about a hidden inwardness—and thus you will have in him an admirer. But meanwhile he will readily see that by means of this hidden inwardness your proclamation of Christianity leaves out one whole side of Christianity, the embattled Christianity, but nothing will be farther from his mind than to harbor any suspicion whatsoever about you, that you might not be fully justified in understanding yourself as having this side in hidden inwardness.

This young man will consider it his task to furnish the complement to your proclamation of Christianity. And he will be happy to take on this work, happy in the foregone conviction of a harmonious relationship with you, he who manifests only devotion to you. He is somewhat melancholy, and therefore it will not even occur to him to take exception to your having appropriated the rewarding side of proclaiming Christianity and he the thankless side—no, in fact that will move him.

Then he begins his work, but from the ground up; therefore it is not immediately apparent where he is going.

No wonder you become aware of him, for he is all attentiveness to you. Now you take a look at him. Perhaps there is a very faint intimation of anxiety, as if there were something inexplicable about the man, but it will vanish promptly. And after having used all your sagacity, the impression you get will be the correct one: This young man is the most unselfishly devoted to me of all.

Then you talk with him once more and express your personal good will to him. You say—and this is after using all your sagacity and therefore what you say is completely true—: We complement each other, we complete each other.

Those were true words—and fateful words. For here is the snare in which you will trap yourself; the young man suspects nothing. He is satisfied devoutly to pursue his task, to actualize the complementarity more and more intensely. And before me he understands this to be his task—consequently nothing is able to hold him back.

Time passes, and the young man has gone ahead with carrying out his task: you, the wise one, perhaps begin to suspect something. But it will not help you, for the young man suspects nothing—otherwise I would not get him to continue without using force.

You, the wise one, now see the snare—but it will not help you to look around for ways to escape it, for you are in it—and the young man suspects nothing. If in "hidden inwardness" you do not have the other side of Christianity but simply want to get rid of it, then you are a deceiver. But whether or not you have it in hidden inwardness cannot be found out directly, for a hidden inwardness is a good hiding place. This is why the complement is introduced outside of you by that enthusiastic admirer of yours, the young man. Now, if you were not a

deceiver, the young man would be able to go on providing the complement as long and as intensely as he wished to; you would continue in
the best understanding, for you possessed the complement in hidden
inwardness. But if you are a deceiver, there will come a moment when
the complement becomes offensive to you—but the young man, he
suspects nothing!—you will be unable to refrain from doing what you
as the wisest one shrewdly did not do for a long time—that is, pass
judgment on the complement, no, you will condemn the complement
as an error. Instantly it will become manifest that your hidden inwardness is not the concealed complement, and it will become apparent to
men (for I the All-knowing can see it more readily) that your proclamation of Christianity is a deception.

It did in fact happen this way, then. For the first time the young
man discovered to his horror that he had prompted what he wanted
least of all. He became so sad over it that he completely withdrew from
the world—for him this was simply a decision "of love."

$$X^6 \text{ B } 226 \quad n.d., \text{ 1852}$$

### « 6834  *To Sit on Twelve Thrones and Judge the Twelve Tribes of Israel*

If I may be permitted to express an opinion on this, I would say
that I am continually amazed that this is presented in the New Testament as something inspiring, something so glorious and blessed that
it ought to inspire the apostles to unprecedented efforts.

I cannot understand this. Suppose that I were not what I nevertheless am, a timorous poet, but that I were able to meet by personal act
the greatest requirement and according to the most exacting standard,
in short, suppose that sitting on the throne and judging Israel was
promised me as a reward for an endeavor I was able to carry out: this
thought would not inspire me in the least but would make me utterly
dejected. I love being a man, I have an unwavering sympathy for all
who suffer—and then qualitatively to be set apart above everybody else
for all eternity!

At the same time I do perceive that this thought, which people
perhaps will find attractive, from the Christian point of view will reveal
my imperfection or what an imperfect Christian I am. For here again
it is apparent that we are pampered from childhood by being brought
up in Christianity, are spoiled by grace, by everything being grace.
This is also the reason that I continually rest in the thought that we
will all be saved. Nowadays we have no inkling of the anxiety, the fear

and trembling, the Christians must have experienced when the either
—or actually applied to them: either to hell or to heaven, their anxiety
about their own salvation, while millions perhaps went to hell. These
millions and millions of Christians, and then from childhood to be
pampered by grace, so that the genuinely earnest expression of respect
for God is lost, which was completely different in other periods—for
example, during the flood, when God scrapped a whole generation.

                                           x⁵ A 46   *n.d.*, 1852

### « 6835 *About "Her"*[3190]

As a regular thing she sees me when Bishop Mynster[3191] preaches
at vespers on Christmas day. It happened again this time.

Frequently I have received by mail letters and the like, effusive
things, some of them from women. It has never entered my mind that
any such letter could be from her, although I have occasionally wondered if it would ever occur to her to do anything like that.

But this Christmas Eve I received a little gift sent by *Flyveposten.*
It pertains to the preface to *Upbuilding Discourses in Various Spirits,* but
also, if I am not altogether wrong, to the two upbuilding discourses of
1843. I do not know why, but it occurred to me—could it be possible
that she could have done this.

Yesterday noon I went to church. I actually had forgotten that
Christmas gift. When I proceeded as usual down the passageway to the
right, she was standing a little farther up in the same corridor. She
stood there, she was not walking, she stood there, obviously waiting
for someone, whoever it was. No one else was there. I looked at her.
Thereupon she walked over to the side door through which I was
about to go. There was something strange about this meeting, a certain forwardness. As she passed me and turned to go through the door,
I made a movement which could have been merely stepping aside to
make room or could also have been a slight bow. She turned quickly
and made a motion. But now there was no opportunity for her to
speak, if she had in fact wanted to do so, for I already was inside the
church. I found my usual place, but I was not unaware that she was
continually looking at me even though she sat some distance away.

Maybe she was waiting for someone else out there in the passage,
maybe she was waiting for me, maybe that little gift was from her,
maybe she wanted to speak with me, maybe, maybe.

God knows how happy I would be to make her happy if this is her
wish, but I dare not. No, I cannot assume the responsibility of ap-

proaching her personally; she must ask for it herself and with her husband's approval.[3192]

x⁵ A 59   n.d., 1852

### « 6836 *Modern Literature*

seems strange to me. I read and read and am still just as wise or just as stupid as I was before. It makes enough noise, but I do not learn anything about what really concerns me. What I retain is the impression of an empty noise which nevertheless made a show of wanting to mean something.

I can illustrate exactly what I mean. I now live[3193] so close to Frue Kirke that during the night I can hear the watchman call every quarter-hour. Sometimes when I wake up at night—now someone might be very interested sometime in finding out what time it is; it is very easy for me—I just need to wait a few minutes and the watchman calls out the quarter-hour. And so he does. He cries in a loud, shrill voice, as clear as if he stood at my side, so loud that he would have awakened me (which I would not want) if I had been asleep. He cries: Watchman— hallo! And after this heroic burst of power his voice sinks and he softly says what time it is. So it goes from quarter to quarter, from hour to hour. If I lay awake the whole night and listened every quarter hour, all I would get to know would be: Watchman, hallo!

x⁵ A 67   n.d., 1853

### « 6837 *My Praying*

There was a time when I believed—it came so naturally, it was childlike—that God expressed his love by sending earthly gifts, happiness, prosperity. How rash my soul was in its desiring and daring—yes, for I thought something like this: One should not himself make an almighty being stingy and petty. I dared to pray about everything, even the most foolhardy things, with the exception of one thing, release from a deep suffering that I had undergone from my earliest years but which I interpreted to be part of my relationship to God. Otherwise I dared to risk even the most reckless prayers. And when everything else (for this suffering, after all, was an exception) went well, how full of gratitude my soul, how blessed it was to give thanks—for my belief that God expresses his love by sending earthly good gifts was unshaken.

This has now changed. How did it happen? Very simply but gradually. Little by little I became more and more aware that all those whom

God actually has loved, the prototypes and others, have all had to
suffer in this world. Furthermore, Christianity teaches that to be loved
by God and to love is to suffer.

But if this is true, then I would not really have dared to pray for
happiness and good fortune, for then indirectly it was as if I prayed at
the same time: O God, will you not stop loving me and let me stop
loving you. When a desire awakened in me and I wanted to pray, it
seemed to be blown away, all my former burning fervor, for it seemed
as if God were looking at me and saying: My little friend, consider what
you are doing; do you really want me not to love you and do you want
to be released from loving me.

To pray outright for suffering, however, seemed to me to be too
high, and I also thought that it could easily be presumptuous, so that
God might, as it were, become angry about it, as if I perhaps wanted
to provoke him.

That is why for some time now my praying has been different,
actually a calm leaving of everything to God, because it still is not really
clear to me how I should pray.

I have been brought up short by this difficulty. But there is still
another difficulty for me here. For even if I did find the bold confidence
to maintain that to be loved by God and to love God is to suffer,
something I have been inclined toward from my early days, I who have
long considered myself chosen for suffering—what about other men!
This is the interpretation I have put on my life. After all, I now live in
melancholy's chamber set apart—but I dare to rejoice upon seeing the
joy of others, and I dare *Christianly* to sanction it. To be loved by a
woman, to live in a happy marriage, enjoying life—this is denied me;
but when I emerge from my chamber set apart I dare to rejoice upon
seeing the happiness of others, I dare to encourage them in their
thought that to rejoice in life and to enjoy life are acceptable to God.
To be healthy and strong, a complete man with the expectation of a
long life—this was never granted to me. But when I emerge from my
solitary pain and move among the happy ones, I believe I dare have
the sad joy of encouraging them in their joy in life. O, but it must be
told that dying to the world, to be loved by God, means to suffer, and
that to love God means to suffer; therefore I must disturb the happiness of all the others, and I cannot have the sad joy of rejoicing in their
happiness, the sad joy of being loved by them.

Therefore this difficulty has brought me up short. If anyone can
show me in Holy Scripture, the New Testament, that to be loved by

God and to love God can be combined with enjoying this life: fine, I will accept this interpretation from the hand of God with unspeakable gratitude, glad for myself but also glad for the others, for I know all too well what men find natural. If anyone could make this clear to me from the New Testament, the game of my cause, if I dare speak this way, is in such excellent condition that with a little worldly wisdom and trust in God it can gain a finite victory. *Aber, aber,* my soul has misgivings about worldly enjoyment and a temporal victory. That is why I do not dare use worldly wisdom—I am almost afraid to have temporal success, for, Christianly speaking, to be loved by God and to love God means to suffer. In any case, in order to have trust in God (for I cannot combine trust in God and worldly wisdom in such a way that, trusting in God, I could use worldly wisdom), I must have the bold confidence *not* to use worldly wisdom, so that if I do gain a temporal victory I dare to say confidently: It was God's will, I placed it all in his hands by renouncing the use of finite prudence.

But if all this is the case and if my relationship to God has changed from what it was formerly, does that mean I am less convinced that God is love? No, no, God be praised, no! As I see it all now, it has become more clear to me that God speaks, as it were, a different language than I do, but all the same he is still infinite love.

And how wonderful it is! Just as I once, in looking back over the past, realized how immensely God had helped me even in the most trifling matters, so I now realize how the very suffering that was sent at a particular time, how everything that went wrong, even the most trifling matters, was designed to wound me in just the necessary way if God was to use me. Infinite love!

To suffer in this world! There was a time when I possessed the external conditions for really enjoying life. At the time I childishly or in adolescent innocence was also of the view that to be loved by God can be expressed by enjoying life; if the thorn in the flesh had not been there at the time, I would have gone ahead, but nothing else ever entered my head. But now—perhaps that thorn in the flesh will be removed, it pains me less; but then something else has also happened: I no longer possess the external conditions for being able to enjoy life, and I also have gained another conception of God.

Yet, as mentioned, I have been brought up short by this difficulty. I still do not dare decide unconditionally that God does not want me to have a temporal victory, that being loved by God means to suffer applies only to the chosen, whereas I and men in general are exempted from it, but then also have a more distant relationship to God; I still am not strong enough to pray myself into suffering.

But I am at a standstill, and in quiet submission to God I await a better understanding. It is so exceedingly high: to be loved by God and to love God means to suffer—and nothing, nothing fills me with such boundless anxiety as the thought of coming too close to God without being called [*ukaldet*].

Otherwise, with regard to the pain of this—to be loved by God and to love God is to suffer—it must be remembered that through the witness of the Spirit God makes it blessed to suffer, without removing the suffering—that is why it never occurred to those glorious ones that helping others to get out into suffering could disturb their joy.

So it is with the prototypes, the glorious ones, the chosen; but right here is "Christendom's" chief malpractice. On a massive scale it has been made far too easy to dispense with the chosen ones, to smuggle them out of the way, to assume that all that creates tension in the N. T. was spoken *specifically* to the apostles, etc. The question is, does the New Testament recognize any other kind of Christian than the "disciple"? For the humility which does not aspire to be an apostle or a disciple—ah, it can so easily be an enormous knavish trick, that is, we want to get out of the suffering the apostles experienced and, as customary in this human thieves' slang, we slyly call it humility and win two advantages: getting out of suffering and being honored for being humble. Not to aspire to the extraordinary gifts of the apostle—well, that may be, yes, it is humility; but that it is "humility" not to aspire to his sufferings, no, that gets to be outright hypocrisy.

$x^5$ A 72   *n.d.*, 1853

« **6838**

N.B. If, instead of bearing the author-signature M. M., the three ethical-religious essays[3194] should have a proper pseudonym, I would call the author Emanuel Leisetritt, a pseudonym I perhaps could use, if not here, if I should ever again have need for a pseudonym.

$x^5$ A 93   *n.d.*, 1853

« **6839**  *What I Have Wanted*
          *As I Can See It Now*

Good Friday

At a very early age I became engrossed in an idea whose origin I cannot account for, an idea which found a model in Socrates, the man with whom I·have had an inexplicable rapport from a very early age long before I really began to read Plato—the idea: How is it to be explained that all those who truly have served the truth get into trouble with their contemporaries while they are alive and no sooner are they dead than they are idolized.

The explanation is quite simple: the majority of men can relate to ideas, the good, the true only by way of imagination. But a dead man has the distance of imagination. A living person, however, who provides actuality (being a nobody he exists for everyone, consequently without the support of illusions)—him they cannot bear, they are offended by him, put him to death, trample on him.

This, again, is what all deceivers, who gamble on the world's wanting to be deceived,[3195] have more or less clearly realized, and they accommodate to it. In their lifetime they are supported by illusions (live in seclusion, take the earthly benefits, offer limited explanations, etc.) and thus make a hit etc. And this gets worse and worse century after century, especially since the press has become a power in society, for it is a definite assistance to living in seclusion (impersonally like a dead man, in a kind of illusion) and operating objectively.

And yet we must move in the direction of gaining personalities.

This, then, is the law: the person who does not want to operate with illusions will unconditionally get into trouble during his lifetime, will be trampled down, sacrificed. On the other hand, as soon as such a person is dead, the deceivers (orators, poets, professors, etc.) promptly take him over and exploit him—and he is idolized by the next generation. And if there is someone in the next generation who does not want to deceive or operate with illusions, well, if he keeps on, the same thing will happen to him as happened to the dead man when he was living.

In this way the actually contemporary generation does not really become aware, it does not attain contemporaneity, for those who kill or trample upon such a person do not really know what they are doing —and those who idolize him are, after all, the next generation and consequently are related to him at the distance of imagination.

Cannot something be done to awaken contemporaneity?

Yes, and it is worth an attempt, and this is the kind of attempt I have made. Use your best years in a prodigious effort but without employing illusions—then you will be well on the way to being trampled down; then stop, withdraw, live in seclusion, and from that vantage point begin pointing out to your contemporaries the past, what has happened, and to which they themselves are witnesses, and show

them what the consequences would have been had you not pulled back
and diminished, point out what is really involved in serving the truth
in truth.

In my opinion it is a matter of gaining the human honesty to take
possession of a past which truly has been in the service of the truth.
But when it is one of those glorious ones who keeps on to the very end
and consequently is trampled down—then deceivers capitalize on
them. And, as mentioned, if there is someone who refuses categorically
to exploit them, perhaps he carries on and eventually becomes one of
those glorious ones himself and becomes the sacrifice—and we do not
get that human integrity I have in mind which interprets serving the
truth in truth.

This is my thought. Everything—time, energy, money—everything
has been spent on it. I have done everything to explode illusions; I
lived on the streets,[3196] was recognized by everyone, took part in the
comedy, etc., etc.

The thought is characteristic and also has been served in such a
way that I would dare present myself to Socrates, and I am convinced
that he would consider it, even though I believe that what he practiced
by sticking it out to the end is infinitely superior.

In the meantime I have found satisfaction in this. A doubt, however, has arisen in me: in eternity will I not repent of it, is it not too
little, is not the only right thing for everyone to do simply to take care
of his own affairs, to take the obedience examination, to be trampled
down, sacrificed, and to leave the rest up to God, not worrying about
whether he has accomplished enough or not. Accomplish enough! Yes,
here it is. That is just what I wanted to do, and I have found satisfaction
in this as a penitent, and therefore I have always joked about accomplishing something, because I am disgusted by the hypocritical rubbish
we constantly hear about accomplishing things, when it is simply egotism wanting to gain something.

So what I really wanted was to accomplish something—and, if I in
profound respect dare have any opinion about those glorious ones,
about a Socrates, it seems to me that the very reason they did not
accomplish as much as they deserved to was that in unconditioned
obedience they were prepared to be trampled down, sacrificed—while,
as stated, the deceivers took possession of them when they were dead,
but the majority were not made aware.

I regard what I have wanted as something far inferior to what those glorious ones intended, because unconditioned obedience, to be trampled down as if one had accomplished nothing, is and continues to be the highest—and precisely what I from a lower level have wanted to point out.

If ethically it is true that there are relative tasks, that no one can assume what has not been given to him—well, then I am happy and satisfied with my own and turn off. But if ethically this does not hold true, if on the contrary it holds true that everyone must regard his life as taking an examination, an examination in obedience, the examination of unconditioned obedience—yes, then I do not dare turn off, but I must continue to steer in the direction of being trampled down.

$x^5$ A 104   March 25, 1853

« **6840** *About Myself*

Second Day of Pentecost

A deep depression has been kept down by writing.

Thus the years went by. Then financial worries[3197] converged on me. And this enormous creativity began to take on the appearance of virtually a splendid distraction.

Well, so it was stopped. That was quite difficult.

For a few years now I have not been writing; so I held to my intention.

As a result, an enormous creativity has accumulated in my head and in my thinking—yes, I believe that right now an abundant variety of professors and poets could be made out of me.

But my difficulty lies elsewhere. In order to indulge this creativity properly, I first of all must make sure of my future and take steps along this line. And there it is again—it seems to me that it is Christianly more valuable to hold out as long as possible without getting material security, far more valuable than if I *first of all* get security and then—write. After all, the essentially Christian thing to do is not to write but to exist [*existerer*]. O, but understood I am not, least of all in our time, when precisely this is what must be emphasized, namely, that Christianity is not a presentation etc. of Christianity while living in other categories oneself.

What I always say in this respect I say again here: My holding back with regard to providing material security may also be a kind of pride. Well, that is why I present myself for the examination, yet always cheerfully trusting in God and resting in the thought that God is love.

$x^5$ A 105   March 28, 1853

« **6841**  *Either/Or*

Every cause which is not served as an either/or (but as a both-and, also, etc.) is *eo ipso* not God's cause, yet it does not therefore follow that every cause served as an either/or is therefore God's cause.

Either/Or, that is, that the cause is served as an Either/Or, is an endorsement similar to "in the royal service."

The symbol for the merely human, for mediocrity, the secular mentality, dearth of spirit, is: both-and, also.

And this is the way Mynster actually has proclaimed Christianity, that is, if consideration is given to his own personal life.

$x^5$ A 119   *n.d.*, 1853

« **6842**  *My Christian Position*

1853                                                               S.K.

First a friendly word to the readers. It is not customary, least of all in journals, to speak in the manner in which I intend to speak and must speak here. Forgive me, then, bear with me, and put the best construction upon it. I cannot speak in any other way, and I must speak, and at this moment it must be in a journal. I do not need to make this excuse to my reader and, indeed, to anyone who is more religiously mature; he will understand that this may and must be said just this way.[3198]

Although I fully realize that as an author I have not had finite, secular, temporal goals, which explains why I have come to stand curiously alien, not to speak of appearing ridiculous, in our clever age in which practically everyone knows all too well what finite, secular, and temporal goals he is striving for, I do, however, as an author have something on my conscience in the strictest sense of the word. Let me accurately describe how I feel about it. There is something very specific that I have to say, and it weighs so on my conscience that I dare not die without saying it. For the minute I die and leave this world, I will then (as I see it) instantly (so frightfully fast does it happen!) I will then instantly be infinitely far from here, at another place, where even that very second (what frightful speed!) the question will be put to me: Have you carried out your errand, have you *very specifically* said the specific something you were to say? And if I have not done it, what then? [*In margin:* But in one sense it has not been this way from the beginning. On the contrary there was a period in the beginning when I hoped to be released from *very specifically* saying this specific thing by death, even if I eventually would say it inasmuch as I would leave it said *very specifically* in writing. Then came a period when it looked like this to me: You will see, you will not die young; instead you will become an old man, and in any case you will live so long that finally you will have to say this specific something in your lifetime; you will have to say it *very specifically*. Then came the last period, which has already lasted for some time now, during which with every month that passes it more and more insistently confronts me thus: I dare not die without having said the specific something very specifically.]

Imagine a servant. He is sent somewhere on a specific errand; there is something specific he has to say and to a specific man. But he is extremely reluctant to say what he has to say, for it is not a happy message, and he is especially reluctant to say it to this particular man. So he makes the journey and arrives at the place; he is at the place—ah, but he lets time go by. He puts it off and puts it off, like a child playing truant from school, so he plays truant from the task—but all the time with anxiety, for he has no idea at all how much time he is going to be given, but he does know and is positively certain that if his recall came, for example, today and he would have to return home and had not taken care of his errand, then, as we say, he is in for trouble.

So it is with me. There is something very specific I have to say. But to be truthful, I am not keen on saying it; on the contrary, I would very much like to see another say it, which would not help me, however, since, after all, as I see it, it was and is my task to say it. But I am not keen on saying it; just the opposite, I have craved and wished and at times almost hoped that I perhaps might get out of saying it. For it is no happy message, this specific something, and there are various persons dear to me who I am positive will be sorry to have it said. Above all, there is one consideration that has constantly held me back, restrained my tongue or my pen, a consideration for this highest clergyman of this Church,[3199] a man to whom I—also in remembrance of a dead father—I feel drawn in an inexplicable, almost morbid, love—and I must believe that he in particular would be very sorry to have it said.

How have I conducted myself then? Let me relate the past briefly but in the historical present, consequently as the situation now.

This is how I conduct myself. I make clear to myself the specific something I have to say. Thereupon—well, whether it be keen discernment, whether it be more or less keen discernment, let others be the judge of that—but what I personally dare say and as truthfully as possible is this: With an extremely *troubled* discernment I seek to find the mildest, gentlest form in which it can be said—and then I send it out into the world. Simultaneously I move over to the other side. I myself do everything to draw attention away from it, and internally I shout and cry (yes, or sigh): Grant, O God, that it all may go off quietly. It is done in such a way, I know, that very few are able to grasp the true situation. Now, if these few are only smart enough to keep absolutely calm and not throw themselves at me to pressure me (for that is what I unavoidably find most abhorrent) the successful outcome would be that I have saved my conscience, that I have said the specific something that had to be said, and that I have saved my love for the old gentleman. I have avoided a collision with the Bishop M., yes, in the eyes of most people I even seem to have strengthened his regime, something in one sense I quite literally am doing.

And so it goes, everything goes off very quietly. Then I am happy; I say to my soul: Be happy, for now you dare to be happy and you have reason to be happy.

But conscience, as the poet says, this blushing, bashful spirit which makes a person utterly restless, conscience is a wonderful thing and marvelously designed for the individual. For while there certainly are various people of whom it might be said that they have a far more sagacious conscience than I have, because in fact they are far more sagacious than I, and while, on the other hand, there also are various ones of whom it might be said that they have a far more limited conscience than I, because they are far more limited than I—the single individual's conscience (what an ingenious divine invention the conscience is, so incomparably designed for the individual) is precisely, just exactly, as sagacious as he is; therefore his conscience will always be just sagacious enough to be able to see through this clever, most clever, invention of his.

I have experienced the truth of this. After some time had passed there came a day when conscience called to me and said: But, my good friend, how about this specific something that you have to say, do you dare say that you have said it? After all, I know just as well as you do how cunningly you are behaving—.

Now this is another story. Now it is no longer: Rejoice, my soul, and be glad. No, I start over again. I make altogether clear to myself that specific something—and I must say that it becomes more and more clear each time. Then I am ready. I sit down and do nothing else from morning until evening than with keen discernment—well, whether it be keen discernment, whether it be more or less keen discernment, let others be the judge of that—I dare truthfully say that it is with an *extremely troubled* discernment that I seek to find the mildest form in which it can be said. Then I send it out into the world. Simultaneously I move to the other side: I do everything to draw attention away from it, internally I shout and cry or sigh etc. etc.

But conscience, this, as the poet says, this blushing, bashful spirit that causes a man nothing but unrest, conscience is something wonderful etc. etc.

Step by step I could point this out through my whole authorship. I believe that I was successful in saying the specific something I have to say, but yet in such a way that it can go off quietly by—I myself help it along. It does go off very quietly—"now I, too, will be happy"—but conscience is wonderfully designed for the individual etc.

But I do not intend to go through the whole authorship in this manner. I will take only the last part.

In 1850 a book came out entitled: *Practice in Christianity.* There the specific something I have to say is actually said.

But, but. In the first place, it got to be a big book, and I know very well that few people read books, especially the bigger ones. In the second place, a pseudonym was used, which almost poetically distances what was said from actuality. In the third place, in a thrice-repeated preface[3200] I let the book recoil upon myself and thereby deflect the attack so that it does not really drive home to actuality. In the fourth place, when the book came out I did manage to lead attention away from it—and those few I mention were, as I secretly wished, quite properly sagacious enough to keep completely calm—it turned out all right, everything went off very quietly.

"Now I will be happy, rejoice in life as I have reason to, for what I thought to be very, very difficult and required rare good luck from the other side turned out all right; I have saved my conscience, I have spoken, have said it—and I have avoided a collision with Bishop M., nothing actually has happened."

But conscience . . . . . yet, no, it did not operate this time just as before. After a short time something else happened. In a little book[3201] (_____) Bishop M. found opportunity in a quick turn to place me as an author on the same level with Goldschmidt of *The Corsair.* What is this, I said to myself; is this the old gentleman, the, to say no more, distinguished, brilliant His Excellency, Bishop M.? In the meantime I surveyed the situation, and I finally concluded that it could be regarded as if nothing had happened—what is a line when one is as attached to a man as I am to Bishop M. Time passed, then conscience spoke up. It said something like this: Do you dare deny that you understand very well what that line signifies, that you can read this hieroglyph only all too well, that it means Bishop M. has ascended the scale of wrath very high since he descends so low as to use such a means, that while his worldly sagacity perhaps told him there really is nothing to do or it is not prudent to do anything against Magister K., that he nevertheless has been so provoked that he—no doubt a rare instance—still has been unable to control his anger and it has to come out in one way or another—have you not understood this, and do you dare let this pass without settling the matter, since it is now clear how at odds he must be with you. —I pondered this. —Time passed, again conscience began wanting to engage me in conversation and about the same matter, also gave the matter a new turn. Suppose, it said to me, that the old gentleman were dead, then do you think it easier to set out and in words get said very specifically, briefly and bluntly, the specific something you have to say. You assume that it is devotedness to the old gentleman—and this I will not completely deny—that holds you back. But watch out, could not this also be a little selfishness, that you want to protect yourself, that you think the matter cannot be either as serious or as painfully exhausting for you as soon as he is gone. O, but think of the accounting! Suppose you dared answer "Yes" to the question "Have you taken care of the errand?" But suppose the question is: Why did you let the moment go unused when you knew that the matter would have become most earnest the moment when that old gentleman representing the opposite stood at the peak of his power, supported by the tradition of his whole life, possessing all the advantages of being an old man, yet still young and energetic? Or did you not realize that you were supposed to see to it that the matter would become as earnest as it is? But this you dodged! [*In margin:* Consequently you cannot truthfully answer "Yes" to the question "Have you taken care of the errand?" but must be silent—and as a reward for not using the time to speak, you can have an eternity in which to be silent, yes, or to sit in despair, brooding over your not speaking.]

Well, so it must be said, bluntly and briefly. And all this business with the big books must have an end. *It must be said briefly, specifically—and my hesitation is not due to inability, for I can do it all right, O, but I will do it so very reluctantly and I would so very much like to be free.

[*In margin:* *What I chiefly have to say will be brief and specific. If Prof. M.[3202] has found me to be too verbose—may I only not be too brief for him now; if Bishop M.—otherwise kindly—has taunted me about using too many devices—may I only not charge him too directly now.]

————

My Christian position is: *Christianity does not exist at all*.[3203]—I speak of Denmark and, of course, within the limits of what is humanly possible to know.

*Christianity does not exist*; but through having the objective doctrine, we are more or less captivated in the fancy, trapped in the illusion, that we are Christians.

O, Luther! And yet in one sense a fortunate situation—at that time there were ninety-five theses and controversy over doctrine—now there is but one thesis: that Christianity does not exist at all.

It is not doctrinal heresy, not a schism, no, it is the most dangerous of all, the most cunning invention of natural human subtlety. It may be the *Fall* from Christianity. It is a mirage, since behind this objectivity which is boasted about and undauntedly appealed to, that we have the objective doctrine and *objectively*, pastors and churches, attention is diverted from what is crucial, the subjective, that we are not Christians. . . .

$x^6$ B 232  *n.d.*, 1853

« 6843  *About Myself*

October 13

No doubt some creativity still slipped into what I jotted down about myself in the journals of 1848 and 1849. It is not so easy to keep such a thing out when one is as poetically creative as I am. It appears the minute I pick up my pen. Strangely enough, in my inner being, I am much clearer and much more concise about myself. But as soon as I want to put it down in writing, it promptly becomes a creative process. Similarly it is also strange that I have no desire to put down the religious impressions, ideas, and expressions which I myself use; they seem to be too important for that. Of these I have a few—but I have produced quantities of them. But only when such a phrase seems to have been consumed,[3204] as it were, can I think of jotting it down or letting it slip into what I write.

Now I nevertheless will again put down a little about myself.

There are two thoughts which I have had so long that I actually cannot determine when they arose. The first is: there are men whose destiny is to be sacrificed, in one way or another to be sacrificed for others in order to promulgate the idea—and because of my cross I was such a person. The second is that I would never have to work for a living, for one thing because I believed I would die very young, and for another because I believed that out of consideration for my particular cross God would withhold from me this suffering and task. Where does one get such thoughts—I just do not know—but one thing I do know, I did not read them or get them from anybody.

Now I will briefly go through my life.

When I left "her" I begged God for one thing, that I might succeed in writing and finishing *Either/Or* (this was also for her sake, because *The Seducer's Diary* was, in fact, intended to repel, or as it says in *Fear and Trembling*,[3205] "When the baby is to be weaned, the mother blackens her breast.")—and then out to a rural parish[3206]—to me that would be a way of expressing renunciation of the world.

I succeeded with *Either/Or*. But things did not go as I expected and intended, that I would be hated, loathed, etc. —O, no, I scored a big success.

So my wish to finish *Either/Or* was fulfilled.

Then I should have gone off to a rural parish as a country pastor. I am bound to admit that after writing so much in such a short time, after the sensation created here at home, I more or less forgot about that idea. Furthermore, such a powerful creativity had awakened in me I could not resist it. Something else happened, too: I became an author but turned in the direction of becoming a religious author.

Soon that second idea popped up again (a rural pastor). I intended to finish writing as quickly as possible—and then become a rural pastor.

With every new book I thought: Now you must stop.

I felt this most strongly in connection with *Concluding Postscript*.

At this point I meant to stop—then I wrote the lines about *The Corsair*.[3207]

From that moment on my idea of what it is to be an author changed. Now I believed that I ought to keep on as long as it was in any way possible; to be an author now, to be here, was such a burden to me that there was more asceticism involved in this than in going out in the country.

Then came 1848.[3208] Here I was granted a perspective on my life that almost overwhelmed me. As I perceived it, I felt that a Governance had guided me, that I actually had been granted the extraordinary.

But simultaneously another thought became clear to me, that if I actually should be the extraordinary, I would have to be required to act appropriately in character, be willing to live in poverty, suffer in a way I had not previously imagined.

That was 1848. Strong I have never been. During that time there were a few reminders of the closeness of death—then I began to think that I should find a man I could initiate into my cause if I died. Professor Nielsen,[3209] who for some time had sought an intimate friendship with me, was selected. (Both the journals and the loose papers contain information on this.)

Here again I was delayed.

Time passed. I thought somewhat like this: If you cannot undertake the extraordinary in character, well, then abandon all the latest works and try to do something about your transitory needs; in that way you will be able to be successful—for I have long believed that I am related inversely to the age, so that if I am going to have temporal success it will have to be by curtailment.

I have always regarded being truthful as essential—well, then, I will direct my endeavor along finite lines.

At the same time thoughts of "her"[3210] awakened, for if there is to be curtailment, if I am to have temporal success, then she must come to the fore.

Occupied by these thoughts, time passed. I suffered very much.

The *Summa Summarum* was that I shrank from the thought of abandoning the idea—and I decided to put out the latest work (*Practice in Christianity*[3211]). I wrote to the printer, who asked to have the manuscript the next day—then Councillor Olsen[3212] dies. How amazing! If I had known the day before, I would not have written to the printer but would have waited longer. Now I regarded the decision as final. But nevertheless there was a curtailment; therefore the last work became pseudonymous.

Again I thought of becoming a rural pastor—but for different reasons now, for now it is a matter of financial help, doing something about making a living.

Here I am brought up short, I am stopped by the thought: As a Christian do I dare make my task a finite endeavor.

As far as "she" is concerned, I cannot do anything. For one thing I must continually consider it enormously risky to disturb the relationship (see entries in the journals of 1848 and 1849); for another, I do not dare do it because it will signify to me that I also am deciding something else, to make my task a finite endeavor. This is why I have not been averse to the thought that if in one way or another she were to request, to seek, a formal and definite reconciliation with me, I would consider it a hint from Governance that I curtail and finitize my endeavor.

I am getting more and more overtaxed—to write seems almost foolish, and to starve, on the other hand, is more likely to be Christianity. For what is Christianity? After all, Christianity is not a sum-total of doctrinal propositions but is service in character.

For half a year now I have altered my way of life; everything is directed to seeing what I can bear.

Yet it seems to me that asceticism is sophistical—and so I come to grace again.

The N. T. clearly rests on the assumption that there is an eternal damnation and—perhaps not one in a million is saved. We who are brought up in Christianity live on the assumption that all of us surely will be saved.

There are moments when it seems to me I must lay hold of the former and then in God's name make a clean break.

I contemplate it and then one thing stops me—she. She has no inkling of this kind of Christianity. If I lay hold of it, if I follow through, then there is a religious disparity between us.

"But then how can you doubt that this means you are not to understand Christianity this way," everyone will say. O, but the N. T. is a terrifying book; for it takes into account this kind of a collision with true Christianity.

This is how I am struggling. And then again there are times when everything is so infinitely mild for me, when I seem to understand expressly that my particular task is to bring truth into our lives so that we make it clear and frankly admit that our Christianity is a modification, that not everyone is asked to be a "disciple."

But I must break off. It wearies me to write. There is a lot of creativity within me, an enormous lot. But something else preoccupies me: Do I dare make my task a finite endeavor, do I dare profit temporally by proclaiming—Christianity, which is renunciation of things temporal.

$x^5$ A 146    October 13, 1853

« **6844** *Bishop M.*

If Bishop M.[3213] were an insignificant person, if—well, then it could readily be shown that what he represents is really not Christianity.

But—in the context of piety—the misfortune is that what he substitutes for decisive, essential Christianity is—in the context of the purely human—so spellbinding—O, so spellbinding, so admirable—O, so admirable. And again it is—in the context of piety—my personal misfortune that I have so much of the esthetic, the poetic, in me that I am far too captivated and impressed with this spellbinding and admirable aspect of him, that I shall not speak of how in filial piety I sincerely am drawn to this significant person.

How relieved and happy I would be if my task had been to depict the remarkable, the grand and glorious, the admirable aspects of this man. But now that it is my sad task to do just the opposite (to show that all this actually is not decisively Christian), I feel victimized, and victimized again because I know that I will distress many people, even if perhaps not one of them could get angry with me for it, since he will more or less clearly understand that Governance is involved here and will more or less clearly realize that Bishop M. also is guilty in this collision, so that even if it ended with total victory for Bishop M. and total defeat for me [*changed from*: my total destruction], I would have suffered an injustice at the hands of Bishop M. inasmuch as he has some guilt in this collision.

But now to the heart of the matter.

Bishop Mynster does not place Christianity into actuality but at imagination's distance from actuality (the poetic). He substitutes the artistic for decisive Christianity; for Christian dignity he substitutes the most beautiful and spellbinding edition of human distinction; he substitutes the most refined prudential concerns and considerations for Christian venturesomeness, the most tasteful worldly culture for Christian heterogeneity with this world, a rare, uniquely refined enjoyment of this world and this life for renunciation and self-denial.

XI² A 283   *n.d.*, 1853–54

« **6845** *Bishop Mynster*[3214]

This must be the nature of the indictment against his whole life.

In a confused, secularized, irreligious age there lives a very shrewd man.

However confused, demoralized, secularized, and irreligious a generation is, there will always be some idea of the earnest, the noble, the elevated, the divine.

That shrewd man understands this—and so he offers the elevated, the noble, the religious at such a bargain price that it becomes the most rewarding thing of all, the most refined refinement, to be the earnest one, the noble one, or to be the earnest one who presents the noble etc. In other words, he exploits the corruption of the age to buy at half-price, yes, at a ridiculously low price, esteem as the earnest one, the noble one—this is most demoralizing, and the person concerned is not the least demoralized.

It is easy to see that a genuinely earnest person in such an age must face a life-and-death collision.

XI² A 288   n.d.,  1853–54

### « 6846 *Actuality—Not Attaining Actuality*

How is actuality attained? Very simply—by speaking specifically and then speaking to the specific persons with whom you live.

Take an example. In every age there are criminals whom the authorities punish. There also are some whom the authorities do not punish, and as the world becomes more and more corrupt, it seems that these are the very ones who take control. Thus particularly in these times and mainly in the large cities there prevails a vice called slander.

Now take a clergyman. If he is to be of any benefit, he must witness against the vices of the day. But probably the majority of clergymen would avoid doing it—anyone who does that—well, he does not attain actuality.

But there was one person, a zealous man—he does not seem to have anything against being given this distinction. He wants to witness against this vice.

Wait a bit. When slander has more or less gained the upper hand, there must be a few specific people who are the instigators.[3215] To attain actuality the thing to do is to aim at these specific people and promptly direct the attack against them, thereby exposing oneself to the inevitability that these specific people, in retaliation for this most specific attack, will direct the whole force of their slander against this specific man: that is how actuality is attained.

But His Reverence[3216] does not conduct himself this way. Let me now show how to produce an appearance of actuality which still remains as far removed as possible from attaining actuality.

There was one specific person in the city who was commonly known to be the instigator—this is very seldom the case, a particularity which should have helped His Reverence if he truly had wanted to reach actuality. Is this a sufficiently easy matter? Yes, if one actually wants to attain actuality.

What does His Reverence do now? This specific person flatters His Reverence, pays him public compliments—and His Reverence preaches "about slander." It was a fine speech, and it also was frightfully far removed from "attaining actuality." His Reverence gains esteem as the zealous man who witnesses against the vices of the age, fearlessly, even against the vice which is no doubt the most dangerous to witness against—"slander." At the same time he secures the personal friendship of the slanderer, and thus also makes sure that the latter will not get it in his head to attack His Reverence.

And this is: not attaining actuality! Regard it as one more example of the objective proclamation of Christianity.

XI$^2$ A 296   n.d., 1853–54

« **6847**

A. Have I had any advantage whatsoever from my relationship to Mynster?[3217]
B. But has Mynster not had even more advantages from my relationship to him.

    (a) I have protected him in literature (the System—Martensen[3218]), made it possible for him to choose Martensen.
    (b) fought against his enemies (Grundtvig,[3219] Rudelbach[3220]).
    (c) taken upon myself tasks he should have done (*The Corsair*[3221]).
    (d) converted the appreciation of my writing into a triumph for him.
    (e) resigned myself to having my proclamation of Christianity, which is far more true than his, labeled as extreme, for his was Christian wisdom; resigned myself to it, yes, even contributed to it, I who was the only one who could oppose Mynster.
    Is it I, then, who am ungrateful to him in my enduring all this these

many years I lived with him and now at last when he is dead must for the sake of truth say an honest word?

Or is it he who has been ungrateful to me, he who throughout all these years perhaps flattered me in private conversations but officially rejected me, showed favors to Martensen, at last even to Gold-schmidt.[3222]

XI[2] A 311   n.d., 1854

### « 6848 *The Story of Bishop M.*[3223]

His character was weak; moreover he had a great sense and fondness for enjoying life, and not the simpler pleasures but the more refined ones, yes, the most refined of all: being honored, esteemed, and respected as a man of earnestness, character, and principles, a man who stands firm when everything shakes, etc.

He was in fact a very gifted man intellectually, an exceptional orator, and definitely was brilliantly [*changed from*: enormously] shrewd.

This combination is Bishop M., and this combination has managed to confuse a whole generation with respect to Christianity. For his weakness of character is never seen, since it is covered up by his brilliant shrewdness; his desire for pleasure is never seen, it is accepted as—a new refinement!—devout freedom of spirit in contrast to pietistic anxiety.

How dangerous to be as brilliantly shrewd as he was, something that is demonstrated in every one of his sermons. Yes, there perhaps is not one man in each generation who has the sharp Christian detective's eye to see and to show the dubiousness of this. It is so deceptive, pure doctrine, and yet perhaps not one of his points has been devoid of some kind of shrewdness—well-intentioned—which has altered Christianity or the way of speaking about Christianity a tiny little bit, so that when all is said and done it is not really Christianity. It is well-intentioned, of that I have no doubt; it is well-intentioned— namely, to win us men to Christianity, but on the other hand it ca-mouflages, one is concealed better by this proclamation than by a Christianly correct proclamation, with which it is so enormously dangerous to get involved, both because it sheds light on the speaker himself (as if in hate toward him) and because it so readily provokes men against the speaker.

In this way his proclamation in word and speech was Christianly confusing, but the other side of the proclamation, the speaker's life was also aided by his brilliant shrewdness. There was a yawning abyss between his personal life and "the quiet devotional hours" (when he was the speaker, the orator, and here boldly ventured much). He knew how to use all his brilliant shrewdness to deflect objectively any contact, to eliminate if possible everything, any situation, any event, etc., that might prompt disclosure of just how much he actually was the man of earnestness, the elevated man of character such as the quiet devotional hours led one respectfully to regard him. And he was a virtuoso in this respect—I could write a whole book and yet fail to mention and describe all the modes and means he had at his command, and always with unquestionable virtuosity.

Such was Bishop M. I make no secret of my feelings: I have been infatuated with the man—alas, that is the way we men are. On the other hand my opinion has been essentially the same from the beginning as it is now. But it was my fate to become unusually aware of the situation with Bishop Mynster (with whom—for I make no secret of my feelings —I have always been infatuated and basically still am) and to be obliged to make every effort to make it manifest.

$XI^2$ A 312   *n.d.,*  1854

### « 6849 *The Disagreement between Mynster*[3224] *and Me*

Mynster believed (perhaps even believed it was acceptable to God) that everything must be done to hide the true state of things, for otherwise everything would fall apart; my idea is that everything must be done to make manifest the true state of things.

Think of a painting: a curtain is hanging in front of it, but this curtain is about to fall to pieces. There are two men, and one of them says: Everything must be done to patch the holes. The other says: The curtain must be ripped off so that we can see the picture. The painting is not altered, but the one wants to hide it and the other wants to have it seen. Thus, at least for the time being, my task is not to change the state of things but to assess it; Mynster's was to do all he could to hide it.

$XI^2$ A 314   *n.d.,*  1854

### « 6850 *Just Measure the Distance*

Consider what once absorbed the Christian with a passion, with a fear and trembling and quaking which nowadays scarcely any poet is able to imagine: the decisiveness of eternity, the accounting, the judgment. Consider this and remember that what preoccupied them was precisely what it was to be a Christian!

And now—now eternity has become a figment of the imagination; poets sit and play around with it, write apocalyptic comedies[3225]

——but we are all Christians. What a distance between being a Christian in that sense and being a Christian nowadays—that is if one can be a Christian in the latter mode, which incidentally is just as strange as someone's being a violinist by virtue of not being able to play the violin.

$XI^2$ A 321   *n.d.*, 1854

« **6851**

The opposition in the realm of the ecclesiastical is not at all in character; it is right, at least partly so, in what it says but is not in character. Therefore the tactic to use against it would be to introduce the ideals, thus forcing it into character or making it obvious that they are without character.

Fenger[3226] of Slotsbjergbye wrote an article in *Nordisk Kirketidende* about eternal punishment, in which he affirms this and scoffs at Christians who imagine that they are Christians without having heaven and hell. From a Christian point of view he is right. But he is positively not in the character of what he says. To believe that there is a hell, that others go to hell—and then get married, beget children, live in a parsonage, think about getting a bigger parish, etc.—that is frightful egotism. But the N. T. is not like that. Anyone who believes that there is a hell, that others go to hell, is *eo ipso* a missionary, that is the least he can do.

Rudelbach[3227] (and Grundtvig[3228] likewise) cries out that it is the state church which ruins Christianity—and both of them remain in their positions in the state church. Grundtvig takes the most desirable one in the whole country, and R. gets a huge salary.

$XI^2$ A 334   *n.d.*, 1854

« **6852**

In our age, which levels[3229] everything, soon not only birth, fortune, etc. will be the object of hatred and envy, but presumably being intelligent and talented, being very industrious, etc. might very well provoke persecution. Just let someone dare to express and insist that he will be eternally saved and the others will go to hell—if it is someone who cannot in smug conceit and superiority be pitied and dismissed as half mad—well, then persecution is inevitable. But nowadays no one is a Christian in character, one is a Christian without the distinction between heaven and hell, we will all be saved together, eternity is simply a leveling—so we think.

XI² A 335   n.d., 1854

« **6853** *Bishop Mynster*³²³⁰

March 1, 1854

Now he is dead.

If he could have been prevailed upon to conclude his life with the confession to Christianity that what he has represented actually was not Christianity but an appeasement, it would have been exceedingly desirable, for he carried a whole age.

That is why the possibility of this confession had to be kept open to the end, yes, to the very end, in case he should make it on his death bed. That is why he must never be attacked; that is why I had to submit to everything, even when he did such a desperate thing as that matter with Goldschmidt,³²³¹ for, after all, no one could know whether this might not be the thing that perhaps could influence him so that, touched by what he had done, he would still come forth with that confession.

Now that he has died without making that confession, everything is changed; now all that remains is that he has preached Christianity firmly and fixedly into illusion.

The relationship is altered also with respect to my melancholy devotion to my dead father's pastor, for it would indeed be too much if even after his death I were unable to speak candidly of him, although I know very well that there will always be something prepossessing for me in my old devotion and my esthetic admiration.

My original desire was to turn everything of mine into a triumph for Mynster. As I came to a clearer understanding later, my desire remained the same, but I was obliged to request this little confession, something I did not covet for my own sake and therefore, as I thought, could very well be done in such a way that it would become a triumph for Bishop M.

After our secret misunderstanding, I hoped that I at least could avoid attacking him during his lifetime; I also considered it possible that I myself might die.

And yet I came very close to thinking that I would have to attack him. I have heard all his sermons except the last, but it was not sickness that prevented me, for I was in church where Kolthoff³²³² preached. I took this to mean: now it must come, you must break the tradition received from Father. It was the last time M. preached. God be praised, is it not like guidance.

If Bishop Mynster could have yielded (something that could, after all, have been concealed from the public, for whom it could have become his triumph), my external situation would also have been much more free from care than it was; for Bishop Mynster, who secretly did indeed make concession enough to me in the intellectual sphere, in his secular shrewdness counted on it ending with my yielding to him in one way or another because financially I would be unable to keep on opposing him. Something he frequently said in our conversations, although not directed at me, was very significant: It does not depend on who has the most power but on who can stick it out the longest.

XI[1] A 1     March 1, 1854

## « 6854 *My Relationship to Bishop Mynster*[3233] *in the Shortest Possible Resume*

---

March, 1854                                              S. Kierkegaard

---

Lest at some time I come to stand in a much too curious light, from a Christian point of view, in the verdict of history because of my characterization of Bishop M., it probably is quite in order for me to give an explanation, something I owe both to Christianity and the circumstances and to my own striving, which in its Christian intent is related to Bishop Mynster's proclamation of Christianity. Now that he is dead,[3234] I can do this. It was my desire, for me a very special desire, to hold it in abeyance as long as he lived—I thank Governance that it was granted. Only I know how difficult it was for me toward the end, how close I nevertheless was to having to deny the fulfillment of my wish.

What led me to take the position I took to Bishop M. was in part something purely personal and in part a Christian concern, and that is why I refrained from saying what I Christianly thought of his proclamation of Christianity, with only one exception[3235] and then guardedly and very briefly.

---

When one considers that Bishop M. reached seventy-eight years of age, one must wonder very much how it came about that this man's proclamation of Christianity never was the object of any attack. Whether it ought to have happened earlier I leave open, but in any case from the very beginning I was, if I may put it this way, his natural opposition.

But I did not express this. On the contrary, I gave expression to something else. When I had completed the esthetic part of my writing, when on the largest possible scale I had made room for Bishop M. (in a postscript to *Concluding Postscript*[3236]), made room for him as the one and only in Denmark, I went to him. I said: I am in complete disagreement with you, as much as is possible. To tackle the matter in that way was personally very satisfying to me. My thinking was: Privately I will tell him how much I am in disagreement with him—I owe that to the truth—but outwardly he is not to be diminished by an attack; on the contrary, he is to be elevated even above his actual worth, for he is a representation of which much must be made.

Bishop Mynster answered: You are the complement to me.

I will not dwell on whether it is not really a strange division that the one, rewarded with all the worldly goods and advantages, takes Christianity in such a way that it provides every possible enjoyment, and that the other, certainly more intensely engaged than any pastor in Denmark, rewarded with ingratitude, even contemned, on his own account must proclaim Christianity, and then the first one does not even put in a word for the second but limits himself to saying it privately to him in his living room. This I will not dwell upon any further. I did not ask to have it otherwise. It was completely satisfying to me; it satisfied my melancholy disposition; it satisfied my devotion to the old man, my late father's pastor; it satisfied my esthetic admiration for all the exceptional qualities in Sjælland's much admired Bishop.

But there is another difficulty involved in this matter of a complement. If it were the case that Mynster's proclamation of Christianity was truly related to a complement, then, whether or not this complement was present, one ought to have been able to detect it in his proclamation, it must, so to speak, have been manifest that it was related to a complement. But such was not the case. On the contrary, Bishop M. had, as they say of a sketcher, rounded off, finalized, his proclamation of Christianity; it was Christianity lock, stock, and barrel, capped and crowned, the true Christianity. —Only when someone comes along who in profound veneration[3237] completely disagrees with him—only then does Bishop M. have his eyes opened and says: It is the complement to me. This is dubious.

And there is something else dubious about this idea of the complement. If my activity is really a complement to his proclamation, then this certainly must be mentioned officially. It is not good enough to say: Officially Bishop Mynster's proclamation of Christianity is true Christianity; privately Magister Kierkegaard is its complement. I do not say this on my own behalf; I require no change. To me it is good just as it is. It satisfies me personally, and whatever Christian motive I may have had could not have anything against it.

Time went on; I was quite satisfied providing the complement.

But it cannot have been long before Bishop M. became wary and said to himself: Despite all this man's honest devotion to me, there is something almost fatal about this complement; at times it seems as if it all must end with the complement's overrunning my proclamation and rendering it false. As far as I am concerned that was not my aim at all, and if it happens I am innocent. If it happens, it has to be the result of the dubiousness of privately having a complement which one does not have officially—otherwise it can never happen.

Time passed, and now we are in the year 1848. It was a catastrophe. In a catastrophe like that, the Christianity Bishop Mynster's proclamation represents is utterly untenable. If in the opposition there is one single man of character, then everything is lost—here I am looking at it from Mynster's side—because what Bishop Mynster represents is not Christianity. From a Christian point of view it is a toning down, a blurring, which can be harmonized with Christianity only by means of a confession. Up to a point Bishop M. has surely seen this, but he probably has thought: There is not one single man of character in the opposition—*ergo,* we do not need to do anything at all.

That was not my view. I believed that Christianly this was not allowed, that Christianity is indeed the truth, and consequently one does not dare avail himself of the accidental circumstance that at the moment there is not a man of character in the opposition. No, one must perceive what truth there may or could be in the opposition and then make an admission. I was perhaps as much in disagreement with Bishop Mynster on how the established should be defended as I was in agreement with him that it had to be defended as vigorously as possible. I believed it should be defended Christianly; he perhaps thought: I will manage with my secular sagacity.

I then turned my attention to the official proclamation of Christianity locally, to Bishop M., to see if he intended to do anything. No, Bishop M. stays put (good-natured journalists have—what cruel satire!

—portrayed this as admirable); while the old world to which he belongs is falling, he stays put, "he fits."

Well, then the complement must do its best. Here lies one of my books, called *Practice in Christianity*. This is from a time of catastrophe such as 1848[3238] and thereafter, with an official proclamation of Christianity resembling the Mynsterian proclamation, the only possible defense for the established. It defends it by making a confession to Christianity, not by concealing or covering up.

Before sending the book into the world, I had tried out of Christian concern to influence the old gentleman in various ways, somewhat like this: "You are an old man now, Bishop M. You have enjoyed life as very few people have done; in all human probability you have only a few years to live—then dedicate these last ones to the service of Christianity—put all your dignity, use all the oratorical power you have, come before the people, but do not address your words to the listeners, no, turn to God in heaven (dare to use your own self [*changed from*: dare to accuse yourself] and then say: The confusion of these times has taught me that I have been too mild in proclaiming Christianity; I have toned it down. I do not owe it to you listeners to say this, but I owe it to you, O God! Do that, do it, and you will see the enormous effect it will have. Do it; you cannot ever rule as long as you have not made this confession to God. But do it—and then take up the reins."

So I sent the book[3239] out. It is a defense of the established, not by concealing and covering up, please note, but my making a confession to Christianity. Properly understood, Christianly understood, this was the only possible defense for the established as well as the most fatal blow to the opposition. However much I wanted to, I did not dare directly advise or ask Bishop M. to declare himself in favor of the book, for then I would have fallen out of my character, because, although it is true that I have provided the complement, it is also true that if there is falsehood in the Mynsterian proclamation, I must become the judge or the very work I am doing must make it manifest.

Bishop M. proved unable to make a decision, to dare boldly to declare himself in favor of this view.

Now then, being incapable of that, there was only one thing left for him to do if he was to continue to be of significance—he could rise up in all his strength and turn against the complement, curse this book to hell as an appalling abomination, "a profane playing with the sacred"[3240]—in his drawing room one no doubt would have detected symptoms of something like this. As far as I was concerned, I was prepared; I had wished it for Mynster's sake if he would not accept the complement. But I was forced to say to myself: M. is too old and too overtaxed by his work for that.

Since he could not decide either to go along with the complement or to cast his weight against it, the complement naturally began to harass him. In the inconsequential meaning of the word he became passionate—alas, perhaps I, even though well-meaning, was responsible for that! In a word of thanks for the article against Rudelbach,[3241] he wrote a line in which he, even though with his customary caution, lined me up together with Goldschmidt.

If anyone were to ask me if I gave Bishop M. up from that moment on, I would answer, "Yes," and thereupon would answer, "No, I almost began to hope, but in a new way; when a man has flared up passionately, he sometimes—if not goaded further—becomes conciliatory afterward, is moved—this was indeed possible." In any case Bishop M. is so important that if he can be brought to make this confession —that what he has represented is not Christianity but a toning down —then for Christianity this is the most desirable turn possible in Denmark, because Bishop M. is a representation that carries a country. That is why he must not be diminished (so he does not become less as a representation), must not be attacked (for this makes it impossible for him to be representative); that is why there must be a waiting period, to the end if possible, which also completely satisfies my devotedness to him.

But he dies without this confession; hence in the interest of Christianity this proclamation must be protested as quickly as possible—and moreover I also owe it to myself—so that we do not remain stuck in it, do not get a flat continuation of it which may even make the Mysterian proclamation the true proclamation, true Christianity. For even if it were admitted ten times and, if you please, ever so honestly, that there was a pious fraud on Bishop M.'s part to tone down and blur Christianity this way for the very purpose of winning men to it, and even if every minute of his life Bishop M. had been inwardly willing to make the confession to God—something I could never doubt—if such a proclamation of Christianity is to be Christianly tenable in any way, it must in one way or another end with making the confession also to men. This must—Christianly—be required. Christianly it makes no difference at all whether his proclamation was artistically peerless, first rate, his "presence creatively evocative, his language unparalleled."[3242]

If Bishop M. could have been prevailed upon, what could not have been achieved, what an awakening! And also how beautifully it could have been achieved, how solemnly, with what an elevating effect, without any commotion, which now perhaps can hardly be avoided, although it still may be only a misunderstanding. And how gently, how peacefully, how reconcilingly, whereas now there perhaps must be a battle and only God knows how violent. How many tears could have been spared which now perhaps will flow even though in secret; how many a sigh could have been prevented, how many a cry of terror which now perhaps will be heard even though against the will of the anxious. It is possible, even though everything may come only through a misunderstanding, but now it is possible. Is it so hard when a man has gotten to be seventy years old, when a man has enjoyed life and all its advantages on such a scale as Bishop M. but still must have had occasional misgivings about whether all this squared with proclaiming Christianity and with his kind of Christian proclamation, is it so hard then in the seventieth year or the seventy-second year or the seventy-sixth year or the day before one dies to make a confession to Christianity—can it be so hard? It must be, since even the man to whom I steadily remain attached in melancholy admiration and devotion could not bring himself to it. But if it can be that hard, then I can scarcely envision how hard is that which those glorious ones consummated, who with a whole life before them proclaimed Christianity, the foolishness of the Gospel, in self-renunciation, twenty, thirty, forty years, perhaps, in self-renunciation, and who were rewarded with hatred, curses, mistreatment, and a martyr's death.

XI$^3$ B 15    March, 1854

« **6855**

You who are dead,[3243] while you lived you had enough who bowed before you—in order to attain something; I attained nothing, yet no one bowed more deeply before you.[3244] — —God be praised that it could last as long as you lived. You knew it; I never concealed it from you. Thank you for the love and sympathy you have shown by kindly being willing to understand it. Forgive me if I almost plagued you by repeating continually (something I did not forget to say while you were living) that what occupied me chiefly (for despite my admiration I am in complete disagreement with Your Grace) was the memory of a late citizen of the city whom you also recalled in print long after his death, that old gentleman who listened to you, your grateful reader, my father!

You who are dead, at your grave there has now been sufficient trumpeting. And as you once jestingly (and who could forget your jesting, no more than one could forget everything else that was soundly and truly remarkable about you), once as you jestingly said to me, "There must be a little trumpeting," so presumably must it be as you said—but is it not true that a little truth must also be heard, a little truth—and without trumpets.

XI³ B 28   *n.d.*, 1854

### « 6856  *The Wretchedness of My Age*

It is an old story that whatever in one way or another is outstanding, a little exceptional, is likely to have a hard time of it in this world, above all that which in some way is related to truth.

But there is a difference. One age is not quite as wretched as another. For example, it is not so bad when the age actually cannot understand the contemporary and therefore *bona fide* persecutes him. However, the mistreatment is infamous in direct proportion to the age's awareness that the person concerned is superior.

But even when this is the case, it is always better if there is a little authentic passion involved, as in antiquity when it was plainly stated:[3245] Aristides is just, the only one who is just—this is exactly what we will not tolerate. But my age is characterized by the most measly wretchedness. In a public way I am mistreated and everything is done to demolish me if possible—and at the same time everyone privately is friendly toward me, and privately I am acknowledged and respected more than usual—but geniuses, they say (and I no doubt am classified among such), must walk a thorny path − − and that is why (what nonsense!) they must do their best to embitter my life. This situation is just about as mean as it can be; in fact, it is possible only in a country which, *summa summarum*,[3246] is a market town.

XI¹ A 6   *n.d.*, 1854

### « 6857  *About Myself—My Brother*[3247]

My manner of living is such that the greatest possible effort is made to make me out to be insane, and for a whole class of people I actually exist as a kind of half-mad person—and then I have a brother who adroitly manages to contrive the opinion that I represent ecstasy[3248] (generally this term means the same to the public as insane and in medical books is used as referring to a kind of insanity)—whereas Martensen[3249] is level-headedness itself.

XI[1] A 47   n.d., 1854

## « 6858 *A Misprint in* Stages on Life's Way

No doubt there are many and various misprints in my books, and I actually have never been very concerned about them. But curiously enough, there is one in *Stages on Life's Way*[3250] which I have not forgotten over the years and which I would like to eradicate.

It is in "The Banquet," in one of the lines spoken by the fashion designer. There it reads: *Pro dii immortales,*[3251] what, then, is a woman when she is not in fashion; *per deos obsecro,*[3252] what is she when she is not in fashion! Obviously there should be no "not" in the second clause; it should read: what is she when she is in fashion.

Oddly enough, indifferent as I am about such things, this misprint has plagued me year after year, and it has always bothered me not to have it corrected. The lines become so very trivial when the "not" is used twice, which certainly was not the case in the manuscript, and on the other hand it is so characteristic if the latter "not" is not there.

In that very phrase is implied the demonic sarcasm as well as the proof that the fashion designer is not a fool who too solemnly believes in the reality[3253] of his craft, as if he solemnly believed that woman amounted to something when she is in fashion. No, "what is she when she is not in fashion" is ironic sarcasm; now comes the far more profound "*per deos obsecro,* what is she when she is in fashion."

XI[1] A 49   n.d., 1854

## « 6859 *Two Things I Have Had to Watch Out For*

Just as the age wants everything up to a point, so it would not have been disinclined to go along (up to a point) with my cause, if only I had conformed to every other endeavor in the age.

But the point is that simply by conforming to the age I would not have benefited the age but instead would have promoted the sickness of the age; it was plainly my task to remain heterogeneous.

The basic evil of the age is that, for one thing, it secularizes and finitizes every higher endeavor—that is, it denies that a higher endeavor truly exists. —This is why it is so important that I maintain my nonconformity, do not form a party, get followers, perhaps even become a sensate power, so that it practically becomes just as advantageous to line up with me as with the established. No, no, no, thank you. Keep on your own side the profit and the decorations and the velvet etc.—I have to watch out so that there is not the least profit in lining up with me; I have to watch out that I do not spiritually weaken my cause by secularly strengthening it.

The other basic evil of the age is that it is demoralized by intellectuality and has become devoid of character. That is why I have to take care lest my cause become, for God's sake—serious!—a scholarly-scientific discussion, in which a random lot of professors and assistant professors et al. could enjoy participating. No, either indirect communication—or in earnest, a matter of life or death if so be it. But above all—not a scientific-scholarly discussion.

$XI^1$ A 56   *n.d.*, 1854

### « 6860 *A Modern Clergyman*

When I think of what, for example in my father's childhood, was understood by a store clerk, a clumsy, uncouth Jutlander—and what is understood by a store clerk today: an adroit, active lad, a gentleman, etc.—this is indeed a kind of progress.

A modern clergyman is just about the same. He is an active, adroit, quick person who knows how to introduce a little Christianity very mildly, attractively, and in beautiful language, etc.—but as mildly as possible. In the New Testament Christianity is the deepest wound[3254] that can be dealt to a man, designed to collide with everything on the most appalling scale—and now the clergyman is perfectly trained to introduce Christianity in such a way that it means nothing; and when he can do it perfectly, he is a paragon like Mynster.[3255] How disgusting! It would be fine if a barber could become so perfect he could shave off beards so lightly one would not notice it—but with respect to what is explicitly designed to deal a wound, to become so skilled in introducing it that it is as far as possible unnoticeable—this is nauseating.

$XI^1$ A 69   *n.d.*, 1854

### « 6861

In a volume of German obituaries in the Athenæum,[3256] perhaps from the year 1854, but more likely for 1851–1852, I find in the obituary of a ducal Saxon minister von Gersdorff the following lines by a poet whom I do not know:

*Wer nur die Wahrheit sieht, hat ausgelebt.*
*Das Leben gleicht der Bühne; dort wie hier*
*Muss, wenn die Taüschung weicht, der Vorhang fallen.* [3257]

$XI^1$ A 71   *n.d.*, 1854

« **6862** *The True Situation*

If a man honestly and in all earnestness and with his whole soul prays God that it might be granted him to find it *blessed* to suffer, to be sacrificed for the truth, God will grant it to him.

But the fact is that from time immemorial there has not been one person living among us who has willed to venture on that scale. Indeed all of us, every single one of us, prefers to be exempt—when it comes right down to it in earnest.

That this is so is all too clearly indicated by the situation in Christendom. We have not dared to venture that way but on the contrary have served Christianity with substitutes and thereby fostered the most enormous confusion.

My proposal is surely the mildest of all—ah, how faint and feeble it is! —My proposal is that we at least disclose the true situation.

When you think of it, how nauseating it all is, these millions who play the game of Christianity, celebrate Pentecost—and now we are going to have a bishop ordained[3258] on Second Pentecost Day, and you can be sure that there will be a lot of rhetoric about "the Spirit"—how nauseating, how revolting, when the true situation is that there is not a single one of us who dares pray for the Holy Spirit in earnest.

What a frightful satire! We believe that it is the Spirit that has helped Christianity to spread, so that now we are all Christians—God in heaven! The true situation is that it happened because the Spirit has departed—and thus the phenomenon of diffusion is easily explained, for diffusion and lack of Spirit go together. And the fact of the matter is that the very minute the Spirit comes again the whole thing will collapse, or it will be demonstrated that there is not one single Christian.[3259]

$XI^1$ A 72   *n.d.,* 1854

« **6863** *Protestantism*

If Protestantism is supposed to be something other than a necessary corrective at a given moment, is it not actually, then, humanity's revolt against Christianity?

If Christianity is to be proclaimed as it essentially is in the gospels, proclaimed as and being: imitation, sheer suffering, misery and wailing, sharpened by a background of judgment where every word must be accounted for—then it is fearful suffering, anxiety, quaking, and trembling. Quite right. But where in the gospels does it actually say that God intends this earthly life to be anything else?

What human nature constantly seeks, however, is—tranquillity—*nil beatum nisi quietum*[3260]—tranquillity, tranquillity in order to be occupied with this finite life, to enjoy life here and now.

Is not Protestantism actually man's revolt against Christianity? We want, we must have tranquillity—we want Christianity to leave us in peace. So we turn Christianity around and get an insipid optimism out of the dreadful pessimism which Christianity is in the New Testament. We insist on tranquillity—then be at peace, because with the help of baptism, infant baptism, and grace, a person is saved by grace alone, yes, it is even presumptuous to want to do the least thing to help—with this we shove Christianity out completely and now things are beginning to hum with all the jobs, begetting children, and finite busyness and enjoyment of life, etc., etc.

XI[1] A 76   *n.d.*, 1854

### « 6864  *Bishop Mynster's*[3261] *Earnestness*

Just as when children play, the parents or some other older person is present to see to it that for God's sake nothing serious happens, so Mynster sat with his great sagacity at the head of things, carefully seeing to it—it must really have been strenuous for him—that for God in heaven's sake Christianity was not taken in earnest. And when he felt assured that things all around the country were just as desired, he felt disposed and ready to play along himself, and he tacitly realized (it was, in fact, true) that he was the one who knew how to play the game most artistically: he attired himself in velvet, he made his appearance with admirable dignity, he had great descriptive powers, he was the consummate orator—he wept, he beat his breast, his very look seemed to be of heavenly origin, etc., etc.

XI[1] A 90   *n.d.*, 1854

### « 6865  *Bishop Mynster*[3262]—*Stephen*

In the sermon on Stephen, among Mynster's sermons during his tenure as Bishop, he makes this point: Let us in this hour strive to repeat after Stephen: I see the heavens open.

To repeat after him! Well, the rest of it does not even remotely resemble Stephen: a man in velvet, rewarded with every earthly good, a connoisseur in enjoying it—and a martyr. But the man in velvet repeats it after him.

Is this not theatrical, and is not this kind of discourse directly related to—theater criticism.

XI[1] A 92   *n.d.*, 1854

« **6866** *Nonsense*

One would think that soon we could be all through with this nonsense: "After all, it is nothing but nonsense."

True enough, but nonsense knows how to mystify: it dresses up in a hundred thousand, a million different forms, and yet it is the same old nonsense.

You stand there, having talked with a man. He was of medium stature, blonde, wearing a brown coat—he was a muddlehead, but you are close to hoping to get rid of him. The minute he leaves along comes another: a tall, heavy, swarthy man in a blue dress coat—but is this not the same man? Certainly not—alas, but it is the same old nonsense.

And so on *ad infinitum.* No animal is as prolific as nonsense, except that nonsense brings forth a hundred thousand, millions of brats—who all look different but still are the same old nonsense.

In a given time so and so many millions live in a country—*essentially* they all say one and the same thing. What is deceptive is that visually they look different.

And then again there is the added danger that nonsense is indeed a sensate power.

\* \*

"Nonsense" is an illusion. Only that which relates to idea and lives primitively is living. All the rest is optical illusion. At death it disappears completely, just as when the comedy is over.

It is this cherished assumption of being saved—just like all the others.

$XI^1$ A 121 *n.d.,* 1854

« **6867** *The Collision in My Public Life*

The collision which is my public life is perhaps rarely experienced; and I dare not expect to be understood by my contemporaries—my life is pitched too high for that.[*] Yes, much too high. This reminds me of the late-departed Bishop Mynster.[3263] It is abhorrent that all his life he assumed the posture of profound Christian earnestness—and his honest objection to me was that my cause was too lofty—and thereupon he even took part personally in the scurrilous meanness toward me.

My collision is this. In a little country, in a limited context, there lives a man of extraordinary talent, favored with independence, with a rare gift to attract individuals to himself.

Then he begins to work. His first piece of work is really sufficient, all the hurdles are surmounted, everything opens up to him or must bow before him.

But now comes the collision: this person is both too depressed and too religious to want to be a success in this world. Furthermore, he has too much love for the ideals and the truly glorious ones who once lived for him to want to allow the idolization of a market town.

So he alienates—always after the calmest and most dedicated reflection, and now the market town becomes more and more enraged over—his pride, arrogance, etc.

The few who have the prerequisites to see the nobility of his conduct are envious of him and therefore exploit the difficulties he creates for himself, this incitement of mediocrity against himself, mediocrity which of course is able to see it only as insanity or pride for someone to defend himself not against derogation but against jubilant elevation, something for which anyone should be slaphappy.

This is the collision. Mynster's many years of ignoble footling proclamation of Christianity, which has gilded mediocrity, naturally has contributed to the fact that in Denmark there presumably is not one single person who is [not] in the power of mediocrity.

This is the collision. My remuneration in this world is suffering. I await in the next the reward that when I see the glorious ones they will concede that I treated them with integrity, that I did not take advantage of the market town to attribute to myself what belongs to them.

Thus I believe that I perhaps will not, as Bishop Mynster wishes, lie in my grave as an honorable man[3264]—for this recognition on the part of my contemporaries I do not expect.[†] But I expect that this will be the verdict on me among those glorious ones.

Inasmuch as Bishop Mynster's wish has come to my mind, let me make a comment on it. His memoirs practically end with this wish. It is like him. In a certain sense, he was a deceiver on a grand scale. Therefore this last insult is also as it should be. It seems to me that when one has defrauded the glorious ones on the scale he did by falsely enjoying a lifetime of esteem as if he were one of the glorious ones— it seems to me that one ought then not be so immodest as to wish to lie in his grave as a man of honor but be grateful that it lasted as long as he lived.

[*]*In margin*: Note. And that posterity will give the appearance of

understanding me is, of course, nonsense, for in contemporaneity posterity would act just the same as the contemporary age.

†*In margin*: Note. That is, I do not expect the present age to understand the extent of my honesty and integrity toward the glorious ones—because dishonesty has not been the charge leveled against me as an author.

XI¹ A 125    *n.d.*, 1854

### « 6868 *The Truth of the Matter*

Speaking purely humanly, Christianity in the New Testament is utter terror; neither Judaism nor paganism has anything as terrifying —this is also the judgment of contemporary paganism and Judaism.

Paced by the founder and the apostles and on the strength of this thrust, it goes for a short time—but soon begins the story that is really the story of Christendom, the story of a cunning way of discarding Christianity, not by revolting, please note—God forbid, no, they dare not do that—but by hypocritically changing it, by contriving an appearance as if what they had was Christianity, although it is just the opposite. Compared with this story of Christendom's lie, all the crime stories in paganism and Judaism are like child's play.

Christianity is the religion in which belonging to the religion means to be a priest (consequently no laymen): to be a Christian means to be a priest.

Furthermore, Christianity is the religion in which to be the priest also means to be a sacrifice oneself (therefore not a priest who offers the sacrifice—to say nothing of living on the sacrifice).

As stated, then, to be a Christian means to be a priest, and consequently to be a Christian means to be sacrificed.

That kind of worship, you see, is not what we men like at all.

So step by step through the long, long history which is called Christendom, the craven and hypocritical attempt to reverse this whole religion has succeeded so that eventually in Protestantism it became a refined enjoyment of life.

What was so terrifying, and so it was at first, that even the toughest masculine nature quaked at venturing out—yes, one shivers to think of it, as a child might plead and beg to get out of something—while God nevertheless calmly ordered to advance, what was so terrifying that even the most honest of men preferred to desert—while God nevertheless ordered him back—this is now—how disgusting!—this is now an idyllic story of begetting children, etc., an idyll in which the pastor, himself a begetter of children and family man, plays the accompaniment for this idyllic nonsense and gets six dozen eggs for every child born in the parish, so that it is especially necessary for the pastor to have learned arithmetic in order to be able to count both the eggs and the other—and this is supposed to be New Testament Christianity.

XI[1] A 128   *n.d.*, 1854

### « 6869 *Just a Word about Prof. R. Nielsen's Books*[3265] *after 1848*

Lest my silence be misinterpreted as consent, just a word: *from my standpoint* I not only cannot give approval but must categorically take exception to Prof. Nielsen's books. Indeed, although I have had various experiences as an author which cannot rightly be called pleasant, still Prof. Nielsen's conduct is the only thing that has distressed me, even deeply distressed me. —This, then, to prevent if possible the misinterpretation of my silence as approval. Incidentally, it will readily be seen that this implies no judgment whatsoever on Prof. Nielsen's books from any other standpoint whatsoever.

Why I must categorically take exception to Prof. Nielsen's books, why Prof. Nielsen's conduct has distressed me, even deeply distressed me, I shall not elaborate. Space does not permit. Moreover, very few have the background that would enable them to understand me regarding this matter. The one best qualified is Prof. Nielsen himself, and this I have repeatedly said to him privately and may do it again.

I can, however, explain briefly why I have been silent until now. In the first place I was always personally prompted to wait and see if the "next book" would be such that from my standpoint I might be able to approve of it. In the second place, Prof. Nielsen is a man of such knowledge and talents that he bears waiting for a while. In the third place, I knew that Prof. N. had enthusiastically spent time studying my writings, by which, linguistically and stylistically, he is as if possessed. In the fourth place, Prof. Nielsen's conduct had brought him unpleasantness from a quite different quarter, and therefore I was unwilling (especially as long as the actual leader of the coterie, the old bishop, was living) to express my judgment when it could not be positive. In the fifth place, on my own account I had to give careful consideration to this step since my own experiences had taught me that to a large extent I would get the blame for it in the city where I live, where I, laughed to scorn—eyes up!—have had the honor to serve Christianity.

XI[3] B 13   *n.d.*, 1854–55

### « 6870 *The Wretched Age*

..... I have made various sacrifices, and if I now carried it to the point of genuine self-denial, would any of my contemporaries, I wonder, be inspired to imitate me? No, no. Something else would happen instead. A few assistant professors would avail themselves of the intellectual output of my life—for lecturing. And since they seem to have an eye for advantages, they would profit from it and consequently would be understood by their contemporaries. And a few poets would avail themselves of the tensions in my life and find in them a motif for poetic portrayal; and since the poets today have an eye for advantages, they would profit from it and consequently would be understood by their contemporaries, who also might have been remotely influenced by my presence. And thus even in my lifetime I would be turned into profit.

Poets today probably have long felt that it would be highly desirable sometime to have an unusual *Erscheinung*[3266] become manifest in actuality—it would help people to believe a little more in the romantic novel; it is so long since anything unusual has been seen that the novel itself is beginning to suffer from it. Just as one longs to get fresh meat after being away at sea for a long time and having only salted meat, so one wants to get the impact of something unusual, not to imitate it, no, no, but to be able to use it for a poem, and so that the public might be more receptive to the poem.

Poetry itself, the modern novel, no longer dares presuppose so much faith in the unusual by the reading public that they are able to believe in it—even in the novel. Actuality is that insipid and flat and wretched. Because the poets have not dared presuppose this faith, it has become common in our day for writers to reverse matters and try to give the effect of actuality: a real-life story, a story of real life, etc.

And, not to omit this point, that was why I turned the relation around and concealed what in substance was from actual life by always using the phrase: psychological experiment.[3267]

$XI^1$ A 131   *n.d.*, 1854

### « 6871 *About Myself*

Among the various ones who have been called out in an exceptional way by Governance, there have perhaps been not a few who have had greater capabilities and gifts, and many have had greater knowledge, and all perhaps have had greater zeal and enthusiasm—but no one, not one has had a more difficult task, not one in Christendom.

To strive against princes, popes—what a relief it is, after all, especially as we come closer to our own time—compared to striving against the masses, the tyranny of peers, against the leering of brainlessness and bestial nonsense and depravity.

Outside of Christianity Socrates stands alone—you noble, simple wise man—you were actually a reformer.

XI$^1$ A 133   *n.d.*, 1854

« 6872 *My Task*

is new in such a way that there literally is no one in Christendom's 1800 years from whom I can learn how to go about it.

For everything that up until now has been of an extraordinary nature has worked in the direction of spreading Christianity; whereas my task is aimed at putting a stop to a mendacious propagation, also at getting Christianity to drop a whole mass of nominal Christians.

Thus none of the extraordinary ones has so literally stood alone as I, even less has understood it to be his task to ward off in order to remain alone, for if there is to be a halt, it is easy to see that the fewer the personnel used for bringing about a halt, the better the task will be done.

Well, well, this will be something for the assistant professors once I am dead. Those infamous rascals! And yet it is futile, even if this, too, is printed and read again and again, it is still futile. —The assistant professors will still make something profitable out of me, will teach directly, perhaps adding: The singular character of this is that it cannot be taught directly.

XI$^1$ A 136   *n.d.*, 1854

« 6873

The real plebians are recognizable as men who are unfit for anything else than to be spectators, who stand and stare and gape or who at most are devoid of character, foolishly wanting to be included in the crowd—to whom it never occurs to want to be themselves the ones who act as individuals in a higher sense.

XI$^1$ A 137   *n.d.*, 1854

« 6874 *The* Berlingske Tidende*'s Review of*
*Martensen's Episcopal Ordination Sermon*[3268]

When one orders, for example, a four-dollar Christmas cake from a baker, one gets not only a much larger cake than one costing one dollar, but the baker feels that at that price he ought to use the best quality butter, many spices, etc.; therefore if a piece were cut from each of the cakes, the one costing a dollar and the one costing four dollars, a connoisseur, such as a baker, could taste which one was from the four-dollar cake. —When one orders a funeral oration costing twenty-five dollars from a clergyman, one gets not only one which is a good deal longer than a ten- or five-dollar one, but the pastor feels that at that price he ought to use the best quality butter and the most sought-after spices; therefore if one took two full sentences, one from the five-dollar and one from the twenty-five-dollar discourse, and submitted them to a connoisseur (a funeral director, for example), he would promptly detect which one was from the twenty-five-dollar discourse.

So, too, with the *Berlingske Tidende*'s review. When an author advances in civil life, he also advances in merchant Nathanson's[3269] critical institute—that is, in the future the criticism of his performances makes use of a better quality butter, or in any case puts the butter on more thickly, so that here again a fine connoisseur, when shown such a review, but without knowing the name of the author being reviewed, would promptly be able to decide the approximate rank of the author from the way it was prepared, from the stylistic flourishes, etc.

Prof. M., as we all know, just became Bishop of Sjælland—immediately he makes a tremendous advance with merchant N. Read this review. There you see what merchant N. is able to do—the finest and most delicate butter—it is the genuine grand style, the kind Mette[3270] speaks of when she says to Johan v. Ehrenpreis: Speak in the grand style. It is the genuine official language; thus, if it would not completely disturb the effect in another way, it should be labeled: Made to order.

XI[1] A 142    *n.d.*, 1854

« **6875 Church Leadership
(Mynster[3271]–Martensen[3272]) and Christianity**

The late Bishop Mynster, everyone must concede, was a master at creating optical illusions, and what he used and excelled in was principally: dignity, exclusiveness, artistic performances, esthetic bravura, etc. By drawing his contemporaries' attention to and fixing their attention upon these qualities that Christianly are completely irrelevant he was thoroughly successful in diverting attention from what Christianly is more important or, more correctly, is the real issue: that Christianity simply does not exist at all.[3273]

Prof. Martensen became his successor, a change, a change so discernible that anyone who has glanced at just the little that has happened will promptly be able to see the change, the new direction, we are now going to have in—optical illusion. Bishop Martensen seems to have understood correctly that what Bishop Mynster used can no longer be used, and this is altogether true. For one thing the repetition of an optical illusion is always extremely dubious, and for another the late Bishop was such a master of his own style that even if Bishop Martensen, the late Bishop's not so deft righthand man, were a good deal more deft in all these aspects than he is, it would still be very risky to have such a reminder as the criterion.

So Bishop Martensen has chosen something new. What he has chosen—and entirely up-to-date—is optical illusion along the lines of what could be called journalistic officiousness, journalistic self-importance and hustle and bustle. Now comes a pastoral letter, now a communication to the pastors, now one to the deans, now one to the parish clerks, now one to the congregational council, all printed, all calculated to interest an esteemed and estimably cultured public, to convince this esteemed public of what a busy church leadership we have, how it is keeping an eye on orthodoxy in our country, how it is doing everything to satisfy the demands of the times—for the big thing is to create official commotion, that there is something official on the move all the time, that there is always something to be discussed, something to do. [*In margin:* somewhat as the French government, when fearing a catastrophe, plans its own diversionary *émeute.*[3274]]

Thus by continually and resourcefully manufacturing new disturbances (incitements) that perpetually draw his contemporaries' attention to what Christianly is completely immaterial, Bishop Martensen perhaps will succeed in drawing all attention away from what Christianly is more important or, more correctly, is the real issue: that Christianity does not exist at all.

And when Bishop Martensen is dead, the same thing will happen to him as happened to Bishop Mynster: there will be one, a possible successor, who will step into the pulpit and in the strongest terms will represent Bishop Martensen as a witness to the truth, one of the authentic witnesses to the truth, a link in the holy chain of witnesses to the truth that stretches from the days of the apostles through the ages[3275]—that is what Martensen did with Mynster. And then perhaps this eulogizer will become Martensen's successor (just as Martensen became Mynster's successor)—and by means of a new version of optical illusion will lead his contemporaries' attention entirely away from what

Christianly is the more important or, more correctly, is the real issue: Christianity does not exist at all.

Perhaps it must go this way, for who indeed is capable of halting Bishop Martensen's momentum, which actually began at the "interment,"[3276] that is, with Bishop Martensen's discourse "the Sunday before Bishop Mynster's interment," in which everyone with a nose for such things promptly smelled a rat.

XI³ B 49   n.d., 1854

## « 6876 *Protestantism, Especially Grundtvigianism*[3277]

In every way the point has been reached that what is called Christianity these days is precisely what Christ came to supersede. This is the case in Protestantism, especially among the Grundtvigians.

Strictly speaking, the Grundtvigians are Jews. I pledge myself to prove that they have a Jewish view of marriage to the degree that they not only regard it as permissible, as Christianity teaches (in contrast to celibacy), not merely as ἀδιάφορον[3278]—no, they believe that one cannot be a real Christian unless he is married, and further, that a flock of children and numerous progeny are the blessing of God, a token of God's pleasure—completely Jewish.

Furthermore, in place of circumcision they have baptism (also an objectivity), which they appeal to quite as the Jews appeal to circumcision.

Furthermore: a genuine Jewish superstition about lineage.

Furthermore: the delusion of being God's chosen people; either that the Christians (the baptized) are God's chosen people or that the Danes are that.

It is Jewish optimism, the most dangerous kind of Epicureanism, that in which the enjoyment of this life becomes the worship of God.

And this is supposed to be New Testament Christianity.

XI¹ A 149   n.d., 1854

## « 6877

To deny God by one's deeds.
Titus 1:16

XI¹ A 153   n.d., 1854

## « 6878 *About My Task*

I would be permitted to say what I have to say in any other way whatsoever (philosophic, as an interesting communication, as witty satire, etc.)—and would make a big success—but not with the character of Christian concern. The present generation knows very well that Christianity does not exist at all,[3279] but it is afraid to have it said and mean that we should then become Christian.

As far as I am concerned, I in fact leaned originally toward carrying out my task by way of dialectical redoubling, not with the character of Christian concern in the strict sense.

But Governance is also in the play and reserves the right to decide in what interest the task is to be carried out.

XI[1] A 171   n.d.,  1854

### « 6879  *About Myself*

It is really abominable. Although I have to put up with living as a caricature, a kind of crazy man, to a whole class of people, I am—but this must not be said—so outstanding to my contemporaries that even while I am still alive minor novelists actually use my life to make their writing interesting.[3280]

Presumably authors of that sort are jovially waiting for me to make a complete mess, collapse, lose my mind, etc.—in order to write about it immediately.

Really and truly, natural scientists are not wrong in pointing to the depressing fact about nature that everything revolves around one creature's eating the other, but perhaps it is reserved to me to call attention to the far more loathesome sense in which men are maneaters.

Preachers and professors eat the dead. Novelists, writers of romances, and minor authors eat even the living. It never occurs to such a scoundrel that he could assist some greater excellence not to succumb. O, no, even if he could, he owes it to his trade not to do it lest he miss out on a poetic motif and the public's eagerness for just that sort of writing.

XI[1] A 177   n.d.,  1854

### « 6880  *Counterfeits*

The counterfeit of using acorns for coffee is easily detected and is not dangerous.

However, an example of more subtle counterfeiting is to use a portion less of the directed amount of meat for the soup and then substitute some seasoning.

That actually was Mynster's brand of counterfeiting,[3281] and it is actually that kind of counterfeiting which is made so much of in just about every age under the name of orthodoxy, whereas it is far more dangerous than all the heresies and schisms.

XI$^1$ A 206   *n.d.*, 1854

### « 6881 *This Sinful World*

This is Christianity's view. Man is a fallen spirit. And just as, for example, in Russia a nobleman who has offended is punished by being put in the army as an ordinary man, so the fallen spirit is punished by being put into the trappings of a slave (the body) and sent to this penitentiary of penance (the world) for the sake of his sins.

But just as the rank and file among whom the nobleman is placed do not notice that it is a punishment but are well satisfied, just so these countless battalions of animal-creatures who lack spirit and among whom the Christian has been placed are very happy and satisfied, find it to be a very nice world, look upon the slave trappings as fancy dress, find it glorious to eat, drink, have a bowel movement, propagate—and just think, mama even got triplets, something the state rewards with a prize, which is just as improper as offering a prize for other bodily functions.

What I am writing here is Christianly so true, so true, and Christianly it has to be said in this way; truly it is high time, for in the name of Christianity all respect for Christianity has been lost on the largest possible scale, and Christianity has been degraded to the lowest paganism.

And yet I can say that what I am writing here is tortured out of me; it is not done intentionally, it is against my will.[*] Alas, I have sympathetically loved men. Generally people who amount to something do not wish to share with others, but that was my life. And my collision came from being unwilling to affiliate egotistically with anyone but, instead, sympathetically loving what it is to be man.

In this manner I went out in the world and got, so to speak, my deserts.

Sad as it is, that is the way it is. Behind the whole thing is a Governance who says: This country is morally corrupt, and as sure as I live they will not escape punishment. For this he will be used ("he" means me). But he will not get off scot-free either, even if he will always have the consolation that I selected him out of love. But he will not go scot-free. In reward for his sympathy, his contemporaries should make his life bitter. That will be good for him, make him tough enough to be rough.

As a rule it is arrogant minds who report to Governance and want to be assigned to shaking things up. Governance cannot use them. No, a sympathetic melancholy disposition is just what guarantees that it is not egotism, and the fact that his contemporaries themselves discipline him by embittering his life is justice's additional solicitude so that what comes will be just exactly what men have deserved.

XI¹ A 209   *n.d.*, 1854

### « 6882

[*]*In margin of 6881* (XI¹ A 209):

Alas, in an earlier period I felt all too deeply the pain that it was made impossible for me to enjoy life, this beautiful human life. The effect on Richard III[3282] was that he decided to make life bitter for others. Not so with me: I intended to conceal my suffering and then make life beautiful for others—who has described marriage[3283] and all these aspects of human existence more beautifully, more charmingly, than I? And then it is men who repay me by embittering my life and thereby, to be sure, bring me farther and farther into Christianity. And then there finally comes a moment when Christianity seems to say to me: My little friend, it was out of love for you that it was made impossible for you to enjoy life. But this had to be hidden from your eyes until you could cope with and bear Christianity, which has a completely different view of this life.

XI¹ A 210   *n.d.*

### « 6883 *Style*

How childish to be duped by such a thing—alas, how true what Socrates[3284] said: Now that I have become seventy years old, it seems to me I ought not embellish my style like a school boy. Although it very seldom occurs to me now, it may awaken, wistfully, my old urge to find delight in word-forms. As a prose writer I believe that simply with word-forms I am able to achieve effects which the poet cannot exceed in truth and beauty.

Let me take as example (and this is the very example which intruded itself upon me today and spoke so beautifully for itself that it actually has gotten me to take pen in hand for the sake of such a childish thing—let me take an in-and-for-itself pregnant thought: Everything disappoints, the hope or—that hoped for. [*In margin:* The

sentence itself—the hope disappoints, or that thing hoped for—is by
Schopenhauer.[3285]] Already there is form here, for the dash is form.
But perhaps the thought is expressed too compactly; therefore let the
thought express itself in such a way that it becomes a somewhat longer
sentence and then a linguistic equation: Everything disappoints: the
hope, what is hoped for does not come, or what is hoped for does come
—and disappoints.[*]

Sometimes I have been able to sit for hours enamored with the
sound of words, that is, when they have the ring of pregnant thought;
I have been able to sit for hours like a flutist entertaining himself with
his flute. Most of what I write is spoken aloud many times, frequently
perhaps a dozen times; it is heard before it is written down.[†] In my
case my sentence construction could be called a world of recollection,[3286] so much have I lived and enjoyed and experienced in this
coming into existence of ideas and their seeking until they found form
or, even though in a certain sense they most often found it at once,
until every detail, even the slightest, was fitted in (for work on the style
was actually a later task—anyone who actually has thoughts also has
spontaneous form) so that the thought could feel, as we say, altogether
suitably accommodated in the form.

—and then the Danish reading public! What has happened is so
true, so true, and so characteristic—my contemporaries have occupied
themselves primarily with the way I dress;[3287] this is the aspect of me
they have understood best. On this point my contemporaries might say
regarding me: They chose the better part. I am not complaining, in one
sense I owe very much to the crudeness of the age; moreover, I think
my experience would have been the same in any age.

XI[1] A 214   n.d.,  1854

« 6884

[*] In margin of 6883 (XI[1] A 214):
The sentence that hope disappoints is a totally ordinary remark;
what must be accentuated is the next sentence. Think of a person who
has passionately experienced that hope disappoints—this very word-
form will either appeal to his passion or bore him. When he hears the
first part (hope disappoints) he will get impatient and think: Are we
going to hear that rubbish again; but then the form of the next sentence will completely satisfy him.

XI[1] A 215   n.d.

« **6885**

[†] *In margin of 6883* (XI[1] A 214):

In another sense most of what I have written has been written *currente calamo*,[3288] as they say, but that comes from my getting everything ready as I walk.

XI[1] A 216   *n.d.*, 1854

« **6886  *The Public—The Daily Press***

Goldschmidt stated someplace in *Nord og Syd*[3289] that if a paper such as *The Corsair* had a sufficient public, it was thereby justified.

Charming! Consequently the public says: We have no responsibility, no guilt; for we are not the ones who write it. G. says: I have no responsibility, for if there is a sufficient public—then etc.

Incidentally, the lines are just as I would have them. They express the sophistry that numbers determine concepts; there is nothing in and for itself, everything is relative, numbers decide the outcome.

But suppose it were utilized this way: If a sufficient public (number) regard stealing as permissible, or if stealing had a sufficient public (number), then it is *eo ipso* also justified. And, after all, one would have the same right to do so, for why should stealing in and for itself be more of a sin than slander, character assassination by means of the press—and furthermore there is, after all, nothing in and for itself; numbers determine the outcome etc.

But the fact is that this cannot easily happen, because the great, great majority of people own a little something and thus are not interested in getting that position established or, as G. says, it cannot get a sufficient public.

It is different with journalistic villainy. Generally speaking, it can be used only against those who in one way or another are somebody, are prominent, for only they can be sniped at. The overwhelming majority are thousands who are nobodies, those lucky people—in our day the only privileged ones—those thousands whom the press cannot attack because they are nobodies and are of no interest to others.

Therefore to these thousands and thousands the press seems a great good—in fact, it is designed to serve their envy without any likelihood of their suffering from it or becoming victimized themselves. That is why journalistic villainy will always have a sufficient public.

This matter of the press is the deepest degradation of the human race, for it encourages revolt from below; a monstrous weapon has been invented that is designed and intended to kill everything that amounts to something, so that only the nobodies are safe; these are by far the most numerous—and thus "the mass" (the evil principle) is installed as the real sovereign.

XI¹ A 242    n.d., 1854

### « 6887  *A Picture of a Strenuous Life*

To be a secret police agent[3290] in the context of regular policemen who are policemen can be strenuous enough. But to be a secret police agent in the context of regular policemen who are thieves—how terribly strenuous!

XI¹ A 258    n.d., 1854

### « 6888  *The Extraordinary*

In one sense it is dreadful, almost fatal, to be the extraordinary under the polemical conditions of the Christian extraordinary. Not merely that it is the greatest possible, an almost superhuman, strain, but this relation of opposition to others and the dimensions of that opposition are almost fatal to all merely human sympathy.

That is why I have steadfastly—sympathy is my passion—desired only to point out the extraordinary.

I recall the words of the dying Poul Møller,[3291] which he often said to me while he lived and which, if I remember correctly, he enjoined Sibbern[3292] to repeat to me (and in addition the words: Tell the little Kierkegaard that he should be careful not to lay out too big a plan of study, for that has been very detrimental to me): You are so thoroughly polemical that it is quite appalling.[*]

Although I am so thoroughly polemical and was so even in my youth, still Christianity is almost too polemical for me.

XI¹ A 275    n.d., 1854

### « 6889

[*]*In margin of 6888* (XI¹ A 275):

I cannot remember exactly whether the dying P. M.[3293] enjoined Sibbern[3294] to say those words to me (You are so thoroughly polemical, etc.), and I am almost inclined to doubt it. But I remember very well the other words he asked S. to tell me the last time he spoke with him before his death. As for the first words (You are so thoroughly polemical), that is what he always said to me while he was living, and S., too, has used them against me several times afterward.

XI[1] A 276   n.d.

### « 6890  *About Myself*

Slight, slender, and frail and, compared to others, with practically none of the physical qualifications making for a whole man, melancholy, sick at heart, profoundly and inwardly ravaged in various ways, I nevertheless was given one' thing: eminent sagacity, presumably to keep me from being completely worthless.

Already as a young lad I was aware of my intellectual gifts and that they constituted my power over these far stronger companions.

*       *

It was precisely sagacity that had to be worked against. Presumably this is why I, who have my work in this area, was equipped with tremendous sagacity.

Alas, but in a certain self-seeking sense I have not had great joy in this power of mine. For this power of mine has been so taken over for religious purposes that by means of more ideal passions and by becoming aware of what Christianity is I saw that the law for the religious is to act against sagacity.

As far as that goes, I am still worthless and weak, for this my power is not used to attain what sagacity usually attains.

But this is precisely why I can also be the preparatory functionary in the area of the religious. I have far, far more sagacity, far, far more resourcefulness than the most sagacious, resourceful person I have known among my contemporaries—ah, but in a certain sense I have all this to make me, humanly speaking, unhappy, make my life difficult, troublesome, and embittered.

But what I have to do I can in fact do; I can obstruct and bring things to a standstill; there is no one alive so cunning and clever that he can devise something so ingenious that my detective eye does not promptly detect it and which my sagacity cannot promptly expose as a trick.

That is why I was so profoundly exasperating to the late Bishop, who undeniably in a finite and self-seeking sense was very sagacious, for he never could understand my sagacity; it never occurred to him to deny that I was sagacious, but the use I made of my sagacity was incomprehensible to him. In fact, I understood the law for his sagacity, but he did not understand the law for mine.

Incidentally, this alone makes it understandable that I must live in the most complete solitariness, for even if I did get someone to understand my sagacity, I would get no one to understand my use of it. Anyone who undertakes to understand me and my life promptly interprets me one exponent lower, does not notice that all the collisions of my life are one exponent higher than those of men generally, that they are voluntarily self-instigated by religiously acting against sagacity, by religiously working against myself. As far as that goes, it is extremely painful for me if anyone takes it upon himself to console me—for he utterly fails to understand the issue. There is a world of difference between these two: someone who happens to be ridiculed against his will and someone who voluntarily demands it of those who idolized him, between someone who despite all effort does not amount to anything in the world and someone who systematically prevents himself from amounting to anything in the world, etc. And worse than all the unpleasantness and nonsense and ruckus and mistreatment, much worse, is the torment of being consoled by someone who utterly misses the point in one's life, especially when this point is so determinative that it makes such a human existence an extreme rarity. I was superior to my contemporaries to an unusual degree. I *voluntarily* exposed myself to mistreatment—and after eight years of this I am presumed to be so weakened that the original qualifying factor may be forgotten now and to be on equal footing with what is seen every day—someone who is trying in vain to make a success in this world. No, poor, miserable market town, no, it will not work. In the interest of truth I have taken care to assemble the various egotisms of the present age in such a way that the truth surely will come to light without my deriving any profit from it, which does not happen to be my aim anyway. But one thing is sure, my report will read that the basest of all is still mediocrity, the most profound damnation is mediocrity—alas, any crime is far preferable to this self-satisfied, smiling, cheerful, blissful demoralization: mediocrity.

$$x^1 \text{ A } 277 \quad n.d., \ 1854$$

« **6891** *Dullness*

Oddly and suspiciously enough, there is a great clamor these days against blasé satiation.

But just look at the actual source of the noise, it actually comes from the self-indulging secular Epicureanism which then wants to declare Christianity to be first and foremost the most dreadful dullness.

As a matter of fact, Epicureanism detects that the shoe pinches, that there is a disintegrating which threatens to disturb the whole dunghill—so it raises a hue and cry about blasé satiation. And to be sure there is much that is nothing but blasé satiation, but it can also be the crisis for Christianity, a breakthrough.

XI[1] A 294   *n.d.*, 1854

### « 6892 *A Picture of Modern Christianity, Especially in Protestantism, Especially in Denmark*

Imagine a country where generally everybody is able to swim—but swimming is understood to mean putting on a life-jacket or tube and then going through the motions of swimming. That is called swimming —and a good deal of attention is paid to who can—as they say—swim the best, make the most beautiful motions, etc. – – –If a swimmer came to such a country, would he not say: You are not swimming at all; this whole business of determining who makes the most beautiful motions is pure nonsense, for not a one of them is swimming.

Similarly when Christianity is preached throughout the whole country by state-appointed officials who make it a livelihood and a career—when the assumption is made that Christianity exists and attention is fixed on who is the greatest orator etc.—is this not nonsense, since Christianity simply does not exist.[3295]

XI[1] A 300   *n.d.*, 1854

### « 6893 *The Way Must Be Changed*[3296]

These words are a stock phrase for my pseudonyms—and strangely enough, they are also entirely appropriate to the meaning of my whole life. There actually is nothing I have touched on that does not bear the secret label with respect to the given: the way must be changed. And in one phrase what is my significance with regard to Christianity, what else but: the way must be changed.

XI[1] A 315   *n.d.*, 1854

### « 6894 *A Genteel Villainy*

Precisely among the most cultured and cultivated of my contemporaries there are some who perceive very well that the rabble persecution and mistreatment I suffer is a mark of my distinction, that I not only am right but that I will also become a celebrity because of it. They are so cultured and cultivated that they see this—and that is why they take part in the ridicule and nonsense and vileness.

Besides being helped by a far higher source, I am helped among other ways by my fortunate objective passion for sleuthing,[3297] the fact that I can completely forget that I am the victim if only I can make a psychological detective discovery.

An objective passion like that is of great help. For example, if someone who is being verbally abused has a similar objective passion for language so that his predominant interest is in the language being used, what a great help it would be.

XI[1] A 378   *n.d.,* 1854

### « 6895 *About Myself*

If my contemporaries could understand how I suffer, how Governance, if I dare say so, maltreats me, I am sure they would be so profoundly shaken that human sympathy would try to wrench me away from Governance (as sometimes is done on behalf of a child mistreated by the parents).

But this is a misunderstanding. For I rest in the conviction that it is out of love, yes, out of love that you do this, O Infinite Love! I know that in your love you suffer more than I suffer, O Infinite Love—even though you cannot for that reason be changed.

But my contemporaries cannot understand this. Even if I were to speak, they could not understand it—even if I were to speak. But as a precautionary measure things are well arranged so I really cannot speak, because I understand that things are so arranged that those to whom I would have to speak would be unable to understand it—a new cruelty, my contemporaries might say, if they could understand it.

Like those in the ox of Phalaris,[3298] whose screams sounded like music—those whom God uses are confined in an even worse way—for all their suffering is always taken by their contemporaries to be arrogance, which means that the contemporaries find joy in bringing more sufferings upon them—because of their arrogance.

But so it must be, O Infinite Love. If a man like that could make himself understood—and then in a weak moment forgot himself and talked out of school: what irreparable loss. That is why, O Infinite Love, you take care to keep such a thing from happening.

XI[1] A 382   *n.d.,* 1854

« **6896** *About Myself*

I was granted a gift, and in such proportions that I may call it genius—this is my gift of being able to converse and talk with any man.

This happy gift was granted to me to hide the fact that I am unquestionably the most silent man in the present age.

Silence concealed in silence is suspect, arouses suspicion; it is almost as if a person betrayed something, at least he betrays that he is silent. But silence concealed in a most striking talent for conversation—that, now, is real silence.

XI[1] A 383   *n.d.*, 1854

« **6897**

. . . . . And when I am dead, how busy all the assistant professors will be stripping me and mine, what competition to say the same thing, if possible, in more beautiful language—as if that were what matters.

How ludicrous an assistant professor is! We all laugh when a Mad Meyer[3299] tugs at a huge boulder which he believes is money—but the assistant professor goes around proudly, proud of his knowledge, and no one laughs. And yet that is just as ludicrous—to be proud of the knowledge by which a man dupes himself eternally.

Yes, you assistant professor, of all the loathsome inhumans the most loathsome, you may very well manage to say the same thing as the religious person has said, perhaps in even more beautiful language, you also may manage to reap worldly advantages with your shrewdness, yes, even honor and esteem such as the authentically religious person never won in this life—but you are duped eternally.

I do not write this as if it could occur to me to hope to convert an assistant professor. How can I hope to influence a person whom Christ's utterances against the Pharisees and against pontificating cannot frighten. Here the verse[3300] applies: They have Moses and the prophets; if they do not believe them, then neither will they believe etc.

XI[1] A 412   *n.d.*, 1854

« **6898** *"Close the Cover"*

So it says in an old hymn.[3301] Close the cover, that is, of the coffin, close it tight, really tight, so that I can really be at peace, well hidden, like a child who is so exceedingly happy when he has found a good hiding place.

Close the cover, close it tight—for I am not lying in the coffin, no, what lies there is not I but what I so very much desire to be rid of, this body of sin, the whole apparatus of the prison I have had to bear.

XI[1] A 423    *n.d.*, 1854

« **6899**

..... It is all too true what people, the practical people, say about me: that I am no good for anything, that I am an utterly impractical man, totally out of place in this practical world.

Alas, yes, I am good for only one thing—and for this I perhaps have an eminent genius—I am only good for loving. Therefore I am completely superfluous, a sheer luxury item in this practical world, yes, maybe even a luxury item that is in the way to boot—so it may end with my getting kicked out of this world.

But love I can! You women, come to me, or to say the same thing in another way, do not come to me. How good are you for loving, you maidens and madams of this miserable generation. No, I am good for loving, and if this were my only genius—it was raised to the second power—concealed in the incognito[3302] that I was the most selfish of all men.

Yes, for loving, that was the only thing I was good for. An object, just an object! But just as the archer whose bow is strung unusually taut has to ask that an object placed at a distance of ten feet for him to shoot at be placed at a distance of 150 or 200 yards, so it was for me. In order to love I had to place the object at a distance!

That was the school in which I was more and more perfected in my one and only genius—to love.

An object, therefore, an object! That was what I looked for and sought.

And then I found it! For you, you, you Eternal Love, you fabulously wealthy one, like all rich men you of course have no need for indispensable articles but, like all rich men, have use only for luxury articles. So you found use for me. In fact, I was the officially acknowledged luxury article in this practical world. You found use for me—and I found the object.

So let the practical age in which I live asininely preoccupy itself with my trousers;[3303] let a trumpeting future preoccupy itself just as asininely with my ideas and books. I have found what I was looking for.

I have found it. "Sure enough," as they say, "but on the mayor's table," meaning that there is something shady about having "found" it. Well, I admit it all right; you, O God, helped me both to seek and to find.

XI[1] A 424   n.d.,   1854

### « 6900

. . . . . I am solitary and alone, I cannot hope to be understood: the young are too young, the old are too stodgy—or, as the beloved poet[3304] of incomparable language has the girl say incomparably of her suitors: "The one is too young to break my wreath, the other too heavy to enter my dance"—except that it does not end for me as for the girl —that I take the third one—no, there was no third one.

XI[1] A 425   n.d.,   1854

### « 6901 *The Difficulty of My Task*

Everything, everything I see around me—but forget it, such things should not concern me—yet everything, everything I have read and heard about (Socrates the only exception, and in Christianity Jesus Christ, for the apostle does not constitute an exception) has constantly construed the task thus: one has something called a cause, or one has a cause in a great, exalted, and profound sense.

So the task, the goal striven for, is to get men interested in it, to win them[3305] to it, to get them to participate, etc. To that end, if I may say so, every sinew, every muscle is strained, or every sail is spread.

This, then, is the task. However, the one striving this way does not at the same time have an equally strong idea that men's interest, participation, etc. are something dubious, are the sure way to travesty, foolishness, and lack of character, that with regard to ideality the participation of men does not increase it, preserve it—no, but rather corrodes it and converts it into meaninglessness, travesty, etc.

It goes like this. One who strives in this way works with all his might to win the support of men—years later (10, 20, or, in proportion to the energy he puts forth, 50, 100, or 200 years) history reveals quite plainly the truth that human support is the way to get ideality destroyed, converted to foolishness and nonsense.

But that striving individual did not have this consciousness when he began. No one, not one of those about whom I have read had at the beginning this perspectival consciousness of what usually comes to light only later with history.

In other words, all the people I have read about (Socrates is the only exception) had only an immediate consciousness of their task, not a reflected consciousness, only an immediate enthusiasm, not a reflected enthusiasm: they stood at the beginning. —History then taught us the end of the story: Socrates[3306] knew the end of the story when he stood at the beginning—he begins there.

But when this is so, the task is (O, Socrates!) strenuous to the second power. That kind of reflected consciousness would kill a merely spontaneous enthusiast, so he would not decide to do anything at all. With loving concern the knowledge of what the end will be is hidden from the eyes of the immediate enthusiast. If he could see the end, his enthusiasm would die.

How appallingly strenuous: at the same time that the task is to relate to men, to be on a divine errand—as Socrates understood his life —and then at the same time to have to guard against men, because one knows as surely as history has ever revealed it with respect to the striving of any long deceased enthusiast that the participation of men is the way to travesty. Alas, yes, so it is; just as every day he lives a man comes one step closer to death (for death is surely certain), so for every man whose participation is won, travesty comes one step closer— travesty, this certainty that is waiting for every ideality.

*          *

But when I think of myself I sometimes can become completely anxious and fearful for myself: where does a young man get a consciousness which would seem to take a long, long life to acquire—that is, if it is acquired that way. "How did he happen to begin?" is the question my pseudonyms constantly raised with reference to the extraordinaries in order to learn something of them. As for me, how did I happen to begin? How sad—as I so often had to say of myself in my younger days—alas, I was never young. When I was a youth I was a thousand years older than an old man! Likewise I must also sadly say of myself: I have never actually been a man! I have never craved social life or had a spontaneous faith in men—and yet (this could be called a contradiction!) yet I am an enthusiast, yes, truly an enthusiast.

*          *

If I were a spontaneous, immediate enthusiast, if I simply had a straightforward task, not a reflected task, what an excellent position my cause would now be in; everything is as favorable as possible to win the support of men.

Look, the Minister of Culture[3307] likes me; Martensen[3308] has become Bishop and he feels strongly that he has been favored as a protégé and has a difficult position—all this disposes him to make everything as easy as possible for me. The attitude among the people is favorable to me, yes, essentially very favorable, because the very fact that I have allowed myself to be ridiculed etc. is beginning to change things for me and to benefit me. As always, in order to bestow its favors on a person properly, the public first of all needs to be allowed to do him wrong. Then, too, in the same vein Martensen's appointment is also advantageous to me, because there is a disposition to let me benefit from being a nobody, from having worked gratis, etc.—that is, I would be able to evoke pathos here.

But when the task is reduplicated, then all this is only an added strain inasmuch as it must be rejected.

No, I have never actually been a man. And there is something inhuman, if you please, in this as well: a young man who—and this idea goes back to my early days—has the idea: there are men whose destiny is to be sacrificed for the others.

XI<sup>1</sup> A 439   n.d., 1854

## « 6902 *To Love God Is to Hate What Is Human*

The human is the relative, the mediocre. Men are at home only in mediocrity. God is the unconditioned. To love God is, then, impossible without hating what is human.

But this hate of the human which Christianity refers to is not something original in any man. No, the baseness and wretchedness of men force it out of one who originally loved men and in a sense continues to love them, that is, in the idea, according to the eternal, but not in the sense of his letting himself be won over to mediocrity.

Sometimes we see a person who is happy and is inclined to what we call loving men. The great rarity, as in my case, is the man who is unhappy and sees that he has to be reconciled to it and then believes that he should be able to help others.

This was my case. But the wretchedness and abjectness of men, which cravenly rewarded my sad, sympathetic desire to help them, taught me, forced me, to seek a closer and closer relationship to God, made it impossible for me to survive without coming to grips with the essentially Christian principle: to love God in contrast to men. I see very well the hand of Governance in this, and Governance must be acceded to in this: it will have its ideas advance, and it knows how to direct.

But this Christian hatred of men is anything but what is usually understood by misanthropy, wishing them ill etc.; no, it is loving them in the idea, ultimately wishing them well.

XI[1] A 445   *n.d.*, 1854

« 6903 *About Myself*

Alas, I have been endowed with the eminent intellectuality of a genius, but I am anything but what might be called a holy man, and anything but one of those deep original religious natures; and an apostle existentially stands a whole quality higher, but in eternity men are ranked existentially.

This is why I feel like a child when I contrast myself to an apostle or even to a figure like Socrates, despite my knowing very well what intellectuality I have compared to that of an apostle, who does not exactly excel intellectually, whereas he existentially stands above Socrates.

I feel like a child. And again on this point an expert would quickly perceive which sphere I belong to, that I belong in the sphere of the geniuses (which at best can be called second rank, and strictly speaking, third rank. Yet there is so much of the existential in me that it cannot be denied that I nevertheless may be said to have suffered for the idea). This belongs to the sphere of genius and is connected with or contributes to the mental depression and unhappiness which is inseparable from genius. Genius is a disproportionate composition. Goethe's comment on Hamlet gives a striking picture of the genius: He is an acorn planted in a flower pot. So too the genius: a superabundance without the strength to bear it.

XI[1] A 460   *n.d.*, 1854

« 6904 *The North*

That the North is the less favored part of the world is seen, among other aspects, in the following two: the harsh climate makes impossible the kind of carefree approach to making a living found in the warm countries, where a philosophical ideality is therefore also more easily attained, a philosophical ideality which does not divide a man so that with philosophy he becomes a professor of philosophy and businessman. For another thing, only in the North do we find this pedestrianism which in so many ways warps the feminine nature and poses problems which simply cannot appear in the South—namely, that a woman is a person who is also useful and profitable. Originally it was not so; originally woman was designed to be a luxury: a companion, an adornment, a decoration. Only in the North does she also have to prove herself useful, and therefore it is also in the North that this question of her emancipation has to arise.

XI[1] A 469   n.d., 1854

### « 6905  *The Sum Total of What I Have Done*

And what is the sum total of what I have done? Quite simply, I have injected just a little bit of *honesty*.

It is like finding something on the road—I would not appropriate it but either let it lie or have it advertised. So with my New Testament in hand I have said: There is something wrong about the way in which we are Christians. Therefore I want to report to you, God! If what Christianity promises actually could be attained on the terms offered these days, no one is more gratefully willing to accept it than I. But I want to report to you and inquire if this all hangs together properly.

But that is scarcely allowed in this—honest (Christian!) world. Dishonesty very cleverly (and I admit that in a certain sense it is clever) maintains the position that the safest thing is to pretend it is nothing at all. Well, yes, that is the safest way, after perhaps having prospered in this world, to be rejected eternally. But I admit that what dishonesty does is, it says so itself, the safest way: "It is the safest way. Above all, let us not meddle at this point. At one time, and happily continued through many generations, there was brilliant success in fooling God and, to use the most affable expression, putting a wax nose on him— so let us not be crazy enough to stir up anything now."

XI[1] A 474   n.d., 1854

### « 6906  *About Myself*

At one time my condition was such that I had the burden of anguish which I may call my thorn in the flesh: a sorrow, a mental anguish related to my late father, a deep grief related to that beloved girl[3309] and everything that was involved. Thus I believed that, compared to the ordinary man, I might be said to be carrying a heavy burden.

Meanwhile I found so much spiritual and mental joy in my work that even the burden of sorrow over sin still did not force me to call my life one of suffering.

Added to all these earlier things, I now have the burden of financial concern[3310] and mistreatment by the rabble.[3311]

Without falsifying or muddling the concept, I may say that my life is a kind of martyrdom, but of a new type. What I as a public person am suffering is best described as a slow death, like being trampled to death by geese, or like pettiness's painful method of execution used in distant lands: being cast to the insects, and the offender is first smeared with honey to whet the insects' appetite—and in the same way my reputation is the honey which really whets the insects' appetite.

Only let it come, the auditing of history—everything is all right, and this includes the fact that this did not just happen, but I *voluntarily* exposed myself to it.

XI<sup>1</sup> A 484    n.d., 1854

### « 6907  *About Myself*

If I would start a movement, form a party, etc., gather numbers —then I would be regarded as being a power. Well, good night! But I still would not be understood. Actually my life is one of the most profound satires on this generation: an altogether solitary man, apparently so weak externally that he scarcely exists—and then an initiation into the secrets of life such as is rarely found, and then only after a long period of time will I really be understood, although I do not mean that men will have become better or different than they are now.

But the satire consists precisely in this that such a little dot has been present, a dot whose influence will prompt a latter generation to reconstruct my life fantastically, rewrite it in order to be able to explain its influence, for the world will always be just as shrewd.

The intensive is always related ironically to the extensive—something along the line of the saying: *"Der Eine hat den Beutel und der Andre hat das Geld."*[3312] Extensity is an enormous mechanism—and intensity, well, the smaller the extensity into which it can be squeezed, the greater the irony. Extensity spreads and sprawls with great complacency—it generally spreads to such a degree that intensity is not permitted to slip in at all with even as much as a little bit of a dot—the situation is all the more ironic—imagine the irony inherent in a huge audience, one so huge that the speaker could not get in the door and could not manage to give his speech at all.

At every moment of actuality, extensity is an enormous mechanism—it does not detect, it has no intimation that it essentially is all played out, that a little dot is to be seen—a dot, yes, esteemed public, a little dot is to be seen. But if it is ludicrous for actors to go on acting after the curtain has fallen, then by rights the given actuality is also ludicrous every time such a dot appears, for the dropping of the cur-

tain means that the comedy is over, and the appearance of the dot
signifies that the given actuality is now over and done with. But, as
stated, the smaller, the more miniscule this little dot can be, if possible
detectable only through a microscope, the more ironic it is. The irony
consists in the disparity between the extensive and the intensive. There
is nothing ironic in routing a given actuality with battalions—that is
sensate power against sensate power, therefore homogeneity, propor-
tionality—but a dot! There is nothing ironic in killing a horse by hitting
it on the head with a club—the quantity of the sensate force corresponds to the size of the horse. But to kill it by sticking it or pricking
it in a particular spot with a sewing needle—there is something ironic
in that. To dispose of an actuality in such a way that it is promptly
apparent that it is finished—there is nothing ironic in that; what has
happened is, after all, apparent. But to dispose of an actuality in such
a way that the last thing anyone suspects is that it is over and done with
—that is ironic, for what has happened is not apparent. No, esteemed
public, what has happened is not apparent. On the contrary, the given
actuality seems to be completely unchanged, the whole mechanism is
in full operation, all the players as busy as usual. And yet something
has happened, but it is not detected; and what has happened is this—
a little dot has appeared. It is visible—that is, actuality does not see it,
but it is to be seen.

XI[1] A 497   n.d., 1854

### « 6908  *The Beginning—the End—the Beginning*

The beginning was: There were no Christians at all.

Then all became Christians—and for that reason there are once
again no Christians.[3313]

That was the end; now we stand at the beginning again.

XI[1] A 505   n.d., 1854

### « 6909

. . . . . Alas, no matter how old I am, when thoughts present themselves I am almost like a child who has been given permission to pick
fruit in the garden and wants so much that he almost transforms joy
into toil and trouble.

XI[1] A 510   n.d., 1854

### « 6910

. . . . . To want to get someone to help me would turn out to be
just as ludicrous as for a darning needle or an awl to want to help do

the finest embroidery for which the sharpest English needle would be too blunt—willing enough, perhaps, but not sharp enough.

XI$^1$ A 543   *n.d.*, 1854

« **6911** *The Specific Character of Corruption in Christendom*

When Christianity entered the world, the depravity against which it had to battle most directly was in the sphere of carnal lusts and cravings, wild unbridled passions, the animality in man.

Then Christianity did enter the world; Christianity was the truth.

The corruption which can follow from this, which is the case with Christendom, is in the nature of the *lie.*

This corruption, in relation to that which has been corrupted, is far deeper than what held sway before Christianity entered the world. Thus the ensuing corruption always corresponds proportionally to what is introduced. For example, asceticism exists to restrain lusts and the flesh. If there is corruption in which asceticism is instrumental or if there is corruption following on the heels of asceticism, it is not sensual lust but unnatural desires.

But the lie is the specific character of corruption in Christendom. Just as the country constable shudders when he comes to the big city and sees the scale of crime there, so a pagan ethicist would shudder at the grandness of the lie which is Christendom; indeed, a pagan ethicist would not have the instruments to measure the depth of this lie which Christendom is.

And the lie is so habitual, such a state of lying that thousands and thousands are *bona fide* thoughtlessly lost in the lie.

It is all a lie, and to such an extent that the only way we try to counteract it is to recognize mutually that it is a lie—to such an extent is the lie official.

What was intended as a blessing but which men themselves have transformed into a curse upon them—Christianity—actually makes liars out of them. This terrible lie—that everyone calls himself a Christian and deludes himself and his neighbor into thinking that both of them are Christians.

How deserved, therefore, the mockery over the human race, this nauseating almost daily telegraph-lie. Rejoice, O human race, that you have invented the telegraph; be proud of your discovery which is so appropriate to the times, calculated to lie on the greatest possible

scale. Just as the Romans branded slanderers with the letter $C$,[3314] so
the telegraph is a brand upon the human race—you liars.

Yes, the lie is the specific character of the corruption in Christendom. Just as in the state of corruption which Christianity found, where
raw lusts and passions were not regarded as sin but rather as something magnificent, so it is now in Christendom with the lie. No one
thinks that lying is something evil; the assumption is rather that it is
just as impossible to live without air—and there is truth in this in the
sense that the very atmosphere of this Christian world is a lie. We
regard lying as unavoidable and we admire the big lie in the very same
way the raw pagans admired violence and plundering on a large scale
and unbridled lusts on a colossal scale.

XI[1] A 551    *n.d.*, 1854

### « 6912 *The Freethinkers' Version of What Christianity Is*

As noted elsewhere [i.e., XI[1] A 161, 162], the state of Christianity
has long been such that one cannot find out what Christianity is in the
so-called Christian church (especially in Protestantism, especially in
Denmark) but has to seek it among the freethinkers. Yet this, too, has
its hazards, because the freethinker, simply because he himself wants
to escape Christianity, sometimes finds a vicious pleasure in exaggerat-
ing Christianity as bitterness. The so-called Church falsifies Christianity by softening it—for we do indeed want to be Christians. The
freethinker, standing on the outside and wanting to bait the Christians,
falsifies Christianity by making it bitter. Of the two, however, the
freethinker's version is closer to the truth than that of the so-called
Christian Church, especially in Protestantism, especially in Denmark.

XI[1] A 559    *n.d.*, 1854

### « 6913

..... In all fairness I cannot ever ask for any help from men,
because I fully realize that the concept of Christianity I represent is not
exactly acceptable to us men right off; on the contrary, it is what we
defend ourselves against with all our might—therefore it is unfair to ask
that they help me. And I must fear this help, however much I wished
to live in harmony with men, I must fear it, for it means that my cause
suffers loss.

On the other hand God cannot help me directly, for then the cause
loses ground; he must help me by knocking me around—and yet it is
out of love, yes, out of love—would only that I were worthy of it.

XI[1] A 560    *n.d.*, 1854

« **6914** *The Prototype*

Bishop Mynster[3315] once thought it strange that the prototype may stand both ahead and behind, as Anti-Climacus[3316] says. He could not get it through his head that the prototype could stand behind. However it is not difficult to understand, as I in fact once understood it. It is similar to a corporal's training of recruits; sometimes he stands in the rear in order to see to it that he has not lost anybody. Otherwise the same thing could happen to him as happened in *Preciosa*[3317] to Pedro the castellan, who marched ahead of his henchmen and when he looked back his henchmen had gone down another road. And this actually is the game Christendom, especially in Protestantism, especially in Denmark, and not least Bishop Mynster, has played: letting the prototype go ahead alone. This, Your Grace, is why the prototype also stands in the rear.

XI$^1$ A 586   *n.d.*, 1854

« **6915**

. . . . . In an age when there is such a craving for originality, there suddenly pops up an originality of such a qualitative character that to be this originality must be a suffering.

This is my situation. Yet I do not complain of the age, for the same thing would happen to me in any age.

A merely quantitative originality is directly recognizable and understandable by way of a given or what is given (and the more inferior, the lesser the originality, the more rapidly and surely it is recognized). Qualitative originality must actually demand faith. But men never wish to put out this effort. When in some future time qualitative originality rests on its results—yes, then it is feted, but then faith is no longer required. Thus a qualitative originality must always suffer more or less, for it cannot possibly begin with its result—and men are incapable of anything more than believing on the basis of the result—that is, they are incapable of faith, they are merely capable of craving —to be deceived![3318]

XI$^1$ A 593   *n.d.*, 1854

« **6916**

. . . . . My life is exceedingly trying; I feel so alien to, so at variance with, what commonly preoccupies men. Day in and day out I detect my heterogeneity in practically every contact and in the most varied ways. Encompassed at all times by curiosity, always a stranger, now envied,

now the butt of laughter, of boorish stares—everything possible is done
to prevent me from being myself and to prevent anyone else from
being himself in relation to me. In every situation I am not actually
treated as a person but as a kind of interesting object, variously understood, something to talk about. If I were to say to a shoemaker: I have
a defect in one foot, could you alter the boot to compensate for it, I
risk that his first concern as soon as he gets home to his family will be
to report: Søren K. has a defective foot. And it may go farther, perhaps
get into the papers; perhaps I may get to read about it in Swedish[3319]
(as I read about my walking), read about it in the papers (just as the
way I dress,[3320] for that matter, is subjected to journalistic circulation),
and then I may have every passerby looking (as they have looked at my
legs and pants for a year now) at my feet and forgetting to get out of
the way although I have the right of way, simply because they must look
at my foot———all that I may achieve, but still the boots would not
be satisfactory.

Certainly this is extremely comical, but it also says something
about how exhausting my life is.

As mentioned, the strain is due, among other things, to my being
altogether different from other men. Either they live solely for finite
goals, and this is the class of men I like best, with whom I would have
been on good terms if the rabble-rousing press had not intervened, or
they pretend to be living for something higher, but this is just a hoax.
In any case the kind of life I lead for the idea is just as different from
the lives men live hereabouts as speaking the Hebrew language is from
speaking Danish—we not only do not share a common effort but in a
sense we do not share a common language insofar as they use the
language fraudulently.

Consider a criminal—his life is different from the life of other men.
But then again there usually are several criminals and together they
form their own world. But imagine being the only criminal—would it
not be exceedingly trying.

Conversely, consider the highest example, the God-man—living in
that manner, knowing that he has come to light a fire[3321]—and it is not
a question of setting fire to a house or two, no, but of setting fire to
the human race— —the appalling strain of being a man and of living
among men and yet being differentiated this way from what it is to be
a man—of this I can form a slight conception.

From this I can also understand what nonsense it is with these
millions of Christians and thousands of clergymen, for if a man has to

experience the tension I do merely to get a slight conception of Christ's suffering—what is it then that the preachers, as the more advanced, preach and the congregations take after.

$XI^2$ A 11   *n.d.,* 1854

« **6917** *An Altogether Unique Kind of Proclamation*

has been entrusted to me, and how strenuous it is to the $n^{th}$ power.

Wherever I look, the law for proclamation until now has always been: If men are willing to accept the proclamation and say to him, "What is it you want us to do? Do you want us to do just what you are doing?"—the answer has always been, "Yes." Not so with me. If all the millions of people alive approached me all together with the greatest receptivity and said: "What do you want us to do? Do you want us to do as you do?"—I would be obliged to answer: "No, there is not one single person alive who shares my task, and, in my opinion, not one person among these millions shares a task with another"— —and precisely this is what I must proclaim. The difference is similar to that between collecting and dispersing; as a rule all proclamation aims at collecting people; mine aims at dispersing them, making them single individuals.

This much is clear. The person who answers "Yes" to the question (Shall we do as you do?) may himself be an individuality, but his proclamation is not the proclamation of individuality. He obviously has a doctrine, and his doctrine does not really make men individualities but specimens.

My proclamation is the proclamation of reduplicated individuality.

But how can I possibly be understood even in the remotest manner in a period when every strategy aims at collecting men and when no one, of course, has any intimation of a strategy aimed at dispersing them or how the one is more strenuous than the other by a whole quality.

Yet this is the path the human race must take.

And my task is this: myself an individuality and keeping myself that (and in infinite love God in heaven keeps an eye on this), to proclaim what boundless reality [*Realitet*] every man has in himself when before God he wills to become himself. But consequently I do not have a stitch of doctrine—and doctrine is what people want. Because doctrine is the indolence of aping and mimicking for the learner, and doctrine is the way to sensate power for the teacher, for doctrine collects men. The proclamation of individuality is: blessedly compensated within oneself —to be sacrificed to men.

In the strictest sense my proclamation is a service of the spirit. Everything proclaimed with the aim of collecting men is connected in one way or other to an animal definition of man. That is why it is so easy. For if the whole thing is just the encompassing of more and more, if specimens are reckoned with and not individualities, then thousands can be had quickly—alas, in a certain sense there are enough of them. But the proclamation of individuality is so slow that just one is already something great, and one must be able to be satisfied with none at all —which in another sense the authentic individual can readily do since he is himself.

My proclamation is similar to someone's declaring: What a beautiful sight the starry evening sky is. Now if thousands were willing to accept his proclamation and said to him: "What do you want us to do, do you want us to memorize what you said"—would he not be obliged to answer: "No, no, no, I want each one to gaze at the starry evening sky and, each in his way—it is possible for him to be uplifted by this sight."

Alas, but man is still an animal-creature, and the indolent inclination to ape and mimic seems to be his second nature. That is why it is so very easy to collect them in a herd; that proclaimer will get thousands who want to learn what he says by rote, perhaps become professors of it—but perhaps not one in ten thousand who himself gazes at the starry evening sky. But are not the proclaimers all too frequently to blame when the whole thing becomes aping and copying, for it is to their earthly and temporal advantage. Be unprincipled, if you will, toward the starry evening sky, make it seem that what is glorious is not the starry evening sky but your conception of it, get a few blaring knights of commerce on your staff, and you will soon get a crowd who will pay a fancy price for your wonderful instruction. Ah, but if you are honest toward the starry evening sky, if you tell the truth and declare that the glory belongs to it and that every man could if he would see its glory in his own way, and that his own way means infinitely much more to him than yours to him or his to you: well, then there is really no occasion for making money or for animal-like crowding together in herds.

Certainly there is no one else in the kingdom of Denmark with the sense for individuality that I have. But there certainly are sufficient semi-intelligent fellows who conceitedly look down on the human throng as lower beings. This truly is not the case with me. A maidservant, a watchman, a cabdriver has had infinite worth to me. I also knew (as no one else in Denmark) how to talk with unconditionally any and every person and idealize them in the conversation. That was my practice (inhuman?)–and that was why I was abandoned to rabble-maltreatment or that was why the rabble's mistreatment took on an utterly distinctive meaning in my case, since I felt that I ought to expose myself to it. What pains me is that I no longer can come in touch with all these people whom I love[3322] but who now either feel obliged to make a fool of me or are afraid that I am making a fool of them.

What a tragedy, these thousands and thousands–every single one could grasp the highest, acquire the infinite worth that is his–but all goes to waste, and everything is also done by the politicians and their like to transform them into specimens. Think of a housewife's shock and distress at seeing good, nourishing food thrown into the gutter– this is but a poor illustration of the shock and distress which must fill the heart of someone who, himself an individuality, sees in every single human being something of absolutely equal significance, something of infinite worth, an individuality–and then sees them wasted by the millions as specimens!

Act as an individuality yourself, engage a half-dozen Corybants, trumpeters, and drummers to proclaim that one becomes an individuality through a relationship to you–it will work like a charm, will soon become a brilliantly successful business. Proclaim the truth that every man, unconditionally every man, is an individuality, becomes that by the relationship to God, who in no way has assigned you to collect his debts–and you will see that it becomes an affair of which one can say (as that woman in *Barselstuen*[3323] tearfully says of the meat which never-theless cost ——— a pound): There is not an ounce of fat on it.

$$\text{XI}^2 \text{ A } 19 \quad n.d., \ 1854$$

### « 6918  *An Apostle—My Inferiority*

An apostle's task is: to spread Christianity, to win men to Christianity.

My task is: to disabuse men of the illusion that they are Christians –yet I am serving Christianity.

Christianity has now existed for 1800 years–show me that this idea has ever been advanced before in Christendom.

My life, like everything else in the sphere in which I belong, for which I work, is in the sphere of the paradox: the positive is recognizable by a negative. Alas, it is true my life is utter sadness, like nighttime (so those words from the Diapsalmata in *Either/Or*[3324] are entirely appropriate: When I die, I will be able to say: *Du bist vollbracht nachtwache meines Daseins*); it is true my life is pain and suffering, and God —lovingly and out of love—tortures me where it hurts the most: yet his negative is a mark of the positive, a primitivity that does not relate to the contemporary age but to coming generations, and a significance which is properly expressed by the fact that I am superfluous to my age.

By and large my age is entirely right in pretending to be ignorant of me as anything else than a caricature recognized by everyone on the street; my age is especially right in not getting involved in judging me. For of course none of my contemporaries has any intimation of my task, even less of the strategy related to the task. But it would be the most ridiculous thing one could ask for: my work (aiming to disabuse men of the idea that they are Christians) judged by the current criterion, the common, trivial, insipid, shabby notion of spreading Christianity. Think of a soldier who knew nothing but offensive tactics, and that perhaps rather poorly, and then he wants to use this criterion to judge a defensive military operation—this would be somewhat analagous: he would have no conception of the strategy that must be used. Another analogy: if someone who could play a game in which the lowest score wins were to see a high-scoring game and then wanted to judge a player's moves, his way of playing, by his own method. It does not help that those who are engaged these days in what is called spreading Christianity are mediocre partners; they do not thereby come any closer to understanding my task, my tactic. It would be more likely to happen if they were distinguished in their own enterprise. For real competence in proclaiming Christianity—and also reflection on the depth of confusion implicit in the concept "Christendom"—might very well lead them to understand my cause or bring them closer to it.

From time immemorial the work has gone on as follows: the more outstanding and competent people have all suspended judgment on whether Christianity exists, on the matter of Christian states and countries and races—and then they thought to remedy deficiencies in details and if possible to bring in a little new life—before they realized the result of their activity, that they fostered the misunderstanding, nurtured the sickness, which was very quick to assimilate weak remedies and transform them into sustenance for itself.

No, no, the matter must be treated basically, the terrain must be cleared, it must be made effectually evident that Christianity does not exist[3325]. . . .

XI² A 21   *n.d.,* 1854

### « 6919   *A View of Christianity*

which, according to my knowledge, has never been advanced is that Christianity is Satan's invention reckoned to make men unhappy through the imagination. Just as the worm and the bird look for the best fruit, so Satan has set his cap for the very superior ones, those with high imagination and feeling, aiming to lure them astray through the imagination, to get them to make themselves unhappy and, if possible, the others along with them.

This view should be listened to. Certainly when that high plateau has been reached where becoming a Christian can actually be said to begin, every single step is such a strain, so dangerous, that it is continually a question of "black or red," whether it is God or it is Satan. To be a Christian, just to approach it, is such an ideality that it continually is: either God or Satan.

But how in the world did we get into this mess of Christendom, these millions of Christians! A harmless, grunting, prosperous bourgeois, provided that he is generous to the pastor, is supposed to be the earnest Christian, typical—but this is really as ridiculous as if the Round Tower[3326] were to pass itself off as an eighteen-year-old dancer.

How is it possible that this confusion came to be! I, of course, attribute it mainly to "the clergyman," because it is to the interest of his trade that there be as many Christians as possible. Suppose a recruiting officer were sent out to recruit and he was promised a specific sum for everyone he recruited and there was no investigation of his recruits—what then? I believe it would end with his recruiting cripples, the bedridden, old crones, in short, those who would be useless in war but whom he could get for the cheapest price—whereupon he would hand in his lists and get paid for each one. So it is with Christendom. The fact that the auditing does not come until eternity has practically the same effect as if there were none—and now the clergyman, himself not a Christian, of course, stakes everything on winning paying souls. Anyone who can pay is a Christian, that is if he is willing to pay—otherwise he is a pagan. If he is willing to pay—fine, then he is an earnest Christian. If the household pets could pay for themselves, I am certain that "the clerygman" would make them Christians as well.

What disgusting nonsense and villainy! Alas, I can certainly see that in a certain sense Bishop Mynster[3327] was right in saying of my position: "It is pitched altogether too high." I really am not very good at dealing with people. What one of my pseudonyms[3328] with a tinge of paganism declares: I dance to the glory of the god, and what I have sometimes said to Professor Nielsen:[3329] My life is a service in the royal court—this is indeed true.

That is how I have lived among men. Among the Danish poets now living there is not one who can ever reach as high in imaginative performance as I do in actuality. A few people, those who are a little more advanced, seem to find it quite amusing to watch me, talk a little with me, otherwise flatter themselves as being more sensible, for my position, after all, is an exaggeration—but there was no one, not one, who could or would venture out. And from the moment I began to withdraw a little from men, so as not to indulge in their nonchalant point of view myself but demonstrate earnestness, even though very slightly, they were offended.

$XI^2$ A 31   *n.d.*, 1854

### « 6920  *"A Better Future"*

There is something naive and undialectical about letting oneself get enthusiastic at the thought of a better future, a future time when one will be better understood—quite as if things did not substantially remain just as bad, or, if there is a change, then for the worse.

A better future, that is, a time when one will be better understood, a future when admiring scoundrel professors and the preacher-rabble turn the life and activity and witness of those who are dead into profit for themselves and their families. Is this a better future, is this becoming better understood.

Take the highest example of all: which misunderstanding is the greater, which must be most loathsome to Christ—that of the Jews who put him to death or of Christendom which turned him into profit? Unquestionably the latter, yes, only the latter must be really loathsome.

And yet all the *men* I have read about who have fought for something (Socrates the only exception) have always been inspired by the thought of a better future when they would be better understood.

This thought does not inspire me in the least, and in my opinion to require an inspiring idea like this (an illusion) is an indirect proof that one is not intrinsically self-possessed in his enthusiasm. In any case this thought does not inspire me; on the contrary, what incites me most of all is to contemplate this knavish posterity. The misunderstanding of the contemporary age is not nearly as embittering or, if you please, as hopeless—no, everything is hopelessly lost and one's life is tortured by misunderstanding when that misunderstanding is devoid of character, is unthinking admiration.

$$XI^2 \text{ A } 32 \quad n.d., \ 1854$$

« **6921** *Christian Auditing*

What money is in the finite world, concepts are in the world of spirit. All transactions are conducted with them.

When it so happens that generation after generation everyone takes over the concepts he got from the previous generation—and then devotes his days and his time to enjoying this life, works for finite goals, etc.—it all too easily happens that the concepts are gradually distorted, become entirely different from what they were originally, come to mean something entirely different, come to be like counterfeit money. Meanwhile all transactions nevertheless continue to be conducted smoothly with them, which, incidentally, does not disturb men's egotistical interests (which is not the case when counterfeit money appears), especially if the concept-counterfeiting is oriented precisely toward human egotism; thus the one who is actually fooled, if I dare say so, is the other partner in the business of Christianity: God in heaven.

Yet no one wants the business of auditing the concepts. Everyone understands more or less clearly that to be employed in such a way in this business is practically the same as being sacrificed, means that a person's life becomes so impounded that he cannot follow his natural inclination to occupy himself with finite goals. No, the human thing to do is to treat the concepts as superficially as possible and to plunge into the concrete details of life the sooner the better, or in any case not to be particularly scrupulous about the concepts, not so scrupulous that one cannot move full speed into the concrete details of life.

Nevertheless auditing is needed, and more and more with each decade.

Therefore Governance must take possession of an individual who is to be used for this purpose.

Such an auditor, of course, is nothing at all like the whole chattering company of preachers and professors—yet he is not an apostle either, but rather just the opposite.

Precisely what the auditor needs is what the apostle[3330] does not really need—intellectuality, superior intellectuality—moreover, he must be extremely familiar with all possible kinds of swindling and counterfeiting, almost as if he personally were the trickiest of all swindlers—in fact, his business is to "know" the counterfeits.

Since all this knowledge is so very shady and equivocal that it could occasion the greatest possible confusion, the auditor is not treated like the apostle. Alas, no, the apostle is a trusted man; the auditor is put under the strictest supervision. Because it is so descriptive, my one metaphor for this is constantly the same. Imagine that the Bank of London became aware that counterfeit notes were in circulation—so well counterfeited that the bank despaired of identifying them with certainty and of protecting itself against future imitation. Despite all the talented bank and police personnel, there was only one with absolute talent in this area—but he was a criminal, one of the condemned. So he is used, but he is not used as a trusted man. He is placed under the most terrifying supervision: with death hanging over his head, he has to sit and handle all that mass of money, he is periodically searched, etc.

It is the same with the Christian auditor. If the apostle has the task of proclaiming the truth, the auditor has the task of discovering counterfeits, identifying them and thereby rendering them impossible. If the apostle's personal attribute is a noble and pure simplicity (which is the condition for being the instrument of the Holy Spirit), the auditor's is this shady, ambiguous knowledge. If the apostle is in the power of Governance in a univocal and wholly good sense, the auditor is completely in the power of Governance in an equivocal sense. If with all his efforts and work the apostle still has no merit before God, the auditor has even less and could not possibly gain any (were it otherwise possible), since he has a negative service to fulfill and thus is essentially a penitent—but essentially both of them are sacrificed and both are chosen in grace by Governance, for it is not in disgrace that the one is chosen as auditor. And as it begins with the apostle, the auditor obviously can come only toward the end, since he has the dissemination as a presupposition. And if the apostle has his name from being sent out because he proceeds from God outwards, the examiner's task is to penetrate the counterfeits and lead back to God.

Apostles can never come again; otherwise Christ also must be able to come again in a way different than his second coming. Christ's life on earth is Christianity. The apostle signifies: Now Christianity has been introduced; from now on you men have to take it over yourself, but with responsibility.

So mankind took it over. And even if it is an everlasting lie that Christianity is perfectible, mankind certainly displayed a mounting perfectibility—in counterfeiting Christianity.

Confronted with this counterfeiting, God—even if he wanted to (and even if there were no other hindrance)—cannot use an apostle, because through its counterfeiting Christendom has so alienated itself from God that a trusting appeal to men, if I dare put it this way, is out of the question. No, as Christendom is a counterfeiting, and since sin nowadays is primarily prudence, on the side of Governance (whom man with his counterfeiting has alienated) all is distrust. Joyous emissaries no longer come from God, any more than we hail the police as such; no, only experts in frauds come, and even these, since they in fact essentially belong to the general fraudulence, are treated by Providence as shady and equivocal characters.

Christendom today is happy and satisfied. Not infrequently we are given the impression that a new epoch is coming, new apostles are coming—because Christendom, which of course has done an excellent job, has so perfectly practiced and appropriated what the apostles introduced that now we must go further. The truth is that Christendom has done the shabbiest, trickiest job possible, and to expect new apostles (if there were any truth to this idea at all) is the most confounded insolence.

$$XI^2 \text{ A } 36 \quad n.d., 1854$$

« **6922**

..... When I so frequently have compared myself to a secret agent,[3331] a doomed person with more than ordinary knowledge of all kinds of counterfeiting[3332] but who is himself placed under the strictest supervision, this is a completely true and very descriptive comparison.

But viewed from another side I am anything but a rogue. On the contrary what I represent is a human integrity which has refused to avail itself of or take part in Christendom's having extracted from Christianity something pleasing to flesh and blood, something entirely different from what it is in the New Testament.

My proposal is always the same: let us be honest, state plainly where we are, but do not counterfeit Christianity. Understood thus, God assists me in order to prevent me from slipping into any illusion. It is not just in connection with Christianity that I compare myself to a doomed person, no, it is in connection with my personal life and what I personally may have on my conscience. And my honesty about Christianity is linked to my desire to do, if possible, something well-pleasing to God precisely because I personally may have much to blame myself for.

$XI^2$ A 40   *n.d.,*  1854

« **6923**

..... Somewhere in these journals [i.e., $XI^1$ A 439] there is something about my never craving a social life, and this is certainly quite true but yet must be understood in a special way.

In one sense there perhaps are few natures as social as I was. Alas, but the miserable plight that has been my lot from my early days made it preferable and a great relief for me to be able to remove myself unsociably from everybody, hiding my pain. In this sense it is true that I have not craved sociality.

In order really to have a relationship to Christianity, most men first seem to have to be plunged into sufferings of which they at present have scarcely any intimation. My life was suffering very early. In contrast to what men normally call the joy in life, my joy in life was to be able to hide it.

$XI^2$ A 44   *n.d.,*  1854

« **6924** *To Proclaim True Christianity,*
*the Christianity of the New Testament*

is in one sense beyond a man's powers; divine authority is required for this, or, more correctly, a divine absorption in the unconditioned.

To take myself, for instance. I actually do have an awareness of what Christianity is—nothing is more certain than that. Humanly speaking, I have had to become fundamentally unhappy in order to remain aware—nothing is more certain than that.

But now when I am supposed to turn toward men and proclaim Christianity to them, the matter is altogether different. My human sympathies cut across—for the fact remains that to become a Christian is to become, humanly speaking, unhappy.

Here it comes—do I have the heart to make men, humanly speaking, unhappy? This is the point! That I have had to become unhappy concerns only me. But others—and that I am the one who is supposed to do it! Thus the whole matter is reversed and it is roughly equivalent to my saying, as I proclaim Christianity: Forgive me, O forgive me for making you, humanly speaking, unhappy. I am also saying something similar in another way when I say: "It is your own fault that the price of being a Christian has to be forced up so high," for here it is as if I were not speaking about a good but almost an evil, which again is bound up with the fact that true Christianity must make a man, humanly speaking, unhappy.

It is different with the apostle;[3333] he is unconditionally absorbed in the unconditioned, blind to everything else, in a certain sense does not see, humanly speaking, what he is doing—namely, making us men, humanly speaking, unhappy.

Incidentally, here again we see the distinguishing marks of this sphere: the positive is recognizable by the negative; Christ is the Savior of the world (the positive), recognized by the negative, by the fact that he, he is the very one who makes us men, humanly speaking, unhappy. It is easy to see that this belongs in the sphere of the paradox, and is something else, of course, than this nonsense about the Savior of the world in which Christendom excels.

$XI^2$ A 45    *n.d.*, 1854

« **6925**

. . . . . If someone who had learned to write as we learn it, from left to right, and had never heard of any other way, saw another person writing from right to left, how could he make head or tail of it? Alas, compared to the lives of most people, my life is like that, all wrong according to the ordinary view—how then can I expect to be understood.

$XI^2$ A 61    *n.d.*, 1854

« **6926** *Eternity's Price (Buying and Selling)*

. . . . . "Studenstrup"[3334] is perfectly right in saying that the city hall and courthouse is a very impressive building and at the trifling price those good fellows would sell it for is almost the best business deal possible. The only thing "Studenstrup" has overlooked is the question of the legal right of those good fellows to sell it—it may in fact be the case that even ten dollars is also too much.

So also with Christianity and eternal salvation. That eternal salvation is an indescribable, invaluable good is, of course, certain—and for the price at which the pastor will dispose of it; well, there is absolutely no doubt that this is still more brilliant business than Studenstrup's would be.

But what makes me suspicious is whether "the pastor" has such a relationship to eternal salvation that he is able to sell it, whether his connection resembles that of the two rogues to the city hall and courthouse—for then even ten dollars is also too much.

Probably it is better, then, not to let oneself be fooled by the pastor's ridiculous price but to apply to him who actually owns and controls eternal salvation—but who certainly does not have a clearance sale.

XI² A 75   n.d., 1854

### « 6927  *Bishop Mynster*[3335]

The reason Bishop Mynster may be said to have been as ill-starred a figure as possible for me was not that he was not what I needed but that he conjured up an appearance of being what I needed. I needed a man of character in the bishopric of Sjælland—the trouble for me was not that Mynster was not that, for that is of little consequence; no, the trouble was that, refining all the rest of his enjoyments, he craftily also passed for a man of character, a governmental leader, although he was only a Sunday orator and, incidentally, a worldly shrewd eudaimonist.

It was impossible for me to attack him while he was living. For my charge simply was: he does not govern, it is an hallucination; he is a journalist, a slave to the public as much as anybody. But to whom should I say this? And on the other hand, I was fighting on the side of the government and therefore could not very well weaken his position. I said that to him privately—but what did he care about the private man; he was afraid only of the public, for he was cowardly.

XI² A 78   n.d., 1854

### « 6928  *Christendom*

If it is correct that we are all Christians, that the first person I meet on the street is a Christian, in short, everyone—then the New Testament is the most ridiculous of books and God as impractical as possible. Can anything more ridiculous be imagined than to set in motion motivations such as eternal punishment and heaven's salvation in order to produce this effect. Can anything more ridiculous be imagined than using a jack to pick up a pin—and likewise to use eternal damnation to bring people to the half-demoralized, more or less harmless fuddyduddyism which is just about what it is to be a human being.

And that this can go on in such a way that no one ever catches on or raises a hue and cry—yes, it just proves again how insignificant men's lives are.

XI² A 79   n.d., 1854

« **6929** *Playing Christianity*

I see by the papers[3336] that the widow of the late Russian Adjutant General for the Marines was named by the Empress to the Order of the Ladies of the Great Martyr Chatarine, Second Class.

Wait a minute! First of all, Chatarine has never been advanced to the class of great martyr. Great martyr—what does that mean? It is nonsense—but of course deliberately intended to broaden the rubric of martyr in such a way that anybody and everybody can come under it. So a real martyr is advanced and called a great martyr—perhaps there is one class still higher: *geheime general ober hof* great martyrs.

Second, to establish an order for aristocratic women who, please note, do not become martyrs but—just the opposite—decorate themselves with a certain kind of ribbon etc., thereby enabling them to make a more ostentatious appearance in the most select salons.

Third, "Second Class"—so there are more classes!

This, you see, is an example of playing Christianity (as if all Christendom were anything else).

Men are constantly engaged in broadening the concepts in such a way that they become child's play, an artifice, the very opposite of earnestness, a refinement.

How dreadfully true are Christ's words[3337] that they who build the tombs of the martyrs are just as guilty as they who put them to death —to me they seem worse, to me there seems to be more humanness in the temper that flares up and kills than in this oafish post-mortem game which hits upon the idea of decorations on the occasion of a martyr's death, and then, decked out in ribbons, one becomes celebrated and distinguished in society. The martyr's death shriek must sound dreadful to his murderer, but it seems to me it sounds even more dreadful in this wretched childish nonsense which shamefully exploits him.

$XI^2$ A 101  *n.d.,* 1854

« **6930**

. . . . . I have a born genius for two things: to be a secret agent[3338] and to be a courtier. Those we call courtiers have no intimation of what it is to represent Majesty in the highest sense, to bow to genuine Majesty; all their festiveness is still only on the regular scale. But to move and express oneself on the scale which is called the reverse scale is something completely different. —And yet what we call the police are limited by the fact that large numbers invalidate or change the concept, that large numbers make them afraid to prosecute a case, yes, where large numbers make wrong into right. But the police force in which I serve regards numbers itself as a crime, and there can be a criminal case in which centuries are guilty.

XI² A 121　　 *n.d.,* 1854

### « 6931　*Christendom*

A metaphor. Imagine a country where the subjects are happy and contented and the one says to the other: We in our country have the great and priceless blessing that if anyone in any way feels he has been wronged or has anything whatsoever on his mind, he may personally approach the King. It is a matter of common knowledge to all of us that unconditionally everyone has free access to His Majesty. That is the kind of life they have. But look, the unvarnished truth is that everyone thinks something like this: But the smartest thing to do, after all, is to avoid a personal approach to His Majesty. After all, it is a very delicate, awkward matter to stand before His Majesty. It opens the door for all sorts of troubles afterward with officials and many others. In short, *summa summarum,* [3339] no one personally approaches His Majesty.

Similarly, Christendom is more or less a society of men who are happily and mutually convinced that unconditionally every single person may personally and individually approach His Heavenly Majesty at any time—but the smartest thing. . . . .

XI² A 134　　 *n.d.,* 1854

## IX. BEYOND ARMED NEUTRALITY
## DECEMBER 1854–SEPTEMBER 1855

« 6932 *The Problem*

So far removed, so distant is Christendom (Protestantism, especially in Denmark) from the Christianity of the New Testament that I continually must emphasize that I do not call myself a Christian and that my task is to articulate the issue,[3340] the first condition for any possibility of Christianity again.

It was incendiarism (this is how Christ[3341] himself describes his commission), it was incendiarism, setting fire to men by evocatively introducing a passion which made them heterogeneous with what is naturally understood to be man, heterogeneous with the whole of existence, an incendiarism which must necessarily cause discord between father and son, daughter and mother—in short, in the most intimate, the most precious relationships, an incendiarism with the intention of tearing apart "the generation" in order to reach "the individual," which is what God wants and therefore the passion introduced was: to love God, and its negative expression: to hate oneself.

It was incendiarism. But it is not always water that is used to put out a fire—however, to keep the metaphor, I could certainly say that Christendom is the water that has put out the fire. But, as mentioned, one does not always use water; sometimes one uses, for example, featherbeds, blankets, mattresses, and the like to smother a fire. And so I say that if Christendom is the bulk that has smothered that fire once lighted, it now has such an enormous layer of the numerical beneath it that Christianity may serenely and safely be made into just the opposite of what it is in the New Testament.

Whoever you are, if it is your purpose, your idea to do your bit to help smother the fire still more, then get busily involved in this massive popularization, doing it under the name of spreading Christianity, and you will do as much harm as you can possibly do. But if you want Christianity again, fire again, then do all you can to get rid of the featherbeds, blankets, and mattresses, the grossly bulky stuff—and there will be fire.

The orders for busyness of that kind are: Away, away with abstractions: the state church, the folk church, Christian countries—for any

549

effort of that kind is treason against the fire; they are the featherbeds and blankets that help smother the fire still more. But efforts of the kind that aims at dispersing, aims at "the individual," are the solution.

It was incendiarism. For the time being forget that, forget that this is Christ's own view of Christianity. Then take Protestantism, especially in Denmark. From what you see to be Christianity here, would it ever even remotely occur to you that it was to set fire that the founder of this religion came to earth, would you not get the overall impression that it must have been to put out fire that he came to the world.

It was incendiarism—and nowadays Christianity is reassurance, reassurance about eternity in order that we may all the better be able to rejoice and enjoy this life.

As we all know, a person can get sick from a fetid stench; there are various other disgusting smells which a man cannot bear, from which he gets sick—but one can also get sick from stupid nonsense. And just as during plague or cholera the surgeon walks about and chews on something to prevent inhaling, so also one may well have a spiritual need for something in the mouth when one has to work incessantly against stupid nonsense. But there is the difference that for the surgeon inhaling may actually be dangerous, and for the other practitioner it is not harmful, may even be beneficial. For while man by nature wishes for what can give him pleasure in life, the religious person on active duty needs a proper dose of disgust with life in order to be fit for his task; disgust with life, taken properly (for the way it is used is crucial), is the best safeguard against getting involved in stupid nonsense.

$XI^2$ A 206   *n.d.,* 1854

### « 6933 *The Christian Coat of Arms*

Just as everything Christian is the direct opposite of the directly human, so this, too. The memory of one's exploits is preserved directly as heraldic insignia—Christianly the memory of one's guilt—so in a way the cock became Peter's symbol—*zum Andenken.*[3342]

$XI^2$ A 213   *n.d.,* 1854

### « 6934

..... How far Christianity is from existing[3343] is seen best in me.

For even with the clarity I have—I still am not a Christian.[3344] Yet it seems to me that, despite the abyss of nonsense into which we are thrust, we all will still be just as fully saved.

This is the result of having gotten the very opposite, so-called Christianity, as a child.

But nevertheless my situation is difficult enough. I am not like a pagan to whom an apostle proclaims Christianity briefly and to the point—no, I am the one who, so to speak, has to discover Christianity himself, work it out of the bewitchment into which it has been hexed.

XI² A 244   n.d., 1854

### « 6935 *Three Things for Which I Thank God*[3345]

(1) that no living person owes me his life

(2) that he prevented me from carelessly becoming a pastor in the sense in which one is a pastor around here these days, which is a mockery of Christianity

(3) that I voluntarily exposed myself to being abused by *The Corsair.* [3346]

XI² A 248   n.d., 1854

### « 6936 *My Task: To Make Room*

I am not an apostle who brings something from God, and with authority.

No, I serve God, but without authority. My task is to make room so that God can have access. [*In margin:* My task is not to make room imperatively but, suffering, to make room.]

From this it is readily apparent why I literally must be a single man and also be kept very weak and frail.

For if that which is supposed to make room came, for example, at the head of a couple battalions—well, humanly speaking this seems a wonderful way to make room, the surest way. But then the very thing which is supposed to make room could occupy the space itself, could occupy so much space that God could not really have access.

My task is to make room—and I am a police detective,[3347] if you please. But in this world the police come with force and arrest the others—the higher ranking police come suffering and ask instead to be arrested.

XI² A 250   n.d., 1854

### « 6937 *Mynster*[3348] *and I*

are the collision between the old and the new.

As a rule the new comes in its own self-interest and wants to stamp out, overthrow, the old—the sooner the better.

I come deferentially, even wanting to play the new into his hands as his last triumph, hiding myself and all my sufferings and sacrifices for the cause in the most obscure incognito, even the incognito of being a laughing stock, while the whole age, I in the lead, has bowed before Mynster as the man.

Governance decreed: Mynster has never deserved that.

And I, too, have surely seen that, but disguise is my life, my element; to suffer, to make sacrifices, etc., that I am willing enough to do, but disguise is a passion with me.

XI² A 251   n.d., 1854

### « 6938 *Ludicrous*

To bury a man who even by proclaiming Christianity has acquired and enjoyed in very large measure all the earthly goods and advantages possible, to bury him as a witness to the truth[3349] is just as ludicrous as burying a virgin who as a matter of fact left three children and was pregnant with the fourth.[3350] Such virgins are regarded as ludicrous, and it does not help a bit, it only increases the laughter if the pastor, perhaps for money (since "fine sand"[3351] has been ordered) adds emphatically: the real virgins, the true virgins.

The fact is that people are very well informed about the creaturely definition of what it is to be a virgin and the like. But they know nothing at all about what a witness to the truth is, simply because they have managed to make Christianity and the world coincide, whereas the "witness to the truth" is related to Christianity's heterogeneity with this world and therefore always suffers, renounces, and misses out in this world.

Basically Martensen has made Mynster ludicrous, but his contemporaries lack the Christian presuppositions to see that he has been made ludicrous.

XI² A 252   n.d., 1854

### « 6939 *On My Being Contemporary with Bishop Mynster*[3352]

What it actually means is this: the question is—was it possible for me, who presumably am naturally equipped for the catastrophic, was it possible for me to become the last defense of the established instead of attacking it.

I had to have time to make up my mind on this question. That was why Governance arranged it so that I had as a contemporary the man at the head of the established order, the man for whose sake I wanted so very much to be adaptable in every way.

How I wanted—for many reasons—to be the last defense. But actually it is Mynster who, by what I have endured because of him and by what I have perceived in him and where he is leading us, has changed me or, more correctly, has contributed to making me more clear about myself.

XI² A 253   n.d., 1854

### « 6940  Mynster[3353] and I

I have rescued Mynster from what he feared more than the most superstitious of men fear crossing a graveyard at midnight—namely, a religious movement.

And I have helped him to achieve what he wanted more eagerly than the vainest of maidens wants to outshine everybody at the Royal Club—namely, to die undiminished.

XI² A 254   n.d., 1854

### « 6941  Mynster[3354]

was, after all, an egotist—even in the following way: I am fairly convinced that he did not (possibly because of the chance that Martensen[3355] would some day succeed him) suggest to him that I actually was a man with a completely different importance and influence than I was believed to have.

Martensen could well have used such counsel. But on the other hand Mynster could not very well give it without giving himself away a little.

XI² A 256   n.d., 1854

### « 6942  Mynster[3356]—Martensen[3357]

Mynster's prudence consisted in refraining altogether from passing judgment on me, for he surely saw how complicated everything gets here. Then, too, my devotion to him[3358] made me try to help him come through all right.

Martensen plunges in headfirst; to say that he is administering the Church is as strange as saying that a man who continually runs headfirst into doors is the boss, although that too takes a little managing.

XI² A 257   n.d., 1854

### « 6943  (Who I Am and) What I Want

Now that the old Bishop is dead,[3359] removing that consideration together with much else that made me keep indefinite (who I really am) what I want, I now can and must and will speak as directly as possible.

I understand it as my very particular task assigned by Governance, for which I was selected very early and was educated very slowly, and which I now for the first time fully embrace, having always understood also that it really would be about the same as having to be a sacrifice —I understand it as my task to undertake a complete auditing of all the Christian concepts, to extricate the Christian concepts from the illusions in which we have entangled them, and in so doing work toward an awakening [*in margin:* which is urgently needed in Denmark, since more than a generation of artistically perfect and secularly sagacious, skillful proclamation of Christianity has hexed us into a kind of esthetic spell] with all the power the Almighty has granted me and with the willingness to suffer which he may have loved forth in my soul both by severity and by gentleness.

But first of all I consider it my responsibility to the established— thus manifesting how I acknowledge an established as an authority— to express my view and opinion of the established as definitely and candidly as possible, thereby in every way enabling the established, if it regards this as justified, to take measures against me with the power and authority it has. [*In margin:* therefore after making every effort over the years to keep from being at the head of a party etc., taking care only to be a solitary (which, after all, is in harmony with my having in the highest sense this very special task)]

My opinion is: compared with the situation when Luther put in his appearance, what at first glance seems to be horrible, that there were ninety-five theses, on closer inspection seems to be an alleviation—for now there is but one thesis: Christianity, the Christianity of the New Testament, does not exist at all.[3360]

In Protestantism, especially in Denmark, the point has been reached of having the very opposite of what the New Testament understands to be Christianity.

The official "proclamation" (taking the word in its double meaning) here in this country, if placed alongside the New Testament, is, in my opinion, a perhaps well-meant attempt to make a fool of God— if one does not avoid this by confessing that it is not the Christianity of the N. T., and in that case the whole proclamation of Christianity used today must be done over completely; everything must not be done to maintain, perhaps with good intentions, the appearance that what we have is the Christianity of the N. T., but, just the reverse, everything must be done to get us to see how in truth we do relate to the Christianity of the N. T.

Of course, I consider it a guilt to take part in an official divine worship of that kind, and the kind of guilt that is the last to be forgiven in eternity, because it is high treason. Therefore I do not take part any longer in the official divine worship and have not done so for some time.

Now it is up to the established to act.

If I am not disturbed [*in margin:* if I am not perhaps prosecuted, arrested, perhaps even executed], I will begin my task along the lines of stripping the costumes and disguises of illusions from the Christian ideas and concepts [*changed from:* auditing the Christian ideas and concepts, stripping them of the disguises of illusions].

I will also work toward an awakening, and the power I will use (as I am led to understand by Governance) is—yes, people will be amazed, but so it is—it is laughter. Governance will no doubt find it appropriate. The situation in the Church is not that the clergy are sunken in dissoluteness and wild debauchery, by no means; no, it is sunken in inanity, in trivial philistinism, and they drag the parishioners down into this flat mediocrity and absence of spirit. Here only one power can be used— the power of laughter. But, please note, divinely dedicated, as it is when I make use of it—and this, you see, is why it pleased Governance that I, idolized by profane grinning mockery, should voluntarily expose myself to become—if you please—a martyr to grinning mockery, in this way consecrated and dedicated by the highest approval of divine governance to becoming a vexing "gadfly," a quickening whip on all this spiritlessness, which in secularized mediocrity has blabbered Christianity down into something meaningless, into being spiritless impotence, suffocated in illusion.

$$XI^3 \; B \; 53 \quad n.d., \; 1854$$

« **6944** *My Program:*

> *Either/Or*
> by
> S. Kierkegaard

$$XI^3 \; B \; 54 \quad n.d., \; 1854$$

« **6945**

*Addition to 6944* ($XI^3$ B 54):

It is laughter which must be used—therefore the line in the last diapsalm in *Either/Or.*[3361]

But the laughter must first of all be divinely consecrated and devoutly dedicated. This was done on the greatest possible scale. Socrates.

An example. From an essentially Christian point of view, Mynster[3362] was comical—like someone about to run a race who then puts on three coats—intending to proclaim him who was mocked and spit upon, to proclaim renunciation and self-denial—and then pompously appearing in silk and velvet and in possession of all earthly advantages and goods. But on the other hand, the comic of this sort is Christianly something to weep over, for it is something to weep over that this has been regarded as earnestness and wisdom.

And this is how the comic must be used. The laughter must not prevail; it must not end with laughter, either—no, it is merely a power which is to throw some light on the trumpery and the illusions so that I might succeed, if possible, "to influence by means of the ideals."[3363]

$XI^3$ B 55    *n.d.,* 1854

### « 6946

*Addition to 6944* ($XI^3$ B 54):

Either/Or! We must examine the implications of the Christian requirement, that whole side of Christianity which is suppressed these days.

We must examine this, and then we must—either/or—*either* our lives must express the requirement and we are then justified to call ourselves Christian, *or,* if our lives express something quite different, we must give up being called Christian, we must be satisfied with being an approximation of what it is to be a Christian, etc.

The latter is my aim[3364] (at least for the time being). But there must be truth in this whole affair—this shirking and suppressing and concealing and blurring must go—divine worship must not be: making a fool of God.[3365]

$XI^3$ B 56    *n.d.,* 1854

### « 6947

*Addition to 6944* ($XI^3$ B 54):

..... So let it be said[3366] (the article[3367] against Prof. Martensen on Bishop M. was "the occasion"); it should and must be said yet again!

It can by no means be denied that the whole official proclamation of Christianity here in this country, when one regards what is said as well as what the teacher's (the pastor's) life expresses, is completely different from what is found in the N. T. It can by no means be denied that the whole official proclamation—to take just one aspect—as a matter of course suppresses and omits a whole side of Christianity, of which the pastor's life is not a reminder, either—namely, dying to the world, voluntary renunciation, crucifying the flesh, suffering for the doctrine. How can we accept this, is not public worship—in which every Sunday a book called God's Word is brought out, on which the sermon is based, as they say, and to which appeal is made—is not the public worship changed into mockery when this Word of God is treated in such an arbitrary way that one leaves out what is inconvenient, while —and is this not again mockery!—the teacher is committed by a sacred oath to the N. T., is ordained to it, which then presumably means that the Holy Spirit is imparted to him in a special way—how can we accept this?

What I have repeated again and again should be kept in mind: "I am without authority, am only a poet,[3368] an average man." I do not claim to be better than others,[3369] only that I am not bound by a pledge to the New Testament and am not an ordained man, either. No, in no way do I pretend to be better than others, but I do want it made known that this is the way we carry on—I want some truth here and want it said honestly, loudly, and clearly. But I do not pretend to be better than others. Therefore what the old Bishop once said to me is not true— namely, that I spoke as if the others were going to hell. No, if I can be said to speak at all of going to hell then I say something like this: If the others are going to hell, then I am going along with them. But I do not believe that; on the contrary, I believe that we will all be saved, I, too, and this awakens my deepest wonder.

But, to repeat, clarity must be brought into this matter, we must have it said—this shirking is abominable. We must—to take just one aspect of it—bring forward again that whole side of Christianity in order to see things in the context of the Christian requirement, see whether one can be a Christian without complying with it. But not this scurvy business of suppressing it.

Bishop M. died at the right time. God be praised that things could go on as long as the old Bishop lived.

He had actually placed Christianity under the determinants: *both-and,* or *also,* both the temporal and the eternal, the eternal and also the temporal. [*In margin:* This is what his life expressed, and it is life, after all, that preaches; what the mouth says is not enough, especially when one never uses the mouth to make the confession, "My life expresses something entirely different."] In order to be examined, Christianity must be brought under the determinant: either/or.

I am without authority, only a poet—but oddly enough around here, even on the street, I go by the name "Either/Or."

The illuminating light is "either/or." Under this illuminating light there must be an examination of the doctrine of the imitation of Christ, the doctrine of grace (whether it can give indulgence for the future, scale down the requirement for the future, or only forgive the past), the doctrine of the Church, whether a relaxed Christianity, established Christianity, is not Judaism.

[*In penciled parentheses:* O, Luther, you had ninety-five theses; in our present situation there is only one thesis: Christianity does not exist at all.[3370]]

Some suggestions by way of a few questions. Can one be a Christian at all without being a disciple, can one also be a teacher of Christianity, committed by a sacred oath to the New Testament and ordained, without being a disciple—can this be done? Can one change Christianity, which in the New Testament, especially in the gospels, is sheer commitment (and this is the conception the early Church had, for that reason even delaying baptism until the deathbed), can Christianity be transformed to pure and simple gift, donation, present, "Be so kind as to take this"—if this can be done, can one in this way be a Christian? Can Christianity, which in the New Testament, especially in the gospels, is about how God wants to be loved, wants to be loved by us, can it be changed around to be simply and solely about how God loves us and be changed to give total protection against being obliged to love God, which undeniably may strike us men as very inconvenient, even to make it presumptuous to want to love God—can one change Christianity in this way and be a Christian? —Can Christianity, which came into the world to strengthen and inspire men morally, be changed in such a way that it demoralizes them with the help of "grace"—can one be a Christian in that manner? Is it all right to take away the possibility of offense which is present in everything essentially Christian, because Christianity realizes that to make men eternally happy it has to make them temporally unhappy (and precisely here is the possibility of offense), is it all right to take away this possibility of offense and encourage men to enjoy this life—is it all right to be this kind of Christian? Is it all right to take from Judaism the promises for this life, which it had because it had no eternal salvation to point to, and to take from Christianity the promises of eternity, which it has because it demands renunciation of this life, and mix these together so it gets to be really bonbon (twice as sweet)—is it all right to call this Christianity and be a Christian in this way. Christianly speaking, can this and this, etc., etc., be done? And if by virtue of "grace" it can be done, must not one thing at least be demanded, that we realize clearly what we have done and how heavily we are drawing upon "grace"?

It must not be forgotten that "I am without authority, only a poet," yes, "only a poet who wishes, if possible, to influence by means of the ideals."

But it was precisely the ideals which the old Bishop with his considerable sagacity—a dangerous power, far more dangerous than riches, which nevertheless are supposed to be so dangerous that it is easier for a camel to go through a needle's eye than for a rich man to enter into the Kingdom of God—it was precisely the ideals which the old Bishop with his considerable sagacity was in the process of abolishing, although he still had sufficient truth in him, I am sure, to be willing to confess that he was not a witness to the truth. Professor Martensen "goes further"—that is to be expected of Prof. M.—he goes further in abolishing ideals and from the pulpit proclaims Bishop M. to be a witness to the truth, one of the authentic witnesses to the truth. Just as in housekeeping sterling silver has been discontinued and silver plate is used—it was not thus in the old days, when one either had silver and it was sterling silver or one did not have it at all, but one did not have something that was supposed to be silver—so now the secular mentality and ambitious enterprise aim to abolish the ideals and introduce plated ideals, thus we get *both-and,* one gets all the earthly advantages and is also a witness to the truth, one of the authentic witnesses to the truth.

XI$^3$ B 57   *n.d.,* 1854

« **6948**

From a strictly Christian point of view, what we men call earnestness in contrast to diversion is often nothing but diversion.

XI$^2$ A 370   *n.d.,* 1854–55

« **6949**  *A View of the Matter*

"In Christendom" we make it appear as if Christianity were a goal that perhaps lies far, far away in the distance, toward which one then strives—and perhaps also these united millions.

We craftily do not want to know the truth that Christianity, after all, lies behind us, has existed, and these mounting millions and their united striving are, from a Christian point of view, a diminution.

XI² A 371   *n.d.*, 1854–55

« 6950

In the New Testament, Christianity is a discharging of "the duty to God," and now it has been decided for a long time that there are no duties to God[3371]—yet we are Christians, yes, precisely this is supposed to be Christianity. And yet all the collisions which hit us in the New Testament are impossible if there are no duties to God.

XI² A 374   *n.d.*, 1854–55

« 6951

Is it Christianity which in exclusive loftiness does not want to have more than those twelve apostles?

Or is it the human race which craftily has exempted itself from being apostles, because we have the idea that it probably is sheer suffering, which we would rather avoid but do so preferably under the hypocritical pretense of humility and modesty.

XI² A 377   *n.d.*, 1854–55

« 6952  *Change the Expression*

[*In margin:* A world-transformation!]

In an ancient author I have read an observation something like this: When we see someone holding an axe wrong and chopping in such a way that he hits everything but the block of firewood, we do not say, "What a wrong way for the woodcutter to go about it," but we say, "That man is not a woodcutter."

Now for the application. When we see thousands and thousands and millions of Christians whose lives do not resemble in the remotest way what—and this is decisive—what the New Testament calls a Christian, is it not peculiar, is it not tampering with the meaning to talk as one does in no other situation and say: "What a mediocre way, what a thoroughly inexpressive way these Christians use to express that they are Christians." In any other situation would one not say: "These people are not Christians."

Now be earnest about it and say: These people are not Christians; let it become ordinary language usage—and you will have a world-transformation.

XI² A 379   *n.d.*, 1854–55

« 6953 *Jamming the Lock*

When there is no religion at all in a country, one cannot say that in a religious sense the lock is jammed.

No, but when making a fool of God[3372] in a refined way is regarded as worship of God and this worship flourishes in the land, then religion is jammed.

To continue the metaphor: when a door is locked, well, one takes his key and unlocks it. But when the lock in a door is jammed—then the locksmith must be summoned, the lock must be picked.

So it is with "Christendom." In "Christendom" Christianity is jammed.

$XI^2$ A 383   *n.d.*, 1854–55

« 6954 *"Mrs. Burmann"*

S. Kierkegaard

In *De Uadskillelige*[3373] there is a conversation between Mr. and Mrs. Burmann which frequently comes to my mind these days.

The topic of their discussion is engagements. Mrs. B. has just said that the importance of an engagement is that the lovers learn to know each other. "But," says Mr. B., "If in learning to know each other the lovers learn that they are unsuited to each other, must they then break the engagement?" "Heavens, no!" "Well, but then they may as well get married right away." "Heavens, no!"

*          *

If, with all the variance of my point of view, I had wanted to attack Bishop Mynster[3374] openly while he lived, Mrs. Burmann would have said: "Heavens, to attack an old man, to embitter an old man's last days!" "All right, let me wait patiently until he is dead. But when in addition an injudicious friend[3375] with his conception of Bishop Mynster later turns his whole life into a falsehood, in fact, a shocking falsehood, which in my opinion was not the case while Mynster lived and is not the case if the claim of his being a witness to the truth is omitted, must I not then make a Christian protest?" "Heavens, no! To attack a dead man—that is terrible."

There is nothing more to say about this than: This is nonsense or this is Mrs. Burmann speaking.

Even when the most earnest cause is to be introduced into this world (of sin and, possibly even more correctly, of nonsense), it is impossible to prevent the greatest power in society, "nonsense," from usurping it immediately and, thousand-tongued as it is, even wanting to transfərm its opinion into earnestness. It is impossible to prevent its usurpation of the cause—the most that can be done is, if possible, to prevent nonsense from becoming victorious to the extent that it becomes earnestness.

XI³ B 93   *n.d.*, 1855

« **6955**

The individual, the single individual, has been replaced by the race. This is the difference between "Christendom's" Christianity and the Christianity of the New Testament.

> That is why "Christendom" itself has to be split apart— the individual introduced—why one can be a Christian only by way of contrast.
>
> XI² A 406   *n.d.*, 1855

« **6956**

The one single thing we have to cling to with regard to an eternal life is one single fact contained in the New Testament—everything else is *about* that thing. Thus we are deluding ourselves—as if the prolixity of these 1800 years has made the matter more certain.[3376]

XI² A 407   *n.d.*, 1855

« **6957  *Why I Used This Newspaper*[3377]**

April 8, 1855

Luther[3378] declares in one of his sermons that preaching actually should not be done inside of churches. He says this in a sermon which as a matter of fact was delivered inside a church. So it was nothing more than talk; he did not carry it out in earnest. But certainly preaching should not be done inside of churches. It is extremely damaging for Christianity and represents a changing (a modifying) of Christianity by placing it at an artistic distance from actuality instead of letting it be heard right in the middle of actuality—and precisely for the sake of conflict (collision), for all this talk about quiet and quiet places and quiet hours[3379] as the proper element for the essentially Christian is upside down.

Therefore preaching should not be done in churches but on the street, right in the middle of life, the actuality of ordinary, weekday life.

Our age might not be ready for this and perhaps must first be prepared for it, but in any case I cannot do it for the simple reason that I lack the physical strength. My assignment is to speak with individuals, to converse, and then to use the pen.

Still I did want to achieve an approximation of preaching in the streets or of placing Christianity, thinking about Christianity, right into the middle of life's actuality and in conflict with its variants, and to that end I decided to use this newspaper. It is a political paper, has completely different interests, concerns itself with a great variety of subjects—but not with Christianity.

Having these little articles printed in this daily paper got them a hearing in a medium quite different from what they deal with; the result corresponds somewhat to listening to a sermon about Christianity on the street. I could not accomplish this effect with a specialized organ.

Another advantage was that I could communicate my thoughts in small doses. If I used a specialized organ, I would have to give considerably more at a time, with the result that it would be read in a different way, sometimes perhaps with greater concentration, but never with the stimulation experienced when, unprepared, one unexpectedly encounters the essentially Christian.

Furthermore, I managed in a simple way to maintain an independence, free from the possibility of becoming a party etc. (something most men surely regard as a great misfortune, the very last thing to be desired, but which I view differently). In a daily paper utterly unassociated with me and my cause, I live, if you please, as a tenant. It does not take sides with me in any way; in fact it accepts articles, even anonymous articles, against me (which I told the editor I did not object to, although I would not like to see the opposite). Thus I also succeeded in using the daily press without contradicting my own views of the press. Part of my objection to the daily press is its being used in such a way as to become a sensate power itself, also to its being used anonymously.

\*     \*

I gladly apologize to the readers of this paper, who may have very little or no interest at all in what so greatly concerns me, for taking up with my articles space that otherwise available for what would be of quite different interest to them.

$XI^3$ B 120   April 8, 1855

### « 6958 *The Christian State "Denmark" and I in It*

May 12, 1855

Of course, in the Christian state all are Christians; and Denmark, of course, is a Christian state.

This is the first point. The second is: what is Christianity, the Christianity of the New Testament? Well, one can say it in many ways but in this way as well: Christianity is the predominance of the outlook of eternity over everything temporal; Christianity grips a man in such a way that because of the eternal he forgets everything of this earth, considers everything of this earth to be "loss,"[3380] exposes himself even to suffering all possible persecution for the sake of the eternal.

Let us now look a bit more closely at life here in Denmark, in this Christian state where we are all Christians; and permit me for illustration to use my own life and what has happened to me in this Christian state.

So, then, in a state where all are Christians, there lives a man who undeniably has considerable talents and gifts and is unusually industrious, uncommonly unselfish. And yet this man must have the experience that to a very great majority of people his life represents a kind of insanity. Why? Because everyone knows that with all my strenuous work year in and year out I do not make any money but put money into it,[3381] and with all my strenuous work year in and year out nothing is achieved except to become a nobody and get into all sorts of ruckus and trouble.

*Ergo* such a life is a kind of insanity.

And this is in a society where all are Christians, where there are 1,000 oath-bound pastors, from whom—yes, that is right, it is only during a three-quarter hour period on Sunday that the congregation learns from these men that Christianity is renunciation of things earthly etc.; for the rest of Sunday and the rest of the week they learn from these men, especially by their example (and it is a familiar fact that example has an influence quite different from that of the tongue) that Christianity and the earnestness of life are to strive for things of this earth, that a life such as mine is a kind of insanity.

And this is a Christian state—we are all Christians.

Now to go on with what I have experienced in this Christian state. When, after persevering for years with perhaps unparalleled patience (also out of filial piety toward my late father[3382]) in bowing and scraping to the velvet lie (Christianly speaking) which was Bishop Mynster's whole life—and when a successor,[3383] who knows personally how untrue it is dares to stand in the pulpit and represent Bishop Mynster as a witness to the truth, one of the sainted procession—then when I finally protest, it is considered Christian to brand my act as a kind of villainy.

And this is a Christian state where all are Christians.

This cannot frustrate me. I do not write it for my own sake but because I think it can be informative for others, for, as I said, it cannot frustrate me. The N. T. is very helpful here, for it explains to me that this world in which I live is a world of tricks and lies. That is precisely it!

$XI^2$ A 399 May 12, 1855

« **6959**

With respect to the cause the same thing
will happen to my contemporaries as
happened to me: they will not escape,
they must go on through.

May 23, 1855
$XI^2$ A 409 May 23, 1855

« **6960**

Articles in *Fædrelandet*[3384]
from Dec. 18, 1854 to May 26, 1855
by
S. Kierkegaard
Reitzel's Publishing House[3385]

$XI^3$ B 128 *n.d.,* 1855

« **6961**

*Addition to 6960* ($XI^3$ B 128):
Contents[3386]

I Was Bishop Mynster[3387] a "Witness to the Truth," One of "the Authentic Witnesses"—Is This the Truth?

II There the Matter Rests.

III A Challenge to Me from Pastor Paludan-Müller.[3388]

IV The Point at Issue with Bishop Martensen;[3389] Christianly a Crucial Issue for the Hitherto Dubious (Regarded from the Point of View of Christianity) Established Church.

XVII Concerning the New Printing of *Practice in Christianity*

XVIII That Bishop Martensen's Silence Is (1) Christianly Indefensible, (2) Ridiculous, (3) Stupid-Shrewd, (4) in More than One Respect Contemptible.

[*In margin:*
To Mr. Schou, typesetter
**N.B.** This article is not on the first page but in the feuilleton, columns 4 and 5.]

$XI^3$ B 129   *n.d.*, 1855

« **6962**

Perhaps you[3391] will be so kind as to undertake the publication of a separate edition of my articles in *Fædrelandet,* which are enclosed.

They are to be printed verbatim.[*] Each article is to have an initial page and number of its own; only in case of a serialized article is the text to be printed directly following the lead article, but with a division line and in smaller type and also with "feuilleton" printed with very small type in parentheses under its title.

In addition, under the number of each article *Fædrelandet,* No. —— d. —— 18—— is to be printed in very small type. For example:

No. I
(*Fædrelandet,* No. 295, Dec. 18, 1854)
Was Bishop Mynster a "Witness to the Truth," One of
"the Authentic Witnesses to the Truth"–Is This True?
in February, 1854.

Another example:

No. XV
(*Fædrelandet,* No. ——, date, year)
A Conclusion

———

A Monologue
(Feuilleton)

"Feuilleton" is to be set in small type.

$XI^3$ B 131   *n.d.*, 1855

« **6963**

[*]*In margin of 6962* (xi³ b 131):
But of course my name which is under each title is to be omitted.

xi³ b 132    *n.d.*

« **6964  Babbling**
         *or*
         **Kjøbenhavnsposten**

May 28

There are various kinds of talk; there is loose talk, flippant talk, stupid talk, good talk, etc. There is also the kind of talk we describe as talking on and on, and perhaps this is the kind that is also called babbling.

When a newspaper, in both prose and poetry, has pronounced a man insane, then this man might venture to expect that, in all fairness, the paper will quit talking about him; and it betrays contempt for its readers when, after declaring a man insane, it goes on chatting with them about him as if he were not insane. This kind of conduct is talking on and on, is babbling.

This is the relation of *Kjøbenhavnsposten* to me. On the occasion of my first article[3392] against Martensen the paper[3393] pronounced me—in both prose and poetry—insane. "Fine," thought I, "so I am free from *Kjøbenshavnsposten*, one less pestering triviality."

But later *Kjøbenhavnsposten*[3394] got other ideas. Without retracting that statement, it now wants to talk about me as if I were not insane. Perhaps that first pronouncement was a test to see if it could be done, something like a bid one makes at an auction to see if he might have the good luck of buying what he is bidding on at such a ridiculously low price.

Incidentally, what it is saying about me now is, if not babbling, nevertheless talk which clearly shows (a) that *Kjøbenhavnsposten* is utterly unqualified to discuss religious matters, (b) that it never reads what it discusses of my writing, something I am not obliged to prove but is merely something that ought to be said, [*in margin*: (c) that its biased articles against me are intended to be vexatious, for which it perhaps is hired by the clergy.]

May I suggest to *Kjøbenhavnsposten* that it get itself a more reliable coworker; if not, that include in its paper a special column for religious matters and caption it "Babbling" and that the editorial staff members write in it themselves. Or if it so happens that as far as politics is concerned the paper also babbles (of this I have no idea since I do not understand politics), the whole paper should take the title "Babbling." The old name of *Kjøbenhavnsposten* need not be dropped; unfortunately, there is enough babbling in Copenhagen, so the paper could well be called *Snik-Snak eller Kjøbenhavnsposten.*

*          *

My motivation for getting mixed up in this right now is religious —because it has so pleased the Almighty, who best knows how loathe I am to do so. They may rage at me as aggressively as they please, but by speaking occasionally I will make sure that I do not avoid whatsoever hubbub it is my duty to expose myself to [*in margin*: but I shall not shirk by keeping silent], and that anyone who pays attention to me will know my opinion on what happens in connection with this affair and me.

$XI^2$ A 411   *n.d.,* 1855

« **6965**

If a person were permitted to distinguish among Biblical texts, I could call this text [James 1:17–21] my first love, to which one generally ("always") returns at some time: and I could call this text my only love—to which one returns again and again and again and "always."[3395]

$XI^3$ B 291:4 August, 1855

« **6966**  *Only a Man of Will Can Become a Christian*

———

Sept. 23, 1855

Only a man of will can become a Christian. For only a man of will has a will that can be broken. But a man of will whose will is broken by the unconditioned or by God is a Christian. The stronger the natural will, the deeper the break can be and the better the Christian. This is what has been described by the expressive phrase: the new obedience. A Christian is a man of will who has acquired a new will. A Christian is a man of will who no longer wills his own will but with the passion of his crushed will—radically changed—wills another's will.

A man of understanding can never become a Christian; the most he can achieve, through the power of imagination, is to play with the Christian problems. And it is this type, if you please, of Christians that produce every possible confusion in Christianity. They become scholars, scientists, make everything copious and complicated, and drown therein the essential point of Christianity. But of course Governance in his compassion can do much to change a man of understanding into a man of will so that he can become a Christian. For the possibility of becoming a man of will lies in every man. The most irresponsible person, the most cowardly, the most phlegmatic, a *raisoneur*[3396] without beginning and end: place them in a situation of mortal danger and they will become men of will after all. It is true that necessity cannot produce freedom, but it can place the freedom within man as close as possible to becoming will.

Consequently Christianity or becoming a Christian is not at all related to transforming the intellect—but to transforming the will. But this transformation is the most painful of all operations, comparable to a vivisection, the right to which is ethically dubious. And because it is so appalling, to become a Christian was changed long ago in Christendom into a remodeling of the intellect (insofar as it is not made into something utterly meaningless, something one is automatically). The asceticism of the Middle Ages of course perceived more correctly (compared to all this scholarly nonsense, all this gibberish about proofs) that the issue is a transformation of the will and approached the matter from that perspective. The mistake made in the asceticism of the Middle Ages was to strike out the specifically Christian suffering: to suffer at the hands of men. The ascetic allowed men to admire him as the extraordinary. In that way the human aggregate got mixed into it; the human aggregate became ordinary Christians. If the ascetic had spoken the truth and said: "There are no extraordinary Christians; what I express is but an approximation of all that is required of all; what I express is but an approximation of what it simply means to be Christian"—he would have been persecuted. One can escape suffering at the hands of men in two ways: by diminishing the Christian requirement and making use of this oneself or by more scrupulously abiding by the Christian requirement oneself but egotistically calling this the extraordinary. Then the human aggregate still comes along and one avoids persecution; in both cases the human aggregate is transformed into the very opposite of what it must become in true Christianity, something one profits from, just plain financial profit etc., or something from which one has the profit of an admiring chorus.

XI² A 436   September 23, 1855

« **6967  *Certainly Bishop Mynster*[3397] *Was a Great Man!***

Sept. 24, 1855

But Christianly he was not great. No, but esthetically he was great: as a forger.

Understood in this way he had esthetically my unqualified admiration; personally he had my whole devotion,[3398] "also out of reverence for my deceased father"; Christianly, in me Governance put the man most dangerous to him on his side.

*        *

Most men have no time at all to have religion, just as a child does not have time to gather his thoughts, simply because he is continuously preoccupied with the abundant variety of sense impressions. In that sense most men have no religion at all. To have a religion, to be a "Christian" in "Christendom", to them simply means to have a pass enabling them to enter into the actuality of this life. They are preoccupied with the abundant variety of life, with sense-impressions, the pressure of business, curiosity, etc., etc. Just as the child cannot stand quietly but hops up and down to get permission as quickly as possible to go out to the hill, over to the playground, so these men are utterly impatient to get into the sensate hustle and bustle of this life. Since the "Christian" state has now (sagaciously!) arranged it so no one can play the game without a certificate from the pastor stating that he is a Christian, all these men are then indeed, yes, indeed, Christians. The pastor's certificate stating that they are Christians has just about the same importance to them as a ticket to Tivoli or for a boat or a bus: it means that they are going along.

Persons who do have some spare time to have religion nevertheless wish to have this matter of religion decided as early and as quickly as possible—so they can get busy enjoying this life. So every once in a while they may have a spare moment also for religion, but on the condition that it be a kind of enjoyment and that it be decided once and for all that they have religion and thus eternal salvation is settled for them.

If there is a clergyman, and if esthetically very gifted, so much the better, and if he is willing to take it upon himself to represent this kind of religion under the name of Christianity—yes, indeed, there is lionizing and swarming; he is loved, revered, adored, etc. For like all other men these men privately have a vague idea that one cannot have religion in this way, neither in such a way that one has no time at all to have religion nor in such a way that every once in a while one has a spare moment for religion, and that it is not at all immoderate of "eternity" to demand all of a man's time. This demand is the one men fear most, for they all love time, which is their element, and fear eternity. That is why they lionize such a teacher.

Such a teacher was Bishop Mynster. He was the bank for a whole generation. How all these men did enjoy life; yet in eternity all of them inevitably will hear to their horror that this is not Christianity, will, if I dare say so, will present a banknote with the signature: Mynster. For Mynster was a bank. In the deepest and most solitary silence in which I speak only with myself, and with my detective information, I used to call Mynster: The National Bank. I was alluding to something specific which the Copenhagen police will understand, for they of course are well aware that a few years ago in north Sjælland there lived (whether he is still living I do not know, but the police do, no doubt) a person well known to the police by the name: The National Bank. His business was making counterfeit notes, and he did a good job.

That was the point of similarity—they both made counterfeit notes. Otherwise there of course was no comparison, especially with respect to the size of the business. On the whole, when it comes to scope and size, there is absolutely nothing analagous to the crimes practiced in the realm of the religious. Even the most experienced and most undaunted secret police agent anywhere in the world will shudder at taking on this case, which involves using false bank notes on eternity to defraud a whole generation throughout its whole life and to defraud them for eternity.

Nor does the rest of the criminal world have anything analagous, anything that could even resemble an analogy to the way these crimes pay off or are paid with gold, goods, everything worldly, and with—idolization.

But perhaps it may be said that Bishop Mynster was never paid adequately, that his age was not sufficiently grateful. Toward the end of his life a trust fund[3399] was collected that was to bear his name. Mynster, always sagacious, found an opportunity to express thanks[3400] for this considerable sum—about 7,000 rix-dollars. By rights, in line with Mynster's proclamation of Christianity, it seems to me that just one of our millionaires ought to have given, and gladly, 30,000 rix-dollars. For the New Testament holds that so exceedingly difficult is it for millionaires to enter the Kingdom that it is just about impossible. But Bishop M. gave them no trouble, and yet, if one is a millionaire, it would be well worth it to give 30,000 rix-dollars. Of course, it is a quite different matter if all Mynster's proclamation of Christianity was an optical illusion and his bank notes on eternity false, for then four shillings is actually too large a contribution to the fund, and three shillings too much for the commemorative monument, if he is being thanked in the capacity of a teacher of Christianity. But [if he is being thanked] as orator, rhetorician or (to recall the *Berlingske Tidende*'s naive but true announcement of his death[3401] which made one completely forget that the reference was to a teacher, a Christian bishop, a spiritual counselor who, after practicing under an eternal responsibility for more years than are normally given a man to live, has now gone to the accounting of eternity) as master stylist, distinguished by "a hitherto unattained use of language" and as an actor distinguished by "his beautifully modeled countenance," then it can be entirely appropriate.

XI² A 437   September 24, 1855

« **6968  Minor Remarks**

Sept. 24, 1855

1.

*A Metaphor for the Suffering of a Christian*

There are people with nervous systems so delicate and sensitive that the weather affects them in an almost appalling way. They are able to detect a change in the weather far in advance, perhaps suffer most from anxiety, restlessness, and torment when a storm is brewing but is preceded by what we call fine weather, but there is something wrong with this fine weather.

All people of animal vigor consider fine weather to be glorious weather—and then there is the unlucky person whom the stronger ones tease and torment and distress because they are unable to understand what he is talking about, how anyone can call such fine weather bad weather.

But this lasts only a few days, and sometimes the man with the frail nervous system has the fringe benefit of others having to acknowledge later that he was right.

But now suppose that this weather lasts and that such an unlucky person has to endure living a whole lifetime in this situation, surrounded by people of animal vigor.

So it is with Christian suffering. In appearance this world seems to be a glorious world, a world that is advancing; in the world of appearance it seems as if Christianity does exist; indeed, all are Christians and there are 1,000 pastors—and now the poor wretched Christian who is so sensitively structured that he perceives that this whole wonderful world is a pack of lies, that its progress is a retrogression, if that is still possible, that this matter of everybody's being a Christian and the 1,000 pastors is an optical illusion, the poor Christian who in fear and trembling orients himself to the accounting of eternity—think what he must suffer by living among men with an entirely different nervous system. If he does not hide the contents of his soul as carefully as possible, these men, to feel their superiority, will avail themselves of the opportunity to taunt him, and if he does not put up with it patiently—which in another sense goads them on—he will be pronounced insane, and if they cannot get the better of him that way, they will kill him.

2.

### The Human Race's Chitchat

Men of ideas, bearers of ideas, achieve absolutely nothing—except immortality—because everyone who patiently, gladly, and gratefully is dedicated solely to carrying the idea is immortal.

But they achieve absolutely nothing. While they are living, their words are drowned in the babbling of the age, and after their death their words are drowned in the babbling of the assistant professors. Their significance actually consists only in giving the human race something to talk about.

Just as a family, a social gathering, a town feel the need to have something to talk about, the human race also feels the same need. The only difference is that town-gossip is carried on by barbers, shopkeepers, etc., the human race's chitchat by professors and pastors, and that a big thing is made of this chitchat, that it is printed, and that sciences develop to maintain an overview of this chitchat.

That the chitchat of the human race has such great status compared to town-gossip is no doubt largely due to the fact that pastors and professors make a living on it. What a man with a family lives on is an earnest matter. If the barbers made a living by carrying on town-gossip instead of sustaining themselves in another way and just making a sideline of town-gossip, their status would also rise. This is seen by the status it actually got when the journalists got hold of it, simply because the journalists make a living on it. People will have respect only for that on which one makes a living.

XI² A 438 September 24, 1855

« 6969 *The Christian Understanding of the Destiny of This Life*[3402]

The destiny of this life is that it be brought to the extremity of life-weariness.

The person who when brought to that point can maintain or the person whom God helps so he is able to maintain that it is God who has brought him to that point—such a person, from the Christian point of view, passes the examination of life and is matured for eternity.

I came into existence [*er blevet til*] through a crime, I came into existence against God's will. The guilt, which in one sense is not mine even though it makes me an offender in God's eyes, is to give life. The punishment corresponds to the guilt: to be deprived of all zest for life, to be led into the most extreme life-weariness. Man wants to dabble in the creator's activity, if not by creating man, at least by giving life. "You certainly must pay for this, because life-weariness is the destiny of this life, yet by my grace, for only to you who are saved do I show the grace of leading you to the extremity of life-weariness. Most men these days are characterized by such absence of spirit and of grace that the punishment cannot even be used for them. Completely wrapped up in this life, they clutch at this life of nothingness and become nothing; their lives are wasted.

The persons in whom there still is some spirit and whom grace still does not disregard are led on to that point where life reaches the extremity of life-weariness. But they cannot reconcile themselves to it; they mutiny against God, and so on.

Only those persons who, brought to this point of life-weariness, are able by the help of grace to maintain that God does it out of love and do not conceal in their souls, in the remotest corner, any doubt about God as love—only those persons are matured for eternity.

God accepts them into eternity. But what, specifically, does God want? He wants souls able to praise, adore, worship, and thank him—the business of angels. Therefore God is surrounded by angels. The sort of beings found in legions in "Christendom," who for a few dollars are able to shout and trumpet to God's honor and praise, this sort does not please him. No, the angels please him, and what pleases him even more than the praise of angels is a human being who in the last lap of this life, when God seemingly changes into sheer cruelty and with the most cruelly devised cruelty does everything to deprive him of all zest for life, nevertheless continues to believe that God is love, that God does it out of love. Such a human being becomes an angel. In heaven it is easy to praise God,[3403] but the period of learning, the time of schooling, is always the most strenuous. Like a man traveling around the whole world with the fixed idea of hearing a singer with a perfect tone, God sits in heaven and listens. And every time he hears praise from a person whom he has brought to the extremity of life-weariness, God says to himself: This is it. He says it as if he were making a discovery, but of course he was prepared, for he himself was present with the person and helped him insofar as God can give help for what only freedom can do. Only freedom can do it, but the surprising thing is to be able to express oneself by thanking God for it, as if it were God who did it. And in his joy over being able to do this, he is so happy that he will hear absolutely nothing about his having done it, but he gratefully attributes all to God and prays God that it may stay that way, that it is God who does it, for he has no faith in himself, but he does have faith in God.

XI² A 439 September 25, 1855

# Bibliography
## Collation of Entries
### Notes

# Bibliography

## KIERKEGAARD'S WORKS IN ENGLISH

Editions referred to in the notes.
Listed according to the original order of publication or the time of writing.

*The Concept of Irony*, tr. Lee Capel. New York: Harper and Row, 1966; Bloomington: Indiana University Press, 1968. (*Om Begrebet Ironi*, by S. A. Kierkegaard, 1841.)

*Either/Or*, I, tr. David F. Swenson and Lillian Marvin Swenson; II, tr. Walter Lowrie, 2 ed. rev. Howard A. Johnson. Princeton: Princeton University Press, 1971. (*Enten-Eller*, I–II, ed. Victor Eremita, 1843.)

*Johannes Climacus or De omnibus dubitandum est*, and *A Sermon*, tr. T. H. Croxall. London: Adam and Charles Black, 1958. ("Johannes Climacus eller *De omnibus dubitandum est*," written 1842–43, unpubl., *Papirer* IV B 1; "Demis-Prædiken," 1844, unpubl., *Papirer* IV C 1.)

*Upbuilding* [*Edifying*] *Discourses*, I–IV, tr. David F. Swenson and Lillian Marvin Swenson. Minneapolis: Augsburg Publishing House, 1943–46. (*Opbyggelige Taler*, by S. Kierkegaard, 1843, 1844.)

*Fear and Tremblimg* (with *The Sickness unto Death*), tr. Walter Lowrie. Princeton: Princeton University Press, 1968. (*Frygt og Bæven*, by Johannes de Silentio, 1843.)

*Repetition*, tr. Walter Lowrie. Princeton: Princeton University Press, 1941. (*Gjentagelsen*, by Constantin Constantius, 1843.)

*Philosophical Fragments*, tr. David Swenson, 2 ed. rev. Howard Hong. Princeton: Princeton University Press, 1962. (*Philosophiske Smuler*, by Johannes Climacus, ed. S. Kierkegaard, 1844.)

*The Concept of Anxiety* [*Dread*], tr. Walter Lowrie, 2 ed. Princeton: Princeton University Press, 1957. (*Begrebet Angest*, by Vigilius Haufniensis, ed. S. Kierkegaard, 1844.)

*Three Discourses on Imagined Occasions* [*Thoughts on Crucial Situations in Human Life*], tr. David F. Swenson, ed. Lillian Marvin Swenson. Minneapolis: Augsburg Publishing House, 1941. (*Tre Taler ved tænkte Leiligheder*, by S. Kierkegaard, 1845.)

*Stages on Life's Way*, tr. Walter Lowrie. Princeton: Princeton University Press, 1940. (*Stadier paa Livets Vej*, ed. Hilarius Bogbinder, 1845.)

*Concluding Unscientific Postscript*, tr. David F. Swenson and Walter Lowrie. Princeton: Princeton University Press for American-Scandinavian Foundation, 1941. (*Afsluttende uvidenskabelig Efterskrift*, by Johannes Climacus, ed. S. Kierkegaard, 1846.)

*The Present Age* [part of *Two Ages: the Age of Revolution and the Present Age. A Literary Review*] and *Two Minor Ethical-Religious Essays* [*Treatises*], tr. Alexander Dru and Walter Lowrie. London and New York: Oxford University Press, 1940. (*En literair Anmeldelse. To Tidsaldre*, by S. Kierkegaard, 1846; *Tvende ethisk-religieuse Smaa-Afhandlinger*, by H. H., 1849.)

*On Authority and Revelation, The Book on Adler*, tr. Walter Lowrie. Princeton: Princeton University Press, 1955. (*Bogen om Adler*, written 1846–47, unpubl., *Papirer* VII² B 235; VIII² B 1–27.)

*Upbuilding Discourses in Various Spirits*. (*Opbyggelige Taler i forskjellig Aand*, by S. Kierkegaard, 1847.) Part One, *Purity of Heart* [*"En Leiligheds-Tale"*], tr. Douglas Steere, 2 ed. New York: Harper, 1948. Part Three and Part Two, *The Gospel of Suffering* and *The Lilies of the Field* [*"Lidelsernes Evangelium"* and *"Lilierne paa Marken og Himlens Fugle"*], tr. David F. Swenson and Lillian Marvin Swenson. Minneapolis: Augsburg Publishing House, 1948.

*Works of Love*, tr. Howard and Edna Hong. New York: Harper and Row, 1962. (*Kjerlighedens Gjerninger*, by S. Kierkegaard, 1847.)

[*The*] *Crisis* [*and a Crisis*] *in the Life of an Actress*, tr. Stephen Crites. New York: Harper and Row, 1967. (*Krisen og en Krise i en Skuespillerindes Liv*, by Inter et Inter, *Fædrelandet*, 188–91, July 24–27, 1848.)

*Christian Discourses*, including *The Lily of the Field and the Bird of the Air* and *Three Discourses at the Communion on Fridays*, tr. Walter Lowrie. London and New York: Oxford University Press, 1940. (*Cristelige Taler*, by S. Kierkegaard, 1848; *Lilien paa Marken og Fuglen under Himlen*, by S. Kierkegaard, 1849; *Tre Taler ved Altergangen om Fredagen*, by S. Kierkegaard, 1849.)

*The Sickness unto Death* (with *Fear and Trembling*), tr. Walter Lowrie. Princeton: Princeton University Press, 1968. (*Sygdommen til Døden*, by Anti-Climacus, ed. S. Kierkegaard, 1849.)

*Practice* [*Training*] *in Christianity*, including "The Woman Who was a Sinner," tr. Walter Lowrie. London and New York: Oxford University Press, 1941; repr. Princeton: Princeton University Press, 1944. (*Indøvelse i Christendom*, by Anti-Climacus, ed. S. Kierkegaard, 1850; *En opbyggelig Tale*, by S. Kierkegaard, 1850.)

*Armed Neutrality* and *An Open Letter*, tr. Howard V. Hong and Edna H. Hong. Bloomington and London: Indiana University Press, 1968. (*Den bevæbnede Neutralitet*, written 1848–49, publ. 1965; *Foranledigt ved en Yttring af Dr. Rudelbach mig betræffende*, *Fædrelandet*, no. 26, January 31, 1851.)

*The Point of View for My Work as an Author,* including the Appendix " 'The Single Individual' Two 'Notes' Concerning My Work as an Author" and *On My Work as an Author,* tr. Walter Lowrie. London and New York: Oxford University Press, 1939. (*Synspunktet for min Forfatter-Virksomhed,* by S. Kierkegaard, posthumously published, 1859; *Om min Forfatter-Virksomhed,* by S. Kierkegaard, 1851.)

*For Self-Examination,* tr. Edna and Howard Hong. Minneapolis: Augsburg Publishing House, 1940. (*Til Selvprøvelse,* by S. Kierkegaard, 1851.)

*Judge for Yourselves!,* including *For Self-Examination, Two Discourses at the Communion on Fridays,* and *The Unchangeableness of God* (tr. David Swenson), tr. Walter Lowrie. Princeton: Princeton University Press, 1944. (*Dommer Selv!* by S. Kierkegaard, 1852; *To Taler ved Altergangen om Fredagen,* by S. Kierkegaard, 1851; *Guds Uforanderlighed,* by S. Kierkegaard, 1855.)

*Kierkegaard's Attack upon "Christendom,"* 1854–1855, tr. Walter Lowrie. Princeton: Princeton University Press, 1944. (*Bladartikler* I–XXI, by S. Kierkegaard, *Fædrelandet,* 1854–55; *Dette skal siges; saa være det da sagt,* by S. Kierkegaard, 1855; *Øieblikket,* by S. Kierkegaard, 1–9, 1855; 10, 1905; *Hvad Christus dømmer om officiel Christendom,* by S. Kierkegaard, 1855.)

*The Journals of Søren Kierkegaard,* tr. Alexander Dru. London and New York: Oxford University Press, 1938. (From *Søren Kierkegaards Papier,* I–XI[1] in 18 volumes, 1909–1936.)

*The Last Years,* tr. Ronald C. Smith. New York: Harper and Row, 1965. (From *Papirer* XI[1]–XI[3], 1936–48.)

*Søren Kierkegaard's Journals and Papers,* tr. Howard V. Hong and Edna H. Hong, assisted by Gregor Malantschuk. Bloomington and London: Indiana University Press, I, 1967; II, 1970; III–IV, 1975; V–VII, 1978. (From *Papirer* I–XI[3] and XII–XIII, 2 ed., and *Breve og Akstykker vedrørende Søren Kierkegaard,* ed. Niels Thulstrup, I–II, 1953–54.) Cited in notes as *J.P.*

———

At various times in recent years over twenty-five paperback editions of twenty Kierkegaard titles have appeared in English translation. For paperback editions currently available, see the latest issue of *Paperback Books in Print,* published by R. R. Bowker Co., 1180 Avenue of the Americas, New York, N.Y.

General works on Kierkegaard are listed in the bibliography, *Søren Kierkegaard's Journals and Papers,* I, pp. 482–88. Studies of a more limited and specific nature are listed in the appropriate section of topical notes in volumes 1–4 of *Søren Kierkegaard's Journals and Papers.*

# Collation of Entries in this Volume With the Danish Edition of the *Papirer* and the *Breve*

Numbers in the left-hand column are the standard international references to the *Papirer*. Numbers in parentheses are the serially ordered references in the present edition.

| Volume IX A | Volume IX A | Volume IX A | Volume IX A |
| --- | --- | --- | --- |
| 8 (6141) | 71 (6167) | 142 (6192) | 189 (6220) |
| 9 (6142) | 72 (6168) | 144 (6193) | 190 (6221) |
| 10 (6143) | 73 (6169) | 150 (6195) | 203 (6222) |
| 18 (6144) | 74 (6170) | 155 (6198) | 205 (6223) |
| 23 (6145) | 81 (6171) | 156 (6199) | 208 (6224) |
| 25 (6146) | 83 (6172) | 159 (6200) | 209 (6225) |
| 26 (6147) | 85 (6173) | 166 (6201) | 211 (6226) |
| 27 (6148) | 86 (6174) | 167 (6202) | 213 (6227) |
| 33 (6149) | 87 (6175) | 168 (6203) | 214 (6228) |
| 39 (6150) | 99 (6176) | 169 (6204) | 216 (6229) |
| 41 (6151) | 100 (6177) | 171 (6205) | 217 (6230) |
| 42 (6152) | 106 (6178) | 172 (6206) | 218 (6231) |
| 43 (6153) | 108 (6179) | 173 (6207) | 219 (6232) |
| 48 (6154) | 122 (6180) | 174 (6208) | 220 (6233) |
| 50 (6155) | 123 (6181) | 175 (6209) | 222 (6234) |
| 53 (6156) | 125 (6182) | 176 (6210) | 223 (6235) |
| 54 (6157) | 128 (6183) | 178 (6211) | 225 (6236) |
| 55 (6158) | 129 (6184) | 179 (6212) | 226 (6237) |
| 62 (6159) | 130 (6185) | 180 (6213) | 227 (6238) |
| 64 (6160) | 131 (6186) | 183 (6214) | 229 (6239) |
| 65 (6161) | 132 (6187) | 184 (6215) | 230 (6240) |
| 66 (6162) | 134 (6188) | 185 (6216) | 236 (6241) |
| 67 (6163) | 135 (6189) | 186 (6217) | 241 (6242) |
| 68 (6164) | 137 (6190) | 187 (6218) | 243 (6243) |
| 69 (6165) | 139 (6191) | 188 (6219) | 251 (6244) |
| 70 (6166) | | | |

| Volume IX A | Volume IX A | Volume X¹ A | Volume X¹ A |
|---|---|---|---|
| 255 (6245) | 488 (6291) | 74 (6325) | 161 (6366) |
| 258 (6246) | 492 (6194) | 77 (6326) | 162 (6367) |
| 262 (6247) | 493 (6196) | 78 (6327) | 163 (6368) |
| 265 (6248) | 498 (6278) | 80 (6328) | 166 (6369) |
| 271 (6249) | 499 (6279) | 84 (6329) | 167 (6370) |
| 276 (6250) | 500 (6280) | 88 (6330) | 169 (6371) |
| 281 (6251) | **Volume IX B** | 89 (6333) | 183 (6372) |
| 283 (6252) | | 90 (6334) | 187 (6373) |
| 285 (6253) | 63:7 (6255) | 92 (6335) | 192 (6374) |
| 288 (6254) | 67 (6292) | 94 (6336) | 199 (6375) |
| 293 (6258) | 68 (6293) | 95 (6337) | 202 (6376) |
| 298 (6259) | **Volume X¹ A** | 100 (6338) | 206 (6377) |
| 307 (6260) | 8 (6298) | 104 (6339) | 228 (6378) |
| 310 (6261) | 9 (6299) | 107 (6340) | 234 (6379) |
| 312 (6262) | 11 (6300) | 110 (6341) | 239 (6380) |
| 321 (6263) | 14 (6301) | 111 (6342) | 247 (6382) |
| 338 (6264) | 15 (6302) | 112 (6343) | 250 (6383) |
| 343 (6265) | 23 (6303) | 113 (6344) | 258 (6384) |
| 371 (6266) | 24 (6304) | 115 (6345) | 260 (6385) |
| 375 (6268) | 33 (6305) | 116 (6346) | 262 (6386) |
| 379 (6269) | 37 (6307) | 118 (6347) | 263 (6387) |
| 381 (6270) | 39 (6308) | 120 (6348) | 266 (6388) |
| 390 (6271) | 41 (6309) | 121 (6350) | 272 (6389) |
| 393 (6272) | 42 (6310) | 123 (6351) | 273 (6390) |
| 408 (6273) | 43 (6311) | 126 (6352) | 281 (6391) |
| 411 (6274) | 45 (6312) | 130 (6353) | 289 (6392) |
| 413 (6275) | 46 (6313) | 131 (6354) | 300 (6393) |
| 416 (6276) | 52 (6314) | 137 (6355) | 309 (6394) |
| 421 (6277) | 53 (6315) | 138 (6356) | 320 (6395) |
| 428 (6281) | 54 (6316) | 139 (6357) | 322 (6396) |
| 432 (6282) | 56 (6317) | 140 (6358) | 323 (6397) |
| 448 (6283) | 58 (6318) | 143 (6359) | 325 (6398) |
| 451 (6284) | 61 (6319) | 146 (6360) | 336 (6399) |
| 458 (6285) | 63 (6320) | 147 (6361) | 338 (6400) |
| 463 (6286) | 67 (6321) | 151 (6362) | 342 (6401) |
| 467 (6287) | 71 (6322) | 152 (6363) | 343 (6402) |
| 471 (6288) | 72 (6323) | 156 (6364) | 351 (6407) |
| 473 (6289) | 73 (6324) | 158 (6365) | 366 (6408) |
| 484 (6290) | | | |

| Volume X¹ A | Volume X¹ A | Volume X² A | Volume X² A |
|---|---|---|---|
| 374 (6409) | 553 (6448) | 10 (6489) | 184 (6528) |
| 377 (6410) | 556 (6449) | 11 (6490) | 191 (6529) |
| 381 (6411) | 557 (6450) | 15 (6491) | 192 (6530) |
| 385 (6412) | 567 (6451) | 20 (6492) | 193 (6531) |
| 402 (6413) | 568 (6452) | 25 (6493) | 195 (6532) |
| 404 (6414) | 569 (6453) | 39 (6494) | 196 (6533) |
| 406 (6415) | 570 (6454) | 40 (6495) | 199 (6534) |
| 422 (6416) | 571 (6455) | 44 (6496) | 204 (6535) |
| 423 (6417) | 576 (6456) | 45 (6497) | 205 (6536) |
| 424 (6418) | 583 (6457) | 48 (6498) | 210 (6538) |
| 425 (6419) | 584 (6458) | 56 (6499) | 211 (6539) |
| 441 (6420) | 586 (6459) | 61 (6500) | 212 (6540) |
| 450 (6421) | 588 (6460) | 66 (6501) | 213 (6541) |
| 469 (6422) | 593 (6461) | 68 (6502) | 214 (6542) |
| 476 (6423) | 594 (6462) | 75 (6503) | 215 (6543) |
| 483 (6424) | 598 (6463) | 88 (6504) | 216 (6544) |
| 488 (6425) | 615 (6464) | 89 (6505) | 217 (6545) |
| 494 (6426) | 616 (6465) | 90 (6506) | 228 (6546) |
| 495 (6427) | 617 (6466) | 92 (6507) | 242 (6547) |
| 496 (6428) | 640 (6467) | 94 (6508) | 251 (6548) |
| 497 (6429) | 643 (6468) | 101 (6509) | 252 (6549) |
| 498 (6430) | 644 (6469) | 105 (6510) | 256 (6550) |
| 510 (6431) | 648 (6470) | 106 (6511) | 260 (6551) |
| 513 (6432) | 653 (6474) | 109 (6512) | 261 (6552) |
| 517 (6433) | 659 (6476) | 110 (6513) | 273 (6553) |
| 519 (6435) | 660 (6477) | 112 (6514) | 275 (6554) |
| 520 (6436) | 661 (6478) | 126 (6515) | 277 (6555) |
| 525 (6437) | 663 (6479) | 134 (6516) | 278 (6556) |
| 529 (6438) | 664 (6480) | 147 (6517) | 280 (6557) |
| 530 (6439) | 665 (6481) | 148 (6519) | 281 (6561) |
| 531 (6440) | 667 (6482) | 150 (6520) | 285 (6562) |
| 535 (6441) | 668 (6483) | 157 (6521) | 298 (6563) |
| 536 (6442) | 670 (6484) | 158 (6522) | 302 (6564) |
| 538 (6443) | 671 (6485) | 163 (6523) | 307 (6565) |
| 541 (6444) | 676 (6486) | 167 (6524) | 315 (6568) |
| 546 (6445) | 678 (6487) | 174 (6525) | 338 (6570) |
| 548 (6446) | **Volume X² A** | 177 (6526) | 345 (6571) |
| 551 (6447) | 3 (6488) | 183 (6527) | 346 (6572) |

| Volume X² A | Volume X³ A | Volume X³ A | Volume X³ A |
|---|---|---|---|
| 352 (6573) | 78 (6617) | 321 (6661) | 635 (6702) |
| 372 (6575) | 86 (6618) | 367 (6662) | 636 (6703) |
| 374 (6576) | 88 (6619) | 381 (6664) | 637 (6704) |
| 375 (6577) | 89 (6620) | 389 (6665) | 647 (6705) |
| 393 (6578) | 90 (6621) | 391 (6666) | 650 (6706) |
| 411 (6579) | 94 (6622) | 399 (6667) | 661 (6707) |
| 413 (6580) | 98 (6623) | 402 (6668) | 663 (6708) |
| 415 (6581) | 99 (6624) | 403 (6669) | 678 (6709) |
| 425 (6582) | 112 (6625) | 404 (6670) | 680 (6709a) |
| 427 (6583) | 115 (6626) | 415 (6671) | 716 (6710) |
| 440 (6585) | 128 (6627) | 416 (6672) | 730 (6711) |
| 459 (6586) | 142 (6628) | 422 (6673) | 742 (6712) |
| 475 (6587) | 144 (6629) | 423 (6674) | 769 (6713) |
| 476 (6588) | 146 (6630) | 434 (6677) | 770 (6714) |
| 488 (6589) | 147 (6631) | 435 (6678) | 771 (6715) |
| 525 (6590) | 152 (6632) | 448 (6679) | 780 (6716) |
| 534 (6591) | 161 (6633) | 450 (6680) | 782 (6717) |
| 544 (6592) | 163 (6634) | 453 (6681) | 789 (6718) |
| 560 (6593) | 164 (6635) | 472 (6682) | 799 (6719) |
| 586 (6594) | 168 (6642) | 483 (6683) | 800 (6720) |
| 596 (6595) | 174 (6643) | 487 (6684) | Volume X⁴ A |
| 601 (6597) | 183 (6644) | 519 (6685) | |
| 605 (6602) | 189 (6645) | 526 (6686) | 6 (6721) |
| 619 (6603) | 190 (6646) | 530 (6687) | 8 (6722) |
| 622 (6604) | 191 (6647) | 550 (6688) | 9 (6723) |
| 627 (6605) | 194 (6648) | 551 (6689) | 14 (6724) |
| Volume X³ A | 204 (6649) | 555 (6690) | 20 (6725) |
| | 210 (6650) | 563 (6691) | 23 (6726) |
| 3 (6607) | 219 (6651) | 564 (6692) | 33 (6727) |
| 4 (6608) | 239 (6652) | 565 (6693) | 36 (6728) |
| 8 (6609) | 249 (6653) | 568 (6694) | 37 (6729) |
| 12 (6610) | 258 (6654) | 569 (6695) | 52 (6730) |
| 13 (6611) | 261 (6655) | 577 (6696) | 53 (6731) |
| 30 (6612) | 265 (6656) | 578 (6697) | 55 (6732) |
| 41 (6613) | 304 (6657) | 591 (6698) | 56 (6733) |
| 67 (6614) | 309 (6658) | 599 (6699) | 57 (6734) |
| 68 (6615) | 310 (6659) | 628 (6700) | 58 (6735) |
| 77 (6616) | 318 (6660) | 629 (6701) | 64 (6736) |

| Volume X⁴ A | Volume X⁴ A | Volume X⁵ A | Volume X⁶ B |
|---|---|---|---|
| 85 (6737) | 390 (6782) | 21 (6826) | 84 (6404) |
| 87 (6738) | 395 (6783) | 33 (6831) | 85 (6405) |
| 101 (6739) | 404 (6784) | 43 (6832) | 86 (6406) |
| 130 (6740) | 408 (6785) | 46 (6834) | 93 (6663) |
| 154 (6741) | 458 (6791) | 59 (6835) | 105 (6475) |
| 166 (6742) | 472 (6792) | 67 (6836) | 121 (6574) |
| 167 (6743) | 474 (6793) | 72 (6837) | 127 (6566) |
| 168 (6744) | 488 (6794) | 93 (6838) | 128 (6596) |
| 195 (6745) | 511 (6795) | 104 (6839) | 130 (6558) |
| 201 (6752) | 512 (6796) | 105 (6840) | 131 (6559) |
| 204 (6753) | 513 (6797) | 119 (6841) | 137 (6636) |
| 228 (6754) | 539 (6798) | 146 (6843) | 145 (6786) |
| 231 (6755) | 540 (6800) | 148 (6471) | 162 (6637) |
| 233 (6756) | 545 (6801) | 149 (6472) | 163 (6638) |
| 270 (6757) | 554 (6802) | 150 (6473) | 164 (6639) |
| 271 (6758) | 557 (6803) | 152 (6331) | 167 (6640) |
| 272 (6759) | 558 (6804) | 153 (6332) | 169 (6641) |
| 285 (6760) | 559 (6805) | 158 (6306) | 171 (6748) |
| 296 (6761) | 566 (6806) | 165 (6584) | 173 (6749) |
| 299 (6762) | 568 (6807) | 166 (6746) | 188 (6750) |
| 300 (6763) | 584 (6808) | 167 (6747) | 194 (6751) |
| 301 (6764) | 586 (6809) | **Volume X⁵ B** | 226 (6833) |
| 302 (6765) | 587 (6810) | | 232 (6842) |
| 303 (6766) | 592 (6811) | 206 (6518) | 245 (6567) |
| 318 (6767) | 603 (6812) | 263 (6675) | 253 (6787) |
| 322 (6768) | 604 (6813) | 264 (6676) | 254 (6788) |
| 323 (6769) | 605 (6814) | **Volume X⁶ B** | 259 (6789) |
| 339 (6771) | 610 (6815) | | 260 (6790) |
| 351 (6772) | 625 (6816) | 4:3 (6770) | **Volume X⁶ C** |
| 353 (6773) | 628 (6817) | 6 (6829) | |
| 358 (6774) | 629 (6818) | 7 (6830) | 1 (6296) |
| 359 (6775) | 646 (6819) | 40 (6256) | 2 (6297) |
| 367 (6776) | 647 (6820) | 41 (6257) | 4 (6827) |
| 373 (6777) | 651 (6821) | 48 (6349) | 5 (6828) |
| 377 (6778) | 661 (6822) | 68 (6598) | 6 (6829) |
| 380 (6779) | 663 (6823) | 69 (6599) | 7 (6830) |
| 383 (6780) | 673 (6824) | 77 (6600) | **Volume XI¹ A** |
| 389 (6781) | 674 (6825) | 82 (6601) | 1 (6853) |
| | | 83 (6403) | 6 (6856) |

| Volume XI¹ A | Volume XI¹ A | Volume XI² A | Volume XI² A |
|---|---|---|---|
| 47 (6857) | 382 (6895) | 101 (6929) | 438 (6968) |
| 49 (6858) | 383 (6896) | 121 (6930) | 439 (6969) |
| 56 (6859) | 412 (6897) | 134 (6931) | **Volume XI³ B** |
| 69 (6860) | 423 (6898) | 206 (6932) | |
| 71 (6861) | 424 (6899) | 213 (6933) | 13 (6869) |
| 72 (6862) | 425 (6900) | 244 (6934) | 15 (6854) |
| 76 (6863) | 439 (6901) | 248 (6935) | 28 (6855) |
| 90 (6864) | 445 (6902) | 250 (6936) | 49 (6875) |
| 92 (6865) | 460 (6903) | 251 (6937) | 53 (6943) |
| 121 (6866) | 469 (6904) | 252 (6938) | 54 (6944) |
| 125 (6867) | 474 (6905) | 253 (6939) | 55 (6945) |
| 128 (6868) | 484 (6906) | 254 (6940) | 56 (6946) |
| 131 (6870) | 497 (6907) | 256 (6941) | 57 (6947) |
| 133 (6871) | 505 (6908) | 257 (6942) | 93 (6954) |
| 136 (6872) | 510 (6909) | 283 (6844) | 120 (6957) |
| 137 (6873) | 543 (6910) | 288 (6845) | 128 (6960) |
| 142 (6874) | 551 (6911) | 296 (6846) | 129 (6961) |
| 149 (6876) | 559 (6912) | 311 (6847) | 131 (6962) |
| 153 (6877) | 560 (6913) | 312 (6848) | 132 (6963) |
| 171 (6878) | 586 (6914) | 314 (6849) | 291:4 (6965) |
| 177 (6879) | 593 (6915) | 321 (6850) | *Letters* |
| 206 (6880) | **Volume XI² A** | 334 (6851) | |
| 209 (6881) | | 335 (6852) | 180 (6197) |
| 210 (6882) | 11 (6916) | 370 (6948) | 192 (6267) |
| 214 (6883) | 19 (6917) | 371 (6949) | 195 (6294) |
| 215 (6884) | 21 (6918) | 374 (6950) | 196 (6295) |
| 216 (6885) | 31 (6919) | 377 (6951) | 213 (6434) |
| 242 (6886) | 32 (6920) | 379 (6952) | 239 (6537) |
| 258 (6887) | 36 (6921) | 383 (6953) | 240 (6560) |
| 275 (6888) | 40 (6922) | 399 (6958) | 243 (6381) |
| 276 (6889) | 44 (6923) | 406 (6955) | 257 (6606) |
| 277 (6890) | 45 (6924) | 407 (6956) | 262 (note |
| 294 (6891) | 61 (6925) | 409 (6959) | 2648) |
| 300 (6892) | 75 (6926) | 411 (6964) | 265 (note |
| 315 (6893) | 78 (6927) | 436 (6966) | 2733) |
| 378 (6894) | 79 (6928) | 437 (6967) | 276 (6799) |

# Notes

The following abbreviations have been used throughout the notes:

*S.V. Samlede Værker* by Søren Kierkegaard, I–XIV, edited by A. B. Drachman, J. L. Heiberg, and H. O. Lange (Copenhagen: Glydendal, 1901–1906).

*Pap. Papirer* by Søren Kierkegaard, I–XI³ (20 vols.), edited by P. A. Heiberg, V. Kuhr, and E. Torsting (Copenhagen: Gyldendal, 1909–1948); 2 ed., I–XI³ and suppl. vols. XII–XIII, edited by Niels Thulstrup (Copenhagen: Gyldendal, 1968–1970). References to entries in the *Papirer* that are not included in *Søren Kierkegaard's Journals and Papers* are prefaced by *Pap.*, e.g., *Pap.*, I A 1. Crossreferences within *J.P.* are by *Papirer* serial number (I A 9) or by footnote number.

*ASKB Auktionsprotokol over Søren Kierkegaards Bogsamling* (Auctioncatalog of Søren Kierkegaard's Book-collection), edited by H. P. Rohde (Copenhagen: Det Kongelige Bibliotek, 1967). This enlarged edition of the auction-catalog contains the basic serially numbered list of books indicated by number (*ASKB* 200), two appendices designated by I and II (*ASKB* II 200), and a section on books otherwise unlisted but in various ways known to have belonged to Kierkegaard, designated by U (*ASKB* U 100).

*Letters Breve og Aktstykker vedrørende Søren Kierkegaard*, I–II (Letters and Documents pertaining to Søren Kierkegaard), edited by Niels Thulstrup (Copenhagen: Munksgaard, 1953).

Notes 1–1805 appear in Volume 5; notes 1806–3403 appear in Volume 6.

1806. Later spelled "Anti-Climacus," which means, not opposed to Johannes Climacus, but superior to or above Climacus. See X¹ A 510.

1807. See Plato, *Symposium*, 201 d–212 c.

1808. Regine Olsen. See notes 637, 2017.

1809. See Philippians 2:7–8.

1810. See Romans 8:18.

1811. Kierkegaard had two German editions of Plutarch's *Moralia:* the Kaltwasser edition (see note 1616) and *Plutarchs Werke, Moralische Schriften*, tr. J. C. F. Bähr, I–III (Stuttgart: 1828). *ASKB* 1178–80. The German text is not from Kaltwasser's edition. The Bähr edition was not available to the editors for checking.

1812. ". . . pipefish and vipers, they say, burst in giving birth, and secrets, when they escape, destroy and ruin those who cannot keep them." "On Talkativeness," 508 c, Plutarch, *Moralia,* Loeb edition, VI, p. 431.

1813. See note 1811.

1814. "It was a witty answer, for instance, that King Archelaüs gave to a loquacious barber, who, as he wrapped his towel around him, asked, 'How shall I cut your hair, Sire?' 'In silence,' said Archelaüs." "On Talkativeness," 509 a, Plutarch, *Moralia,* Loeb edition, VI, p. 435.

1815. One of the early sketches, eventually developed and published September 27, 1850, as *Practice in Christianity.*

1816. At a distance, you unholy ones!

1817. See J. P. Mynster, *Prædikener holdte i Aaret 1848* (Copenhagen: 1849), pp. 68–69. *ASKB* 232.

1818. Ibid., pp. 284–85, 302–4. See note 3023.

1819. See note 1818.

1820. Ibid., pp. 79 ff.

1821. Appearance. See $x^6$ B 171.

1822. Ecclesiastes 3:7.

1823. See Mark 14:61, 15:5.

1824. See *For Self-Examination,* pp. 1–3.

1825. I would have perished, had I not perished. See *Stages,* p. 187.

1826. This entry eliminates or renders dubious P. A. Heiberg's and others' autobiographical (father looking for unknown child) interpretation of "A Possibility" in *Stages,* pp. 258–68.

1827. On this theme, see introductory essay, *Armed Neutrality* and *An Open Letter,* pp. 3–24. The idea was not carried out.

1828. See *The Point of View,* p. 103.

1829. *The Corsair* repeatedly caricatured Kierkegaard's physique and his clothes and thereby prompted some to taunt Kierkegaard on the street.

1830. Regine Olsen, now Mrs. Frederik Schlegel. See notes 637, 1712, 2017.

1831. Ibid.

1832. Kierkegaard's father, Michael Petersen Kierkegaard, died August 9, 1838, a few months after their reconciliation. See IX A 71 and notes 18, 460.

1833. See II A 20.

1834. This is not a rejection of history or of the "historical Jesus" but a rejection of the falsification of substituting historical accommodation and historical information for the contemporaneity of encounter with Christ. See *Fragments,* pp. 68–139.

1835. Jacob Peter Mynster (1775–1854), since 1834 Bishop of Copenhagen. See notes 547, 943, 1343, 1534.

1836. Ibid.

1837. Ibid.

1838. See Samuel Warren, *Passages from the Diary of a Late Physician* (Edinburgh, London: 1854), p. 24.

1839. See *Practice [Training] in Christianity*, p. 17, on human sympathy.

1840. Kierkegaard's brother, Peter Christian Kierkegaard (1805–88). See note 1.

1841. See notes 1783, 1796, 2692.

1842. See *Dansk Kirketidende*, I, 1846, col. 193 ff.

1843. See note 1832.

1844. See notes 1783, 1796, 2692.

1845. In English the meaning is perfectly clear but a nice bit of word-play in the Danish is lost: "father in his place" [*Sted*] and "stepfather" [*Stedfader*].

1846. See note 1811.

1847. See II Corinthians 12:2,7.

1848. Regine Olsen. See note 637.

1849. Ibid.

1850. End or purpose.

1851. See note 1848.

1852. Presumably Kierkegaard had completed at some level Part One of *Practice in Christianity*, which eventually was published September 27, 1850.

1853. *Dansk Kirketidende*, 148, July 9, 1848, col. 710.

1854. The *Corsair* affair.

1855. See *J.P.*, III, note 372.

1856. Prior conduct of life.

1857. Humor according to Kierkegaard is not the funny, the comic, but is the sadly benevolent recognition of difference in sameness, sameness in difference, born of radically penetrating insight into temporal actuality in the context of the eternal. Humor is the borderland between the ethical and the religious.

1858. See *Upbuilding Discourses in Various Spirits*, Part Three [*The Gospel of Suffering*, p. 136].

1859. Frederik Christian Sibbern (1785–1872), professor of philosophy, University of Copenhagen, 1813–70. See note 701.

1860. The reference is to the main character in Holberg's *Mester Gert Westphaler eller Den meget talende Barbeer* [Master Gert Westphaler or the Very Talkative Barber].

1861. *Nyt Aftenbladet*, 164, July 15, 1848.

1862. The series of articles began in *Nyt Aftenbladet*, 50, February 29, 1848. The July 15, 1848, article has the superscription: XXXVII.

1863. A new journal established by M. Goldschmidt after his return to Denmark.

1864. See note 1860; ibid., sc. 8. See also notes 193, 1259, 1567.

1865. F. C. Sibbern, "Fra den unge Genialitets Side," *Nyt Aftenbladet*, XXXVII (article serial no.), July 15, 1848. See note 1859.

1866. Kierkegaard had few close friends. Pastor Emil Boesen was a lifetime friend (see note 468); Professor Poul Martin Møller, a friend from the university (see note 438); Professor Rasmus Nielsen, a confidant for a time and Kierkegaard's potential literary executor (see note 1939); and Professor J. L. A. Kolderup-Rosenvinge, a later and older friend. Kolderup-Rosenvinge (1792–1850) was professor of law and history of law. Councilor of Conference (*Conferentsraad*) is an honorific title. Like Kierkegaard, he was an omnivorous reader and liked to walk. The two walked together rather regularly and also carried on a sizable correspondence for two persons who lived in the same area and visited frequently. The *Letters* contain nine letters from Kierkegaard and nine letters to Kierkegaard, the earliest dated September 30, 1847.

1867. See note 1860; ibid., sc. 4.

1868. Comic power.

1869. There was considerable interest at the time in the invention and construction of copying and typesetting machines.

1870. A short street from the square between the University and Vor Frue Kirke and Købmagergade. Kolderup-Rosenvinge lived at number 33 (now 11).

1871. Kolderup-Rosenvinge's daughter.

1872. See *J.P.*, III, note 372.

1873. In Danish: *Kiøbstad.* Copenhagen (*Kjøbenhavn*) means literally "market-harbor."

1874. *Fædrelandet*, 904, June 12, 1842. See *S.V.*, XIII, pp. 397–406.

1875. See J. L. Heiberg, "*Litterær Vintersæd,*" *Intelligensblade*, 24, March 1, 1843, pp. 285 ff.

1876. Kierkegaard's newspaper articles are to be found in *S.V.*, XIII, pp. 1–39, 397–485, which includes two disputed pieces (a series of three letters and "Literary Quicksilver"), pp. 460–85. Kierkegaard omits from his own list "Expression of Thanks to Professor Heiberg," *Fædrelandet*, 1168, March 5, 1843, signed "Victor Eremita." See IX A 186, 432.

1877. *Kjøbenhavns Flyveposten*, 34, December 17, 1834, signed: A. *S.V.*, XIII, pp. 5–8. The title is reminiscent of the title of a book Kierkegaard had, Henr. Cornelii Agrippa ab Nettesheim, *De nobilitate et præcellentia foeminei sexus* [On the Nobility and Pre-excellence of the Feminine Sex] (Frankfurt and Leipzig: 1622). *ASKB* 113. See *Stages*, pp. 128–29.

1878. Ibid., 86, February 18, 1836, signed: B. *S.V.*, XIII, pp. 9–15.

1879. Ibid., 82, March 12, 1836, signed: B. *S.V.*, XIII, pp. 16–27.

1880. Ibid., 87, April 10, 1836, signed: S. Kierkegaard. *S.V.*, XIII, pp. 28–39.

1881. *Fædrelandet*, 905, June 12, 1842, signed: S. Kierkegaard. *S.V.*, XIII, pp. 397–406.

1882. Ibid., 1162, February 27, 1843, signed: A. F. . . . . . *S.V.*, XIII, pp. 407–10.

1883. Ibid., 1236, May 16, 1843, "A Little Explanation," signed: S. Kierkegaard. *S.V.*, XIII, pp. 416–17.

1884. *Fædrelandets Feuilleton*, 1890–91, May 19–20, 1845, signed: A. *S.V.*, XIII, pp. 447–56.

1885. *Fædrelandet*, 1883, May 9, 1845, signed: S. Kierkegaard. *S.V.*, XIII, pp. 418–21.

1886. "The Activity of a Traveling Esthetician . . ." and "The Dialectical Result of a Literary Police-Operation," ibid., 2078, December 27, 1845, and 9, January 10, 1846. *S.V.*, XIII, pp. 422–35. See note 1328.

1887. The Danish is *han*, third person singular masculine. The reference is to T. Olsen, Regine's father.

1888. See VII¹ B 211.

1889. By mid-1848 there had been three reviews of the *Postscript* in Copenhagen papers and one by P. L. Møller (*Kritisk Skizzer*, Copenhagen: 1847, II, pp. 253–68). Therefore the statement here is numerically incorrect. If, however, the reference is to serious, perceptive reviews, the statement is correct, for none of the reviews betrays a penetrating reading of the work.

1890. Falsification or a pious fraud.

1891. See note 1932.

1892. See note 1899.

1893. Johanne Luise Pätges Heiberg (1812–90), wife of writer J. L. Heiberg and the leading actress in Denmark.

1894. See *Stages*, pp. 133–34 fn. Anna Helene Brenøe Nielsen (1803–56) was the only actress comparable to Mrs. Heiberg at the time.

1895. Jens F. Giødwad or Gjødwad (1811–91), journalist, editor of *Fædrelandet*, and Kierkegaard's middle-man between him and the printer and the bookseller of the pseudonymous works.

1896. Two of Kierkegaard's parallel lines of writing, the esthetic works and the ethical-religious works (the journals were the third), made their appearances in the form of more or less simultaneous publication of a work or works from each of the two lines. See notes 979, 1110, 1177, and Chronology.

1897. See *Practice [Training] in Christianity*, p. 75.

1898. Ibid., p. 5.

1899. See IX A 175. The piece was finally published in *Fædrelandet*, 188 – 91, August 24–27, 1848.

1900. See note 1895.

1901. This is not the concept and possibility of offense as Kierkegaard usually presents it (see *Practice in Christianity*, passim), but the possibility that publication of "The Crisis . . ." might offend some people. See IX A 175, 178.

1902. See note 1899.

1903. Kierkegaard regarded all differentiating talents as esthetic differences. Genuine equality among men is found only in the realm of ethical-religious possibility independent of personal gifts. With regard to differentiation in the authorship itself, see note 1896, IX A 175.

1904. The remainder of the entry is an addition.

1905. The J. L. Heibergs. See IX A 175.

1906. The *Crisis and a Crisis in the Life of an Actress, Fædrelandet,* 188–91, June 24–27, 1848. See IX A 175, 178, 179, 180.

1907. This plan was not carried out. In 1857, however, Rasmus Nielsen published the newspaper articles under the title *S. Kierkegaard's Bladartikler.* See IX A 167, 432.

1908. On the intention to stop writing, see notes 1359, 1367, 1827.

1909. See note 1906.

1910. See notes 962, 1443, 1876, 1893, 2760.

1911. See note 1906.

1912. The occasion for "The Book on Adler" [*Authority and Revelation*]. See notes 1018, 1472, 1473, 1647, 1656, 1657, 1658.

1913. See notes 1659, 1969, 2116.

1914. See *J.P.,* III, note 372.

1915. See note 1906.

1916. A. G. Rudelbach (1792–1862), theologian and writer. See *Armed Neutrality* and *An Open Letter,* pp. 30–31, 47–55.

1917. See note 1835.

1918. See notes 1674, 2474.

1919. See note 1453, 1605.

1920. See notes 1333, 1590, 1829.

1921. See notes 1783, 1796, 2692.

1922. See note 1906.

1923. See note 1827.

1924. See note 1921.

1925. Literal translation of *elsker op. Opelske* means to raise, cultivate, encourage, and to Kierkegaard "to love forth." See *Works of Love,* p. 206. *Opdrage* means to raise, to bring up, to educate (*Opdragelse,* education).

1926. See note 1932.

1927. See *For Self-Examination,* pp. 15–16.

1928. See *Practice* [*Training*] *in Christianity,* pp. 75–144 and passim; also note 1901.

1929. See note 1906.

1930. Ibid.

1931. See note 1939.

1932. See, for example, VI A 40, VIII² B 186, IX A 42, in which there are indications that Kierkegaard was considering the possibility of some kind of direct statement about the aim of his work. Later this took the form of *On My Work as an Author,* published August 7, 1851, *The Point of View for My Work as an Author* (written 1848, posthumously published, 1859), and *Armed Neutrality,* written 1849, unpublished except as *Pap.*, x⁵ B 107 until the first Danish edition in 1965.

1933. See *Armed Neutrality* and *An Open Letter,* p. 42.

1934. See note 2173.

1935. See note 1906.

1936. The last two pieces constitute Part One and Part Two of *Practice* [*Training*] *in Christianity.*

1937. See note 1939.

1938. See *Works of Love,* p. 149; *Two Discourses at the Communion on Fridays,* together with *Judge for Yourselves!* p. 5. See also x¹ A 247.

1939. For a time it seemed as if Rasmus Nielsen (1809–84), professor of philosophy, University of Copenhagen, would be permitted to be a "follower" of Kierkegaard (see, for example, IX A 220 and x¹ A 406), but this incipient exceptional relationship ended, mainly for the reason indicated in the present entry. See *Letters,* no. 247.

1940. See note 1899.

1941. The two discourses of 1843, published within three months of *Either/Or.* See note 1896.

1942. See [*The*] *Crisis* [*and a Crisis*] *in the Life of an Actress,* pp. 82–83.

1943. See *Pap.* IX A 227.

1944. See *The Concept of Anxiety* [*Dread*], ch. V, pp. 139–45.

1945. See note 1932.

1946. See note 1835.

1947. See note 1906.

1948. See IX A 229.

1949. See *Armed Neutrality and An Open Letter,* p. 54 fn.

1950. See *Practice* [*Training*] *in Christianity,* Part One.

1951. See note 982.

1952. See J. P. Mynster, *Prædikener,* I–II (I, 3 ed., Copenhagen: 1826, II, 2 ed., 1832), I, p. 198. *ASKB* 228.

1953. The opening lines of stanza 2 of H. A. Brorson, *"Nu jeg har vunden"* (see note 1788), p. 706.

1954. See note 1939.

1955. See note 1906.

1956. Regine Olsen Schlegel. See notes 637, 1712, 2017.

1957. Rasmus Nielsen. See note 1939.

1958. Regine Olsen's father.

1959. Ole Kold. See note 1313; *Letters,* no. 120a.

1960. See note 1932.

1961. See no. 1 in IX A 255; *Practice* [*Training*] *in Christianity,* pp. 151–56. Kierkegaard delivered this sermon in Vor Frue Kirke on September 1, 1848.

1962. The possibility of a renewal of a friendly relationship was always in Kierkegaard's mind, but out of consideration for Regine and Johan Frederik Schlegel he did not want to take the first step. The closest he came was a letter to Schlegel (November 19, 1849) accompanied by a letter (written and rewritten many times) to Regine after her father's death (June 26, 1849). Schlegel returned unopened the letter addressed to Regine. See *Letters*, no. 239.

1963. Like, along the lines of.

1964. See *Practice [Training] in Christianity*, pp. 174–77.

1965. From a much altered and reworked draft of *'The Single Individual' Two 'Notes' Concerning My Work as an Author*, published posthumously together with *The Point of View* (see p. 130 of present English edition). On the themes of this entry, see SOCIAL-POLITICAL THOUGHT. *J.P.* IV; *Letters*, no. 186.

1966. See *Fragments*, p. 2. The motto is from *Twelfth Night*, I, 5, via the Schlegel and Tieck German translation into Danish which has been literally translated. The commentary is from *Postscript*, p. 3.

1967. See Part One of *Upbuilding Discourses in Various Spirits*, "An Occasional Discourse" (*Purity of Heart* in present separate English edition), passim.

1968. See *The Point of View*, pp. 70–71.

1969. This and the following entry are from versions of the unused preface to "A Cycle of Ethical-Religious Essays," which was published May 19, 1849, as *Two Minor Ethical-Religious Essays*. See note 1659. See *Pap.*, IX B 9–11 for other versions (dated October 1848).

1970. Kierkegaard frequently used the expression "without authority" to express the fact that he wrote as an individual, as a poet, and not as an ordained man or appointed teacher or as one specially called.

1971. See note 1969.

1972. See note 1970.

1973. Written in 1848 and published posthumously, 1859, by his brother Peter C. Kierkegaard. See note 2209.

1974. See note 1973. Eventually the appendix contained two parts. Part Three was to have been "Preface to 'The Friday Discourses'" (IX B 63:14) and Part Four the present entry.

1975. See VIII$^1$ A 640, 645, IX A 222.

1976. See *The Point of View*, p. 68.

1977. See John 6:68.

1978. Johan Arndt, *Sämtliche geistreiche Bücher vom wahren Christenthum* (2 ed., Tübingen: 1777). *ASKB* 276.

1979. If otherwise the head and not the feet rule in the land.

1980. The postscript (IX B 24, written October, 1848) was not used in the published work (May 19, 1849). Kierkegaard's version is that the political point of departure is *"from below, from that which is lower than the established order"* (pp. 323–24).

1981. S. M. Trier (1800–63), professor of medicine, 1847–63, and chief physician at Frederiks Hospital 1842–60.

1982. See note 2454.

1983. See VIII¹ A 227; also notes 1631, 1796.

1984. The corner of Rosenborggade and Tornebuskegade 156 (now 7) at 295 rix-dollars annually, later six rooms at 400.

1985. *Christian Discourses* was published April 26, 1848, the month Kierkegaard moved. See note 1984.

1986. Anders Christensen. See notes 593, 1797.

1987. See IX A 390; note 2118.

1988. See note 1939.

1989. The *Corsair* affair.

1990. See *Upbuilding [Edifying] Discourses*, I, pp. 32–33; IX A 498.

1991. See Luke 16:19–31.

1992. Eventually published separately July 30, 1849.

1993. Eventually published September 27, 1850, as Part I of *Practice in Christianity*.

1994. Ibid., Part II.

1995. See note 1932.

1996. See note 1970.

1997. Part III of *Practice in Christianity*, pp. 144–254.

1998. Regine Olsen. See notes 637, 2017.

1999. See notes 991, 1037, 1712.

2000. Kierkegaard's brother, Peter C. (1905–1888). See note 1.

2001. See III A 113, VIII¹ A 485.

2002. See *Tillæg til den evangelisk-christelige Psalmebog* (Copenhagen: 1845), 610, Appendix, p. 51. The author's name is not given.

2003. Although this promising plan (see IX A 498–500) was not carried out, the essential contents of it flowed into *The Sickness unto Death*, pp. 208–62.

2004. See notes 2002, 2003.

2005. Part Two of *Christian Discourses*.

2006. See IX A 379.

2007. Eventually Part III of *Practice [Training] in Christianity*, pp. 193–94. See IX A 390.

2008. See VIII¹ A 300, 302, 500.

2009. See notes 2002, 2003.

2010. See note 2002.

2011. See note 1817; ibid., I, pp. 105–31.

2012. They err.

2013. On March 21, 1848, as the result of earlier events, movements, and an enormous demonstration at Christiansborg, King Frederik VII (King Christian VIII had died January 28, 1848) agreed to the dissolution of the ministries. Thereupon the March government, the Moltke-Hvidt government, was formed and Frederik VII declared that he now regarded himself as a constitutional monarch.

2014. Meïer Goldschmidt, editor of *The Corsair*. See notes 1329, 1529, 1531, 1748.

2015. "The Activity of a Traveling Esthetician" and "The Dialectical Result of a Literary Police-Operation," *Fædrelandet*, 422, 432, December 27, 1845, January 10, 1846. See notes 1328, 1329.

2016. See IX A 167, 186.

2017. Regine Olsen. See note 637. This is a fair epitome of Kierkegaard's two main reasons for breaking the engagement: his love for Regine in the context of an awareness that he most likely would burden her and his sense of a life-task that would preoccupy him.

2018. See notes 1333, 1590, 1829.

2019. The *Corsair* affair.

2020. Literally, "crows' corner"; backwater, the sticks.

2021. See $x^2$ A 3.

2022. See notes 991, 1037, 1712.

2023. As a companion piece to *The Crisis and a Crisis in the Life of an Actress* (see note 1906), Kierkegaard wrote "Phister as Scipio" in honor of the Danish actor Joakim Ludvig Phister (1807–96). The role concentrated upon was that of Captain Scipio in *Ludovic*, by J. H. Vernoy de St. Georges, translated by T. Overskou (Copenhagen: 1834), with music by L. J. F. Herold and J. F. Halevy. The piece was presented numerous times during 1834–41 and the last time during Kierkegaard's life on June 11, 1846. The manuscript on Phister was brought up to publishable form but was not printed. See English translation by Stephen D. Crites in a volume entitled *Crisis in the Life of an Actress* (New York: 1967).

2024. See note 2023.

2025. Julie Augusta Thomsen (1810–84), daughter of M. A. Kierkegaard, cousin of Kierkegaard's father. *Letters* contains two other letters to Julie (no. 148 and no. 197).

2026. Presumably William Baggesen Thomsen (1843–91).

2027. N. E. Balle, *Lærebog i den Evangelisk-christelige Religion* (Copenhagen: 1824). *ASKB* 183. Chapter I, para. 2 has the heading: Under the name "world" are commonly included both heaven and earth and everything contained therein.

2028. "Six Go out into the World." Kierkegaard had *Kinder- und Haus-Märchen*, I–III (Berlin: 1819–22), no. 71, I, pp. 378–85. *ASKB* 1425–27. The third edition of a Danish translation was published in 1844. The story appears on pp. 339–45.

2029. Hans Peter Kierkegaard (March 1, 1815–April 22, 1862), son of M.

A. Kierkegaard, who was a cousin of Kierkegaard's father. Although crippled, he occasionally visited Kierkegaard, who frequently visited him. No doubt Hans Peter was in S.K.'s mind during the writing of a portion of "Purity of Heart" about suffering and of Chapter VII, Part Two, of *Works of Love*, "Mercifulness, a Work of Love, Even if It Can Give Nothing and Is Capable of Doing Nothing." *Purity of Heart*, pp. 148–69; *Works of Love*, pp. 292–305.

2030. Hans Peter was severely crippled from birth.

2031. Ecclesiastes 12:13.

2032. Michael Andersen Kierkegaard (1776–1867), son of Andreas Christensen Kierkegaard, a brother of Søren Kierkegaard's grandfather Peder Christensen Kierkegaard (1718–99).

2033. The Royal Library in Copenhagen has two copies of the same edition of the New Testament that Kierkegaard read intensively and marked. See VIII² C 3. The dating of Kierkegaard's use of this volume is conjectural.

2034. See VII¹ A 154.

2035. *Berlingske Tidende*, 320, 323, December 27, 30, 1848.

2036. Par excellence.

2037. See *Either/Or*, I, p. 19; II, pp. 214–15.

2038. See Plato, *Republic*, 600 e, 605 b–c, 608 a.

2039. Rasmus Nielsen. See note 1939.

2040. See note 2039.

2041. Regine Olsen. See note 1962.

2042. See note 2041.

2043. See VIII¹ A 447. On December 29, 1848, Johan Frederik Schlegel, thirty-one years old, was appointed head of the Colonial Office of the Ministry of Finance.

2044. J. P. Mynster, *Prædikener paa alle Søn- og Hellig-Dage i Aaret*, I–II (Copenhagen: 3 ed., 1837), I. *ASKB* 229–30.

2045. Summary of summaries, quintessence.

2046. The voice of the people; the voice of God.

2047. See *Postscript*, pp. 297–99; VII¹ A 139.

2048. Michael Petersen Kierkegaard was fifty-six when Søren was born. See note 18.

2049. Christian VIII (1786–1848), Denmark's last absolute monarch (1839–48). See note 2013.

2050. Royal summer residence north of Copenhagen.

2051. François Pierre Guillaume Guizot (1777–1874), French politician and historian. See *Berlingske Tidende*, 153, 171, 189, July 5, 26, August 16, 1847.

2052. Sorø Academy, the Danish Eton, with an attached academy for outstanding scholars and poets.

2053. March 13, 1847, also the publication date of *Upbuilding Discourses in Various Spirits*, by S. Kierkegaard.

2054. The delegates to the meeting of Scandinavian natural scientists were royal guests in July, 1847. See *Fædrelandet* 158, 160, July 9, 12, 1847; *Berlingske Tidende*, 160, July 13, 1847.

2055. See note 537.

2056. *Works of Love*, pp. 137–38.

2057. Student Assembly, which held a meeting December 3, 1839, and sent two petitions to the king.

2058. Eggert C. Tryde (1781–1860). See note 2790. There is no other trace of the incident in the *Papirer*.

2059. Smørum is a district in northeast Sjælland above Copenhagen. Upper Smørum and Lower Smørum are two very small villages of the district. The witticism apparently consists in the pun on the name *Smørum* understood as *Smøren* (scribbling) with the suffix *um*, which comes out fairly well in English: *Scribbleby*.

2060. F. W. J. Schelling (1775–1854), German philosopher whose lectures (III C 27) Kierkegaard (and Engels and Jakob Burckhardt and many others from outside Germany) heard during his first Berlin visit October 25, 1841–March 6, 1842. See notes 688, 700, 727, 730.

2061. The text has "*jo bedre,*" which the Danish editors suggest be read as "*jo mindre*" as here translated.

2062. See IX A 390.

2063. Kierkegaard seriously considered quitting writing. See notes 1359, 1367.

2064. Martin Hammerich (1811–81), writer and educator, principal of Borgerdydskolen Christianshavn, from 1842.

2065. F. L. Høedt (1820–1885), poet and actor, at the time teacher of Danish in Borgerdydskolen, Christianshavn. See *Corsaren*, 208, 209, 211, September 6, 13, 27, 1844.

2066. See note 1939.

2067. H. A. Brorson, *Psalmer og aandelige Sange*, ed. J. A. L. Holm (Copenhagen: 2 ed., 1838). *ASKB* 200.

2068. See Song of Solomon 6:13.

2069. See note 2067.

2070. A monument more enduring than bronze.

2071. See *Armed Neutrality*, pp. 33–34, 36–39, 44–45.

2072. Still life, an analogy to a type of painting.

2073. *Ludwig Tieck's sämmtliche Werke*, I–II (Paris: 1837) II, pp. 748 ff. *ASKB* 1848–49.

2074. *Virtu*osity as written carries the double meaning of *virtue* and *skill* or *talent*, that is, for Mynster his virtuosity was not virtuosity but a virtue.

2075. See note 2000.

2076. The reference cannot be explicated by any extant letters from the period (January, 1849), and Peter's speech at the Roskilde ministerial conference came later (October 30, 1849); see $x^2$ A 256, 273, 280. The most pertinent albeit unspecific entry is IX A 483.

2077. For examples, among many throughout the various works, of sympathetic passion, of the love and sympathic concern that enabled Kierkegaard to live into the lives of others and to present their own concerns, see *Works of Love*, pp. 292–305; Part One of *Upbuilding Discourses in Various Spirits* [*Purity of Heart*, pp. 160–64]; *Letters*, no. 161, 167.

2078. See note 2072.

2079. Robert Greene (1560–92), dramatist, writer, and repentant debauchee. Shortly after his death Henry Chettle published a pamphlet written by Greene, entitled "Greene's Groat's-worth of Wit Bought with a Million of Repentance."

2080. See note 2073.

2081. See note 2014.

2082. *Dansk Kirketidende*, 175, February 4, 184, col. 324.

2083. Schøller P. V. Birchedahl (1809–92).

2084. *Either/Or*, II, pp. 165–66.

2085. See *Fear and Trembling*, p. 129.

2086. Matthew 8:22.

2087. Mark 8:33.

2088. See II Corinthians 12:7.

2089. *Stages*, pp. 304–5.

2090. Anon., *China, historisch, romantisch, malerisch* (Carlsruhe: n.d.). *ASKB* 2036.

2091. See *Letters*, no. 154, 156, 157.

2092. See notes 1796, 2692.

2093. "A Cycle of Ethical-Religious Essays," "The Point of View for My Work as an Author," including "Armed Neutrality" and "Three Notes." Only the first, limited to two essays, was published by Kierkegaard.

2094. See note 1359.

2095. See *The Point of View*, pp. 7, 80, 82.

2096. Ibid., pp. 75, 103, 155.

2097. Ibid., p. 87; see *J.P.*, III, note 372.

2098. *The Sickness unto Death* and the three parts of *Practice in Christianity*.

2099. See note 1932.

2100. Kierkegaard's father lived to be eighty-two years old.

2101. See note 2098.

2102. Luther, *En christelig Postille*, tr. Jørgen Thisted, I–II (Copenhagen: 1828), II, pp. 137–43. *ASKB* 283. In 1849 Septuagesima Sunday was February 4.

2103. "Three Notes" and "Armed Neutrality." See note 2093.

2104. The final part of *Either/Or*, I, and the final part of *Stages*, respectively.

2105. See *Stages,* p. 363.

2106. Ibid., pp. 37–38, 76–80.

2107. See notes 899, 1008.

2108. See note 1912.

2109. See VII A 9.

2110. See IX B 10–22.

2111. See no. 2 of original "A Cycle of Ethical-Religious Essays," eventually chapter I of "The Book of Adler" [*Authority and Revelation,* pp. 19–56]. See notes 2116, 2474, 2483.

2112. See note 1939.

2113. See note 1835.

2114. See note 1827.

2115. See notes 1783, 1796, 2692.

2116. The envisioned work "A Cycle of Ethical-Religious Essays" originally had the following parts (see *Papirer,* IX B 2); Preface; no. 1, "Something on What Might Be Called 'Premise-Authors' "; no. 2, "The Dialectical Relations: the Universal, the Single Individual, the Special Individual"; no. 3, "Has a Man the Right to Let Himself Be Put to Death for the Truth?"; no. 4, "A Revelation in the Situation of the Present Age"; no. 5, "A Psychological Interpretation of Magister Adler as a Phenomenon and as a Satire upon Hegelian Philosophy and the Present Age"; and no. 6, "On the Difference between a Genius and an Apostle." *Two Minor Ethical-Religious Essays,* by H. H., published May 19, 1849, contains a preface and nos. 3 and 6 of the above. "The Book on Adler," which remained in manuscript form, included a preface (Kierkegaard wrote eight different prefaces for it), no. 1, no. 2, and no. 5 of the above. See *Authority and Revelation* (title of "The Book on Adler" in the present English translation).

2117. An explanation in the sense that the Seducer is a negative instance of the special individual.

2118. "The Sickness unto Death," "Practice in Christianity," "A Cycle of Ethical-Religious Essays," "Armed Neutrality," "The Point of View." Whether the estimate "most valuable" applies to all of them is not clear, but statements in IX A 375, 390, $x^1$ A 147, 202, 510, and $x^2$ A 66 indicate that it applies at least to *The Sickness unto Death* by Anti-Climacus (published July 19, 1849) and *Practice in Christianity,* by Anti-Climacus (September 27, 1850). See note 2486.

2119. As you like it.

2120. See *Two Ages, S.V.,* VIII, pp. 79–82 (*The Present Age,* pp. 27–47).

2121. See note 1939.

2122. Ibid.

2123. See notes 2474, 2483.

2124. See note 2116.

2125. See $x^1$ A 43.

2126. See note 2123. The "little thing" alluded to is no. 2 of the envisioned publication "A Cycle of Ethical-Religious Essays." See note 2116.

2127. See note 2116.

2128. The introduction and chapter I of "The Book on Adler." See *Authority and Revelation*, pp. 3–56. These were originally considered as parts of "A Cycle of Ethical-Religious Essays" but were omitted from *Two Minor Ethical-Religious Essays*, published May 19, 1849. See note 2116.

2129. The "Three Notes Concerning My Work as an Author" intended as appendices to "The Point of View" were (1) "Concerning the Dedication to 'that Single Individual,' " (2) "A Word on the Relation of My Work as an Author to 'that Single Individual,' " and (3) "Preface to the 'Friday Discourses.' " Eventually no. 3 was omitted. See *The Point of View*, pp. 105–38; IX B 63. A shortened version of no. 3 was used as the preface to *Two Discourses at the Communion on Fridays* (1851), together with *Judge for Yourselves!* p. 5. See note 2209.

2130. Published April 26, 1848.

2131. See *Letters*, no. 154, 156, 157.

2132. See note 2063.

2133. See *Armed Neutrality*.

2134. See note 1329.

2135. Marshal Michel Ney (1769–1815), general of the army against Napoleon after Elba, went over to Napoleon and was executed in Paris. He himself gave the order to the firing squad.

2136. See *Postscript*, pp. 19, 545–46.

2137. See x⁶ B 48.

2138. See notes 1327–1330, 1529, 1531, 1748, 3289.

2139. See note 2015.

2140. *Tausend und eine Nacht*, tr. G. Weil, I–IV (Stuttgart and Pforzheim: 1838–41), IV, p. 353. *ASKB* 1414–17. Quoted in German in *Pap.*, VII¹ A 60.

2141. *Goethe's Werke*, I–LX (Stuttgart and Tübingen: 1828–33). *ASKB* 1641–68.

2142. See note 1329.

2143. *ASKB* 264.

2144. See note 1827.

2145. *Upbuilding Discourses in Various Spirits, Works of Love*, and *Christian Discourses*.

2146. See *The Point of View*, p. 126.

2147. See *Stages*, pp. 179–444.

2148. See note 2116.

2149. No. 3 in the envisioned "A Cycle of Ethical-Religious Essays" and finally published as no. 1 of *Two Minor Ethical-Religious Essays*, May 19, 1849. See note 2116.

2150. Philippians 1:21.

2151. This term, seemingly inconsistent here, is a sample of Kierkegaard's penchant for using words in their elementary meaning. The Danish words for *art* and *artistic* are *Kunst* and *kunsterisk* derived from the root *kunne*, to be able (see *Pap.*, v b 59:29, p. 120; viii² b 83). See *Postscript*, pp. 312–22: for example (p. 314), "The subjective thinker is not a scientist, but an artist. To exist is an art". In this elemental sense, then, the art is to live, the existential thinker's life is a being-able, a making, a doing, an embodying in personal being of what he understands.

2152. Hans Christian Andersen, who, for example, clearly used his own personal history in "The Ugly Duckling."

2153. See *Letters*, no. 154, 156, 157.

2154. See note 1827.

2155. The last two titles are of pieces that eventually became Parts I and II (of three) of *Practice in Christianity*, published September 25, 1850.

2156. See note 2118.

2157. *The Sickness unto Death*, published July 30, 1849. Entry x¹ a 147 is from late February or early March, and the manuscript of *The Sickness unto Death* was delivered around June 28 (x¹ a 510).

2158. See *Fragments*, notes, pp. 148–49.

2159. See x⁶ c 2.

2160. See note 2129.

2161. See *Postscript*, p. [554]. Not accurately quoted in the entry.

2162. Ibid., pp. 224–66.

2163. Pp. 330–43.

2164. Ibid., pp. 341–42.

2165. See *The Present Age*, p. 42 fn.

2166. See note 1993.

2167. See John 9:22.

2168. See John 7:48.

2169. See notes 1783, 2013.

2170. See note 1835.

2171. See ix a 288.

2172. See note 1329.

2173. See ix a 226, x² a 106; "The Accounting," together with *The Point of View*, p. 144; ibid., pp. 38, 42–43, 96.

2174. See *Fragments*, p. 65.

2175. See *Letters*, no. 154, 156, 157.

2176. See notes 1631, 1796, 1983, 2692.

2177. See notes 1984, 2454.

2178. Published April 26, 1848.

2179. See note 1783.

2180. Ibid.

2181. See note 2118.

2182. See note 2045.

2183. See notes 1329, 1529, 1531, 3289.

2184. A novel by Goldschmidt, published Copenhagen, 1845. *ASKB* 1547.

2185. Alas, woe is me.

2186. See notes 1008, 1329, 1531; V B 72:22, VI B 225.

2187. See note 1835.

2188. See note 1829.

2189. Johan Christian Lund (1799–1875), who also happened to be a clothing merchant, husband of Nicoline Christine Kierkegaard (1799–1832).

2190. Bishop Jakob Peter Mynster. See note 1835. The allusions to recollection and memory are prompted by Mynster's privately printed book, *Om Hukommelsen* [On Memory] (Copenhagen: 1849; *ASKB* 692) and Kierkegaard's distinction between memory and recollection (see *Stages*, pp. 27–36).

2191. By *The Corsair* and subsequently by others. See note 1531.

2192. See note 1329.

2193. See notes 1329, 1529, 1531.

2194. See note 1938.

2195. A blessed leap into eternity. See *Fear and Trembling*, p. 53 fn.

2196. See note 2129.

2197. See note 1973.

2198. *The Lily of the Field and the Bird of the Air, Three Godly Discourses*, published on the same day as the second edition of *Either/Or*, May 14, 1849, in present English edition together with *Christian Discourses*, pp. 311–56.

2199. See note 1476.

2200. See *Armed Neutrality* and *An Open Letter*, Introduction, pp. 31, 32.

2201. See note 1329.

2202. See note 2760.

2203. See note 1829.

2204. Tivoli, the now world-famous amusement park in the center of Copenhagen, opened August 1843. The Casino, a winter amusement building to complement the summer Tivoli, was opened February, 1847, and was changed into a theater December, 1848.

2205. See note 1783.

2206. See notes 1659, 1969, 2116. The plan entertained here was not carried out except for the two by H. H. See next note.

2207. Only one of these pseudonyms was eventually used: *Two Minor Ethical-Religious Essays*, by H. H. See note 2116; $x^1$ A 535, $x^6$ B 167.

2208. The three parts of *Practice in Christianity*, eventually published September 27, 1850.

2209. "The Accounting," published later, August 7, 1851, as part of *On My Work* [*Virksomhed*] *as an Author*. In the present English edition this appears together with, but is not to be confused with, *The Point of View for My Work* [*Virksomhed*] *as an Author*, published posthumously (1859). See note 2129.

2210. See note 2198.

2211. See *Letters*, 154, 156, 157; note 2198.

2212. See note 2198.

2213. Regine Olsen's. See note 637.

2214. Johannes Climacus. See *Postscript*, p. 132 fn.

2215. *Two Upbuilding Discourses*, published May 5 (Kierkegaard's birthday), 1843. See *Edifying Discourses*, I, p. 5.

2216. See note 2209.

2217. See *Upbuilding Discourses in Various Spirits*, Part One [*Purity of Heart*, pp. 180–82].

2218. See note 1964.

2219. See Matthew 27:39; Mark 15:29.

2220. Socrates. See, for example, *For Self-Examination*, pp. 1–3; *Postscript*, pp. 143, 161, 204–5, 207, 316.

2221. Mark 9:49.

2222. See *Postscript*, p. 184. Platonic recollection.

2223. Here again is an exploitation of elemental word meanings: *forloves* (passive; is engaged or pledged) and *for-lovet* (past participle; before-promised, pledged or engaged earlier).

2224. See Luke 7:47.

2225. See IX A 106. The two preceding paragraphs constitute Kierkegaard's thumbnail autobiography: his Christian upbringing and vision of Christ, Socrates, his engagement, the *Corsair* affair, his father, all in the context of his sense of vocation, penitence, and mature religious life.

2226. To Kierkegaard "to step forth in character" meant to reduplicate an idea or vision in a personal act, which is qualitatively different from poetizing the vision. See X$^1$ A 281, 385.

2227. See notes 1783, 1796.

2228. Potentially.

2229. See *Armed Neutrality*, pp. 33–39.

2230. See *Either/Or*, II, pp. 3–58; *Stages*, pp. 95–178.

2231. See *Either/Or* I, p. 19.

2232. A. S. Ørsted (1778–1860), leading jurist in Denmark at the time, author of *Prøvelse af de Rigsforsamlingen forlagte Udkast til en Grundlov og en Valglov*, vol. III of which appeared April 26, 1849. *ASKB* 924.

2233. See Plato, *Apology*, 25 a; *Works of Love*, p. 217, also p. 219.

2234. See *Fædrelandet*, 95, April 25, 1849.

2235. See *Stages*, p. 373; *Two Ages* [*The Present Age*, p. 25].

2236. A play by the French dramatist, A. E. Scribe, *Puf eller Verden vil Bedrages*, tr. N. C. L. Abrahams, presented March 21, 30, April 11, 14, 23, 1849. See note 1476.

2237. A French interjection: "all right."

2238. See I A 333, also X$^1$ A 448.

2239. See *Either/Or*, I, p. 20.

2240. The two Danish words are *Gave* and *Gene*.

2241. "Has a Man the Right to Let Himself Be Put to Death for the Truth?"

2242. *Evangelietroen og den moderne Bevidsthed. Tolv Forelæsninger holdte ved Universitet i Kjøbenhavn i Vinteren 1849–50* was published in Copenhagen, May 19, 1849. *ASKB* 700. See note 1939.

2243. See note 1939.

2244. See x¹ A 343.

2245. The pseudonymous author of *Fragments* and *Postscript*.

2246. See *Postscript*, pp. 551–52.

2247. See note 2136.

2248. See p. 47.

2249. I, pp. 3–15.

2250. *Postscript*, title page.

2251. See note 2245; *Fragments*, pp. 46–60; *Postscript*, pp. 183–209.

2252. See LEAP and PARADOX.

2253. See, for example, *Fear and Trembling*, pp. 91–129.

2254. Ibid., pp. 49–52, 86–89, also *Postscript*, p. 447 fn.

2255. See note 2242; ibid., p. vi–vii.

2256. Ibid., p. 198.

2257. See note 1939.

2258. *Two Minor Ethical-Religious Essays*, by H. H., published May 19, 1849.

2259. "The Accounting." See note 2209.

2260. See note 2129.

2261. See note 2209.

2262. *Three Discourses at the Communion on Fridays*, by S. Kierkegaard, was published on November 14, 1849.

2263. Subtitle of *The Lily of the Field and the Bird of the Air*. See note 2198.

2264. See note 2258.

2265. A character in L. Tieck, *Der gestiefelte Kater*, tr. A. Oehlenschläger, *Digtninger af Ludwig Tieck*, I–II (Copenhagen: 1838–39), I, pp. 11–48. See *From the Papers of One Still Living*, *S.V.*, XIII, p. 26; *The Concept of Irony*, p. 97.

2266. Kierkegaard's father and Regine Olsen.

2267. Anon. [J. C. Hauch], *Søstrene paa Kinnekullen* (Copenhagen: May 14, 1849), presented April 26, 29, 30; May 5, 8, 9, 25, 1849.

2268. See I, p. 30.

2269. See Luke 2:37–38; Romans 8:25; *Upbuilding [Edifying] Discourses*, III, pp. 37–63.

2270. See Luke 12:32, text for May 27, 1849. As a royally appointed member of the Constitutional Assembly, Mynster was one of ten who abstained from voting on the constitution, May 25, 1849.

2271. Presumably a reference to J. L. Heiberg's articles in his paper *Den flyvende Postens Interimsblade* (1836–37) against the "liberal movement" and to his presentation of its leaders and institutions as constituting a hell of triviality in Act 3 of *En Sjæl efter Døden* (Copenhagen: 1840).

2272. See J. P. Mynster, *Prædikener holdt i Aarene 1849 og 1850* (Copenhagen: 1851), pp. 54–66. *ASKB* 233.

2273. See note 2038.

2274. See note 2226.

2275. *Either/Or*, second edition, published May 14, 1849.

2276. Pseudonymous editor of *Either/Or*.

2277. Adam G. Oehlenschläger (1799–1850), leading Danish poet and dramatist of the period.

2278. R. V. Christian F. Winther (1796–1876), Danish poet.

2279. Henrik H. Hertz (1797 or 1798–1870), Danish writer.

2280. See note 1939.

2281. See note 2116. The three referred to in this entry are numbers 1, 2, and 4.

2282. See note 2129.

2283. Carl A. Reitzel (1789–52), Copenhagen bookseller and publisher.

2284. See note 1997.

2285. See note 1827.

2286. Part IV of *Christian Discourses*, published April 26, 1848.

2287. See notes 1783, 1796, 2692.

2288. See note 1903.

2289. *Two Minor Ethical-Religious Essays*, together with *The Present Age*, p. 81.

2290. See note 2208.

2291. See *The Lily of the Field and the Bird of the Air*, together with *Christian Discourses*, p. 350.

2292. I Peter 5:7.

2293. See note 1827.

2294. Danish: *det Deriverende*, that which de-rives, takes away, diverts, from Latin: *derivare*, to lead off. The form of the word is like that of *sedative*, signifying not a product but that which produces something.

2295. See note 1827.

2296. See x¹ A 422.

2297. *Fenelons Werke religiösen Inhalts*, tr. Matthias Claudius, I–III (Hamburg: 1823), I, pp. 220–21. *ASKB* 1914. "It is the wonderful forbearance of God's goodness that he never forces us inwardly to sacrifice something that till then we have loved and possessed, without giving us insight into it, and that he never gives us insight into this sacrifice without giving us the power for that purpose."

2298. *Auswahl aus Gerhard Tersteegens Schriften,* ed. Georg Rapp (Essen: 1841), p. 141. *ASKB* 729.

2299. See note 1827.

2300. J. N. Madvig (1804–86), Danish philologist and politician, at one time Minister of Church and Education.

2301. See notes 547, 943, 1343, 1835.

2302. See note 2242.

2303. See note 2258.

2304. See note 1827.

2305. Kierkegaard is still wrestling with the question of publishing "The Point of View" and with the question of "The Collected Works of Consummation" (see IX A 390).

2306. For Kierkegaard's own distinction between "upbuilding" and "for upbuilding," see IV B 159:6.

2307. See note 2136.

2308. Demonic in the sense of wanting to reform the world instead of oneself.

2309. Rasmus Nielsen. See note 1939.

2310. See *Letters,* no. 212.

2311. All is to be doubted.

2312. The pseudonymous author of *Fear and Trembling.* See p. 25.

2313. *The Sickness unto Death,* published July 30, 1849.

2314. See IX A 390, X$^1$ A 116.

2315. See IV B 159:6. The title page of the first edition had both "upbuilding" and "awakening," as does the current English edition.

2316. *The Sickness unto Death,* p. 142.

2317. Ibid., pp. 208–11.

2318. Pp. 227–31.

2319. See *Pap.,* X$^4$ B 16–23.

2320. See note 2315.

2321. Ibid.

2322. See *The Sickness unto Death,* p. 143.

2323. See note 2136.

2324. See *Postscript,* p. 533.

2325. Ibid., p. 547.

2326. The eulogy was originally part of the intended "Three Minor Ethical-Religious Essays" but later became part of "The Book on Adler" (*Pap.* VII$^1$ B 235, pp. 43–45). See *Authority and Revelation,* pp. 36–37. See notes 2116 and 2258.

2327. The pseudonym envisioned for "Three Minor Ethical-Religious Essays." See X$^1$ A 263, 422.

2328. Johannes Climacus. See note 2136.

2329. See *Dansk Kirketidende*, November 19, 1848, May 13, 20, July 8, 1849, col. 132 ff., 537 ff., 562 f., 688.

2330. About himself.

2331. See *Fear and Trembling*, p. 21; *Repetition*, p. 149; *The Concept of Anxiety*, p. 15 fn.

2332. Kierkegaard considered this to be the task of Anti-Climacus in *The Sickness unto Death* and *Practice in Christianity*, See also *Fear and Trembling*, pp. 129–32; x¹ A 546. *Postscript* was the "hint".

2333. Bishop J. P. Mynster was in the highest rank (Grand Cross) of the Order of Dannebrog. See viii² B 116, 118.

2334. See note 2332.

2335. Anti-Climacus; see note 2332.

2336. *Two Minor Ethical-Religious Essays*.

2337. *Dansk Kirketidende*, July 22, 1849, col. 718–19. See x¹ A 351.

2338. See AUTHORITY.

2339. H. L. Martensen's *Den christelige Dogmatik* was published July 19, 1849. *ASKB* 653.

2340. Ibid.

2341. See IV B 159:6.

2342. See note 2313.

2343. See note 2208.

2344. Terkild Olsen, Regine's father, died the night of June 25–26, 1849.

2345. Bianco Luno (1795–1852), who did Kierkegaard's printing.

2346. See note 2344.

2347. Regine Olsen. See notes 637, 1712.

2348. See note 1962.

2349. See note 2344.

2350. Johan Frederik Schlegel, her husband. See note 1712.

2351. July 22, 1849.

2352. Ernst William Kolthoff (1809–90).

2353. A "book" that eventually became Part III of *Practice in Christianity*. The idea of a dedication to Terkild Olsen was not carried out.

2354. See note 2344.

2355. See note 2339.

2356. See note 1889.

2357. See note 1829.

2358. See note 2339.

2359. See notes 1993, 1994.

2360. See notes 1359, 1367, 1908, 2063.

2361. The reference may be to Part IV of *Christian Discourses*, but it could also be to "Three Discourses at the Communion on Fridays," ready for publication in that year (November 19, 1849). See x¹ A 351, 678, x² A 148.

2362. Anti-Climacus, pseudonymous author of *The Sickness unto Death* and *Practice in Christianity* (published later, September 27, 1850).

2363. See IV B 159:6, x¹ A 510.

2364. *The Sickness unto Death* and Part I of *Practice in Christianity*. See note 1028.

2365. See IX A 9, x¹ A 510, 530.

2366. See note 2362.

2367. See note 2332.

2368. See note 2339.

2369. See CORRECTIVE.

2370. See Acts 26:14.

2371. Regine Olsen. See note 637.

2372. See x¹ A 568, 569, note 2344.

2373. See note 1962.

2374. See IX A 262.

2375. Regine's assertion at the time the engagement was broken. See V A 88, VIII¹ A 447, x¹ A 648, x² A 105, x⁵ A 149:12.

2376. Regine Olsen. See note 637.

2377. See notes 499, 1711.

2378. The family of Peter Rørdam (1806–83), a fellow university student. See note 354. Hanne Mourier, a close friend of Regine Olsen Schlegel in her later years, wrote an account (March 1, 1902) of their conversations about Kierkegaard, whose books Regine read and approved. It appears as an appendix to Hjalmar Helweg, *Søren Kierkegaard* (Copenhagen: 1933), pp. 385–92, and contains the following portion about the first meeting at Rørdam's, pp. 386–87.

> You recall having seen S. Kierkegaard the first time when you were 14–16 years old. You met him then at Widow Rørdam's (mother of the well-known pastor Peter Rørdam) house to which you had been invited to a party for a girl of your age (Thrine Dahl from Roskilde) who was visiting there. Kierkegaard called on the family, and his vivacity of mind made a great impression upon you, which, however, you did not let on. You remember that he talked incessantly, that his talk seemed to pour out and was extremely fascinating, but after these many years you do not recall the content any more. You think that perhaps the passage in the *Efterladte Papirer* (p. 123, May 8, 1837), "... My God, why should the inclination awaken just now! O, *how alone* I feel!" etc., refers to the meeting with you, where he, too, got his first impression of you, as you did of him.

2379. See note 570.

2380. See IX A 131.

2381. See note 578.

2382. See note 2378. Hanne Mourier, p. 387, gives Regine's account of this meeting:

> Kierkegaard gave you some music but otherwise must not have paid special attention to you, for one day when he met you on the street and wanted to walk you home, and you replied that no one was at home, you scarcely noticed that he ignored your reply and walked along with you anyway. Having arrived home, you proposed playing the piano for him—as you were accustomed to do, since he did like music, but after a little while he shut the music book in front of you and declared that that was not why he had come; then he confessed his love for you. You became utterly speechless and without a word or any explanation got him out the door as quickly as possible. —Your strange way of reacting to the situation made Kierkegaard worried about you. He immediately sought out your father at his office and recounted the entire scene for him. —Your father mentioned nothing to you, but the following day when Kierkegaard came again, you gave him your assent, but only after you had mentioned that there was a teacher from your school days whom you liked very much and whom you thought cared for you. To this Kierkegaard paid no attention, for, as he said later, "You could have talked about Fritz Schlegel till doomsday—it would not have helped, because I *wanted* to have you!" You were eighteen years old then.

2383. See notes 1830, 2382.
2384. Earlier life or life prior to the act.
2385. See *Stages*, p. 50.
2386. Ibid., pp. 304–7.
2387. Ibid., p. 340.
2388. Ibid., p. 351.
2389. Emil Boesen (1812–81), Kierkegaard's closest friend from childhood and throughout his life. See *Letters* for extensive correspondence.
2390. Gustav A. Bürger, *Lenore, Bürgers Gedichte* (Gotha, New York: 1828), I, pp. 48 ff. See I A 25.
2391. See *Repetition*, p. 100.
2392. See *Letters*, nos. 49, 54, 62, 68.
2393. See *Either/Or*, I, pp. 297–440.
2394. *Upbuilding [Edifying] Discourses*, I, p. 5.
2395. Ibid. May 5, 1843, Kierkegaard's thirtieth birthday.
2396. Ibid., p. 3.
2397. See note 1859.
2398. See note 991.
2399. See notes 1830, 2435.
2400. See note 1962; *Letters*, no. 239.
2401. Nørregade 230A (now 38).
2402. See note 982. The Danish *Piedestal* accounts for occasional translations of the term as pedestal. The tall palisander (or rosewood) cupboard may be seen in the Kierkegaard room of the Copenhagen City Museum.

2403. See IV B 140.

2404. See note 2043.

2405. Elise D. Dencker (1801–?), housekeeper in the family of Kierkegaard's sister Nicoline, Mrs. Johan Christian Lund.

2406. Cornelia Olsen, Regine's older sister. See VI A 12, X³ A 769.

2407. See note 2135.

2408. Friederike Brion, "Friederike von Sesenheim" (1752–1813). After Goethe left her at the end of his Strasbourg student days, she had numerous suitors but never married. Goethe wrote about her in *Dichtung und Wahrheit.*

2409. See note 1830.

2410. See notes 354, 2378.

2411. See *Fear and Trembling*, pp. 103–8.

2412. Kierkegaard had thought the better journalists would have supported him during the *Corsair* affair.

2413. A pious wish.

2414. See note 2014.

2415. Ibid.

2416. Peder Ludwig Møller (1814–65), writer involved in the *Corsair* affair. See notes 1328–29.

2417. See, for example, VIII¹ A 107, 125, 214, VIII¹ A 163.

2418. See notes 1796, 2692.

2419. See H. L. Martensen (see note 2339), pp. 546–50.

2420. See *Attack*, p. 42; *Visebog indeholdende udvalgte danske Selskabssange* (Copenhagen: 1814), pp. 86–87. *ASKB* 1483.

2421. See, for example, *Postscript*, pp. 372, 435–36, 465, 467–68, 480 fn., 493–94, 499, 535 fn., 538; X¹ A 617.

2422. Alteration.

2423. Fredrika Bremer (1801–65), Finnish-Swedish writer and traveler who visited Denmark for about a year in 1848–49. *Liv i Norden* was published in Copenhagen, September 12, 1849. See pp. 36–78, see *Letters*, no. 201, 203, 204.

2424. See note 3269; *Berlingske Tidende*, 205, August 30, 1849.

2425. Ibid., 126, May 28, 1845. See *Pap.* VI B 191; "The Individual," together with the *Point of View*, p. 125.

2426. *Jeppe paa Bjerget*, II, 3.

2427. Regine Olsen.

2428. See note 1916.

2429. See note 2332.

2430. See note 2294.

2431. Regine Olsen.

2432. Johan Frederik Schlegel, the husband of Regine Olsen.

2433. Regine Olsen.

2434. Regine's father, Terkild Olsen.

2435. Johan Frederik Schlegel (1817–96), whom Kierkegaard had displaced, and who later married Regine (November 3, 1847).

2436. Johan Frederik Schlegel.

2437. Regine Olsen.

2438. See *Stages*, pp. 179–444.

2439. October 11, 1841.

2440. Regine Olsen.

2441. See note 2198.

2442. See note 2208.

2443. Published July 30, 1849.

2444. See note 1974.

2445. See note 2129.

2446. See note 1997.

2447. See note 1932.

2448. *Pap.* IX B 67–72. See note 3160.

2449. See note 2361.

2450. Regine Olsen.

2451. See note 2435.

2452. Journal NB.[12] See note 1384.

2453. Anders Christensen; see notes 593, 1797.

2454. The census register for February 1, 1850, lists Frederik C. Strube, Icelandic-born cabinet-maker, his wife, and two daughters, as living in Kierkegaard's apartment on the corner of Rosenborggade and Tornebuskegade. See entry 6267 (*Letters*, no. 192) to the physician S. M. Trier in appreciation for what he had done for Strube.

2455. See notes 1796, 2692.

2456. C. A. Reitzel (1789–1853), publisher, on an honorarium basis, of Kierkegaard's books after August 1847. See note 1630.

2457. See note 1984.

2458. See note 1962.

2459. See note 1939.

2460. See note 2242.

2461. See note 2474; *Fear and Trembling*, pp. 30–31.

2462. See note 2423.

2463. See notes 1329, 1333, 1448, 1590, 1829.

2464. See notes 1796, 2692.

2465. Hans Lassen Martensen (1808–84), professor of theology and later Bishop Mynster's successor. See notes 3258, 3275.

2466. Just Henrik V. Paulli (1809–65), J. P. Mynster's son-in-law, Royal Chaplain from 1840.

2467. See note 2760, also 1910.

2468. See note 2014.

2469. See note 2416.

2470. See note 2339.

2471. This is the beginning of what eventually was published as *Two Discourses at the Communion on Fridays,* September 12, 1851. No. 3 was omitted, and in the manuscript entry the last two lines are crossed out.

2472. Should be I Peter 4:8.

2473. Par excellence.

2474. "Poetic" in the sense that it is not accurately descriptive of the one who writes but is an ideal presentation, and "partially poetic" in the sense that the one who writes is striving toward what is presented ideally. See $x^2$ A 184, 281; *The Point of View,* p. 74 fn.; *Armed Neutrality,* pp. 37, 44; *The Sickness unto Death,* pp. 208–9.

2475. See notes 1008, 1329, 1448, 1531.

2476. See note 3299.

2477. See note 3125.

2478. M. Goldschmidt. See note 1529.

2479. See $x^1$ A 584.

2480. See $x^2$ A 48; notes 1008, 1531.

2481. Transition or change into another sphere.

2482. See note 1531.

2483. See *Armed Neutrality,* pp. 33, 36–37, 39, 43; notes 1674, 2332, 2474.

2484. Ibid.

2485. See *Either/Or,* II, pp. 3–157; *Stages,* pp. 95–178; *Three Discourses on Imagined Occasions,* II (*Thoughts on Crucial Situations in Human Life,* pp. 43–74).

2486. *Practice in Christianity,* on which Kierkegaard worked at the same time as he worked on *The Sickness unto Death.* See note 2118.

2487. Anti-Climacus was the pseudonym used.

2488. See note 2483.

2489. See notes 1796, 2692.

2490. See note 1827.

2491. See note 2226.

2492. See note 2487.

2493. Publication of the Anti-Climacus works under his own name, inasmuch as he himself did not correspond to the ideality which they presented. See note 2483.

2494. Regine Olsen. See notes 637, 1712.

2495. See note 1962.

2496. See note 2435.

2497. See note 2102; ibid, I, p. 124.

2498. See note 1835.

2499. See note 2483.

2500. See note 1531.

2501. "Practice in Christianity," "Armed Neutrality," "The Point of View," "Three Discourses at the Communion on Fridays."

2502. See note 1939.

2503. See note 2483.

2504. See note 1997.

2505. Presumably the "also" refers to the role Kierkegaard considered that Governance had in his work and to his own double understanding of his work at the time and in retrospect.

2506. See Part III of *Practice [Training] in Christianity,* pp. 75 and 227–50. On Kierkegaard's various special expressions for his writings see note 1028.

2507. See note 2474; $x^2$ A 393.

2508. See note 2483.

2509. As a result of the repeated caricaturing of Kierkegaard by *The Corsair,* not only his legs and clothing became occasions for ridicule and harassment on the streets but also his name "Søren," which lent itself as a taunt word because in popular Danish usage it also means "devil."

2510. See notes 1333, 1448, 1590, 2509.

2511. Meïer Goldschmidt, who had been editor of *The Corsair.* See note 1863.

2512. See note 2375.

2513. See $x^1$ A 95, $x^2$ A 66.

2514. See note 2474.

2515. See note 2173.

2516. *The Point of View,* which was "as good as ready" in November 1848. See IX A 293; notes 2129, 2209.

2517. Please, please.

2518. See note 2262.

2519. See note 1806.

2520. Peter C. Kierkegaard. See note 1.

2521. See note 2517.

2522. Easy.

2523. See note 1694.

2524. See IX A 390.

2525. See $x^1$ A 497; notes 2300, 3213.

2526. See note 2344; $x^1$ A 568, 569.

2527. See $x^2$ A 126.

2528. Both the signed and the pseudonymous lines of the authorship involve repetition. *Either/Or* is repeated on a higher level in *Stages.* The theme of the lily and the bird is treated three times, each time on a higher level. The preface to *Three Discourses at the Communion on Fridays* "repeats" the preface to the first two discourses of 1843, and later the preface to *Two Discourses at the*

*Communion of Fridays* states: "A graduated forward-moving authorship, which began with *Either/Or*, seeks here its crucial resting place, at the foot of the altar." See $x^2$ A 217.

2529. See note 2483.

2530. For example, the young man and Constantin in *Repetition*, Quidam and Frater Taciturnus in *Stages*. See also *Upbuilding Discourses in Various Spirits*, Part One (*Purity of Heart*, p. 95).

2531. See notes 1796, 2692.

2532. See note 3213.

2533. See *Practice [Training] in Christianity*, p. 71.

2534. See $x^2$ A 163.

2535. Of L. Feuerbach's works, the Auction-catalog of Søren Kierkegaard's Book-collection includes *Geschichte der neuern Philosophie* (Ansbach: 1837); *Das wesen des Christenthums* (Leipzig: 1843); *Abelard und Heloise* (Ansbach: 1834). *ASKB* 487, 488, 1637.

2536. Advice from the enemy.

2537. Evil genius, evil daimon.

2538. Pseudonymous author of *Philosophical Fragments* and *Concluding Unscientific Postscript to Philosophical Fragments*. The reference is primarily to the second work.

2539. Thomas à Kempis, *Om Christi Efterfølgelse*, tr. J. A. L. Holm, introduction by A. G. Rudelbach (Copenhagen: 1848). *ASKB* 273.

2540. See note 2483.

2541. See notes 1674, 2474.

2542. See $x^1$ A 497.

2543. See $x^2$ A 10.

2544. See note 2344.

2545. See notes 1674, 2474.

2546. In *The Sickness unto Death*, the first work by the idealized pseudonymous writer Anti-Climacus.

2547. See note 1993.

2548. See no. 4 in Part IV of *Christian Discourses*, pp. 283–88.

2549. See note 2096.

2550. See IX A 390, $x^1$ A 45.

2551. Ibid.

2552. See, for example, *Fear and Trembling*, pp. 22–23, 27, 43, 79, 98, 130–32; *Fragments*, pp. 14, 25, 29, 139.

2553. See note 2332.

2554. See note 2483.

2555. See note 2096.

2556. See IX A 262.

2557. The drafts of the letters to Regine Olsen Schlegel and to her husband, Johan Frederik Schlegel, are in *Letters,* no. 235–38. The following four paragraphs were not sent as part of the letter to Regine. The following letters and additions are from Kierkegaard's copies.

2558. Regine Olsen Schlegel. See notes 637, 991, 1037, 1712, 1962.

2559. Johan Frederik Schlegel. See note 2435.

2560. See note 2344.

2561. Francois Boieldieu and Eugene Scribe, *La dame blanche,* tr. Thomas Overskou (*Den hvide Dame*), presented at the Royal Theater on October 12, and 18, 1841.

2562. Emil Boesen. See note 2389.

2563. See note 1835.

2564. Alexander Dumas, *Kean, ou Désordre et Genie,* performed October 21, 1841, with F. F. Printzlau in the title role.

2565. See *Letters,* no. 49. The date 10/31 six lines above refers to this Berlin letter.

2566. See *Letters,* no. 239; IX A 276; note 2557.

2567. Schlegel's reply is noted in *Letters,* no. 239; see X³ A 769.

2568. See note 982.

2569. See note 1962.

2570. See X² A 212.

2571. See note 2528.

2572. See note 2375.

2573. For particular entries see Index (*J.P.*, vol. 7.): Olsen, Regine.

2574. See note 1962; *Letters,* no. 239.

2575. See *Letters,* no. 239.

2576. Kierkegaard's working places included a stand-up desk (Danish: *Pult*) which helped alleviate the obvious occupational hazard of sitting at one desk too long. The high desk is now in the Kierkegaard room in the Copenhagen City Museum.

2577. See note 2344.

2578. See X² A 427. The paper is not extant.

2579. Regine Olsen.

2580. See X² A 210.

2581. See notes 991, 1037.

2582. See note 2528.

2583. See note 2014.

2584. See VII¹ A 233.

2585. See *Postscript,* p. [552]. The pages of "The First and Last Declaration" were deliberately unnumbered in the original edition and also in the present English edition.

2586. See note 2465.

2587. See VII¹ B 5, A 99, A 214.

2588. See notes 1329, 1529.

2589. See *Works of Love*, pp. 185–92, 196; *Practice [Training] in Christianity*, p. 217.

2590. See note 2096.

2591. See note 2226.

2592. See note 1329.

2593. See notes 1327, 1330.

2594. Kierkegaard's brother, Peter C. See note 1.

2595. Pastoral convention in Roskilde, October 30, 1849. Six years later, on July 5, 1855, again in Roskilde, three months before Søren Kierkegaard died (see note 3402), Peter C. Kierkegaard gave another address, under the title "Remarks on the Famous Pseudonyms of the Day and the Theology of Their Author," in which Peter discussed the "misgivings I, for my part, have long entertained against the theology, or what could better be called the non-theology, that an academy of pseudonyms has developed these last years in the literature of our fatherland.·. . ." (Otto Holmgaard, *Exstaticus*, Copenhagen: 1867, p. 57.) In the *Papirer* there is no reference to this second Roskilde address, but it was the occasion of the rift between the brothers during the last days of Kierkegaard's life.

2596. See *Dansk Kirketidende*, V, 219, December 16, 1849, col. 171–93. See also 22, May 29, 1881. Entries $x^2$ A 256, 273, and 280 must have been written after Peter's visit in December (see $x^2$ A 280). After the visit Kierkegaard read the printed version of Peter's talk and wrote all three entries.

2597. See notes 1875, 1889, 2851.

2598. See note 2509.

2599. Emilie Carlén, *En Nat ved Bullar-Søen*, *Berlingske Tidende*, 43–206, February 20–September 4, 1847.

2600. See note 2465.

2601. Matthew 8:22.

2602. See notes 2594–96.

2603. II Corinthians 5:13; see note 2465.

2604. Soundness of mind.

2605. See note 2594.

2606. Rasmus Nielsen. See notes 1939, 2242.

2607. See $x^2$ A 256.

2608. See notes 1796, 2692.

2609. See note 2594.

2610. See $x^2$ A 256.

2611. See note 2606.

2612. Pseudonymous author of *Two Minor Ethical-Religious Essays*, published May 19, 1849.

2613. I Corinthians 3:22.

2614. Kierkegaard was meticulous about this in the journals, giving hundreds of titles, usually with full bibliographical information. For this reason a reconstitution of his library (the same editions) is a great asset to one working with the journals and papers.

2615. See note 2594. This reply to Peter's address was not published.

2616. See notes 2595, 2596.

2617. Johannes F. Fenger (1805–61).

2618. See note 2339.

2619. See note 2596; ibid., especially col. 179.

2620. See note 2615.

2621. See note 2596.

2622. See note 2595.

2623. See note 2594.

2624. See note 2596.

2625. See note 2465.

2626. See *Postscript*, p. [552]; $x^6$ B 127, 245.

2627. See Matthew 3:3; Mark 1:3.

2628. See note 2483.

2629. See note 2474.

2630. See note 2096.

2631. See note 2612; $x^2$ A 280.

2632. See note 2596; ibid., col. 191; *Two Minor Ethical-Religious Essays*, in present English edition together with *The Present Age*, pp. 82–83.

2633. Ibid., p. 129.

2634. Combiner, or weaver of dialectical strands.

2635. See note 1939.

2636. December 3, 1841, H. L. Martensen (see note 315), nominated by J. P. Mynster, had been made a member of *Det kongelige danske Videnskabernes Selskab.* R. Nielson became a member in 1876.

2637. No. 306, December 28, 1849.

2638. *Spirit in Nature*, by Hans Christian Ørsted (1777–1851), physicist and brother of A. S. Ørsted, the jurist, and best known for his discovery of electromagnetism.

2639. N. F. S. Grundtvig (1783–1872), Danish pastor, poet, historian, and politician. See note 73.

2640. See *Postscript*, pp. [551–52].

2641. Ibid., p. [552]. See *Letters*, no. 240.

2642. I. M. Hjorth. Review of R. Nielsen, *Evangelietroen og den moderne Bevidsthed. Nyt Theologiske Tidsskrift*, I, 1850, p. 137.

2643. See note 1939.

2644. R. Nielsen's *Mag. S. Kierkegaards "Johannes Climacus" og Dr. H. Martensens "Christelige Dogmatik"* was published October 15, 1849.

2645. See note 2626.

2646. See notes 1008, 1329, 1448.

2647. See notes 118, 951, 952, 1127, 1448, 1606.

2648. The letter is not extant. See VI B 222. The reply from Henrik Lund (see note 17) reads as follows.

Odense, April 12, 1850

Dear Uncle,

You will, I hope, forgive me for not having written to you for such a long time when you take into consideration the extensive task you assigned me in your last letter: to provide you with an outline of the time of arrival of the most important migratory birds. In order to answer it fairly completely, I have both explored the local woods myself and gathered information from several farmers and zoologists about their experiences. Here are the results of my investigations up to date: [*two pages of data on various birds*].

Your devoted nephew,
Henrik

*Letters*, no. 262   April 12, 1850

2649. In 1846 Peter C. Kierkegaard was involved with Bishop Mynster in a controversy over baptism in the established Folk Church of Denmark.

2650. Provisional title of what eventually was named *Practice in Christianity*. See $x^2$ A 346.

2651. See note 1939.

2652. Peter M. Stilling (1812–69), assistant professor (*privatdocent*), University of Copenhagen 1846–50, author of *Om den indbildte Forsoning af Tro og —Viden, med særligt Hensyn til Professor Martensens "Christelige Dogmatik"* (Copenhagen: 1850). *ASKB* 802.

2653. See notes 2538, 2644.

2654. See note 2481.

2655. See *Postscript*, pp. 19, 545, 548.

2656. See note 1939.

2657. C. E. Scharling (1803–77) wrote a long review of Martensen's *Christelige Dogmatik* (Copenhagen: 1849) with specific reference to Kierkegaard, P. M. Stilling, and R. Nielsen. *Nyt theologisk Tidsskrift*, 1850, I, pp. 348–75.

2658. See note 2652.

2659. Unofficial oddities. The noun and the adjective above are German, and the noun has a Danish ending.

2660. See note 2339; ibid., I.

2661. See note 2369.

2662. See note 2242.

2663. Presumably Johannes Climacus, pseudonymous author of *Fragments* and *Postscript*.

2664. Socrates.

2665. See note 1276; $x^1$ A 584.

2666. See note 1788.

2667. See note 2096.

2668. See note 2474; $VIII^1$ A 347.

2669. See note 2332.

2670. See note 2007.

2671. See *Practice* [*Training*] *in Christianity*, pp. 227–31.

2672. See $x^2$ A 90.

2673. The *Corsair* affair. See note 1531.

2674. Common shipwreck.

2675. Sophie, wife of Peter Christian Kierkegaard. See note 1666; *Letters*, no. 161, 167.

2676. Johan Christian Lund. See note 17.

2677. See $x^2$ A 256, 273.

2678. See note 1796.

2679. See *Upbuilding Discourses in Various Spirits*, Part One (*Purity of Heart*, pp. 197–205).

2680. Regine Olsen.

2681. See $x^2$ A 215.

2682. "The Point of View," "The Accounting," and "Three Notes."

2683. The inner story of his engagement to Regine Olsen. See notes 637, 2017.

2684. See *Postscript*, p. 49, for a sample from an earlier time.

2685. See note 1276; $x^1$ A 584.

2686. Philosophical questions and positions.

2687. See note 2652.

2688. In every way.

2689. P. M. Stilling's book was *Den moderne Atheisme eller den saakaldte Neohegelianismes Consequentser af den hegelske Philosophie* (Copenhagen: 1850). *ASKB* 801.

2690. See *Fear and Trembling*, pp. 116–21.

2691. See $x^1$ A 41.

2692. See note 1796. In the later years of his life, Kierkegaard became more stringent about his expenses. He divided what he had into units, which were placed in the custody of his brother-in-law Henrik Ferdinand Lund of the National Bank. Shortly before his death he drew out the last portion. See $VII^1$ B 211.

2693. *Either/Or*, I–II, was published February 20, 1843, and *Two Upbuilding Discourses*, May 16, 1843, in a parallel pattern of pseudonymous and signed writing and publishing that was continued through 1850.

2694. See note 1939.

2695. The *Corsair* affair.

2696. See note 1827.

2697. See note 2345.

2698. See note 1328.

2699. See notes 1327, 1330, 2511.

2700. See note 2465.

2701. See $x^1$ A 187.

2702. See note 2339.

2703. It goes from mouth to mouth.

2704. *Speculativ Rettroenhed, fremstillet efter Dr. Martensens "Christelige Dogmatik"* (Copenhagen: 1849).

2705. Ibid., p. 108.

2706. See *Postscript*, pp. [551–54].

2707. Theophilus Nicolaus (Magnus Eiríksson, 1806–81), author of *Er Troen et Paradox og "i Kraft af det Absurde"? et Spørgsmaal foranlediget ved "Frygt og Bæven, af Johannes de Silentio"* . . . (Copenhagen: 1850). *ASKB* 831. See note 2704.

2708. See note 2136.

2709. Good faith.

2710. See note 2707.

2711. The entry was intended for possible publication in some paper, but it remained unpublished.

2712. See note 2136.

2713. See *Fear and Trembling*, p. 43.

2714. Magnus Eiríksson (pseudonym, Theophilus Nicolaus), *Tro, Overtro og Vantro* (Copenhagen: 1846).

2715. See *Fear and Trembling*, pp. 64–77.

2716. Ibid., pp. 78–91.

2717. Ibid., pp. 52–53.

2718. *Is Faith a Paradox and "by Virtue of the Absurd," a Question Prompted by "Fear and Trembling" by Johannes de Silentio, Answered with the Help of the Confidential Communications of a Knight of Faith, for the Mutual Edification of J e w s, C h r i s t i a n s, and M o s l e m s, by the Above-mentioned Knight of Faith's Brother, Theophilus Nicolaus.* See note 2714.

2719. See notes 2707, 2714.

2720. Ibid.

2721. See note 2718.

2722. See note 2714.

2723. See note 2713.

2724. See note 2014.

2725. See *Nord og Syd*, ed. M. Goldschmidt, 1850, III, p. 276.

2726. Remarkableness. See note 2659.

2727. See note 2692.

2728. See *S.V.*, VIII, pp. 100–2.

2729. See IX B 63:7.

2730. The last section of *Stages,* pp. 178–444.

2731. Rasmus Nielsen. See note 1939. In all there are extant seventeen letters or notes from Kierkegaard to Nielsen.

2732. See notes 2242, 2644. A third work was published April 6, 1850: *Evangelietroen og Theologien,* of which Kierkegaard had a gilt-edged presentation copy from Nielsen. *ASKB* 702.

2733. Rasmus Nielsen. See note 1939. Although Kierkegaard was disappointed in that relationship, his vivacious friendship with Emil Boesen continued, as is indicated by this whimsical wedding invitation from Boesen.

Dear friend,
     You are hereby invited to my wedding on Wednesday afternoon (May 1) at 6 p.m. (or 7) at Frue Kirke. I cannot call on you myself, because I have caught a bad cold and must try to get rid of it quickly again.
     R.S.V.P. It would give us great pleasure if you would come.

Yours
Emil Boesen.

Copenhagen, April 29, 1850

[Address:]
To
Magister Kjerkegaard
45 Nørregade

*Letters,* no. 265   April 29, 1850

2734. See note 2652.
2735. See note 1829.
2736. See note 2509.
2737. See note 1939.
2738. See *Letters,* no. 257.
2739. See note 2242.
2740. See note 1531.
2741. Ibid.
2742. John 16:23–28, text for the fifth Sunday after Easter.
2743. See notes 1939, 2738.
2744. See note 62.
2745. *The Corsair.*
2746. See note 1895.
2747. See note 1328.
2748. See note 2014.

2749. See note 2760.

2750. See note 1835.

2751. See note 1328.

2752. See note 2014.

2753. See note 1328.

2754. Parmo Carl Ploug (1813–94), writer, politician, and editor of *Fædrelandet*, together with J. F. Giødwad.

2755. See note 1895.

2756. Nørregade 43 (now 35), where Kierkegaard lived between the customary annual April Moving Days 1850 and 1851.

2757. See notes 1783, 1796, 2692.

2758. See *Either/Or*, II, pp. 343–56.

2759. Georg J. B. Carstensen (1812–57), founder of Tivoli (1843) and founder-publisher of *Portefeuillen* (1839–41), *Figaro* (1841–42), *Ny Portefeuille* (1842–44), and *Dansk Album* (1845).

2760. J. L. Heiberg (1791–1860), the foremost Danish writer and critic of the time and exponent of Hegelian philosophy.

2761. See notes 897, 905, 1276; $x^1$ A 584, $x^3$ A 99.

2762. See $x^1$ A 42.

2763. Israel Levin (1810–83), philologist and writer, assisted Kierkegaard at times in the preparation of final manuscript copy (particularly the pseudonymous works) and proofreading in the 1840s. Levin contributed greatly to the *Ordbog over det danske Sprog* and was in part responsible for the extraordinarily large number of Kierkegaard quotations now contained in it. See note 3402.

2764. V. J. Bjerring (1805–79), philologist and politician, professor of French, University of Copenhagen, 1848–74.

2765. See note 2762.

2766. See *Stages*, p. 276; note 547. Kierkegaard recommends this practice to his reader (*Purity of Heart*, p. 27; *For Self-Examination*, p. iii).

2767. The *Corsair* affair.

2768. Tornebuskegade and Rosenborggade.

2769. See note 2756.

2770. See note 2454.

2771. See notes 593, 1797. Presumably the same Anders.

2772. The sentence is incomplete, and the entire paragraph is crossed out in the manuscript.

2773. See note 2692.

2774. See notes 1939, 2738.

2775. See note 1141.

2776. See IX A 365.

2777. See note 2465; $x^3$ A 164.

2778. See Luke 18:18.

2779. Some time after the publication of his *Dogmatics* (see note 2339), H. L. Martensen replied to various criticisms (particularly R. Nielsen's and P. M. Stilling's) in an occasional piece entitled *Dogmatiske Oplysninger* (Copenhagen: June 14, 1850). See p. 7.

2780. See note 2652.

2781. See Mark 7:1–8.

2782. See note 2779.

2783. Ibid., p. 10.

2784. See note 2423.

2785. See note 2779; ibid., p. 13.

2786. Carl Emil Scharling (1803–77), theologian, professor of theology, University of Copenhagen, from 1834.

2787. See note 2760.

2788. See note 2652.

2789. See notes 1939, 2738.

2790. Eggert C. Tryde (1781–1860), pastor, friend of J. L. Heiberg, and after 1854 the Royal Chaplain.

2791. See, for example, Johannes Climacus, *Fragments*, Preface, pp. 3–7.

2792. Bishop J. P. Mynster. See note 547.

2793. See *Prefaces*, by Nicolaus Notabene, *S.V.*, V, pp. 35–38, 44.

2794. See *S.V.* XIII, pp. 397–406.

2795. See note 2339; ibid., Preface, p. III.

2796. A bosom friend.

2797. This and a number of other pieces [*Pap.*, x⁶ B 103–43] were prepared as part of the controversy, but none of them was published.

2798. See VIII¹ A 415; VIII² B 116, 118.

2799. See note 2779.

2800. See notes 1939, 2644.

2801. This contemplated eulogy to Bishop J. P. Mynster was not used. See *Bogen om Adler*, *Pap.*, VII² B 235, pp. 43–45 (in present English translation under the title *Authority and Revelation*, pp. 36–37).

2802. See J. P. Mynster, *Prædikener*, I–II (Copenhagen: 3 ed., 1826; II, 2 ed., 1832), I, p. ix. *ASKB* 228.

2803. This dedication was used in the gift copy of *Works of Love* to Bishop J. P. Mynster. See *Breve og Aktstykker*, I, p. 339; VIII² B 118.

2804. See note 2207.

2805. His father, Michael P. Kierkegaard.

2806. Regine Olsen.

2807. Christian Scriver, *Seelen-Schutz*, I–V (Leipzig: 1723). *ASKB* 261–263. The reference has not been located.

2808. Particularly *Practice in Christianity*.

2809. See notes 2483.

2810. By itself, or precisely thereby or for that reason.

2811. See, for example, *Fear and Trembling,* pp. 78–80.

2812. See *Armed Neutrality,* p. 42 and note. The distinction here is "the wise" and "lovers of wisdom."

2813. See note 1835.

2814. Peter Wilhelm Lund (1801–80), natural scientist, brother of Johan C. and Henrik F. Lund (married to Kierkegaard's sisters Nicoline C. and Petrea S). See note 92.

2815. See note 1835.

2816. See note 2102; ibid., I, p. 513.

2817. *Postscript,* p. [551] (ed. tr.).

2818. Part of *On My Work as an Author,* together with *The Point of View,* pp. 138–51. See note 2209.

2819. See note 2465.

2820. See $x^3$ A 164, $x^6$ B 137.

2821. See $x^1$ A 615, $x^2$ A 66, 106, 126, 147, 148, 177, 184.

2822. See $x^1$ A 568.

2823. See note 1962; *Letters,* no. 239.

2824. A motto of the Grundtvigians was "the living [spoken] word," rather than the written word. See note 75.

2825. See note 1827, 1908.

2826. See note 1468; ibid., II, pp. 208–9.

2827. See *For Self-Examination* (published the next year, 1851), p. i.

2828. See note 1939.

2829. See, for example, IX A 229.

2830. See $x^1$ A 343.

2831. In the public domain.

2832. Remarkable. A German word with a Danish ending. On the following German phrase, see note 2659.

2833. See notes 1939, 2738.

2834. *Practice in Christianity,* published September 27, 1850.

2835. See VIII$^1$ A 581, $x^1$ A 323.

2836. See *Practice in Christianity,* pp. 247–49.

2837. August 9, 1838.

2838. See note 2102; ibid., II, pp. 248–55.

2839. James 1:17–21.

2840. See note 2834.

2841. See Romans 8:18–23.

2842. September 8, 1840, the day of proposal; Regine accepted the proposal on September 10.

2843. Matthew 6:24–34.

2844. See note 1835.

2845. See *Fragments*, p. 137; *Postscript*, p. 251; VII¹ A 107, VIII² B 88, IX A 72, X² A 457, X³ A 395.

2846. See *Stages on Life's Way*, p. 419; *Practice [Training] in Christianity*, pp. 229–30.

2847. Anti-Climacus, pseudonymous author of *The Sickness unto Death* and *Practice in Christianity*.

2848. See note 2842.

2849. See Matthew 6:24–34.

2850. A German hymn by Paul Gerhardt, "*Befiel du deine Wege*," no. 573 in *Gesangbuch* (Berlin: 1829; *ASKB* 205), translated into Danish by E. Stevensen, 42, Roskilde-Konvents *Psalmbog* (Copenhagen: 1850; *ASKB* 198). The full text in English (tr. Henry Mills, *Evangelical Lutheran Hymnal*, 411 [Columbus, Ohio: 1888]) reads:

> Commit thy way, confiding,
>    When trials here arise,
> To Him whose hand 'is guiding
>    The tumults of the skies.
> There clouds and tempests, raging,
>    Have each their path assigned;
> Will God, for thee engaging,
>    No way of safety find?

> 2   Trust in the Lord! His favor
>        Will for thy wants provide;
>     Regard His word!—and ever
>        Thy work shall safe abide.
>     When sorrows here o'ertake thee,
>        And self-inflicted care,
>     Let not thy God forsake thee!
>        He listens for thy prayer.

> 3 Should Satan league his forces,
>       God's purpose to withstand,
>    Think not their rage and curses
>       Can stay His lifted hand!
>    When He makes known His pleasure,
>       The counsel of His will,
>    That, in its utmost measure,
>       Will He at last fulfill.

> 4 Hope on then, weak believer,
>       Hope on, and falter not!
>    He will thy soul deliver

From deeps of troubled thought.
Thy graces will He nourish,
With hope thy heart employ,
Till faith and hope shall flourish
And yield their fruits of joy.

5   Well blest, His grace receiving,
God owns thee for a son!
With joy, and with thanksgiving,
Behold the victor's crown!
Thy hand the palm-branch raises,—
God gives it thee to bear;—
Then sing aloud His praises,
Who has removed thy care.

6   The sorrows, Lord, that try us,
O bring them to an end!
With needed strength supply us!
Thy love to us commend!
That we, till death pursuing
Thy best, thy chosen way,
May then, our life renewing,
Praise Thee in endless day.

2851. Hans Peter Kofoed-Hansen (1813–93), curate at Frelsers Kirke, 1849–54, author of *Dialoger og Skizzer* (under pseudonym Jean Pierre) and various other works for which Kierkegaard was the greatest single influence and at times the subject. He wrote perhaps the first penetrating review of a Kierkegaard work (*Either/Or*) in *For Literatur og Kritik*, 1843, I, pp. 377–405. See H. P. Jørgensen, *H. P. Kofoed-Hansen (Jean Pierre)* (Copenhagen: 1920).

2852. Not published until August 7, 1851. See note 2209.

2853. Kierkegaard considered the possibility of a cryptic dedication to Regine. See x⁵ B 263, 264; see the dedication to *Two Discourses at the Communion on Fridays*, together with *Judge for Yourselves!* p. 3.

2854. See note 2852.

2855. See note 2834.

2856. See notes 637, 1712. Another version of the dedications below and of x⁵ B 264 was used in *Two Discourses at the Communion on Fridays*. See note 2853.

2857. Ibid.

2858. See note 1835.

2859. See note 2465.

2860. See note 1835.

2861. The world *wants* to be deceived. See note 1476.

2862. The *Corsair* affair. See note 1329.

2863. See notes 1008, 1329, 1448.

2864. See note 1835.

2865. Ibid.

2866. King of France (1830–1845).

2867. Over the years Kierkegaard's father and Kierkegaard himself were regular readers of Mynster's sermons. See notes 547, 2766.

2868. See *For Self-Examination* (published September 10, 1851) pp. 87–90.

2869. *Practice* [*Training*] *in Christianity*, p. 137.

2870. See note 2102; ibid., I, pp. 65–66.

2871. See note 2790.

2872. See *Practice* [*Training*] *in Christianity*, pp. 227–30. Bishop Mynster had written a work entitled *Betragtninger* [*Observations*] *over de christelige Troeslærdomme*, I–II (Copenhagen: 1833). *ASKB* 254–55 (2 ed., 1837).

2873. Pp. 98–100. *ASKB* 695.

2874. See *The Sickness unto Death*, pp. 212–13.

2875. Johannes Climacus and Anti-Climacus, the pseudonymous authors of *Fragments* and *Postscript*, *The Sickness unto Death* and *Practice in Christianity*, respectively.

2876. See note 2466.

2877. Literally, in good love; on good terms.

2878. See $x^3$ A 530.

2879. See note 2465.

2880. See note 2466.

2881. See note 2834.

2882. See note 1835.

2883. Ibid.

2884. See *Practice* [*Training*] *in Christianity*, pp. 45–55.

2885. See note 2466.

2886. See note 2000.

2887. See note 1859.

2888. See $x^3$ A 568.

2889. See *On My Work as an Author*, in present English translation together with *The Point of View*, pp. 142–50; note 2209.

2890. A. Neander, *Der heilige Bernhard und sein Zeitalter* (Berlin: 2 ed., 1848), pp. 158–60.

2891. See $x^2$ A 285.

2892. See note 1. On December 29, 1849, Peter was elected to the *Landsting* and was active on various political and ecclesiastical issues.

2893. Clara Raphael [Mathilde Fibiger], *Tolv Breve*, edited by J. L. Heiberg (Copenhagen: 1851). *ASKB* 1531. See $VII^1$ A 9. This review was not published.

2894. Magnus Eiríksson, *Om Baptister og Barnedaab* (Copenhagen: 1844).

2895. See *Either/Or*, I, pp. 247–75.

2896. A character in J. L. Heiberg's *Aprilsnarrene*, sc. 29. See *The Moment*, 4, in *Attack*, p. 144 and note.

2897. See *Postscript*, pp. 163–64.

2898. Holberg's *Perseus*, II (Copenhagen: 1838) contains the promise of a system of logic. *ASKB* 569. See "Prefaces," *S.V.*, V, pp. 17, 51–52.

2899. See J. L. Heiberg, *"Det Astronomical Aar," Urania* (Copenhagen: 1844).

2900. See note 2339; ibid., pp. 546 ff., especially p. 550.

2901. H. A. Brorson, *Psalmer og aandelige Sange* (Copenhagen: 2 ed., 1838), p. 623. *ASKB* 200.

2902. Kierkegaard's father, M. P. Kierkegaard, and J. P. Mynster had been long-time friends.

2903. See note 2483, $X^2$ A 375.

2904. Regine Olsen.

2905. See *Letters*, no. 239; note 1962.

2906. See note 1176. Note spelling of name here.

2907. See note 2875.

2908. See note 2905.

2909. See note 1835.

2910. See J. P. Mynster, *Prædikener holdte i Aarene 1851 og 1852* (Copenhagen: 1853), pp. 3–16. *ASKB* 234. This sermon was given on January 19, 1851.

2911. See *For Self-Examination* (published September 10, 1851), pp. 12–18.

2912. See note 1835.

2913. See *For Self-Examination*, pp. 10–23.

2914. *Practice [Training] in Christianity*, p. 7.

2915. See the preface to *Two Discourses at the Communion on Fridays*, together with *Judge for Yourselves!* p. 5, para. 1.

2916. See note 1835.

2917. See note 2639.

2918. See note 1916.

2919. See *For Self-Examination* (published September 10, 1851), pp. 22–23.

2920. See note 2483.

2921. See *For Self-Examination*, pp. 23–54.

2922. See Preface to *Practice [Training] in Christianity*, p. 7.

2923. See notes 1329, 1531.

2924. See *An Open Letter*, together with *Armed Neutrality*, pp. 50–51.

2925. Ibid.

2926. See note 1835.

2927. Niels Møller Spandet (1788–1858), Danish jurist and politician who in 1850 introduced a bill in the lower house to establish civil counterparts of marriage, baptism, and confirmation. This was supported by Grundtvig and most of the Venstre (left) party but was strongly opposed throughout the country and in the upper house. See *Dansk Kirketidende*, V, November 24, 1850, col. 977 ff., December 1, 1850, 1011 ff., December 8, 1850, 1019 ff.; *Berlingske Tidende*, 282, 300, December 2, 1850, December 24, 1850 (Supplement).

2928. See note 1916.

2929. See note 2924; ibid., pp. 48–55; $x^6$ B 171 (3).

2930. J. P. Mynster. Despite his criticism (see note 1534) of Mynster, Kierkegaard saw more reason to support him than the reformers of ecclesiastical machinery.

2931. See the preface to *Fragments*, p. 7.

2932. See *Practice [Training] in Christianity*, p. 221, where the same meaning is found, although not the exact phrase. See also pp. 214–15, 243–44, 249–50.

2933. Ibid., p. 7.

2934. See Matthias Claudius: *"Die Mutter bey der Wiege,"* oder *Sämmtliche Werke des Wandsbecker Bothen*, I–IV (Hamburg: 1819), $I^{1-2}$, pp. 35–36. *ASKB* 1631–32.

2935. See note 2932.

2936. See note 2930.

2937. See note 2639.

2938. Delivered in Copenhagen in the spring of 1810.

2939. See *For Self-Examination*, pp. 27–30.

2940. See note 2639.

2941. See note 2938.

2942. See note 2932.

2943. See note 2639.

2944. See note 2483.

2945. See note 2209.

2946. See *On My Work as an Author*, in the present English version with *The Point of View*, p. 155. See note 2096.

2947. See note 2509.

2948. To base an argument on what another has stated.

2949. See notes 2474, 2483.

2950. See *The Point of View*, pp. 5, 16, 39, 44–45, 62.

2951. F. Böhringer, *Die Kirche Christi oder die Kirchengeschichte in Biographien*, I, 1–4; II, $1-4^{1-2}$ (Zürich: 1842–53). *ASKB* 173–77 (lacking II, $4^{1-2}$).

2952. See *Armed Neutrality*, p. 41, for partial analogy.

2953. See note 2014.

2954. The honor of praising Goldschmidt as "one of our most talented writers" and using for Kierkegaard a term (*Fremtoning*) coined by Goldschmidt. See note 2967; J. P. Mynster, *Yderligere Bidrag til Forhandlingerne om de kirkelige Forhold i Danmark* (Copenhagen: 1851), p. 44.

2955. Ludvig Holberg, *Det lykkelige Skibbrud*, III, 3.

2956. See note 2954.

2957. Ibid.

2958. Ibid.

2959. Ibid.

2960. See note 2483.

2961. See *Postscript*, p. 549; VIII$^1$ A 415, VIII$^2$ B 116, 118, X$^6$ B 163, 164, 169, X$^4$ A 377; note 2801.

2962. See note 1835.

2963. *De la Rochefaucault's moralische Maximen* (Vienna, Leipzig: 1784), 14. *ASKB* 739.

2964. See note 2954.

2965. See note 1835.

2966. See note 2954.

2967. In *Nord og Syd*, V, 1849, pp. 143–44, Meïr Goldschmidt coined a word, *Fremtoning*, as the Danish equivalent of the German *Erscheinung*, commonly translated into Danish as *Phænomenon*. To express the novelty of the new Danish word and its combining of *frem* (forth) and the double meaning of the verb *tone* (to sound and to appear), *phono* and *phenomenon* have been conflated in phonomenon as the English translation. See *O.D.S.*, V, col. 987 (*Fortone*, I, Para. 1, and II), col. 1031 (*fremtone* and *Fremtoning*). For further discussion in *Nord og Syd*, see V, 1849, pp. 299–303; VI, 1849, pp. 266–68.

2968. See *An Open Letter*, with *Armed Neutrality*, pp. 49–52.

2969. See note 1748.

2970. See note 2961.

2971. See X$^1$ A 53.

2972. Jakob Peter Mynster's pseudonym, formed from the middle consonant of each name.

2973. Restitution to its pristine state; in this case.

2974. See notes 2954, 2967.

2975. Memorial, record.

2976. A play on the name of Goldschmidt's journal, *Nord og Syd* (*North and South*). See notes 1748, 3289.

2977. See note 2961.

2978. Can you force a smile?

2979. I swear by the gods, why by Goldschmidt!

2980. Publicly.

2981. New Harbor, the sailors' haunts, off Kongens Nytorv.

2982. A narrow alley of dubious reputation, leading onto Strøget near Kongens Nytorv.

2983. See notes 1875, 1889, 2851.

2984. No. 904, June 12, 1842. See *S.V.*, XIII, pp. 397–406.

2985. See note 2760.

2986. Date etc. omitted: 1883, May 9, 1845. See *S.V.*, XIII, pp. 418–21.

2987. See Appendix, p. [549].

2988. See *Either/Or*, I, pp. 104, 108, and 129. The volume also includes a review of Heiberg's translation of Scribe's *The First Love*, pp. 229–77.

2989. No. 24, March 1, 1843, p. 290.

2990. H. L. Martensen (1808–84), professor of theology, University of Copenhagen, whose lectures Kierkegaard heard and who was also his tutor for a time. On April 15, 1854, Martensen was named Mynster's successor as Bishop of Sjælland. See notes 315, 1661, 2339, 2465, 2779, 3258, 3275.

2991. An academic title most closely approximated by "Assistant Professor."

2992. See note 2339.

2993. See note 1827.

2994. Ibid., pp. 19–20.

2995. The *Corsair* affair. See note 1329.

2996. Frederik Paludan-Müller (1809–76), poet, author of *Adam Homo*.

2997. See note 2483.

2998. See note 2483.

2999. See note 2995.

3000. See note 1529.

3001. See note 2954.

3002. See notes 1748, 3289.

3003. The above article was not published.

3004. See note 1827.

3005. See *Practice* [*Training*] *in Christianity*, by Anti-Climacus, p. 7.

3006. *On My Work as an Author* was published the same day as *Two Discourses at the Communion on Fridays*, on August 7, 1851. See note 2209.

3007. See x³ A 265, x⁴ A 373.

3008. See note 1329.

3009. See note 2483.

3010. Ibid.

3011. No. 38, February 14, 1851.

3012. *Fædrelandet*, 37, 38, February 13, 14, 1851. See x⁵ B 128, in *Armed Neutrality* and *An Open Letter*, pp. 109–15.

3013. See pp. 7, 77, 149.

3014. See notes 2954, 2967.

3015. See note 2954.

3016. The above portion is from an article entitled "An Expression by Bishop M.," written for possible issue in a journal but not submitted or published.

3017. See x⁶ B 171 (2).

3018. See notes 2954, 2967.

3019. See note 2950.

3020. See *J.P.*, III, note 372.

3021. See note 2919.

3022. See note 1835.

3023. By "quiet hours" [*stille Timer*] is not meant periods of quiet reflection, meditation, and prayer (see SILENCE, QUIET) but rather the formal occasions of public worship insofar as they are isolated practically from the rest of the day and week. See note 1818.

3024. See note 2483.

3025. Ibid.

3026. See note 2954.

3027. See note 1835.

3028. August Petersen, *Die Idee der Kirche*, I–III (Leipzig: 1839–46). *ASKB* 717–19.

3029. Ibid.

3030. Anti-Climacus, See note 2875.

3031. See note 2918.

3032. See note 2954.

3033. See x⁶ B 171, para. (3) and (5).

3034. Ibid.

3035. See *Works of Love*, p. 29.

3036. See note 2954.

3037. See note 1835.

3038. Pessimism is the corruption of optimism.

3039. See note 2875.

3040. See note 2692.

3041. See notes 1939, 2738.

3042. See note 2454.

3043. See x⁶ B 173, x⁴ B 373.

3044. See note 1962; *Letters*, no. 239; x³ A 789, x⁴ A 323.

3045. See note 2300; x¹ A 497.

3046. See note 1835; x¹ A 497.

3047. See x¹ A 494.

3048. See note 2345.

3049. See note 2344.

3050. The three parts eventually published under the title *Practice in Christianity* (see notes 1993, 1994, 1997, 2208) had been regarded by Kierkegaard as separate works. Hence, for example, the repetition of the preface before each of the three parts. In 1849, Kierkegaard had even considered a subscription series beginning with these three works (see *Pap*, x⁵ B 40–41).

3051. See note 3044.

3052. See note 2402.

3053. See note 2768.

3054. See *Practice* [*Training*] *in Christianity*, p. 7.

3055. See note 3007.

3056. See x³ A 265.

3057. See note 3048.

3058. See note 3049.

3059. See note 2756.

3060. See note 2454.

3061. See x⁴ A 299.

3062. See note 1962; *Letters*, no. 239.

3063. Ibid.

3064. May 18, 1851, in Citadelskirken. See x⁴ A 323.

3065. See x⁴ A 322.

3066. See note 3064.

3067. See, for example, *Three Upbuilding Discourses in Various Spirits*, Part One (*Purity of Heart*, pp. 27, 178–80).

3068. Regine Olsen Schlegel.

3069. See x⁴ A 318.

3070. See note 3065.

3071. *Prædikener paa alle Søn- og Hellig-Dage i Aaret*, I–II (Copenhagen: 3 ed., 1837), I, pp. 191–203. *ASKB* 229–30.

3072. See note 2692.

3073. Written as the preface to *For Self-Examination*, but not used.

3074. See note 2173.

3075. See notes 1783, 1796, 2692.

3076. Regine Olsen Schlegel.

3077. *On My Work as an Author* and *Two Discourses at the Communion on Fridays*, published August 7, 1851.

3078. See Luke 5:8–9.

3079. See note 1835.

3080. Ibid.

3081. Ibid.

3082. Ibid.

3083. See note 3077.

3084. The extended review of Thomasine Gyllembourg-Ehrensvärd's *Two Ages* is the chief instance of Kierkegaard's implementation of an idea for ceasing to be an author without ceasing to write (see vii¹ A 9, x¹ A 90, x⁴ A 373). His first book, *From the Papers of One Still Living*, a long review of Hans Christian Andersen's *Kun en Spillemand* (*Only a Fiddler*) was of the same order, although prior to his idea formulated in vii¹ A 9.

3085. See note 2994.

3086. See note 2954.

3087. See note 1835.

3088. See note 2954.

3089. See *Practice* [*Training*] *in Christianity,* pp. 7, 77, 149; note 3050.

3090. See note 2961.

3091. See $x^6$ B 163, 164.

3092. See note 1939.

3093. See note 2300; $x^1$ A 497.

3094. See note 1916.

3095. See note 2954.

3096. See note 3007.

3097. Previous life or life prior to the act. See notes 1329, 1529.

3098. See note 3077.

3099. No. 181, August 7, 1851.

3100. See L. Holberg, *Erasmus Montanus,* I, 4.

3101. No. 187, August 9, 1851.

3102. *On My Work as an Author,* published August 7, 1851. See note 2209.

3103. See note 2481.

3104. See notes 1329, 1531.

3105. See note 1534.

3106. The world wants to be deceived; see notes 1476, 2236.

3107. See note 1008.

3108. See note 2692.

3109. See note 1008.

3110. See note 3296.

3111. See note 2932.

3112. No. 215, September 16, 1851.

3113. See note 1342.

3114. Together with *The Point of View,* p. 148.

3115. See note 3089.

3116. See *The Moment,* August 23, 1855, no. 6, in *Attack,* p. 182.

3117. Ibid., p. 181.

3118. Ibid.

3119. Hans Lassen Martensen. See notes 1661, 2990.

3120. The play on the Danish *rørt* and *tørt* is lost in the translations "movingly" and "dryly."

3121. I Corinthians 1:28.

3122. See L. Holberg, *Ulysses von Ithacia,* II, 3.

3123. See $x^6$ B 253.

3124. Danish: *Mundharpen,* mouth-harp.

3125. See Isaiah 3:4, also Ecclesiastes 10:16. Kierkegaard presumably has made his own translation of the expression from the Hebrew. See *The Point of View,* p. 55.

3126. See note 2402.

3127. See $x^4$ A 338.

3128. Silhouette-cutting was a popular and earnest minor art at the time. Hans Christian Andersen is now the best known Danish practitioner from that period.

3129. See note 1835.

3130. See note 1697.

3131. See *Either/Or*, I, p. 19.

3132. See Luke 11:47.

3133. II, ch. 32.

3134. See *Rousseaus Bekjendelser*, I–II (Copenhagen: 1798), IV, pp. 6–7. *ASKB* 1922–25.

3135. See note 286.

3136. See note 1835.

3137. See reference to Kts (Mynster's pseudonym), *Postscript*, p. [553]. See note 1343.

3138. "Purity of Heart."

3139. See note 2692.

3140. See note 2954.

3141. M. P. Kierkegaard read Mynster's sermons regularly; Søren Kierkegaard appreciatively and rewardingly continued this practice. See x⁶ B 173; notes 547, 2766.

3142. See note 2961.

3143. See note 3213.

3144. See note 2768.

3145. See note 2208.

3146. Henrik S. Lund (1825–89), son of Kierkegaard's sister Nicoline Christine and Johan Christian Lund. See note 17.

3147. Regine Olsen Schlegel. See notes 637, 1712, 1962. Between April 1851 and April or October 1852 Kierkegaard lived at Østerbro 108A (since torn down).

3148. See note 2466. Paulli preached in Slotskirken May 9, 1852, on James 1:17–27.

3149. See note 1859.

3150. See notes 1783, 2013.

3151. See note 3213.

3152. See note 2466.

3153. See *The Sickness unto Death*, p. 224; *On My Work as an Author*, with *The Point of View*, p. 164; *The Moment*, no. 2, in *Attack*, p. 113.

3154. See note 2692.

3155. *Two Ages* (*The Present Age*, p. 63).

3156. See note 2096.

3157. See note 2692.

3158. See note 2878.

3159. See note 2466.

3160. Joachim L. Phister (1807–96), a prominent Danish actor whose work Kierkegaard admired. See "Herr Phister as Captain Scipio," with *Crisis in the Life of an Actress*, pp. 110–26; *Either/Or*, I, p. 237.

3161. See Matthew 10:38, 16:24; Mark 8:34; Luke 9:23, 14:27.

3162. See note 2932.

3163. See x³ A 152; x⁴ A 582, 609.

3164. See note 3061.

3165. See note 2692.

3166. Regine Olsen, daughter of Terkild Olsen referred to in the next paragraph. See notes 637, 2344.

3167. See note 3213.

3168. See note 2692.

3169. See note 3213.

3170. See note 2878.

3171. *Geschichte des Agathon, C. M. Wielands sämmtliche Werke*, I–LX (Leipzig: 1794–98), I, pp. 173–74, 182–83.

3172. See note 2878.

3173. The source has not been located.

3174. See Psalms 39:6; Luke 12:20. In the Kalkar edition (Copenhagen: 1847; *ASKB* 8–10), Psalm 39 has the heading, "Before God Man Is always in the Wrong"; see *Either/Or*, II, p. 343.

3175. No. 185, August 9, 1852.

3176. See Plato, *Crito*, 52–53 a.

3177. See note 3100.

3178. See note 2692.

3179. Ibid.

3180. See note 2483.

3181. See note 2848.

3182. Of the two Lund brothers (Johan Christian, 1799–1875, who married Kierkegaard's sister Nicoline, September 24, 1825, and Henrik Ferdinand, 1803–1875, who married Petrea, October 11, 1828), it more likely was National Bank office-manager Henrik Ferdinand Lund, who was custodian of Kierkegaard's apportioned dwindling assets in the last years (see note 2692) and whose home Kierkegaard visited frequently.

3183. The book titles listed in x⁶ c 6 and x⁶ c 7 are in a separate small pamphlet. The titles are of books in the University Library, various books Kierkegaard had been reading, and books selected from the catalog of the Athenæum.

3184. *ASKB* 913–14.

3185. *ASKB* 268.

3186. *ASKB* 154–55.

3187. Matthew 10:37; Luke 14:26.

3188. See note 3213.

3189. Presumably the entire entry alludes to J. P. Mynster and the relation between him and Kierkegaard. See note 1835.

3190. Regine Olsen. See notes 637, 1712, 1962; *Letters*, no. 239.

3191. See note 3213.

3192. See note 3190.

3193. Klædeboderne 5–6 (now Skindergade 38), Kierkegaard's address from April 1 or October, 1852, to the time of his death, November 11, 1855.

3194. The three remaining essays from the "Cycle," after the publication of *Two Minor Ethical-Religious Essays* by H. H. (May 19, 1849) and the exclusion of no. 5 (on Adler). See notes 2116, 2128.

3195. See notes 1476, 2236.

3196. See note 1008.

3197. See note 2692.

3198. In the manuscript the initial paragraph is crossed out.

3199. See note 3213.

3200. See note 3089.

3201. See note 2954.

3202. H. L. Martensen. See note 2779; ibid., p. 13.

3203. See note 3360.

3204. See $x^4$ A 651.

3205. Pp. 28–29.

3206. See note 1827.

3207. See note 1329.

3208. See notes 1783, 1796, 2013.

3209. See notes 1929, 2644, 2732, 2738.

3210. Regine Olsen Schlegel. See note 1962; *Letters*, no. 239.

3211. It should be *The Sickness unto Death*. See $x^4$ A 299.

3212. See note 2344.

3213. Jakob Peter Mynster, Bishop of Sjælland. See notes 547, 943, 1534, 1835, 2961.

3214. Ibid.

3215. The allusion is presumably to Meïr Goldschmidt, editor of *The Corsair*, and his collaborators. See notes 1329, 1529.

3216. The allusion is presumably to Bishop J. P. Mynster. See note 3213.

3217. See note 3213.

3218. See note 2990.

3219. See note 2639.

3220. See note 1916.

3221. See notes 1329, 1529, 1531.

3222. See note 2954.

3223. See note 3213.

3224. See note 3213.

3225. See J. L. Heiberg, *En Sjæl efter Døden. En Apocalyptisk Comedie*, in *Nye Digte* (Copenhagen: 1841). *ASKB* 1562. Perhaps the reference is also to Frederik Paludan-Müller's *Adam Homo*, I–III (Copenhagen: 1842–1848), III, song 12. Although this work is not listed in *ASKB*, Kierkegaard most likely had it and read it with care, because the two writers shared a common concern, man and his becoming.

3226. P. A. Fenger, *"Til Læserne af evangelisk Ugeskrift,"* *Dansk Kirketidende*, VIII, 417, October 2, 1853, col. 635.

3227. See note 1916.

3228. See note 2639.

3229. See note 2120.

3230. See note 3213. Bishop Mynster died January 30, 1854.

3231. See note 2954.

3232. Ernst Wilhelm Kolthoff (1809–1890), associated with Helligaandskirke, Copenhagen, 1845–80.

3233. See note 3213.

3234. See note 3230.

3235. Presumably the reference is to *Practice in Christianity*. See note 2878.

3236. See note 2961.

3237. Ibid.

3238. See notes 1783, 2013.

3239. See note 2208.

3240. See $x^3$ A 563.

3241. *An Open Letter*, with *Armed Neutrality*.

3242. The phrases are from an obituary of Mynster in *Berlingske Tidende*, 25, January 30, 1854.

3243. See note 3230. Mynster (Kts) was the author of an article in which reference is made to Kierkegaard's father. *Intelligentsblade*, I–IV (Copenhagen: 1842–44), IV, pp. 111–12. *ASKB* U56.

3244. See note 2961.

3245. See "Aristeides," *Plutarks Levnetsbeskrivelser*, tr. S. Tetens, I–IV (Copenhagen: 1800–11), III, p. 342. *ASKB* 1197–1200. See *Stages*, p. 170.

3246. See note 2045.

3247. See note 1840.

3248. See $x^2$ A 256; notes 2595, 2596.

3249. See note 2990.

3250. See p. 78.

3251. See note 1441.

3252. I swear by the gods.

3253. Danish: *Realiteten*, which is characteristically used by Kierkegaard to denote genuineness, essential significance, authenticity.

3254. See, for example, Part III of *Christian Discourses*, "Thoughts That Wound from Behind—for Upbuilding," pp. 167–250.

3255. See note 3213. *Mønsteret* (paragon) is spelled *Mynsteret* (Mynster) and has been translated in a phrase as a play on words.

3256. The Athenæum, a book society founded in Copenhagen in 1824, had a superb collection of about 40,000 volumes from which Kierkegaard frequently borrowed (see note 153). The Athenæum catalog of 1857, *Fortegnelse over Selskabet Athenæums Bogsamling*, II, p. 57, lists F. A. Schmidt and B. F. Voigt, *Neuer Nekrolog der Deutschen*, XXX, 1852 (Weimar: 1854).

3257. He who sees only the truth has ceased to live.
Life resembles the stage; there as here
Must the curtain fall when the illusion retreats.

3258. H. L. Martensen was named as J. P. Mynster's successor on April 15, 1854, and was ordained as Bishop on June 5, 1854. See note 2990.

3259. See note 3360.

3260. Nothing is happy that is not at rest. In Cicero, *De natura deorum*, I, 20, 52, a similar expression, *nisi quietum nihil beatum est*, is found in a formulation of the philosophy of Epicurus. See article in *Fædrelandet*, 10, January 12, 1855, in *Attack*, p. 18.

3261. See J. P. Mynster, *Prædikener holdte i Aarene 1846 til 1852* (Copenhagen: 1853), pp. 166–78, p. 169 in particular. *ASKB* 234.

3262. See note 3213.

3263. See note 3230.

3264. See J. P. Mynster, *Meddelelser om mit Levnet* (Copenhagen: 1854), which concludes on p. 291 with the quoted line: "So that with an honorable name I may lie in my grave." No doubt Kierkegaard had this volume, but it is not listed in *ASKB*.

3265. The occasion for this entry (which was not published) presumably was the publication of Rasmus Nielsen's *Om personlig Sandhed og sand Personlighed* [On Personal Truth and True Personality], May 27, 1854. In the preface Nielsen states: "That there are works in our literature which deal with the task on a scale not employed in my contribution, I have previously pointed out and, it seems to me, quite emphatically." In *Kjøbenhavnsposten*, 138, June 18, 1854, an anonymous review of Nielsen's book declared Nielsen to be Kierkegaard's apostle. Kierkegaard cared neither for Nielsen's use of his works (and their conversations) nor for Nielsen's appearing to be a collaborator and exponent. See IX A 229, X$^1$ A 343, X$^6$ B 93, 121, *Letters*, no. 257.

3266. Manifestation. See notes 2954, 2967.

3267. See subtitles of *Repetition, The Concept of Anxiety* [*Dread*], *The Sickness unto Death; Stages*, subtitle of " 'Guilty?'/ 'Not Guilty?' " p. 179; *Postscript*, pp. 230, 235–36, 240, 257.

3268. *Berlingske Tidende*, 141, June 21, 1854. The sermon, on the text John 3:16–21, was printed in *"Bispevielse i Frue Kirke paa anden Pinsedag den 5te Juni 1854"* (Copenhagen: 1854).

3269. Mendel Levin Nathanson (1780–1868), merchant, writer on trade and finance, and from 1838–1858, 1865–66 editor of Denmark's oldest and largest newspaper, *Berlingske Tidende*.

3270. J. H. Wessel, *Kjærlighed uden Strømper* (Copenhagen: 1772), IV, 5.

3271. See note 3230.

3272. See notes 2990, 3258, 3275.

3273. See note 2932.

3274. Disturbance.

3275. A repetition of phrases in Bishop Martensen's eulogy of the late Bishop Mynster (February 3, 1854, the Sunday before Mynster's funeral). See Kierkegaard's later article in *Fædrelandet*, 295, December 18, 1854 (in *Attack*, pp. 5–9), which was the beginning of his open criticism of the established order.

3276. Ibid.

3277. See note 73; *Postscript*, pp. 36–45.

3278. Adiaphoron, a matter of indifference.

3279. See note 3360.

3280. For example, H. C. Andersen, *Lykkens Kalosker;* Henrik Hertz, *Stemninger og Tilstande;* C. Hostrup, *Gjenboerne, En Spurv i Tranedans.*

3281. See note 1534.

3282. See Shakespeare, *The Tragedy of King Richard the Third,* I, 1.

3283. See note 2485.

3284. See Plato, *Apology,* 17 c; *For Self-Examination,* pp. 1–3.

3285. See A. Schopenhauer, *Die Welt als Wille und Forstellung,* I–II (Leipzig: 2 ed., 1844), II, ch. 46. *ASKB* 773–773a.

3286. On memory and recollection, see *Stages,* pp. 27–36.

3287. See notes 1829, 2509.

3288. With flowing pen.

3289. I, January–March, 1848, p. 227 fn. In 1848, after his return to Denmark, Aaron Meïr Goldschmidt, former editor of *The Corsair* (see notes 1329, 1529) founded *Nord og Syd,* a cosmopolitan journal devoted to politics, the theater, and literature. On June 7, 1843, the Supreme Court had placed him under lifetime censure. On January 24, 1848, he was granted amnesty by the king while the first quarterly issue of *Nord og Syd* was at the printer. Thereupon Goldschmidt publicly declared himself to be the responsible editor of *Nord og Syd.* See I, January–March, 1848, pp. 272–73.

3290. See *J.P.,* III, note 372.

3291. Poul Martin Møller (1794–1838), Kierkegaard's favorite professor, a good friend, and a great influence on his life. See note 438.

3292. See note 1859.

3293. See note 3291.

3294. See note 3292.

3295. See note 3360.

3296. "Way" or "method" or "the how" for Kierkegaard means not technique but rather the *mode* of a person's relation to what he understands or envisions (subjectivity is truth) and the mode of his expression of what he understands or envisions (reduplication, imitation, religious jest). See, for example, among the pseudonymous writings, *Fear and Trembling*, pp. 22, 24; *Philosophical Fragments* (the "how" on the title page and the "if . . . then . . ." structure of the entire work); *Postscript*, pp. 80, 104–5, 115, 169–224, 287, 324–75 fn., 442, 481, 508–9, 535–44.

3297. See *J.P.*, III, note 372.

3298. See *Either/Or*, I, p. 19.

3299. Presumably Edvard Meyer (1813–80), journalist, founder of the humor paper *Kjøbenhavns Morskabsblad* (1842), a competitor of Goldschmidt's *Corsaren*. Meyer himself and his activities had something of a comical cast, and he was the object of jokes by students and others. See *Corsaren*, 407, July 7, 1848, col. 11.

3300. See Luke 16:29–31; John 5:45.

3301. Line 8 (*Luk Døren til*) of the first stanza of *"Eet Sovekammer er min Grav,"* in *Gamle og Nye Psalmer*, ed. P. Hjort (Copenhagen: 2 ed., 1840), p. 301. *ASKB* 202.

3302. See note 2950.

3303. See notes 1829, 2509.

3304. Christian Winther, *"Tre Beilere,"* in *Digtninger* (Copenhagen: 1843), p. 246.

3305. See *For Self-Examination*, p. i.

3306. Ibid., pp. 1–3.

3307. A. S. Ørsted (1778–1860), brother of the physicist Hans Christian Ørsted, jurist; in 1853 named Prime Minister and also Minister of Culture and Minister of the Interior.

3308. See note 3258.

3309. Regine Olsen. See notes 637, 2017.

3310. See note 2692.

3311. The *Corsair* affair. See notes 1329, 1531.

3312. "One has the purse and the other has the money."

3313. See note 3360.

3314. The letter *C* for *calumnia* (English: calumny), false accusation, slander, or *calumniator*, perpetrator of the foregoing, who was punished by the loss of accusatory rights in court and by the brand mark *C*.

3315. See note 3213.

3316. See *Practice [Training] in Christianity*, p. 232.

3317. See P. A. Wolff, *Preciosa*, tr. C. J. Boye (Copenhagen: 1822), pp. 78–79.

3318. See note 3106.

3319. See note 2423; ibid., p. 54.

3320. See notes 1829, 2509.

3321. See Luke 12:49.

3322. See *Pap.* VII$^1$ A 69.

3323. L. Holberg, *Barselstuen*, II, 12. The beef, even at a high price, is so stringy lean that she must add pork to it for proper soup.

3324. P. 35. You are fulfilled, nightwatch of my life.

3325. See note 3360.

3326. A landmark on Købmagergade in Copenhagen.

3327. See XI$^1$ A 125.

3328. See *Fragments*, p. 6.

3329. See note 1939; X$^4$ A 36.

3330. See "The Difference between a Genius and an Apostle," in *Two Minor Ethical-Religious Essays,* with *The Present Age,* pp. 139–63.

3331. See *J.P.*, III, note 372.

3332. See XI$^2$ A 36.

3333. See note 3330.

3334. A character in Ludwig Holberg's *Den ellevte Junii* involved in a plan to mortgage the city hall (III, 6). See "A Monologue", an article in *Fædrelandet,* 107, May 10, 1855, in *Attack,* p. 50.

3335. See note 3213.

3336. See *Berlingske Tidende,* 267, November 15, 1854.

3337. See Matthew 23:29–32.

3338. See *J.P.*, III, note 372.

3339. See note 2045.

3340. See *Armed Neutrality,* passim.

3341. See note 3321.

3342. In remembrance.

3343. See note 3360.

3344. See note 3340.

3345. See *Stages,* pp. 67–68, for Victor Eremitas' version and also that of Plato and of Thales.

3346. See note 1329.

3347. See *J.P.*, III, note 372.

3348. See note 3213.

3349. See note 3275.

3350. See article ("There the Matter Rests!") by Kierkegaard in *Fædrelandet,* 304, December 30, 1854; in *Attack,* p. 11.

3351. A reference to lines by Per Degn in L. Holberg's *Erasmus Montanus,* I, 3. See *Fear and Trembling,* p. 119.

3352. See note 3213.

3353. Ibid.

3354. Ibid.

3355. See note 3258.

3356. See note 3213.

3357. See note 3258.

3358. See note 2961.

3359. See note 3230.

3360. See note 2932; "A Thesis—Only a Single One," an article in *Fædrelandet,* 74, March 28, 1855, in *Attack,* pp. 32–33.

3361. I, pp. 41–42.

3362. See note 3213.

3363. See note 2483; *For Self-Examination*, pp. 12–13, 18.

3364. See XI[1] A 206.

3365. See article, "Is This Christian Worship," in *Fædrelandet*, 68, March 21, 1855, in *Attack*, 26–27.

3366. See *This Has To Be Said*, in *Attack*, pp. 57–66.

3367. "Was Bishop Mynster a 'Witness to the Truth' . . . ?" in *Fædrelandet*, 295, December 18, 1854, in *Attack*, pp. 5–9.

3368. See note 2483.

3369. Ibid.

3370. See note 3360.

3371. See, for example, *Fear and Trembling*, pp. 78–91.

3372. See note 3365.

3373. J. L. Heiberg, *De Uadskillelige* (Copenhagen: 1827), sc. 5.

3374. See note 3230.

3375. See XI[3] B 57; note 3275.

3376. See, for example, *Postscript*, pp. 45–47.

3377. Between December 18, 1854, and April 11, 1855, thirteen articles by Kierkegaard were printed in *Fædrelandet*; eight more appeared by May 26, 1855. They constituted Kierkegaard's open criticism of the established order of the Church and were followed by ten numbers of a pamphlet series called *The Moment*. No. 10 was published posthumously in *Efterladte Papirer*, ed. H. Gottsched (Copenhagen: 1881), Vol. VIII, pp. 593–609. See XI[3] B 128.

3378. See note 2102; ibid., II, p. 66; *For Self-Examination*, p. 14.

3379. See note 3023.

3380. See Philemon 3:7–8.

3381. See note 1796.

3382. See note 1832.

3383. See note 3275.

3384. See note 3377. The plan to publish in book form the articles printed in *Fædrelandet* was not carried out until *Søren Kierkegaard's Bladartikler*, a more inclusive volume edited by Rasmus Nielsen, appeared in 1857.

3385. See note 2456.

3386. In *S.V.*, XIV, the numbering runs I–XXI instead of I–XVIII as in the *Papirer*. Number IV here is IV and V in *S.V.*, number XIII is XIV and XV, and number XV is XVII and XVIII. The doublets here are given single numbers because in each case the two pieces appeared in the same issue of *Fædrelandet*.

3387. See notes 3213. 3275, 3277.

3388. J. Paludan-Müller, *Dr. Søren Kierkegaards Angreb paa Biskop Mynsters Eftermæle* (Copenhagen: 1855).

3389. See notes 3258, 3275.

3390. Signed N-n, *Fædrelandet*, April 3, 1855.

3391. Reitzel, the printer. The letter was not sent. See note 3384. Article no. I, written in February, 1854, was held until December, eight months after Martensen had been named Mynster's successor as Bishop. See notes 3258, 3367.

3392. See notes 3367, 3391.

3393. *Kjøbenhavnsposten*, 300, December 24, 1854, an article signed *Aesculap*.

3394. Ibid., 120, May 26, 1855.

3395. Entry deleted from manuscript of *The Unchangeableness of God*.

3396. A chattering know-it-all. See *The Present Age* (p. 58), where *at raisonere* is understandably but erroneously translated as "to reason." A *Raison-*[n] *eur* (Ludwig Meyer, *Fremmedordbog*, 1844; *ASKB* 1034) is one who "chatters about everything," "who uses his mouth." See *Pap.*, VII$^1$ B 110.

3397. See note 3213.

3398. See note 2961.

3399. See *Berlingske Tidende*, 154, July 7, 1851.

3400. Ibid., 207, September 6, 1851.

3401. Ibid., 25, January 30, 1854.

3402. This entry of September 25, 1855, written on loose sheets, is Kierkegaard's last piece of writing. On September 3, 1855, the discourse *The Unchangeableness of God* was published. No. 8 and no. 9 of *The Moment* appeared on September 11 and September 24, 1855.

Never particularly strong, Kierkegaard became progressively ill the latter part of September. One attack came at a party at J. F. Gjødwad's (see note 1895). Falling to the floor, he winked and said to the friends around him, "Oh, leave it-let-the maid-sweep it up-in the morning." (Reported by his one-time amanuensis, Israel Levin, *Hr. Cand. Israel Levins Udtalelser om S. Kierkegaard 1858 og 1869, D. PK. 5, Læg 31, Søren Kierkegaard Arkivet, Kongelige Biblioteket*, Copenhagen; see note 2763).

A few days later he collapsed on the street. After a time in his quarters at Klædeboderne 5–6 (see note 3193), he was taken to Frederiks Hospital on October 2, where he died November 11, 1855.

3403. See the end of *The Point of View*, p. 103: "... the author, who historically died of a mortal disease, but poetically died of longing for eternity, in order to do nothing else than uninterruptedly to thank God."